Transformations
of
Kinship

SMITHSONIAN SERIES IN ETHNOGRAPHIC INQUIRY

William L. Merrill and Ivan Karp, Series Editors

Ethnography as field work, analysis, and literary form is the distinguishing feature of modern anthropology. Guided by the assumption that anthropological theory and ethnography are inextricably linked, this series is devoted to exploring the ethnographic enterprise.

ADVISORY BOARD

Richard Bauman (Indiana University), Gerald Berreman (University of California, Berkeley), James Boon (Princeton University), Stephen Gudeman (University of Minnesota), Shirley Lindenbaum (City University of New York), George Marcus (Rice University), David Parkin (Oxford University), Renato Rosaldo (Stanford University), and Norman Whitten (University of Illinois).

Transformations
of
Kinship

Edited by

MAURICE GODELIER,
THOMAS R. TRAUTMANN,
AND FRANKLIN E. TJON SIE FAT

SMITHSONIAN INSTITUTION PRESS
Washington and London

The Suger Conference on which this volume is based was held in Paris
in 1993 and received generous support from the Suger Foundation

Copy editor: Vicky Macintyre
In-house editor: Ruth Spiegel
Designer: Kathleen Sims
Indexer: Andrew L. Christenson
Illustrations and typesetting: John Hamer

Library of Congress Cataloging-in-Publication Data
Transformations of kinship / edited by Maurice Godelier, Thomas R.
Trautmann, and Franklin E. Tjon Sie Fat.
    p. cm. — (Smithsonian series in ethmographic inquiry)
    Product of a roundtable held in the Maison Suger in June 1993.
    Includes bibliographical references and index.
    ISBN 1-56098-791-X (cloth : alk. paper). — ISBN 1-56098-768-5
(pbk. : alk. paper)
    1. Kinship—Congresses. 2. Social structure—Congresses. 3.
Social evolution—Congresses. 4.Social change—Congresses.
I. Godelier, Maurice. II. Trautmann, Thomas R.
III. Tjon Sie Fat, Franklin Edmund, 1947- . IV. Series.
GN487.T725 1998
306.83—dc21   97-39955
                                                CIP

British Library Cataloguing-in-Publication Data available

Manufactured in the United States of America
05 04 03 02 01 00 99 98   5 4 3 2 1

∞ The recycled paper used in this publication meets the minimum
requirements of the American National Standard for Information
Sciences—Permanence of Paper for Printed Library Materials ANSI
Z39.48-1984

Contents

Preface **vii**
Acknowledgments **x**
Kinship Notation **xi**
Glossary **xii**

1   Introduction **1**
MAURICE GODELIER, THOMAS R. TRAUTMANN, AND
FRANKLIN E. TJON SIE FAT

SETTING THE STAGE
2   "Dravidian," "Iroquois," and "Crow-Omaha" in North American
Perspective **27**
THOMAS R. TRAUTMANN AND R. H. BARNES
3   On the Formal Analysis of "Dravidian," "Iroquois," and "Generational"
Varieties as Nearly Associative Combinations **59**
FRANKLIN E. TJON SIE FAT

NORTH AMERICA
4   Developmental Processes in the Pre-Contact History of Athapaskan,
Algonquian, and Numic Kin Systems **94**
JOHN W. IVES
5   Kinship and Dravidianate Logic: Some Implications for Understanding
Power, Politics, and Social Life in a Northern Dene Community **140**
MICHAEL ASCH
6   Dravidian Nomenclature as an Expression of Ego-Centered Dualism **150**
EMMANUEL DÉSVEAUX AND MARION SELZ

SOUTH AMERICA
7   Serial Redundancy in Amazonian Social Structure: Is There a Method for
Poststructuralist Comparison? **168**
ALF HORNBORG
8   Jivaro Kinship: "Simple" and "Complex" Formulas: A Dravidian
Transformation Group **187**
ANNE-CHRISTINE TAYLOR
9   Taking Sides: Marriage Networks and Dravidian Kinship in Lowland South
America **214**
MICHAEL HOUSEMAN AND DOUGLAS R. WHITE

10   On Double Language and the Relativity of Incest: The Campa Sociology of
     a Dravidian-Type Terminology **244**
     FRANCE-MARIE RENARD-CASEVITZ

ASIA
11   Dravidian and Iroquois in South Asia **252**
     ROBERT PARKIN
12   Transformations of Kinship Systems in Eastern Indonesia **271**
     JEAN-FRANÇOIS GUERMONPREZ

THE BIG PICTURE
13   The Synchro-Diachronic Method and the Multidirectionality of
     Kinship Transformations **294**
     M. V. KRYUKOV
14   The Prehistory of Dravidian-Type Terminologies **314**
     N. J. ALLEN
15   Dravidian and Related Kinship Systems **332**
     EDUARDO VIVEIROS DE CASTRO

16   Afterword: Transformations and Lines of Evolution **386**
     MAURICE GODELIER

Bibliography **414**
Index **444**

Preface

The essays in this volume come out of a roundtable on kinship systems organized by Maurice Godelier and held in the Maison Suger in June 1993 under the sponsorship of the Maison des Sciences de l'Homme, the Ecole des Hautes Etudes en Sciences Sociales, and the Centre National de la Recherche Scientifique. The purpose of the conference was to explore the transformations of kinship systems, with an emphasis on whether such transformations are reversible or irreversible, and whether there is an overall directionality of change, or an evolutionary drift that cumulates transformations in a particular way.

The conception for the Maison Suger conference arose from Godelier's review of more than two thousand articles and books on kinship during two years of research leave in Berlin. This work had strengthened his conviction that, contrary to the claims of the evolutionist anthropology of the past, there is no simple, direct connection between types of kinship and the political and social regime of any given society. It became equally clear to him that in order to determine the relation of kinship to property, rank, and gender—beyond the implication that it is a complex and indirect relation—one must first understand the logic of kinship transformations themselves. Godelier also was struck by the still unexplained fact that all kinship terminologies are but variations of a small number of basic types.

The conference itself was the result of a fortunate conjuncture. In the fall of 1992, when Godelier was returning to Paris, he learned from Jean-Claude Galey that Thomas Trautmann was to teach in Galey's seminar the following spring, by virtue of an exchange program of long standing between the Ecole and the University of Michigan. Just the previous April, Michael Kryukov had held a conference in Moscow on kinship in Asia at which N. J. Allen, John Ives, Robert Parkin, and Trautmann, among others, had presented papers, copies of some of which Godelier had obtained from Parkin in Berlin. Godelier began organizing a conference on kinship, with help from Galey, Anne-Christine Taylor, and (by fax) Trautmann. First contacts were made in January 1993, and the "Colloque Systèmes de parenté Dravidiens, Iroquois et Crow-Omaha" was held on June 3–5 at the Maison Suger. The invitation elicited a completely unexpected rush of interest. It seemed to have tapped a hidden fountain of pent-up interest in kinship analysis.

At the time the conference was first mooted, Trautmann and R. H. Barnes had been engaged for some time in a collaboration to revisit the original data on kinship terminologies collected from North American groups by Lewis Henry Morgan in the 1850s and 1860s, stimulated by David Kronenfeld's (1989) provocative reexamination of the relations among systems of Dravidian, Iroquois, and Crow-Omaha kinship types. Indeed, Kronenfeld's paper served, together with the Moscow conference papers, as an important prior text for the Maison Suger roundtable, determining indirectly which of the main kinship types came to be discussed there. Trautmann and Barnes took this opportunity to discuss the results of their research. The essay, published here (chapter 2), was circulated to others in March.

Franklin Tjon Sie Fat, who had brought out a book on mathematical models for kinship systems in 1990, then decided to apply an algebraic treatment to the central contrast in Trautmann and Barnes's paper, namely, the difference between kinship terminologies of the types called Dravidian (or Dravidianate, or Type A) and Iroquois (or Iroquoian, or Type B). His formal analysis, which appears in chapter 3, was also circulated to participants in advance of the Maison Suger conference. The two essays together defined the starting-point of the conversation that then ensued.

By early May, a flood of new papers from other participants had begun to arrive in Paris. In response to a stream of faxes from Godelier asking authors to discuss further issues they had not covered, no less than six of the papers were rewritten and circulated a second time prior to the Maison Suger meeting. The conversation was well under way before the roundtable actually took place.

The overall shape of the assembled papers had other surprises. The first was that South America emerged as a central area of discussion. A half-century earlier the kinship systems of South America were practically unknown to anthropologists, and Claude Lévi-Strauss, whose specialty was South America, had been obliged to turn to Asia and Oceania for materials for his work, *Les Structures élémentaires de la parenté* (1949). Now South America is a whole world unto itself, a world to which it is no accident that the *Structures* remains very pertinent. South America contains abundant examples of all the systems that enter into Lévi-Strauss's seminal work: Dravidian, Iroquois, Crow-Omaha, and Australian (including marriage sections). Furthermore, the South Americanists are avid about kinship and proud of the ethnographic wealth of the continent. Anne-Christine Taylor says that "canonical Dravidian" as defined by Louis Dumont is better exemplified in Amazonia than in South India; Eduardo Viveiros de Castro has become so Amazocentric as to propose that the system of Dravidian-speakers in India be called Amazonate! The high quality of the new South American materials and the kinship analyses of them make these aggressive claims increasingly difficult to deny.

Another surprising development was the abundance of relevant contributions from the classic field of North America. The richness of the North American ethnography was evident in 1937, as reflected in the excellent collection of North

American kinship studies, *Social Anthropology of the North American Tribes*, inspired by Radcliffe-Brown and edited by Fred Eggan. That work is still unequaled. The essays in the present volume show, however, that North America has by no means been fully explored and that its possibilities are far from exhausted. There are still new things to be discovered, partly by mining the archives (as Trautmann and Barnes demonstrate in chapter 2 and John W. Ives does in chapter 4), partly by undertaking new fieldwork (as reported by Michael Asch in chapter 5 and Emmanuel Désveaux and Marion Selz in chapter 6).

Paradoxically, the Maison Suger conference did not devote as much attention to the Dravidian land itself, which was its point of departure. Anthony Good (1993) developed his earlier work (1980, 1981) on the ethnography of marriage between elder sister's daughter and mother's younger brother, arguing that it is the dominant pattern in South India. In this volume Robert Parkin (chapter 11) explores the differences between North and South Indian kinship systems and the relation of Central Indian systems to both, while Michael Kryukov's investigation (chapter 13) ranges from China to Europe. Southeast Asia is also covered by Kryukov, and by Jean-François Guermonprez (chapter 12). Work on New Guinea had figured in Tjon Sie Fat's 1990 book, and he includes some of the New Guinea cases in his analysis of the "Type B alliance structure" published here (chapter 3). Another New Guinea example, the Yafar, appeared as a variant form of crossness in the essay of Viveiros de Castro (chapter 15) and in Tjon Sie Fat's hypercube (chapter 1). Australia is discussed in the contributions by N. J. Allen (chapter 14) and Viveiros, and in an essay by Testart (1993; see also 1992).

In the end, Dravidian kinship was found all over the world, which is not to say, of course, that it occurs everywhere. There are many blank spaces on our map of the world: Africa, Europe, the Arctic, and Central America are scarcely touched. In typological terms, employing quasi-Murdockian categories, discussions at the Maison Suger conference focused on Dravidian, Iroquois, the grab-bag of contested forms called Crow-Omaha, and what Viveiros dubs Normal Australian. Little was said about the Sudanese, Eskimo, and Hawaiian types of kinship terminology.

The conversation continues, well after the Maison Suger roundtable, by post, fax, and e-mail. Some entirely new studies appeared after the conference, notably an important analysis of kinship patterns in South America by Paul Henley, and a response, to be published elsewhere, by David Kronenfeld to Trautmann and Barnes's essay. And the next-to-last paper of this volume (chapter 15) by Eduardo Viveiros de Castro largely recasts, post-conference, his invaluable insights into South American kinship systems and projects them upon a worldwide ethnological screen.

The discussion of particular issues bubbles along even after the papers have settled into their final form. As a result, this volume is very much the product not only of the conference itself but of the second fermentation in its aftermath. As such, it is both somewhat less than a record of the Maison Suger roundtable and something more and other: less because it does not reproduce all the papers, nor the discussion of them; more and other because it reflects the conception of the editors as it has continued to evolve in discussions following the roundtable itself. It is a record, if anything, of a renewed and vigorous interest in kinship analysis.

Acknowledgments

The editors wish to record their thanks to a number of institutions and individuals who made this volume possible: the Maison des Sciences de l'Homme, the Ecole des Hautes Etudes en Sciences Sociales, and the Centre National de la Recherche Scientifique for support of the Maison Suger conference and for the translation of papers; Helena Meininger and Hoscham Dawod for administrative assistance; Jean-Claude Galey and Anne-Christine Taylor for contributions to the planning of the conference; the International Institute and the Institute for the Humanities, University of Michigan, for travel support; Julia Routson, for secretarial help with the manuscript; and, for support for making the figures and tables, the Office of the Vice-President for Research and the LSA Faculty Fund of the University of Michigan.

William Merrill, Series Editor of the Smithsonian Series in Ethnographic Inquiry, gave his strong support to this project and his close reading of the manuscript led to many improvements, for which the editors are very grateful. For the various aspects of transforming the manuscript into a book they are indebted to Daniel Goodwin, Robert Lockhart, Vicky Macintyre, Ruth Spiegel, and John Hamer.

Kinship Notation

A	aunt
B	brother
C	cousin
Ch	child
D	daughter
F	father
H	husband
M	mother
N	nephew or niece ("nibling")
Pa	parent
S	son
Sb	sibling
Sp	spouse
U	uncle
W	wife
Z	sister

e	elder, e.g., FeB = father's elder brother; e(FBS) = father's brother's son, older than ego
y	younger
♂ (to the left)	or m.s. (to the right): male or male speaking, e.g. ♂Z = mZS = ZS (m.s.) a male's sister's son or sister's son (male speaking)
♀	or f.s.: female or female speaking
ss or s.s.	same sex
os or o.s.	opposite sex

G^2 or G^{+2}	grandparents' generation
G^1 or G^{+1}	parents' generation
G^0	ego's generation
G^{0e}	ego's generation, elder than ego
G^{0y}	ego's generation, younger than ego
G^{-1}	childrens' generation
G^{-2}	grandchildren's generation

Glossary

affines — People related by marriage, in-laws.

agnates — People related through male linking relatives; patrilineal kin.

agnatic ties — Relationships through male linking relatives; patrilineal relationships.

asymmetric alliance system — Kinship system having a positive marriage rule (prescription) that is asymmetrical in that it requires opposite-sex siblings to marry into different groups. Hence the reciprocal exchange of persons of the same sex in marriage between groups is forbidden. Also known as a system with indirect or generalized exchange.

cognates — People related through common ancestors, by linking relatives of either sex.

complex systems — Kinship systems that have only a negative marriage rule, proscribing marriage with specified kin and that lack a positive rule prescribing marriage within a specified category of relatives, such as the rule of cross-cousin marriage.

consanguines — People related by blood, that is, by descent from common ancestors.

crossness — The distinction of relatives into two kinds, cross and parallel. There are two main varieties of crossness reckoning: Type A (associated with Dravidian terminologies) and Type B (associated with Iroquois terminologies).

Crow-Omaha — Type of kinship terminology strongly influenced by unilineal descent (matrilineal: Crow; patrilineal: Omaha), such that certain kinship categories of different generations but falling in the same line of descent are merged. The merger of categories across generations is called "skewing" or "unilineal equations." For example, in a Crow system the FZD and FZDD may be merged with the FZ (that is, all are a kind of "aunt") and in Omaha systems the MBS and MBSS with the MB (as "uncles"). In ego's generation, siblings and parallel cousins (FBCh, MZCh) are merged.

Dravidian — Type of kinship terminology associated with a rule of cross-cousin marriage; historically related kinship systems of South India and Sri Lanka. Such terminologies exhibit a distinction of "crossness," dividing relatives into "cross" and "parallel" sets (Type A), and the merger of affinal with consanguineal kin.

elementary — Kinship systems having a positive marriage rule, that is, one that prescribes marriage within a specified category, such as that of cross cousins.

Eskimo — Type of kinship terminology that distinguishes collaterals (uncle, aunt, cousin, nephew, niece) from lineals (father, mother, brother, sister, son, daughter); also called "lineal." English kinship terminology is an example of the Eskimo type.

Hawaiian — Type of kinship terminology that merges kinship categories within the same generation, assimilating collateral relatives to the lineals (father and mother, brother and sister, son and daughter). Also called "generational."

Iroquois — Type of kinship terminology exhibiting crossness similar to that of Dravidian terminologies, but differing in detail (Type B); and lacking the merger of affines and consanguines characteristic of the Dravidian type.

nepotic — Concerning nephews and nieces (sometimes collectively called "niblings").

oblique marriage — Marriage between persons of different generations. An example would be the marriage of a woman to her MyB or of a man to his eZD, which is a pattern found in some parts of South India and elsewhere that feature Dravidian terminologies.

prescriptive — Used of kinship systems having a positive rule of marriage, such as a rule prescribing the marriage of cross cousins, and not just a negative marriage rule, prohibiting the marriage of siblings and other specified kin.

reciprocal sets — Paired sets of kinship categories that are the referents of one another, such as H/W (husband and wife), or F + M / S + D (father and mother, son and daughter). Different kinship terminologies have different underlying reciprocal sets.

semicomplex — Kinship systems intermediate between elementary and complex, having a purely negative marriage rule but one that is so extensive as to leave a somewhat delimited category of marriageable kin. In the work of Lévi-Strauss (whose terms these are) such a regime of marriage is generally associated with Crow-Omaha terminologies.

skewing/unilineal equations — The merger of kin of different generations and same descent line, as in terminologies of Crow-Omaha type.

Sudanese — Type of kinship terminology in which collaterals are distinguished from lineals, as in the Eskimo type, but in which collateral kin are not merged among themselves, so that the different kinds of uncles (FB, MB) and aunts (FZ, MZ) have separate terms, and likewise the cousins and "niblings." Also called "bifurcate collateral."

symmetric alliance system — Kinship system having a positive rule of marriage (prescription) that is symmetrical, requiring opposite-sex siblings to marry into the same group. Hence the reciprocal exchange of persons of the same sex in marriage between two groups is prescribed. Also known as a system with direct or restricted exchange.

teknonymy — Naming a person by reference to that person's child, for example, Rahulamātā, "Rahula's mother."

uterine kin — People related through the same mother, or through female linking relatives; matrilineal kin.

1
Introduction

MAURICE GODELIER, THOMAS R. TRAUTMANN, AND
FRANKLIN E. TJON SIE FAT

For much of its history anthropology has seemed unable to live without kinship analysis, which is, after all, its own invention, dealing with a subject-matter uniquely its own. Today, in the face of a rapidly shrinking world and the disappearance of kin-based societies, the importance of kinship analysis is no longer so clear. Does kinship analysis have a future? The answer this volume gives to that question is a resounding "yes." The various chapters remind us how much anthropology has accomplished in the study of kinship. They also show how much remains to be discovered and how much of the diversity of humanity will perish without record if anthropologists refuse this calling. To understand the current role of kinship analysis one must go back to the circumstances of its origin.

This volume may be thought of as the continuation of a conversation about kinship begun in the mid–nineteenth century. Lewis Henry Morgan was seeking information about the structure of the Iroquois League in the New York State records at Albany, when he encountered the young Ely S. Parker, or Hasanoanda, serving as interpreter to his Seneca elders in talks with the governor. Their meeting led to a research collaboration and the publication of *League of the Iroquois* (1851), "the fruit of our joint researches," as Morgan called it. In discussion with Parker, Morgan came to see that the kinship system of the Iroquois (of which the Seneca Nation is a part) had an integrity and logic of its own that was entirely different from that of English-speaking Americans and of Europeans.

What particularly intrigued Morgan was that the Seneca did not distinguish between the father and the father's brother, labeling both with a single term that Morgan translated as "father"—"The father's brother is equally a father," was how he put it. Furthermore, membership in each of the eight Iroquois clans was determined by descent traced through women, that is, they were matrilineal, a principle that Morgan found new and puzzling.

Morgan's work on Iroquois kinship raised fundamental questions about what precisely a "father" is and what "paternity" might mean in societies where the same

1

term labeled the father and the father's brothers—and, as Morgan later discovered, in other American Indian societies such as the Omaha, where the "father" category could even include men of different generations. It also raised doubts about whether the European concept of consanguinity—which held that a person shared blood or other bodily substances with his or her father and mother—had universal meaning.

These decentering findings launched Morgan on a worldwide comparative study of kinship. The results of this ambitious project were published by the Smithsonian Institution in 1871 as *Systems of Consanguinity and Affinity of the Human Family,* one of the truly original works of the nineteenth century. Through this book, Morgan created the domain of kinship as an analytical category and forged the tools for its scientific study (Godelier 1995).

Morgan went on to use his discoveries to construct a speculative vision of the evolution of human society, in the book *Ancient Society* (1871).[1] In it Morgan proposed that human society had risen by stages from savagery through barbarism to civilization, the latter exemplified for him by the Euro-American society of his day, whereby the West was made the mirror and yardstick of development. This scheme allowed him to "domesticate" the exotic findings that had launched his inquiry; but in the movement from decentering to recentering, things were not restored to their initial condition, and his conclusions also challenged many basic assumptions of Euro-American society, for example, the idea that the patriarchal family known from biblical or early Roman days was the starting point of human development. Morgan argued that this structure was preceded by a series of different family types, including the matrilineal. In doing so, he dealt a mortal blow to the patriarchal theory of human history, "denaturalizing" both modern monogamy and ancient patriarchy by giving them a completely exotic prehistory (see Godelier 1995).

Morgan's problematic, reformulated by W. H. R. Rivers in his *Kinship and Social Organisation* (1914), led to a golden age of kinship study in the early twentieth century. There was a second golden age in the 1950s and 1960s, stimulated by the publication in 1949 of Claude Lévi-Strauss's *Les Structures élémentaires de la parenté* (published in English as *The Elementary Structures of Kinship*). Two decades later—and a century after Morgan's great work was published—negative critique was the rise, and it seemed as if the possibilities of the paradigm had been exhausted. Leading kinship practitioners published a number of skeptical essays, most notably Rodney Needham (1971) and David Schneider (1972, 1984). Adopting a radically relativistic perspective, Schneider challenged the legitimacy of kinship studies as a whole, arguing that the boundaries of the kinship domain and its relations to other domains are unstable and different from one society to the next. Anthropology's view of kinship "does not correspond to any cultural category known to man" (1972:50) and is essentially concocted by Morgan.

E pur si muove—and yet it moves! That kinship analysis has survived its age of uncertainty is certain: one need only examine the bibliography of kinship studies published in the 1970s, 1980s, and 1990s to see that it is so. Although the required kinship course has by and large disappeared in America, it remains important in other anthropological traditions, as may be seen in the appearance of new manuals for kinship research, such as those of Barnard and Good (1984) in England and

Zimmerman (1993) in France. In France, especially, kinship continues to be an area of ambitious theoretical studies. Leading instances include Pierre Bourdieu's 1977 [1972] analysis of parallel cousin marriage; Françoise Héritier's studies of Crow-Omaha, incest, and other topics, and the four volumes of essays on Crow-Omaha systems that she and her colleagues have produced (Héritier 1981, 1994a, 1994b; Héritier-Augé and Copet-Rougier 1991–94); and Lévi-Strauss's formation of the concept of "house societies," first presented in his 1979 book *La Voie des masques,* which was further developed by Macdonald (1987) and Carsten and Hugh-Jones (1995).

Anthropology is changing, of course, and the objects of its inquiry are changing with it. While the number of anthropologists increases, the world shrinks, and the kin-based societies that have been anthropology's classic focus are turning into something else. Before the world-shaping processes of global production, global markets, and global communications, "there" and "here" no longer keep to their places. Growing numbers of anthropologists now write dissertations on tourism in Greenland, the effects of gambling casino ownership on the Ojibwa, and the lives of Southeast Asian refugees in America or Turkish *Gastarbeiter* in Germany.

The family will continue to be a focus of anthropological study in the foreseeable future, but what has made anthropological kinship analysis distinctive—and different from sociological, historical or social-psychological studies of the family—is that kinship has always been something more than the family. In the classic societies, that "something more" has been the whole of social organization articulated by kinship-based structures such as clans, castes, moieties, or marriage classes. However, such kin-based structures appear to be disappearing before the forces making for large-scale integration, leading one to think that in the future families (and their fragments) may find themselves articulated with one another not by kinship structures but by quite different principles.

What then? The usefulness of kinship analysis will not come to an end even if the kin-based societies that have been the classic objects of kinship studies slip wholly and irrevocably into the past. The human past is a vast territory and whatever aids in illuminating it will be of permanent value. Kinship has long suggested itself as a tool for the elucidation of the ancient civilizations of China (Granet 1939; Kryukov 1972) and India (Held 1935; Trautmann 1981); and Jack Goody's book, *The Oriental, the Ancient, and the Primitive: Systems of Marriage and the Family in the Pre-industrial Societies of Eurasia* (1990), illustrates what may be accomplished when the analysis of kinship takes the long view from the paleolithic to the present. The archive that ethnography has created is large and there is limitless material awaiting elucidation by the anthropological analysis of kinship.

Thus a limitless future for kinship analysis is ensured, if only for the study of the past. Moreover, announcing the demise of kin-based societies surely is premature. There remain numerous societies in the world that are suffused by kinship, especially in New Guinea and South America, where previously unknown types and variants of kinship systems continue to appear, as the chapters that follow abundantly show. Anthropologists in these and other areas of the world still find themselves expected to become kin and to master kinship terms and the etiquette of

kinship prestations as a condition of their living among the peoples of their research. Jamous (1991) found it to be so among the Meo of India, as did Ahearn
(1994) among the Magar of Nepal. Moreover, from time to time the real world hits
the general public on the head with the importance of kinship, as when the frustrat-
ing confrontation of UN forces and the Somali "clan" leaders demonstrated on tele-
vision newscasts the persistent power of kinship. We now have Ioan M. Lewis's
book *Blood and Bone: The Call of Kinship in Somali Society* (1994) to help us
understand.

Even as anthropology moves off in new directions, students who have not had
the benefit of training in kinship analysis clearly will be at a disadvantage in their
efforts to understand societies of classic type. Equally important, they will be poorly
equipped to contribute to the development of theory within a changing anthropology. At the head of all the forces of transformation within the discipline in recent
decades we would have to put the influence of feminism. The intellectual power it
gives to the study of gender and the body as a site of social inscription has led to
some of the best recent work in kinship analysis, which is implicated in these inquiries. Indeed, Collier and Yanagisako (1989) have called for the theorization of
kinship and gender as a single domain. It is no accident that much of the best recent
work in kinship is directed to the new interest in gender and the body.

APPROACHING THE ANALYSIS OF KINSHIP

In view of these various changes, it is all the more important to have a firm grasp of
the classic problems of kinship. To this end it remains useful to divide kinship,
following Needham, into three parts: behavior, rules, and categories, or the kinship
terminology. Behavior and rules are the domains of the "is" and the "ought," the
behavioral and the moral realms, respectively. Kinship behavior is what people actually do and thus is amenable to statistical treatment. Kinship rules, in contrast, are
amenable to mechanical modeling because they indicate what people *should* do.
The domain of rules has an idealizing, even ideological, character. Through the
rules (of descent and marriage, for example) we see most clearly the way in which
the family extends itself into larger kinship groupings (lineages, clans, moieties,
and so forth) that constitute social organization. In the end it is impossible to say
where exactly kinship ends and social organization begins.

Anthropological thinking about the domain of kinship rules has undergone considerable change of late. In the past, anthropologists regarded the domain of rules as
one of consensus and clarity as opposed to the fuzzy indeterminacy of individual
behavior. They assumed that, in principle at least, a single informant could provide
a book of kinship rules, identical copies of which were carried around in the heads
of every rational adult member of the society in question. Nowadays, however, anthropologists tend to see the domain of rules as one of variations, contested meanings, hegemony, and resistance. The prevailing notion is that public symbols are
argued over and manipulated in the pursuit of private advantage. This changed conception makes the realm of rules a kind of fulcrum for kinship studies, a Janus-

faced center, which, looking right (toward behavior), sees the region of "hot" kinship, the kinship of practice—kinship red in tooth and claw; and, looking left (toward kinship terminology), finds the region of "cool" kinship, of calm, lucid, exact, mathematical beauty.

This book pulls leftward, so to speak, toward the cool side of kinship study, focusing on the kinship categories or terminologies and dealing with rules and behavior as they relate to terminologies. It does so not out of a sense that terminology is the true or superior side of kinship, but, if anything, from a feeling that this is the side of kinship analysis that has been comparatively neglected of late and is most in need of collective attention. We believe that this restorative development is important for a more profound understanding not only of "cool" kinship but of "hot" kinship as well.

The discussions that follow build upon three fundamental ideas about the nature of kinship terminologies, ideas—first proposed by Morgan—that have held up very well over the last century or so of kinship analysis. First, kinship terminologies do not exist in a vacuum but are influenced by the marriage rules of the societies in which they are found. Second, the thousands of systems of kinship terminology in human societies around the world are but variants of a limited number of different types. And third, the different types of kinship terminology can be shown to be transformations of one another. The question that remains open is whether there is an overall directionality to such transformations.

Each kinship type is a representation of two things: (a) principles of classification, which assign individuals to different kinship categories, and (b) rules that define relationships of consanguinity and affinity ("blood" and marriage) among these individuals. Each specific set of principles and rules generates corresponding types of terminology. And each type of terminology has its own specific logic as well as a capacity to transform into other types along one or several paths.

At this point one is tempted to ask: Do such types of kinship terminology really exist or are they merely constructs of the anthropologist? On the surface the answer is not difficult at all. Kinship terminological types are evidently mental constructs and are not discovered empirically but, on the contrary, are imposed by anthropologists upon empirical instances to mass them into classes. However, when we say that types of kinship terminology are not "discovered" empirically but are constructed, that does not mean that the construction is arbitrary and that the human mind is not guided by empirical facts. One example would be the itinerary of Morgan himself, who needed time and effort to understand the Dravidian type of crossness and even then was not able to recognize it as a type in its own right but as a blemish or a deviation from the Iroquois model from which his researches had begun. The kinship terms, together with the principles of classification and the rules of relationships that constitute the different types of kinship terminology, are historical and sociological facts created and applied by the human mind in specific historical contexts. They are not the invention of scholars.

Although the different types of kin terminologies have a real existence in some sense, the number and definition of the types, let alone their names, are scarcely agreed upon. To the contrary, typologies and names are matters of continual debate, and for a good reason: we are still in the age of discovery, and new discovery is constantly unsettling received typologies.

The typology of kinship terminologies is by no means settled, then, and is still very much a work in progress. Nevertheless, the assumption upon which this volume is predicated is one that has held up very well over the last century or so of kinship analysis: that types of kinship terminologies do exist, that the number of types is limited, and that whatever the number should finally turn out to be, it is much less than the number of languages. The variants of the kinship system known as "Dravidian" are found not only among Dravidian-speaking people of South India and Sri Lanka and some of their near neighbors, but also among certain American Indian societies in South America and North America, even though their language families are entirely different—as are their political and economic systems. This is a capital fact, the implications of which are enormous but partly still obscure.

What do similarities among the kinship systems of such unrelated societies mean? Why does a particular type of kinship terminology exist in distant parts of the world where direct contact and historical relatedness can be ruled out as causes? Much of this book is devoted to exploring alternative solutions to these fundamental problems, which raise basic questions about how human societies can be understood.

At the outset, the patchy and recurrent distribution of kinship types around the globe obliges us to distinguish between two principles of grouping, which we will call propinquity and form. Relationships of propinquity, on the one hand, serve to classify the kinship terminologies of societies sharing common origins or languages or living adjacent to one another into larger groups containing many instances, all of which must be taken into consideration to understand any one instance. Thus, the kinship system of any single community in South India or Sri Lanka is not an absolute datum, self-contained and explicable in and of itself but is best understood by comparison with kinship systems of neighboring communities that, taken together, constitute a field of variation whose unity derives from the historical relatedness of communities speaking (for the most part) related languages. Analysis of such geographically and historically contiguous instances takes place within a culture area.

The principle of form, on the other hand, applies when numerous examples of kinship systems that are formally quite similar to those of the Dravidian region of India are found in societies as distant as the Americas, where quite different language families exist. The geographical and linguistic distances suggest that there is no direct historical connection between these societies. In such instances, the set of Dravidian terminologies is established not by propinquity but by form alone. Accordingly, at this level comparison of kinship terminologies making up the type is conceptualized quite differently; identity of the type of kinship terminology between distant regions cannot be attributed to historical connections and must be explained in relation to general properties of the human mind.

At the outset of kinship studies Morgan was impelled to a different conclusion and mingled the two levels of analysis. Morgan viewed the entire universe of kinship systems as so many points on a single family tree, with two main branches, the classificatory and the descriptive. He labeled as classificatory those kinship systems that merged lineal and collateral relatives (for example, the father and the father's brothers) and as descriptive those systems that used separate terms for lineal and collateral relatives. Because he could show that his classificatory type existed in both the Old and the New Worlds, while the descriptive type was restricted to Europe and the Near East, Morgan believed that Asian and American Indian terminologies were historically linked, thereby proving the Asian origin of the peoples of the Americas.[2] Essentially, the method of Morgan was the method of propinquity, but he applied it, wrongly, across very large distances of the globe.

Another founder of modern anthropology, E. B. Tylor, brought a sharply contrasting perspective to the study of the global distribution of traits of many kinds. In his *Primitive Culture,* published in the same year as Morgan's *Systems of Consanguinity and Affinity of the Human Family,* Tylor (1889 [1871]:10) wrote: "The phenomena of culture, as resulting from widely-acting similar causes, should recur again and again in the world." For Tylor, the preeminent cause of far-flung cultural similarities was a basic human nature shared by all of mankind. To discover human universals and general laws of human will and conduct, he searched far and wide for regularities that occurred among societies so distant from one another that they could be presumed to be historically independent of one another.[3]

Morgan's method starts with contiguous (especially linguistically related) societies and explains similarities among them by assuming that they are historically linked. As the circle of contiguous societies expands, the presumption of historical relatedness is pressed harder and harder, and the generalizations based on it grow less certain. Tylor's method, on the other hand, begins with societies so distant from one another that their historical independence can be assumed, and it explains similarities among them as the result of shared structures of the human mind and other human universals. As more societies are included in the comparison, the likelihood increases that at least some of them will be historically linked, and the presumption of their independence becomes increasingly difficult to sustain.

It is evident that the two methods complement one another, and that each is useful in different situations. When anthropologists examine the kinship systems of societies that are linguistically related or geographically contiguous, they are following Morgan's method. Alternatively, when they compare the kinship systems of widely separated societies, presumed to be historically independent of one another, they adopt Tylor's method, which focuses more on logical rather than historical relations among systems.

THE DRAVIDIAN AND IROQUOIAN SYSTEMS

The studies of kinship terminologies in this volume focus on two systems traditionally conceived as being related but distinct: the Dravidian and the Iroquoian systems. The Dravidian system looms large in anthropological discussion because it is an especially lucid case of the union of kinship terminology and a marriage rule, in this case the rule of cross-cousin marriage. Under this rule, a brother and sister may not marry, but their children *should* marry (see figure 1-1). The semantics of kinship

Figure 1-1
The Marriage of Cross Cousins

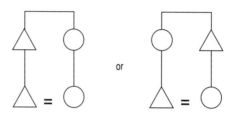

terms in this kinship system presume that everyone marries according to the rule, so that, for example, a person's "father-in-law" and "mother-in-law" are simultaneously his or her "uncle" and "aunt," and a "son-in-law" or "daughter-in-law" is simultaneously a "nephew" or "niece."

In the Dravidian kinship system, all consanguineal kin (i.e., "blood" relatives) in one's own generation and the generations of one's parents and children (which we label as G^0, G^{+1}, and G^{-1}, respectively) are classified as either "cross" or "parallel." "Cross" and "parallel" are the two values of a dimension that, for want of a better word, we call "crossness." We illustrate, beginning with my parents' generation (G^{+1}). I use the terms for "uncle" and "aunt" to label my parents' opposite-sex siblings, that is, my mother's brothers (MB) and father's sisters (FZ). In contrast, I call my parents' same-sex siblings by the terms for "father" and "mother"; these are my father's brothers (FB) and mother's sisters (MZ). In my own generation (G^0), I call the children of all of my "fathers" and "mothers" my "brothers" and "sisters." In addition to my own full siblings, these "brothers" and "sisters" are my father's brother's children (FBCh) and my mother's sister's children (MZCh), who are my parallel cousins and therefore are unmarriageable. I call the children of my "uncles" and "aunts" by a different term, equivalent to "cousin." They are my cross cousins and therefore marriageable. In my children's generation (G^{-1}), I call the children of my same-sex siblings my "sons" and "daughters;" these are my brothers' children (σBCh) if I am a man and my sisters' children (φZCh) if I am a woman. Children of my opposite-sex siblings are my "nephews" and "nieces." Using these Dravidian redefinitions of the English words, we can say that cross kin consist of all uncles, aunts, cousins, nephews, and nieces, while parallel kin are all fathers, mothers, brothers, sisters, sons, and daughters. Thus these three generations (G^0, G^{+1}, and G^{-1}) are completely divided or "bifurcated" by the principle of crossness, which sorts kin into two grades of nearness: near (parallel) and far (cross).

By taking into account the relationships by marriage, Dumont (1953) showed that the Dravidian contrast of parallel versus cross is in fact a contrast of kin versus affines. The kinship terminology of English is also bifurcated into the same two sets of words, but in their ordinary English meaning, by a different principle, that of lineality (lineal versus collateral kin), involving a quite different logic of "near" and "far" relatives.

Figure 1-2
Typologies of Kinship Terminology

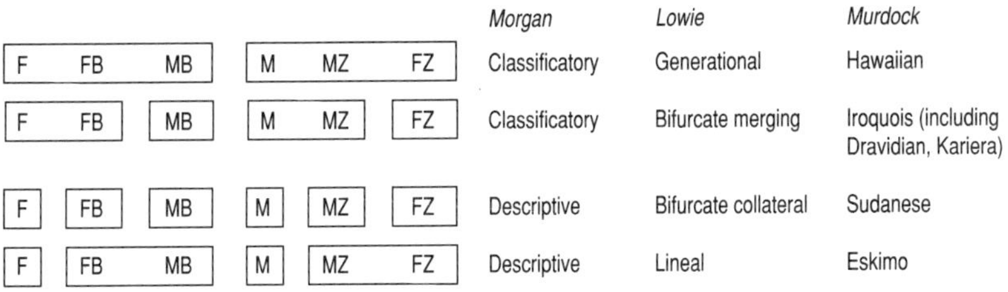

						Morgan	Lowie	Murdock
F FB MB			M MZ FZ			Classificatory	Generational	Hawaiian
F FB MB			M MZ		FZ	Classificatory	Bifurcate merging	Iroquois (including Dravidian, Kariera)
F	FB	MB	M	MZ	FZ	Descriptive	Bifurcate collateral	Sudanese
F	FB	MB	M	MZ FZ		Descriptive	Lineal	Eskimo

Source: Trautmann (1981).

Turning to Iroquois, the semantic order is identical to the Dravidian so long as we confine ourselves to immediate kin, but the Iroquois and Dravidian systems classify certain, more distant kin in opposite ways. These more distant kin are (1) the people my "parents" call "cousin" and (2) the children of the people I call "cousin." Members of each set are reciprocals of members of the other (parents and children are reciprocal kin of one another, for example; uncles and aunts are reciprocal kin to nephews and nieces, and vice-versa; and so forth).

In both the Iroquois and Dravidian systems, people call the children of their parents' same-sex siblings their "brothers" and "sisters" while they call the children of their parents' opposite-sex siblings their "cousins." Obviously, such "cousins" can be either male or female. In the Iroquois system, I consider my "parents'" same-sex "cousins" to be my parallel kin and my "parents'" opposite-sex "cousins" to be my cross kin. In the Dravidian system it is the opposite: my "parents'" same-sex "cousins" are my cross kin and my "parents'" opposite-sex "cousins" are my parallel kin. Similarly, in the Iroquois system, I consider my same-sex "cousin's" "child" to be parallel kin and my opposite-sex "cousin's" "child" to be cross kin. In the Dravidian system, I regard an opposite-sex "cousin" as a potential or presumed spouse, according to the rule of cross-cousin marriage, and so I classify that person's child as my "child" (parallel kin). The reversal of this and the other classifications in the Iroquois system suggests that the rule of cross-cousin marriage does not operate as an ordering principle in it.[4]

The difference in the classifications for crossness in Iroquois and Dravidian remained invisible to anthropologists for a very long time. Although Morgan was aware of differences in details between the two systems, he regarded them as essentially the same system and lumped them together in the supersystem called Classificatory (i.e., systems that merge FB with F, and so forth), as opposed to the Descriptive supersystem (systems that do not merge collaterals with lineals). In their typology, Robert Lowie (1928) and Paul Kirchhoff (1932) divided the entire universe of kinship terminologies into four categories—*generational, bifurcate merging, bifurcate collateral,* and *lineal*—on the basis of whether kin of the parents' generation were merged or not (see figure 1-2). In their scheme, Dravidian and Iroquois kinship terminologies again fall together, into the bifurcate merging class.

George Murdock devised a typology (1949) with similar properties, but he divided the universe of terminologies into six types rather than four. His Hawaiian, Iroquois, Sudanese, and Eskimo types correspond to the Lowie-Kirchhoff types of generational, bifurcate merging, bifurcate collateral, and lineal, respectively, but he added two additional types, which he called Crow and Omaha. Crow and Omaha are distinguished from the other types by the merging of unilineal kin of *different* generations and from one another by "skewing," in a matrilineal (Crow) or patrilineal (Omaha) direction. In Murdock's typology Dravidian terminology again falls into the Iroquois class.

Floyd Lounsbury (1964a) was the first scholar to clearly differentiate Iroquois and Dravidian as separate types, largely defined by the differences in crossness. More recent work on variation in crossness classifications has subdivided the semantic neighborhood of Dravidian and Iroquois still further. In 1959, Reay (1959, cited by Scheffler 1971) established the kinship system of the Kuma of Melanesia as an intermediate type of crossness between Dravidian and Iroquoian. In this volume, Viveiros de Castro (chapter 15) adds the kinship systems of the Yafar of New Guinea and the Ngawbe of Central America and provides the first comparison of the operation of crossness in all five systems (Dravidian, Iroquois, Kuma, Yafar, and Ngawbe).

At the same time as newly described variants are dividing the space between Dravidian and Iroquois crossness, Dravidian itself is being subdivided. The Dravidian system appears to have two major varieties, depending on whether crossness is lost or maintained in the grandparents' and grandchildren's generations (Trautmann 1981). In addition, Good (1980, 1981) has proposed the existence of a skewed variety of Dravidian characterized by the marriage of the elder sister's daughter (eZD) with the mother's younger brother (MyB). Normal Australian, formerly thought to be identical with Dravidian, now appears to be different, as Viveiros de Castro shows (chapter 15). Similarly, Iroquois appears to have four distinct variants, although the variety is probably less than meets the eye: one variant appears to be the same as Yafar, another the same as Ngawbe (see chapters 2, 3, and 15).

The growing number of variants obliges us to reconsider the types and to ask: Should these variants be regarded as distinct types in their own right or are some of the types mere variants of others? How do we decide the boundaries between types?

The work of Viveiros de Castro and Tjon Sie Fat provides the foundation for arriving at answers to these questions. Viveiros de Castro argues that there are sixteen possible classifications of cross cousins, of which only five have been recorded ethnographically: Dravidian, Iroquois, Kuma, Yafar, and Ngawbe. What are the relations among them? Tjon Sie Fat (1994) has recently suggested a way of conceptualizing the relations among four of these types of classifications (he omits Ngawbe) by modeling patterns of crossness in an abstract space represented by a hypercube (see figure 1-3).

In the hypercube, the sixteen variants of crossness that are theoretically possible form the nodes or vertices of the figure. Iroquois and Dravidian are two of these variants, located at a maximal distance from each other.[5] Note that this is not the usual three-dimensional diagram. Instead it has four dimensions that reflect the op-

Figure 1-3
Hypercube Modeling Sixteen Variants of Iroquois/Dravidian Crossness

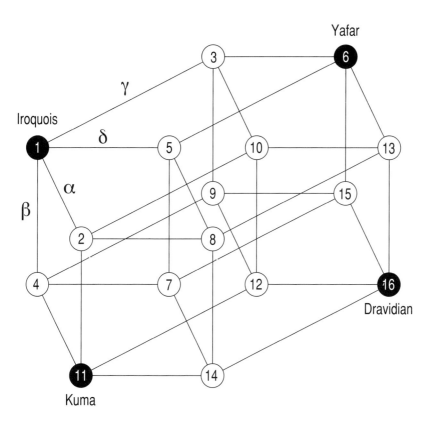

posite ways that the Iroquois and Dravidian systems assign crossness to four pairs of relations in the class of "parents'" "cousins" and "cousins'" "children." The distance between Iroquois and Dravidian is four steps; to transform one into the other, the crossness of four pairs of relations must be changed. Each step between nodes on the hypercube represents one reversal of crossness. The journey between Iroquois and Dravidian can take many routes—twenty-four to be exact. Two of these paths pass through two ethnographically attested variants, Kuma and Yafar. These two variants lie exactly two steps, or midway, between Iroquois and Dravidian along two of the twenty-four possible paths, but they do not lie on the same path. In other words, to travel between Iroquois and Dravidian, one can pass through Yafar or Kuma, or neither, but not both. Seen from another angle, Yafar and Kuma lie four steps apart from one another, with Dravidian and Iroquois between and equidistant from both, along two of the twenty-four minimal paths that connect them.

The Dravidian, Iroquois, Yafar, and Kuma systems provide ethnographic examples of four of the sixteen nodes, but what of the other twelve nodes? The types of crossness that correspond to these twelve nodes all contain some reciprocals that are inconsistent with respect to crossness. This feature suggests that Dravidian, Iroquois, Yafar, and Kuma may be stable types whereas the others are not; empirical examples of them might therefore be scarce. If, in fact, there are no actual cases that correspond to the remaining twelve nodes, we can conclude that variation among the different types is not limitless and that the four ethnographically attested types do not shade off into one another.

As this exercise of the hypercube suggests, the world of mathematical realities is round, and the trajectories among differing structures are ideally reversible. However, reversibility seems to be a rare phenomenon in the real world of sociological facts. Kinship terminologies change through time and over the long run, such changes seem to be irreversible. In the shorter term, however, a particular type of terminology can move in several directions out of a limited number of possible directions. The hypercube illustrates the possibility of such movements well, but it does not establish an overall directionality to the transformations. To discover such directionality, it would seem that we must look elsewhere. The essays in this volume suggest ways of doing so.

THE ESSAYS

The book is divided into five sections. The first sets the stage. The next three are devoted to specific regions: North America, South America, and Asia. And the concluding section discusses the overall direction of change in kinship terminologies.

The first two essays in the volume set the terms of the discussion. In chapter 2, Thomas R. Trautmann and R. H. Barnes return to Morgan's kinship data of the 1850s and 1860s. They develop the difference between Dravidian (Type A) and Iroquois (Type B) crossness and show that the latter is well grounded in Morgan's ethnography for North America. Next, Franklin Tjon Sie Fat gives an algebraic treatment of this distinction, establishing a gradient of associativity that is not quite fully achieved in Dravidian (full associativity being complete path-independence of kinship categories found in patrimoieties, for example). He confirms Trautmann and Barnes's claim that Dravidian, but not Iroquois, is based on bilateral cross-cousin marriage, but he further demonstrates for the first time several variant models of Iroquois and shows that Iroquois terminology, like Dravidian, is compatible with a positive marriage regime, in other words, with specific marriage rules. Systems such as Yafar and Mundugumur of New Guinea and Ngawbe of Central America find a place in his elaboration of the Iroquois structure.

Chapter 2 and the essays in the North American section cover most of the kinship systems found among Indian kinship systems in the United States and Canada. They show that if Morgan's travels had taken him further northwest to various Athapaskan-speaking peoples or to Ojibwa-speakers further to the north of those he reached in northern Michigan, he would have encountered Dravidianate systems that reflect symmetrical prescriptive marriage rules (in this case, bilateral cross-cousin marriage) instead of only Iroquois-like ones.

In chapter 4, John Ives finds Dravidian-like systems in his survey of the vast area comprising interior and southern Alaska, western Canada, and the western noncoastal areas of the United States, areas largely complementary to those from which Morgan derived his data. Ives shows that different "principles of group formation" act upon the Dravidian form to produce quite different social structures.

In chapter 5 on the Canadian Dene (northern Athapaskan) kinship systems, Michael Asch begins with the important point that kinship is not reducible to the terminology. He demonstrates that we must understand the kinship terminology in order to understand the structure of Dene society, which tends to divide into factions, and further that this knowledge is a source of power to the old women who monopolize it. His essay builds upon his earlier work among the Beaver (1972), which established the Dravidianate model for Athapaskan speakers of Canada, subsequently extended and elaborated by Ives in *A Theory of Northern Athapaskan Prehistory* (1990) and here in chapter 4.

Chapter 6, by Emmanuel Désveaux and Marion Selz, analyzes the kinship system of northern Ojibwas of Big Trout Lake in northwestern Ontario on the basis of ongoing fieldwork. Like Trautmann and Barnes, they accept a difference between Dravidian-like and Iroquois-like types among northern and southern Ojibwa-speakers respectively, Big Trout Lake being similar to Dravidian. They give this Dravidianate terminology an "alliance" interpretation in an exceptionally strong form, one in which the logic of the distinction between consanguines and affines is so overpowering that the "descent" perspective is reduced to zero, such that relations of co-descent have no role in crossness. Is such a system viable, or do all systems have both alliance and descent features? Whatever the answer, taking the argument to the limit, as they have, has the virtue of helping to clarify the interpretive choices by revealing their consequences.

The South American section opens with an essay by Alf Hornborg (chapter 7). His earlier study, *Dualism and Hierarchy in Lowland South America* (1988), was a useful synthesis of the expanding ethnography of the region, and his 1993 article on "Panoan marriage sections" made the case that the Panoan section-like systems are transformations of Dravidian systems—a point that converges with the views of Viveiros de Castro. Here, Hornborg develops the concept of "serial redundancy" to show how different kinship systems are intertwined in geographical space, and his concluding model of congruities or possible transformations of kinship systems resembles the overlapping fibers in a thread, the metaphor with which he opens his essay.

Anne-Christine Taylor demonstrates in chapter 8 that despite their many differences the seven groups belonging to the Jivaro-Candoa language family constitute a vast series of structural transformations of a single model, which is typically Dravidian in character. She focuses on three cases: Achuar and Aguaruna of the Jivaro branch, Kandoshi of the Candoa branch. Here the ideal marriage rule is one of symmetrical restricted exchange, but its application ranges from the elementary formula of local exchange of marriage partners among "close" people to the complex formula of distant marriages of a man with the "father's father's sister's daughter's daughter" (FFZDD) within wider and wider areas, which constitute political units. This widening is accompanied by the emergence of several distinctions that supplement the Dravidian structure: a twofold distinction of lineal and collateral, and a threefold distinction of true consanguines, potential affines and affinal consanguines, and true affines. To arrive at these findings, Taylor develops an analytical strategy that promises to be of great value, which involves close comparison of the reference terminology (kinship terms that people use when referring to one another) with the address terminology (those they use when addressing one another), showing how some kinship categories in the reference terminology change polarity in respect of the consanguine/affine distinction, so to speak, in the address terminology. Kinship and language act together, Taylor argues, as diacritics that mark tribal identities among peoples whose kinship systems and languages are, at a deeper level, unitary.

In chapter 9 Michael Houseman and Douglas R. White develop a new method of representing Dravidian-like kinship systems that visually renders both empirical cases and ideal-type models—the "statistical" and "mechanical" models of Lévi-Strauss's well-known discussion (1969:xxvii ff.)—in the same register, so that they can be directly compared. They introduce into the discussion of Dravidianate systems a rigorous graphic modeling of actual marriage networks that is based on their concept of "sidedness," which occupies a middle ground between the egocentric structure of the kinship terminology and sociocentric structures of social groupings, such as moieties and marriage sections. Their elegant new instrument has a number of promising possible applications in kinship studies.

The section on South America concludes with chapter 10 by France-Marie Renard-Casevitz, who focuses on the Campa of Peru. The Campa have two languages of kinship, one for males and one for females, and they regard the male language to be superior. In some ways, the Campa case is the inverse of the Dene described by Asch (chapter 5), for whom kinship knowledge is a female privilege. Renard-Casevitz's essay is one of a growing number of studies that demonstrate the need for sophisticated descriptions of the kinship systems of single societies in order to do justice to the variability inherent in them.

The section titled "Asia" focuses on India and Indonesia. It opens with Robert Parkin's essay (chapter 11), which reports on the first Iroquois-like system to be discovered in South Asia, which he described previously in his 1992 synthesis of the Munda kinship systems. Parkin uses the Dravidian/Iroquois distinction to rethink the kinship history of the entire Indian subcontinent in its three distinct linguistic groupings: Munda, Dravidian, and Indo-Aryan.

Jean-François Guermonprez then takes the discussion to eastern Indonesia in chapter 12. He offers a new view of the directionality of change that sets the conventional (Needhamite) wisdom on its head. Guermonprez argues that asymmetric (nonreciprocal) prescriptive terminologies of that region develop out of bilateral (cognatic) systems rather than moving from symmetric (reciprocal) systems toward cognatic systems.

The last section, "Big Picture," opens with Michael Kryukov's essay (chapter 13), much of which is germane to the regional survey of Asia in the preceding section. In his earlier work on the history of kinship in China (1972), Kryukov showed a symmetric prescriptive (Dravidian-like) ancient past for Chinese kinship, one that subsequently developed into a terminology of the Sudanese type. In his essay in this volume, he analyzes kinship systems of the Southeast Asian borderland of China according to methods for the historical analysis of kinship systems pioneered in the nineteenth century by P. A. Lavrovski, whose work is introduced to the West for the first time here. Kryukov suggests that if kinship relationships previously distinguished by different terms are moving in the direction of fusion under a single term, then the change will start at ego's generation (G^0). Alternatively, if the change is going in the opposite direction—from a single term to different terms— the change will start at the first ascending generation (G^{+1}). By way of example, he describes the transformation of a symmetric prescriptive system (in which marital exchanges are reciprocal) into an asymmetric one (in which one group of kin provide spouses for another kin group but do not receive any spouses from them in return). He also gives a contrary example, in which a Dravidian-like prescriptive system is transformed into an Iroquois-like non-prescriptive system.

In chapter 14, N. J. Allen develops what he calls a "tetradic" theory of kinship terminology by imagining the most economical kinship terminology possible, one that has only four terms (or eight if the distinction of sex is added in). He then considers the relations of all other types of terminology to the tetradic standard. In its weak form, his theory simply clarifies the logical relations among kinship terminological types, but the strong form presented here offers a comprehensive evolutionary model of kinship systems. According to this model, the overall direction of change in these systems involved the breaking down, or breaking open, of an original tetradic system, and with it a proliferation of kinship categories and terms. Dravidian and Australian systems are close to the tetradic starting point; others are farther away from it, since the historical process is the largely irreversible one of the rupture of equations, such as the Dravidian equation MB = FZH = SpF (i.e., a single term for mother's brother, father's sister's husband and spouse's father) decaying into separate categories (that is, separate terms for uncle and father-in-law in post-Dravidian systems).

In contrast to Allen, who moves in a world of pure models, Viveiros de Castro in chapter 15 pursues the Dravidian system and its structural relatives in real-world settings around the globe. His project can perhaps be best described as the third step in the analysis of the same-but-different Dravidian and Iroquois forms of crossness. In the first step (represented in this volume by Trautmann and Barnes, chapter 2), the two systems are shown to differ primarily in the presence (Dravidian) or absence (Iroquois) of a rule of cross-cousin marriage. In the second step (Tjon Sie Fat, chapter 3), the variability of the Iroquois type of crossness and its compatibility with some form of a rule of cross-cousin marriage are demonstrated. In the third step, Viveiros de Castro attempts to show that *all* types of "crossness" can be associated with some set of marriage rules, even if these rules do not involve prescriptive cross-cousin marriage. His "metaterminological" account attempts to find a single generalized structure that encompasses all types of crossness, from Dravidianate to Crow-Omaha, under a single structural law. In his scheme, the symmetric exchange of marriage partners that took place in the parents' generation creates an opposition between consanguines and affines. This opposition in the parents' generation and its power to define alliances in subsequent generations remain constant in all the types of crossness. Finally, in the Afterword (chapter 16) Maurice Godelier brings the volume to a close by examining the place of kinship terminologies within the domain of kinship and in relation to the classic problem of kinship studies, the origin of the incest tabu.

FUTURE RESEARCH

Where do we go from here? What next steps offer the best prospects for advancing the inquiry into the transformations of kinship systems? Taken together, the studies in this volume suggest that we should turn our attention to the unevennesses of our subject—that is, to describing and explaining the uneven distribution of kinship types across the various regions of the world, and to repairing the uneven development of analysis of the different types.

The Uneven Distribution of Kinship Types

One result of the Maison Suger discussions is a greater appreciation of the variety and relatedness of systems that are in the "near vicinity" of the Dravidian. The hypercube (figure 1-3) seems to imply that a world in which Dravidian and Iroquois exist is a world that also contains its intermediate types, Yafar and Kuma. At this stage of analysis, we employ the method of Tylor, and invoke the possibilities of the human mind in general at a more structural level. Turning to Morgan's North American data, one can identify Red Knife as the North American counterpart of Yafar and model the variation among Morgan's eighty North American peoples as a band of variation along the face of the hypercube that extends between Iroquois and Yafar (see the appendix to this chapter). Doing so employs the method of Morgan and assumes historically related systems within a culture area. But we now know that just beyond the area in which Morgan collected his data, systems exist that are similar to the Dravidian, and both Iroquois- and Dravidian-like systems are found within a single linguistic group, the Ojibwa. Our hypercube functions at several levels, modeling not only the whole world of kinship systems but also the North American world and the Ojibwa-speaking populations as a subset of it. Does the model imply that, since we find Iroquois-, Dravidian-, and Yafar-like systems in North America, we should expect also to find instances of Kuma-like ones there? Or again, if we find Iroquois-like and Dravidian-like phases among Ojibwa-speakers, should we also find intermediate (Yafar and Kuma) phases in the intermediate ranges?

Probably not. The world is full of unevennesses, and the beauty of the hypercube is that it provides a perfectly symmetrical baseline of possibilities against which to evaluate the data that we encounter. It tells us what to look for, but we must determine through empirical research which types actually exist and then explain the significance of the presence or absence of specific types. What does it mean for

India, for instance, to find that Ojibwa-speakers have both Dravidian-like and Iroquois-like phases of their kinship system? To begin with, the appearance of the two kinship systems in distinct but historically linked northern Athapaskan communities suggests that Iroquois-like systems might also be encountered in South Asia alongside the Dravidian systems traditionally associated with this region. The Maison Suger conversations stimulated Parkin to undertake such a search, which resulted in his discovery of the first Iroquois-like system there. But does this discovery mean that many more Iroquois-like systems will be found in South Asia? If not, what does the scarcity or absence of Iroquois- (and Yafar- and Kuma-) like systems in South Asia mean? And how can we explain the situation in Africa, where Iroquois-like systems appear to be abundant and Dravidianate systems absent? These questions are difficult to answer. Any attempt to do so must, as a first step, undertake regional inventories, especially in the regions not covered in this volume, most notably, Africa and Europe.

The Uneven Development of Kinship Analyses

The study of kinship types is itself uneven. The kinship phenomena on which the essays in this volume focus are the same as those that have attracted the attention of anthropologists since the invention of kinship analysis: Dravidian, Australian, and the cross-cousin rule of marriage. Crow-Omaha, the subject on which Françoise Héritier and her associates have written so extensively, weaves in and out of this book, but only at its margins. We know next to nothing about the kinship systems that fall under Murdock's classes of Sudanese and Hawaiian, largely because little research has been conducted on these types since the 1960s. The next step here, at least in principle, should be to investigate and illuminate those systems that previous analysis has tended to neglect.

A final consideration for the future direction of research comes from a problem posed by the kinship terminologies of three peoples of the Apachean language group—the Navajo, the Western Apache, and the Jicarilla Apache—in a study by Donald and Tighe (1986). All three terminologies show an Iroquois-like crossness in which the terms for same-sex siblings are merged, as are some terms for lineal and collateral relatives. However, two of these systems (Navajo and Western Apache) also show the matrilineal skewing found in the Crow type. The skewing is limited in scope and the resulting merging of terms across generations within matrilines is so infrequent that scholars have not recognized these systems as being like Crow. Nevertheless, the skewing rule in these systems is structured just like Lounsbury's Crow III rule (Lounsbury 1964b). Thus one may say that all three linguistically related terminologies have Iroquois-like crossness, and two of them also have a Crow-like skewing.

How should a case that has both Iroquois and Crow features be classified? Donald and Tighe suggest that all systems that contain a skewing rule, however limited in scope, should be classified as Crow-Omaha. If their position is accepted, Navajo and Western Apache cease to be classified as Iroquois and are reclassified as Crow, while Jicarilla Apache remains Iroquois.

We draw a different conclusion. For us, the mixing and coexistence of such features within single systems should not compel us to place them in one category or the other. Indeed, doing so tends to obscure rather than consolidate the progress of the study of variations among related kinship systems. What one wants to know is not which category is more appropriate but what features can combine in various ways to form concrete systems in the real world.

For these and other purposes, it may be helpful to shift the project of classification from the "atomic" level of the six Murdockian types to the "subatomic" level of the constituent particles (generation, gender, crossness, skewing, and so on) that join in different combinations to form the types. Donald and Tighe stress the importance of further research, both empirical and theoretical, on the range of variation within and among (Murdockian) categories such as Crow, Omaha, and Iroquois. As their chapter and this book as a whole suggest, such research will probably lead to an erosion or realignment of the boundaries and defining characteristics of the orthodox categories, and to a better understanding of their transformations.

APPENDIX: CONSTRUCTING THE HYPERCUBE

All current discussion of crossness takes as its point of departure the classic essay by Louis Dumont (1953), "The Dravidian Kinship Terminology as an Expression of Marriage." In it Dumont shows that the cross/parallel distinction derives from the distinction between consanguines and affines.[6]

Trautmann (1981:177–85) confirms Dumont's argument by devising rules of composition, that is, rules for determining crossness of a relative's relative, within Dravidian systems. A person's primary consanguines (C) are that person's father, mother, brothers, sisters, sons, and daughters; her husband or his wife is the primary affine (A). The universe of these primary relatives' relatives consists of the consanguines' consanguines (CC), the consanguines' affines (CA), the affines' consanguines (AC), and the affines' affines (AA). These relatives' relatives are themselves classified as consanguines or affines by application of the rules, and the outcomes are equivalent to parallel or cross respectively in Dravidian classifications (see figure 1-4).[7] In the notation, the operators C and A often have to be further specified as of the senior (+) or junior (-) generation and of the same (=) or opposite (≠) sex as the relative to the left, which in the limiting case is ego.

In table 3-1, Tjon Sie Fat presents this algebra as a 12 × 12 table of compositions, that is, as a kind of multiplication table in the form, relative × relative = relative's relative. This multiplication table contains 144 cells that give the crossness of a relative's relative as either cross (A) or parallel (C), which correspond to affines and consanguines, respectively. Further, he gives a table of compositions for Iroquois (table 3-2) that is comparable to the one for Dravidian, implying that Iroquois crossness, too, is in some sense a particular configuration of the distinction between consanguines and affines.

Figure 1-4
Equivalence Rules for Crossness (after Trautmann, 1981)

1.1 $A^0C^0 \to A^0$
1.2 $A^0A^0 \to C^0$
1.3 $C^0A^0 \to A^0$
1.4 $C^0C^0 \to C^0$

2.1 $C^+\left(\begin{array}{c}C^0_{\neq}\\A^0_{=}\end{array}\right) \to A^+$

2.2 $C^+\left(\begin{array}{c}C^0_{=}\\A^0_{\neq}\end{array}\right) \to C^+$

2.3 $A^+\left(\begin{array}{c}C^0_{\neq}\\A^0_{=}\end{array}\right) \to C^+$

2.4 $A^+\left(\begin{array}{c}C^0_{=}\\A^0_{\neq}\end{array}\right) \to A^+$

3.1 $A^+C^- \to A^0$
3.2 $A^+A^- \to C^0$
3.3 $C^+A^- \to A^0$
3.4 $C^+C^- \to C^0$

4.1 $\left(\begin{array}{c}C^0_{\neq}\\A^0_{=}\end{array}\right)\ C^- \to A^-$

4.2 $\left(\begin{array}{c}C^0_{=}\\A^0_{\neq}\end{array}\right)\ C^- \to C^-$

4.3 $\left(\begin{array}{c}C^0_{\neq}\\A^0_{=}\end{array}\right)\ A^- \to C^-$

4.4 $\left(\begin{array}{c}C^0_{=}\\A^0_{\neq}\end{array}\right)\ A^- \to A^-$

5.1 $A^0C^+ \to A^+$
5.2 $A^0A^+ \to C^+$
5.3 $C^0A^+ \to A^+$
5.4 $C^0C^+ \to C^+$

6.1 $\left\{\begin{array}{c}(C^-C^+)_{\neq}\\(C^-A^+)_{=}\end{array}\right\} \to A^0$

6.2 $\left\{\begin{array}{c}(C^-C^+)_{=}\\(C^-A^+)_{\neq}\end{array}\right\} \to C^0$

6.3 $\left\{\begin{array}{c}(A^-C^+)_{\neq}\\(A^-A^+)_{=}\end{array}\right\} \to C^0$

6.4 $\left\{\begin{array}{c}(A^-C^+)_{=}\\(A^-A^+)_{\neq}\end{array}\right\} \to A^0$

7.1 $A^-C^0 \to A^-$
7.2 $A^-A^0 \to C^-$
7.3 $C^-A^0 \to A^-$
7.4 $C^-C^0 \to C^-$
8.1a $A^+C^+ \to A^{++}$
8.2a $A^+A^+ \to C^{++}$
8.3a $C^+A^+ \to A^{++}$
8.4a $C^+C^+ \to C^{++}$
9.1a $A^-C^- \to A^{--}$
9.2a $A^-A^- \to C^{--}$
9.3a $C^-A^- \to A^{--}$
9.4a $C^-C^- \to C^{--}$

8.1b $C^+\left(\begin{array}{c}C^+_{\neq}\\A^+_{=}\end{array}\right) \to A^{++}$

8.2b $C^+\left(\begin{array}{c}C^+_{=}\\A^+_{\neq}\end{array}\right) \to C^{++}$

8.3b $A^+\left(\begin{array}{c}C^+_{\neq}\\A^+_{=}\end{array}\right) \to C^{++}$

8.4b $A^+\left(\begin{array}{c}C^+_{=}\\A^+_{\neq}\end{array}\right) \to A^{++}$

9.1b $\left(\begin{array}{c}C^-_{\neq}\\A^-_{=}\end{array}\right)\ C^- \to A^{--}$

9.2b $\left(\begin{array}{c}C^-_{=}\\A^-_{\neq}\end{array}\right)\ C^- \to C^{--}$

9.3b $\left(\begin{array}{c}C^-_{\neq}\\A^-_{=}\end{array}\right)\ A^- \to C^{--}$

9.4b $\left(\begin{array}{c}C^-_{=}\\A^-_{\neq}\end{array}\right)\ A^- \to A^{--}$

The number of all possible transformations of the crossness of one of these tables of compositions is a horrendously large number (2^{144}, or 2.23×10^{43}), which, though less than the number of particles in the universe (10^{87}), is nevertheless greater than the number of grains of sand at Coney Island (10^{20}) (Kasner and Newman, in Wells 1986). In order to keep the numbers of features manageably small, the discussion of types of crossness must focus closely on a few features that empirical study shows to be salient.

If we ask how we might move between Iroquois and Dravidian in the fewest possible steps, it becomes apparent that only 4 pairs of compositions out of the 144 in each table constitute the difference between the tables of the two polar types, which are identical with respect to the other cells. Using the "plain English" form previously introduced, the four pairs of kin that differ between the Dravidian and Iroquois tables will be the "parents'" "cousins" and the "cousins'" "children," which of course are reciprocals of one another.

If all eight cells of the Dravidian composition table are changed to the opposite value of crossness, the Dravidian model is transmuted into the Iroquois, and vice versa. Since the eight transformations are four pairs of reciprocals, which must vary together in order to maintain reciprocal consistency, they may be treated as four transformations, constituting a four-dimensional universe with sixteen entries or possible types of crossness (table 1-1).[8]

In table 1-1, four types of crossness are ethnographically attested out of sixteen possible types. The canonical Iroquois form is no. 1 and the canonical Dravidian is no. 16. Between them are fourteen variants, but not all of these variants necessarily fall on the same path or trajectory. The Iroquois outcomes (unshaded) are parallel (consanguineal) for the first four terms, cross (affinal) for the second four. The Dravidian pattern (shaded) is the reverse. The variants that lie between are similar to both but identical to neither Iroquois nor Dravidian, as one may see by looking at the patterning of unshaded (Iroquois-like) and shaded (Dravidian-like) outcomes.

Two further ethnographic identifications of the theoretical possibilities may be made: the Yafar pattern is no. 6 and the Kuma pattern is no. 11. These types were found by reconstructing each of the sixteen variants, deriving the crossness pattern for a range of $G^{\pm 1}$ and G^0 kin types for all sixteen variants, and then searching through the ethnographic record. Examination of these sixteen variant kin types shows that the Iroquois, Yafar, Kuma, and Dravidian types have fully consistent reciprocals, whereas all the other theoretical types have some reciprocals that are inconsistent with respect to crossness. All of this seems to say that the Iroquois, Yafar, Kuma, and Dravidian are stable types, whereas the other possibilities are not; empirical examples of the latter might therefore be scarce.

One can model the entire configuration of sixteen variants as the vertices, or nodes, of a four-dimensional Boolean hypercube, or tesseract, with sixteen vertices, thirty-two edges, twenty-four faces, and eight cells (figure 1-3). Each node or theoretical variant type of crossness reckoning is directly connected to four neighbors by an edge, constituting the shortest distance between them along the hypercube, a journey of a single step so to speak, representing a change of crossness in one pair of the eight diagnostic compositions. There are multiple paths connecting any two

Table 1-1
Diagnostic Compositions for Sixteen Variants of Iroquois/Dravidian Crossness

Cell	1 (I)	2	3	4	5	6 (Y)	7	8	9	10	11 (K)	12	13	14	15	16 (D)
α_1	$C_=^{-1}$	$A_=^{-1}$	$C_=^{-1}$	$C_=^{-1}$	$C_=^{-1}$	$C_=^{-1}$	$C_=^{-1}$	$A_=^{-1}$	$C_=^{-1}$	$A_=^{-1}$	$A_=^{-1}$	$A_=^{-1}$	$A_=^{-1}$	$A_=^{-1}$	$C_=^{-1}$	$A_=^{-1}$
α_2	$C_=^{+1}$	$A_=^{+1}$	$C_=^{+1}$	$C_=^{+1}$	$C_=^{+1}$	$C_=^{+1}$	$C_=^{+1}$	$A_=^{+1}$	$C_=^{+1}$	$A_=^{+1}$	$A_=^{+1}$	$A_=^{+1}$	$A_=^{+1}$	$A_=^{+1}$	$C_=^{+1}$	$A_=^{+1}$
β_1	$C_{\neq}^{-1}$	$C_{\neq}^{-1}$	$C_{\neq}^{-1}$	$A_{\neq}^{-1}$	$C_{\neq}^{-1}$	$C_{\neq}^{-1}$	$A_{\neq}^{-1}$	$C_{\neq}^{-1}$	$A_{\neq}^{-1}$	$C_{\neq}^{-1}$	$A_{\neq}^{-1}$	$A_{\neq}^{-1}$	$C_{\neq}^{-1}$	$A_{\neq}^{-1}$	$A_{\neq}^{-1}$	$A_{\neq}^{-1}$
β_2	$C_{\neq}^{+1}$	$C_{\neq}^{+1}$	$C_{\neq}^{+1}$	$A_{\neq}^{+1}$	$C_{\neq}^{+1}$	$C_{\neq}^{+1}$	$A_{\neq}^{+1}$	$C_{\neq}^{+1}$	$A_{\neq}^{+1}$	$C_{\neq}^{+1}$	$A_{\neq}^{+1}$	$A_{\neq}^{+1}$	$C_{\neq}^{+1}$	$A_{\neq}^{+1}$	$A_{\neq}^{+1}$	$A_{\neq}^{+1}$
γ_1	$A_{\neq}^{-1}$	$A_{\neq}^{-1}$	$C_{\neq}^{-1}$	$A_{\neq}^{-1}$	$A_{\neq}^{-1}$	$C_{\neq}^{-1}$	$A_{\neq}^{-1}$	$A_{\neq}^{-1}$	$C_{\neq}^{-1}$	$C_{\neq}^{-1}$	$A_{\neq}^{-1}$	$C_{\neq}^{-1}$	$C_{\neq}^{-1}$	$A_{\neq}^{-1}$	$C_{\neq}^{-1}$	$C_{\neq}^{-1}$
γ_2	$A_{\neq}^{+1}$	$A_{\neq}^{+1}$	$C_{\neq}^{+1}$	$A_{\neq}^{+1}$	$A_{\neq}^{+1}$	$C_{\neq}^{+1}$	$A_{\neq}^{+1}$	$A_{\neq}^{+1}$	$C_{\neq}^{+1}$	$C_{\neq}^{+1}$	$A_{\neq}^{+1}$	$C_{\neq}^{+1}$	$C_{\neq}^{+1}$	$A_{\neq}^{+1}$	$C_{\neq}^{+1}$	$C_{\neq}^{+1}$
δ_1	$A_=^{-1}$	$A_=^{-1}$	$A_=^{-1}$	$A_=^{-1}$	$C_=^{-1}$	$C_=^{-1}$	$C_=^{-1}$	$C_=^{-1}$	$A_=^{-1}$	$A_=^{-1}$	$A_=^{-1}$	$A_=^{-1}$	$C_=^{-1}$	$C_=^{-1}$	$C_=^{-1}$	$C_=^{-1}$
δ_2	$A_=^{+1}$	$A_=^{+1}$	$A_=^{+1}$	$A_=^{+1}$	$C_=^{+1}$	$C_=^{+1}$	$C_=^{+1}$	$C_=^{+1}$	$A_=^{+1}$	$A_=^{+1}$	$A_=^{+1}$	$A_=^{+1}$	$C_=^{+1}$	$C_=^{+1}$	$C_=^{+1}$	$C_=^{+1}$

Key:
$\alpha1$ Same-sex "cousin's" same-sex "child."
$\alpha2$ Same-sex "parent's" same-sex "cousin."
$\beta1$ Same-sex "cousin's" opposite-sex "child."
$\beta2$ Opposite-sex "parent's" same-sex "cousin."
$\gamma1$ Opposite-sex "cousin's" same-sex "child."
$\gamma2$ Same-sex "parent's" opposite-sex "cousin."
$\delta1$ Opposite-sex "cousin's" opposite-sex "child."
$\delta2$ Opposite-sex "parent's" opposite-sex "cousin."

nodes situated at a distance of more than one unit. There are exactly two paths connecting any pair of variants situated at distance two; six distinct paths between variants at distance three, and twenty-four paths linking variants at the maximal distance of four units. The distance between Iroquois and Dravidian in this figure is four steps, and Yafar and Kuma lie equidistant from both at two steps in between. In making the shortest walk between Iroquois and Dravidian, Yafar and Kuma lie midway along two of the twenty-four possible paths, but they do not lie on the same path. Relations among the pairs of four systems is such that Yafar and Kuma also lie four steps apart, with Dravidian and Iroquois in between and equidistant from both, along two of the twenty-four minimal paths that connect them.

The hypercube, as the abstract landscape or substratum on which the sixteen types and variants are situated, invites investigation into the sociological constraints on the logically possible walks among them. As already mentioned, the full consistency of reciprocals of the four types and the partial inconsistency of the other twelve are logical characters that may point to sociological stability and instability, respectively. Other variant systems of crossness reckoning with inconsistencies in G^0 (not included in the foregoing study of sixteen variants) might indicate that a further structural switch to a more fully generational pattern would be the next step. But such a conclusion is highly speculative at this point.

Other ways of employing the hypercube to model relations among kinship types suggest themselves. Instead of identifying each separate node of the hypercube with a distinct terminology or society, one could also consider the possibility of a society spanning or encompassing the range of variation represented by an edge (two adjacent nodes), a face (four vertices), or any other subset of nodes on the hypercube. Under this interpretation, different individuals, the members of different sociological categories (children and adults, males and females, adjacent segmentary lineages), and so forth might defend or explicate different variants of a basic model. Examples are the two or three patterns for the Yafar mentioned by Juillerat (1977), and reports of the coexistence of skewed and unskewed terminologies among the Fanti by Kronenfeld (1980). Viveiros de Castro (chapter 15) also gives an example of this kind of internal variation in the Dravidian/Australian models, which he shows to coexist in the kinship universe of the Amazonian Panoans. Anthropologists should not continue to attempt to reduce all variation in such information within a given society to a unitary system. Better technical means of recognizing and modeling such variation are needed, and the hypercube seems to offer this.

Consider one further elaboration of the model. Morgan published eighty North American Indian terminologies in table II of his *Systems of Consanguinity and Affinity* (1871), giving classifications for more than two hundred genealogical positions. Trautmann and Barnes (chapter 2 and 1991) considered these classifications in terms of twenty of the numbered genealogical positions that distinguished between canonical Iroquois and Dravidian patterns for crossness. None of the eighty North American terminologies in Morgan's table shows a Dravidian pattern, so the variation among them pulls toward the Iroquois node of the hypercube given in figure 1-3. Tjon Sie Fat (chapter 3) identifies Trautmann and Barnes's Iroquois Type B-variant 2 with the fully consistent Yafar model (node no. 6 of the hypercube). A more specific range of variation can be depicted by focusing on the face of the hypercube bounded by the vertices 1, 3, 5, and 6 (the uppermost parallelogram in figure 1-3) and zooming in. This is done by holding constant the "Iroquois" or Type B values for two of the four pairs of compositions and allowing maximal transformations of the others, which now no longer vary as pairs, such that the consistency of reciprocals is not maintained in all cases (see table 1-2). In effect, the area around the four nodes numbered 1, 3, 5, and 6 are blown up to make a *new* hypercube of sixteen vertices, representing sixteen possible types of crossness reckoning, but one in which the "Iroquois" (no. 1) and the original "Yafar" (no. 6) nodes are now situated at a maximal distance of four units (figure 1-5).

Looking at the patterning for close $G^{\pm 1}$ kin types, we find something approximating the full range of possible variation exemplified in the eighty North American kinship terminologies reported in Morgan's *Systems of Consanguinity,* table II, as analyzed by Trautmann and Barnes:

1. Hypercube node no. 1 ("Iroquois") now covers the Seneca (1), the Dakota (10–17), the Cree (37–39), the Ojibwa (40–44), the Blackfoot (57–58), the Micmac (59) and the Etchemin or Malisete (60). The Dakota-Isauntie (9) differ slightly from node no. 1 on the

Table 1-2
Diagnostic Compositions for Sixteen North American "Iroquois" Variants Reported in Morgan, *Systems of Consanguinity* (1871: Table II)

Cell	1 / I	22	23	24	25	3	27	28	29	30	5	32	33	34	35	6 / Y
α_1	$C^{-1}_{=}$	$C^{-1}_{=}$	$C^{-1}_{=}$	$C^{-1}_{=}$	$C^{-1}_{=}$	$C^{-1}_{=}$	$C^{-1}_{=}$	$C^{-1}_{=}$	$C^{-1}_{=}$	$C^{-1}_{=}$	$C^{-1}_{=}$	$C^{-1}_{=}$	$C^{-1}_{=}$	$C^{-1}_{=}$	$C^{-1}_{=}$	$C^{-1}_{=}$
α_2	$C^{+1}_{=}$	$C^{+1}_{=}$	$C^{+1}_{=}$	$C^{+1}_{=}$	$C^{+1}_{=}$	$C^{+1}_{=}$	$C^{+1}_{=}$	$C^{+1}_{=}$	$C^{+1}_{=}$	$C^{+1}_{=}$	$C^{+1}_{=}$	$C^{+1}_{=}$	$C^{+1}_{=}$	$C^{+1}_{=}$	$C^{+1}_{=}$	$C^{+1}_{=}$
β_1	$C^{-1}_{\neq}$	$C^{-1}_{\neq}$	$C^{-1}_{\neq}$	$C^{-1}_{\neq}$	$C^{-1}_{\neq}$	$C^{-1}_{\neq}$	$C^{-1}_{\neq}$	$C^{-1}_{\neq}$	$C^{-1}_{\neq}$	$C^{-1}_{\neq}$	$C^{-1}_{\neq}$	$C^{-1}_{\neq}$	$C^{-1}_{\neq}$	$C^{-1}_{\neq}$	$C^{-1}_{\neq}$	$C^{-1}_{\neq}$
β_2	$C^{+1}_{\neq}$	$C^{+1}_{\neq}$	$C^{+1}_{\neq}$	$C^{+1}_{\neq}$	$C^{+1}_{\neq}$	$C^{+1}_{\neq}$	$C^{+1}_{\neq}$	$C^{+1}_{\neq}$	$C^{+1}_{\neq}$	$C^{+1}_{\neq}$	$C^{+1}_{\neq}$	$C^{+1}_{\neq}$	$C^{+1}_{\neq}$	$C^{+1}_{\neq}$	$C^{+1}_{\neq}$	$C^{+1}_{\neq}$
γ_1	$A^{-1}_{\neq}$	$C^{-1}_{\neq}$	$A^{-1}_{\neq}$	$A^{-1}_{\neq}$	$A^{-1}_{\neq}$	$C^{-1}_{\neq}$	$C^{-1}_{\neq}$	$C^{-1}_{\neq}$	$A^{-1}_{\neq}$	$A^{-1}_{\neq}$	$A^{-1}_{\neq}$	$C^{-1}_{\neq}$	$C^{-1}_{\neq}$	$C^{-1}_{\neq}$	$A^{-1}_{\neq}$	$C^{-1}_{\neq}$
γ_2	$A^{+1}_{\neq}$	$A^{+1}_{\neq}$	$C^{+1}_{\neq}$	$A^{+1}_{\neq}$	$A^{+1}_{\neq}$	$C^{+1}_{\neq}$	$A^{+1}_{\neq}$	$A^{+1}_{\neq}$	$C^{+1}_{\neq}$	$C^{+1}_{\neq}$	$A^{+1}_{\neq}$	$C^{+1}_{\neq}$	$C^{+1}_{\neq}$	$A^{+1}_{\neq}$	$C^{+1}_{\neq}$	$C^{+1}_{\neq}$
δ_1	$A^{-1}_{=}$	$A^{-1}_{=}$	$A^{-1}_{=}$	$C^{-1}_{=}$	$A^{-1}_{=}$	$A^{-1}_{=}$	$C^{-1}_{=}$	$A^{-1}_{=}$	$C^{-1}_{=}$	$A^{-1}_{=}$	$C^{-1}_{=}$	$C^{-1}_{=}$	$A^{-1}_{=}$	$C^{-1}_{=}$	$C^{-1}_{=}$	$C^{-1}_{=}$
δ_2	$A^{+1}_{=}$	$A^{+1}_{=}$	$A^{+1}_{=}$	$A^{+1}_{=}$	$C^{+1}_{=}$	$A^{+1}_{=}$	$A^{+1}_{=}$	$C^{+1}_{=}$	$A^{+1}_{=}$	$C^{+1}_{=}$	$C^{+1}_{=}$	$A^{+1}_{=}$	$C^{+1}_{=}$	$C^{+1}_{=}$	$C^{+1}_{=}$	$C^{+1}_{=}$

hypercube by classifying Morgan 104 as 0 "daughter" instead of 1 "niece."

2. At the opposite pole, node no. 6 ("Yafar") is occupied by the Red-Knife (66) who, merging all G^{-1} kin in the positions examined with parallel kin ("sons" or "daughters"), appear to follow the full "Yafar" pattern. The Hare Indians (65) are a close approximation, with only the entry for Morgan 107 diverging ("nephew" instead of "son").

3. All other relevant terminologies of Morgan's table II are situated somewhere in between, namely, the remaining five nations of the Iroquois: the Cayuga, Onondaga, Oneida, Mohawk, and Tuscarora (2–6), the related Two Mountain Iroquois (7) and Wyandotte (8), and also the Mohegan (61), the Delaware (62), the Munsee (63), and the Slave Lake Indians (64). It should be possible to allocate these to specific nodes on the hypercube.

4. This model predicts that all variants of the hypercube, from "Iroquois" to "Yafar" or "Seneca" to "Red Knife," should classify Morgan kintypes 132, 134, 106, 108, 127, 129, 101, and 103 as parallel kin ("son," "daughter," or "stepchild"). *There are no exceptions in the data.*

These "walks around the hypercube" are not the only way to formalize or visualize the pattern of relations between various types of crossness or the empirical terminologies that manifest them. The thought-experiment of the hypercube, motivated by a desire to understand the transformations of kinship systems, comes out of a

Figure 1-5
Hypercube Modeling Sixteen Variants of Crossness among Eighty North American
Systems Reported in Morgan, *Systems of Consanguinity* (1871: Table II)

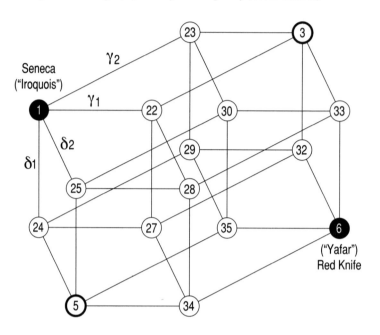

meditation on some of the issues that evolutionary biologists have addressed in
their discussions of evolutionary "walks." Evolutionary biologists seem to be concerned with a number of related questions: the structure of "genotypic" space, the
structure of "phenotypic" space, and the construction of theories relating genotype
to phenotype and to changes or variation in both. Their goal is to be able to map
families of possible morphologies and their transformations onto the underlying
developmental mechanisms and laws of structure. In our case the variety of models
of crossness, abstracted from empirical terminologies and algebraized in a certain
fashion, are situated in an abstract space (of which the hypercubes given here are to
be interpreted as specific subspaces) underlying the morphologies of kinship systems. The hypercube examples are predicated on a specific algebraization of crossness
that reflects the choice of a specific kind of formal model. It is not the only possible
model, and it may not be the best one. One evident weakness of the model is that it
tells nothing of the directionality of change; its model of the world of kinship is
perfectly round.

This said, we are prepared to defend the conclusion that the algebraic model in
question provides the best-articulated framework for comparing the varieties of
crossness as generative models. It is able to incorporate Kuma and Yafar patterns,
which, together with the Dravidian and Iroquois types, generate the only stable or

reciprocally consistent patterns of kinship structure. And in revealing the reciprocally inconsistent territory that lies between each pair of the four types, it seems to show that the generative principles behind kinship systems do indeed form a limited set of discontinuous types rather than being infinitely various. This gives us reason to think that the continuing discussion of typological issues is capable of genuine progress.

NOTES

1. Morgan's evolutionary project fascinated Marx, who took extensive notes on *Ancient Society,* including the most technical aspects of its kinship analysis (Marx 1972). After Marx's death, Engels (1972 [1884]) published a radical reading of Morgan's evolutionary scheme. It was also a touchstone for later social evolutionism in American anthropology, especially that of Leslie White, Elman Service, and the early Marshall Sahlins. Morgan's legacy is multivalent; it both celebrates the institutions of the West as the acme of evolution and denaturalizes them by giving them a past that is their negation.
2. Morgan's proof was directed against older views that the New World peoples may have originated from Europe or from the lost tribes of Israel. His belief that they came, rather, from Asia is of course the mainstream view today, but anthropologists no longer believe that the similarities between distant Asian and American Indian kinship terminologies are such that the terminologies must be historically related.
3. Such a view is consistent with, among other things, a statistical treatment, and it is not coincidental that Tylor (1889) published the first statistical analysis of the newly created field of kinship. This piece is a precursor of Murdock's cross-cultural surveys and the Human Relations Area Files, both of them examples of the method of Taylor and both subject to the problem of ensuring the independence of the societies included in the sample.
4. Changes in G^{+1} kin terms will of course generate changes in the classification of their children in G^0 and imply corresponding changes in their reciprocals in G^{-1}. As a result, all three medial generations are affected by the difference between Iroquois and Dravidian.
5. Viveiros de Castro's sixteen types of crossness reckoning and the sixteen of Tjon Sie Fat are not identical. For an explanation of the differences between the two sets, see note 8.
6. This discussion of the hypercube makes reference to analyses given in other chapters in this volume, specifically chapters 2, 3, and 15. One may wish to read them first.
7. Figure 1-4 corrects an error in equation 6.4 as given in Trautmann (1981:179), where the second line has "=" for "≠."
8. These sixteen possible types of crossness are somewhat different from the sixteen types identified by Viveiros de Castro (in chapter 15 in this volume). Viveiros de Castro's typology is of all possible definitions of crossness for second cousins, that is, kin at the G^0 level, the criteria being two binary features: relative sex (same sex or opposite sex) of the ancestral sibling pair in G^{+2} and of the parents in G^{+1}, giving 2^2 (or four) possible combinations for each type of crossness, which combine with the binary feature cross/parallel in G^0 to yield 4^2 (or sixteen) combinations. What is proposed is a general (binary) scheme for the classification of second cousins, a scheme not particularly constrained by or limited to the class of Iroquois/Dravidian patterns. Tjon Sie Fat's scheme, on the other hand, rests on criteria of difference between Iroquois and Dravidian in the multiplication tables, which differentia are found to reside in G^{+1} and G^{-1} and define the space between the two models of crossness. The resulting scheme of sixteen types is complementary to that of Viveiros, each focusing on different parts of the pattern of variation. For example, in the hypercube, Ngawbe and all Iroquois-generational systems are not differentiated from Iroquois because they exhibit identical

Iroquois patterns of crossness at the G^{+1} and G^{-1} levels, but not, of course, at G^0, where all kin are "brothers" and "sisters." For this reason, Ngawbe appears in Viveiros de Castro's scheme as a separate type. The hypercube model could and should be extended to compositions of affines and consanguines that lead to variation at G^0. It could also take in affinal variations at the three medial levels and be extended to encompass various other classes of models, such as Crow-Omaha, Eskimo, and the like.

SETTING THE STAGE

2

"Dravidian," "Iroquois," and "Crow-Omaha" in North American Perspective

THOMAS R. TRAUTMANN AND R. H. BARNES

The nature of the cross/parallel distinction among the Iroquois was elucidated by Floyd Lounsbury (1964a) using the kinship terminology of the Seneca Iroquois as published by L. H. Morgan in *Systems of Consanguinity and Affinity* (1871). In what must be the most famous footnote in anthropology, Lounsbury overturned the established anthropological view concerning the nature of the Iroquois type of kinship system: namely, that the Iroquois type classifies kin by membership in unilineal descent groups, more specifically (in the case of the Iroquois themselves) by exogamous matrilineal moieties. Although Lounsbury did not speak of Dravidian systems directly, his demonstration is equivalent to a showing that Iroquois and Dravidian systems possess crossness of quite different types. Moreover, this showing holds for all systems of Iroquois type in Morgan's table, from rereading which, Lounsbury discovered the pattern in question. At the very same time, halfway round the world, his colleague Leopold Pospisil happened upon the identical pattern among the Kapauku Papuans (Pospisil 1959–60; Lounsbury 1964a:n. 4).

Following the Lounsbury-Pospisil discovery, the distinction between cross and parallel kin became the focus of attention of numerous studies (Kay 1965, 1967; Tyler 1966; Scheffler 1971; Héritier 1981: annex 1; Trautmann 1981:48–62, 82–89). Recently, Kronenfeld (1989) approached the issue from a new perspective, that is, the relation of Iroquois- and Dravidian-type crossness to unilineal (skewed) systems of Crow and Omaha type. He did so by revisiting the original fund of data on North American kinship systems collected by Morgan and published in his massive table II of the *Systems*. In the course of his analysis, Kronenfeld raised some questions about the reliability of Morgan's data.

Kronenfeld's discussion is based on a comparison of Morgan's and Dorsey's data on the kinship terminology of the Omaha. He submits both sets to a formal semantic analysis, consisting of the identification of kernal kintypes and the formulation of reduction rules that will reduce all other reported kintypes to the kernal

Table 2-1

Classification of Twelve Kin in Omaha and Sauk-Fox Systems as Reported by Morgan, Dorsey, and Tax

Kintype	Omaha: Morgan	Omaha: Dorsey	Sauk & Fox: Morgan	Fox: Tax
176. FFZD (m.s.)	aunt	niece	aunt	niece
177. FFZDS (m.s.)	nephew	grandson	nephew	grandchild
178. FFZDD (m.s.)	niece	granddaughter	niece	grandchild
186. MMBS	uncle	grandfather	uncle	grandfather
187. MMBSS (m.s.)	uncle	grandfather	NR	grandfather
188. MMBSD (f.s.)	mother	grandmother	NR	NR
189. MMBSSS (m.s.)	uncle	grandfather	uncle	NR
190. MMBSSS (f.s.)	uncle	grandfather	uncle	NR
191. MMBSSD (m.s.)	mother	grandmother	mother	NR
192. MMBSSD (f.s.)	mother	grandmother	mother	NR
193. MMBSSSS (m.s.)	uncle	[grandfather]	uncle	NR
194. MMBSDDD (m.s.)	niece	[sister]	NR	NR

NR = no report.

kintype with which they are classed. He discovers thereby a number of discrepancies between Morgan's and Dorsey's data, some of them minor and episodic in character, but twelve of them major and systematic. Since Morgan and Dorsey collected their material from the Omaha, a small community, within a few years of each other, it is unlikely that variation in personal usage or historical change would account for these differences. Moreover, Dorsey's fieldwork lasted longer and he had far better linguistic credentials than Morgan, so that his version surely merits greater credence.[1] Finally, since Morgan's version of the classification of the twelve kin in question introduces a nonuniformity of reciprocals into his set, whereas Dorsey's set is internally consistent, the decision clearly goes to Dorsey in this matter.

Kronenfeld is right in finding that Morgan is here in error. Moreover, the error is systematic in a double sense. Not only are the twelve wrongly classified genealogical positions interrelated, but the error extends to the same genealogical positions in other unilineal systems in Morgan's table II that are of Omaha type,[2] and analogous errors appear among those of Crow type.[3] Thus against these twelve kin Morgan's table II shows a uniformity of error for the unilineal or skewed systems.

An outside source that corroborates Kronenfeld's finding is Tax's report on the (Omaha-like) kinship terminology of the Fox. Table 2-1 shows the twelve discrepant terms in question, giving Morgan's and Dorsey's version of Omaha classifications, and Morgan's and Tax's version of (Sauk and) Fox classifications.[4]

In Morgan's table II, the twelve genealogical positions fall into two series of contiguous entries: the descendants of the FFZ (nos. 176–78) and the descendants of the MMB (nos. 186–94). Morgan's classifications differ from Dorsey's, although it must be said that Dorsey does not actually report on the last two, and the classifications we attribute to him are consistent with the overall pattern of the terminology as he reported it, and as Kronenfeld analyses it. Column 3 of table 2-1 shows Morgan's report on the Sauk and Fox terminology, which coincides with his report on Omaha except for three (no report) positions. As column 4 indicates, Tax reports on five of the positions for Fox, all of which agree with those reported by Dorsey but not by Morgan.

What bearing do these differences have on the nature of the cross/parallel distinction? Kronenfeld argues that the unilineal (skewed) systems (i.e., those of the so-called Crow-Omaha type) presuppose some form of crossness—whether of Iroquois, Dravidian, or other type—and that the errors of Morgan's report on Omaha imply an underlying crossness of Iroquois type, whereas Dorsey's more accurate data presuppose an underlying crossness of Dravidian type. In Kronenfeld's view, Morgan's report for Omaha and other unilineal systems in his table II is inadvertently biased toward the Iroquois pattern of crossness as a result of his work among the Iroquois. According to Kronenfeld, "The findings regarding skewed systems raise the possibility that Morgan might also have imposed an Iroquois-type cross/parallel distinction on his unskewed terminologies (including those of the Iroquois tribes) where the actually occurring distinction might have been a Dravidian-type one" (1989:100). Such a view is tantamount to a finding that crossness of Iroquois type is an anthropological fiction, attributable to Morgan. Kronenfeld is unable to find evidence from North America to test that suggestion. In the end, he rejects it because Iroquois-type crossness is demonstrated beyond doubt in Oceania. Nevertheless, without direct evidence for North America, a doubt lingers. Anxiety rises when one recalls that Lounsbury's elicitation of the Iroquois type rests on Morgan's data.[5]

Kronenfeld's article, then, raises fundamental questions about the integrity of Morgan's data with respect to kinship terminologies of North American groups, particularly about whether crossness of the Iroquois type existed in North America and, if so, what its relation to systems of Dravidian, Crow, and Omaha type may be.[6] What is especially alarming about the notion that Morgan's published kinship terminologies for North American groups may be seriously in error is that his data for the eighty groups of table II have not been superseded by subsequent field studies, as is the case for his collections from other parts of the world. Moreover, many of the groups no longer exist as such, and all of them have been greatly changed by the effects of the dominant Euroamerican society.

Reliable evidence is now available to resolve all of these issues. This chapter gives proof that crossness of Iroquois type did exist in North America, and it (and not the Dravidian type) is the direct precursor of unilineal or skewed systems there.

TYPE B CROSSNESS IN MORGAN

Although the symmetries of kinship terminologies lend themselves to an exact, algebra-like treatment, there are occasions when a naive, "plain English" approach is an advantage, and this is one of them. What surprised Morgan most about Iroquois kinship terminology when he first encountered it was that "the father's brother is equally a father," and likewise the mother's sister is a mother. As he would say, "father" is the "translation" of the Iroquois "vocable" applied to the father and his brother.

There are two reasons why this kind of description is possible at all. First, a kinship terminology as Morgan conceived it is not a list of words but an abstraction: a pattern of meanings of which its vocables (or lexica) are only the markers (see also Lounsbury 1956, 1964a). Second, whereas the English pattern has a semantic dimension of lineal versus collateral kin, the Iroquois pattern lacks such a dimension but has something else in its place. This something else is the semantic dimension we call crossness or bifurcation, or the cross/parallel distinction. It is only by virtue of this complementarity that Morgan can say that the father's brother is a father, but the mother's brother is an uncle. This enables him to describe the semantic organization of Iroquois in a plain English form, speaking of fathers, mothers, uncles, aunts, and the like to stand for Iroquois semantic categories.

The distinctive feature of crossness is the merger of the father's brother with the father and the mother's sister with the mother or, more generally, the merger of same-sex siblings. In the formalization invented by Lounsbury, this principle is represented as the "merging rule," or the rule of "same-sex sibling merging." The principle in question provides that in the three medial generations there are parallel kin consisting of "fathers," "mothers," "brothers," "sisters," "sons," and "daughters" and cross kin who are "uncles," "aunts," "cousins," "nephews," and "nieces"— and that quotation marks are used to indicate that the English term in question is redefined by same-sex sibling merging to represent Iroquois semantic categories and not English ones.

Up to this point, the description suffices for Iroquois and for Tamil or other instances of the Dravidian systems of South India. Indeed, Morgan found the similarity between Iroquois and Dravidian classifications so striking that he took it to be proof of the Asiatic origin of the American Indians. But in the classification of more distant kin, the Dravidian and the Iroquois differ in a systematic way. We prefer to avoid culturally specific labels, however, and call these two forms of crossness Type A and Type B, rather than Dravidian and Iroquois type. We do so to avoid the question of which of the variable cases of Dravidian and Iroquois should be the type cases. Another reason is to avoid the paradox of asking whether the Iroquois have Iroquois-type crossness. Type B crossness is illustrated in figure 2-1.

The kin circled in figure 2-1 are those for whom Type B classifications are the opposite of the more familiar Dravidian-like Type A. The differences between Types A and B begin to appear at a certain distance from Ego, namely, among the children of "cousins," and among the parents' "cousins," their children (second cousins), and children's children. For Type A, the rule of bilateral cross-cousin marriage as a principle of classification clearly comes into play at this point. For example, since the terminology classifies my opposite-sex "cousin" as a spouse, his or her children are my "son" and "daughter," and since it classifies my same-sex "cousin" as a "spouse's sibling," his or her children are classified as my "nephew" and "niece," and are marriageable to my children. (This principle of classification must override to some extent the distinction between consanguines and affines.) For Type B, on

Figure 2-1

Type B Crossness: Shaded Kintypes Are Classified in the Opposite Way in Type A Systems

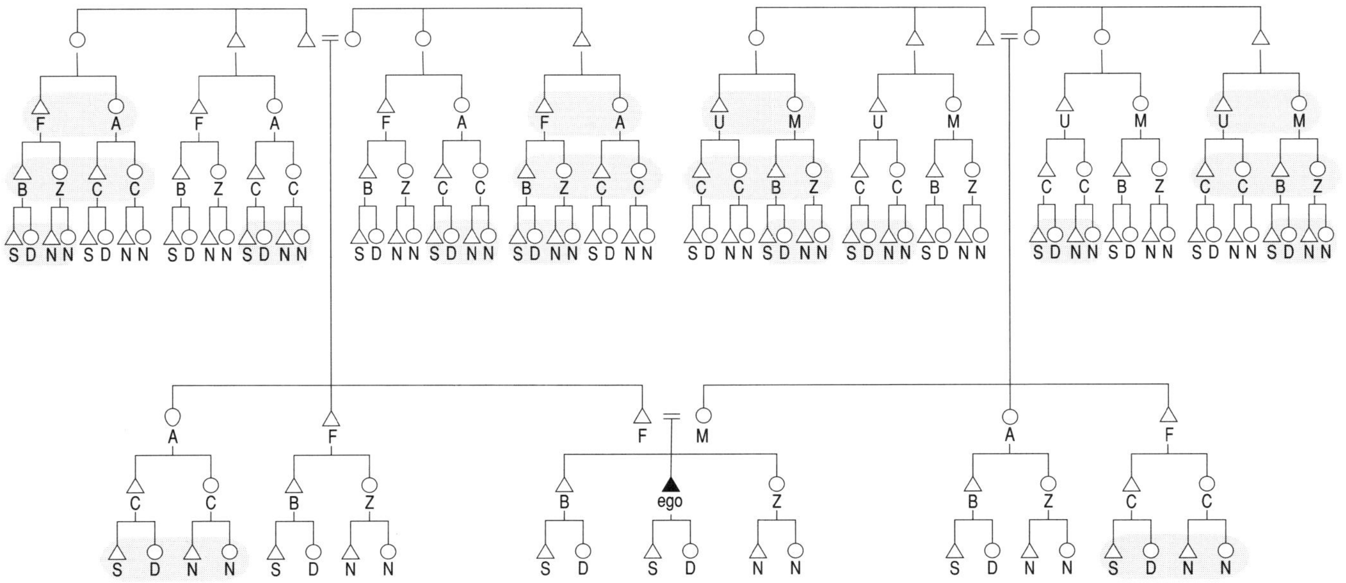

Table 2-2

Diagnostics of Type A and Type B Crossness in Morgan, Table II

Table II kintype	Type B	Type A
101. FZSS (m.s.)	son	nephew
102. FZSS (f.s.)	nephew	son
103. FZSD (m.s.)	daughter	niece
104. FZSD (f.s.)	niece	daughter
105. FZDS (m.s.)	nephew	son
106. FZDS (f.s.)	son	nephew
107. FZDD (m.s.)	niece	daughter
108. FZDD (f.s.)	daughter	niece
127. MBSS (m.s.)	son	nephew
128. MBSS (f.s.)	nephew	son
129. MBSD (m.s.)	daughter	niece
130. MBSD (f.s.)	niece	daughter
131. MBDS (m.s.)	nephew	son
132. MBDS (f.s.)	son	nephew
133. MBDD (m.s.)	niece	daughter
134. MBDD (f.s.)	daughter	niece
176. FFZD (m.s.)	aunt	mother
177. FFZDS (m.s.)	cousin	brother
178. FFZDD (m.s.)	cousin	sister
186. MMBS	uncle	father
187. MMBSS (m.s.)	cousin	brother
188. MMBSD (f.s.)	cousin	sister

the other hand, the rule of cross-cousin marriage is violated by these classifications and cannot be present. For example, the children of my opposite-sex "cousin" are my "nephews" and "nieces," like the children of my opposite-sex sibling, which they could not be under a rule of cross-cousin marriage. The principle that is at work can more easily be seen by considering how I classify my parents' "cousins." My father's male cousin is equally a "father," just as my father's brother is; whence his children are my "brother" and "sister." Thus, in certain contexts, there may be said to be a rule that has the effect of merging opposite-sex siblings, as well as the rule, shared by both variants, of merging same-sex siblings. We note for later discussion that Type B appears to be incompatible with the kinds of merger of affines and consanguines that one expects for Type A.

Morgan's table II does not have all the genealogical positions in figure 2-1, but it does contain twenty-two of them that are diagnostic of the difference between the two types of crossness (see table 2-2).

The diagnostics are unevenly distributed across the three medial generations: there are only two for G^{+1}, four for G^0, and sixteen for G^{-1}. Evidently Morgan did not devise his kinship table with our problem in mind. The various Iroquois nations reported in table II conform to Type B expectations on each diagnostic, for the very good reason that Type B is an abstraction of the pattern Lounsbury derived from Morgan's data on the Seneca Iroquois. The Dravidian kinship systems Morgan reports on in table III of the *Systems*—namely, Tamil, Telugu, and Canarese (or Kannada)—conform to the expectations of Type A in most instances but are mistaken on the last three of the list. That is, Morgan's entries wrongly show the Type B pattern of "uncle, cousin, cousin" for the last three entries of table 2-2. This appears to be an instance of Iroquois bias imposed on his Dravidian entries. How this error came about is explained later in the chapter.

Inspection of the twenty-two diagnostics in table II shows that, aside from (Crow-Omaha type) systems with unilineal equations (skewing) and those for which the requisite information is not reported, Type B and not Type A pervades the systems of Iroquoian, Dakotan (or Siouan), and Algonquian language families given in the table, and perhaps Athapaskan. That is to say, the crossness is regularly of Type B, but one can see that there is a good deal of variation in the realization of this dimension in the three medial generations. Four variants on the Type B theme are discernible:

1. Type B crossness may be extended throughout the three medial generations (Seneca, Wyandotte, Dakota, Cree-Ojibwa-Ottawa, Piegan, possibly Mohegan).
2. It may be lost in women's speech for G^{-1} kin, with reciprocal partial loss in G^{+1} (other Five Nations Iroquois, possibly Delaware).
3. It may be lost in G^0 altogether; that is, all of Ego's generation are "brothers" and "sisters," and there are no "cousins" (Two Mountain Iroquois, Cheyenne, Micmac, Slave Lake; also, Arapaho and Gros Ventres, according to Eggan (1955b), or partially lost in G^0 (Etchemin/Malisete).
4. It may be partially lost in G^{+1} and G^{-1}, and also fully lost in G^0. That is, there may be a combination of patterns (2) and (3) (Munsee).

Other imaginable variants— such as complete loss of crossness in G^{+1} and G^{-1} (no "cousins" without "uncles" and "aunts," the inverse of variant (3) above), and complete loss of crossness in all three medial generations—do not occur. That is to say, there is no wholly generational system in Morgan's table II. What is certain is that variation is not between Type B and Type A; every case of apparent conformity to Type A turns out on inspection to be nonsignificant, as in variant (3) above, where all G^0 diagnostics show sibling terms because crossness is lost in this generation and there are no "cousins." Variation within nonunilineal systems of table II is between presence and absence of Type B crossness in the three generations. What remains uncertain is whether that should be considered variation between Type B and a generational (Hawaiian type) pattern, since the latter does not occur in pure form among these North American groups.

No discussion of Iroquois and Dravidian crossness would be complete without some mention of affines. Lounsbury talks about an affinal terminology separate

from that for consanguines, and that is a major difference from Dravidian terminologies, but neither he nor Kronenfeld include affines in their analyses. It is easy
to show that for fifty-four affinal terms in Morgan's tables, the three Dravidian
terminologies merge the greater part of them with consanguineal kin, while the
American terminologies of table II show a rich affinal terminology and limited
merger with consanguineal kin. The patterns remain widely different even though
neither embodies the pure type of complete merger or nonmerger. In particular, the
North American terminologies most often merge the spouses of G^{+1} kin with the
four consanguines—MBW with FZ, FZH with MB, FBW with MZ, MZH with
FB—which would be consistent with Type A crossness. All too often, equations of
this kind are hastily taken as evidence of cross-cousin marriage and a Dravidian
pattern. Since the overall patterning of the affinal terminology is considerably different from that for the Dravidian systems, the logical conclusion is that mergers of
this kind are compatible with both Type A and Type B.[7]

In sum, the semantic patterning of Morgan's North American terminologies in
relation to Type B crossness and affinal terms suggests a field of variation among
culturally and historically related systems, much as the Dravidian systems of South
India and Sri Lanka present themselves as a field of variation upon Type A crossness,
no single instance being more "Dravidian" than the others. One striking difference
should be mentioned, however: the North American cases are distributed across
several language families. This makes the similarities all the more noteworthy. We
now turn to the possibility, arising from Kronenfeld's work, that the strong similarity among the components of table II did not come from Morgan's informants, but
from Morgan himself, and is in error.

EXTERNAL EVIDENCE OF TYPE B IN NORTH AMERICA

External evidence for the existence in North America of Type B crossness is not
abundant, but some of it is persuasive. It comes in large part from Eggan's *Social
Anthropology of North American Tribes* (1955 [1937]). This volume not only contains Sol Tax's study of the Fox but shows its value in providing outside substantia-
tion, if somewhat indirect, for Dorsey's version of Omaha. Furthermore, we find
clear instances of Type B crossness among the Cheyenne, Arapaho, and Gros Ventre in the chapter by Eggan and in McAllister's Kiowa-Apache and Opler's
Chiracahua Apache. Figure 2-2 illustrates Eggan's Cheyenne and Arapaho.

The kin circled in figure 2-2 are those whose classification is diagnostic of the
difference between Type B and Type A crossness: here, the crossness is Type B in
each instance. This is a case of variant (3) just discussed, that is, one in which ego's
generation has only "brothers" and "sisters" and not "cousins." In a sense, this makes
more evident the logic of the classification of their children: the children of cross
cousins are treated in the same way as the children of "brother" and "sister," because they *are* the children of "brother" and "sister."

Further outside confirmation for Type B in North America comes from the Morgan Papers, which we have been studying closely and which are the principal re-

Figure 2-2

Cheyenne and Arapaho: Shaded Kintypes Are Diagnostic of Type B

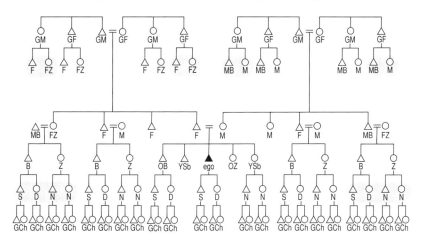

Source: Eggan (1955).

source for this study. Morgan preserved his manuscripts and field notebooks, including the printed schedules of kinship terminology on which he had written the information originally elicited for each group at the end of the 1850s and the beginning of the 1860s. From these he constructed the three massive tables of the *Systems*. Morgan bequeathed his papers to the University of Rochester, in whose library they may be seen. Few anthropologists seem to be aware of this invaluable collection, and only a handful have studied the original schedules.[8]

One of the gems of that collection is the schedule for Ojibwa returned by the Reverend Edward Jacker, a Catholic missionary at Houghten, in the upper peninsula of Michigan. For the most part, Morgan was disappointed with the returns of schedules he had posted to Indian missions, and he himself collected the greater part of the schedules on which table II is based. But Father Jacker's return is one that he singles out as specially full and accurate (his notation on the back: "Splendidly done"), and inspection of the original confirms that this confidence is well placed. Like many of the schedules, it is difficult to make out since it is printed on thin paper, front and back, and entries on either side bleed through to the other. Nevertheless a patient reading reveals all. The schedule shows many points at which Father Jacker went beyond the questions of Morgan's schedule, introducing additional distinctions within genealogical positions printed on the schedule that were necessary to an exact understanding of the semantic pattern of the Ojibwa community he served. For example, Morgan's schedule asked for the word and "translation" for MMMZGrGrD (m.s.), and Father Jacker's entry stipulates that she is a "sister" (more exactly, elder sister or younger sibling, depending on her age in relation to Ego), "if by her mother," that is, if she is MMMZGrDD, since for this out-

Table 2-3

Ojibwa Kinship Terminology, from Edward Jacker

Term	Translation	Kintype
1. *nindanike-nimishomiss*	GrGrF	FGrF, FGrFB, FGrMB, FGrGrF
2. *nindanike-nokomiss*	GrGrM	FGrFZ, FGrM, FGMZ, FGrGrM
3. *nimishomiss*	GrF	FF, FFB, FMB, HGrF
4. *nokomiss*	GrM	FFZ, FM, FMZ, MMMZD (m.s.), WGrM
5. *noss (nin baba, nin dede)*	F	F
6. *ninga (nin mama, nimama)*	M	M
7. *nimishome*	StF	FB, FeB, FyB, MZH, FFZS (m.s.), StF
8. *ninoshe (nimwishe)*	StM	FBW, MZ, MeZ, MyZ, MMZD (m.s.), MMMZGrD (m.s.), StM
9. *ninsigoss (nisigoss)*	A	FZ, MBW, FFZD (m.s.)
10. *nizhishe*	U	FZH, MB, MMZS (m.s.)
11. *nin (ni) widigemagan* (*nin wabem*)	my cohabitant, my man	H
12. *nin widigemaga* (*nin wijiwagan*)	my cohabitant, my associate	W
13. *ninsiniss (nisiniss)*	F-in-law	HF, WF
14. *ninsigosiss (nisigosiss)*	M-in-law	HM, WM
15. *nissaye*	eB	eB (m.s.), eB (f.s.), FBS (m.s.) if older, FBS (f.s.) if older, MZS (m.s.) if older, MZS (f.s.) if older, FFZSS (m.s.) if older, MMZDS (m.s.) if older, HfB if older
16. *nimisse*	eZ	eZ (m.s.), eZ (f.s.), FBD (m.s.) if older, FBD (f.s.) if older, MZD (m.s.) if older, MZD (f.s.) if older, FFZSDD (m.s.) if older, MMZDD (m.s.) if older, MMMZGrGrD (m.s.) older, if by her M, HfZ if older
17. *nishime*	yB	yB (m.s.), yB (f.s.), FBS (m.s.) if younger, FBS (f.s.) if younger, MZS (m.s.) if younger, MZS (f.s.) if younger, FFZSS (m.s.) if younger, MMZDS (m.s.) if younger, HfB if younger
	yZ	yZ (m.s.), yZ (f.s.), FBD (m.s.) if younger, FBD (f.s.) if younger, MZD (m.s.) if younger, MZD (f.s.) if younger, FFZSD (m.s.) if younger, MMZDD (m.s.) if younger, MMMZGrGrD (m.s.), younger, if by her M, HfZ if younger.
18. *nitawiss*	C	FZS (m.s.), MBS (m.s.), FFZDS (m.s.), MMZSS (m.s.)
19. *ninimoshe*	C	FZS (f.s.), FZD (m.s.), MBS (f.s.), MBD

Continued on next page

Table 2-3 continued

Term	Translation	Kintype
		(m.s.) [wrongly niece], FFZDD (m.s.), MMZSD (m.s.), MMMZGrGrD (m.s.) if by her F
20. *nidangoshe*	C	FZD (f.s.), MBD (f.s.) [wrongly niece]
21. *nita*	B-in-law	FBDH said by a male, FZDH said by a male, MZDH said by a male, MBDH said by a male, ZH (m.s.), WZH, WB
22. *ninim*	B-in-law	FBDH said by a female, FZDH said by a female, MZDH said by a female, MBDH said by a female, HB, ZH (f.s.), HZH
	Z-in-law	FBSW said by a male, FZSW said by a male, MZSW said by a male, MBSW said by a male, WZ, BW (m.s.), WBW
23. *nindangwe*	Z-in-law	FBSW said by a female, FZSW said by a female, MZSW said by a female, HZ, BW (f.s.), HBW
24. *nindangoshe*	Z-in-law	MBSW said by a female
25. *ningwiss*	S	S
26. *nindaniss*	D	D
27. *nindozhim* (*odozhiman*)	StS	BS (m.s.), FBSS (m.s.), FZSS (m.s.), MZSS (m.s.), MBSS said by a male, FFZGrGrS (m.s.) if by his F, StS said by a male
28. *nindozhimiss* (*odozhimissan*)	StS	ZS (f.s.), FBDS (f.s.), FZDS (f.s.), MZDS (f.s.) [wrongly step-daughter], MBDS said by a female, StS said by a female
29. *nindozhimikwem* (*odozhimikweman*)	StD	BD (m.s.), FBDS (f.s.) FZDS (f.s.) MZSD (m.s.) MBSD said by a male, FFZGrGrD (m.s.) if by her F, MMMZGrGrGrD (m.s.) if by her F, StD said by a male
30. *nindozhimiss* (*odozhimissan*)	StD	ZD (f.s.), FBDD (f.s.), FZDD (f.s.), MZDD (f.s.), MBDD said by a female, StD said by a female
31. *niningwaniss* (*oningwanissan*)	Nephew	ZS (m.s.), BS (f.s.), FBSS (f.s.), FBDS (f.s.), FZSS (f.s.), FZDS (m.s.), MZSS (f.s.) MZDS (m.s.), MBSS said by a female, MBDS said by a male, FFGrGrS (m.s.) if by his M
32. *nishimiss* (*oz[s]himissan*)	Niece	ZD (m.s.), BD (f.s.), FBSD (f.s.), FBDD (m.s.), FZSD (f.s.), FZDD (m.s.) MZSD (f.s.) MZDD (m.s.), MBSD said by a

Continued on next page

Table 2-3 continued

Term	Translation	Kintype
		female, MBDD said by a male, FFZGrGrD (m.s.) if by her M, MMMZGrGrGrD (m.s.) if by her M
33. *niningwan* (*oningwanan*)	S-in-law	BDH (m.s.), ZDH (m.s.), ZDH (f.s.), BDH (f.s.), S-in-law
34. *nissim* (*ossimin*)	D-in-law	BSW (m.s.), ZSW (m.s.), ZSW (f.s.), BSW (f.s.), D-in-law
35. *nozhishe* (*ozhisheyan*)	GrCh	GrS, GrD, BGrS (m.s.), BGrD (m.s.), ZGrS (m.s.), ZGrD (m.s.), ZGrS (f.s.), ZGrD (f.s.), BGrS (f.s.), BGrD (f.s.), FBGrGrS (m.s.), FBGrGrS (f.s.), FBGrGrD (m.s.), FBGrGrD (f.s.), FZGrGrS, FZGrGrD, MZGrGrS (m.s.) MZGrGrS (f.s.), MZGrGrD, MMMZGrGrS (m.s.), MMMZGrGrD (m.s.)
36. *nind anikobijigan* (*odanikobijigan*)	GrGrCh	GrGrS, GrGrD, GrGrGrS, GrGrGrD, BGrGrS (m.s.), BGrGrD (m.s.), BGrGrS (m.s.), ZGrGrD (m.s.), ZGrGrS (f.s.), ZGrGrD (f.s.), BGrGrS (f.s.), BGrGrD (f.s.), FBGrGrGrS, FBGrGrGrD, FZGrGrGrS, FZGrGrGrD, MZGrGrGrS, MZGrGrGrD, MBGrGrGrS, MBGrGrGrD

come the logic of Type B requires that Ego's parent and alter's parent be of the same sex; but she is a "cousin," Father Jacker says, "if by her father"—that is, if she is MMMZGrSD—since in that case ego's and alter's parents are of the opposite sex.

The detail and exactness of Father Jacker's return—it is, we are certain, the most extensive original record of an Ojibwa terminology—has made it worthwhile to decipher and reassemble it in a more readily comprehended form (see table 2-3). (Table II, like the schedules on which it is based, gives Amerindian words and "translations" against genealogical positions; here we give the reverse arrangement, collecting all instances of each word and giving "translations" and all genealogical positions for each.)

In this terminology, a parent's same-sex siblings are not merged with the parent; F and M have their own specific terms, and their same-six siblings are given terms whose "translation" is "stepfather" and "stepmother." Otherwise, the logic is clearly that of Type B: that is, a parent's "siblings" and "cousins" of the same sex are classed with the stepparent, and those of the opposite sex with the "uncle" and "aunt." G^{-1} exhibits a similar pattern: "stepson" and "stepdaughter" terms collecting the children of same-sex "siblings" and "cousins," "nephew" and "niece" terms collecting children of opposite-sex "siblings" and "cousins," as in the Type B model.

G^0 has no comparable category of "stepbrother" and "stepsister," and parallel kin become "siblings" of either sex, older or younger than ego, with cross kin becoming "cousins" by Type B logic. Consistent with this picture, there are several affinal terms, though here, as generally in Morgan's table II, we find the usual equations, compatible, apparently, with both Type A and Type B, namely, FB = MZH, MZ = FBW, FZ = MBW, and MB = FZH. The existence of Type B crossness among the members of at least one Ojibwa community must be regarded as definitely established by this evidence.

This is a matter of some moment because subsequent Ojibwa ethnographies by Hallowell and Landes promote a Dravidian-like interpretation of Ojibwa crossness, attributing it to cross-cousin marriage. Ethnographies of other Central Algonquian groups in Canada lend support to this view of Ojibwa (Hallowell 1928b, 1937; Strong 1929; Landes 1937, 1969 [1938]; Graburn 1975). The discrepancy within Ojibwa ethnography is a difficult problem that can be resolved only in stages. Furthermore, it is a clear reminder that although external sources indicate that Type B exists in North America within the orbit of Morgan's table II (including Ojibwa) and cannot therefore be a fiction of Morgan's invention, no steps have yet been taken to determine whether the near ubiquity of Type B in the table is due to the operation of an Iroquois bias. This is a genuine question, for an Iroquois bias is, at a minimum, discernible in the errors we have found in Morgan's Dravidian. What is more, the presence of Type A in Canada at least has been shown not only for northerly Algonquian speakers but also for Athapaskan-speaking groups in Ives's (1990) study, a finding recently extended to other groups (see chapter 4 of this volume).

To determine the scope of an Iroquois bias in Morgan's table II, we must again resort to his manuscript schedules of kinship terminologies for the light they throw on the question, beginning with his gradual discovery of Type B, continuing with his partial recognition of Type A, and finishing with his errors in reporting unilineal systems.

MORGAN'S MANUSCRIPT SCHEDULES OF KINSHIP

The Ojibwa kinship terminology played a crucial role in the genesis of Morgan's kinship project. Morgan had published the *League of the Iroquois* in 1851 and would always regard the kinship system of the Seneca Iroquois as the standard from which all other Indian types were deviations. But his remarks about Iroquois kinship in that book deal mainly with the system of matrilineal clans, and with a handful of terms among which he discerned in part the principle of same-sex sibling merger: the father's brother is a father, and so on. By his own admission, it was the Ojibwa kinship system that generated his vast program of comparative study, which was "born in an Indian cabin in Michigan" in the summer of 1858. That is, he found among the Ojibwa the same principle of same-sex sibling merger that he had among the Iroquois, although they belong to distinct language families, whose relationship philology is unable to demonstrate. Kinship, by contrast, does show the unity of the Indians and thus can be considered a "new instrument for ethnology." Ojibwa was the crucial second case that made the study of kinship a comparative study; and it was the encounter with Ojibwa that obliged Morgan to return to the terminology of the Iroquois and investigate it more extensively.

At each step in the process Morgan widened the network of genealogical positions in which he hoped to capture what he called the principles of the system. Thus his field notebooks for Ojibwa terminology show successive lists of eight, fourteen, and forty-six terms, the last with many additions and corrections, followed by a list of Latin terms alongside slightly more than one hundred genealogical positions. All this revealed to him the shortcomings of his knowledge of Iroquois terminology, and so in November he returned to the Seneca of Tonawanda Reservation and collected information on more than two hundred genealogical positions, on the basis of which he drew up a schedule of kinship for printing.

Morgan was soon faced with the problems of classifying the more remote genealogical positions, in respect of which, needless to say, errors are easily made (and which are also at the center of this inquiry). In the years that followed, Morgan issued three versions of the kinship schedule (which we call those of 1859, 1860a, and 1860b), undertook four field trips to the American and Canadian West (in the summers between 1859 and 1862), and carried on a voluminous correspondence with missionaries, American consuls, and scholars around the world. Through these activities he amassed the material for the three kinship tables of the *Systems*. Morgan's manuscript and published material for this period indicate that he was not yet aware of the Type B pattern during his November 1858 visit to the Seneca, but that it gradually became apparent sometime in 1859, perhaps during the first of his western field trips, to Nebraska and Kansas Territories in May and June. It was not until then that he had found the right questions to detect its existence. During his first encounter with Tamil and Telugu kinship systems in August 1859, he believed these systems to be identical with the Iroquois and did not encounter Type A differences of Dravidian systems from Iroquois until the end of his fourth field trip in 1862.

Morgan's growing awareness of Type B and his late and partial recognition of Type A are reflected in his changing view of the classification of cross cousins' children, a problem that he had grappled with ever since the November 1858 visit to the Seneca of Tonawanda. Consider the following two patterns for children of my cousins (parents' siblings' children's children):

FBSS (m.s.)	S	FZSS (m.s.)	N
FBSS (f.s.)	N	FZSS (f.s.)	S
FBSD (m.s.)	D	FZSD (m.s.)	N
FBSD (f.s.)	N	FZSD (f.s.)	D
FBDS (m.s.)	N	FZDS (m.s.)	S
FBDS (f.s.)	S	FZDS (f.s.)	N
FBDD (m.s.)	N	FZDD (m.s.)	D
FBDD (f.s.)	D	FZDD (f.s.)	N

Under Type B crossness, the children of all cousins, cross and parallel, are classified for crossness as in column 1. Under Type A crossness, children of parallel cousins are classified as in column 1, and children of cross cousins are classified in the opposite way, as in column 2. Sex of ego is necessary to the pattern of both.

Morgan published two articles on kinship in the form of a circular letter to accompany the schedules of kinship that he posted to missionaries and others from whom he hoped to acquire information on kinship terminologies. The first, dated January 1859, shows no understanding of the Type B pattern or of the relevance of sex of ego; the second, dated October 1, 1859, shows the full Type B pattern. The first of these circular letters explains clearly the principle of classification of near kin but stumbles on the children of "cousins":

But the descendants of a brother and the descendants of a sister continued, in like manner, to be cousins; this last degree being as far asunder as it was possible for the descendants of brothers and sisters to fall, under the system of the Iroquois. In case one was farther removed from the ancestral head than the other, the rule which changed the collateral into the lineal line at once applied: thus the son of the son of my father's sister, or my cousin's son, becomes my nephew, and the son of this nephew becomes my grand-son. In like manner, the son of the son of my mother's sister becomes my nephew, although his father was my brother.

The following are among the examples he lists from Seneca:

FZSS	N	MZSS	N
FZSD	N	MZSD	N
FZDS	N	MZDS	N
FZDD	N	MZDD	N

Thus, from his November 1858 collection of information from the Seneca, Morgan derives the principle that the child of a cousin, parallel or cross, is a "nephew" or "niece," a principle that conforms to neither Type B nor Type A, because it lacks the distinction of sex of ego, which both types employ in the classification of these kin. Morgan was not yet asking the right questions and was not getting the information that would show him that he must consider the differences between classifications of males and females among these kin.

In the second version of the circular letter, formulated at the end of the summer of 1859, his examples include the distinction of sex of ego for classification of the children of cousins, again from the "Seneca dialect of the Iroquois language":

FBSS(m.s.)	S	FZSS(m.s.)	S
FBSS(f.s.)	N	FZSS(f.s.)	N
FBSD(m.s.)	D	FZSD(m.s.)	D
FBSD(f.s.)	N	FZSD(f.s.)	N
FBDS(m.s.)	N	FZDS(m.s.)	N
FBDS(f.s.)	S	FZDS(f.s.)	S
FBDD(m.s.)	N	FZDD(m.s.)	N
FBDD(f.s.)	D	FZDD(f.s.)	D

This is the Type B pattern we have abstracted from his Seneca, as published in the *Systems* and analyzed by Lounsbury.

It appears that up to April 1859 Morgan was getting what would have seemed contradictory answers to the question of how to classify the children of cousins for the Seneca, principally because he was not yet aware that one had to specify sex of ego to uncover the pattern.[9] The full Type B pattern appears on two other schedules, one of them for Seneca dated November 1, 1859, and another identified generically as Iroquois and undated.[10]

There is ample evidence in Morgan's manuscript schedules for his summer field trip to Nebraska and Kansas that he was becoming aware of the need to distinguish the sex of ego to get at the pattern for the children of cousins. His classifications for children of all first cousins among nonunilineal systems, and children of parallel cousins among unilineal ("skewed," Crow-Omaha type) systems in the collection of that season often include the sex of ego in schedules for Kaw, Wyandotte, Iowa, Stockbridge or Mohegan, and Ottawa. To this list we must add Winnebago, the schedule for which Morgan collected in Washington, D.C., before embarking on his field trip in May. The Wyandotte schedule is particularly intriguing as a close linguistic relative of Iroquois; the full Type B pattern is given for FBChCh, and the rest is consistent with it. Morgan did not add sex of ego to these entries in his inadequate 1859 schedule for Dakota, Delaware, Shawnee, and Kaskaskia, but in the last-named schedule he shows an awareness of it when he notes, against the descent line of the FB, "A man's brother's son is his son but his sister's son is his nephew. The rule should apply here? Here a man's son is a woman's nephew and vice versa"; and, in the descent line of MZ, "Same as father's brother's son—double. Reverse for man & woman." This verbalizes the Type B pattern nicely.

The effects of Morgan's new understanding of Seneca may be seen in his exchanges concerning Dakota with the Reverend S. R. Riggs, a missionary and the compiler of a Dakota dictionary and grammar. The Morgan Papers contain three schedules for Dakota terms completed by Riggs. In the first, dated March 1859, the children of "cousins" are identified as "nephews" and "nieces" for ego, without reference to the sex of ego, which of course the 1859 schedule does not take into account. (This is different from the Seneca pattern as given in Morgan's January 1859 circular letter.) In the second, 1860a schedule (dated January), Riggs gives the children of "cousins" as "grandchildren," surely a simple error of generation, for ego of either sex. In the third, also of 1860a vintage (dated May), he clearly gives the Type B pattern, at least for the FZChCh. His letters show that his understanding of the Dakota principles of classification changed under Morgan's questioning and in response to Morgan's changing understanding of Seneca. In a letter of March 8, 1860, Riggs represents the Dakota pattern as follows: My father's brother is my father, whether I am a man or a woman; consequently my father's brother's children are my brothers and sisters, whether I am a man or a woman; so my FBSS will be my son, and that too whether I am a man or a woman. "Do I understand you to say that, if *I am a woman,* he will be *my nephew* in Iroquois?" The same relationships hold in regard to my MZS and MZSS, whether I am a man or a woman. On the other hand, FZCh and MBCh are my "cousins," and my "cousins'" children are "nephews" and "nieces": "That is the rule. . . . At the same time I think that some Dakotas will say my male cousins children are my children I being a man—and of course my female cousins children are my children, I being a woman. But in this regard there does not appear to be uniformity." In a subsequent letter, written on April 17, Riggs accepts the Type B pattern for Dakota that Morgan had found for Seneca:

Your letter is received with the schedule partly filled up. Since receiving it I have reexamined the subject and find you right. You have gotten the victory and I thank you for it. I was led into that last error by forgetting, for the time being, that a man's sister's children are not the same to him as his brother's children, and vice versa.

Now I believe we have the general principles thus;—viz;

1. My fathers brothers (I being a man or a woman) are all fathers—and my mother's sisters are all mothers—while my mother's brothers and my father's sisters are uncles and aunts.

2. All the children of my fathers and of my mothers (understood as above) are my brothers and sisters, whether I am a man or a woman—and all the children of my uncles and aunts, (understood as above) are my cousins.

3. All the children of my brothers (understood as above, and I being a man) are my children—and all the children of my sisters are my nephews and nieces.

4. All the children of my sisters (I being a woman) are my children—and all the children of my brothers are my nephew and nieces.

5. All the children of my male cousins (I being a man) are my children—and all the children of my female cousins are my nephews and nieces.

6. All the children of my female cousins (I being a woman) are my children—and all the children of my male cousins are my nephews and nieces.

The same principles run on through remote relationships. Principles (5) and (6), of course, are the Type B pattern.[11]

At about the same time, Morgan received the schedule of Ojibwa kinship terms from Reverend Jacker. These filled out and fixed his conception of the principles underlying the terminology with which his project had begun. Thus, by the spring of 1860, he had strong evidence for the existence of Type B among representatives of three disparate language families: Iroquoian, Dakota or Siouan, and Algonquian. The schedules he filled in during his second field trip to the West in the ensuing summer are strongly patterned in the Type B manner.

The second schedule that Morgan drew up that year (1860b) was published by the Smithsonian Institution, whose sponsorship Morgan now accepted. The question can now be raised, How are the three schedules related to one another and to table II of the *Systems* with respect to Type A/Type B diagnostics?

The diagnostics (mapped in table 2-4) indicate that the 1859 schedule failed to add a sex-of-ego distinction, which was required to uncover the Type A or Type B pattern. The 1860a schedule made good this deficiency for one of the "cousins" but not the other; 1860b did so for both, and the pattern is carried over into table II. Among the parents' "cousins" and their children, the 1859 schedule gives only the line of the MMB and 1860a and 1860b give only the line of FFZ, while table II gives both lines, though fewer of each.

The schedule was not an iron cage; as we have pointed out, Morgan, Father Jacker, and some others wrote in the sex-of-ego distinction in the 1859 and 1860a schedules when they were aware of the need to do so to render the pattern truly. These and other improvisations in the field became the improvements for the next recension of the schedule.

Venturing further afield in the following two summers, Morgan traveled along the Red River of the North in 1861 into the vicinity of Winnipeg in Canada, and up the Missouri in 1862 to Fort Benton in Dakota Territory, in what is now Montana. On both trips he used the 1860b schedule. The way in which he fills the schedules is revealing. If the Type B pattern was evident to him, as it was in most cases, he filled in the descent line of the FB, but for the descendants of MZ, and of FZCh and MBCh, he simply wrote "same as father's brother's son above."[12] Having mastered the Type B principle, he no longer needed to fill in every repeat of the pattern. Indeed, the pattern is more readily seen in the schedules under this practice than they would be if every blank were filled in. Thus the schedule in its three recensions enabled him to uncover the principles underlying the classifications, and was not merely a means of recording the classifications in themselves.

Table II of the *Systems* was the final form in which Morgan displayed these principles for his readers. It is huge, consisting of 80 rows of different Indian nations and 268 columns for the genealogical positions, and thus contains more than 20,000 cells. In fact, there are twice that number of cells, since for every column Morgan gives both the word or "vocable" and its "translation." The table often goes beyond the entries in the schedules. Not only is it more extensive than any of the schedules of which it is made (1859: 206 genealogical positions; 1860a: 204; 1860b: 218), but the schedules themselves have many blanks, in some cases because of a lack of information and in some because Morgan was sure that he was observing a repeating pattern. Not every cell of table II is filled, but where Morgan believed he had sound evidence of the pattern, he filled the blanks accordingly. In short, the entries in table II represent Morgan's best judgment of the nature of the vocabulary and the principles by which it classifies kin, and are not records of questions asked and answered in mechanical fashion.

These points can, of course, be inferred from the very size of the final table, but they need to be mentioned because they are germane to the central issue in this chapter. The question here is whether the complete absence of Type A terminologies from table II reflect the state of things on the ground, or whether it is an artifact of Morgan's methods and the state of his understanding.

By the time of the third schedule, Morgan apparently had an instrument perfectly capable of registering Type A terminologies if they came his way. And some did, namely, those for Dravidian languages of South India. Morgan specifically targeted Tamil and other Dravidian languages at the outset of his project, and he learned the rudiments of the Tamil and Telugu terminology from a returned missionary in the fall of 1859. He saw at once the structural similarities with Iroquois that are due to same-sex sibling merger and strongly believed in their essential identity as proof that the American Indians had come from Asia. In his October 1, 1859, circular letter, he announced this supposed identity. He listed the principle features of these systems so far as he knew them and went on to say:

Table 2-4

Comparison of Morgan's Schedules and Table II on Diagnostics of Crossness, Type A and Type B

1859	1860a	1860b	Table II
73. FZSS	91. FZSS (m.s.)	95. FZSS (m.s.)	101. FZSS (m.s.)
	92. FZSS (f.s.)	96. FZSS (f.s.)	102. FZSS (f.s.)
74. FZSD	93. FZSD (m.s.)	97. FZSD (m.s.)	103. FZSD (m.s.)
	94. FZSD (f.s.)	98. FZSD (f.s.)	104. FZSD (f.s.)
75. FZDS	95. FZDS (m.s.)	99. FZDS (m.s.)	105. FZDS (m.s.)
	96. FZDS (f.s.)	100. FZDS (f.s.)	106. FZDS (f.s.)
76. FZDD	97. FZDD (m.s.)	101. FZDD (m.s.)	107. FZDD (m.s.)
	98. FZDD (f.s.)	102. FZDD (f.s.)	108. FZDD (f.s.)
97. MBSS	128. MBSS	136. MBSS (m.s.)	127. MBSS (m.s.)
		137. MBSS (f.s.)	128. MBSS (f.s.)
98. MBSD	129. MBSD	138. MBSD (m.s.)	129. MBSD (m.s.)
		139. MBSD (f.s.)	130. MBSD (f.s.)
99. MBDS	130. MBDS	140. MBDS (m.s.)	131. MBDS (m.s.)
		141. MBDS (f.s.)	132. MBDS (f.s.)
100. MBDD	131. MBDD	142. MBDD (m.s.)	133. MBDD (m.s.)
		142. MBDD (f.s.)	134. MBDD (f.s.)
	150. FFZS (m.s.)	162. FFZS (m.s.)	
	151. FFZD (m.s.)	163. FFZD (m.s.)	176. FFZD (m.s.)
	152. FFZSS (m.s.)	164. FFZSS (m.s.)	
	153. FFZSD (m.s.)	165. FFZSD (m.s.)	
	154. FFZDS (m.s.)	166. FFZDS (m.s.)	
	155. FFZDD (m.s.)	167. FFZDD (m.s.)	
			177. FFZDS (m.s.)
			178. FFZDD (m.s.)
153. MMBS			186. MMBS
154. MMBD			
155. MMBSS			187. MMBSS (m.s.)
156. MMBSD			188. MMBSD (f.s.)
157. MMBDS			
158. MMBDD			

If, in addition to these particulars, the grandfather's and grandmother's brothers and sisters, are all alike, grandfathers and grandmothers; if the grandsons of a man's brothers and sisters are his grandsons; and *if the son of a man's female cousin is his nephew,* and the son of this nephew is a grandson, then all the radical features of the American Indian are present in the Telugu and Tamilian system of relationship. (Emphasis added)

It was not until Morgan returned from his last western field trip in the summer of 1862 that he received a fully worked out schedule (second version, of 1860a) for

Tamil from the Reverend Ezekiel C. Scudder that forcibly drew his attention to the failed prediction about the child of a "cousin" (see figure 2-3). For the children of the FZS and FZD, Scudder's reply gives the Type A classifications, and he adds, "The names of these relationships & some others result from the laws of intermarriage & are the reverse of what you have indicated," referring to the statement and examples in Morgan's circular letter. Crossed lines ending in pointing hands join Tamil terms with English translations that show the reversals of Morgan's expectations. Again, for children of MBS and MBD, he gives Type A responses and notes, "Reversed again here."

Morgan duly noted these departures from the expected pattern in the *Systems,* referring to them as a kind of blemish rather than as a principled difference (1871:391):

It is a little singular that the children of my male cousins, *Ego* a male, should be my nephews and nieces, instead of my sons and daughters, and that the children of my female cousins should be my sons and daughters instead of my nephews and nieces, as required by the analogies of the system. It is the only particular in which it differs materially from the Seneca-Iroquois form; and in this the Seneca is more in logical accordance with the principles of the system than the Tamilian. It is difficult to find any explanation of the variance.

The explanation of the variance had, of course, been given to him by Reverend Scudder: "the laws of intermarriage" or the cross-cousin rule, which Morgan did indeed consider but rejected for "want of generality." It may be that Morgan tended to minimize evidence that cross-cousin marriage was the organizing principle of Dravidian terminologies because he himself, as it happened, had married his cross cousin (Trautmann 1987:241–45); but even without that happenstance, his belief in the essential identity of these systems would have prevented him from arriving at a full appreciation of their differences. Accordingly, in table III (which contains the Asian systems of classes called Turanian and Malayan), Morgan duly records the classifications for the Dravidian terminologies he had acquired from his missionary correspondents on the second (Tamil, Telugu) and third (Canarese or Kannada) schedules. Because these schedules lack questions for the MMBS, MMBSS, and MMBSD, however, Morgan had to decide how to classify them and in doing so he followed Seneca, or Type B, principles—which explains the errors in his Tamil classifications on these diagnostics. Morgan failed to recognize that the Dravidian languages departed from the Iroquois in classifying a parents' cousins and his or her descendants, and he imposed an Iroquois pattern in the blanks of table III not filled by the schedules.

This, then, is definite evidence of an Iroquois bias affecting the table III entries at the margin. Furthermore, the fact that Morgan did not become aware of the Type A pattern until after his western field trips raises the possibility that if he had encountered American Indian terminologies with Type A classifications he would not have registered them as such. Rather, expecting Type B classifications, he would have recorded them under that rubric. For the moment, this must remain a blank

Figure 2-3

Tamil Kinship Terminology, as Reported to Morgan by E.C. Scudder

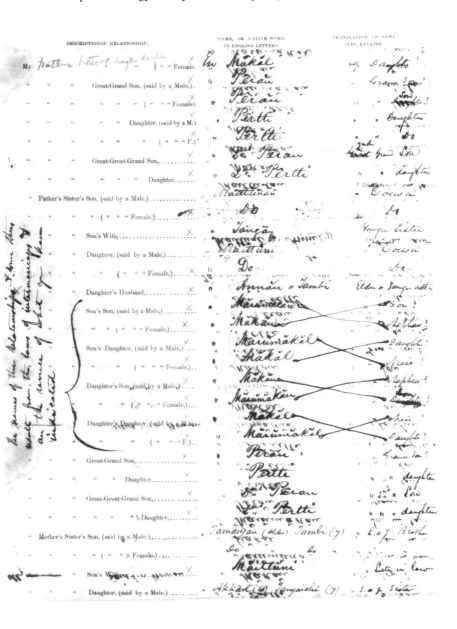

Source: Morgan Papers, University of Rochester.

Table 2-5

Comparison of Morgan's Schedules and Table II on Twelve Kintypes

1859	1860a	1860b	Table II
	151. FFZD (m.s.)	163. FFZD (m.s.)	176. FFZD (m.s.)
	154. FFZDS (m.s.)	166. FFZDS (m.s.)	177. FFZDS (m.s.)
	155. FFZDD (m.s.)	167. FFZDD (m.s.)	178. FFZDD (m.s.)
153. MMBS			186. MMBS
155. MMBSS			187. MMBSS (m.s.)
156. MMBSD			188. MMBSD (f.s.)
159. MMBGrGrS			189. MMBSSS (m.s.)
			190. MMBSSS (f.s.)
160. MMBGrGrD			191. MMBSSD (m.s.)
			192. MMBSSD (f.s.)
			193. MMBSSSS (m.s.)
			194. MMBSDD (m.s.)

space of possibility without content; all that can be said in this regard at the moment is that Morgan had indeed found reliable evidence for Type B in Iroquois, Ojibwa, and Dakota terminologies.

OMAHA AND OMAHA-LIKE SYSTEMS IN MORGAN

The raw data of schedules and the field notes can also be used to address Kronenfeld's problem: the genesis of the systematic, twelve-term error in Morgan's version of Omaha, and of Omaha-like systems in table II. A comparison of the schedules with table II (see table 2-5) shows that the schedules contain only three or five of the twelve table II terms, and none of them contain both the descendants of MMBS and of FFZD. This suggests that entries for these twelve terms are based on little raw data, as confirmed by the original schedules. Morgan was clearly extrapolating from information in hand and his understanding of the principles of the system. And the error he made in this regard has been generalized throughout the table II entries on these twelve terms for unilineal or skewed systems, perhaps from a single system. The question is, which one?

Morgan had encountered unilineal (skewed) systems of the Omaha kind right at the beginning of his project, while he was still sorting out the Type B characteristics for Seneca. As early as April 1859, he had collected substantial information on Winnebago terminology from a Winnebago delegation while on a trip to Washington, D.C. In the schedule he gives characteristic "Omaha" equations such as MBS "uncle," MBSS and MBSSS "little uncle"; MBD and MBSSD are, incorrectly, "aunt," but MBSD, correctly, "little mother." FZS appears as "nephew" and "FFFZS as "little nephew." In short, Morgan gives a good record of an Omaha-like system. Of the twelve table II terms that Kronenfeld examines, Morgan's schedule for Winnebago gives "Lit. G.F." (little grandfather) for MMBS, MMBSS, and MMBGrGrS, and "L.G.M." (little grandmother) for MMBD, MMBSD, and MMBGrGrD. This is essentially what Dorsey gives for Omaha (more exactly: "grandfather" and "grandmother" without the "little"), and contradicts what Morgan gave for Omaha, Winnebago, and other such systems in table II! In table II, Morgan "corrects" the Winnebago "little grandfather," changing it to "little uncle" and "little grandmother" to "little mother."

Morgan's notebook on his interview of the Winnebago delegation—his first encounter with the Omaha principle—shows how baffling it was to him.

In the schedule it will be seen that the children of a brother and of a sister are not cousins, but the one is uncle to the other, and in a different sense from uncle in other cases. He has authority over his nephew and can command his services in a sense in which his own father could not, and this authority reaches to his posterity. The idea is expressed in the schedule by superior uncle & inferior nephew. The same thing to some extent appears in the Shawnee system. The idea on which this special deviation rests is not very apparent. As descent was in the male line it may have been an attempt to exalt the male and depress the female line. (Morgan Papers)

In retrospect, when Morgan was writing the *Systems,* it seemed to him that the decisive breakthrough in recognizing the principles of the Omaha type systems came not from Winnebago, but the following month, during his first western field trip, from the Kaw or Kansa: "My mother's brother is my uncle . . . and calls me nephew; his son is my uncle again, and calls me nephew; and his descendants in the male line are severally my uncles, theoretically in an infinite series."

Of the actual existence and daily recognition of these relationships, as stated, novel as they are, there is no doubt whatever. I first discovered this deviation from the typical form while working out the system of the Kaws in Kansas in 1859. The Kaw chief from whom I obtained it, through a perfectly competent interpreter, insisted upon the verity of these relationships against all doubts and questionings; and when the work was done I found it proved itself through the correlative relationships. Afterwards in 1860, while at the Iowa reservation in Nebraska, I had an opportunity to test it fully, both in Iowa and Otoe, through White Cloud a native Iowa well versed in English. While discussing these relationships he pointed out a boy near us, and remarked that he was his uncle, and the son of his mother's brother who was also his uncle. (Morgan 1871:179 n.)

In the original schedule of the Kaw or Kansa terminology Morgan gives "uncle" for MMBS and MMBSS, and "mother" for MMBD, in conformity with the erroneous table II pattern for the twelve terms. On the next page, he adds relevant specifications "in the female line," that is, for MMBDDS as an interpretation of MMBGrGrS of the printed schedule. At the top of the page, he writes, "If [crossed out: the son has] the uncle has a son he is also an uncle," which reflects his discovery of the

Omaha principle, but in the wrong descent line. Obviously, there was some confusion between himself and his informant and, on the assumption that this version was right, he generalized it to other Omaha type systems in table II.

The systematic character of the twelve errors arises from the fact that they are a series, or rather two series, descending from the MMB and the FFZ. Since the first of the series was wrong, for whatever reason, the rest, generated by analogy, would also be wrong, in a systematic way. The crucial mistake recorded in the schedule for Kaw is that MMBS is "uncle," whence the other classifications follow by analogy and on the Omaha principle that the son of the uncle is an uncle. If MMBS is "uncle," then it is reasonable to suppose that FFZD is "aunt."

Are these errors attributable to an Iroquois, Type B bias? The answer may be "yes," in the simple sense that in Type B the MMBS is "uncle" and the FFZD is "aunt," the starting points of the twelve-term error. But at the time Morgan was discovering the Omaha principle he was only beginning to clarify the Type B pattern for Seneca. In the April 23, 1859, Seneca schedule he had not yet done so, but in the November 1 schedule he had. So it is unlikely that the bias could have been in operation at the time he first encountered systems of Omaha type, namely, the Winnebago and the Kaw.

Even if we suppose what seems unlikely—namely, that Kronenfeld is right in saying that Morgan's errors for Omaha type systems in table II are based on Iroquois (or Type B) crossness—we still must ask: Is he also right in saying that Dorsey's Omaha is based on crossness of a Dravidian (Type A) kind? We think not, and must now say why.

OMAHA AND THE TWO TYPES OF CROSSNESS

If Morgan's published and unpublished material were the only record available for North American systems of kinship, Kronenfeld's proposition would have to be rejected for the compelling reason that the systems of unilineal equations Morgan records, both of Omaha and of Crow type, are entirely systems of Type B. There are no Type A systems at all in the record. Consequently, Type B must be the ground from which Omaha and Crow type systems arise, although the evidence to this effect is more complicated than Morgan's material would imply. This complexity can be illustrated with reference to post-Morgan collections of material from among Central Algonquian speakers, which show the existence of Type A.

There is a sort of fatality about the way in which Morgan learned kinship. Certain consequences attach to the specifics of the precise angle at which he approached the kinship systems of American and other peoples, as well as the trajectory and timing of his movement through the masses of information that came to him. Starting from the Seneca and proceeding to Ojibwa, Tamil, and others, he constructed an initial model according to which the children of all cousins are "nephews" and "nieces." However, he quickly abandoned this model as he developed a clear conception of Type B, taking it to be the standard from which all other forms were deviations. Once his sense of the principles underlying the logic of Type B had become robust, it seems to have prevented him from understanding the different logic of Type A. For anthropologists of the twentieth century, the reverse has been the case. Following Tylor and Rivers, Type A and the principle of cross-cousin marriage that is its logical operator become transparent and normal, whereas Type B virtually disappears from view until Lounsbury and Pospisil rediscover it as a distinct type. Even then, it remains difficult to discern and more difficult still to account for. Lounsbury shows that, after Morgan, a Type A bias overtook even the way in which Iroquois kinship was read.

Type A was eventually discovered among Central Algonquian speakers because anthropologists were looking for it. The well-known studies that led Hallowell to cross-cousin marriage among the Ojibwa were inspired by Rivers's sociological approach to kinship terminologies. At first, Hallowell (1928a, 1928b) uncovered evidence of cross-cousin marriage exclusively in the past, through old (seventeenth- and eighteenth-century) dictionaries for Abenaki, an Eastern Algonquian group, and Ojibwa. These showed Dravidian-like equations of uncles and aunts: MB = FZH; FZ = MBW; FB = MZH; MZ = FBW. (Anthropologists in search of cross-cousin marriage do not seem to have considered that these equations hold for their own English kinship terms, in which the wife of an uncle is an aunt and the husband of an aunt is an uncle. We have in any case seen how insufficient such evidence is to rule out Type B.) Hallowell presents these findings diffidently, pointing out that "contemporary ethnological inquiry has not produced any evidence of the practice of cross-cousin marriage among Algonkin, Ottawa, and Ojibway-speaking peoples, or, for that matter, among any other Algonkian. . . . Moreover, the marriage of cousins is actually viewed with abhorrence by some present-day Algonkin tribes" (1928b:521). Subsequently, Hallowell (1937) found the contemporary practice of cross-cousin marriage at a high frequency among Ojibwa in the Lake Winnipeg area. Ruth Landes (1937, 1969 [1938]) confirmed these findings in her ethnographies of Ojibwa at Emo, Ontario. As for the linguists, Hockett (1964) reconstructed cross-cousin marriage for Proto-Central Algonquian through a comparison of lexica, and Wheeler (1982) argued with him only over which type of cross-cousin marriage it was to have been.

In retrospect, a weakness of the pre-Lounsbury Ojibwa and Central Algonquian ethnology, fine as it is in other respects, is that it is not aware of the Type B alternative as it develops the case for a "Dravidian" interpretation. Furthermore, it does not probe the diagnostic points of the kinship space. Indeed, it is only rarely aware that Morgan's tables are at cross-purposes on this matter with what becomes the dominant view in the absence of opposition.

Nevertheless the existence of Type A among some Ojibwa seems to be established securely enough from other indications: the reported merger of affinal terms with consanguines (that is, beyond the uncle and aunt terms); the practice, or memory of the practice, of cross-cousin marriage; and the joking relations of a ribald, erotic nature current among cousins (see chapter 6). Moreover, limited but unmistakable evidence of Type A comes from related, northerly members of the Central Algonquian group, Cree (Montangais and Naskapi: Strong 1929; Graburn 1975). Indeed, the phenomenon is a distinctly northern one, confined to Canada.

This evidence, together with Father Jacker's evidence for Type B among Ojibwa of Upper Michigan and the rest of Morgan's collections, shows that all three corners of Kronenfeld's problem are found in the Central Algonquian group, distributed from north to south: Type A (Cree, Northern Ojibwa), Type B (Southern Ojibwa, Ottawa), and Omaha (Miami, Peoria, Piankeshaw, Kaskaskia, Weaw, Sauk and Fox, Menominee, Kikapoo, Shawnee, perhaps Potawatomi). This distributional pattern confirms that Type B and not Type A is the immediate context in which systems of Omaha (and Crow) type arise. Ojibwa speakers are distributed along both sides of the Type A/Type B divide.

As already explained, an inspection of the classifications indicates that Type B lacks cross-cousin marriage as a principle of classification. That it lacks the rule or practice of cross-cousin marriage is established ethnographically as well. With regard to Jacker's (Type B) Ojibwa, he writes to Morgan, "The intermarriage between persons belonging to the same tribe [i.e., clan] was not allowed, but the Indians living in the proximity of the white man have yielded to the power of the example and to the pressure of necessity (the greater part of whole settlements belonging to the same tribe) so far that even marriages between second cousins occur" (Jacker to Morgan, May 30, 1860, Morgan Papers). As to the Dakota, it is well known that the marriage of cousins was prohibited; Riggs confirms that this was the case in the middle of the nineteenth century (Riggs to Morgan, March 1, 1859, Morgan Papers): "There is no prohibition to marriage except within the same degree of relationship; among which are *cousins,* some of which are counted by them as *brothers* and *sisters.* There are among the Dakotas two *clans* or *villages* called Ke-ya'-ksa, *Breaking something of their own*—so named from their transgressing this law."

Callender's 1962 survey, *Social Organization of the Central Algonkian Indians,* posits the same threefold division of Central Algonquian speakers without benefit of Lounsbury's elucidation of Type B (see figure 2-4). In the North-Central group consisting of the dialects of Southern Ojibwa, he finds partial terminological equations of affinal and consanguineal terms; in the Northern group, "complete equating of affinal and cross kin" that can be explained "by assuming a more consistent practice of cross-cousin marriage"; and, in the Central group, strong unilineal clans and systems of Omaha type. In a later publication (Callender 1978), he posits two configurations for Algonquians and Siouans of the Great Lakes region, varying between Omaha- and Iroquois-type terminologies.

Ives's theory of Athapaskan prehistory demonstrates the widespread existence of Type A terminologies among Athapaskan speakers of Canada (Ives 1990), and also among other groups (chapter 5 of this volume). His study area just touches the margin of Morgan's area of collection, at the same latitudes as the Type A Central Algonquians to their east. He shows how Athapaskan Type A terminologies and cross-cousin marriage are related to the formative principles that govern small hunting bands thinly scattered across vast hunting territories in this region. But to the south, where a denser demography is sustained by different conditions and techniques, we find the exogamy of cousins and Type B terminologies among Algonquians, Siouans, and at least some Athapaskan speakers, namely, Kiowa-Apache (McAllister 1937) and Chiricahua Apache (Opler 1937), and also, of course, systems of Crow and Omaha type.

Figure 2-4
Distribution of Central Algonquian Languages

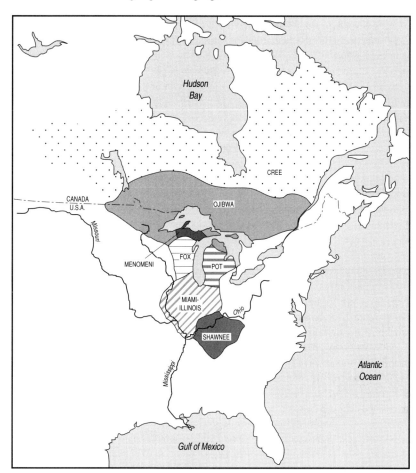

Source: Callendar (1962).

CONCLUSION

This study leads to three principal conclusions, concerning the integrity of Morgan's ethnographic record, the ethnology of kinship in North America, and the relevance of it to other parts of the world.

Since ethnography is the lifeblood of ethnology, it is essential to determine whether the "supply" is pure and uncontaminated. To this end, the findings of Kronenfeld have provided a valuable impetus to further investigations of the integrity of Morgan's record. That impetus is all the more important when one considers that, for many of the Indian nations in Morgan's table II, his record is the main record, or even the only record, available, and that, occurring as they do at the point of the "invention of kinship," both Morgan's errors and his discoveries have no doubt had a large and long-lasting effect on subsequent studies of kinship.

With respect to the issues we have examined, we can say, first, that Kronenfeld has correctly identified twelve systematic errors in Morgan's record for Omaha-type terminologies for North America. However, because of the evident superiority of Dorsey's record for the Omaha themselves, it became the standard for discussion from as early as 1897 (e.g., in the analyses of Kohler and Durkheim; discussed in Barnes 1975, 1984). Moreover, later discussions (e.g., those of Lounsbury 1964b; Radcliffe-Brown 1968 [1941]) have taken as their basis Tax's (1937b) report on Fox or Lounsbury's version of Morgan's table II report for Republican Pawnee— from which Lounsbury has cleaned the record of the very errors Kronenfeld has identified (Lounsbury 1954; analyzed in Barnes 1995). In short, the ethnological discussion of Omaha-type terminologies in North America has not been contaminated by Morgan's errors.

Second, Morgan's small but significant errors in reporting Dravidian terminologies have had no adverse effect on discussion, because Dravidianists have had easy recourse to abundant original data and have developed a well-formed notion of the principles of Type A crossness that differ from those of Morgan. These few errors appear to be reported here for the first time.

Third, the case of the Type B pattern in North America is more complicated. The Type B pattern for Seneca rests on many kintypes, but of those in Morgan's table II, only twenty-two are diagnostic of the difference of the two types of crossness, and most of these pertain to the children of "cousins." Since Lounsbury's 1964a study, Type B has been given considerable attention in ethnology. But Lounsbury's Seneca data are taken from Morgan's table II, so that the question of integrity is of greater moment here. Moreover, Lounsbury's table of Seneca terms contains forty-one genealogical specifications not found in table II but presumably generated from reciprocals (in the manner made explicit in his discussion of Republican Pawnee, which also augments Morgan's table II entries in this way: see Barnes 1995). These additional specifications include most of the second-cousin types that Trautmann (1981:87), for example, relies on to illustrate the Dravidian/Iroquois, or Type A/Type B, difference. However, it can easily be shown that Lounsbury's augmentations are consistent with the organization of the terms explicitly given in table II.

The critical question is whether the Type B pattern in table II is ethnographically well grounded. Although the first two Seneca schedules (of November 1858 and April 1859) do not show it (having a pattern that is neither Type A nor Type B), subsequent Seneca and other Iroquois schedules in the Morgan Papers do show Type B. Furthermore, Type B among other groups in table II is corroborated by contemporary (e.g., Jacker, and Riggs) and twentieth-century (Eggan et al.) reports. Type B is therefore ethnographically well attested for various North American groups, and the ethnography on this question is sound.

Our ethnological conclusions with respect to North America are as follows: (1) Type B is the ground from which unilineal systems, whether Crow or Omaha in type, arise; that is, the direct precursors of unilineal systems in North America are systems with crossness of Type B. (2) The relation of systems with Type A crossness to systems with unilineal equations (i.e., Crow-Omaha type) is mediated by systems with Type B crossness. (3) Type A systems lie to the north, those with Type B or unilineal patterns to the south. The latter are associated with larger aggregations of population. (4) Type B crossness lacks cross-cousin marriage as a principle of classification and is associated with the exogamy of cousins. Thus, without presuming any particular direction of change, it is safe to say that in North America both Type B and the unilineal (Crow-Omaha) systems are associated with an opening out of affinal ties (4) and larger agglomerations of people (3) as compared with Type A.

Here the interaction of landscape, economic technique, social organization, and semiotics seems to be governed by a logic particular to their conjuncture, and quite foreign to, for example, the conditions under which terminologies with Type A crossness occur in South India and Sri Lanka. What, then, do North American hunting bands have in common with South Indian agriculturalist castes? The answer is Type A, and little else.

As to the general ethnological significance of these North American results, the first lessons they give are methodological. Comparison has been bedeviled by the use of cultural labels and type cases. Although it makes some sense to speak of Iroquois, Crow, and Omaha types within North America, and Dravidian within India and Sri Lanka, problems arise when these names are used for cross-cultural types. When these names are used outside their proper places of origin, they create considerable confusion over the two distinct senses in which they have come to be used: as cultural-historical sets of related but varying terminologies, on the one hand, and as structural types having a set of properties that is limited and fixed, on the other. In the case of the "Iroquois" type, the confusion has been compounded by Murdock's global typology, which puts all the world in one of six types, according to the treatment of siblings and first cousins (namely, Hawaiian, Iroquois, Sudanese, Eskimo, Crow, and Omaha), a practice that lumps Type A and Type B as "Iroquois." It is far better to use severely structural types and names to prevent the intermixture of the structural and the contingent. Rather than "Dravidian," "Iroquois," and "Crow-Omaha," we prefer "systems with Type A crossness," "systems with Type B crossness," and "unilineal systems" or "systems with unilineal equations," or even "systems with skewing."

As to substantive ethnological conclusions on the significance of the North American results cross-culturally, they would have to be founded upon areal surveys, which we have not made. Nevertheless, a few points merit further discussion.

One has to do with Africa and comes from an unexpected source there: Kronenfeld's (1973, 1980a, 1980b) report on the kinship terminology of the Fanti. According to Kronenfeld, the Fanti have not one terminology, but two. One of them is "Crow"—or in our terms a system based on matrilineal equations. But there is also an "unskewed" terminology in simultaneous use among the Fanti, who can and do discuss the one in terms of the other. We have been gratified to find that Kronenfeld's genealogical chart of the unskewed terminology shows that it is of Type B and not of Type A crossness. If nothing else, this is further evidence—from his own hand!—against Kronenfeld's claim that unilineal systems are based on crossness of "Dravidian" type. We notice frequent reference to "Iroquois-" type systems in the literature on Africa, which, in view of the influence of the Murdockian scheme mentioned above, is ambiguous on the face of it; but perhaps it would be a good place to look for the juxtaposition of Type B and the unilineal systems found in North America.

The second point has to do with Southeast Asia. Despite the encouraging result of the Fanti case, it would be foolhardy to claim that the mediating position of Type B is necessary, especially in view of the contrary evidence of empirical association and theoretical discussion of the succession of types, ready made, as it were, to generate unilineal systems from prescriptive ones in the absence of the still shadowy and elusive Type B. Southeast Asia would seem to supply such counterevidence in abundance. Even so, a Type B has been reported from Mentawai, an island south of Sumatra (Schefold 1988). So even Southeast Asia with its abundance of Type A and unilineal terminologies has at least one Type B case. We need to search for others. Parkin (chapter 12 of this volume) finds the first Type B case reported from South Asia.

The paradox of Type B is that it was abundantly recorded by Morgan and his contributors when kinship became the focus of study, but thereafter it fell into an obscurity so complete that it was confused with Type A and associated with the logic of exogamous moieties or cross-cousin marriage. Even after Lounsbury's article rescued it from oblivion, it remained poorly known. The grand theories of evolutionary succession all fix upon systems of Type A crossness as the starting point of development from elementary to complex (Lévi-Strauss 1949), prescriptive to nonprescriptive (Needham 1966b, 1967, 1973), or tetradic to the successive products of its dissolution (Allen 1989a, and chapter 14 of this volume). Structuralism in its many forms deserves credit for every modern advance in the study of kinship, but admittedly it has not illuminated Type B brightly enough that we may see it clearly. The time has come to put it under the spotlight.

NOTES

The authors thank the Rush Rhees Library of the University of Rochester for access to the Morgan Papers and permission to publish the photograph that appears in figure 2-3. We especially thank Karl S. Kabelac, curator of the Morgan Papers, for his help. We are grateful for a British Academy Travel Grant (to R. H. Barnes), and thank the LSA Faculty Fund of the College of Literature, Science, and the Arts, University of Michigan (Thomas R. Trautmann) for research and travel support.

1. Kronenfeld makes the additional point that in Morgan's Omaha, unlike Dorsey's, "reciprocals are not totally consistent." But the point is not compelling. He says, "One's mother's brother's son is in the same 'uncle' terminological category as one's mother's father's brother's son, while the reciprocal expression, one's father's sister's daughter's child is in the 'grandchild' category, and not the 'nibling' category that one's father's brother's daughter's child is in." But one of the elements of this four-cornered comparison is not in Morgan's table II at all: the MFBS. Moreover, reciprocals are not in every instance constant. See Barnes (1984:138, 142).

2. Ponca, Omaha, Iowa, Oto, Kaw (Kansa), Winnebago. Morgan does not report on the twelve

kin for one other Omaha-like group in table II (Osage) and for Mandan (type uncertain).

3. Chocta, Chickasa, Creek, Cherokee, Pawnee. Morgan gives no report on the twelve kin for Crow and Arikaree.

4. Kronenfeld does not give a list of the twelve genealogical positions, but he does give the reductions rules that identify them. Trautmann identified the twelve by working out the formulas in kintype terms, and Barnes arrived at the same list independently, through an empirical comparison of the Morgan and Dorsey tables. In addition to the twelve, there are a further eight on which Morgan and Dorsey differ and that fall outside this set of systematic differences between the two—48: BDH(w.s.) = S-in-law (Morgan), HB (Dorsey); 88: FZH = uncle (M); WB/HB/ZH (D); 235: WF = old man (M), GrF (D); 236: WM = M-in-law (M), GrM (D); 258: WZH = e/yB (M), [eB/yB] (D); 259: HZH = B-in-law (M), GrF (D); 264: HBW = A-in-law (M), Z (D); 265: WBW = GrM (M), SW (D). There is considerable variation on the last five for Omaha systems in Morgan's table II.

5. In addition, Lounsbury's version of Morgan's Seneca kinship terminology contains forty-one genealogical specifications that are not found in table II, as discussed at the end of the chapter.

6. We omit details of Kronenfeld's comparative analysis of Iroquois and Dravidian, which, in its recourse to unilineal exogamous descent groups and a distinction of "side" (father's/mother's) to explain terminologies, adopts the very analytical devices that Lounsbury (1964a) set aside—one would have thought—so effectively. The attempt to explain categories in terms of social institutions has the faults exposed some time ago by Dumont (1961).

7. Evidence from which these generalizations about variation among Type B patterns for consanguines and about merger of consanguines and affines are drawn can be found in Trautmann and Barnes (1991).

8. Some exceptions: Norbeck's (1963) work on Japanese kinship terms in Morgan; DeMallie's (1979) important study of variation in Dakota kinship terminology; Trautmann's (1987) analysis of the genesis of the *Systems of Consanguinity and Affinity;* and Tooker's (1992) new findings on Morgan's kinship project.

9. A fuller treatment of the sources than we can give here would discuss the characteristics of the November 1858 Seneca terminology and Morgan's comments. Briefly, Morgan's original question calls for the grandson and granddaughter (i.e., not differentiated as SS, SD, DS, DD) of FB, FZ, MZ and MB, and he finds they are all "nephew" and "niece"; this, then, is the preliminary stage of the inquiry and is consistent with the January 1859 statement. At a later point, he differentiated the grandchildren into son's and daughter's children, but without yet specifying sex of ego. Interestingly enough, the answers given are consistent with Type B if we assume a *female* ego, which suggests that his informant was Caroline Parker of the Parker family of Tonawanda (for details of Morgan's relations with the Parkers, see Trautmann 1987). The April 1859 schedule for Seneca, attributed to Caroline Parker and her brother Isaac Newton Parker, gives classifications that are opposite for crossness, that is, consistent with Type B if for a male ego (perhaps presuming Morgan as the point of reference?). We have also omitted from our analysis a series of sixteen questions on the printed schedules pertaining to the relations obtaining between descendants of sister-sister, brother-brother, and brother-sister pairs. These were worded in a very complex way (e.g., "The son, of the son, of a brother, to the daughter, of the daughter, of the brother's sister"), and Morgan eventually gave up trying to collect information on them. These are, of course, part of his attempt to uncover the pattern of classifications for cousins and their children and to make his point that in the "Classificatory" system all consanguines eventually merge with the lineal line as grandchildren, no matter how distant.

10. The first of these, in spite of its 1859 date, is entered on the (1860a) schedule with the date 1860 printed on it, which presumably had been printed by then. It is bound in the first volume of the "Record of Indian letters," Morgan Papers. The second is also on the 1860a schedule.

11. Could this record be interpreted the other way? Could there have been variation between

Types A and B on the ground, and could Morgan by powers of suggestion have caused the field ethnographer to suppress that variation in the final version of the ethnography? DeMallie (1979) gives a clear and careful account of Dakota variation and Morgan's tendency to correct variations out of table II, which on the face of it encourages this view. But against the bare possibility of the interpretation mentioned, we must consider that there is no positive evidence for Type A classifications (on points diagnostic of the difference from Type B) in the unpublished records of Riggs and Morgan, and in the published literature on Dakota kinship terminology, including especially the work of DeMallie, who was looking for variation, and also that of Walker (1914), Lesser (1928), and Hassrick (1944). What variation Riggs speaks of is not between Types A and B, but between a pattern in which children of "brothers" and "sisters" are "sons" and "daughters," and the children of "cousins" are "nephews" and "nieces," which he takes to be the dominant pattern, and a variant which is the Type B pattern. The first agrees neither with Type B nor with the Seneca pattern as given in Morgan's circular letter of January 1859 and is not otherwise attested for Dakota.

12. This practice is also found in the 1860a schedule for Yankton Dakota, which Morgan singles out as a type case for Dakota.

3

On the Formal Analysis of "Dravidian," "Iroquois," and "Generational" Varieties as Nearly Associative Combinations

FRANKLIN E. TJON SIE FAT

In the view of Eugene Wigner (1960), one of the striking features of mathematics is its "unreasonable effectiveness." Mathematical concepts turn up in entirely unexpected connections, often permitting an unexpectedly close and accurate description of phenomena. Why, Wigner asks, should this be the case? Moreover, how does one know whether a theory formulated in terms of mathematical concepts is uniquely appropriate? Whether mathematics is *unreasonably* effective remains an open question.[1] Any scientific enterprise is selective: when building models (mathematical or otherwise), one often disregards certain information and focuses narrowly on data deemed relevant to some particular theory. Mathematics is undoubtedly effective in that it enables us to formulate hypotheses and to represent phenomena in a precise manner. At the same time, a theory formulated in terms of mathematical concepts is not necessarily uniquely appropriate. Mathematics is about structure. It is effective because it captures the abstract form underlying the many apparently dissimilar patterns exhibited in the physical or social world (MacLane 1990:121).

The present study applies mathematics to the similarities and differences between "Dravidian" and "Iroquois" types of kin classification in an effort to shed some light on the generalization of cross/parallel distinctions. My intention is to explore the possibility of providing a formal, mathematically unambiguous class of related models for the structural comparison of Dravidian and Iroquois variants. This objective is broadly similar to the goal set out in Scheffler's (1971) analysis of Melanesian systems.

However, I adopt a different theoretical framework, reconceiving Dravidian and Iroquois classifications as algebraic structures, not as systems of kin classification to be analyzed by means of equivalence rules applied to focal kintypes under the assumptions of extensionist theory. For Scheffler (1971), Dravidian, Iroquois, and certain other types should be considered structural variants of one another, inasmuch as they are identical with regard to the primary meaning of their kinship terms (i.e., the semantic dimensions underlying their focal kintypes) and differ only in the manner in which the cross/parallel distinction forming the base of all such systems is extended (by means of suitable equivalence rules) to more distant kin. In contrast, I define a new class of structures by recasting the seminal model advanced by Trautmann (1981:177–200) into the language of universal algebra. This approach leads to an economy of presentation, allows for a direct comparison of variants, and yields significant new information on the relationship among several seemingly different types of kinship structure.

Trautmann devised his formal model in the course of his reconstruction of the proto-Dravidian kinship system. Its purpose was to help articulate the wide range of terminological patterns and marriage rules found in the data from historically related, localized kinship systems of South India and Sri Lanka. Central to this model is the assumption that the characteristically Dravidian cross/parallel discrimination within ego's generation also operates at the level of ego's parents and children, thus constituting a single unifying semantic dimension. Trautmann's real innovation is the series of equivalence rules he devised to assign all kintypes correctly to the cross or parallel category. These rules are formulated directly in terms of specific combinations of cross and parallel relational symbols and not (as in the more familiar Lounsbury-Scheffler formalization) as equivalence rules operating on kintype strings (Trautmann 1981:179).

Trautmann's scheme lends itself to a direct representation as an algebra, that is, as a mathematical structure defined as a family of finitary operations (unary, binary, or otherwise) on a nonempty underlying set of relations. This is the line of research I propose to explore.

After a short technical introduction, I demonstrate that the algebraic reformulation of Trautmann's Dravidian model may be fruitfully extended and applied to the analysis of Iroquois and "generational" types of classification for crossness. The first step is to define the canonical Dravidian and Iroquois structures, by furnishing partial multiplication tables for the binary operation determining whether the relative of a relative is cross or parallel (consanguineal kin only). I then demonstrate that these canonical structures are "nearly" *associative*. That is, the cross/parallel allocations in the kinship structure are, roughly speaking, independent of the particular genealogical path chosen for their composition. But in certain other variants of these basic structures, the binary composition of relations is *nonassociative:* one must specify the admissible subset of genealogical paths. Moreover, by simply varying the constraints on associativity, one can generate a variety of generational types, such as structures with the standard Iroquois pattern of cross/parallel kin classification in the parents' and children's generations, but with the possibility of merging all first, second, and third cousins in ego's own generation as "siblings." I show how a further series of generational variants may be derived in which the Iroquois pattern of crossness is transformed in G^{-1}, and reciprocally in G^{+1}, by modifying key entries in the canonical multiplication table. These results are summarized later in the chapter in a series of genealogical diagrams. Because these partial models represent the pattern of crossness for consanguineal relations only, no algebraic equivalent to a rule of bilateral cross-cousin marriage is required for their formulation.

The discussion then turns to the algebraic structure corresponding to Trautmann's full set of "Dravidian A" equivalence rules through which the articulation of consanguineal and affinal relations is expressed. This structure is indeed compatible with a rule of sibling exchange and with the logic of bilateral cross-cousin marriage, extending the properties of my partial models. However, Trautmann's full model is shown to be underdetermined, requiring further specification of the rules for the composition of cross/parallel relations. The chapter concludes with a few words about the possibility of mapping a marriage rule based on the direct exchange of "sisters" onto certain Iroquois-generational-like systems and suggests avenues for further research.

ASSOCIATIVITY AND THE COMPOSITION OF KINSHIP RELATIONS

A binary operation * on a set S is described as *associative* if, for all a, b, and c in S, $(a * b) * c = a * (b * c) = a * b * c$, that is, if the binary operation has the property that the bracketing of its arguments may be disregarded. Not all binary operations are associative, of course. For example, the associative law holds for addition and multiplication of the real numbers, but not for subtraction or division. Thus, $(8 + 4) + 2 = 8 + (4 + 2) = 14$, and $(8 \times 4) \times 2 = 8 \times (4 \times 2) = 64$, but $(8 - 4) - 2 = 2$, while $8 - (4 - 2) = 6$, and $(8 \div 4) \div 2 = 1$, while $8 \div (4 \div 2) = 4$.

Similar observations hold for the composition of kinship relations. For example, the kintype MBD representing the composition of the relations "mother," "brother," and "daughter" subsumes two possible bracketings or ways of parenthesizing the expression (see figure 3-1): (MB)D and M(BD). The specific shape of the bracketing may also be conveniently visualized as a *tree* structure in which the order of composition is represented by the order of branching. Differences of bracketing may indeed be highly relevant in the composition of kinship relations. Although (MB)D and M(BD), glossed, respectively, as *"uncle's daughter"* and *"mother's niece"* are both equivalent to *"cousin"* in the English terminological system, different paths may lead to different evaluations in other systems. For example, Kronenfeld (1980b:157) mentions the following alternate patterns for the reduction of the string *na n'nua banyin n'ba* (MBC): either (1) *na n'nua (banyin)n'ba* (M(BC)), reduced to *na n'ba* (MC) and to *nua,* "sibling"; or (2) *wofa n'ba* ((MB)C) and then to *ba,* "child."

The number U_n of bracketings associated with some sequence $x_1 x_2 x_3 \ldots x_n$ of n factors is given by

$$U_n = \frac{1}{n} \binom{2n-2}{n-1}$$

Thus $U_3 = 2$, $U_4 = 5$, $U_5 = 14$, $U_6 = 42, \ldots, U_9 = 1{,}430$, and so forth, with the number of possible bracketings rapidly proliferating.[2]

The following summary notation may be used to represent different kinds of bracketing (see, e.g., figures 3-1 to 3-3). Let [*xyz*] stand for the two possible

Figure 3-1
Distinct Bracketings for the Kintype MBD and the Corresponding Tree Structures

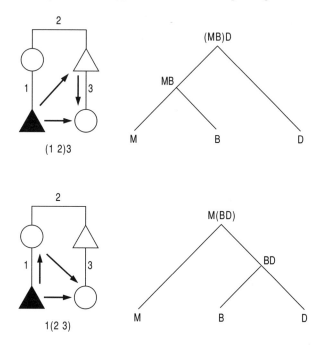

bracketings of three elements, $(xy)z$ and $x(yz)$. The notation may be nested: $[a[xyz]b]$ equals $(a[xyz])b$ and $a([xyz]b)$, summarizing the four possibilities $(a((xy)z))b$, $a(((xy)z)b)$, $(a(x(yz)))b$, and $a((x(yz))b)$.

There have been numerous applications of nonassociative structures in pure mathematics (see, e.g., Schafer 1966; Zhevlakov et al. 1982). These structures were introduced to population genetics mainly through the work of Etherington (1939a, 1939b, 1941a, 1941b [reprinted in Ballonoff 1974]). Some studies have also emphasized the significance of nonassociativity for kinship theory (Atkins 1974a, 1974b, 1974c; Greechie and Ottenheimer 1974; Lehman and Witz 1974). For the most part, however, kinship modeling has relied on mathematical structures such as groups and semigroups that embody the axiom of associativity (see Tjon Sie Fat 1990). Boyd (1991:9) is among those who have used the associative axiom for their models: "Without associativity, the idea of a 'path' is undefined; instead, one would have to use the more intractable and complicated evaluation trees that correspond to each way of parenthesizing a sequence of relations." This is indeed the crux of the matter. As I now demonstrate, the necessary insertion of parentheses in the composition of cross and parallel relations may affect the denotation of the expression, allowing for a more discriminating analysis of the variant systems of kin classification. (The problem of nonassociativity is also discussed in Boyd 1991, which is the source of the example in figure 3-1.)

DRAVIDIAN AND IROQUOIS STRUCTURES

For practical reasons, this discussion concentrates on the classification of selected kin at the $G^{\pm 2}$, $G^{\pm 1}$, and G^0 levels, particularly on the three medial generations of G^{+1}, G^0, and G^{-1}. As a first approximation, "crossness" is defined for the domain of consanguineal relations, and no particular marriage rule or alliance structure is assumed.

Following Atkins (1974a, 1974b, 1974c), for two persons e (ego) and a (alter) in a genealogical network, let the statement "*a is a consanguine of e*" be defined as "person a is a jth-remove descendant of some person b, who in turn is an ith-remove ancestor of person e" notation: eQ^iP^ja, with i and j nonnegative integers. In this approach, a consanguineal relation is traced through the nearest common ancestor, "removal" referring to the number of generations up (i) and down (j), the links joining the ancestor with ego and alter, respectively. P is the dyadic, asymmetric, nontransitive, and many-many relation glossed as "*is a parent of*," that is, the relation of the common ancestor to ego. Q is the relational converse "*is a child of*," that is, the relation of the common ancestor to ego. Person b is the "nearest" common ancestor of a and e, and is identical with a (respectively, e) for $j = 0$, $i \geq 1$ (or $j \geq 1$, $i = 0$). Define $P^0 = Q^0 = I$, the *identity* relation, so that eQ^0P^0a means that e and a are the same person. Also, eQ^1P^1a means that e and a are *siblings,* since they have a parent (i.e., a direct ancestor at one generation of removal) in common.

In order to ensure that all intervening relatives in the consanguineal paths thus defined are distinct from one another and that the paths do not involve a "doubling back" of genealogical connections, Atkins defines the compositions of the basic relations P and Q as a *nonassociative* operation called the *geneaproduct.*

Let R_k stand for P or Q. Then $eQ^iP^ja = eR_1R_2 \ldots R_na$ (with $n = i + j$) is defined as $\{(e, a)|$ there exist $x_0, x_1, \ldots, x_n$ such that (x_{k-1}, x_k) is in R_k, $x_0 = e$, $x_n = a$, and if $x_m \neq x_p$, then $x_m \neq x_q$, where $1 \leq k \leq n$ and $1 \leq m \leq p \leq q \leq n\}$.

For example, under the geneaproduct, the expression eQ^2P^2a asserts unambiguously that a is a first cousin of e, effectively ruling out that eQ^1P^1a or eQ^0P^0a also hold, and thus the possibility that a and e are either also related as siblings or that a and e are the same person (Atkins 1974a:31–32; 1974b:3–4; 1974c:2–4). Unless otherwise stated, I restrict the range of genealogical relations examined to those defined by the following combinations of generational removal: $j = 0$ and $i = 1, 2$; $j = 1$ and $i = 0, 1, 2, 3$; $j = 3$ and $i = 1, 2, 3, 4$; $j = 4$ and $i = 2, 3, 4$. These will suffice to capture the variations of cross/parallel classifications of consanguines in the three medial generations. They are the relations represented in figures 3-2 to 3-8.

I now introduce the algebraic counterpart to Trautmann's (1981:179) Dravidian equations for determining the crossness of a relative of a relative (the complete list of his rules is reproduced in figure 1-4 of this volume).[3]

Let $U = \{C^i_p, A^j_q\}$ for all i, j in $G = \{-1, 0, +1\}$ and p, q, in $S = \{=, \neq\}$. I retain Trautmann's symbols for ease of comparison. Thus, C is glossed as "*parallel*" and A as "*cross.*"[4] The superscripts in G denote *generation* (following, same, previous) and the subscripts in S denote *sex* (same, opposite), both relative to ego, or in the case of composite relations, relative to the super-and subscript values of the imme-

Table 3-1

Table of Compositions for the Canonical Dravidian A Structure

	$C_=^0$	$C_{\neq}^0$	$A_=^0$	$A_{\neq}^0$	$C_=^{-1}$	$C_{\neq}^{-1}$	$A_=^{-1}$	$A_{\neq}^{-1}$	$C_=^{+1}$	$C_{\neq}^{+1}$	$A_=^{+1}$	$A_{\neq}^{+1}$
$C_=^0$					$C_=^{-1}$	$C_{\neq}^{-1}$						
$C_{\neq}^0$					$A_{\neq}^{-1}$	$A_=^{-1}$						
$A_=^0$					$A_=^{-1}$	$A_{\neq}^{-1}$						
$A_{\neq}^0$					$C_{\neq}^{-1}$	$C_=^{-1}$						
$C_=^{-1}$					$C_=^{-2}$	$C_{\neq}^{-2}$						
$C_{\neq}^{-1}$					$C_{\neq}^{-2}$	$C_=^{-2}$						
$A_=^{-1}$					$A_=^{-2}$	$A_{\neq}^{-2}$						
$A_{\neq}^{-1}$					$A_{\neq}^{-2}$	$A_=^{-2}$						
$C_=^{+1}$	$C_=^{+1}$	$A_{\neq}^{+1}$	$A_=^{+1}$	$C_{\neq}^{+1}$	$C_=^0$	$C_{\neq}^0$	$A_=^0$	$A_{\neq}^0$	$C_=^{+2}$	$C_{\neq}^{+2}$	$A_=^{+2}$	$A_{\neq}^{+2}$
$C_{\neq}^{+1}$	$C_{\neq}^{+1}$	$A_=^{+1}$	$A_{\neq}^{+1}$	$C_=^{+1}$	$C_{\neq}^0$	$C_=^0$	$A_{\neq}^0$	$A_=^0$	$C_{\neq}^{+2}$	$C_=^{+2}$	$A_{\neq}^{+2}$	$A_=^{+2}$
$A_=^{+1}$					$A_=^0$	$A_{\neq}^0$						
$A_{\neq}^{+1}$					$A_{\neq}^0$	$A_=^0$						

Note: The analogous table for the Dravidian B structure can be obtained by transposing the values of the cross/parallel symbols in the shaded areas.

diately preceding relation in the genealogical path. Thus $♀C_=^0$ is a female ego's same-generation, same-sex parallel relative; is to be read as a male ego's previous-generation, same-sex parallel relative's same-generation, opposite-sex cross relative, and so forth.

Let X_p^i and Y_q^j be elements of U. Then my objective is to specify suitable multiplication tables for the composition of Dravidian and Iroquois cross/parallel relations, that is, tables with entries Z_r^k defined as the composition of X_p^i by Y_q^j. Composition of superscripts is by simple addition, that is, $k = i + j$; composition of subscripts follows binary multiplication, with = x = and ≠ x ≠ equal to =, while = x ≠ and ≠ x = both equal ≠. Both of these composition operations are associative.

Table 3-2
Table of Compositions for the Canonical Iroquois Structure with Cross/Parallel
Distinction Neutralized at the G^{+2} Generation Levels

	$C^0_=$	$C^0_{\neq}$	$A^0_=$	$A^0_{\neq}$	$C^{-1}_=$	$C^{-1}_{\neq}$	$A^{-1}_=$	$A^{-1}_{\neq}$	$C^{+1}_=$	$C^{+1}_{\neq}$	$A^{+1}_=$	$A^{+1}_{\neq}$
$C^0_=$					$C^{-1}_=$	$C^{-1}_{\neq}$						
$C^0_{\neq}$					$A^{-1}_{\neq}$	$A^{-1}_=$						
$A^0_=$					$C^{-1}_=$	$C^{-1}_{\neq}$						
$A^0_{\neq}$					$A^{-1}_{\neq}$	$A^{-1}_=$						
$C^{-1}_=$					$X^{-2}_=$	$X^{-2}_{\neq}$						
$C^{-1}_{\neq}$					$X^{-2}_{\neq}$	$X^{-2}_=$						
$A^{-1}_=$					$X^{-2}_=$	$X^{-2}_{\neq}$						
$A^{-1}_{\neq}$					$X^{-2}_{\neq}$	$X^{-2}_=$						
$C^{+1}_=$	$C^{+1}_=$	$A^{+1}_{\neq}$	$C^{+1}_=$	$A^{+1}_{\neq}$	$C^0_=$	$C^0_{\neq}$	$A^0_=$	$A^0_{\neq}$	$X^{+2}_=$	$X^{+2}_{\neq}$	$X^{+2}_=$	$X^{+2}_{\neq}$
$C^{+1}_{\neq}$	$C^{+1}_{\neq}$	$A^{+1}_=$	$C^{+1}_{\neq}$	$A^{+1}_=$	$C^0_{\neq}$	$C^0_=$	$A^0_{\neq}$	$A^0_=$	$X^{+2}_{\neq}$	$X^{+2}_=$	$X^{+2}_{\neq}$	$X^{+2}_=$
$A^{+1}_=$					$A^0_=$	$A^0_{\neq}$						
$A^{+1}_{\neq}$					$A^0_{\neq}$	$A^0_=$						

The "Dravidian" and "Iroquois" canonical structures are defined as partial algebras in tables 3-1 and 3-2, with the permitted bracketings for all relevant compositions of the basic cross and parallel relations indicated in figures 3-2 and 3-3.

There are two main areas in which the composition tables differ (these are marked with heavy borders): (1) compositions of the form $A^0_p C^{-1}_q$, that is, one's same-generation cross relatives' parallel descendants; (2) conversely, compositions of the form $C^{+1}_p A^0_q$, that is, one's previous-generation parallel relatives' same-generation cross kin. In both instances, the Iroquois entries in the table are of opposite crossness to the Dravidian ones and may be obtained from the corresponding Dravidian compositions by a simple transposition of the cross and parallel symbols, that is, by the transformation $T: C^k_r \leftrightarrow A^k_r$.

The entries in table 3-1 defining the cross/parallel classification of kin at the G^{+2} and G^{-2} levels correspond to a subset of the equations used by Trautmann to define

Figure 3-2

Permitted Bracketings for the Composition of Cross/Parallel Relations in All Structures

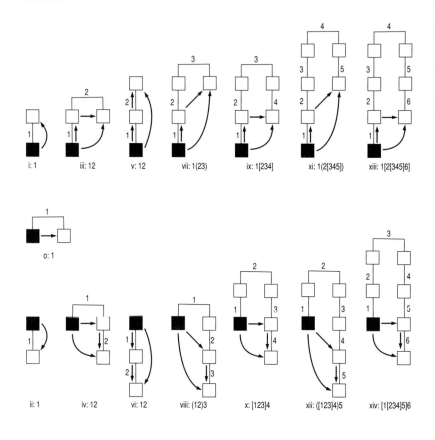

his "Dravidian A" model (1981:190). Thus: (3) $C_p^{+1}C_q^{+1} = C_r^{+2}$ and conversely $C_p^{-1}C_q^{-1} = C_r^{-2}$; that is, one's previous-generation parallel relatives' previous-generation parallel kin, and one's parallel descendants' parallel descendants are parallel. Also: (4) $C_p^{+1}A_q^{+1} = A_r^{+2}$ and conversely, $A_p^{-1}C_q^{-1} = A_r^{-2}$; that is, one's previous-generation parallel relatives' previous-generation cross kin, and one's cross descendants' parallel descendants, are cross. Trautmann's "Dravidian B" model (1981:192–93) is a simple variant. It can be obtained directly from the Dravidian A structure by applying the transformation T defined earlier to the shaded entries in table 3-1. These two Dravidian variants differ mainly in the manner in which crossness is defined for $G^{\pm 2}$ kin.[5] Either option could easily be implemented in an analogous Iroquois variant. In table 3-2, however, I propose a more general Iroquois model in which the cross or parallel categorization of $G^{\pm 2}$ kin remains undefined or (under an alternative interpretation) in which the cross/parallel distinction is considered to be

Figure 3-3

Permitted Bracketings for the Derivation of G^0 Cross/Parallel Classifications for Canonical Dravidian and Iroquois Structures, and for the Iroquois-Generational Variants

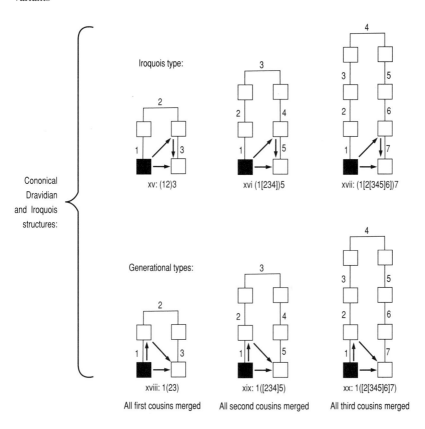

Cononical Dravidian and Iroquois structures:

Iroquois type:

xv: (12)3

xvi 1([234])5

xvii: (1[2[345]6])7

Generational types:

xviii: 1(23)

xix: 1([234]5)

xx: 1([2[345]6]7)

All first cousins merged   All second cousins merged   All third cousins merged

neutralized at the $G^{\pm 2}$ levels. This is indicated by the use of symbols (see the shaded areas in table 3-2), differentiated only by their superscripts (+2 or -2) and subscripts (= or ≠). This assumption may be easily amended.

The canonical Dravidian and Iroquois models are completely identical with regard to all further entries in their multiplication tables. Thus, (5) $C^0_= C^{-1}_q = C^{-1}_r$ and $C^0_{\neq} C^{-1}_q = A^{-1}_r$. That is, one's same-sex, same-generation parallel relative's parallel descendants are parallel kin, but an opposite-sex, same-generation parallel relative's parallel descendants are cross kin. Conversely, (6) $C^{+1}_p C^0_= = C^{+1}_r$ and $C^{+1}_p C^0_{\neq} = A^{+1}_r$. That is, one's previous-generation parallel relatives' same-sex, same-generation parallel kin are parallel, but the previous-generation parallel relatives' opposite-sex, same-generation parallel kin are cross. Also, (7) $C^{+1}_p C^{-1}_r = C^0_r$. That is, one's previous-generation parallel relatives' parallel descendants are parallel. Finally, (8) $C^{+1}_p A^{-1}_q = A^0_r$. That is, one's previous-generation parallel relatives' cross-kin descendants are cross. Conversely, $A_p^{+1}C_q^{-1} = A_r^0$. That is, one's previous-generation cross relatives' parallel descendants are cross kin. These last two series of entries are bordered with double lines in the tables; they will play a crucial role in the "generational" variants discussed below.[6]

If one compares the overall structure of both tables, the Iroquois pattern could be judged "less complex" than the Dravidian pattern in the sense that it contains a number of replications: it is more highly ordered. For example, the blocks of entries corresponding to (1) $A_p^0C_q^{-1}$, and (5) $C_p^0C_q^{-1}$, and conversely, to (2) $C_p^{+1}A_q^0$, and (6) $C_p^{+1}C_q^0$, are identical for the Iroquois structure but differ for the Dravidian model. Indeed, the compositions described under (1) and (2) are precisely those entries that are distinctive, and through which the models are differentiated (see the bordered areas in tables 3-1 and 3-2).[7] As a corollary, structures "intermediate" between the two canonical structures will show a different pattern at one or more of the eight bordered cells.[8]

Turning now to the constraints on associativity, composition of relations for the canonical Dravidian and Iroquois models is associative *where defined:* all bracketings in figure 3-2 (0 to xiv) and in figure 3-3 (xv to xx) are permitted and lead to consistent derivations.[9] In this respect, both models are similar. I shall demonstrate that this is not the case for the "Iroquois-generational" variants defined below.

To complete the model, the basic cross/parallel relations C_p^i and A_q^j must be mapped onto the genealogical paths defined earlier under the assumptions of Atkins's nonassociative geneaproduct. It would in fact suffice to make only *two* direct identifications, mapping C_p^{+1} and C_q^{-1} onto, respectively, the generating relations Q and P of the geneaproduct (with relative sex specified). Since under the geneaproduct rule of composition all consanguineal paths are given an unambiguous definition, compositions of the form $C_p^{+1} \ldots C_q^{-1} \ C_r^{-1} \ldots C_s^{-1}$ provide a sufficient and unambiguous classification of all cross and parallel relations (assuming, of course, that the multiplication tables and the constraints on parentheses introduced above have been defined).

Comparison of the algebraic models with equivalence-rule analysis will be easier if one further identification is made: that is, if one's siblings (the children of one's parents) are mapped onto the parallel relation C_p^0 (specified for relative sex). Thus, since $Q^1P^1 \leftrightarrow C_p^{+1}C_q^{-1} = C_p^0$, all consanguineal paths will now be traced through an *ancestral sibling pair* and not (as defined under the geneaproduct) through some single common ancestor.

This formal mapping establishes a correspondence between primary genealogical relations and the basic symbols introduced above. For the entire class of Iroquois and Dravidian models introduced here, primary kin relations are defined as "parallel": for example, for male ego, F, M, S, D, B, and Z are identified with, respectively, $C_=^{+1}$, $C_{\neq}^{+1}$, $C_=^{-1}$, $C_{\neq}^{-1}$, $C_=^0$, and $C_{\neq}^0$ (for female ego the values of the relative-sex subscripts are inverted). Note that there is no direct designation of specific nonprimary kin relations as affines (e.g., ♀FZS = H = ♀$A_{\neq}^0$, or ♂MBD = W = ♂$A_{\neq}^0$). "Crossness" is introduced through the binary operation defined in tables 3-1 and 3-2. In other words, there is no *necessary* assumption of marriage rules or of specific alliance strategies that would, in any case, introduce the very multiplicity of alternative

Table 3-3
Cross/Parallel Classifications for Second and Third Cousins

Second Cousins

DRAVIDIAN	IROQUOIS parallel	IROQUOIS cross
parallel	MMZDCh	**MMBSCh**
	MFBDCh	**MFZSCh**
	FMZSCh	**FMBDCh**
	FFBSCh	**FFZDCh**
cross	**MMBDCh**	MMZSCh
	MFZDCh	MFBSCh
	FMBSCh	FMZDCh
	FFZSCh	FFBDCh

Third Cousins

DRAVIDIAN	IROQUOIS parallel		IROQUOIS cross	
parallel	MMMZDDCh	FMMZDSCh	MMMZSSCh	FMMZSDCh
	MMMBSDCh	**FMMBSSCh**	**MMMBDSCh**	**FMMBDDCh**
	MMFZSDCh	**FMFZSSCh**	**MMFZDSCh**	**FMFZDDCh**
	MMFBDDCh	FMFBDSCh	MMFBSSCh	FMFBSDCh
	MFMZSDCh	FFMZSSCh	MFMZDSCh	FFMZDDCh
	MFMBDDCh	**FFMBDSCh**	**MFMBSSCh**	**FFMBSDCh**
	MFFZDDCh	**FFFZDSCh**	**MFFZSSCh**	**FFFZSDCh**
	MFFBSDCh	FFFBSSCh	MFFBDSCh	FFFBDDCh
cross	MMMZSDCh	FMMZSSCh	MMMZDSCh	FMMZDDCh
	MMMBDDCh	**FMMBDSCh**	**MMMBSSCh**	**FMMBSDCh**
	MMFZDDCh	**FMFZDSCh**	**MMFZSSCh**	**FMFZSDCh**
	MMFBSDCh	FMFBSSCh	MMFBDSCh	FMFBDDCh
	MFMZDDCh	FFMZDSCh	MFMZSSCh	FFMZSDCh
	MFMBSDCh	**FFMBSSCh**	**MFMBSSCh**	**FFMBDDCh**
	MFFZSDCh	**FFFZSSCh**	**MFFZDSCh**	**FFFZDDCh**
	MFFBDDCh	FFFBDSCh	MFFBSSCh	FFFBSDCh

Note: Kintypes with an ancestral pair of opposite-sex siblings indicated in bold.

genealogical paths linking consanguines that is *excluded* under the geneaproduct. I shall return to this important issue in a later section.

The formal algebraic mechanism of my model has now been assembled. I apply the model to generate all relevant cross/parallel classifications.[10] The main results are summarized in figure 3-4 (for the canonical Dravidian structure) and in figure 3-5 (for the canonical Iroquois structure). Cross-kin symbols are filled in; symbols representing parallel kin are left open. Positions where the cross/parallel classification is undefined or where the distinction is assumed to be neutralized (e.g., at the $G^{\pm 2}$ levels in figure 3-5) are marked with shading. The genealogical nodes encircled in both figures indicate kin positions for which the Dravidian and Iroquois classifications are transposed under the transformation $T: C_p^i \leftrightarrow A_p^i$. All derivations are from the viewpoint of a male ego; for a female ego, the values at the G^{-1} and G^{-2} levels should be transposed. For further ease of comparison, table 3-3 summarizes the classifications of second and third cousins.

This procedure generates results fully compatible with the patterns for "crossness" reported in previous accounts of Dravidian and Iroquois systems.[11] The algebraic structures are thus *possible models,* that is, valid alternative representations for these systems insofar as they reproduce the classifications described in the ethnographical data. A few computational examples may help to clarify how I obtained the full set of cross/parallel classifications from the models.

Figure 3-4
Canonical Dravidian: A Pattern of Crossness for Male Ego

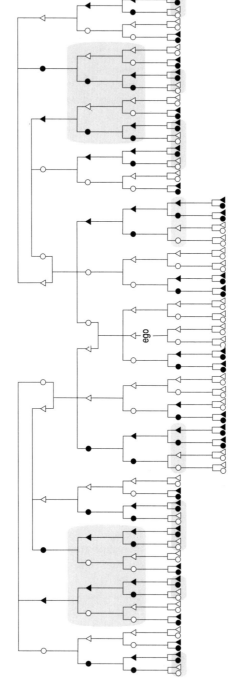

Note: Cross relatives black, parallel relatives white. Shaded nodes indicate kin positions diagnostic of the difference between Iroquois and Dravidian.

Figure 3-5
Canonical Iroquois Pattern of Crossness for Male Ego

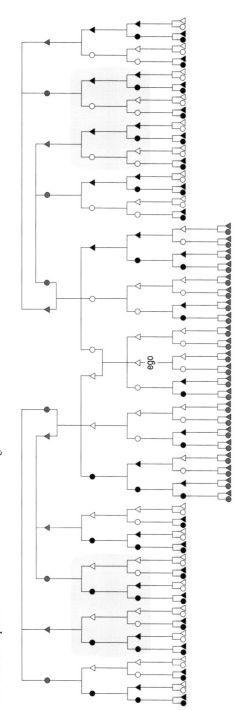

Note: Cross relatives black, parallel relatives white. The dimension of crossness is neutralized for G^{+2}. Shaded nodes indicate kin positions diagnostic of the difference between Iroquois and Dravidian.

Example 1: σFFZ

Here the key entries in the multiplication tables as well as the permitted bracketings (vii) are similar for the Dravidian and Iroquois structures (see tables 3-1 and 3-2). Substitution of the algebraic symbols for the kintype notation gives

$$\sigma\text{F(FZ)} = \sigma C_{=}^{+1}(C_{=}^{+1}C_{\neq}^{0}) = \sigma C_{=}^{+1}A_{\neq}^{+1} = \sigma A_{\neq}^{+2}$$

and thus a *cross* classification of σFFZ for the Dravidian A structure (note that σFFZ is a *parallel* relative for the Dravidian B model since $\sigma C_{=}^{+1}A_{\neq}^{+1} = \sigma C_{\neq}^{+2}$). However, $\sigma C_{=}^{+1}A_{\neq}^{+1} = \sigma X_{\neq}^{+2}$ under the canonical Iroquois assumptions of table 3-2, neutralizing the cross/parallel distinction at this generation level.

Example 2: σMBD

Two possible bracketings (xv and xviii) are permitted, both giving an identical result for each structure: following (xv),

$$(\sigma\text{MB})\text{D} = = \sigma A_{=}^{+1}C_{\neq}^{-1} = \sigma A_{\neq}^{0}$$

For (xviii),

$$\sigma\text{M(BD)} = \sigma C_{\neq}^{+1}(C_{\neq}^{0}C_{\neq}^{-1}) = \sigma C_{=}^{+1}A_{\neq}^{-1} = \sigma A_{\neq}^{0}$$

with the identical result.

Example 3: σMBDS

Here again two bracketings (summarized as [1 2 3]4 in diagram x of figure 3-2) are allowed for each structure. Fortunately, one is not obliged to carry out the fairly tedious procedure of composition for these relational paths of length four. Under the assumptions of the canonical models, bracketing is a nested operation, and the results for some kin path of length $n + 1$ may be obtained directly (by pre- or postmultiplication) from earlier results derived for paths of length n (see the diagrams in figures 3-2 and 3-3). Building on the results from the previous example, σMBDS = [σMBD]S leading to $\sigma A_{\neq}^{0}C_{\neq}^{-1} = \sigma C_{=}^{-1}$ for the "Dravidian" structure, but to $\sigma A_{=}^{-1}$ under the Iroquois table of compositions.

"GENERATIONAL" VARIETIES

As defined above, in certain instances the canonical Dravidian and Iroquois models permit the use of several distinct genealogical paths in deriving the crossness of relations. However, this does not lead to inconsistent results under the constraints on associativity (i.e., the permitted bracketings; see example 2) specified for these structures. Both models are also consistent with regard to the "reciprocal" or "converse" entries in their tables of composition. For example, $A_p^{+1}C_q^{-1}$ as well as $C_p^{+1}A_q^{-1}$ are defined as A_r^0. That is, for both models, one's previous-generation cross relatives' parallel descendants, as well as one's previous-generation parallel relatives' cross-kin descendants are all classified as zero-generation cross kin. The entries for these relations are bordered with double lines in tables 3-1 and 3-2. Nevertheless, as illustrated by Kronenfeld's Fanti example previously discussed, such formal criteria for perfect consistency appear to be too stringent: the classification of specific kin may be dependent on the genealogical path chosen (the bracketing), as well as on the rules for the composition of cross/parallel categories (the multiplication table). By varying these assumptions, I now introduce a further series of models that articulate aspects of the canonical Dravidian and Iroquois structures with a generational pattern of kin classification at G^0.

Table 3-4 defines the compositions for one such "Iroquois-generational" model. This particular model has been obtained from the canonical structure merely by changing the values of the entries in the area outlined in bold. Thus in table 3-4, $C_p^{+1}A_q^{-1}$ is now defined as C_r^0 (i.e., as parallel kin) and not (as in the canonical Iroquois model of table 3-2), as A_r^0 (i.e., cross). The set of permissible bracketings must also be redefined. Bracketings 0 to xiv (see figure 3-2) are allowed (as is the case with the canonical models). With regard to the classification of G^0 kin, however, relational composition has become "less" associative: one must now select a subset of bracketings from figure 3-3 (xv to xx) to ensure consistent results.

Consider the relation $\male$MBD. If one applies the order of parentheses under (xv), then

$$(\male\text{MB})\text{D} = -(\male C_{\neq}^{+1}\ C_{\neq}^0)C_{\neq}^{-1} = \male A_{=}^{+1}C_{\neq}^{-1} = \male A_{\neq}^0,$$

that is, *cross*. However, under (xviii),

$$\male\text{M}(\text{BD}) = \male C_{\neq}^{+1}(C_{\neq}^0 C_{\neq}^{-1}) = \male C_{=}^{+1}A_{\neq}^{-1} = \male C_{\neq}^0,$$

which is *parallel*. These observations may be generalized as follows: for the Iroquois-generational model of table 3-4, the classification of zero-generation kin (e.g., ego's first, second, and third cousins) conforms to the canonical Iroquois pattern (see figure 3-3) if the evaluation is made from the point of view of *the cousins' parent* (see diagrams xv, xvi, and xvii in figure 3-3). In contrast, if *ego's parent* is taken as the position of reference (as in diagrams xviii, xix, and xx of figure 3-3), then all first cousins (respectively, second or third cousins) will be merged with ego's siblings as parallel kin.

Let Ir(xv, xvi, xvii) stand for the Iroquois-generational variant that reproduces the canonical Iroquois pattern of crossness at all generation levels. Then, depending on the choice of alternative bracketings, there are *seven* additional variants with some form of generational classification at ego's generation (roman numerals indicate the bracketings selected; see figure 3-3):

1. Ir(xviii, xvi, xvii)   Only first cousins merged with siblings
2. Ir(xviii, xix, xvii)   First and second cousins merged

Table 3-4

Table of Compositions for the Family of Iroquois Structures with Zero-Generational Merging

	$C^0_=$	$C^0_\neq$	$A^0_=$	$A^0_\neq$	$C^{-1}_=$	$C^{-1}_\neq$	$A^{-1}_=$	$A^{-1}_\neq$	$C^{+1}_=$	$C^{+1}_\neq$	$A^{+1}_=$	$A^{+1}_\neq$
$C^0_=$					$C^{-1}_=$	$C^{-1}_\neq$						
$C^0_\neq$					$A^{-1}_\neq$	$A^{-1}_=$						
$A^0_=$					$C^{-1}_=$	$C^{-1}_\neq$						
$A^0_\neq$					$A^{-1}_\neq$	$A^{-1}_=$						
$C^{-1}_=$					$X^{-2}_=$	$X^{-2}_\neq$						
$C^{-1}_\neq$					$X^{-2}_\neq$	$X^{-2}_=$						
$A^{-1}_=$					$X^{-2}_=$	$X^{-2}_\neq$						
$A^{-1}_\neq$					$X^{-2}_\neq$	$X^{-2}_=$						
$C^{+1}_=$	$C^{+1}_=$	$A^{+1}_\neq$	$C^{+1}_=$	$A^{+1}_\neq$	$C^0_=$	$C^0_\neq$	$C^0_=$	$C^0_\neq$	$X^{+2}_=$	$X^{+2}_\neq$	$X^{+2}_=$	$X^{+2}_\neq$
$C^{+1}_\neq$	$C^{+1}_\neq$	$A^{+1}_=$	$C^{+1}_\neq$	$A^{+1}_=$	$C^0_\neq$	$C^0_=$	$C^0_\neq$	$C^0_=$	$X^{+2}_\neq$	$X^{+2}_=$	$X^{+2}_\neq$	$X^{+2}_=$
$A^{+1}_=$					$A^0_=$	$A^0_\neq$						
$A^{+1}_\neq$					$A^0_\neq$	$A^0_=$						

3. Ir(xviii, xix, xx)	First, second, and third cousins merged
4. Ir(xv, xix, xx)	Second and third cousins merged
5. Ir(xv, xvi, xx)	Third cousins merged
6. Ir(xv, xix, xvii)	Second cousins merged
7. Ir(xviii, xvi, xx)	First and third cousins merged

Iroquois-generational variants 1 and 2 are depicted in figures 3-6 and 3-7. The patterns generated by the formal model are fully compatible with descriptions of generational or "bifurcate generation" systems in North America (e.g, the Cheyenne and Arapaho; see Eggan 1955b:43, fig. 1), South America (the Kuikuru; Dole 1969), and Melanesia (the Binumarien; Hawkes 1976).[12]

A few remarks to round off this discussion of generational variants are also in order. First, the Iroquois-generational model presented above was obtained by re-

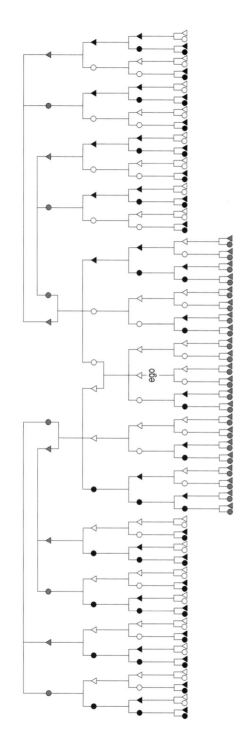

Figure 3-7
Iroquois-Generational Pattern of Crossness for Male Ego: Variant 2 with Merging of All First and Second Cousins

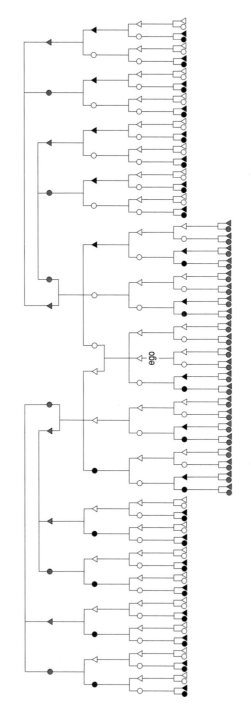

defining the "cross" entries $C_p^{+1}A_q^{-1}$ in the canonical Iroquois table (table 3-2) as "parallel." A formally equivalent structure can be derived if, instead, the "converse" entries $A_p^{+1}C_q^{-1}$ in table 3-2 are redefined as "parallel," retaining the original "cross" evaluation for $C_p^{+1}A_q^{-1}$.[13] If one decides to change the evaluation of $C_p^{+1}A_q^{-1}$ as well as $A_p^{+1}C_q^{-1}$ from "cross" to "parallel," the resulting model is consistent with the full set of parentheses in figures 3-2 and 3-3, generating Iroquois classifications at G$^{\pm1}$ while allocating *all* G^0 kin to the "parallel" category (the resulting pattern is identical to that obtained from the Iroquois-generational variant 3).[14]

What is perhaps more interesting is the fact that the class of structures generated by my Iroquois-generational model seems to articulate (at a formal level) much of the variation described by Trautmann and Barnes (chapter 2) for the North American terminologies. It may be modified to represent a variety of systems in which the canonical Iroquois-type crossness is either fully extended throughout the three medial generations or is retained for G$^{\pm1}$ kin but partly or completely lost at the G^0 level.

For example, Trautmann and Barnes also describe an Iroquois variant in which the canonical pattern of "crossness" is lost in women's speech for G^{-1} kin (with reciprocal partial loss in G^{+1}). Moreover, if one uses the diagnostics of Type A (Dravidian) and Type B (Iroquois) crossness that they present in figure 2-3 of this volume (see also the summary of Morgan's data in Trautmann and Barnes 1991), along with Morgan's numerical identification for kintypes, the Cayuga, the Onondaga, the Oneida, and the Mohawk (all Five Nations Iroquois) exhibit the following pattern: 102. ♀FZSS, 106. ♀FZDS, 128. ♀MBSS, 132. ♀MBDS: "son"; 104. ♀FZSD, 108. ♀FZDD, 130. ♀MBSD, 134. ♀MBDD: "daughter." The data on reciprocals are less detailed: 176. ♂FFZD: "mother."

This classification clearly varies between the Dravidian (102, 104, 128, 130, and 176) and the Iroquois pattern (106, 108, 132, 134) and thus raises a number of formal and substantive points directly related to the question of historical transformations from one pattern to the other.[15] First, the pattern of crossness described for the Cayuga, Onondaga, Oneida, and Mohawk terminologies may be modeled as part of a fully consistent, "stable" algebraic structure: there is no *formal* reason to treat these systems as "degenerate" or "marginal" variants.[16] the multiplication table for such a structure appears in table 3-5. The entries for the compositions $C_p^{+1}A_{\neq}^0$ and $A_{\neq}^0C_q^{-1}$, reciprocally, now follow the Dravidian pattern (see tables 3-1 and 3-2). The derivations for female ego are provided in figure 3-8, with deviations from the standard Iroquois classification marked in outline. The range of permitted bracketings is identical to that of the canonical Dravidian and Iroquois models introduced earlier.

At the G^{-1} level, all kin are now merged with a woman's own children, with the exception of the children of "near" or "distant" brothers. Reciprocally, at G^{+1}, father's female cross cousins and mother's male cross cousins are merged, respectively, with mother and father, superimposing Dravidian-like features onto a basic Iroquois pattern (there are also Dravidian-like mergings of second cousins at G^0). This leads to the second point: the pattern summarized in table 3-5 and figure 3-8 is not merely a formal possibility. It is fully realized in the terminological structure of the Yafar, a

Table 3-5

Table of Compositions for Trautmann and Barnes's Type B, Variant 2 Structure

	$C_=^0$	$C_{\neq}^0$	$A_=^0$	$A_{\neq}^0$	$C_=^{-1}$	$C_{\neq}^{-1}$	$A_=^{-1}$	$A_{\neq}^{-1}$	$C_=^{+1}$	$C_{\neq}^{+1}$	$A_=^{+1}$	$A_{\neq}^{+1}$
$C_=^0$					$C_=^{-1}$	$C_{\neq}^{-1}$						
$C_{\neq}^0$					$A_{\neq}^{-1}$	$A_=^{-1}$						
$A_=^0$					$C_=^{-1}$	$C_{\neq}^{-1}$						
$A_{\neq}^0$					$C_{\neq}^{-1}$	$C_=^{-1}$						
$C_=^{-1}$					$X_=^{-2}$	$X_{\neq}^{-2}$						
$C_{\neq}^{-1}$					$X_{\neq}^{-2}$	$X_=^{-2}$						
$A_=^{-1}$					$X_=^{-2}$	$X_{\neq}^{-2}$						
$A_{\neq}^{-1}$					$X_{\neq}^{-2}$	$X_=^{-2}$						
$C_=^{+1}$	$C_=^{+1}$	$A_{\neq}^{+1}$	$C_=^{+1}$	$C_{\neq}^{+1}$	$C_=^0$	$C_{\neq}^0$	$A_=^0$	$A_{\neq}^0$	$X_=^{+2}$	$X_{\neq}^{+2}$	$X_=^{+2}$	$X_{\neq}^{+2}$
$C_{\neq}^{+1}$	$C_{\neq}^{+1}$	$A_=^{+1}$	$C_{\neq}^{+1}$	$C_=^{+1}$	$C_{\neq}^0$	$C_=^0$	$A_{\neq}^0$	$A_=^0$	$X_{\neq}^{+2}$	$X_=^{+2}$	$X_{\neq}^{+2}$	$X_=^{+2}$
$A_=^{+1}$					$A_=^0$	$A_{\neq}^0$						
$A_{\neq}^{+1}$					$A_{\neq}^0$	$A_=^0$						

Note: Equivalent to the "Yafar" structure (based on information in Juillerat 1977). Areas of difference with the canonical Iroquois structure of table 3-2 outlined; these entries are Dravidian-like.

Melanesian society described in detail by Juillerat.[17] A reexamination of the North American terminologies in the light of these remarks may lead to a better understanding of the transformational possibilities linking all of these variant structures.[18]

Some of the most intriguing descriptions of anomalous or inconsistent terminological systems combining a variety of Dravidian, Iroquois, and "Hawaiian" or generational features with a range of affinal terms and extensive marriage prohibitions pertain to the Western Desert peoples of Australia. From Elkin's descriptions (1939, 1940), the Kukata or "Southern Aluridja" articulate an Iroquois pattern for G^{+1} (with father's parallel and cross cousins classified as "father" and "father's sister," and mother's parallel and cross cousins classified as "mother" and "mother's brother"), with a generational merging of first and second cousins at G^0. At the G^{-1} level,

Figure 3-8

Type B, Variant 2 or Yafar Pattern of Crossness for Female Ego

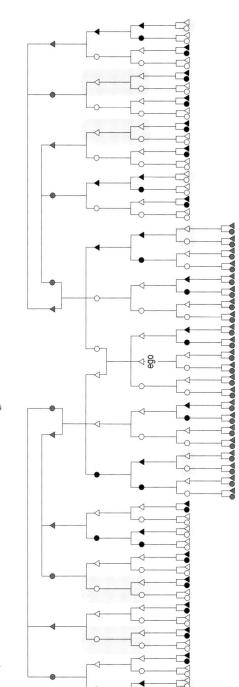

crossness is partly lost: male ego has no separate term for his sister's children to distinguish them from own children. The "Northern Aluridja" (Elkin 1939) also apply the terms for "father" and "father's sister" to father's parallel cousins. However, father's cross cousins and mother's parallel and cross cousins are now all classified as "mother" and "mother's brother." (Put differently, all of father's cousins follow the Dravidian pattern; all of mother's cousins follow the Iroquois classification.) The G^0 mergings are similar to those of the Southern Aluridja, but at the G^{-1} level the Northern Aluridja do differentiate between own children and children of opposite-sex siblings. According to Elkin (1939), the Wirangu classification is similar to that of the Southern Aluridja, with one important difference: only one term, "mother," is used for all women of the first ascending generation.

Further variants have also been reported. A case in point is that of the Pintupi. Their traditional homeland was situated in the Western Desert, but they moved eastward and apparently adopted a sociocentric system of classification similar to that of the Warlpiri. The Pintupi terminological patterning for the first ascending generation is basically Dravidian: a father's cross cousin is classified as "mother" or "mother's brother," a mother's cross cousin as "father" or "father's sister"—but only for male ego. In contrast, a woman classifies her parent's cross cousin as a "parent" or "parent's opposite-sex sibling," that is, according to the canonical Iroquois pattern (Myers 1986:204–8). Here again, the G^0 classification is generational.

Scheffler's (1978:88–118, 419–22) analysis of the Pitjantjara (one of Elkin's Aluridja-type systems) is interesting to the extent that it departs from his earlier (1971) treatment of Iroquois-type systems and of the relations between them and the Dravidian-type systems.[19] Although Scheffler acknowledges a number of similarities between the Pitjantjara and Iroquois-type systems, he concludes that "the similarities are largely superficial and should not be misinterpreted as reflecting an underlying structural identity" (1978:114). The main problem appears to arise from the Pitjantjara generational classification by which cross cousins are merged with siblings. Scheffler proposes a distinctive Pitjantjara "sibling merging rule" (PSb → P) = (SbC → C) to neutralize the opposition between "siblings" (including parallel cousins) and "cross cousins" at the level of ego's parents. "In other words, the opposition between lineal (and colineal) and collateral kin relevant to the definitions of the primary senses of the kin terms are neutralized, and the classes they designate are expanded to include all collateral kin of the same generation as the class foci" (Scheffler 1978:419). Consistent with the assumptions of his extensionist theory, Scheffler then argues that this points to a fundamental difference with Iroquois-like systems (and other Australian systems) that feature distinct MB and FZ classes and a more limited same-sex sibling merging rule (1978:113–18). In a curious twist, the Pitjantjara are thus seen as even *less* similar to the Iroquois system than the Kariera-like systems (i.e., systems generally described as Dravidian) "whose structures are readily understandable as simple permutations of the structure of Iroquois-like systems" (Scheffler 1978:118).

In line with the more general conclusions of Trautmann and Barnes (chapter 2), the Western Desert cases can be considered a variation among culturally and historically related systems, in which further analysis might illuminate the interaction of Iroquois-like principles of crossness with the more famous Kariera or Dravidian-like forms associated with the "elementary" logic of cross-cousin marriage.[20]

OBSERVATIONS ON THE FULL DRAVIDIAN MODEL

All Dravidian systems, according to Trautmann, embody two related principles: (1) a rule of cross-cousin marriage of a particular kind, and (2) a specific pattern of cross/parallel classification. Both principles are maximally consistent if bilateral cross-cousin marriage is assumed (Trautmann 1981:3, 200–206, 214). Trautmann's full set of equivalence rules (1981:177–97; see also figure 1-4 in this volume) are developed in accordance with these two principles.

Up to this point, I have ignored certain issues central to the discussion of Dravidian and Iroquois classifications: the status of a rule of (bilateral) cross-cousin marriage (formulated as a prescription, or as an ideal, or posited as a structural equivalence between specific kintypes), and the existence of a special "affinal" terminology. Under the prevailing view, the canonical Dravidian classification (as represented in figure 1-4) merges consanguineal relations so that the resulting pattern is compatible with, or even isomorphic to, the equivalence of kintypes established through the application of a rule of bilateral cross-cousin marriage. The kin universe is, ideally, closed, with the dimensions of consanguinity and affinity interdependent (at least in a formal sense).[21] Where the structural possibilities are more fully implemented (as perhaps in the classical descriptions of certain Australian systems), the ego-centered paradigm of terminological classification may be mapped onto a nested hierarchy of "sociocentric" categories (e.g., moieties, alternate generations, classes, subsections, and so forth).

In contrast, Iroquois systems are of a more "open" nature. There is no rule of bilateral cross-cousin marriage; indeed, the Iroquois pattern of crossness is not compatible with the specific equivalences induced by such a rule. Consanguinity and affinity are relatively independent dimensions, marked by the use of separate subsets of the kinship terminology. Thus, when the canonical diagrams of figures 3-4 and 3-5 are compared, the comparison is between the complete Dravidian model (i.e., the consanguineal cum affinal classification), and the partial Iroquois model representing only the consanguineal pattern.

Trautmann's full set of Dravidian rules goes beyond the specific constraints on the tracing of consanguineal paths implied by Atkins's geneaproduct. His goal is to formulate not only the *shortest consanguineal* path for the composition of cross and parallel categories (as I have done), but to generate *all possible paths* (through consanguineal as well as affinal relationships). The implicit assumption is that such a model will be fully consistent.

Table 3-6 provides an algebraic representation of Trautmann's full set of rules using the formal notation and conventions introduced earlier. There is no loss of information: the multiplication table is a complete and concise rendering of all binary compositions implied by Trautmann's equivalence rules. Table 3-6 illustrates Trautmann's Dravidian model A (generated by his rules 1 to 7 and 8A and 9A). His

Table 3-6

Table of Compositions for Trautmann's Dravidian A Model

	$C^0_=$	$C^0_{\neq}$	$A^0_=$	$A^0_{\neq}$	$C^{-1}_=$	$C^{-1}_{\neq}$	$A^{-1}_=$	$A^{-1}_{\neq}$	$C^{+1}_=$	$C^{+1}_{\neq}$	$A^{+1}_=$	$A^{+1}_{\neq}$
$C^0_=$	$C^0_=$	$C^0_{\neq}$	$A^0_=$	$A^0_{\neq}$	$C^{-1}_=$	$C^{-1}_{\neq}$	$A^{-1}_=$	$A^{-1}_{\neq}$	$C^{+1}_=$	$C^{+1}_{\neq}$	$A^{+1}_=$	$A^{+1}_{\neq}$
$C^0_{\neq}$	$C^0_{\neq}$	$C^0_=$	$A^0_{\neq}$	$A^0_=$	$A^{-1}_{\neq}$	$A^{-1}_=$	$C^{-1}_{\neq}$	$C^{-1}_=$	$C^{+1}_{\neq}$	$C^{+1}_=$	$A^{+1}_{\neq}$	$A^{+1}_=$
$A^0_=$	$A^0_=$	$A^0_{\neq}$	$C^0_=$	$C^0_{\neq}$	$A^{-1}_=$	$A^{-1}_{\neq}$	$C^{-1}_=$	$C^{-1}_{\neq}$	$A^{+1}_=$	$A^{+1}_{\neq}$	$C^{+1}_=$	$C^{+1}_{\neq}$
$A^0_{\neq}$	$A^0_{\neq}$	$A^0_=$	$C^0_{\neq}$	$C^0_=$	$C^{-1}_{\neq}$	$C^{-1}_=$	$A^{-1}_{\neq}$	$A^{-1}_=$	$A^{+1}_{\neq}$	$A^{+1}_=$	$C^{+1}_{\neq}$	$C^{+1}_=$
$C^{-1}_=$	$C^{-1}_=$	$C^{-1}_{\neq}$	$A^{-1}_=$	$A^{-1}_{\neq}$	$C^{-2}_=$	$C^{-2}_{\neq}$	$A^{-2}_=$	$A^{-2}_{\neq}$	$C^0_=$	$A^0_{\neq}$	$A^0_=$	$C^0_{\neq}$
$C^{-1}_{\neq}$	$C^{-1}_{\neq}$	$C^{-1}_=$	$A^{-1}_{\neq}$	$A^{-1}_=$	$C^{-2}_{\neq}$	$C^{-2}_=$	$A^{-2}_{\neq}$	$A^{-2}_=$	$A^0_{\neq}$	$C^0_=$	$C^0_{\neq}$	$A^0_=$
$A^{-1}_=$	$A^{-1}_=$	$A^{-1}_{\neq}$	$C^{-1}_=$	$C^{-1}_{\neq}$	$A^{-2}_=$	$A^{-2}_{\neq}$	$C^{-2}_=$	$C^{-2}_{\neq}$	$A^0_=$	$C^0_{\neq}$	$C^0_=$	$A^0_{\neq}$
$A^{-1}_{\neq}$	$A^{-1}_{\neq}$	$A^{-1}_=$	$C^{-1}_{\neq}$	$C^{-1}_=$	$A^{-2}_{\neq}$	$A^{-2}_=$	$C^{-2}_{\neq}$	$C^{-2}_=$	$C^0_{\neq}$	$A^0_=$	$A^0_{\neq}$	$C^0_=$
$C^{+1}_=$	$C^{+1}_=$	$C^{+1}_{\neq}$	$A^{+1}_=$	$A^{+1}_{\neq}$	$C^0_=$	$C^0_{\neq}$	$A^0_=$	$A^0_{\neq}$	$C^{+2}_=$	$C^{+2}_{\neq}$	$A^{+2}_=$	$A^{+2}_{\neq}$
$C^{+1}_{\neq}$	$C^{+1}_{\neq}$	$C^{+1}_=$	$A^{+1}_{\neq}$	$A^{+1}_=$	$C^0_{\neq}$	$C^0_=$	$A^0_{\neq}$	$A^0_=$	$C^{+2}_{\neq}$	$C^{+2}_=$	$A^{+2}_{\neq}$	$A^{+2}_=$
$A^{+1}_=$	$A^{+1}_=$	$A^{+1}_{\neq}$	$C^{+1}_=$	$C^{+1}_{\neq}$	$A^0_=$	$A^0_{\neq}$	$C^0_=$	$C^0_{\neq}$	$A^{+2}_=$	$A^{+2}_{\neq}$	$C^{+2}_=$	$C^{+2}_{\neq}$
$A^{+1}_{\neq}$	$A^{+1}_{\neq}$	$A^{+1}_=$	$C^{+1}_{\neq}$	$C^{+1}_=$	$A^0_{\neq}$	$A^0_=$	$C^0_{\neq}$	$C^0_=$	$A^{+2}_{\neq}$	$A^{+2}_=$	$C^{+2}_{\neq}$	$C^{+2}_=$

Note: The full table for Trautmann's Dravidian B model can be obtained by transposing the values of the cross/parallel symbols in the shaded areas.

"Dravidian model B" (also generated by rules 1 to 7, but now in combination with rules 8B and 9B) is obtained by a simple transposition of the cross and parallel values in the shaded entries of table 3-6.

With $U = \{C^i_p, A^j_q\}$ for all i, j in $\{-1, 0, +1\}$, and p, q in $\{=, \neq\}$, and composition $=$ as defined earlier, Trautmann's rules are mapped onto the entries of table 3-6 as follows:

$$\text{rule 1} \Leftrightarrow X^0_p Y^0_q; \quad \text{rule 2} \Leftrightarrow X^{+1}_p Y^0_q; \quad \text{rule 3} \Leftrightarrow X^{+1}_p Y^{-1}_q;$$
$$\text{rule 4} \Leftrightarrow X^0_p Y^{-1}_q; \quad \text{rule 5} \Leftrightarrow X^0_p Y^{+1}_q; \quad \text{rule 6} \Leftrightarrow X^{-1}_p Y^{+1}_q;$$
$$\text{rule 7} \Leftrightarrow X^{-1}_p Y^0_q; \quad \text{rule 8} \Leftrightarrow X^{+1}_p Y^{+1}_q; \quad \text{rule 9} \Leftrightarrow X^{-1}_p Y^{-1}_q.$$

More precisely, my canonical Dravidian A model of table 3-1 is embedded in Trautmann's full model of table 3-6. It corresponds to the entries in rows $C_=^{+1}$ and $C_{\neq}^{+1}$, and in columns $C_=^{-1}$ and $C_{\neq}^{-1}$ and to Trautmann's rules 2.1, 2.2, 3.1, 3.3, 3.4, 4.1, 4.2, 8.3A, 8.4A, 9.1A, and 9.4A.

This leads to the following observations. First, the partial structure of table 3-1 is a necessary and sufficient model for generating the correct Dravidian A pattern of crossness. However, its range of application is restricted to consanguineal relations (as defined under the geneaproduct), and no particular marriage rule is assumed. Second, my partial structure appears as a proper subset of Trautmann's Dravidian model A, a model that *does* presume the existence of a (bilateral) cross-cousin marriage rule (or its semantic equivalent). Therefore, by "subtracting" my partial model from the full model A structure of table 3-6, one might be able to focus more clearly on those features of Trautmann's model directly associated with the marriage rule.[22] This chain of reasoning is incorrect. One cannot really point to any particular (sub)set of Trautmann's rules as the embodiment of a "bilateral cross-cousin marriage principle." The logic of the marriage assumptions is a global logic, articulating the "consanguineal" and "affinal" entries of the full table (including certain key compositions in my partial "consanguineal" model).

Having said this, one can point to areas in the Dravidian table that are highly ordered and may be treated as a substructure in their own right. One such set of entries pertains to the composition of zero-generation relations (the area in the upper left-hand corner of table 3-6, corresponding to Trautmann's rule 1). The four relations $C_=^{0}$, $C_{\neq}^{0}$, $A_=^{0}$, and $A_{\neq}^{0}$ represent an algebraic group of order four isomorphic to the *Klein group*. This commutative group articulates the structure of a double opposition (cross/parallel; same-sex/opposite-sex). More to the point, it generates a consistent bipartition of the zero-generation kinship universe. According to Trautmann (1981:180), the basic series of equations (I): $AC = CA = A$ and $CC = AA = C$ (glossed as "one's affine's consanguine and one's consanguine's affine are one's affine"; "one's consanguine's consanguine and one's affine's affine are one's consanguine") show that WB, WZ, HB, HZ, and BW and ZH are affines, whereas WBW, WZH, HBW, HZH, and BB and ZZ are consanguines, classifications obviously compatible with a dual organization or with a rule of sister-exchange and bilateral cross-cousin marriage.[23] These equations are in fact also compatible with asymmetric cross-cousin marriage if the connubial cycles close with any *even* number of links.[24] Moreover, the set of equation (I) does not appear to be specific to a Dravidian type of classification.

Another fundamental set of entries follows from the necessity of linking marriage with descent: one's parent's spouse is one's parent of the opposite sex; conversely, one's spouse's child is one's own child. With child defined as $C_=^{-1}$ or $C_{\neq}^{-1}$, parent as or $C_=^{+1}$ or $C_{\neq}^{+1}$, and husband or wife as $A_{\neq}^{0}$ (that is, as an opposite-sex, same-generation cross relative), the following equations are necessary:

$$\text{(II)} \quad C_=^{+1}A_{\neq}^{0} = C_{\neq}^{+1} \quad \text{and} \quad C_{\neq}^{+1}A_{\neq}^{0} = C_=^{+1},$$

and conversely

$$A^0_{\neq} C^{-1}_{=} = C^{-1}_{=} \text{ and } A^0_{\neq} C^{-1}_{\neq} = C^{-1}_{=}$$

These four entries are situated in the crucial areas bordered in tables 3-1 and 3-2, which define the differences between the canonical Dravidian and Iroquois structures. The equations obviously do not hold for the latter model. Instead, the analogous Iroquois compositions are

$$\text{(II$'$) } C^{+1}_{=} A^0_{\neq} = A^{+1}_{\neq} \text{ and } C^{+1}_{\neq} A^0_{\neq} = A^{+1}_{=},$$

and conversely

$$A^0_{\neq} C^{-1}_{=} = A^{-1}_{\neq} \text{ and } A^0_{\neq} C^{-1}_{\neq} = A^{-1}_{\neq},$$

which are difficult to interpret as consistent marriage assumptions. In this context, it is important to note that the relevant entries (cf. II and II$'$) for the Iroquois-Yafar model of table 3-5 are Dravidian-like and thus compatible with a minimal marriage assumption.

There are two further series of equations that are generally assumed to be compatible with both canonical structures (see chapter 2). These are (III) FB = MZH, MZ = FBW (i.e., replication of same-sex sibling marriage in G^{+1}, and (IV) FZ = MBW, MB = FZH (i.e., replication of opposite-sex sibling marriage in G^{+1}). If complete associativity is assumed, the following compositions are required: from (III)

$$C^{+1}_{=} C^0_{=} = C^{+1}_{=} \text{ and } C^{+1}_{\neq} C^0_{=} = C^{+1}_{\neq}$$

(which hold for both canonical structures), and

$$C^{+1}_{=} A^0_{\neq} = C^{+1}_{\neq} \text{ and } C^{+1}_{\neq} A^0_{\neq} = C^{+1}_{=}$$

(true for the Dravidian model but *not* for the canonical Iroquois structure). From (IV)

$$C^{+1}_{=} C^0_{\neq} = A^{+1}_{\neq} \text{ and } C^{+1}_{\neq} A^0_{\neq} = A^{+1}_{=}$$

(again, true for both structures), and

$$A^{+1}_{=} A^0_{\neq} = A^{+1}_{\neq} \text{ and } A^{+1}_{\neq} A^0_{\neq} = A^{+1}_{=}$$

(true for the full Dravidian model and not incompatible with the Iroquois canonical structure of table 3-2). (Equation (I) is also presumed to apply.) Hence the canonical Iroquois model is not compatible with equation (III). If this equation is to hold, a transformation of the relevant entries to a more Dravidian-like pattern is required.

Finally, the crucial equations: (V) W = MBD, H = FZS, and (VI) W = FZD, H = MBS. Solving them under the assumption of full associativity leads to $C^{+1}_{\neq} C^0_{\neq} = A^{+1}_{=}$, $C^0_{\neq} C^{-1}_{\neq} = A^{-1}_{=}$, and $C^{+1}_{\neq} A^{-1}_{=} = A^{+1}_{\neq}$ and $C^{+1}_{\neq} A^0_{\neq} = A^{+1}_{=}$ (from (V)); these results are compatible with both canonical structures. (VI) gives $C_{=}^{+1}C_{\neq}^{0} = A_{\neq}^{+1}$, $C_{\neq}^{0}C_{=}^{-1} = A_{\neq}^{-1}$, and $C_{=}^{+1}A_{\neq}^{-1} = A_{\neq}^{+1}C_{=}^{-1} = A_{\neq}^{0}$, again consistent with both canonical structures. These perhaps surprising results should be carefully interpreted. What they do *not* imply is that the global Iroquois classification is compatible with cross-cousin marriage. This is easily seen if one refers to the entries for ♂MBDC and ♂FZDC (i.e., ♂$A_{\neq}^{0}C_{=}^{-1}$ cross). These are parallel for the Dravidian model, but cross for the Iroquois structure and hence in the latter case are inconsistent with the definition of ego's children as parallel kin. Equations (V) and (VI) only admit to the fairly trivial conclusion that the classification of MBC and FZC is similar (i.e., cross) for both canonical types. As stressed at the beginning of this section, the consistency of the marriage assumptions must be analyzed at the level of the global structure of the table.

In fact, it is precisely at this global level that Trautmann assumes that his rules allow for an unambiguous derivation of the cross/parallel classification of all kintype relations in Dravidian systems, operating not only through consanguineal links but also through affinal links. Although he acknowledges the possibility of reducing certain kin relations in more than one way, his basic premise is that the evaluation of crossness is path-independent; that is, his Dravidian model is fully associative. In discussing relations of the type WBWF, he asserts:

We see here and elsewhere that some kintypes can be reduced in more than one way, an effect that formal analysts generally try to avoid by reducing the number of rules or (if all else fails) imposing an order of operation by fiat. Because the outcome is in every case the same, and correct, however, the effect is harmless and may be ignored. (Trautmann 1981:182–83)

If associativity is *not* perfect (and this is what I shall argue), however, then restrictions on the derivations are not merely a whim of the formal analyst but a necessary delimitation of the model. Curiously, the problem of dealing with incompatible derivations is central to Trautmann's discussion of the Dravidian grandkin classifications. For example (1981:190), FF and MF are parallel relatives (by rule 8.4A), but when described as MHF and FWF, they are cross kin (by rule 8.3A). Citing a number of similar cases for relatives at the $G^{\pm 2}$ levels, Trautmann concludes that the dimension of crossness is neutralized in these generations. Indeed, the problem of dealing with such "double classifications" is one reason for introducing his "model B," a hypothetical Dravidian variant conforming to the Kariera terminology and which generates unambiguous classifications of all grandkin (1981:190–93, 434–37).[25]

Trautmann's problematic "double classifications" are caused by the fundamental nonassociativity of his full model. For example, ♂FF equals ♂$C_{=}^{+1}C_{=}^{+1} = $ ♂$C_{=}^{+2}$ and hence a parallel relative. However, the alternative formulation ♂MHF will only be classified as cross if one assumes the bracketing

$$♂\text{M(HF)}: ♂C_{\neq}^{+1}(A_{\neq}^{0}C_{=}^{+1}) = ♂C_{\neq}^{+1}A_{\neq}^{+1} = ♂A_{=}^{+2}.$$

The other possible bracketing (σMH)F (apparently not considered by Trautmann) leads to a classification *consistent* with that of

$$\sigma_{FF} : (\sigma C_{\neq}^{+1}A_{\neq}^{0})C_{=}^{+1} = \sigma C_{=}^{+1}C_{=}^{+1} = \sigma C_{=}^{+2}.$$

Trautmann's rules 8A and 9A therefore only generate "double classifications" and the necessity of neutralizing cross/parallel distinctions at the grandkin level if the full Dravidian A model is assumed to be associative. It is not.

The inconsistencies occur when multiple paths are traced across generations through certain combinations of consanguineal and affinal links: Trautmann's model is underspecified with regard to their composition. These observations are not intended to be a fundamental critique of Trautmann's seminal Dravidian analysis. As already indicated in the case of the Iroquois-generational variants, specifying more stringent constraints on the associativity of relational composition is not necessarily a bad thing. As an important source of structural variation, it may lead to an enrichment of the original model.

CROSS/PARALLEL CLASSIFICATIONS AND THE IMPOSITION OF MARRIAGE RULES

The previous remarks touch upon the fundamental relationship between the modes of cross/parallel classifications and the range of models developed (mostly under the now classic paradigm of Lévi-Straussian theory) for the analysis of marriage rules and alliance structures.[26] There are fundamental methodological difficulties relating to the comparison and integration of anthropological theories based upon disparate or even possibly incommensurable assumptions. The following examples show how specific alliance structures might intersect with the cross/parallel and generational classifications defined earlier.

The Ngawbe or Western Guaymí are a Chibchan-speaking people at present inhabiting the three westernmost provinces of the Republic of Panama. Young (1970, 1971) describes the primary kin group as cognatic, with a core of patrilineally related males residing together in a hamlet. The terminology appears to be a variant of what I have described as Iroquois-generational, with an Iroquois patterning at the $G^{\pm 1}$ levels, and with all first cousins and siblings merged.[27] There is a cross/parallel classification of second and third cousins that is neither strictly Iroquois nor Dravidian. The preferred form of marriage is a direct (symmetric) exchange of women between two kin groups, with men ideally exchanging "sisters" (or "sister's daughters"; Young 1970:87). A spouse is generally a second or third cross cousin classified as a cross relation.

According to Young (1970:92–94), kindred membership is based on the notion of "symmetric filiation": while all individuals receive patrifiliation from their father and matrifiliation from their mother, a man passes on only his patrifiliation to his children, and a woman only her matrifiliation. Young states the following marriage prohibitions: (1) If two individuals share either patri-or matrifiliation, they may not marry; (2) if a woman shares filiation with either parent of a man, she may not marry him, and conversely, if a man shares filiation with either parent of a woman, he may not marry her (1970:92). If these rules are combined with (3), the ideal of sister exchange, then the closest marriageable kin are the second cousins descended from opposite-sex siblings, that is, the kintypes indicated in boldface in table 3-3 (top).

Young also reports a preference for marriage with a man's FFZDD; if such marriages were carried out in a systematic manner, given the assumption of direct exchange, the simplest model is a four-line structure with the marriage cycle repeating after three generations (Young 1970:89). In addition, the Ngawbe recognize the option of reestablishing an initial alliance after only two generations: in this case, the preferred marriage is with a man's MMBDD. These marriage strategies are complementary: the Ngawbe forbid marriage with a person who is *both* FFZDD and MMBDD to male ego (1970:91–93).

Figure 3-9 illustrates the simplest "elementary" representations of the two Ngawbe marriage structures; the cross and parallel classifications are also indicated. A number of conclusions follow. First, the modified Iroquois-generational scheme is compatible with both alliance structures, the two-generation model (figure 3-9, left; marriage with MMBDD, MFZDD, FMBSD, and FFZSD, i.e, Dravidian-cross kin), and the three-generation structure (figure 3-9, right; marriage with FFZDD, FMBDD, MMBSD, and MFZSD, i.e., kin that are Iroquois-cross).[28] If interpreted as a principle of "crossness," this G^0 classification constitutes an independent type in which the relative sex of an apical or ancestral sibling pair is the defining factor, not (as in the case of the Iroquois) the relative sex of G^{+1} kin, or (as for the Dravidian mode of reckoning), the relative sex of all linking relatives. Cross cousins are descended from opposite-sex siblings, parallel cousins from same-sex siblings. Furthermore, this mode of classification is fully consistent with a rule or ideal of sister exchange, with marriage exchanges repeating in two or more generations, not (as in the Dravidian-type systems) in consecutive generations. Finally, the classifications in G^0 constitute a bipartition of kin such that the logic of the fundamental equations identified by Trautmann (1981:180) is obeyed: (I) $AC = CA = A$, and $CC = AA = C$.

A second example is taken from McDowell's recent (1991) Mundugumor reconstruction. The Mundugumor terminology is again an Iroquois-generational variant; here the G^0 parallel classification is not only extended to all first cousins (as in the Ngawbe example), but also to all second cousins. (For a relevant selection of the terminology, see the appendix to this chapter.) Furthermore, according to McDowell the Mundugumor marriage system is based on a form of third bilateral cousin marriage and brother-sister exchange. Descendants of an original brother-sister pair are reunited in marriage in the fourth generation. These marriages are supposed to reunite two "lines" that have been performing ritual services for each other or have been exchanging with each other for two generations; in each generation, these exchanges should take place between classificatory brother-sister pairs. After she has ruled out various possibilities, McDowell (1991:266–78) proposes a

Figure 3-9

Ngawbe Two- and Three-Generation Structure

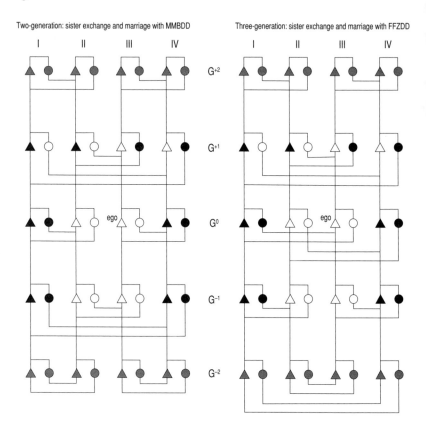

Two-generation: sister exchange and marriage with MMBDD   Three-generation: sister exchange and marriage with FFZDD

partial model in which a man marries his FMMBSDD, who is also his FMFZSDD, or his MFMBDSD, equal to his MFFZDSD.

Figure 3-10 introduces an exchange structure compatible with McDowell's analysis of the Mundugumor terminology and marriage rules.[29] Here again, as in the Ngawbe example, the Iroquois-generational classification is compatible with the exchange structure, the G^0 cross relations are all third cousins linked through an ancestral pair of opposite-sex siblings (see table 3-3, bottom), and the equations $AC = CA = A$, and $CC = AA = C$ apply to all zero-generation positions.

Finally, the Yafar system introduced earlier as an Iroquois variant also exemplifies the use of an optional mode of classification (applied mostly by the younger men). According to Juillerat (1986:336, note 7), crossness may be determined by reference to an ancestral pair of opposite-sex siblings. Moreover, the exchange of "sisters" (one of the permitted forms under a wide range of prohibitions) combines with the ideal of a man marrying his FFFZDDD, repeating the system of exchanges after four generations (Juillerat 1986:285–328). If conceived of as an "elementary"-

Figure 3-10
Mundugumor Four-Generation Structure: Sister Exchange and Marriage with FMMBSSD

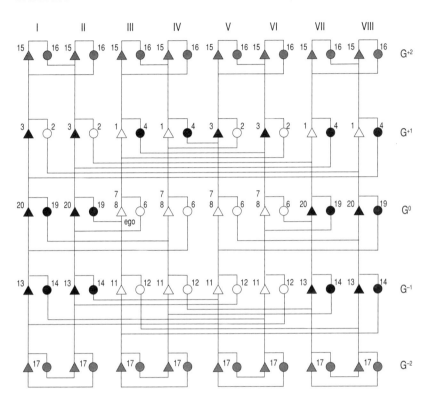

type scheme, it leads to an elementary type alliance model similar to the "Mundugumor" structure discussed above.

These brief observations do not, perhaps, provide much basis for generalization. The most that may be said is that Iroquois-generational terminologies are compatible with specific alliance models of the type generally associated with elementary systems of restricted exchange. Under the marriage prohibitions and the ideal of "sister" exchange, marriageable kin are limited to cross relatives defined through an ancestral pair of opposite-sex siblings; this category (see table 3-3) intersects with the canonical Iroquois and Dravidian classifications for G^0 kin. Moreover, if such systems tend toward the implementation of a "global" classificatory logic, the fundamental cross/parallel equations (i.e., $AC = CA = A$, and $CC = AA = C$) are realized at the zero-generation level.

These remarks suggest an alternative to Scheffler's (1971:248–50) interpretation of the Kuma terminology. In his analysis, the Kuma system is seen as neither a Dravidian nor an Iroquois type, but one with the same structural base (i.e., the same semantic dimensions underlying the focal kintypes), though with a different mode of extending the cross/parallel distinctions. A cross relationship is defined through an ancestral opposite-sex sibling pair and extended across the generations to "all descendants of any cross-cousin" (Reay 1959:xv). Scheffler (1971:250) concludes: "However Kuma society may be ordered, it seems certain from Reay's description that it is not ordered as a symmetric alliance or two-section system, and Kuma kinship terminology certainly does not owe its structure to, or 'express,' Kuma 'rules' of marriage."

Scheffler does not mention one feature of the Kuma system stressed by Reay (1959:57–61): that the direct exchange of "sisters" is the ideal. Furthermore, a man is specifically prohibited from marrying close kin, and from marrying into clans that are traditional enemies. "The only cognates with whom a union can be contracted are the descendants of cross-cousins, too distantly related to be considered part of the kindred at all" (Reay 1959:57).

Although it cannot be said that the Kuma terminology is in any way *generated* through a marriage rule, the Kuma mode of defining crossness through an opposite-sex sibling pair might well be a necessary covariant of the ideal of sister exchange (and an extensive series of marriage prohibitions). Under this interpretation, the terminological patterning seems formally consistent with the imposition of the logic of symmetrical exchange onto an underlying Iroquois-like terminology.[30]

Further analysis of systems with Iroquois-like terminologies and zero-generation crossness of the Ngawbe, Mundugumor, Yafar, or Kuma types and a range of marriage prohibitions might forge a link between theories about kinship terminology and the ongoing discussion on "semicomplex" structures of alliance.[31] To cite Scheffler (1971:253–54): "Instead of typologies of total social systems we need a series of relevant structural elements and structural subsystems defined analytically, . . . independently of their particular forms of realization and conjunction in real social systems." The alternative Dravidian, Iroquois, and other algebraic models submitted here constitute some such structural elements. The exploration of alternative connections may lead to surprising results.

APPENDIX: SUBSET OF THE MUNDUGUMOR KIN TERMS USED IN FIGURE 3-10 (ADAPTED FROM MCDOWELL 1991:168–80)

1. *Avbang:* F, FB, FFBS, FFZS, FMBS, FMZS, and so on. Ego applied this term to father and to anyone his or her father called brother (which included father's first and second male cross and parallel cousins); MH, or any man married to a woman ego called *ume* (mother).

2. *Ume:* M, MZ, MMZD, MMBD, MFBD, MFZD, and so on. Ego applied this term to mother and to anyone his or her mother called sister (which included mother's first and second female cross and parallel cousins); FW, or any woman married to a man called *avbang* (father).

3. *Gumi:* MB, MMZS, MMBS, MFBS, MFZS, and so on. Ego applied this term to mother's brother and to anyone his or her mother called a brother (which included mother's first or second male cross and parallel cousins); FZH, or any man married to a woman called *unyenya* (father's sister).

4. *Unyenya:* FZ, FFBD, FFZD, FMZD, FMBD, and so on. Ego applied this term to father's sister and to anyone his or her father called sister (which included father's first and sec-

ond female cross and parallel cousins); MBW, or any woman married to a man called *gumi* (mother's brother).

6. *Shemi:* (male ego only) Z, MZD, MBD, FBD, FZD, and so on. Ego applied this term to all female siblings and first and second cross and parallel cousins.

7. *Weih:* (male ego only) elder B and any male first or second cross or parallel cousins who were senior to ego.

8. *Kakai:* (male ego only) younger B and any male first or second cross or parallel cousins who were junior to ego.

11. *Fok:* generally, S and S of a sibling of the same sex.

12. *Alep:* generally, D or D of a sibling of the same sex.

13. *Mivafo:* generally, S of sibling of the opposite sex.

14. *Miva'alep:* generally, D of sibling of the opposite sex.

15. *Ungwasak:* MF, FF, and all males of this generation to whom kinship was traced.

16. *Weyak:* MM, FM, and all females of this generation to whom kinship was traced.

17. *Afun:* grandchild or SS, DS, SD, DD; reciprocal for *ungwasak* and *weyak*.

19. *Mi:* (male ego only) W, BW, and so on. A man applied this term to his own wife and to any woman married to men he called brother (*weih, kakai*), again including his first and second cross and parallel male cousins.

20. *Ovambu:* (male ego only) WB or any man ego's wife called brother; ZH, or any man married to someone ego called sister (*shemi*); thus, a reciprocal term between brothers-in-law.

NOTES

This is an amended version of the paper presented at the 1993 Paris workshop on Dravidian, Iroquois, and Crow-Omaha kinship. I owe many improvements to the critical discussion at this meeting. I would like to extend special thanks to Maurice Godelier, Tom Trautmann, and Eduardo Viveiros de Castro for their many suggestions and incisive comments on successive drafts of the manuscript. They are, however, in no way responsible for any of the remaining shortcomings. The Ecole des Hautes Etudes en Sciences Sociales and the Maison Suger provided generous support for a short period of research in Paris in February 1994.

The formal model initially developed in this essay for the analysis of the Dravidian and Iroquois family of structures (including the Kuma, Yafar, and generational variants) has since been greatly extended. Interpreted as a more general class of binary operator algebras or tree automata, it has now been implemented as a series of programs in APL 68000-II-3. The generalized model has successfully been applied to a much more extensive range of terminologies (e.g., Crow and Omaha types, the Fanti, the Navajo). The results of this analysis can be found in Tjon Sie Fat (1995).

1. See the recent discussion in Mickens (1990).

2. For a discussion of the combinatorics involved in deriving this formula, see van Lint and Wilson (1992:116–31) on Catalan numbers.

3. The subscript "=" in the second line of Trautmann's rule 6.4 in the original publication (Trautmann 1981:179, appendix A) is an obvious printing error.

4. In Trautmann's model, the symbols *C* and *A* derive from the "consanguineal" versus "affinal" distinction but are used to elaborate a classification in "parallel" and "cross" relations. These two dichotomies are not necessarily identical and may relate to different principles of organization (see Trautmann 1981:97–106).

5. In "model B," for example, ego's FF and MM are classed as parallel kin and opposed to MF and FM, who are cross; in "model A," all four grandparents are parallel.

6. The compositions $C_p^{+1} C_q^{-1} = C_r^0$ and $A_p^{+1} C_q^{-1} A_r^0$ correspond to Désveaux and Selz's *homogeneity constraint* (*a*") (chapter 6 of this volume). However, these compositions

do not figure exclusively in Dravidian logic (as Désveaux and Selz appear to argue), and the second equation is not essential to certain Dravidian variants with generational classifications at the G^0 level.

7. "Complexity" is a slippery term meaning different things to different people. However, my observations seem compatible with the more orthodox representations of Iroquois/Dravidian crossness. Thus, Scheffler (1971:242), following Lounsbury (1964a), defines crossness for G^0 kin in an "Iroquois" system solely by reference to the relative sex of linking kin in G^{+1} (ego's and alter's parents); information on linking kin in all higher generations is irrelevant. In contrast, to determine G^0 crossness in a Dravidian-type system, one must consider the relative sex of linking kin at *all* generational levels. Here again, if "complexity" is taken to reflect high information content, the Dravidian criteria are the "more complex."

8. There are $2^8 = 256$ possibilities; if consistency of reciprocals is assumed, however, this number is reduced to $2^4 = 16$, giving only fourteen possible models (including the Kuma and the Yafar) "intermediate" to the canonical Dravidian and Iroquois structures. The transformational possibilities linking these variants have been analyzed in more detail elsewhere (see Tjon Sie Fat 1994, and the "hypercube" model sketched in the introduction to this volume). Further variation may, of course, be obtained by modifying the entries in other cells. See Tjon Sie Fat (1995).

9. Generally, the bracketings in these two figures are only some subset of the number of all *possible* bracketings for genealogical paths of length *n*.

10. I follow Trautmann in assuming that there is some underlying dimension of "crossness" operating at least throughout the three medial generations. This is the rationale for defining the formal composition of relations. It is, however, not necessary to assume that the semantic content of such underlying dimensions is identical for different kinship systems: the algebraic representations permit a direct comparison of a wide variety of structural forms. See the analysis in Tjon Sie Fat (1995).

11. See Pospisil (1959–60), Lounsbury (1964a), Kay (1975), Scheffler (1971), and Trautmann (1981). See also the chapters 2, 6, and 15 in this volume. Note however, that certain authors propose other definitions of crossness that are dependent on a rule of descent. See Kay (1965, 1967), Tyler (1966), Buchler and Selby (1968:219–46), and Kronenfeld (1989). (There are a number of unfortunate typographical errors in Kronenfeld's figures 8 and 9.)

12. See also the diagram reproduced in chapter 2. My Iroquois-generational variants seem to model the empirical cases subsumed under "variant 3" of that chapter.

13. The only difference between these two options is an inversion of the roles of ego's parent and parent of ego's cousin as the point of reference, and thus of the two sets of bracketings xviii, xix, xx and xv, xvi, xvii. Further analysis of ethnographical cases might provide criteria for choosing the most appropriate model.

14. An analogous range of Dravidian-generational structures is also possible. Although a full discussion is beyond the scope of this chapter, preliminary analysis indicates that such variants will require even more specific constraints on the permitted bracketings (i.e., on the choice of genealogical paths).

15. This is a fundamental issue discussed in many of the other chapters in this volume.

16. See the remarks by Kronenfeld (1989:102, note 7).

17. See especially Juillerat (1977, 1981, and 1986). See also the remarks on the Yafar by Viveiros de Castro in chapter 15 of this volume. Juillerat (1977) describes the Yafar system as "Dakota-Iroquois," although he stresses that the definition of the cross/parallel classification is different from the definitions given by Pospisil and by Lounsbury for the Kapauku and Seneca.

18. I sketch such an analysis in Tjon Sie Fat (1994).

19. A point acknowledged in a note (1978:537–38, note 5).

20. Preliminary analysis suggests that at least some of the variation can be generated by formulating a further Iroquois-generational variant in which the entries $C_=^{+1}A_q^0$ and $A_q^0C_=^{-1}$ follow the Dravidian pattern.

21. Alternatively, one might assume a maximal correspondence between the affinal/consanguineal and the cross/parallel dichotomies.

22. See Scheffler (1971:235–37), where reasons for rejecting any such marriage rule as a defining characteristic of Dravidian systems are discussed. Trautmann (1981:55–56) uses a spouse-equation rule in his initial equivalence rule analysis.

23. Désveaux and Selz (chapter 6) present a similar analysis of the "binary logic" of Dravidian systems. Contrary to Trautmann, however, they argue that there is no necessary linkage of the classificatory logic (seen as egocentric and largely conceptual) with the occurrence of positive marriage rules.

24. Under this interpretation, the basic equations represent the "consanguineal/affinal" logic at G^0. They are also an alternative realization of the principle of bipartitioning defined by Houseman and White (chapter 9) as *dividedness*. However, Trautmann's complete set of equations and the full algebraic structure of table 3-5 do not yield a globally consistent bipartite structure *in terms of C and A* (for a technical definition of bipartite graphs, see chapter 9). For example, while both of one's parents are defined as parallel kin, they are cross relations of each other; hence no consistent bipartite clustering of the three relations is possible. However, the models most probably do represent bipartite *marriage structures* under the formalization introduced by Houseman and White.

25. The Kariera or Dravidian B model is certainly more consistent than the Dravidian A variant. However, I have not ascertained if it is *fully* associative: that is, if all possible paths (and not only the bracketings defined in figures 3-2 and 3-3) lead to consistent derivations.

26. See the references in Tjon Sie Fat (1990). See especially Héritier (1981).

27. This is a minimal and highly selective sketch. For a more complete description of the terminology, see Young (1971).

28. Analogues of the Aranda and Bardi structures formulated for Dravidian-like Australian systems; see Tjon Sie Fat (1990:189–200). See also Gell (1975) for a discussion of an identical three-generation model for the Umeda of Papua New Guinea. Gell's analysis, in which he presents the Umeda system as a "complex" structure, is discussed in Barnes (1984:208–10). In relation to the analyses of Houseman and White (chapter 9) it is perhaps relevant to observe that the two-generation structure exhibits "sidedness," but the three-generation structure does not. Any analysis based entirely on the patterning of actual Ngawbe marriages might therefore produce ambiguous results. For other relevant remarks on the Ngawbe, see Viveiros de Castro (chapter 15).

29. There is one possible discrepancy: my model equates ego's spouse with his FFFZDDD, FFMBDD, MMMBSSD, and MMFZSSD, in addition to the third-cousin kintypes mentioned by McDowell. She appears to rule out these possibilities (1990:274). See also the remarks on the Yafar, where FFFZDDD is recognized as an ideal marriage. A similar marriage structure has been proposed by Lucich (1987, 1991) for the Kukata and Aluridja in Australia and by Pfeffer (1982:79–88) for the Ho in India. For a fundamental critique of Pfeffer's analysis, see Parkin (1993).

30. The formal relationships between the Dravidian, Iroquois, Yafar, and Kuma models are discussed in Tjon Sie Fat (1994).

31. See Héritier (1981) and the series on *Les Complexités de l'alliance* edited by Héritier and Copet-Rougier (1990: vol. 1; 1991: vol. 2). See also Tjon Sie Fat (1993).

4

Developmental Processes in the Pre-Contact History of Athapaskan, Algonquian, and Numic Kin Systems

JOHN W. IVES

There is a paradox in the study of kinship in hunter-gatherer societies. Kinship is often accorded a central role in this field, yet, when kinship assumes that role, it frequently becomes the subject of generalizations that mask important variability in hunter-gatherer social structures. Thus, although kinship is said to be vital in hunter-gatherer societies, the details remain elusive.

In many ways, this paradox stems from the dominance of cultural ecological and evolutionary ecological approaches in hunter-gatherer studies during recent decades. Were one to parse through this literature, some dominant trends would quickly become evident. There is, for instance, a strong sense that hunter-gatherer bands are kin-connected, although rather amorphous. Kinship is implicated in the flexibility or fluidity that bands need in order to deal with conflict resolution or the unequal distribution of resources. Bands are often viewed as self-regulating entities, always returning to stable size ranges, which are in turn closely connected with "optimal foraging strategies," or similar concepts.

This chapter builds the case for a different view of hunter-gatherer band societies. The central question here is not how bands stay the same, but how they are formed. That is, what *principles of group formation* are applied by different hunter-gatherer societies? The answer, at least for many North American Indian societies, appears to be that bands are not simply kin connected, but *kin structured,* particularly in the arrangement of sets of siblings within bands. The combined effects of the principles of group formation and kin-structuring trigger characteristic developmental processes for these societies.

These topics are of interest in their own right, but I have another reason for pursuing them. In the Maison Suger conference, Maurice Godelier raised the fascinating question of whether the logical transformations that can be made of mathematical or other models of kin systems are essentially endless, or whether they have a directionality. When viewed in an ecological evolutionary sense, hunter-gatherer societies do appear to be relatively invariant, archetypal "cold" societies that are not too susceptible to important historical change. When viewed as the outcome of various developmental processes, however, these elementary social structures appear to have considerable potential for real historical transformation in particular settings.

In this discussion, I examine kinship and principles of group formation for several band societies in North America with this perspective in mind. The time scales are of relevance to ethnographic study but may also be of interest to archaeologists and historical linguists. One time scale will involve the developmental processes governing the creation, existence, and disappearance of bands over generations; the other involves the key thresholds at which socioeconomic transformations take place in the historical development of different social formations. These changes occur at the scale of centuries or millennia, in the realm of language family origins, dispersals, and adjustments to different political and physical environments.

Consistent with these interests, the methodology employed here will follow that of controlled comparison, essentially as advocated by Eggan (1955a:498–99), for the Athapaskan, Algonquian, and Numic language families. The assumption here is that some form of historical connection links the member dialects and languages of a language family. The analysis opens with the kin terminologies and principles of group formation found in some key examples within a language family. It then proceeds to the distribution of different kin systems within each language family. Terminological variability in kin lexica is assessed against the political and economic settings throughout which a language family is found. In order to inject a temporal dimension into the discussion, I also resort to the best available reconstructions of kin lexica for the protolanguages involved. This is undertaken to gain insight into the social transformations likely to have affected societies of the more distant past.

There is a bias in this approach, and it is one I wish to make evident from the outset. Many of the ideas presented here flow from my interest in the social and economic organization of peoples living in Subarctic North America. Although the Subarctic has been successfully settled for ten millennia or more (e.g., Ives 1993), ecological conditions render it a challenging region in which to live. Northern hunter-gatherers were traditionally arranged in a series of regional groups, or regional marriage isolates (see Ives 1990:61–65 for a summary discussion). Regional groups were focused on large-scale physiographic features (often major segments of river drainages). Subarctic population densities are among the lowest in the world, commonly dipping to one person for every 150 to 400 square kilometers. This is a reflection of the dispersion and relatively low density of Subarctic game and fish resources. Regional groups generally approached that "magic number" of five hundred individuals so widely reported for hunter-gatherer regional groups. The reasons for this are undoubtedly certain biological realities for human populations, such as the demographic persistence of population aggregates of this size range in the face of stochastic processes, as shown by Wobst (1974, 1976).

Large-scale social gatherings (approaching the size of regional marriage isolates) could only take place once or twice a year, at times and places with resources sufficient to support large groups of people. Regional marriage isolates were, in fact, composed of a series of smaller local groups or bands, which might number anywhere from ten to a hundred or more. Such groups were generally composed of sibling sets. Local groups were vital in the day-to-day economic activities that dispersed people across the Subarctic landscape in highly mobile residential groups. Subarctic food resources can be notoriously unpredictable in their abundance; generally speaking, extremely broad kin networks were essential in providing individuals with a variety of options and rights in joining other local groups in order to counter these fluctuations.

Consequently, kinship in these societies is intimately tied to very small social groups, especially to the affinal arrangements made between the different sets of siblings comprising the nuclei of local groups or bands. Group-forming principles in the Subarctic are constantly applied in the creation of truly elementary social groups, which take shape, persist for one or a few generations, and disappear. This is in decided contrast to settled villages (such as might be found in southern India or parts of South America), where increasingly elaborate kin systems, stable co-residential groups, cycles of exchange, and related phenomena can appear. The bias is to begin by learning—from the subtle dynamics in simpler hunter-gatherer band societies.

The playing out of developmental processes also has important consequences for the distribution of people in band societies across the landscape and through time. This should in turn structure the archaeological record. An understanding of such developmental processes is essential in devising socially, politically, and economically realistic models through which archaeologists can assess the material record of the past. Since it is more than likely that the Americas were first populated by hunter-gatherers, the elementary social dynamics of band societies are also an inherently attractive place to look for developmental processes that could lead to increasing social complexity (as in the tribal societies of the Plains, or the settled villages of northwestern North America). Models developed in this area can also be valuable in exploring key socioeconomic transformations in the history of language families, an area of mutual interest to archaeologists and historical linguists.

MACKENZIE BASIN DENE

Kin systems founded upon the logical implications of bilateral cross-cousin marriage have been recognized in North America for the better part of this century. As early as 1914, Rivers thought that this form of marriage was likely to exist among the Cree and had probably affected the Athapaskan (Dene) Red Knife kin terminology as well (see figure 4-1 for a map of Athapaskan societies).[1] The logical patterning for the Red Knife was imperfect, however, and Rivers (1968 [1914]:69) observed that "the terminology had arisen in some other way, or that there has been some additional social factor in operation which has greatly modified a nomenclature derived from cross cousin marriage." He was quite correct in these suspicions; an explanation for the patterning in question, which is widespread in North America (e.g., Spier 1925), is provided below.

Figure 4-1
Distribution of Athapaskan Speakers in Northwestern North America, with
Information on Kin Terms for Cousins

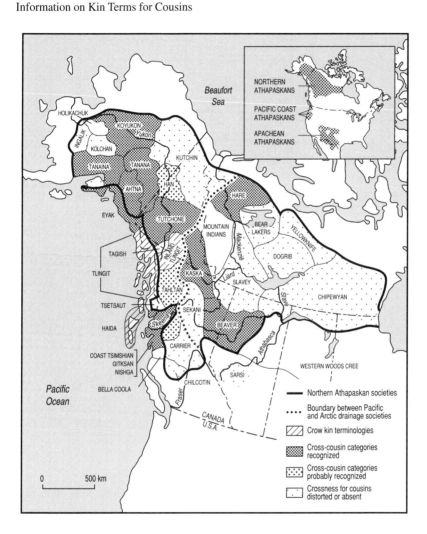

Although the Mackenzie Basin of northern Canada is a useful place to begin
discussion, it cannot proceed without a well-documented kin terminology and clearly
established principles of group formation (this is a necessarily abbreviated version
of Ives 1985, 1987, 1988, and 1990). Asch (1972, 1988, and chapter 5 of this volume) has provided these for the Wrigley Slavey. In its key elements, the Wrigley kin
schedule (figure 4-2) fits neatly within the paradigm Trautmann (1981) developed
for South Indian Dravidian systems. Cross/parallel kin distinctions are well represented in the three medial generations. Terms equating consanguines with affines

Figure 4-2
Wrigley Slavey Kinship Terminology

	♂		♀	
	x	//	//	x
G^2	*ehtsée* FF, MF		*ehtsi* MM, FM	

		♂			♀	
G^1		*se?eh* MB, FZH, SpF	*gotáa* FB, MZH	*setá* F	*semo* M	*emǫo* MZ, FBW	*ehmbée* FZ, MBW, SpM

		♂		♀	
G^0 e	*segheh* MBS, FZS, WB	*gojnde* eB, e(FBS), e(MZS), FZDH, MBDH	*sembae* eZ, e(FBD), e(MZD), FZSW, MBSW	*selah* MBD, FZD, WZ, MZSW
G^0	*selah* MZDH		ego	*sets'éke* W
G^0 y	*sedené* H	*sechia* yB, y(FBS), y(MZS), FZDH, MBDH	*sedea* yZ, y(FBD), y(MZD), FZSW, MBSW	

	♂		♀	
G^{-1}	*sebaa* ♂ZS, ♀BS, ♂DH, ♂FZSS,♂MBSS, ♂FBDS,♂MZDS,♀MBDS, ♀FZDS, ♀MZSS,♀FBSS *sedo* ♀DH	*sezhaa* S, ♂BS, ♀ZS, ♂FBSS, ♂MZSS, ♂FZDS, ♂MBDS, ♀MZDS, ♀FBDS, ♀FZSS, ♀MBSS	*setié* D, ♂BD, ♀ZD, ♂FBSD,♂MZSD, ♂FZDD, ♂MBDD, ♀MZDD, ♀FBDD, ♀FZSD, ♀MBSD	*sendaa* ♂ZD, ♂SW, ♂MBSD, ♂FZSD, ♂FBDD, ♂MZDD *secháa* ♀BD,♀SW, ♀FBSD, ♀MZSD, ♀ZSW

G^{-2}	*sepii* ♂SS, ♂DS, ♂DD, ♂SD *secháa* ♀SS, ♀DS, ♀DD, ♀SD	

Source: Asch (1972: 47–60, 1988: 37–47).

(hereafter, "affinal equations"), consistent with a model of symmetrical or bilateral cross-cousin marriage, are pervasive. More distant relatives (e.g., as given in G^{-1}) are correctly classed for Dravidian-type (and not Iroquoian) crossness.

The Dravidian structural properties Asch identified for the Wrigley Slavey have profound implications for the sibling cores of Mackenzie Basin local groups, as seen in figure 4-3A. In figure 4-3Ai, a brother and a sister are married to a brother and a sister, while in figure 4-3Aii, two brothers are married to two sisters. Beyond

Figure 4-3

Variations in the Composition of Affinal Implications of Different Sibling Cores for
Local Groups or Bands

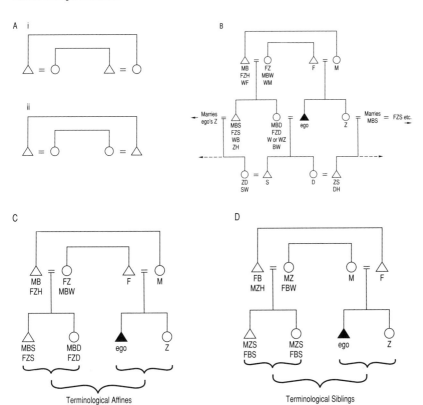

Terminological Affines

Terminological Siblings

that single difference, no amount of analytical rigor can help to distinguish between
the two sibling cores. Each group has the same number of individuals, each has the
same number of men and women, each individual has one sibling tie but two ties by
marriage, and so forth. Most anthropologists looking at these sibling cores have
concluded that they represent essentially the same thing.

As Trautmann (1981) has shown, Dravidian structural systems equate parallel
relatives with consanguineal or blood relatives, whereas cross relatives are actual or
potential affines. These terminological systems are driven by the notion of bilateral
cross-cousin marriage, as shown in figure 4-3B. Everyone in the social universe of
such systems is therefore either an affine or consanguine. It is this conjunction of
factors that reveals the real difference between the two sets of sibling cores in figure
4-3A. In figure 4-3Ai, cross relatives are present, with the consequence that in the
next generation, cross cousins will live together (as in figure 4-3C). These children
can marry. In figure 4-3Aii, parallel relatives are present; that generation's children

will be parallel cousins and, in fact, siblings to each other (figure 4-3D). These children *must not* marry. It is precisely these nuances that many Northern Athapaskans explored in their principles of group formation.

In his study of the Wrigley Slavey, Asch (1980, 1988) reported three critical findings:

1. The entire population of Wrigley was marked by a cross/parallel distinction between consanguineal and affinal relatives.
2. Wrigley residents gave a rule of "unilocality" for residence, in which siblings or classificatory siblings of one sex remained together, at a single location, while siblings of the opposite sex departed. The sex of the siblings who departed was not specified.
3. Marriage outside the local group was strongly favored.

Asch (1980, 1988) had some compelling proofs for the operation of these principles. That all members of the community should be partitioned into cross and parallel relatives went far beyond coincidence, especially given the torturous genealogical tracings necessary to maintain this appearance. He also found that fully thirteen of fourteen marriages had taken place between relatives of the cross and parallel categories. The single exception caused such controversy that it may be said to have proved the rule. For the nine marriages for which there was information, eight had involved a spouse from another local group.

The Wrigley Slavey deliberately fashioned same-sex sibling cores that enforced local-group exogamy in the first descending generation. The entire logic of this framework is to keep potential affines outside the local group. The Slavey impetus to exogamy is so powerful that it can in fact distort the semantic structure of the terminology. Asch found a distinct tendency to call even cross cousins by sibling terms, widening the field for marriages.

As Asch (1988:106) has pointed out, this strong emphasis on exogamy provides an explanation for Leslie Spier's (1925:67–77) Mackenzie Basin "type" of terminology (see also Ives 1992). In what he referred to as a strictly empirical classification, Spier (1925:71) used generational attributes to identify terminological forms. Mackenzie Basin terminologies are distinguished by G^0 terms in which all cousins (parallel or cross) are siblings (Spier:76–77). Here, I am particularly concerned with the Mackenzie Basin variant in which there is a bifurcate merging pattern in G^{+1} accompanied by cross/parallel distinctions for children and nepotic relatives in G^{-1}.

Spier's classification was not particularly helpful to later researchers, even for those working among Mackenzie Basin Dene. Helm (MacNeish 1960) puzzled over Dene terminologies in which first ascending and descending generation cross reckoning was present, but where crossness in ego's generation was absent ("Hawaiian" cousin terminologies). Despite the frequency of cross-cousin marriage among neighboring Algonquians, despite the equation of cross relatives in G^{+1} and G^{-1} in the Dene terminologies, and even despite the fact that some informants would produce cross-cousin terms, Mackenzie Basin Dene only rarely engaged in cross-cousin

Figure 4-4
Lynx Point Slavey Kinship Terminology

		♂			♀		
		x	//	//	x		
G^2		*etsi* FF, MF			*etsu* MM, FM		
G^1		*se'e* MB, FZH, SpF / *etsia:* SpF	*eta* FB, MZH	*seta* F	*semó, ene* M	*emo* MZ, FBW	*ehmbe* FZ, MBW, SpM / *etsu* SpM
G^0	e	*gunde, sunde* eB, e(FBS), e(MZS), FZS, MBS / *seye* FZS, MBS, ZH, WB, HB / *sedene* H			*emba* eZ, e(FBD), e(MZD), FZD, MBD / *seye* FZD, MBD, BW, WZ, HZ / *setzeke* W		ego
	y	*seče* yB, y(FBS), y(MZS), FZS, MBS			*sede* yZ, y(FBD), y(MZD), FZD, MBD		
G^{-1}		*saze* ♂ZS, ♂DH, ♀BS / *seto* DH	*seža* S, ♂BS, ♀ZS		*setue* D, ♂BD / *sede* ♀ZD(?)	*saze* ♂ZD, ♂SW / *sede* ♀BD / *setθue* ♂SW / *seča* ♀SW	
G^{-2}		*seča, setθue* DD, SD, SS, DS					

Source: Helm, in MacNeish (1960: 280–81).

marriage. Helm (MacNeish 1960:290–92) suggested that this form of terminology might arise from acculturative processes but did not seem satisfied with this idea.

Elsewhere (Ives 1990:88–93), I have argued that the history of one of the Slavey communities in which Helm (1961) conducted ethnographic research, Lynx Point, can illuminate the processes creating the Mackenzie Basin pattern. The consensus terminology for Lynx Point is presented in figure 4-4; it is similar to that for the Wrigley Slavey, but crossness is lacking in ego's generation. Not surprisingly, marriages were local-group exogamous, and a number of Helm's (1961:66) informants thought it inappropriate to marry too close in a genetic sense. Lynx Point was nevertheless one of the Mackenzie Basin Dene communities creating flux in cousin terms in Helm's sample of schedules, and cross-cousin terms were occasionally mentioned. Helm's (1961:67) most thoughtful informant actually indicated that cross-cousin marriage, sister exchange, the sororate, and the levirate were "all good things to do."

When Lynx Point formed as a community in 1911, it was small and had essentially a same-sex sibling core (of three sisters), with a high density of dyadic consanguineal ties. By the time of Helm's ethnographic work, it had grown to be one of the largest bush communities in the Mackenzie Basin. Brother-brother dyadic ties were now more common, but the overall density of consanguineal links had dropped noticeably. The next most common dyadic ties were brother-sister ones. At this stage of its existence, Lynx Point was beginning to have a plethora of legitimate local-group endogamous marriage possibilities.

Kin terms are subject to a variety of moral and tactical usages (e.g., Murphy 1967; Bloch 1971), and therein lies the root cause of the variability Helm observed. Cousin and nepotic terms are key points of tension in Dravidian-type systems, and the form in which they are represented can do a great deal in affirming or contradicting affinal potentials. A Mackenzie Basin style of terminology reflects Dravidian structural antecedents and sibling exchange marriages, but shows equally a strong proclivity for local-group exogamy. Immanent in the fully articulated crossness and affinal equations of a Dravidian-type terminology is the possibility of local-group endogamy. Since the social, political, and economic ramifications of such choices are important in Subarctic settings, it is not surprising that the manner of representing a kin terminology could be subject to considerable (conscious or unconscious) debate. I believe that Dene terminologies of Mackenzie Basin "type" are the outcome of strong pressures for local-group exogamy; they render the composition of sibling cores immaterial by casting the children of either same-sex or opposite-sex sibling cores as siblings themselves. This is precisely the "additional social factor" that Rivers wondered about.

Not all Northern Athapaskan communities adopt a high degree of local-group exogamy as a strategy. Ridington's (1968, 1969) analysis of the Beaver of northeastern British Columbia shows contrasting principles of group formation operating with another attested Dravidian-type kin terminology. There, crossness is not distorted, although there is an intergenerational skewing of terms for female cross relatives. This stems from a tendency toward intergenerational marriages between older men and younger women.

The most critical contrasts reside in the composition of sibling cores. Among local Beaver groups, sibling cores with brothers and sisters married to brothers and sisters are common. Furthermore, a high proportion of marriages occurs between children in the next generation, as Ridington's (1968) genealogies showed. The Beaver place a premium upon tightly knit, highly endogamous local groups, from which children are less likely to leave. They do so as part of a competitive political environment, in which differences in the supernatural powers between men receive

Figure 4-5
Developmental Processes of Beaver (A) and Slavey (B) Local Groups

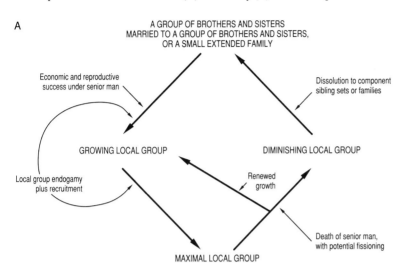

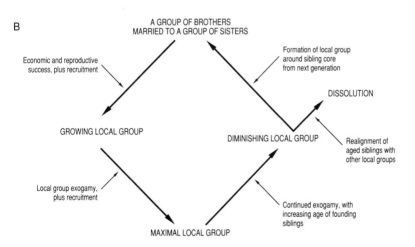

freer expression than is the case with the Slavey. Therefore, while the Slavey take a Dravidian logic and use it to segregate cross and parallel kin, the Beaver do not have a preference for unilocal residence, and they do not spatially segregate cross kin who are potential spouses. Even at extremely small group sizes, local-group endogamy becomes possible and is favored as a strategy.

These principles of group formation set in motion distinctive developmental processes (see figure 4-5a). Ridington's (1968:60–81) band histories show that local groups could arise from even a single conjugal pair. Usually, a senior man headed up a band consisting of his wife, their married children, and perhaps widowed women and their children. Bands experienced vicissitudes of economic and reproductive success. They might fail altogether, or they might more or less maintain their smaller size with a net balance in forces of natality, mortality, endogamy, and exogamy. If the band was economically viable, however, the senior man could recruit additional people. Moreover, with an opposite-sex sibling core, children in the first descending generation could take part in completely endogamous marriages. Although exogamy could certainly occur, recruitment of kin and nonkin from outside the band, the influx of new spouses through affinal alliances, and marriage of children within the group each counteracted the loss of personnel. Bands in these later stages of development could grow to ten to twenty families and associated relatives.

Three factors could truncate these processes. First, food resources in boreal forest environments are irregular and cyclical. Difficult conditions there could cause dissolution of growing or stable bands. Second, the Beaver sociopolitical environment was a competitive one, and supernatural conflict between men could also cause growing local groups to fission. Third, death of the senior man in such groups could lead to fissioning along sibling lines. Thus the Beaver preserved essential terminological elements of crossness along with bilateral cross-cousin marriage. Their successful local groups tended to grow and persist with endogamous marriages. Yet socially isolated endogamous groups were more prone to the ecological dislocations of the Subarctic, since they did not form as broad a net of kin alliances with neighboring groups.

Quite another pattern occurs among the Wrigley Slavey (figure 4-5b). Slavey bands may begin in a similar fashion and may also experience economic and reproductive success. In this case, personnel loss is caused by two other factors. The principal one is local-group exogamy: at least half the children of the sibling core generation are enjoined to marry out. Aging of the sibling core causes attrition. Older people, especially once widowed, leave so that they can be cared for by their children in other bands. Local Slavey groups tend to fluctuate within a size range of two to eight or ten conjugal pairs, plus ancillary relatives. According to Asch, local Slavey groups also tend to disappear with the passing of a generation.

For the Wrigley Slavey, then, the preference for unilocal residence (linking sets of same-sex siblings) fits well with a Dravidian-type logic because it carefully segregates cross and parallel relatives. Only the latter are found within the ideal local group. Although local groups remain small and tend to disappear with regularity at the time scale of generations, this kind of system "pumps" individuals out because of its focus on local-group exogamy. This practice, in turn, has a critical bearing on the creation of a broad geographic network of kin ties, giving both individuals and local groups options and rights in dealing with the fluctuating resources typical of the boreal forest. In fact, local-group exogamy is sufficiently important that other Slavey force the issue from the outset. The cousin terminology is shifted so that all are siblings; this renders the composition of sibling cores irrelevant because the entire thrust of the strategy is to push the boundary for incest outside the local group altogether.

Figure 4-6
Variability in Size and Temporal Persistence of Beaver and Slavey Local
Groups

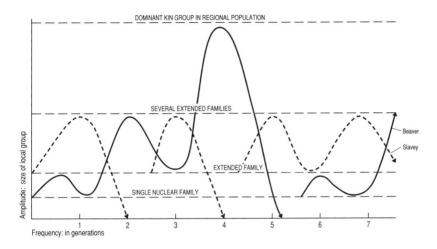

Figure 4-6 portrays the variability in local-group size and temporary persistence of local Beaver as opposed to local Slavey groups. Local Beaver groups show greater swings in amplitude, even to the extent of approaching the size of an incipient regional population. Local Slavey groups fluctuate in size within a narrower range, and they tend to dissolve with each generation.

The contrasts between the Beaver and Slavey cases provide some insight into what Rivers suspected of the Red Knife. Chipewyan kin terminologies are not well reported but encompass a considerable range of variability. They run from the well-preserved Dravidian-type patterning of the Cold Lake Chipewyan (Elford and Elford 1981; Ives 1990:209–14) to the significantly altered patterning of the Red Knife schedule given by Morgan (1871) in his table II. That terminology preserves some crossness in the first ascending generation, especially for usages such as FZ = MBW = HM = WM, but sees crossness being obliterated in ego's and the first descending generations.

The Mission and Snowdrift Caribou Eater Chipewyan terminologies depart even further from the pattern, in that crossness is virtually absent from the schedules, and the remaining distinctions are of a lineal-collateral nature (e.g., siblings are distinguished from all cousins) (VanStone 1965:70–71; Sharp 1979:11; Ives 1990:209–12). This is quite likely the result of Caribou Eater Chipewyan local-group dynamics, in which same- and opposite-sex sibling cores both occur (Ives 1990:221–23). Such a circumstance almost certainly erodes affinal equations because Caribou Eater Chipewyan local groups are highly exogamous. By the same token, local groups frequently fission along the sibling lines between brothers at characteristic points in their developmental cycle, consistently removing parallel cousins from domestic groups. Under these circumstances, cross cousins need not be cast as affines, and parallel cousins are not the necessary equivalent of siblings. This suggests that full-fledged Dravidian structural distinctions can also break down in the direction of "Eskimoan" terminologies.

Proceeding in another way, crossness is well represented in the Hare terminology, and affinal equations remain quite common (Hara 1980:245–46; Ives 1990:203). Even so, the incidence of cross-cousin marriage among the Hare is negligible (12 of 457 cases over a sixty-six year period researched by Helm 1968b:216). The Hare seem to use Dravidian-type principles to unite relative strangers in very small local groups that will not persist after a generation.

These distinctions remain useful even when we move beyond the ambit of the Mackenzie Basin Dene to other Northern Athapaskans. On the opposite side of the continental divide, crossness, precise affinal equations, and frequent bilateral cross-cousin marriage are typical of Athapaskans such as the Ahtna. The Ahtna alternated between relatively sedentary village camps along the Copper River (in which salmon fishing and storage was important) and upland camps for communal caribou hunting (De Laguna and McClellan 1981; see Ives 1990:242–48 for a summary). The Upper Tanana described by Guedon (1974) are similar in both economy and intensive cross-cousin marriage between localized siblings; there is at least one trace of Dravidianate patterning for more distant relatives in the genealogies Guedon presents (a MFZSS classed as a sibling). The Eyak (who spoke the only other language with a genetic relationship to Athapaskan languages) also lived a comparatively sedentary village life on the lower Copper River, where they could hunt sea mammals hunting and harvest salmon. Marriages took place between exogamous moieties. The Eyak terminology has extensive crossness with affinal equations, as well as the presence of cross reckoning in G-2 (Krauss n.d.; Ives 1990:248–53).

The Sarsi—Athapaskans who became allied with the Blackfoot of Alberta and Montana—have perhaps the most significantly different kin system among Northern Athapaskans. Their kin terminology is not well known, but the information provided by Jenness (1938:24) indicates that crossness is lacking in all three medial generations.[2] Little has been reported of Sarsi marriage practices, but they do have a reputation for extensive outmarriage (Curtis 1928:102).

THE SITUATION FOR ALGONQUIANS

Kin systems founded on symmetrical cross-cousin marriage were first confirmed in North America for northern Algonquian peoples, again as Rivers (1914) suspected. Hallowell (1928b) initially suggested that such marriage systems existed on historical grounds, but it was Curtis (1928:70, 156) who first described the prevalence of cross-cousin marriage among westerly Woods Cree in more recent times. Subsequent reports from Strong (1929), Landes (1937), Flannery (1938), and Rossignol (1938), among others, noted a significant incidence of bilateral cross-cousin marriage for several peoples, including the Ojibwa, Cree, and Montagnais-Naskapi.

However, a full range of diagnostic points along the semantic dimensions for crossness are seldom recorded for these terminologies, with the result that one often cannot discriminate Type A from Type B crossness. For proximal kin, however, affinal equations are common and precise. Moreover, Hallowell's (1975 [1937]) more detailed work with Cree and Saulteaux in the Lake Winnipeg area leaves little doubt that Dravidian-type cross reckoning is involved: not just first- but second-cross-cousin marriage was common in this region (see also chapter 6 of this volume). Many individuals involved in these marriages were multiply related to each other as first or second cross cousins, or both. The second cross-cousin categories represented (MMBDD, MMZSD, MFBSD, MFZDD, FFBDD, FFZSD, FMBSD, and FMZDD) are all of Dravidian and *not* Iroquois-type (Hallowell 1975 [1937]:320). Similarly, Rogers (1962:B10–12, B50) reported consistent Dravidianate crossness for more distant G^{-1} relatives for the highly endogamous Round Lake Ojibwa in northwestern Ontario (e.g., for a man speaking, FZSS, MBSS, FBDS, and MZDS are referred to by a term for son-in-law or sister's son, whereas FBSS, MZSS, FZDS, and MBDS are called "brother's son").

Meyer's (1984) historical analysis of the Red Earth and Shoal Lake communities near the Pasquia Hills in east central Saskatchewan provides insight into the group-forming principles at work. He recorded the formation of a regional marriage isolate in this region, beginning in the mid–nineteenth century. The fourteen couples in the founding generation of the group came from Swampy Cree speakers formerly oriented toward the Pas region to the east, or from Plains Cree speakers formerly oriented toward the Fort à la Corne region to the west. The individuals involved seemed intent on isolating themselves from increasing Euro-Canadian influence. The next generation (Meyer's Generation One, ca. 1870–1900) saw continued intense social and ceremonial interaction (notably for the Goose Dance), coupled with a marriage pattern in which 64.3 percent of all marriages took place within the region. The population had grown to 178 persons. By Generation Two (1900–1930), the population had grown to 220 persons, and regionally endogamous marriages had reached a rate of 85 percent. The rate of endogamy held steady as the population grew to 325 persons in Generation Three (1930–60).

Meyer has described a situation in which a small number of people, approximately the size of a local group, isolated themselves from neighboring groups. Featuring high rates of endogamy and a great degree of socioeconomic independence, this group met with success and grew into the size range of a regional marriage isolate or deme. Meyer (1984:9) held that the social processes connected with the formation of a regional marriage isolate were common for more easterly Cree and Ojibwa. The overall pattern is quite similar to that of the Beaver.

Although full-fledged distinctions for medial generation crossness are common for Subarctic Algonquians, the Montagnais-Naskapi (close linguistic relatives of the Cree) of Labrador and Quebec make a series of terminological shifts reminiscent of the Dene cases discussed earlier. Strong (1929:279–82) reported differences between the Barren Ground and Davis Inlet bands where, for the former band, cross cousins were recognized and equated with affines in the terminology and cross-cousin marriage was favored. In contrast, in the latter band all cousins were siblings and cross-cousin marriage was not practiced unless there were no other available partners.

Similar patterns can be traced among Plains Algonquian peoples. The Plains Cree, whose ancestors in the late part of the prehistoric period lived at the Plains margin in western Canada, became increasingly involved in the emerging Plains horse culture during the last two hundred years of the historic period. Mandelbaum's (1979:124–26) terminology for Plains Cree shows such Dravidianate features as MB = SpF, FZ = SpM, FZS = MBS = ZH and ZHB, and FZD = MBD = ZHZ. This is intriguing for despite the persistence of affinal equations, cross-cousin marriage had lapsed among most of Mandelbaum's informants, although it persisted among the Calling River people (Mandelbaum 1979:127).[3] Mandelbaum observed that a cross-cousin marriage principle shaped the Plains Cree kin system, except that

in many instances there are two terms which may be utilized—thus, sister's daughter's husband may be called *nikosis,* son, or another term may be applied to this relative. It is *ntosim,* which is now used specifically for cross-niece's husband. Lacombe defines this term as "brother's son" which is consistent with the cross cousin marriage principle, although the term is not at present used for that relationship. *It seems as though a set of extraneous terms had been added to a consistent system based on cross cousin marriage.* In some cases the "extraneous" terms have entirely supplanted the "older" terminology. (Mandelbaum 1979:124; emphasis added)

If Mandelbaum is correct about the Plains Cree circumstance, then his remarks are all the more fascinating in the light of patterns among other Plains Algonquians. Cheyenne and Arapaho social organization strikes a familiar chord (Eggan 1955a). Their custom of matrilocal residence gave rise to an extended domestic family, or "camp" comprised of several lodges. These involved a man and wife, their married daughters and the daughters' husbands, their unmarried sons, their daughters' children, and other dependents, in other words, some fifteen to twenty-five individuals (Eggan 1955a:61, 83). It was common and desirable for households to exchange brothers and sisters in marriage. Sororate and levirate marriages were common.

Cheyenne bands were composed of a series of extended families that operated for much of the year as a political and economic unit under a chief. Band affiliations were somewhat weaker than family affiliations; women generally remained with their natal band, with husbands coming from elsewhere. Rivalry between bands was pronounced, and chiefs would encourage endogamy to maintain the size and strength of the band. This was balanced by general tribal advantages conferred by band exogamy. Age-graded societies such as the Dog Soldiers crosscut these other social entities.

The dominant features of Arapaho kin terminology given by Eggan (1955a:42–49) are one again of the Mackenzie Basin pattern. Crossness with affinal equations is clearly represented in the parent's generation (e.g., F = FB = MZH, M = MZ = FBW) and in the children's generation. In fact, close linguistic analysis of the Arapaho terminology led Salzmann (1959) to suspect that they had once practiced cross-cousin marriage, as Eggan (1955b:531) himself had suggested. Specifically,

Salzmann equated MB = FZH with WF, and FZ = MBW with WM. Likewise, he equated the term for cross niece with the term for SW, and cross nephew with DH. Yet in ego's generation, all cousins are referred to as siblings, and cousins could not be married. There are some specific differences for the Cheyenne and Gros Ventre, but the fundamental pattern is the same.

In terms of group-forming principles, this is not so surprising. Here is a society in which extended domestic families tend to be formed from same-sex sibling cores, the entire thrust of which forces exogamy. Powerful chiefs of bands might encourage endogamous marriages, but even bands had a strong predilection for exogamy in favor of tribal unity (Eggan 1955b:84).

It is important to note, however, the exact nature of the cross reckoning exhibited here. Although the Arapaho affinal equations might be construed as the residue of a system of bilateral cross-cousin marriage founded on distinctions of Dravidian structural type, the cross reckoning is actually of Iroquois type, as demonstrated by Trautmann and Barnes (1991, and chapter 2 of this volume) (second-cousins pattern in Iroquois fashion).[4]

The Algonquian Plains groups provide one further example of interest. Blackfoot—represented by the Pikuni (Peigan), Siksika (Blackfoot Proper), and Kainai (Blood)—is generally regarded as the most divergent of all the Algonquian languages. Some anthropologists suspect that the Blackfoot peoples were on the Plains longer than any other Algonquians. As table 4-1 shows, Blackfoot also has the most divergent Algonquian kin terminology observed thus far (see Wissler 1911:15; Michelson 1916; and Hanks and Hanks 1945). There is scarcely a vestige of crossness anywhere in these schedules, and a decided tendency toward a generational semantic framework. Hanks and Hanks (1945:29–31) Siksika schedule is further marked by relative age distinctions that override generation, especially for males in ego's father's family (e.g., the series *naa'xs*[a], *nin.'a*, *ni's*[a], *nisis.'*[a], *nuxku'a*, *nis.xku'y*[a]). Furthermore, intergenerational skewing is prominent (e.g., a married woman elevates members of FZ's line by a generation, while depressing those of MB's line by two generations). Hanks and Hanks (1945:25) observed that "the woman's system of relating herself to other women is very similar to the Crow kinship structure."

Each of the Blackfoot tribes was composed of a series of named bands or local groups that undertook subsistence pursuits. For the Blood, bands historically ranged from 18 to as many as 200 lodges (bands totaling about one hundred to several hundred people) (Dempsey 1982:94). According to Wissler,

When a band begins, it may be a group of two or three brothers, fathers and grandfather, or a small family band (which means the same thing); later, friends or admirers of the head man in this family may join them until the band becomes very large. Bands may split apart in dissention, one part joining another or forming a new one. (Wissler 1911:19)

Bands were largely exogamous. Although marriage within the band was not desirable, it was reluctantly allowed if no trace of blood relationship could be found. There was always a suspicion, however, that some blood relationship might have

Table 4-1

Sisika (Blackfoot) kin terms

naa'xs[a1]	FF, FFB, FFW, FFBW, FFZ, FFZH; FM, FMH, FMZ, FMZH; MF, MFB, MFZ, MFW, MFBW, MFZH; MM, MMZ, MMH, MMZH
ni's[a]	♀ (married) MMB

G[1]

naa'xs[a]	FeB, FeBW, FZ, FZH; WM, WF, WFB, WFZ, WFBW, WFZH; WMZ, WMZH
nin.'a	F, F's comrade; MZH; ♂ (or unmarried ♀) speaker, for all the following: MMZDH, MMBDH, MFZDH, MFBDH; ♀ (unmarried) speaker, for all the following: MMZDH, MFZDH, MFBDH
niksis'ta	M, M's co-wife, MZ, W of F's comrade; ♀ (married) speaker, for all the following: MFBD, MFZD, MMZD; ♂ (or unmarried ♀) speaker, for all the following: MFBD, MFZD, MMBD, MMZD
ni's[a]	♀ (married) for all the following: MB, e(MFBS), e(MFZS)
nitax'soku'	HBF, HBM, HZF, HZM, WBF, WBM, WZF, WZM; kinsman to SP's sibling

G[0]

ni's[a2]	eB, e(MZS), e(F's comrade's S); e(FYBS), e(FYZS); e(MBS), e(MFBDS), e(MFZDS), e(MMZDS)
nin'sta[3]	eZ, e(MZD), e(F's comrade's D); ♂ (or unmarried ♀) speaker, for all the following: e(FBD), e(MBD), e(FZD); ♂ (or unmarried ♀) speaker, for all the following: e(FBD), e(FZD)—but not M(eB)D; FyZ, older than ego
naa'xs[a]	much older eZ; ♂ (member of husband's family older than husband; spouse of same); WM, WF, WFB, WFZ, WFBW, WFZH; FZS, FZD (rare with male referent), FZDH
niskən.'a	♂yB, ♂yZ; ♂y(FBS), ♂y(FZS), ♂y(FZD), ♂FyZ, younger than ego
nisis.'a[4]	♀yB, ♀yZ; ♀y(FBS), ♀y(FBD), ♀y(FZS), ♀y(FZD), ♀FyZ, younger than ego; ♀y(F's comrade's Ch)
nom.a'	H
nitxhi.'man	W
nitotoyom.'a	"Distant" H, ZH, comrade's H
nitotɔ'xhi.man	"Distant" W, ZW, comrade's W
nitak.'a	WZH, "comrade"
nistamo'	♂ZH
nistamox'kua	♂WB
nii'mpsa	♂ (or unmarried ♀) YBW, ♀ (married) BW
nitax'soku'	SWF, SWM, DHF, DHM, or kinsman of S's or D's SP

G[-1]

nuxku'a	S, WZF, ♀ZS, comrade's S
nitan.'a	D, WZD, ♀ZD, comrade's D
nii'mps[a]	SW
nis.a	DH
naa'xs[a]	FZDS

Continued on next page

Table 4-1 continued

G⁻²

nis.xku'ᵃ	SS, DS, yBS; ♀ (married) MBS; ♀WHCh
nis.otan'ᵃ	SD, DD
nii'mpsᵃ	SSW, DSW
nis.a	DDH, SDH
naa'xsᵃ	FZDSS

Source: Hanks and Richardson (1945:29-31).

[1] Hanks and Richardson indicate that this applies to a male of father's family or its collateral who is older than father, or a female of father's family or its collateral who is of father's generation or antecedent generations.

[2] Includes male of father's family or its collateral younger than father but older than ego.

[3] For a male or unmarried speaker, includes a female older than ego in ego's generation of mother's family, father's family, or their collaterals.

[4] For a female speaker, includes a person younger than ego in father's family or its collateral who is a first generation descendant of ego's senior.

been overlooked (Wissler 1911). Dempsey (1982:95) was told that "the leading man was usually the father of all the members, so that he did not want the children to marry each other." Bands tended to be patrilocal, but matrilocality was common where the woman was from an affluent band (Dempsey 1982). Once again, the evidence suggests a strong impetus to exogamy, band compositions with a tendency toward same-sex sibling cores, and a terminology in which crossness is completely lacking.

These Subarctic and Plains Algonquian examples lend further weight to the thesis suggested earlier for the Mackenzie Basin Dene. Subarctic Algonquian societies have local groups similar to those of the Subarctic Athapaskans; the extended domestic families and small bands of the Plains Algonquian societies are formed in very similar ways. Local-group endogamy, cross/parallel distinctions, and bilateral cross-cousin marriage are correlated for a number of Subarctic groups, but "Mackenzie Basin" patterning can also occur in this region. A pattern quite like the Mackenzie Basin style is also common for Plains Algonquians, although documented instances of it feature Iroquoian and not Dravidian precepts for crossness. In the Blackfoot example, crossness is completely absent, save for pronounced intergenerational skewing reminiscent of Crow terminologies. In both of the latter patterns, local-group exogamy is vital to extended domestic families and bands.

NUMIC SPEAKERS

Numic societies are distributed in a large, fan-shaped arc anchored in southeastern California and encompassing almost all of the Great Basin, as well as some immediately adjacent areas (figure 4-7). They consist of three distinct groups, associated with the northern, central, and southern segments of this area (Miller 1986). Two languages are spoken in each of these subdivisions: these pairs are Mono and Northern Paiute (sometimes called Paviotso) in the northern segment, Panamint and Shoshone in the central segment, and Kawaiisu and Ute in the southern zone. The nearest Uto-Aztecan neighbors of the Numic languages are the adjacent Tubatulabal of south-eastern California and the Puebloan Hopi of Arizona.

Ethnographically, Numic speakers are among the better-known peoples in North America. Many researchers have contributed to this record, but none so prominently as Julian Steward. His ethnographic research covered some thirty Numic-speaking groups and about sixty informants (Steward 1938; Thomas 1983:61). Not only did Steward record cultural ecological variability, but he also took a census of social behavior, marriage practices, and kin terminologies in most of these cases. Since then, few regional ethnographic surveys have achieved such comprehensive coverage.

Steward's early ethnographic work with the Shoshone shaped his view of cultural ecology, and they became the archetype of his family level of sociocultural integration (Steward 1955). It is with some degree of irony, then, that in his later statements of cultural ecological principles (e.g., in *Theory of Culture Change,* 1955), Steward tended to synthesize Great Basin socioeconomic variability toward a western Shoshone norm (see Thomas 1983). This later work, Thomas (1983) argued, failed to express the full spectrum of Great Basin economic patterns, which ranged from small, highly mobile groups in low and high desert conditions to less nomadic groups with a higher population density. The Shoshone, for example, lived in desert or semidesert regions in which mountain ranges separate a series of valleys. They gathered wild grass seeds, pinyon nuts, and roots and hunted game, including rabbits and antelope. Clusters of three to five families formed winter "villages" or camp groups that moved seasonally from valley floors to high elevations. More sedentary groups such as the Owens Valley Paiute practiced irrigation, lived in quite populous, exogamous, and relatively sedentary villages, and worked inherited seed plots and pinyon groves; they had fairly powerful positions of leadership (Steward 1933; Bettinger 1983:48).

Steward, it has also been pointed out, vacillated in his emphasis on the self-sufficiency of the individual family (Eggan 1980:174). Eventually, he acknowledged that the winter "village" or camp group cluster of interrelated families was actually the central social entity. What is particularly interesting about these groups is their fluid composition: the Shoshone not only adopted levirate and sororate practices, but they expected several brothers to marry several sisters, or a brother and sister to marry a sister and a brother (Steward 1938:244).

As might be expected for local groups typically composed of same-sex or opposite-sex sibling sets, Steward's (1938:297–306) thirty Northern Paiute, Shoshone, Gosiute, and Southern Paiute kin terminologies reveal two fundamental glosses. One trend approaches a pattern resembling that for the Battle Mountain Shoshone (figure 4-8), who exhibit cross/parallel distinctions throughout the three medial generations and numerous affinal equations. The fourfold terms used by grandparents seem to be the product of a reckoning of father's side / mother's side, but the reciprocal terms for grandchildren are the product of cross-reckoning: one's son's chil-

Figure 4-7
Distribution of Numic Languages and Adjacent Societies in the Southwestern
United States

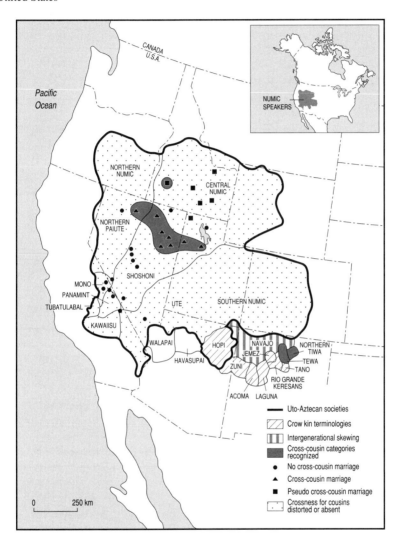

Source: Information of Great Basin cousin marriage practices comes from Steward (1938) and Hoebel (1939).

dren are distinguished from one's daughter's children. Not enough data are available (e.g., for second cousins) to determine conclusively if these are fully Dravidian-type kin schedules, but they may well be, especially in view of the correlation between this terminological pattern and the presence of actual cross-cousin marriage

Figure 4-8
Battle Moutain Shoshone Kinship Terminology

	♂			♀	
	x	//		//	x
G²	dogo MF	guno FF		gago MM	hutsi FM

G¹	ada
	MB, FZH,
	HF, WH
		natsugu
		FB,
		MZH,
		StF
			apu
			F
				bi biatsi
				M MZ,
				    FBW
				    fiatsi
				    StM
					baha
					FZ, MBW, HM,
					WM

G⁰ e	detc, dui FZS, MBS dej: WB, ZH nanadej ♂SWF, ♂DHF	bavi eB, e(FBS), e(MZS) dui e(MZS), e(FBS)		badzi eZ, e(FBD),e(MZD) sauwüpü e(FBD), e(MZD)	auwasauwüpü FZD, MBD nanabahambia ♀SWM, ♀DHM, HZ, ♀BW
G⁰ y	nanadainump ♀SWF, ♀DHF guhɔp H, ♀ZH nagahaguhɔp HB	ego dami yB, y(FBS), y(MZS) dui y(FBS), y(MZS)		nami yZ, y(FBD), y(MZD) sauwüpü y(FBD), y(MZD)	nanadainump ♂SWM, ♂DHM gwuhü W nagagwüh WZ hangwüh ♂BW
G⁻¹	ada ♂ZS baha ♀BS monɔp DH	dua S, ♀StS, ♀ZS due, naduivitci StS, ♂BS,/ZS		bedüpü D bedu, nanaivi StD, ♂BD, ♀ZD	ada ♂ZD baha ♀BD: hutsombia SW
G⁻²	hutsi ♀SS dogo ♂DS	guno ♂SS, ♂SD gago ♀DS,♀DD			hutsi ♀SD dogo ♂DD

Source: ▪ Steward (1938).

or pseudo cross-cousin marriage (marriage with a stepchild of a cross uncle or aunt) in Steward's (1938:284) Great Basin data.[5] For the Battle Mountain Shoshone themselves, the preferred marriage was with a pseudo cross cousin.

The alternate pattern is of a Mackenzie Basin configuration and is exemplified in the carefully considered Hɜkandika (Seed Eater) Shoshone of Idaho and Comanche (figure 4-9) terminologies collected by Hoebel (1939). Crossness is well preserved in G⁺¹ and G⁻¹, where it is accompanied by a number of affinal equations (e.g., MB = FZH = SpF or, for a man speaking, S = BS = ZDH = WZS for Hɜkandika); it

Figure 4-9
Comanche Kinship Terminology

		♂		♀	
		x	//	//	x
G²		*tɔk* MF, MFB!, MMB, MMZH, MFZH!	*kønu* FF, FFB, FMB!, FFZH, FMZH!	*kaku* MM, MMZ, MFZ!, MMBW, MFBW!	*hutsi* FM, FMZ!, FFZ, FMBW!, FFBW
G¹		*aʃa* MB, FZH *yahixpia* HF, HFB, HMB *nɜmɜtɔk* WF, WFB, WMB	*ap'* F, FB, MZH	*pia* M, MZ, FBW	*baha* FZ, MBW *yahixpia* HM, HMZ, HFZ *nɜmɜkagu* WM, WMZ, WFZ
G⁰	e	*paβi* eB, FZS, FBS, MZS, MBS *kuap'* H, ZH, ZHB, HB *tɜts* WB, ♂ZH *haints* WZH, WZHB		*pazi* eZ, FBD, FZD, MBD, MZD *kwɜhɜ* W, BW, BWZ, WZ *haipia* ♂BW, WZ *bahapia* ♀BW, HZ	
		ego			
	y	*tami* yB, FZS, FBS, MZS, MBS, WZH, HZH		*nami* yZ, FBD, FZD, MBD, MZD, WBW, HBW *tɜ:i* HBW	
G⁻¹		*aʃa* ZS, WBS *baha* ♀BS, HZS *monapɜ* DH	*tua* S, ♂BS, WZS, ♀ZS, HBS *monap* ♂ZDH!, ♀BDH!	*bɜt* D, ♂BD, WZD, ♀ZD, HBD *hutsipiap* ♂ZSW, ♀BSW	*aʃa* ZD, WBD *baha* ♀BD, HZD *hutsipiap* SW
G⁻²		*tɔk* ♂DCh, ♂ZDCh, ♂BDCh *hutsi* ♀SCh, ♀BSCh	*konu* ♂SCh, ♀ZSCh, WBSCh, WZSCh *kaku* ♀DCh, ♀BDCh, HBDCh, HZDCh		*tɔk* ♂DCh, ♂ZDCh, ♂BDCh *hutsi* ♀SCh, ♀BSCh

Note: Crossness is absent in G⁰ but is well developed in G¹ and G⁻¹. Reciprocal cross/parallel distinctions also exist in G² and G⁻², although the patterning in the second ascending generation is imperfect for Dravidian crossness.

Source: Hoebel (1931: 441–42).

is retained even for grandchild reciprocals. Cross/parallel distinctions are absent in ego's generation, however, where all are siblings. This pattern usually does not occur where there is cross-cousin marriage, although it can appear where pseudo cross marriage is present (Steward 1938:284).

Interestingly, the correlations in Steward's data between marriage form and terminological structure are not perfect. Steward (1938:285) himself wrote: "In certain instances there was a possible choice of several terminologies any of which would have been consistent with social usage." Of the two Gosiute Shoshone groups Steward (1938:140, 284, appendix C) reported on, Deep Creek had bilateral cross-cousin marriage, whereas Skull Valley preferred patrilateral cross-cousin marriage (discussed below). Even so, Steward reported two variants of the Skull Valley kin system: one discriminated FZD and FZS; the other treated all cousins as siblings. Deep Creek cousin terms actually have a strong lineal/collateral distinction. Shapiro (1986:626) noted parts of this, but added a personal communication from Miller, who had recorded a "bifurcate merging cousin terminology" among Gosiute.

Hoebel (1939:446), too, wrote that "inter-familial exchange underlies the entire structure of the Shoshone and Comanche systems" but of course concluded that the implication of the underlying structure for cousins, cross-cousin marriage, was not put into practice. What puzzled him was that informants explicitly regarded any cousin marriage as incestuous, yet stated that first ascending generation affinal equations (for parents-in-law with aunts and uncles) arose because one should marry one's aunt's daughter (Hoebel 1939:453). The latter form of marriage almost never took place. Hoebel (1939:455) concluded that there were two "distinctive systems" or models for the Hɜkandika terminology, and that both had likely arisen from cross-cousin marriage. This origin he attributed to borrowing from other Shoshoneans.

This is precisely the kind of ambiguity reported for Mackenzie Basin Dene. Where cross/parallel distinctions are made, cousin terminology is *the* pivotal facet in the semantic domain of kinship that can be seized upon for a variety of strategies generally connected with local-group exogamy. Even when terminologies shift toward the Mackenzie Basin form, however, first ascending and first descending generation crossness and affinal equations loom in the background, full of meanings that suggest the possibility of bilateral cross-cousin marriage. The nature of the variability, the frequency of terminological alternatives, and the kind of paradoxes reported in Steward's and Hoebel's ethnography flow from similar-sounding choices.

I submit that Great Basin Numic speakers typically made a variety of "plays" on cross/parallel (and perhaps Dravidianate) distinctions in selecting different social, economic, and political strategies. These strategies are susceptible to a number of generalizations. Before following Eggan's (1980) lead in this, it is important to remember that the conceptualization of kin systems may vary not only between communities but within them. Variability of both forms has, I think, helped obscure the underlying pattern.

Eggan (see 1980:175–85) explored Shoshone socioeconomic variability against an array of environmental circumstances. The southern Shoshone lived in severe desert conditions near Death Valley: their population density here was low (one person for every 16–72 square kilometers) and local-group mobility was high. There was preferential brother-sister exchange, and all cousins were treated as siblings in the terminology. Eggan (1980:177) thought this important in creating an extensive kin network for sharing information on food resources. The Central Shoshone had access to more food resources spread across better-watered and more diverse life zones in an area with greater mountainous relief. Population densities increased to one person for every 5–8 square kilometers. With a greater range and abundance of food resources available in each valley, the pattern of brother-sister exchange marriages persisted into bilateral cross-cousin marriage of the resulting children. This increased the density of alliances within communities, while reducing links to neighboring areas. Full-fledged cross/parallel distinctions with affinal equations predominated in terminologies for this region.

Populations of the Gosiute Shoshone of adjacent Utah dropped again to about one person for every 65 square kilometers, but valleys were also isolated from one another by deserts. Intermarriage within a valley was encouraged, and bilateral cross-cousin marriage was favored at Deep Creek Valley. At Skull Valley, however, an incipient preference for marriage with FZD existed, perhaps as a consequence of the generally perceived responsibility of a man toward his sister (the man's son would take care of his father's sister and her daughter) (Eggan 1980:179). As already discussed, several terminological models seemed to be in play among Gosiute, including treatments for cousins where cross-cousins were distinguished, where the matrilateral cross cousins became siblings but patrilateral cross cousins were distinguished; all cousins were siblings; and lineal/collateral distinctions were recognized (for most of these variants, see Steward 1938).

North of the Humboldt River, salmon and bison became elements of the subsistence pattern in various areas. Population densities remained low, but as the horse became prominent between A.D. 1700 and 1750, larger and more permanent bands took shape. Emphasis shifted from cross-cousin marriage to pseudo cross-cousin marriage. In a number of cases, cross cousins were treated terminologically as siblings, and affinal terms were applied to pseudo cross cousins. Eggan (1980:181) concluded that cross-cousin marriage was too restrictive in fashioning a broader network of ties linking families together within the larger bands required for bison hunting and defense against typical Plains raiding. This pattern had been in existence for some time: Comanche had been seen on the southern Plains by the Spanish as early as A.D. 1706 and probably moved onto the Plains around the end of the seventeenth century (Eggan 1980:182).

ELEMENTARY STRUCTURES, DEVELOPMENTAL TRAJECTORIES, AND SOCIAL COMPLEXITY

Eggan's review of Shoshonean socioeconomic variability led him to conclude: "There is a whole world of social structures 'underneath' Claude Levi-Strauss' 'Elementary Structures of Kinship' " (Eggan 1980:188). Speaking just of the Mackenzie Basin Dene, this is certainly true. There one sees Dravidian-type terminologies associated with endogamous bilateral cross-cousin marriage (the Beaver), Dravidian-like terminologies where cross-cousin marriages almost never occur (the Hare), Dravidian-type terminologies where there is a strong imperative for exogamy (the Wrigley Slavey), and Mackenzie Basin terminologies where exogamy is mandatory

Table 4-2

Contrasts in Developmental Processes for Bands

Local Group Growth Alternative	Local Group Alliance Alternative
• Like sex sibling cores; if unlike sex sibling cores, "Mackenzine Basin" or other terminologies where crossness is compromised are present	• Unlike sex sibling cores; comprehensive cross/parallel distinctions
• Strong emphasis on exogamy	• Agamy to significant endogamy
• "Pumping Out"—Individuals circulate widely in regional marriage isolate	• "Implosive"—Restricted circulation of individuals in regional marriage isolate
• Broad net of external alliances	• Inward focus in alliance formation
• Local groups within regional marriage isolate have short duration (one or two generations)	• Local groups in regional marriage isolate have longer duration or can grow into regional marriage isolate size range
• Political and economic accomodations to external environment achieved by linking local groups together	• Political and economic accomodations to external environment achieved by fostering local group growth

(Lynx Point Slavey, various Chipewyan groups). Asch (1988:105–6; chapter 5 of this volume) gave further shape to Eggan's idea by suggesting that Lévi-Strauss's program of analysis actually lacked a logical category: one composed of societies that do not have unilineal descent but that *do* have positive marriage rules.[6] An important aspect of the variability in elementary structures can be accounted with the aid of this general category of society.

The Athapaskan, Algonquian, and Numic societies mentioned earlier in the chapter have three important factors in common. First, each language family maintains a cross/parallel distinction. Second, sets of siblings (whether of the same sex or of the opposite sex) play a central role in alliance formation and in shaping the nuclei of local groups in their various forms—bands, extended domestic families, village clusters, and so on. Third, these two features combine to form two distinct configurations, which covary in all three language families: (1) opposite-sex sibling cores, cross/parallel distinctions in ego's generation, and endogamy; and (2) same-sex sibling cores, absence of crossness in ego's generation, and local-group exogamy. In addition, all three language groups exhibit terminological fluidity in their key kin categories, especially in the representation of cousins and siblings; this fluidity is observed both within and between communities.

These common features can be used to explore developmental processes in hunter-gatherer band societies. To do this, I construct two idealized models (table 4-2) for principles of group formation and developmental processes affecting hunter-gatherer societies in these language families. Two assumptions are required to begin. First, I posit that principles of group formation have primary reference to local groups or bands, which in turn exist within the context of broader regional marriage isolates. This is an empirical reality for virtually all nomadic hunting and gathering societies. Second, I assume that a cross/parallel distinction underlies the social structure of the groups in question. It is simplest to conceive of this in Dravidianate terms, but the basic reasoning requires primarily that cross categories be linked with notions of affinity and alliance (this treatment relies heavily on Ives 1990:298–328).[7]

The premise that local groups generally form about affinally united sibling sets (as opposed to other analytical categories found in the literature, such as nuclear families or conjugal pairs) make it possible to see how cross/parallel distinctions can guide the arrangement of affines and consanguines in different directions. One trend in the diversity of elementary structures examined in this chapter can be termed a *local-group growth* alternative. Where opposite-sex sibling cores are allowed or favored, local groups will be predisposed toward endogamy. When endogamy does prevail, it conveys a significant growth potential to local groups. Retention of band members through endogamy can combine with recruitment in such a way that a band comes to have a large number of people. At the same time, a greater degree of endogamy may mean that there are insufficient affinal ties available to fashion systematic external alliances. People in local-group growth systems therefore tend to seek political and economic accommodations to their external environments by increasing the size of the local group itself.

Among Northern Athapaskans, the Beaver are an example of a local-group growth system. The Beaver preserved essential terminological elements of crossness and practiced bilateral cross-cousin marriage. Local groups tended to grow and persist through endogamous marriages. Smaller local groups could certainly act as "foragers" in boreal forest environments. But local-group growth could also be harnessed to exploit different opportunities, such as communal game hunting (of woodland caribou or wood bison) or novel political situations created by the fur trade (large groups headed by Big Men figures). However, socially isolated endogamous groups were more prone to the ecological dislocations of the Subarctic, since they did not form as broad a net of kin alliances with neighboring groups. Starvation and population dislocations, for example, play a noticeably more prominent role in Beaver oral tradition than seems characteristic of other Northern Athapaskans (Goddard 1916; Ives 1990:194–95).

The alternative trend in elementary structures is toward what may be called *local-group alliance* systems. These systems favor same-sex sibling cores and virtually ensure local-group exogamy through incest taboos based on cross/parallel distinctions. Local groups in these circumstances have attritional as well as structural limitations over their growth. Nevertheless, the outward orientation of the affinal ties typical of these groups provides the basis for either intensive or extensive external alliances. Growth of the local group itself is limited, but surrounding local groups within the regional marriage isolate provide a ready source of people for different political and economic strategies, as illustrated by the Wrigley Slavey.

The Wrigley Slavey preference for unilocal residence links sets of same-sex siblings and carefully segregates cross and parallel relatives. Only the latter are found within the ideal local group. Although local groups remain small and tend to disappear with regularity at the time scale of generations, this kind of system "pumps" individuals out through its focus on local-group exogamy. In turn, this has a critical bearing on the creation of a broad geographic network of kin ties, giving both individuals and local groups options and rights in dealing with the fluctuating resources typical of the boreal forest. Alternative economic and political strategies requiring larger groups of people are not out of the question. The solution in this case comes from linking together a series of allied local groups.

I contend that terminological variability in hunter-gatherer band societies can best be understood in this larger context of the social and biological reproduction of succeeding generations. Here, kinship intersects the domains of human biological reproduction, economic organization, and polity. In the societies examined in this chapter, different forms of sibling exchange are dominant and may, as others argue in this volume, set up the affinal equations seen in G^{+1}. In many respects, it is G^0 and G^{-1} that are more interesting, however. Cross/parallel partitioning triggers a series of choices about what to do with prospective affines in descending generations. Obviously, what children learn to call members of their own generation (at the instigation of their parents) will have profound effects on the possibilities for future exchanges. Cousin and nepotic terms are terminological points of tension precisely because they provide the "leverage" required to shift some basic tenets of socioeconomic reproduction in one direction or another.

Note, too, that these models abstract two polarities in developmental processes for local groups with principles of group formation founded on cross/parallel distinctions. Between these two poles are many shades of variability. Endogamy can, for instance, lead to local-group growth, but it can just as well serve as a prescription for relative social isolation. This was the pattern McDonnell (1975:48) reported for the Ross River Kaska. Opposite-sex sibling core local groups (in which parents wanted their children to marry) tended to remain small in size and to be inwardly focused. Similarly, there are many glosses possible for local-group alliance alternatives. For example, the ideal Wrigley Slavey pattern, involving sets of same-sex siblings, does tend to concentrate external affinal alliances. These external alliances could also be externally dispersed, a pattern explored by some Chipewyan groups (Ives 1990:221).

Inasmuch as the local-group growth and alliance models reflect divergent potentialities for hunter-gatherer band societies, they can also be helpful in creating meaningful archaeological models. Prehistoric societies organized along similar lines should leave behind characteristic signatures in the material record of their existence. To continue with Athapaskan examples, one would predict somewhat different approaches to communal game hunting. For a local-group growth system, one would seek evidence of a growing local group, decreasing its diet breadth and increasing its degree of sedentism about key hunting locations. The internal dynamic that allows for larger numbers of people is nevertheless irregular in nature and should lead to episodic communal hunting as local groups succeed, grow into a larger size range, and ultimately fission. A shift to communal hunting in a local-group alliance system should be sought in the increasing duration of seasonal gatherings of local groups at strategic hunting locations. Because this means of forming groups is founded on more extensive external alliances, episodes of communal hunting ought to be conducted more regularly.

Local-group growth and alliance alternatives should also have different long-term occupancy characteristics. That is, as generations elapse in the different systems, different patterns of land use should emerge over larger regions. A feature of local-group alliance systems, on the one hand, is that some local groups tend to dissolve in the course of a generation and leave portions of the landscape unoccupied. Successful bands in local-group growth systems, on the other hand, tend to persist through more than one generation and thereby create greater continuity in the occupancy of ranges within a regional marriage isolate.

These models for stylistic variability have certain test implications. Archaeologists generally assume that face-to-face contact between individuals has a direct bearing on the transmission of the stylistic variability seen in artifacts. Here again, the two alternatives differ. The circulation of people within and between regional marriage isolates in a local-group growth setting will be inherently more limited. One would therefore expect such settings to yield enclaves in which artifact styles reflect a greater degree of isolation and there is a greater chance for "drift" to affect artifact styles. Because they characteristically circulate individuals more widely, local-group alliance systems should produce greater stylistic homogeneity across a regional marriage isolate, and perhaps beyond.

Lest these archaeological test implications sound too abstract, it should be emphasized that archaeologists and physical anthropologists do work with data sets that can provide persuasive illustrations of such premises. Hanna (1984) made a convincing case for local-group endogamy in carefully conceived chemical and mineralogical studies of ca. 800-year-old Duck Bay Ware ceramics from west central Manitoba (an area historically inhabited by Algonquian speakers such as Cree and Saulteaux, as well as the Assiniboine). The pattern she describes strongly resembles the stylistic enclave mentioned above, centering on a region especially productive of diverse resources. Resorting instead to human osteological analysis, Kennedy (1981) was able to infer the presence of band exogamy for an Archaic burial population from Port au Choix, Newfoundland. Metric and nonmetric trait analysis for cranial and infracranial remains from forty-three individuals revealed levels of genetic variability consistent with nonspecific exogamy for female members of a village population roughly 4,000 years old.

Figure 4-10 summarizes the logical transformations that can affect kin systems in the three language families. It provides a basis for exploring developmental pathways affecting kin systems. Any of the patterns present there can and should be construed as elementary structures from which further transformations could take place. The local-group growth and local-group alliance models provide an effective means of conceptualizing how and why such shifts may occur. These models can therefore assist in assessing ethnographic and archaeological information for hunter-gatherers throughout the three language families, particularly those in band societies. They could also be applied in comparing the southern Shoshone (who typify the local-group alliance in severe desert conditions), for example, and the central Shoshone (who typify local-group growth, with valley endogamy in regions with

Figure 4-10
Logical Transformations of Kin Systems Based on Principles of Cross Reckoning
with Representative Cases from the Athapaskan, Algonquian, and Numic Families

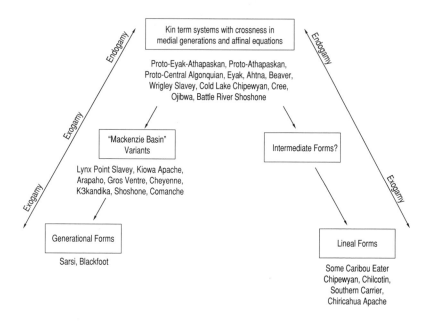

richer resources). Furthermore, such models might be used to ascertain how greater socioeconomic complexity arises. What happens, for instance, when local-group growth and alliance systems occur in association with rich salmon harvesting locales (see Ives 1988, 1990), or prime but restricted horticultural land?

SPACE, TIME, AND HISTORICAL PROCESSES

Figure 4-10 leads directly to a central question. The very presence of these trends among closely related societies within language families raises the intriguing prospect that the pathways there may trace real historical trajectories. It cannot be assumed, of course, that the transformations in the figure recapitulate historical development in any simple way. There is simply not enough information on cross/parallel distinctions for more distant relatives of North American bands and tribes to determine how prevalent different forms of crossness really are on a continental scale. At the same time, as the Maison Suger symposium showed admirably, there are many logical and mathematical models for cross/parallel distinctions, and ethnographic manifestations for virtually all of them can be found at the global level. Thus it would be imprudent to narrow the horizon for historical antecedents without good reason.

Nevertheless, one of the purposes of this discussion is to explore ways in which anthropological methods might be used to provide a richer sense of the history of aboriginal peoples in North America. Too often, any sophisticated sense of history for aboriginal peoples is relegated to the Contact period, after Euro-Canadian or Euro-American mercantile interests arrived on the scene. Against the danger of inferring little more than conjectural history, I am inclined to balance a desire to make use of existing information from which temporal dynamics can be derived. With due caution, then, I would like to explore independent reconstructions of kin lexica for prototypical speech communities, as well as distributions of key features of societies within language families. The resulting information may give some indication of the scale and scope of historical processes affecting earlier Athapaskan, Algonquian, and Numic societies.

NORTHERN ATHAPASKAN PREHISTORY

To this point, the situation for Athapaskans has been explored through individual examples. The more one examines the individual cases, however, the more it seems that different glosses in the direction of local-group growth or local-group alliance alternatives could result from variations upon a theme. The lexical reconstructions of the proto-Athapaskan kin terminology offered by Dyen and Aberle (1974) and Krauss (n.d.) can shed some light on this possibility. Crossness is well represented in all three medial generations, and affinal equations are common (e.g., FB = MZH, MZ = FBW, FZ = MBW = SpM, and MB = FZH) (see figure 4-11). The affines of affines might have been classed as siblings (Dyen and Aberle 1974:69). Absolute confirmation of the presence of a Dravidian structural type would require documentation of Dravidian-style cross reckoning (not Iroquoian or other varieties) for more distant relatives, such as second cousins. This last form of evidence is difficult to find for the great majority of ethnographic accounts in North America, so that it generally does not inform reconstructed kin terminologies. Thus there is suggestive evidence that the proto-Athapaskan kin system was of Dravidian structural type, although one cannot be absolutely certain of this. It is certainly a viable hypothesis that Dravidian cross reckoning and persistent bilateral cross-cousin marriage formed the basic pattern in early Athapaskan prehistory.

Current linguistic, human biological, and archaeological evidence all point to a proto-Athapaskan homeland somewhere in the region of southern Alaska, the southern Yukon, and northern British Columbia (Dyen and Aberle 1974:380–83; Krauss and Golla 1981:68; Ives 1990). This area is the site of the most profound linguistic differences in the Athapaskan languages and of the only genetically related non-Athapaskan language, Eyak. Linguists surmise that Eyak became separated from all Athapaskan on the order of 3,000 years ago. Sometime prior to 1,500 years ago, Pacific Coast Athapaskans departed this homeland, ultimately reaching northern California. About 1,200 years ago, a second movement out of the Athapaskan homeland took place. This distributed Canadian Athapaskan speakers across the Subarctic east of the Rockies and set the stage for the movement of Apachean Athapaskans

Figure 4-11
Proto-Athapakan Kin Terms

		♂	♂	♀	♀
		X	//	//	X
G²		*-tšə̃ỹə̀ — MF	*-ʔay — FF(?)	*tšu — MM	*tšᵐʷ∂nə̀ — FM
G¹		*-zə̀ʔə — MB, FZH; *-(z)ɔ(n)ts'ᵐæ? — SpF	-tɔ́yə̀ — FB, MZH ‖ *-tɔ? — F	*-ɔn — M ‖ *-ɔ(n) -q'ey(?)ə — MZ, FBW	*-wætš̃ᵐæ? — FZ, MBW, SpM
G⁰	e	*-zæ̃də̀ — ♀FZS, ♀MBS; *-udæ — ♂FZS, ♂MBS; *-qaỹ? — H	*-unə̀və̀ — eB, e(FBS), e(MZS); *-lɑG~-lɑx — WZS, ?BWB	*-ɔdæ — eZ, e(FBD), e(MZD); *-lɑG~-lɑx — WBW, HBW	*-zæ̃də̀ — ♀FZD, ♀MBD; *-udæ — ♂FZD, ♂MBD
G⁰	y	*-tɬ∂n — WB, ♂ZH; *-yæ̥ — HB, ZH	*-kə̀tl'ə — yB, y(FBS), y(MZS)	*-dæ̃džo(?) — yZ, y(FBZ), y(MZD)	*-ʔɔd — W; *-yæ̥ — BW, HZ, WZ
G⁻¹		*-ɔš̃ᵐ~ — ♂ZS, ♀BS; *-van?donə̀n — DH	*-yʔə — ♂S, ♂BS; *-yɔž̃ᵐə — ♀S, ♀ZS	*-tsæ?(e) — ♂D, ♂BD; *-yoʼs'æ?(e) — ♀D, ♀ZD	*-ɔš̃ᵐ~ ♂ZD, ♀BD; *-yɔš̃ᵐ?ɔd ♀SW; *-yV?əd ♂SW
G⁻²		*tsuye ♂SS, ♂DS, ♂SD, ♂DD ‖ ḳɔ̃ỹə ♀SS, ♀DS, ♀SD, ♀DD			

(ego is located at the center of the G⁰ row, between the // columns.)

Source: Reconstructed by Krauss (n.d.).

toward the Plains and the Southwestern United States. Two catastrophic volcanic eruptions, which led to the massive White River Ash falls of roughly 1,900 and 1,250 years ago, might have triggered these exoduses from the proto-Athapaskan homeland (for an assessment of this idea, see Ives 1990:42–46). Whatever the case may be, it is quite likely that pre-Contact Athapaskan history involved two or more episodes of expansion out of a homeland in northwestern North America during the last two millennia.

Figure 4-1 illustrates the geographic distribution of tendencies in cousin terminology in northwestern North America. Among Athapaskan speakers, it shows a central area where cross-cousin marriage is common and in which cross cousins are always recognized, as well as an outer "ring" in which the cross/parallel distinction for cousins commonly breaks down. The most frequent shift is of Mackenzie Basin form, with all cousins being equated with siblings, but lineal-collateral distinctions crop up again among interior British Columbian groups such as the Southern Carrier. In a more detailed analysis presented elsewhere (see Ives 1985, 1990), I have argued that terminologies in which crossness in ego's generation is eroded are implicated in one of three circumstances:

1. The creation of alliance ties over great geographic areas, providing a support network to counter the vicissitudes of boreal forest resource fluctuations.
2. An impetus to strong local-group exogamy and the formation of widespread alliances in groups using treeline intercept strategies to exploit Barren Ground caribou.
3. Athapaskan presence in near-coastal social settings in which bilateral kindreds are vital in the definition of crest groups that control ceremonial activity and resource harvesting (especially Pacific salmon) prerogatives (see Ives 1990).

Variations on an original theme of bilateral cross-cousin marriage quite probably arose in conjunction with Athapaskan expansion into a wide variety of social, economic, and political settings in western North America. At least among Northern Athapaskans, then, Spier's Mackenzie Basin type is not simply a static type, but rather the outcome of an antecedent Dravidian structural pattern that is systematically modified by social, economic, and political processes intimately tied to imperatives for widespread alliance formation. These processes are revealed by the absence of G^0 crossness, which in turn forces local-group exogamy and the outward extension of alliances. This modified form (although it has its own internal tensions) is itself an effective and stable social organization in a wide variety of settings.

The case can also be made that the more complex social structures of the Haida, Tlingit, and Tsimshian have their historical antecedents in social formations like those of Athapaskans, who engaged in bilateral cross-cousin marriage (Rubel and Rosman 1983; Ives 1987, 1990). The Tsimshian, who practiced matrilateral cross-cousin marriage and lived in populous towns at the mouth of the Skeena River, had a terminology marked by cross reckoning and a number of affinal equations (Rubel and Rosman 1983; Ives 1987, 1990:329–33). The terminology would otherwise seem at odds with the marriage practice. Haida and Tlingit kin systems are marked by Crow skewing. It is not clear from existing Northwest Coast information if there could be a historical link between systems of Dravidian structural type and more complex kin systems, although that is conceivable.

ALGONQUIAN ANTECEDENTS

Trautmann and Barnes (chapter 2) refer to a geographic divide in Algonquian kin systems. On the one side are Dravidian-type systems that have crossness, have affinal equations, and are strongly associated with cross-cousin marriage. On the other side are kin systems that may have crossness and affinal equations, but the crossness is demonstrably of Iroquois-type, or the kin systems have Omaha or Omaha-like terminologies (as is the case for the Sauk, Fox, Menominee, Winnebago, Illinois, Miami, and Potawatomi). Fanning out to the north, northwest, and northeast are various Cree, Ojibwa, and Montagnais-Naskapi groups in which cross cousins are recognized (and cross-cousin marriage often occurs). Davis Inlet Naskapi treat all cousins as siblings and many eastern Algonquians (such as the Micmac and Delaware) also distort crossness in G^0.

For northern Algonquians, the point of division appears to come with nineteenth-century Ojibwa of the Upper Peninsula of Michigan, where Father Edward Jacker's terminology (as provided to Lewis Henry Morgan) reveals distinctly Iroquoian crossness (Trautmann and Barnes, chapter 2). Eggan (1955a:531) thought it possible that the Gros Ventre and Arapaho might once have "had a cross cousin marriage system which was modified and gradually given up as they adjusted their social structures to the new conditions of Plains life." The question arises, then, as to what the parent Algonquian kin system might have been like.

In this respect, we can turn to Hockett's (1964) reconstruction of proto-central-Algonquian kin terms, which was based upon Cree, Ojibwa, Potawatomi, Menomini, Fox, and Shawnee. Crossness is well represented in the medial generations, and there are affinal equations. Both MB and FZ appear to be diminutives of SpF and SpM, respectively (Hockett 1964:248 dissents from this, but Hickerson's 1967 rebuttal is compelling). For a man speaking, MBS = FZS = ZH = WB. Cross nieces and nephews and children-in-law, on the one hand, are distinguished from children and parallel nieces and nephews, on the other. For reasons that are not clear, Hockett (1964:256) chose to conclude that "cross cousin marriage of the stricter type (man with mother's brother's daughter)" prevailed in the proto-central-Algonquian speech community. This is hardly warranted from the reconstruction itself, and Hickerson (1967:363) was quite correct to counter that a bilateral cross-cousin marriage system (with neither descent nor residence known) was the most reasonable inference.

Wheeler (1982), elaborating upon Hockett's work, reached the conclusion that his own reconstruction could serve for proto-Algonquian more generally (see also Goddard 1978:583). Wheeler's reconstruction had MB = FZH = WF, FZ = MBW = HM, and ♂ZS = ♀BS = DH as well as ♂ZD (man speaking) = ♀BD = SW (figure 4-12). Naturally, he inferred from this that proto-Algonquian kin terms were predicated on a system of bilateral cross-cousin marriage.

There is insufficient information to determine conclusively whether the proto-Algonquian kin system might have had Dravidian or Iroquois-type formal semantics. Still, crossness is present in conjunction with affinal equations for proximate relatives of the medial generations. These findings keep the following set of propositions viable as explanations:

Figure 4-12
Proto-Algonquian Kin Terms

	♂		♀	
	X	//	//	X
G²	*nemeso:ha, etc.:* FF, MF		*no:hko, etc.:* FM, MM	
G¹	*nesihSa, etc.:* MB, FZH,WF	*no:θko:* F, FB, MZH	*nekya* M *neθwihsa* MZ, FBW	*nesekwihsa, etc.* FZ, MBW, HM

		♂ X	♂ //	♀ //	♀ X
G⁰	e	*ni:?taiwa* ♂MBS, FZS, ♀WB *ni:θemwa* ♀MBS, ♀FZS, HB, H (before marriage)	*ne?θ-* eB, e(FBS), e(MZS)	*nemihsa* eZ, e(FBD), e(MZD)	*ni:θemwa* ♂MBD, ♂FZD, WZ, W (before marriage) *neta:nkwa* ♀MBD, ♀FZD, HZ
	(ego)				
	y	*-a:nkw* WB *ona:pe:mali* H	*nehSima, etc.* yB, yZ, y(FBS), y(FBD), y(MZS), y(MZD)		*-a:nkw* HZ *ni:wa* W

	♂ X	♂ //	♀ //	♀ X
G⁻¹	*neθenkwaθa, etc.* ♂ZS, ♀BS, ♀DH *naha:nka* DH	*nekiwi?sa* S *neto:sima* ♀BS, ♂ZS	*neta:na, etc.* D *neto:simeθkwe:wa* ♂BD, ♀ZD	*ne?θem-, etc.* ♂ZD, ♀BD, SW *naha:nkaniθkwe:wa* SW
G⁻²	*no:hsihsa* SS, SD, DS, DD			

Source: As reconstructed by Wheeler (1982). For terms where Wheeler has reconstructed more than one closely related form, I have given a single term, followed by "etc."

1. That early Algonquian kin systems featured crossness and affinal equations founded on bilateral cross-cousin marriage.
2. That some daughter systems retained the very same features, much as is the case in the northern Subarctic groups today.
3. That other systems underwent regular transformations in the direction of Spier's Mackenzie Basin type, or beyond. Some (e.g., Arapaho) betray traces of the antecedent condition through G⁺¹ and G⁻¹ crossness and affinal equations, though G⁰ cross reckoning is obliterated. Others (e.g., Blackfoot) have proceeded much farther,

rendering the antecedent condition unrecognizable and hinting of intervening terminological structures (with intergenerational skewing).

These propositions elaborate—but are consistent with—positions adopted by authors such as Eggan (1955a) and Callender (1962, 1978). They may founder, however, on the observation about the nature of cross reckoning recorded earlier for Arapaho and Cheyenne, namely, that cross reckoning is Iroquois in form. It is more difficult to sustain the historical and developmental sequence I have outlined for Algonquians because of these instances.

There may be an alternative explanation, however. Although Algonquian prehistory is the subject of considerable debate, the ranges of flora and fauna known in the protolanguage suggest a homeland between Georgian Bay and Lake Ontario. As the proto-Algonquian-speaking nucleus expanded some 2,500 to 3,000 years ago, it fragmented into the forerunners of the three Plains languages, roughly six central languages, and proto-eastern Algonquian (Goddard 1978:586). However divergent the different anthropological theories of Algonquian prehistory, they often share a common feature, namely, that at an early date in the southeastern part of the Algonquian homeland, a wedge of Iroquoian speakers was interposed between the Great Lakes (or central) and coastal (or eastern) Algonquians (Goddard 1978:586; Proulx 1984:394; Fiedel 1987:1). Goddard (1978:586–87) observed that the linguistic break between eastern and central Algonquians is so sharp as to require an early intervention of Iroquois-speakers, and that Algonquian languages do show borrowing of Iroquoian tribal names.

These data contain the seeds of a somewhat different interpretation. Some early Algonquian speakers may have been involved in developmental processes that were transforming their kin systems away from straightforward bilateral cross-cousin marriage. These transformations were in the direction of extinguishing crossness in ego's generation in connection with pressures for local-group exogamy. This "Mackenzie Basin" shift begins the process of *disengaging* the terminology from the strict logic and affinal equations associated with bilateral cross-cousin marriage. These Algonquian systems may have been particularly susceptible to a change in the modality of cross reckoning because of their own internal development (i.e., shifts to Iroquois cross reckoning or intergenerational skewing were ongoing within Algonquian), or because they were in proximity to Iroquoian speakers who had developed or were developing an alternative mode of cross reckoning that was not directly founded on principles of bilateral cross-cousin marriage.

Archaeologists working on the Northwestern Plains argue convincingly that the terminal Late Prehistoric Period saw an exodus onto the Plains of Siouan-speaking peoples (e.g., Assiniboine, Crow, and Hidatsa) and Algonquian-speaking peoples (e.g., Cheyenne, Arapaho) from the middle Missouri River region (e.g., Vickers 1994). Such evidence even includes a protohistoric (ca. A.D. 1730s) village (Cluny Village, possibly the result of a Hidatsa splinter group) complete with moat and palisade as far northwest as south-central Alberta (Forbis 1977). In significant measure, these situations likely had to do with the historical disruptions eastern North America underwent as consequence of expanding European settlement. I am therefore inclined to read Iroquois crossness among the Cheyenne, Arapaho, and Gros Ventre as a historical residue of a more easterly origin in this time frame.

By the same token, this is hardly the first evidence of intensive contact (including population movements) involving the Plains, middle Missouri River trench, and Eastern Woodland regions. People emanating from these regions during the last two or more millennia originally possessed or had been influenced by more complex social structures to the east and southeast (including sophisticated centers such as Cahokia). Beginning about 1,000 years ago, intrusive archaeological complexes appear in southern Manitoba and adjacent Saskatchewan, featuring evidence of corn horticulture, ceramics with links to the east and southeast, and earthwork burial mounds (Hanna 1976; Nicholson 1994a, 1994b). Quite possibly the Besant Phase (extant from roughly 2,000 to 1,100 years ago) and certainly the related Sonota Complex (ca. 2,000 to 1,400 years ago) on the northern Plains have links to the middle Missouri River region.

Eggan (1966:65–66) suggested that the Crow kin terminology was beginning to break down: terms of reference remained Crow in form, but direct vocative usages were becoming generational (see also Maxwell 1979). Eggan saw this and the loss of Crow clans as an adjustment to Plains life from a previously village horticultural existence along the Missouri. This raises an interesting point in connection with the intergenerational skewing present in Blackfoot. What would a Crow terminology look like after centuries of life in a Plains environment stressing significant exogamy, with much more fluid social groups? Would it not resemble the Siksika one in table 4-2, which would then reveal an even more distant past of more easterly origin?

To be certain, these remarks are of a speculative nature. Yet no one need speculate about the significance of such shifts for Plains peoples. The Plains political environment was highly competitive and featured intense raiding activity. The staff of life on the Plains was the bison, an animal effectively hunted communally, by large groups of people. As Eggan observed:

The conditions of Plains life demanded a local-group small enough to subsist by hunting and gathering but large enough to furnish protection against hostile war parties and raids. The extended family was adequate for the first condition but was at the mercy of any war party; the tribe, on the other hand, was too unwieldy to act as an economic unit for very long. The band proved an adequate compromise; this is perhaps the most important reason for its almost universal presence in the Plains area. (Eggan 1955a:85)

There are few more effective ways to link local groups into cohesive bands than to place a premium on local-group exogamy, tying local groups together through affinal alliances.

NUMIC PREHISTORY

The fan-shaped distribution of Numic languages is suggestive of what might have happened in Numic prehistory. This distribution led Lamb (1958) to develop an influential hypothesis to explain their spread across the Great Basin. He suggested that three distinct speech communities had developed in a Numic homeland in southeastern California (centered approximately on Death Valley) by about 2,000 years ago. After about 1,000 years ago, each of these speech communities was able to spread rapidly to the north and east, creating the three segments in the fanlike shape.

Several lines of linguistic evidence support Lamb's ideas about a Numic expansion. Limited language and dialect diversity is found at the northern and eastern periphery of Numic distribution. The greatest language diversity (for Mono, Panamint, and Kawaiisu) occurs in the southwest corner of the Great Basin. Mono and Panamint (though not modern Kawaiisu) also exhibit the greatest dialect diversity; similarly, the greatest dialect diversity for Northern Paiute, Shoshone and Ute is also found in areas nearest to Mono, Panamint, and Kawaiisu, respectively (Miller 1986:102). The greater degree of linguistic diversity in or near the proposed homeland, coupled with limited linguistic diversity at the periphery of the fan, accords well with Lamb's view of Numic expansion.

Following up on this reasoning, Miller (1986:103) argued that place names nearest the Numic homeland ought to be opaque or least susceptible to linguistic analysis, whereas Numic place names farthest from the homeland ought to be most transparent. This is indeed the case. Numic plant and animal names suggest a similar pattern. Fowler (1972), through analysis of the ecological tolerances of species such as oak and pine, submitted that shared Numic terms for these species implied a homeland in southeastern California, though in a larger area including locales such as the better-watered Owens Valley. Where Nez Perce neighbors of the Numic in Idaho have single and unanalyzable words for common fish in that region (e.g., trout and sturgeon), Northern Paiute and Shoshone speakers have compound, descriptive names.

Although a majority of anthropologists working in the Great Basin seem to favor this general point of view, alternative views on Numic prehistory have certainly been offered (e.g., Goss 1977; Lathrap and Troike 1984; Aikens and Witherspoon 1986; Gruhn 1987). In general, these authors have suggested that Numic speakers originated earlier within the central Great Basin, possibly even 5,000 years ago. Some key points in these discussions have been that (1) it is difficult to conceive of successful population expansion out of a region so difficult to live in as Death Valley (Lamb's locus for the Numic homeland); (2) flexible adaptation to Great Basin ecological conditions involved constant population flux, which would have tended to homogenize language over large areas; (3) the archaeological record for the Great Basin shows considerable continuity over this period; and (4) the expansion hypothesis does little to account for whoever might have been displaced from the Great Basin.

Since there appears to be no reconstructed version of early Numic kin terms, one must rely on Shimkin's (1941) treatment of the earlier Uto-Aztecan system of kin terms (Numic being a part of the larger Uto-Aztecan language grouping). His assessment is different from the reconstructed kin terms for proto-Athapaskan or proto–Central Algonquian in that he did not provide a set of reconstructed terms and meanings but rather offered sixteen probable characteristics of Uto-Aztecan (based on their frequency in ten Uto-Aztecan languages). To Shimkin, the prominent features of Uto-Aztecan were as follows: (1) four grandparent terms were used reciprocally with grandchildren; (2) G^{+1} had terms for F, M, FZ, and MB, with FeB = yBCh and MyZ = eZCh; (3) terms for older brother and older sister were extended to all cousins, and similarly for younger siblings; (4) affinal terms existed for H, W, son-in-law, and parent-in-law, with teknonymous usages for other affines. Shimkin (1941:234) considered northern Shoshone–northern Paiute to be a divergent grouping among Uto-Aztecan speakers and remarked on the ostensible Plains origin of the following attributes: M = MZ, F = FB, BCh = Ch (man speaking), ZCh = Ch (woman speaking), father-in-law = MB, WF (among other usages such as MF).

There is little evidence for crossness and affinal equations in Shimkin's reconstruction. I am nevertheless inclined to agree with Eggan (1980:184) in his suggestion that "the influence of Plains tribes may not be the whole story" for the divergent Numic features. Eggan (1980) thought that pseudo cross-cousin marriage might have existed in Uto-Aztecan, which would explain some of this patterning. Whether or not that is the case, that crossness of one or more varieties may have been more fully expressed in Uto-Aztecan than Shimkin allowed. There is a trace of it in the distinction of son's as opposed to daughter's child as a reconstructed element. And even without the benefit of a comprehensive survey of Uto-Aztecan kinship terminologies, cross reckoning simply crops up too often to be a recent innovation.

Crossness is well attested in Numic terminologies across the Great Basin, where cross/parallel distinctions are frequently associated with affinal equations. The patterns of another linguistic relative, Tubatulabal, closely resemble those of Shoshonean kin systems of Mackenzie Basin form, with crossness and some affinal equations in G^{+1}, G^{-1}, and G^{-2}, but no G^0 crossness (Gifford 1917). Cross/parallel distinctions also exist among southern California Uto-Aztecan groups such as the Serrano, Cahuilla, and Luiseno (Gifford 1922:54–62). The Serrano, for example, have cross reckoning for grandchildren, do distinguish cross cousins, and have G^{+1} equations such as FZ = MBW, MB = FZH, MyZ = FyBW, MeZ = FeBW and FyB = MyZH. Finally, the Hopi kin system is Crow in form, so that crossness exists along with intergenerational skewing (Eggan 1950).

Although it is difficult to say much more than that Uto-Aztecan in all likelihood had crossness in one or more forms, the patterning for Numic is consistent enough to allow somewhat better defined propositions. Since at least some Numic kin systems have fully developed crossness, abundant affinal equations, and bilateral cross-cousin marriage, it is conceivable that the antecedent system had this form, too. This would mean that a fully Dravidian-type pattern persisted in some areas, but that there were widespread shifts toward Mackenzie Basin–style patterning over the remainder of the Great Basin and in groups such as the Comanche, who departed for the Plains. In fact, the Mackenzie Basin pattern is so pervasive (also occurring among the Tubatulabal) that I am inclined to suggest another alternative: that is, that the proto-Numic kin system actually *was* Mackenzie Basin in form.

By themselves, distributional information and kin reconstructions certainly do not explain how Numic speakers came to occupy the Great Basin (i.e., whether emanating from southeastern California, or from within the central Great Basin itself). These two sources of information may provide some baseline scenarios, however. If Numic speakers emanated from the central Great Basin, then one would expect the systems making G^0 cross/parallel distinctions and engaging in endogamous bilateral cross-cousin marriage to have a long history there, predating any outward expansion. This should mean a longer history of local-group growth characteristics for the central Great Basin. Outside of this zone, one would anticipate local-group alliance alternatives to be explored in the more severe desert conditions faced by groups such as the southern Shoshone, where exogamy is especially adaptive.

If the point of origin was southeastern California and the antecedent was the Mackenzie Basin type, the scenario would be different. One would expect a horizon with widespread expansion of local-group alliance systems over much of the Great Basin. This would in time give way to emerging local-group growth systems in the central Great Basin, as Mackenzie Basin systems shifted back in the direction of endogamy and bilateral cross-cousin marriage.

On the basis of current evidence, something more akin to Lamb's version of Numic expansion seems more likely. It is difficult to believe that population flux can serve as an adequate explanation for the leveling of linguistic diversity for as much as *five* millennia of prehistory. And as long as southeastern California more generally (i.e., the foothills of the Sierra Nevada and the Mojave Desert, and not Death Valley specifically) is thought to contain the Numic homeland, there is considerably less difficulty in seeing it as a point of origin for expanding populations. Owens Valley Paiute, for instance, practiced irrigation of inherited seed plots; lived in quite populous, exogamous, and relatively sedentary villages; and had fairly powerful (i.e., less egalitarian) positions of leadership (Steward 1933). Traces of a similar pattern may have an early onset in the Owens Valley archaeological record (Bettinger 1983:51). Regions and socioeconomic systems like this *could* produce expanding populations. Molecular genetic evidence may some day help in resolving this issue. Smith et al. (1995) studied serum albumin phenotypes in Stillwater Marsh (west central Nevada) human skeletal remains, dating between 2,265 +/-70 and 290 +/- 80 years B.P. Kaestle (1995) undertook mitochondrial DNA studies for the same population. The results from both studies were inconclusive, however, and further data will be required to determine if there is genetic evidence for a later Numic expansion.

These several sources of information might suggest a thumbnail sketch of Numic socioeconomic history along the following lines. The Numic homeland lay in southeastern California in the southern Sierra foothills and Mojave Desert; it included areas such as Owens Valley. Numic diverged into three distinct speech communities by about 2,000 years ago. The kin system was Mackenzie Basin in form, in response to pressures for local or kin group exogamy. First ascending and descending generation cross/parallel distinctions and affinal equations nonetheless remained essentially intact.

The antecedent sociopolitical system might have been of a simpler Shoshonean variety, as Eggan (1980:185–87) thought, or it might even have been like that of the Owens Valley Paiute. This would have involved a Mackenzie Basin–style terminology (similar to that of the Owens Valley Paiute), a strong emphasis on exogamous marriage beyond ego-centered kindreds in semisedentary villages, and a productive economy based on seed and pinyon nut harvesting (see Steward 1933; Liljeblad and Fowler 1986). Socioeconomic conditions in such a system would have enabled the Numic population to grow and expand into the Great Basin, beginning about 1,000 years ago.

A Mackenzie Basin terminological model would work well for small same-sex and opposite-sex sibling core groups expanding into severe desert conditions and requiring extensive kin networks to cope with fluctuating resources. Under more favorable basin and range environmental conditions in the central Great Basin, relatively endogamous local-group or valley population isolates could have developed. It would have been a relatively straightforward matter for comprehensive Dravidian-type logic to reappear, since it already existed residually in G^{+1} and G^{-1}, and only needed to be expressed again in ego's generation. At the periphery of the Numic fan, a Mackenzie Basin model would have remained viable (as it was for many people near or on the Plains). Pseudo cross-cousin marriage emerged as a means of extending kin relations more widely, although there were strong political and economic pressures for band exogamy altogether. The expansionary process continued into the historic period with the arrival of the horse and the dominance of the Comanche on the southern Plains.

I have attributed some significance to the Owens Valley Paiute as an analogue for an early Numic antecedent because simpler Shoshonean sociopolitical systems can just as easily be derived from it, and because it would have some demographic potential to drive a Numic expansion. Attention to the Owens Valley situation is hardly novel in the Great Basin literature. Eggan (1950, 1980), Thomas (1983), and Bettinger (1983) each comment on it, but in a somewhat different light. Eggan saw in the Owens Valley Paiute a useful analogue for the antecedent of another, more complex Uto-Aztecan social system, that of the Hopi. This, too, is highly plausible, and it is regrettable that Eggan (1980:168) was apparently unable to complete his intended work of developing additional Great Basin models for the development of Hopi and Western Puebloan social systems.

DISCUSSION

What light can the distribution of kin systems and lexical reconstructions of protokin systems shed on historical development in the three language families? Trautmann and Barnes (chapter 2) see a clinal trend for Dravidian (Type A) and Iroquois (Type B) crossness in North America. The former systems are found to the north, in relatively simple hunting societies, whereas the latter systems occur in the south, where population densities are greater. It is legitimate to argue, therefore, that Dravidianate systems arise and succeed under these more marginal circumstances but are otherwise rare.[8]

Where Trautmann and Barnes see a clinal trend from north to south for Dravidianate and then Iroquoian systems, I see another, more provocative pattern.

North America has several regions exhibiting a nexus of interrelated features, including linguistic diversity, complex social structures, high population densities, and highly productive economies (be they founded on intensive horticulture, salmon fishing, or acorn harvesting). For the language families considered in this discussion, the northern Northwest Coast, the Eastern Woodlands, the Southwest, and California are of particular interest.

Northwestern North America has a central zone in which intergenerational skewing of terminologies, asymmetrical cousin marriage, and unilineal descent are the norm, as exemplified by the Haida, Tlingit, and Tsimshian (figure 4-1). Outside this central zone, there is a ring of Athapaskan or Eyak societies in which Dravidian-type distinctions and bilateral cross-cousin marriage predominate in mixed hunting and salmon-harvesting economies. Beyond this, Dravidian-type distinctions are distorted and cross-cousin marriage is rare. A similar pattern exists among the Algonquians and in eastern North America. There is a central zone in which intergenerational skewing of terminologies (Crow and Omaha) and unilineal descent dominate, in economies that engaged in some horticulture or wild rice harvesting. Outside that zone is a ring of societies in which Dravidian-type distinctions and bilateral cross-cousin marriage again predominate. In the farther reaches of the Subarctic, and especially on the Plains, these distinctions disappear and Mackenzie Basin or even generational forms are common.

In the Southwest, the Numic case reveals a similar though slightly different pattern (figure 4-7). Adjacent Puebloan societies, including the Uto-Aztecan horticulturalist Hopi, once again feature intergenerational skewing of terminologies with unilineal descent. To the north and west, the second group of societies is essentially Mackenzie Basin in form with some instances of Dravidian-type systems in the central Great Basin. Note that Gifford's (1922) mapping of kin terms for California, including that for cousin terminologies, revealed a gross pattern rather like Athapaskan and Algonquian, but for several language families.

These patterns clearly show a "center and periphery" phenomenon for the geographic distribution of kin systems in North America. Trautmann and Barnes (chapter 2) have also concluded that Iroquois or Type B systems formed the ground on which Crow-Omaha systems were raised in central North America and that these same systems may have mediated between Dravidian-type systems and systems with intergenerational skewing. Elsewhere in the world, and possibly North America, they saw some capacity for Type A systems to move more directly toward the Crow-Omaha spectrum of terminologies. This suggests another explanation for the center and periphery pattern observed: perhaps the geographic distribution of kin systems in North America does not reflect antecedent social structures and historical processes within language families. That is, the deepest historical antecedents of Crow-Omaha and Iroquois systems may be Dravidianate in form, and historically intense processes associated with emerging social complexity may have obliterated that pattern, so that it persists only outside the central zones.

Although much more information would be needed to prove that this is indeed the case, it does seem highly likely. The entire pattern, in conjunction with the lexical reconstructions, leaves little doubt that antecedent Athapaskan, Algonquian, and Numic kin systems featured a cross/parallel distinction. Beyond this, there is a prima facie case for beginning with Dravidianate assumptions. The Athapaskan and Algonquian reconstructions have extensive affinal equations in all three medial generations, and in a good number of cases these features coexist with documented bilateral cross-cousin marriage. Proto-Eyak-Athapaskan probably featured crossness that extended to grandparent and grandchild generations. These characteristics square well with Dravidianate prototypes. Because there are not documented instances of Iroquoian crossness accompanied by affinal equations and bilateral cross-cousin marriage, it is reasonable to suppose that antecedent forms for the three language families could have shared a Dravidianate logic.

Since the precise variety of crossness has not yet been established, however, it would be wise to consider other alternatives. The most likely error for North American cases would be to conflate Iroquoian with Dravidian crossness, as the Arapaho and Kiowa Apache cases should warn. The originating kin systems might therefore have had an Iroquois logic, with the implication that Dravidianate systems represent a specific historical shift in crossness that can occur in more marginal circumstances. That possibility does not sit well with the Athapaskan evidence, but it should not be ruled out for Algonquian and Numic. At least this scenario would reinforce the notion that there is an intimate connection between Iroquois and Dravidianate forms.

Suppose, now, that this issue were turned around. Since Dravidianate systems are known to occur in Subarctic settings, could Dravidianate systems arise and function in somewhat more complex social settings where there are sedentary villages? The answer is clearly positive for North America and elsewhere. But can Iroquoian systems of crossness arise and function normally in marginal environmental circumstances? In this case, the answer is not so straightforward. There is absolutely no doubt in my mind that a "Mackenzie Basin" style of terminology with explicitly Iroquois crossness (like that of the Arapaho) would do every bit as well as a Dravidianate counterpart in even the most marginal environments. It is quite likely that such instances will yet be documented in these language families.

The difficulty comes with the issue of origins. The tone of technical analysis in this volume (see chapters 2, 3, and 15) for Iroquoian systems is that they may ultimately be related to Dravidian systems. Viveiros de Castro argues that crossness retains an affinal dimension in Iroquoian systems, but that this affinal connection is indirect and derives from intergenerational cycles of alliance. It is safe to say that intergenerational cycles of alliance cannot arise or be maintained over most of the Subarctic (or, for that matter, much of the Great Basin and Plains regions). Identifiable co-residential groups in these settings are highly fluid–in a number of cases, they are virtually programmed to disappear within a generation or two, and necessarily so. Longer cycles of exchange simply are not feasible under these circumstances. While I am anxious to avoid facile attributions of historical significance to one kin system or another, it is difficult to see how historical influences can be ruled out for Iroquoian instances in areas where co-residential groups are unlikely to persist across several generations. A Dravidianate point of origin is more parsimonious and sustainable for the three language families under consideration.

The great majority of archaeologists will argue that the Americas were first populated by hunter-gatherer bands, and that it was not until several millennia ago that more complex social formations appeared. Given the incidence of cross/parallel distinctions in both North and South America, it would be quite surprising if the Paleo-Indians did not bring kin systems with cross/parallel distinctions into the New World 12,000 or more years ago. What form these distinctions might have taken is difficult to know. Yet, if linguistic calculations can be considered rough estimates of times of divergence for language communities, the available evidence hints that Dravidian-type systems had widespread currency in the last 2,000 years, when proto-Athapaskan, proto-Algonquian, and proto-Numic began to break up. This may even be true of the middle reaches of New World prehistory (3,000 to 4,000 years ago), the time range when entities such as proto-Eyak-Athapaskan and Uto-Aztecan began to diverge. Generally speaking, material traces of social complexity in the regions under discussion began emerging 3,000 to 5,000 years ago. It is not difficult to conceive of Dravidian-type systems existing or arising in earlier circumstances. If Iroquoian crossness really does owe its ultimate logical genesis to intergenerational cycles of alliance, however, then it ought to have appeared later in time, when longer-term social arrangements were economically feasible.

CONCLUDING REMARKS

The primary purpose of this chapter has been to show that band-level hunter-gatherer societies in the Athapaskan, Algonquian, and Numic language families employ regular sets of group-forming principles in fashioning bands within regional marriage isolates. The semantic patterning that accompanies cross/parallel distinctions is remarkably flexible in its application to small-scale social settings. It serves to unite sibling sets through persistent bilateral cross-cousin marriage as well as to unite strangers.

Fluid though these local groups may be, people in these societies have made deliberate choices in structuring kin relationships within and between bands. Conjugal pairs and nuclear families are commonly employed in analyses of the social organization of hunter-gatherers, but the ethnographic testimony of case after case reveals that sibling sets are of paramount importance in a wide array of circumstances. The interplay that follows between sibling set arrangements and cross/parallel distinctions sets in motion different developmental processes, showing that bands may have distinctive longitudinal trajectories over the course of one or more generations. These developmental processes, which diverge along the local-group growth and local-group alliance lines, can provide insight into a variety of phenomena, ranging from terminological variability to the strategies that underlie particular forms of socioeconomic organization.

If this analysis is correct, it would also be true to say that the pre-Contact history of Athapaskan, Algonquian, and Numic societies ought to be made up of myriad development processes and transformations through time. Despite the uncertainty that exists in exploring this temporal dimension, it does provide a glimpse of the fabric of aboriginal historical development in North America.

This is not to say that the anthropological tools currently in use are without shortcomings. The very nature of lexical reconstruction, for example, carries with it certain simplifying assumptions about the past that are useful as heuristic devices but are unlikely to be true in many cases: one such assumption is that protolanguages existed as relatively homogeneous entities within bounded homelands. This leads one to discern language family histories that involve expansion (often conceived as migration) out of homelands. If one heads too far in this direction, one loses sight of the significance of heterogeneity within original populations, of the importance of borrowing and wave-like diffusionary expansion of language and culture, and of the neighboring languages and (perhaps not so clearly bounded) societies any prototypical speech community would have possessed (see Moore 1994).

If no anthropological thought is devoted to these areas, however, much of the richness of aboriginal history will simply elude human understanding. Young and Bettinger (1992) construct a computer model of Numic expansion into the Great Basin during the last two millennia. The model hinges on their belief that Numic expansion involved a competitive ecological advantage Numic speakers gained in the time-consuming harvest of wild seeds and similar resources that pre-Numic peoples were not using. As these authors say, only further archaeological research can resolve such questions. No matter how well the computer models might match the final language distributions, however, it is difficult to share the sentiment that this "is a problem of human ecology closely analogous to the problem of two mobile, competing animal species" (Young and Bettinger 1992:86).

Far more can be done in contextualizing human understanding of the past through the use of realistically derived models of social and economic organization. No archaeologist will ever find a kin system from the past, but archaeologists do like to think that societies organized in different ways can leave archaeological signatures diagnostic of certain socioeconomic characteristics (such as the examples of endogamy, exogamy, stylistic variability, and long-term range occupancy touched upon above). Similarly, it would be useful to have more studies like Hill's (1992) elegant reconstruction of the importance of flower symbolism in Old Uto-Aztecan. She uses ethnological, linguistic, and archaeological information to recreate the chromaticism, tropes, gender connections, and spiritual dimensions likely to have characterized the Flower World of Old Uto-Aztecan.

It is only in this fashion that anthropologists will be able to phrase increasingly acute hypotheses about the past. The challenge is to continue to hone the tools for assessing the past that are available in the subdisciplines of anthropology; the incentive to do so is the prospect of linking historically specific findings with a more general theory of elementary structures as these are found in hunting and gathering and tribal societies. Armed with these understandings, anthropologists could search for endogamous village systems giving way to exogamous bison hunters along the eastern and northeastern periphery of the Plains; could ask how local-group growth and local-group alliance systems might evolve in northwestern North American settings where salmon harvesting sites are subject to political control and where there are genuine incentives to move down drainage stems toward the coast (Ives 1988); and could contemplate the socioeconomic dynamics that would affect small groups becoming increasingly involved in horticulture and irrigation in the Southwest.

NOTES

1. Dene is an Athapaskan word for "people," having also the modern political connotation of Dene Nation in reference to Athapaskan peoples of the Mackenzie Basin and Barren Grounds. It can be used to refer to the Slavey, Mountain, Hare, Bear Lakers, Dogrib, Chipewyan, and easternmost Kutchin. The Red Knife were also known as Yellowknife and are now commonly thought of as a Chipewyan group that lost its distinct identity about the turn of the century (Helm and Gillespie 1981).
2. Sarsi kin terms in all likelihood parallel those of Blackfoot, discussed in the next section. Generational qualities and overriding age distinctions predominate there.
3. Hallowell (1976:331–32) made a similar observation, although he had a report from a Father Moulin that Plains Cree at Hobbema, Alberta, engaged in frequent marriages to second cross cousins.
4. There is an Apachean Athapaskan parallel for the Arapaho and Cheyenne situation. The Kiowa Apache are a southern Plains group that historically took part in a formal alliance with the Kiowa. McAllister (1937:165–69) did not provide a great deal of information about sibling groups, but the group-forming principles he described are familiar. The most important social segment was the *kustcae,* an extended domestic family comprised of several tipis. Each tipi consisted of an elementary family and some more distant relatives. Residence was matrilocal, and levirate and sororate marriages were both practiced. Because of the prevalence of raiding, several kustcae invariably camped together in a larger gathering called a *gonka.* The latter represented several extended families that normally camped together year after year under a leader. There was a degree of fluidity, however, and groups could align themselves differently following each year's Sun Dance. Age-graded societies, some with typical Plains police functions, crosscut the first two kinds of social groups in the tribe.

    In the Kiowa Apache kin terminology, crossness is present in G^1, where MB = FZH and FZ = MBW, and F = FB = MZH = StF and M = MZ = FBW = StM. SpF and SpM are treated separately (McAllister 1937:103–111). G^0 crossness is effectively obliterated. Siblings and all cousins are denoted by a single term for either brother or sister, and affinal relatives receive separate terms. Note that although marriage was tribally endogamous, it was prohibited for any immediate, classificatory, or fictive kin relations where children would be considered siblings (McAllister 1937:145). Cross reckoning reappears in G^{-1}, where men and women refer to children of same-sex siblings as S or D but distinguish children of opposite-sex siblings as nieces and nephews. Again, a separate affinal terminology is followed for DH and SW.

    The gross form of the terminology resembles the Mackenzie Basin type and that for the Lynx Point Slavey. It differs from the latter in two respects: Affinal equations are present in G^1 and G^{-1} for Slavey, but they are lacking in Kiowa Apache. Moreover, McAllister accurately recorded a broad range of kin terms. As Trautmann and Barnes (1991) have observed, these terms pattern for crossness, but *not* for Dravidian-type crossness. Second cousins, for instance, pattern in Iroquois structural fashion.
5. Eggan (1980:181) likens this to second-cross-cousin marriage, and it does seem to inject genealogical distance as a prime criterion in selecting a marriage partner.

6. Dyen and Aberle (1974:133) touched upon, but did not pursue, this theme when they queried if the Barren Ground Naskapi, Beaver, and some Sinhalese systems might not represent a "relatively stable type" that has gone largely unnoticed because of the tendency to impute lineality to systems featured by cross-cousin marriage, whether they represent the aftermath of unilineal systems that have lost unilineality, or whether they may represent both the antecedents and the aftermath.

Even before this, Yalman (1967) made a similar recognition with his detailed study of kinship and marriage in Sri Lanka. Yalman (1967:334) created a series of transformational models from a basic pattern of bilateral cross-cousin marriage.

7. At this juncture, I am asking the reader to accept a larger proposition. The proposition (articulated in far more detail in chapters 2, 3, and 15 of this volume) would be that the dimension of crossness has several modalities (Dravidian, Iroquoian, Australian, Kuman, etc.). These modalities are not completely different but are instead more like dialectical variation in a "language" of crossness (an analogy for which I thank Asch, personal communication 1993), which in every case has an affinal implication.

The Dravidian case is the more straightforward one because of its logical connection to symmetrical bilateral cross-cousin marriage. If it turns out that other modalities in crossness are logically connected with other (more complicated) alliance regimes, there remains the sense that crossness itself has inherent affinal qualities (as argued in chapter 15). This more generalized sense of affinity connected with crossness is sufficient for generating the models that follow. Just which form of crossness is involved for a given society is a matter of historical specificity that is addressed at the end of the chapter.

8. In fact, Dravidian systems are comparatively rare among Subarctic Athapaskan societies. If anything, they may be more prone to ecological dislocation because endogamy forgoes outward-looking alliances. It is the Mackenzie Basin variants that are common in the Athapaskan case, though Dravidian overtones are not far beneath the surface for them, as is evident with the Lynx Point Slavey (for Chipewyan, Dogrib, and Bear Lake examples of the same phenomenon, see Ives 1990).

5

Kinship and Dravidianate Logic:
Some Implications for Understanding Power, Politics, and Social Life in a Northern Dene Community

MICHAEL ASCH

This chapter focuses on the ways in which conceptualizing kinship from a structural perspective, in particular as a Dravidianate form, has helped elucidate the politics and social life of Northern Dene (Athapaskan-speaking) communities. The discussion retraces the arguments advanced by Lévi-Strauss (1965) in favor of a conceptual understanding over one that derives from an examination of "empirical" behaviors. At the same time, it is argued that how people behave in the political and social realms of life is crucial to the analytical frame. An attempt is also made to examine approaches, such as those of June Helm (1965) and Julian Steward (1955), in which kinship, per se, is understood as merely a reflection of individual behaviors and is intrinsically unproblematic. Here, the argument runs counter to the presumptions of the "ecological-evolutionary" and "cultural materialist" schools, which, despite the rigorous and successful critiques by Godelier (1972), Friedman (1974), and others, still hold a dominant position within North American anthropology.[1]

The argument here rests on what might seem to be a small point: the use of sibling terms to describe all cousins within a system in which cross- and parallel-kin differentiation occurs in the first ascending generation. From a Dravidianate perspective, this practice provides some insight into several aspects of Dene social organization: (1) the means of structuring flexibility in kinship and group formation reckoning; (2) the role played by endogamy and exogamy; (3) the methods used by nonunilineal societies to structure the identity of the "local band of orientation" (i.e., family of orientation); (4) sources of women's power and its practice; and (5) the way politics is structured and practiced in general.

SLAVEY DENE KINSHIP

Kin terms among the Slavey Dene reflect a system of the following form:[2]

1. In the parent's generation (G^{+1}), the father and father's brother are merged and distinguished from the mother's brother, and the mother and mother's sister are merged and distinguished from the father's sister, as in the Dravidian system.
2. In ego's generation (G^0), however, all cousins are called by the sibling terms, so that there is no distinction of cross and parallel cousins.
3. In the children's generation (G^{-1}), the cross/parallel distinction is picked up again, merging one's children with one's same-sex sibling's children, and distinguishing them from one's opposite-sex sibling's children, as in the Dravidian system.

This kinship system became known as the Mackenzie Basin type (Spier 1925) and formed the basis for Helm's (1960, 1961, 1965, 1969a, 1969b) analyses of Dene kinship and band organization. One hypothesis considered by Helm, particularly in "Kin Terms of the Arctic Basin Dene: Hare, Slavey, Chipewyan" (1960), was that perhaps the cross/parallel distinction once existed in ego's generation, too, but then was suppressed, possibly through the influence of missionaries who would have opposed cross-cousin marriage from their first arrival in the Mackenzie region in the mid–nineteenth century. Eventually, Helm herself rejected this notion, noting that since the "Mackenzie Basin type" terminology appears in the earliest missionary reports (in the mid–nineteenth century), there had not been enough time to "convert" the Dene. The issue, she concluded, was an unanswerable conundrum.[3] Nonetheless, her work reinforced an impression that the Dene were "highly adaptable" and "easily influenced" by contact with Europeans, even to the point of making wholesale changes in their institutions. This viewpoint was first expressed in a footnote in "Tappers and Trappers," by Murphy and Steward (1956), and was later reinforced in Service's (1971) *Primitive Social Organization*, in which he describes the Dene as "debt-peons" of the fur trade virtually from the outset of contact and uses as evidence, among other factors, the presumed, easily undermined use of cross-cousin terms and cross-cousin marriage found in Helm's analysis.[4]

Notwithstanding the evidence collected over the years from many Dene, including much information obtained by my own inquiries, Slavey Dene kinship appears to have a basically Dravidianate form, in that a Dravidianate opposition between cross and parallel cousins underlies the Dene use of generational terms of reference in ego's generation. Ives (1985; and chapter 4 of this volume) has provided further insights that indicate that the information I found at Wrigley is appropriate for understanding kinship in the Mackenzie as a whole.[5] He has, in fact, expanded and deepened this analysis to indicate its value in understanding all Northern Dene kinship from the Mackenzie Basin to the Pacific Coast. In short, the case for approaching Dene kinship from a Dravidianate angle has been established and these steps need not be retraced here.

THE CROSS/PARALLEL DISTINCTION IN EGO'S GENERATION

Rather, the critical question to ask at this point is in what way is the generational form of kinship nomenclature reported by missionaries, fur trade agents, and anthropologists consistent with a Dravidianate logic (Dumont 1953; Trautmann 1981)? To answer that question, one must differentiate, following Lévi-Strauss (1965), between the empirical (as identified both in behavior and in statements) and the underlying model, or between the information provided and the theoretical understanding of it.[6]

Most Dene interviewed for this study provided terms that reflect the "Mackenzie Basin" form when these terms were elicited either in the abstract or with reference to particular relatives. Most people, in fact, provide information on the system as they use it in everyday life and, presumably, as it is given to them by members of their society.

At the same time, as Rushforth (1977) found at Fort Franklin, a few individuals within the population do provide an alternative to this form of kinship nomenclature. Some of these alternative terminologies contain (as in Rushforth's case) certain "anomalies." For example, one out of a hundred speakers may use a standard Dravidianate form to describe kin relations in ego's generation.

Are these anomalies merely statistical aberrations to be footnoted but otherwise disregarded? Or do the individuals using a Dravidianate kinship terminology represent, perhaps somewhat like Galileo, individuals who see, as it were, that the earth travels around the sun while living in a world where conventional wisdom indicates that the sun travels around the earth? In line with the statistical majority, most anthropologists appear to have concluded that the Mackenzie Basin type applies and that those who provide Dravidianate (and other) forms are "deviants" whose views of the world may need to be noted but not taken seriously. Extensive work with a Dene individual leads me to dispute that view, and to propose that the Mackenzie Basin form rests on a Dravidianate logic, as explained in the next section.[7]

KINSHIP, RESIDENCE, DESCENT, AND MARRIAGE

From the insights of Lévi-Strauss (1965, 1969 [1949]) and Dumont (1953), it seems clear that, at one level, certain kinship terminologies are about marriage possibilities and impossibilities. Some populations also treat marriage as a means of joining groups together. In Lévi-Strauss's model, kinship systems fall into three fundamental kinds: elementary, Crow-Omaha, and Complex. These systems are distinguished on the basis of lineality and marriage rules: Elementary structures have unilineal descent and positive marriage rules; Crow-Omaha have unilineal descent and negative marriage rules; and Complex have neither unilineal descent nor positive marriage rules. In this scheme, Slavey Dene could only fit into the "Complex" category, for they do not have unilineal descent and do not appear (on the surface) to have positive marriage rules, because they use only a generational term for cousins. Therefore, it would be difficult to determine through Lévi-Strauss's approach how Slavey kinship might work to organize and unite groups through descent and marriage. However, if it is assumed that his paradigm misses an essential kind of structure, one in which there is a positive marriage rule but no unilineal descent, the picture changes, and the Slavey Dene can be said to have a "Bilateral-Dravidianate system" (see Asch 1980).

The primary difficulty for such an analysis is not the possible existence of a positive marriage rule, for it will follow once the Dravidianate nature of the system is described (as discussed below). Rather, the problem is how to determine the group of "orientation." In a unilineal world, at the most basic level, this may be determined by descent, as Lévi-Strauss (1969 [1949]) suggests. The Slavey Dene are decidedly not unilineal and do not appear to use descent in this manner in order to organize the group of orientation. Therefore to understand how this group is organized it is necessary to consider factors other than descent.

As an aside, note that it would be useful at some point to review the ideas of Eggan (1955 [1937]) and Radcliffe-Brown (1965 [1935]), among many others in the 1920s and 1930s, concerning the relative significance of the principles of descent and of residence in the social organization of groups of orientation among indigenous nations in North America. Clearly, many of the theorists of social organization of that time held that residence played a more significant role, even in unilineal situations, than did Radcliffe-Brown, at least in his 1935 study.

For the purposes of this discussion, however, it is only necessary to state that, whereas descent plays a limited role in the organizing of the group of orientation, residence is crucial. Indeed, among Slavey Dene, one's group of orientation is primarily the group in which one resides, and more particularly the residence group in which one is raised until marriage. Furthermore, there is a strong orientation to remain, throughout one's life, with siblings of the same sex and, ultimately, to live in different residence communities from one's siblings of the opposite sex. Thus there is a tendency among the Dene to conceptualize that it is most appropriate to construct a group of "procreation" with a male's brothers or a female's sisters, but much less appropriate to construct this group from a group that consists of both brothers and sisters.[8] Therefore the "generational shifts" can be said to occur not at the death of members of the senior generation but rather at the time of marriage and thus to move from a set of adults in generation one to a different set of adults in generation two.

These three ideas can now be applied to the presumed anomaly of generational terms existing in ego's generation within what otherwise appears to be Dravidianate logic. The idea around which the "group of orientation" is constructed conceptually consists of a group of men who are terminologically (and perhaps biologically) brothers to each other and who are married to a group of women who are terminologically (and perhaps biologically) sisters to each other. In such a world, the group of orientation is constructed around the assumption that all of the children would be terminologically considered "siblings" to each other —whether or not the underlying terminological structure were generational or Dravidianate. This means, if Dravidianate logic applies, that no person raised within the group of orientation is marriageable with another member and hence the assumption fosters an exogamous approach to marriage. Exogamy is considered appropriate among Slavey Dene (Asch 1988).

The difficulty for Slavey Dene organization arises when, for whatever reason, siblings of both sexes form a residence group together after they are married.[9] In such cases, were the Dravidianate paradigm expressed directly, some of the children in such a group of orientation would be "marriageable" to other children. Hence, the situation of marriage based on an endogamous principle would arise. At this point, society needs to make a choice on a systematic basis. Were the society to choose to emphasize the Dravidianate aspect of the kinship in ego's generation, then it would tend to allow normal expression of endogamy, as is the case among the Beaver Dene (see Ives 1985, 1990:100). The Dravidianate nature of Beaver Dene terminology is expressed conventionally in ego's generation, and endogamy is considered an appropriate form of marriage.

From the Slavey Dene perspective, at least at this time, exogamy is a more highly valued convention. In this case, the use of Dravidianate terms in ego's generation would be in conflict with the convention of exogamous marriage. One solution to this problem has been to automatically transform the cross-cousin term to the sibling term in situations where children of siblings of both sexes co-reside after marriage and to apply this solution conventionally to any situation in which one is describing the children of one's parent's cross-sex sibling (or terminological equivalent)—hence, the development in conventional speech of what is presumed to be a Mackenzie Basin type of kinship nomenclature.[10]

The fact that the terminology is Dravidianate, then, cannot be seen by asking about kinsmen. Rather, it is best seen when asking about marriages, particularly about how married people are related to each other. As I have indicated elsewhere (Asch 1980, 1988), Slavey Dene conventionally say that it is wrong to marry "too close" but do not say one should marry a cross cousin. At the same time, whenever I asked a person who has theoretical knowledge of the system about marriages that had already occurred, the relationships were, with one exception, invariably explained as cross-cousin marriages. Indeed, in that one case, I was told that this marriage was completely inappropriate and caused much turmoil within the community. This marriage was, in fact, between individuals who were related as "parallel cousins" but were not biologically "close." I also saw an instance in which there was an attempt to recast as "cross cousins" two individuals who were previously seen as "brother and sister," once their romantic interest was discovered. Finally, I witnessed a discussion between two women in which one woman, who wanted a marriage between her family of orientation and that of the second woman, addressed the latter as "my sister-in-law," while the second woman, who did not want the marriage, addressed the first as "my sister." These examples provide a solid indication that the Dravidianate logic of the system can be seen when it is examined from the perspective of marriage and that in fact a person only becomes a cross cousin to another person permanently when that relationship is confirmed through marriage.

WOMEN'S POWER

In the social world constructed by the Slavey Dene, people are entangled in kinship relations of many and often contrasting sorts. In the cases just cited, there were attempts to recast various kinship relations into new ones. This was accomplished principally by utilizing different pathways to trace out actual relationships. This approach appears to be used conventionally whenever social circumstances make it necessary to change an individual's status, for example, from that of a "sibling" to a "cross cousin" or, in other terms, from an unmarriageable kinsman to a marriageable ally. Despite the lack of factual evidence in this regard, it may be that such wholesale recalculations of kinship relations are not as easily constructed within unilineal systems, where, for better or worse, lineality itself provides a means to forget "mistakes" and "contradictions" that are bound to arise within any system. Slavey Dene do not seem to view the world that way. The "mistakes" and "contradictions" are an essential element that can be used to construct their social universe. People therefore find it important to be aware of them and to know how to use them. They use this information to structure not only marriage but also hunting groups, residence groups, and so forth.

But who controls this knowledge? It is the women, particularly the most senior women. As many anthropologists can attest, senior women have prodigious knowledge about kin relations (Helm 1961). Generally, these women know about relations within and between bands stretching across a vast territory and going back perhaps through three generations. Such women also know the theory that underlies the way in which kinship terms are expressed in everyday life. This base of information provides them with the materials to identify various pathways that might be used to construct very different social universes out of the same constellation of individuals. In fact, this is the very operation that took place in the social construction of the community of Wrigley two years before my first contact with them. Prior to that time, the people of Wrigley had lived in three bands and at two lakes. Intermarriage took place regularly between these bands and each was understood to be, in anthropological terms, a marriage isolate. With the move into Wrigley, the three bands had to make a decision about their social composition now that they were co-resident. One option was to maintain them as three distinct entities.[11] However, it was apparently decided (how, I do not know) that every effort would be made to reconstruct these three groups of orientation into a single group. This was apparently done successfully. As a consequence, however, many people who were potentially marriageable in the older situation now became "siblings" and hence unmarriageable. In fact, there is a generation of individuals who were young adults at the time of the move who never married or set up any permanent partnerships. Today, conventionally, young adults do marry, but they generally find their marriage partners in other Dene communities.

In sum, it is the women—particularly the senior women—who have the information and the theoretical framework to construct the social universe. This is a significant source of their political power, and it is conventionally withheld from men. I once asked the primary elder with whom I worked, Jessie Hardisty, how she would talk to her sons about kinship. She said she would only tell them who their father's brothers were and who their mother's brothers were (which, of course, would be the basis for knowing which individuals were in their group and with whom they might intermarry–given a Dravidianate logic). That was all they needed to know. I asked what she would do if they persisted. She replied that she would tell them it was just women's gossip and not important for them to know.[12] In short, kinship knowledge and kinship theory provide significant power—power that is central to the construction of Slavey Dene social and political life. At the same time, like much power, it is hidden from the casual gaze. Thus it is not surprising that most Slavey Dene tend to use the conventional system—that is, a system of the so-called Mackenzie Basin type—when responding to anthropologists.

IMPLICATIONS AND CONCLUSIONS

The view that kinship is a peripheral and easily understood phenomenon needs to be reassessed in the light of evidence suggesting that kinship is powerful and hard to apprehend. This latter suggestion clarifies many aspects of Slavey Dene social and political life, particularly the source of tension within social life. In Helm's universe, marriage and group formation is essentially unproblematic. As mentioned earlier, her focus rests, as does Steward's, on how material existence is reproduced and structured. Under the approach advocated here, marriage and group formation are the central problematic of Slavey Dene society.

Furthermore, this approach creates certain implications for political legitimacy. In a statistical world, in which kinship is unproblematic and political units are constructed around "big men" with large followings (such as nodal kindreds), numbers count. Chiefs, for example, can claim legitimacy on the basis of having a larger following than others and, in this time of internal colonialism, the person who is "elected" by the largest number of individuals within the community is certified by the Canadian federal government ipso facto as the legitimate leader. If the world is constructed on a Dravidianate basis, however, it is families, regardless of size, that matter. In such a world, a central question becomes whether families retain intergenerational legitimacy in a situation where people reside permanently in one large community. That is, does descent now count? Should it be constructed out of patrilineal last names? This is the world of problematics that Dene leaders face. The lines of demarcation are around whether or not numbers and elections count and what the alternatives might be. Seeing the possibility of a Dravidianate logic within the system helps explain the dynamics of this situation and may play a practical role as well, especially with respect to deriving alternative political systems in the Canadian Northwest Territories.[13]

One final implication concerns the educational system. Slavey Dene children are compromised in two ways by the insistence on an elementary education based, uncritically, on Western values. In the first place, the English kinship terminology of the so-called Eskimo type appears in Dene texts as "THE KINSHIP SYSTEM," thereby providing them, at an early age, with a system that competes with their own. This system has an internal logic that is both very different from the Dravidianate system and is internally consistent. At the same time, because the kinship logic that underlies the system they are being taught at home is not transparent, there is a tendency for both teachers and children to believe it is "illogical" or "broken down." This view is often reinforced by educators. At the same time, given that kinship is a source of women's power, it would be inappropriate to teach the entire logic of the system in a world where most people, but men in particular, are supposed to know only what they are told about who their fathers' brothers and mothers' brothers are. This problem needs to be addressed soon if that access to power is to be maintained. For some scholars, it is essential to determine whether a kinship system has particular formal properties and whether certain presumed kinship systems, such as "Dravidianate," actually exist in the abstract. Such efforts do indeed contribute to a better understanding of the fundamental nature of kinship and many other theoretical matters.

It is equally important, however, for anthropologists to situate themselves in a "real world" or "practical" problematic and determine to what extent the tools they have developed are helping them to understand, explain, and act within the dynamics of that problematic. A case in point concerns the internal dynamics of Dene (and other First Nations) social and political organization. In investigating how state ideology and institutions act in a manner compatible or competitive with indigenous ideology and institutions, I have found that a knowledge of Slavey Dene kinship has enhanced my understanding of some of the complexities, dilemmas, and issues that are addressed in Slavey Dene social and political life. Viewing Slavey Dene kinship from the perspective of an underlying "Dravidianate" logic has provided a better tool for understanding these matters than did one provided by a presumed Mackenzie Basin type. It is in this sense, then, that Nonetheless, this premise, like all others, is undoubtedly only in part "correct," and discussion of theoretical issues regarding kinship logic in general and about Dravidianate systems in particular must press forward if scholars are to find more appropriate ways of understanding the social and political life of Slavey Dene, as well as of other societies.[14]

NOTES

I acknowledge SSHRCC for its support of research I undertook in developing this chapter.

1. For discussions on this topic, see overview essays by O'Laughlin (1975) and Myers (1988), as well as comments in Leacock and Lee (1982) and Wilmsen (1989).
2. "Slavey Dene" is one appropriate term used to describe those Dene who live in what is known as the Deh Cho region. Deh Cho means "big river" and is the term used to describe the Mackenzie River. However, the Deh Cho region does not include all Dene who live along the Mackenzie River. A more precise term to describe the people with whom I have worked most extensively would be "South Slavey–speaking Dene." However, I know through discussions with others that many of the matters discussed in this chapter apply to all Slavey speakers and may apply to other regions as well. I use "Slavey Dene" as shorthand and for convenience only.
3. That this is a conundrum, it must be mentioned, also derives from the manner in which Gertrude Dole (1969), and to a lesser extent Ellen Basso (1970), analyze Xingu Carib

kinship, which is reported to have a kinship terminological system similar to the Mackenzie Basin type and that may exist as well in many other societies where similar kinds of kinship nomenclature are reported. See, for example, Shoshone kinship as reported by Eggan (1980:174–76).

4. Helm (1989) recently repeated her view of the presumed conundrum of Dene cousin terminology and marriage rules in a discussion of my analysis (Asch 1988) of Slavey Dene kinship terminology. She suggests that my analysis of Slavey Dene kinship fails because I am unable to account for the shift, early in Dene post-Contact history, from a cross/parallel cousin terminology to a generational form. Her point really is a non sequitur with respect to my analysis, as I am arguing that the use of a "generational" form to mask a cross/parallel distinction exists independently of the influence of "contact."

5. Wrigley is the English name of the Slavey Dene community in which I conducted my most extensive primary research on the topic of kinship.

6. This theoretical understanding may take place either from an emic or an etic point of view. In the instance I describe here, I would say that my understanding derives from both theoretical perspectives, in that I worked with someone within the culture who had a solid theoretical grasp of the kinship logic and I was also following what I had learned as an anthropologist about kinship logic in general.

7. To use another convention, and one with which I am much more comfortable, I was honored to have had the opportunity to work with an elder of the community whose knowledge and experience about this matter and many others was highly respected and valued by community members. She taught me a great deal. I am certain, and I hope this is not seen as false modesty, that I only learned a little. Still, it left me feeling grounded in my understanding of the kinship.

8. Elsewhere (Asch 1980), I have called this form of residence "unilocal."

9. I have heard a number of reasons why this might occur. The sons-in-law, for example, might prove to be poor hunters, and so there is a belief that a son should remain; or in case of the early death of a senior male, it is necessary to bring a man into the group who otherwise, after a brief period of bride service, would have taken the woman he would marry with him.

10. It is possible, but would be highly speculative, to move this approach one step further. One way to look at it is this. As Dumont (1953) has shown, the term "cross cousin," in the Dravidianate view, can be used to signify "other" or "potential ally." Marriage, therefore, becomes a means to produce an "ally." In a unilineal world, and perhaps particularly in a world where moiety structures are central, it would seem by deduction that convention produces a situation in which half of the world is conceptualized "self" (and therefore not marriageable) and the other half "other" (and therefore marriageable). In this sense, one is related to all members of the society either by "identity" or by "marriage." In my understanding, the social world might feel somewhat different in a nonunilineal society, especially in one where "residence" rather than descent is a foundational principle. Here, one is only certain that one is "related to" individuals called "kinsmen" by the Dravidianate system. This is because nonkin are not conceptually a homogenous group of "marriageables," as seems to be the case in unilineal situations, especially ones that have moieties. Marriage must take place within the category "other," but given that all of the "others" do not constitute a single "group," the question is the degree to which such a marriage provides a link that is adequate to bind one to the "half" of the population that belongs to "the other side." In my understanding of Slavey Dene society, the group generated by a marriage link is not assumed to be coextensive with all of the people "on the other side." Indeed, the group generated by a marriage is conceptualized as being much smaller. In cases where such a world exists conceptually, there may be individuals to whom one is not linked either by kinsmen designation who are also not linked by marriage. Looking at such a society strategically from the perspective of any individual ego, it seems that (at least in the

case of the Slavey Dene), there is a tendency to try to maximize the use of "kinsmen" ties so as to increase the sphere of relatives. One way of conceptualizing the difference between the two systems is this: in a unilineal system with a moiety structure, there is a presumption that 50 percent of the population is kin and 50 percent ally. In a nonunilineal situation, at least 50 percent of the population is conceptualized as "kin." However, the ally group is unknown in size. Therefore, when encountering others, unless one knows that one is in an "ally" relationship with those individuals, it may be best to try to try to forge a "kinsman" link. Therefore, it may be best to attempt to realize a social universe in which everyone, except for the group into which one marries, is a "kinsman." Hence, unlike unilineal systems with moieties where the ideal is that 50 percent of the population is kin and the other 50 percent is ally, here it is best to conceptualize the ideal world as consisting only of kin, except for those specific groups into which one marries. This results in an ideal in which, in percentage terms, on the order of 90 percent of the population would be conceptualized as "kin," while only 10 percent would be conceptualized as "ally."

11. This may have taken place at Fort Resolution (Driedger 1989) almost a hundred years ago when the bands of that community first moved into a central location. It may yet happen in Wrigley.

12. I also asked her why she was explaining all of this to me. She said that it was clearly important to me but did not go into further detail. As matters actually happened, while I might ask a question, Mrs. Hardisty would ignore me completely and only answer my wife, Margaret. I think, at the same time, she was somewhat surprised that we might understand that there was an underlying logic to the kinship terminology and was therefore comfortable to provide us with further information. For that insight, I must thank Lévi-Strauss and the fact that I had the opportunity to read the English edition of his book (1969 [1949]), *The Elementary Structures of Kinship,* in galley just before our trip to the Canadian North.

13. For example, Dene have articulated an approach to governance that would account for political legitimacy among both indigenous and nonindigenous Northerners. One version of this system has seats allocated to nonindigenous Northerners regardless of their size within the total population. It also calls for representation by "family." However, as mentioned above, much effort is now expended on defining what "family" might be in a situation with permanent residence. It is the nonindigenous, in a sense, who adopt the "nodal kindred" and "big man" approach, for they argue, in communities where they are a majority, that only the majority should rule and hence that indigenous people, where they are a minority, have to "back a single candidate" or, at worst, not have any representation.

14. I need to add this comment. My experience has convinced me that looking at Dene kinship through Dravidianate logic has been much more helpful to me than relying on a Mackenzie Basin typology. At the same time, I know that my knowledge and experience are limited and limiting. I do not claim to fully or even greatly "understand" Slavey Dene kinship. At one level, I am content to say that perhaps I know it as well as a three-year-old Dene child does, but one who has been instructed by people well-educated and knowledgeable in both Slavey Dene and Western cultures. For this reason I am comfortable with what I discuss here but realize that what I say may be more wrong than right, and certainly I am looking forward to any criticisms or corrections that may prove helpful in revising or further developing my understanding of the principles of kinship or Dene social and political life.

6

Dravidian Nomenclature as an Expression of Ego-Centered Dualism

EMMANUEL DÉSVEAUX AND MARION SELZ

Until recently, anthropologists knew little about the northwestern tip of Canada's province of Ontario. It was long thought that this immense space was occupied entirely by Cree-speaking peoples, but this is true only of the perimeter. The interior belongs to the Ojibwa zone and is divided among several distinct groups.[1] The nomenclature presented here comes from the northernmost group,[2] whose members have no special name for themselves, except with reference to Big Trout Lake, the largest of their communities.[3] The terminology was collected from the oldest group of informants who were in no doubt that they were speaking of an ideal object.

A SUCCESSFUL BINARY LOGIC

This Dravidian (or Dravidianate) nomenclature is remarkable for its regularity (see figures 6-1 and 6-2). Male parallel cousins are classificatory brothers, in other words, consanguines; cross cousins are assimilated to affines. Thus *nishishes* means "my uncle" (MB or FZH) and "my father-in-law," and *nisekoos,* "my aunt" (FZ or MBW) and "my mother-in-law," and so forth. Since two perfectly separate fields (*doshem* and *nin'akshem*) are available to the generation of ego's children, the categories of cross cousins and brothers- or sisters-in-law are made up by opposition to those of siblings and parallel cousins. This rule allows considerable horizontal extension, which is discussed later in the chapter. For the time being, it is sufficient to note that affines of affines are included in the social circle embraced by the nomenclature. By a simple mechanical process, these fall into the category of parallels: for example, the wife's brother's wife's brother will be considered a brother. The logical distribution of positions according to the two major categories of consanguinity and affinity is fully consistent. The only time this binary classificatory logic is violated is in the case of ego's direct ascendants and descendants, who are distinguished from other kin. The terminology appears to be of canonical Dravidian type. Nevertheless, two points about this nomenclature call for further attention.

Figure 6-1
Big Trout Lake Northern Ojibwa Terminology: Male Speaking

	♂				♀	
	x	//			//	x
G^2	*nomoshom* FF, MF				*nokom* MM, FM	
G^1	*nihishes* MB, FZH, SpF	*nomoshomis* FB, MZH	*nidada* F	*nimama* M	*n'doses* MZ, FBW	*nisekoos* FZ, MBW, SpM
G^0 e	*nitaoos* FZS, MBS, FBDH, MZDH, WB, WZHZH	*nishikwese* B, FBS, MZS, FZDH, MBDH, WZH, WBWB	*(ni)dawema* Z, MZD, FBD, MBSW, FZSW, WBW, WZHZ			*nimen* MBD, FZD, MZSW, FBSW, WZ, WBWBW
G^0 y		*nijimish* B, Z, FBS, FBD, MZS, MZD	ego			*niwijihakan* W
G^{-1}	*nin'akshem* ZS, FFDS, FZSS, MZDS, MBSS, BDH, FBSDH, FZDDH, MZSDH, MBDDH, SpBS, SpZS	*doshem* BS, FBSS, FZDS, MZSS, MBDS, ZDH, FFDDH, FZSDH, MZDDH, MBSDH	*goses* S	*danes* D	*doshem ikwem* BD, FBSD, FZDD, MZSD, MBDD, ZSW, FFDSW, FZSSW, MZDSW, MBSSW	*nin'akshem ikwem* ZD, FFDD, FZSD, MZDD, MBSD, BSW, FBSSW, FZDSW, MZSSW, MBDSW, SpBD, SpZD
G^{-2}	*noses* SS, DD, DS, SSSp, DDSp, DSSp, SDSp					

First, at Big Trout Lake, the terms in ego's generation vary not as a function not only of the sex of the person addressed but also of the sex of the speaker, or addressor. While a man calls his brother (assimilated to his male parallel cousin) *nishikwese* and his brother-in-law (equivalent to his male cross cousin) *nitaoos,* a woman will call them, respectively, *nishimes* and *nijimoos.* Similarly, while a man calls his sister (and his female parallel cousin) *nidawema,* and his sister-in-law (equivalent to his cross cousin) *nimen,* a woman will call them, respectively, *nimises* and *nijakoos.* This type of terminological reduplication at G^0 as a function of the addressor's sex and not only as a function of the sex and genealogical position of the addressee, as is the case in G^{+1} and G^{-1}, maximizes the classificatory logic un-

Figure 6-2

Big Trout Lake Northern Ojibwa Terminology: Female Speaking

	♂		♀	
	x	//	//	x
G²	*nomoshom* FF, MF		*nokom* MM, FM	
G¹	*nihishes* MB, FZH, SpF	*nomo-shomis* FB, MZH	*nidada* F	*nimama* M	*n'doses* MZ, FBW	*nisekoos* FZ, MBW, SpM
G⁰ (e / y)	*nijimoos* FZS, MBS, FBDH, MZDH, HB, HZHZH	*nishimes* B, FBS, MZS, FZDH, MBDH, HZH, HBWB — *nijimish* B, FBS, MZS	ego	*nimises* Z, MZD, FBD, MBSW, FZSW, WBW, WZHZ	*nijakoos* MBD, FZD, MZSW, FBSW, HZ, HBWBW — *niwijihakan* H
G⁻¹	*nin'akshim* BS, FBSS, FZDS, MZSS, MBDS, ZDH, FFDDH, MZDDH, MBSDH, SpBS, SpZS	*doshem* ZS, FFDS, FZSS, MZDS, MBSS, BDH, FBSDH, FZDDH, MZSDH, MBDDH	*goses* S	*danes* D	*doshem ikwem* ZD, FFDD, FZSD, MZDD, MBDD, BSW, FBSSW, FZDSW, MZSSW, MBDSW	*nin'akshim ikwem* BD, FBSD, FZDD, MZSD, MBDD, ZSW, FFDSW, FZSSW, MZDSW, MBSSW, SpZD, SpBD
G⁻²	*noses* SS, DD, DS, SSSp, DDSp, DSSp, SDSp				

derlying all Dravidian terminologies. G⁰ is the level that exhibits the most distinctive markers, in complete accordance with the spirit of a resolutely ego-centered nomenclature, since this is the reference level. Note, too, the discrepancy in the expression of the addressee's sex: for the generations above ego, sex is signified by distinct forms (*nomoshom, nokom* for G⁺²; *nomoshomis, n'doses, nishishes, nisekoos* for G⁺¹), whereas for the generations below ego, it is signified by a mere derived form for G⁻¹ (*doshem, doshem ikwem; nina'akshem, nina'akshem ikwem*), and it is not discriminated at all for G⁻² (*noses*).[4] Here, too, one can see the consistency of a nomenclature that reserves a strong marking of sex where it is crucial for ego, in particular because such marking determines his genealogical position—and therefore his reference position—and that suppresses its expression, where it becomes indifferent, as is the case for nephews, nieces, sons-in-law, daughters-in-law, and a fortiori for grandchildren.[5]

The intrinsic logical "criteria" of the Big Trout Lake nomenclature can be summarized as follows:

G^{+2} sex
G^{+1} sex, crossness
G^{0} (sex, crossness) sex of addressee
G^{-1} crossness
G^{-2} [no distinctions]

This schema gives an even better picture of just how far this nomenclature goes toward perfecting Dravidian logic in the area of terminology. It becomes clear that the additional specification, which by way of the sex of the addressee characterizes G^{0}, is in no way justified by function (for instance, by prescription of, or preference for, a certain type of marriage). It turns out to be a sort of additional refinement made possible by the very logic of the terminological system, a sort of variation on the theme of sexual difference as generator of binary oppositions. This purely gratuitous variation suggests that nomenclature, as a logical-linguistic object, is relatively independent insofar as it does not conflict with the other rules of a sociological order operating in the group.

Second, within the category of consanguines at the G^{0} level, the nomenclature discriminates between elder and younger. Although a man distinguishes between his older brother (*nishikwese*) and his older sister *nidawema*), he assimilates his younger brothers and sisters to one another in a single category (*nijimish*). As for a woman speaking, there is just one word for all her sisters (*nimises*), but she distinguishes between her older brothers (*nishimes*) and her younger brothers (*nijimish*). One may notice that this is the same term used by a man to designate all his younger brothers and sisters. This suggests a kind of "desexualization" when it comes to younger siblings. And the process is even stronger when ego is a male. A recurring feature of Algonquian Dravidian terminologies and classic terminologies elsewhere, this can be interpreted, in the Algonquian context, as the expression of a certain general terminological bias in favor of the male, a fairly weak reflection of what is on the whole only a relative primacy accorded by the social organization to a certain form of patrilineal structure (Désveaux 1988a:189 *passim*). Moreover, it seems reasonable to connect with this bias the derivation of the diminutive term used to designate the parallel uncle, *nomoshomis,* from the term for grandfather, *nomoshom.* The derivation could be read as a highly attenuated form, like a faint echo, of the generational merging rule.

That being said, a more abstract view suggests another interpretation of the elder/younger distinction. Owing to this device, two brothers do not occupy identical positions: one calls the other elder, while the latter reciprocates with younger (it is only when a sibling group contains three or more brothers that the risk of redundancy arises). The distinction between elder and younger brothers could thus be explained as yet one more way of expressing the ego-centered principle (discussed later in the chapter) that characterizes this terminology, at the cost of a sort of local arrangement of the one space that is not covered by the global classificatory logic.[6]

ETHNOGRAPHIC EVIDENCE AGAINST THE MIRAGE OF FIRST-CROSS-COUSIN MARRIAGE

In its rule of absolute bipartition of all kin into parallels (forbidden as spouses) and crosses-affines in the three medial generations, Big Trout Lake nomenclature is not unique.[7] Based on a lexicon combining Ojibwa and Cree borrowings, it closely resembles the systems reported for the other Ojibwa-speaking subgroups of northwestern Ontario and the adjacent regions of Manitoba—Berens River and Island Lake (Hallowell 1975 [1937]; Dunning 1959:74, 110), Pekangekum (Rogers 1962:B 12), and Weagamow Lake[8]—as well as the nomenclature of the nearby Shamattawa Cree (Turner and Wertman 1977:69–71).[9] Here is a compact set of "purely" Dravidian nomenclatures, a veritable North American center of the phenomenon, to which should be added a much smaller group identified by Strong (1929) and made up of the northernmost of the Naskapi "bands."

Without going clear back to Morgan and Tylor, one can find demonstrated in chapter 1 of Rivers's *Kinship and Social Organization* a Dravidian-type nomenclature (in today's sense of the term) as the expression of a cross-cousin marriage rule that must exist or have existed in North America. As grounds for his argument, Rivers invoked a fragment of Cree nomenclature and a report mentioning the existence of a positive marriage rule among the Haida (Rivers 1968 [1914]:69–74). Since then, all of the authors who have had anything to do with Algonquian Dravidian nomenclatures—with the noteworthy exception of Turner and Wertman—have interpreted them in terms of this paradigm.[10] This group consists not only of Strong, Hallowell, Dunning, and Rogers, as already mentioned, but also the team of physical anthropologists comprised of Gibson, Thames, and Molohon (1991). To be sure, all of these authors encountered, as Désveaux did himself at Big Trout Lake, marriages between first cross cousins in their respective areas.

Before going on, we need to make one point clear about the relationship between Dravidian nomenclature and marriage type. Marriage between first cross cousins is the only kind that can logically be taken into account once it is assumed that a rule of marriage is the causal explanation for a nomenclature that assimilates certain close kin types (cousin, uncle, aunt, etc.) to real or potential affines (spouse, brother-in-law, sister-in-law, father-in-law, mother-in-law, etc.). It is hard to imagine that the first cross cousin could be denoted by extension or by inclusion in a category built on the second or third cross cousin. The latter are, in effect, necessarily defined with respect to the former, unless an inclusive category of "cross cousins" as it appears in the nomenclature is defined at the outset. But how can it be defined if not by marriage with the first cross cousin?

The ethnographic reality is that marriages between first cross cousins have indeed been recorded in northwestern Ontario. The question is whether these marriages are found in sufficient numbers to justify setting up this marriage as the reference type that thus dictates the entire logic of the nomenclature. To our minds, the answer is no. But let us examine the facts.

In the 1930s Hallowell visited Berens River and Island Lake. He never published any of his figures on Berens River, and the only mention he made of first-cross-cousin marriages was highly suggestive: "Probably no more than 25 percent of the marriages were between individuals as closely related as this [first cousins]" (Hallowell 1992:56). He did publish his results for Island Lake: 33 out of 152 marriages (or nearly 22 percent) were between first cross cousins (1975 [1937]:232). However, this information came from a single informant, and the genealogical record pertained to essentially his own "kindred." The average therefore did not represent the marriage norm for the whole group. The members of certain families may have had a particular propensity for marrying close kin. But in our Big Trout Lake genealogies, higher intermarriage "zones" are weighted by other segments of the population in which the individuals seem to have a more adventuresome attitude toward marriage. In short, Hallowell's data cannot be taken at face value.

Let us see what our other sources have to say. Dunning (1959:151), who spent time in the 1950s at Pekangekum, calculates an average of 16.8 percent for first cross-cousin marriages. For Weagamow Lake, Rogers (1962:B49) gives 4 marriages out of 41, or slightly less than 10 percent. Gibson et al. (1991:148–50), whose data come from two anonymous communities in northwestern Ontario, find only 10 marriages between first cousins, out of several hundred in all. As for Big Trout Lake and the neighboring communities, computer processing of our genealogical corpus produces 9 marriages of this type out of 104 (or a rate of less than 9.5 percent).[11] This much is clear, then: the rate of first-cross-cousin marriage in northwestern Ontario is low, and in the adjacent part of Manitoba it is less than 20 percent in both cases.[12]

The argument that this low rate of occurrence stems from demographic happenstance and irregularities—not everyone has a cross cousin of marriageable age at the right moment—does not stand up. For although the Indians of the groups we are dealing with do indeed tend to marry within their own age class, the past fifty years have seen a veritable population boom because of improved health conditions throughout the Subarctic area. Sibling groups everywhere prove to be large, with sometimes as many as ten members. In such conditions, the chances of finding the "ideal" partner—whether this is a "conscious" ideal or not—are increased. The number of cross-cousin marriages should therefore have gone up, which is nowhere the case; rather, it tends to fall as the populations increase. This decline can be explained fairly satisfactorily by the fact that spousal choice increases in proportion to the population of the endogamous group. Marriage with a close kinsman becomes less of a necessity. In other words, first-cross-cousin marriage is above all a reflection of a restricted endogamous zone and not vice versa. Dunning (1959:152), who speaks of "availability of spouses," concurs with this analysis, and Rogers (1962:B48), too, envisages the possibility.

Some say that history may also play a role (Hallowell 1932). That is to say, first-cousin marriages may decline in response to acculturation, particularly missionary influence. Dunning (1959:118) found that the only people in Pekangekum who declared first-cross-cousin marriage to be improper were those who had lived away from the community and who unambiguously espoused the teaching of the Anglican Church. This suggests that ideas running contrary to local principles had only limited influence at the time of Dunning's fieldwork. According to our elderly informants at Big Trout Lake, the Anglican missionary there had little power over the choice of marriage partners.[13] They laugh about how, in the 1930s and 1940s, he was still tracking down cases of polygamy. It is only today that the younger generations, visibly influenced by the evangelical churches—and not the Anglican Church, whose clergy is largely native-born—are beginning to regard first-cross-cousin marriages as out of place. In short, in northwestern Ontario, the trend away from this type of marriage is quite recent; we are witnessing it firsthand.[14] It did not take place in some bygone time. An explicit cross-cousin marriage rule, corollary to this terminology, did not prevail a century or two ago and then disappear without a trace.[15]

Indeed, the main argument against the correlation between Dravidian nomenclatures and cross-cousin marriage is that informants do not mention this type of marriage as being the preferential or, a fortiori, prescribed form of marriage. In spite of his own theoretical convictions, Hallowell (1992:57) admits that "consequently, although marriages of actual cross cousins do occur, these cannot be regarded as preferential marriages." Dunning (1959:151) says the same thing in nearly the same terms: "There is therefore no stated preference for first-cousin marriage." Rogers (1962:B48), who takes a very factual ethnographic approach, states merely that the question did not seem particularly relevant to his informants.[16] This was also Désveaux's experience when he questioned his Big Trout Lake informants.

But if the question, framed in terms of cross cousins, made little sense to them, this does not mean that the a marriage ideal does not exist. Having explained that marriage used to be arranged by the fiancé's parents, our informants told us that, in the case of a woman, they tried to find a man who was *awijimoosh,* in other words, who, with respect to her, belonged to the category of "cross cousin/brother-in-law." Significantly, at that very moment, the female informant spontaneously illustrated the fact of belonging to the right category, not with a consanguineous relationship ("being cross cousins") but with a previous marriage relationship: "For example, there had already been a marriage between these two families, a brother from one and a sister from the other had already married each other." This informant's words found a greater echo in the marital statistics than if she had spoken of marriage between cross cousins. In fact, marriages between sibling groups at Big Trout Lake account for 41 marriages out of 244,[17] or close to 17 percent (compared with less than 9.5 percent for marriages between cross cousins).[18] There is no paradigm for the marriage relationship other than marriage itself. Marriage, as the basis for the consanguinity/affinity dichotomy, encompasses the parallel/cross difference but also goes beyond (since affines of affines are considered to be siblings, as our informants have confirmed).

Trivial though it may be, this statement makes an important point. Its validity can be measured indirectly by looking at the terminological adjustments resulting from each marriage. As a girl, our informant (now over eighty) was in a relation of affinity with one sibling group, but one generation removed: consequently she called the three men of the group *nin'akshim,* "my cross nephew, son of my brother- or sister-in-law," and she called the one woman *nin'akshim ikwem,* "my cross niece, daughter of my brother- or sister-in-law." Then her own sister married one of the brothers, who all therefore became her *niwijimoosh,* "my cross cousin, my brother-in-law," whereas the woman's term (i.e. "my cross niece") remained unchanged. The terminological adjustment concerns only the opposite sex, in other words, those with whom the question of a potential marriage subsists, or even becomes more salient in the wake of intervening changes.

One final series of ethnographic remarks may now be made. At Big Trout Lake, the affinal relationship is underscored by ribald jokes and insinuations. This consists of assigning any individual a "boyfriend" or a "girlfriend" (*omoshomen; nimoshom,* "my boyfriend/ my girlfriend"). In this constant game, the most varied and unlikely suppositions are advanced, particularly about the ages of the individuals involved, as long as they remain affines. Likewise, gifts of material goods are made between affines. These are not subject to reciprocity and therefore are embarrassing for the receiver. Nowadays they take the form of currency (Désveaux 1984:113). At Pekangekum, the gift-giving has a ceremonial character (Dunning 1959:158).[19] Sex and the circulation of money: how better to symbolize the spirit of affinity than by the two "crudest" components of the reality of marriage?

To sum up, when the ethnography of the largest North American center of "pure" Dravidian terminologies is examined in detail, it appears that neither the facts nor ideology substantiate the existence of privileged links between the terminological phenomenon and first cross-cousin marriage. This type of marriage is found purely and simply because it is compatible with Dravidian nomenclature. What does emerge is the existence of a social reality that is entirely focused on marriage and cuts society into two equivalent parts, doing so without any reference to descent groups. Hallowell (1975 [1937]:101, 1992:52), Dunning (1959:73), Rogers (1962:B10), and Turner and Wertman (1977:56) all perceived, to a greater or lesser extent, this radically ego-centered dualism. Ridington (1969:465–66), too, observed it among the quasi-Dravidian Beaver (Ives 1990:95–100): "The cross and parallel categories may be seen as moieties of the mind, for they remain egocentric and conceptual." Yet not one of these authors seems to have drawn the conclusions that were obvious from this ethnography, namely, envisaging the Dravidian nomenclature is not an expression of the practice of cross-cousin marriage but a cognitive device both engendering and reflecting ego-centered dualism of consanguines versus affines.

FORMAL ANALYSIS

Our formal analysis confirms the ethnographic reality. The question we pursued is as follows: Given an initial classification by generation, is there any way other than a Dravidian nomenclature (division into parallel and cross, assimilation of the latter to affines) of dividing—potentially ad infinitum[20]—the spheres of consanguinity and affinity into two parts as equivalently as possible from the logical and statistical standpoints, where ego is the absolute reference?[21]

Discrimination by rank (elder versus younger) is not taken into account. It is incompatible with the statistical requirement that the sibling group of a given individual must always contain an equal or superior number of persons of rank 1 as of rank X, independently of the individual's own position.

We will begin with G^0. Two and only two principles satisfy our criteria of bipartition. Either the division is based solely on difference of sex, in the absolute (men on one side, women on the other) or combined with a criterion of likeness of sex with ego (individuals of the same sex as ego on one side, those of opposite sex on the other), or it is based on (real or potential) marriage. Not only does the last hypothesis distinguish between siblings (brothers, sisters) and affines (brothers-in-law, sisters-in-law), but it potentially embraces the entire social field, giving rise to alternating membership by virtue of the logical rule that affines' affines are nonaffines; that is, they fall into the category of siblings (a principle whose operant validity has been verified in the field).

Given A, ego's division, and B, the alternate division:

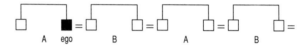

Division by sex and division stemming from marriage are statistically equivalent. We choose marriage as the relevant factor here because, following Lévi-Strauss, it is synonymous with the establishment of social order. A distinction founded solely on sex at G^0 would leave us in limbo concerning the state of society. Recall the strong implication of marriage as the first rule of an ego-centered bipartition. Ego is supposed to marry within the alternate division to his or her own; the incest taboo applies to all individuals in ego's category. This half of society is therefore forbidden to him or her.

But what about the cousins? Let us wait a bit before classifying cousins; contrary to appearances, there is no rush. Let us, rather, respect the practice of our predecessors and turn to G^{+1}: ego's uncles and aunts:[22]

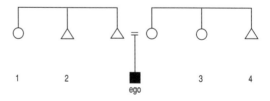

There are three possible two-class groupings that satisfy the stated statistical requirement:

α. [1] [2] versus [3] [4]. Paternals are on one side, maternals on the other.

β. [1] [3] versus [2] [4]. Individuals are grouped solely by sex, women on one side, men on the other.

γ. [1] [4] versus [2] [3]. Individuals are grouped according to whether each is of the same or opposite sex of each of ego's parents (i.e., his/her mother and father). This is called the parallel/cross formula, which prevails in reality.

Since, a priori, no argument favors one of these formulas over the others, we consider G^{-1}. These are ego's children, his nephews and nieces, as well as his sons- or daughters-in-law (as in the case of G^0, we temporarily ignore the children and children-in-law of ego's cousins).

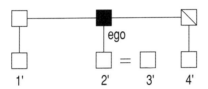

Note that we are looking at elements whose sex is indeterminate. Of course, it would be possible to envisage bipartition by sex (men on one side, women on the other), but it must be rejected because membership in [3'] does not depend on ego, but on the sex of ego's child [2']. We do not respect the constraint of ego-centeredness.

This leaves three possible ways of making up two classes:

α'. [1'] [2'] versus [3'] [4']. Ego's child and the child of his same-sex sibling are on one side, and his son- or daughter-in-law and the child of his opposite-sex sibling are on the other. This is called the parallel/cross solution, which prevails in reality.

β'. [1'] [3'] versus [2'] [4']. Ego's child and the child of his opposite-sex sibling are on one side, and his son- or daughter-in-law and the child of his same-sex sibling are on the other.

γ'. [1'] [4'] versus [2'] [3']. Children and their spouses are on one side, nephews and nieces on the other.

The last possibility (γ') can be discarded out of hand because of its statistical irregularity. An individual usually has fewer children and children-in-law than nephews and nieces (to whom must be added their spouses by virtue of the logic of this solution).

What now distinguishes (α') from (β') and makes it possible to prefer one solution to the other? It appears that (α') is more compatible with the discriminating criterion operating at the level of G^0, namely, marriage. Here the argument takes a cognitive turn that makes it more coherent: it is, in effect, more "natural" for the child of the opposite-sex sibling to "fall" into affinity. Although this sibling represents the prime taboo with respect to social order, he or she is nonetheless the embodiment of the most eloquent image, in the state of nature, of the definition of marriage: a social mode of existence that organizes the natural functions of individuals' sexual reproduction.[23]

Now we can return to G^{+1}. Of the three previous possibilities, solution (γ) is the obvious choice because it is the only one that is logically consistent with the solution that turned out to be relevant for G^{-1}: both discriminate in terms of likeness or unlikeness of sex between siblings.[24]

As for G^0 and the cousins, classification by sex must be rejected since it conflicts with the criterion retained for the rest of the members of G^0. The strong constraint here is the homogeneity of the whole generation involved. This leaves only two possibilities:

α''. The children of uncles or aunts classified as parallel are assimilated to siblings, and children of uncles or aunts classified as cross are assimilated to affines, which is the situation that prevails in reality.
β''. Conversely, the children of so-called parallel uncles or aunts are assimilated to affines and those of so-called cross uncles or aunts are assimilated to siblings.

The primacy of solution (a") is not based on the rule that an individual and his or her ascendant should belong to the same category (this does not work, for example, in the case of a child of an opposite-sex sibling), but on the principle of likeness or unlikeness of sex. However, the principle cannot operate on its own genealogical level, for that would be the same as establishing a simple division by sex, which was excluded above. It therefore operates at the level of the preceding generation, as it does in G^{-1}. Furthermore, this principle is what makes it possible to extend the nomenclature beyond the circle of first-degree kin.

The last individuals to be classified receive their respective places through two types of analogy:

1. *Terminological.* The parents-in-law belong to the alternate division from ego, as do the parents of cross cousins, since the latter are equated to brothers-in-law; cousins' children are classified in the same way as the children of a same-sex sibling or an opposite-sex sibling, depending on whether their parent who is consanguineous with Ego is assimilated to one or the other.
2. *Systematic.* Spouses of so-called parallel uncles and aunts are parallel and those of cross uncles and aunts are cross. If this were not so, all of these couples would be incestuous; it would be as though they comprised, terminologically speaking, siblings (in this case ego's paternal or maternal uncle and aunt). This permutation, which applies equally to parents-in-law, is the hardest for the mind to grasp because it places in the same virtual moiety individuals linked by

marriage. Nevertheless, in this case, too, the twofold constraint that we imposed in our formal analysis—ego-centeredness (the marriage of these individuals therefore does not enter into consideration here) and bipartition—is perfectly respected.[25]

These solutions are so economical from a logical standpoint that it seems difficult to think of any other solution for these cases. The +2 generation, that of the grandparents, has only one classification by sex. G^{-2}, the grandchildren, has none at all. This brings us back to marriage as the basis for bipartition. These generations stand at the edge of the very affinal classification they neutralize. The two-generation space is enough to make it irrelevant, the reason being that, except for individual accidents, ego is not supposed to find a spouse in one of these. It could also be noted that, from a formal standpoint, an ego-centered classification of these individuals would require a cumbersome set of rules and would therefore be contrary to the spirit of the system described up to this point (which, in the end, uses only three rules: marriage, likeness of same-sex siblings, and terminological alignment).

Dravidian reasoning now appears as a binary cognitive structure, a corollary of the invention of marriage as the basis of culture. The opposite-sex sibling plays a crucial role in its structuring, since he or she stands at the articulation between the two spaces defined by the logical mechanism inherent in this nomenclature. In effect, while this sibling is born of the same alliance as ego, namely, the marriage of their common parents (genitors)—and therefore is in a way engendered by the same closure of the affinal field—, he or she almost immediately reopens the field of affinity to the opposite-sex sibling by the intermediary of his or her own children, who are already cross kin. In this respect, the few Amazonian societies that regularly practice oblique marriage with the sister's daughter are exemplary in that they exploit this potentiality of Dravidian nomenclatures (Dreyfus-Gamelon 1993). That being said, the fact that these marriage practices are restricted to a fairly small culture area is in turn evidence of the relative autonomy of the forms of marriage actually contracted in societies with Dravidian nomenclatures.

CORRELATES

In uncovering the Dravidian substratum underlying Dene nomenclatures, Asch (chapter 5) and Ives (1990, chapter 4 in this volume) have dusted off the old classification of North American kinship systems established by Spier (1925) and shaken up the cultural ecologism that has dominated interpretations of Mackenzie River social organizations. Even more significant, their work has revealed a continuity between the two major linguistic blocs of North America that share the immense Subarctic zone: Algonquian and Athapascan. In this area, as Asch and Ives point out, social organization is based on residence, or, more accurately, on the overall social entity being split up into small bands of individuals—co-residents—who hunt together for the better part of the year. The formation of hunting bands (residential units even though they often move) comes out of interaction between individuals of the same generation according to a potentially variable underlying principle, which

Asch brings out in his ethnography of the Wrigley Dene and which he shows to be thoroughly consistent with Dravidian logic. These Indians have a negative rule for constituting winter bands: adult brother and sister must not reside together. This explicit and apparently new formulation states the only two conceivable possibilities of association: either the band forms around the nucleus comprised of two brothers, which is the most frequent one and is illustrated by the Wrigley Dene; or around that comprised of two brothers-in-law (i.e., by a brother and a sister), which is much less frequent, but the prevailing choice among Big Trout Lake Indians (Désveaux 1988a). It is striking to see how closely band formation fits the deep logic of Dravidian nomenclature: preeminence of generation and ego-centered dualism based on radical opposition of relations between same- or opposite-sex siblings.[26]

One is thus forced to bow to the evidence that descent reckoning plays only a minor role, if any at all, in Subarctic social organizations. The terms "bilaterality" or "cognatism," normally conjugated with "flexibility," abound in all of the literature on the Subarctic. Yet a closer examination of these repetitions leaves something wanting, as though use of these ambiguous notions did not mean much more than the inability of ethnologists to come up with any alternative to residence as an organizing principle.[27] In effect, the question of bilaterality arises only in conjunction with that of unilineal descent. But the ego-centered logic just examined does not involve a unilineal descent rule, at least not of necessity: our entire approach up to this point has been to show that a Dravidian system refers uniquely to ego and his affinal group. How far we are from Dumont's (1975:48–49) theory, which rests entirely on the assumption that ego's position, especially with regard to his affines, is inherited, in other words is relative to that of his parents. For us, ego's place in society in no way implies that the position is inherited, unless the transmission is considered to be ensured by nature, which would deprive the concept of kinship of all meaning, something neither Dumont nor any other *social* anthropologist would wish. And if this is so, must we not renounce the necessity of descent reckoning, just as we gave up that of cross-cousin marriage? It is symptomatic in this respect that, when we were attempting earlier to identify the descent rules of Big Trout Lake Indians, our analysis always brought us directly back to the management of space and that, behind this, sooner or later we would come up against the various marriage practices (Désveaux 1988a:284–90). "Pure Dravidian" logic is the *degré zéro* of descent reckoning.

SUGGESTIONS

How does one get from Dravidian systems to the Iroquois or the Crow-Omaha, from either a purely formal standpoint or in an evolutionistic perspective? The results we have obtained—the ego-centered nature of the nomenclature, absolute primacy of the antecedence of marriage practices, even to the detriment of the emergence of descent reckoning—enable us to formulate a few working hypotheses for further reflection.

In a Dravidian system such as the one we have described, cross-cousin marriage is neither recommended nor forbidden. According to Lévi-Strauss's (1949) classification, this marriage model belongs to the class of complex structures. As long as marriages are more or less evenly distributed over the endogamous reference area, the structural superiority of wife-givers over wife-takers tends to be dissolved in the social body. This is a neutral situation both in terms of rank and of the division of society into moieties or clans.[28] But what happens, on the formal level, when cross-cousin marriage assumes special importance, becomes preferential?

When cross cousins are encouraged to marry, the tension between givers and takers of wives rises, owing to the concentration of the one or the other within a limited space of consanguinity. This marriage rule harbors potent destructive powers. It therefore tends to be tempered by a bias (from a male ego's standpoint) either toward the maternals or toward the paternals.

Matrilateral cross-cousin marriage, though a part of generalized exchange, creates a de facto imbalance in favor of the maternal side. From the standpoint of its sociological effects, it still bears a close resemblance to nonspecific bilateral cross-cousin marriage, and one may wonder precisely to what extent these forms of marriage do not finally merge on the ethnographic horizon. Two solutions are available that mitigate the disadvantages inherent in these forms, which engender both a loss of dualism and the introduction of rank.

The first solution is to forbid marriage between cross cousins in order to avoid the ensuing imbalances. The effects are considerable: as the paternals are no longer structurally inferior to the maternals, they can emerge and assert their lines, whence the appearance of exogamous patrilineal clans. Another advantage of this prohibition is that the clans remain equal among themselves—the earlier ideal is preserved on this register—just as the earlier dualism subsists and is simply transposed to another level. Only the ego-centered nature of the system is lost.

This abstract situation corresponds exactly to that of the central Algonquian groups that form the territorial and linguistic continuation of the "pure" Dravidian center of northwestern Ontario and the adjacent part of Manitoba. For instance, the Menomini had a clan division that was subsumed by moieties whose function was largely ceremonial. But it is particularly the Sauk, Fox, Kickapoo, and Potawatomi whose dual arrangements are most exemplary. These groups had institutions that integrally preserved the principle of statistical regularity inherent in Dravidian ego-centered dualism. Here an individual's moiety membership did not depend on the descent group but on the individual's birth order. Among the Fox, the two moieties, called *kishkoha* and *tohkan,* were composed according to a rule of alternating births: the first-born belonged to the father's alternate moiety, the second-born, to the father's own moiety, and so on. This is a particularly effective method of distribution for preserving equal numbers in the moieties, in that the advantage introduced in the first generation (by the fact that there are more elder than younger siblings) is made up in the next generation, where the ranking is reversed.

The alternating dualist formula of the Potawatomi is statistically somewhat more rigid, since the first-born is always assigned to the same moiety, *askasa,* and the second, to the opposite, *ki'sko'ha;* but being totally separate from descent reckoning, this formula eased the integration of individuals from outside the group. It is thought that the Sauk had a system midway between that of the Fox and that of the Potawatomi. Among the Kickapoo, membership depended on naming: the child belonged to the moiety of the person designated to choose his or her name (Callender 1962:32 ff.).

Our hypothesis for "exiting" the Dravidian system via prohibition of cross-cousin marriage is compatible with the formal side of Trautmann and Barnes's transformation sequence. We recognize the concomitance between prohibition of this type of marriage, modification of the nomenclatures with crossness, skewing of nomenclatures, and appearance of "totemic" patrilineal descent groups (see chapter 2), not forgetting disaffection for the residence rule (a clan being by nature unaffected by this factor).[29] The early stages of this logical transformation—changeover from A- to B-type crossness, which these authors isolated—is illustrated within the Ojibwa family by the nomenclature collected in the last century by Jacker. The parallel with South America is striking. The same dichotomy can be found among the nonunilineal societies of Amazonia having a Dravidian nomenclature—where the residential factor is determining—and in central Brazilian societies in which unilineal descent rules go hand in hand with strong residual dualism in the institutions (Hornborg 1993).[30]

The second solution is to forbid matrilateral marriage in favor of patrilateral unions. Here, the wife-giver's situation is given a lasting advantage over that of the wife-taker's. This induces the emergence of matrilineality accompanied by ranking of family lines, unless, in order to avoid such an imbalance, exchange becomes more restrictive, with women being returned as rapidly as possible, in the following generation. In the latter case, the lines automatically form into two moieties, and the dualism lost in the preceding stage is "resurrected." Without going into the details of Athapaskan ethnography, but taking our inspiration from Rubel and Rosman's (1983) reading, we find that the matrilineal societies of the Rocky Mountains and the Pacific Coast, contrary to the still largely "Dravidian" groups of the Mackenzie Basin, oscillate between these two formal possibilities. At times they appear to be governed by a dual regime with strict conditions of matrimonial and ceremonial reciprocity (Tutchone, Kaska, Eyak, Ahtna), at times by economic competition or political rivalry between clans (Haida, Tlingit) and at times by both.[31]

CONCLUSION

The original Dravidian model—that of the Indian subcontinent—states a positive marriage rule: marriage with the cross cousin, linked to a kinship terminology based on the parallel/cross distinction and the complete assimilation of affines to cross kin. This rule reflects nothing more than the presence of already constituted lines engaged in restricted exchange with each other, as both Lévi-Strauss and Dumont have shown. Trautmann and Barnes (chapter 2) argue in favor of a methodological requisite that would distinguish the "original" Dravidian systems from those found in other parts of the world, particularly the New World. They are right, and perhaps we should go even farther and deplore, from a North Americanist point of view, the fact that Morgan was introduced to the Asian Indian model too soon. In effect, this led to a great deal of confusion, sending subsequent anthropologists chasing after a veritable mythical beast, namely, this famous rule of cross-cousin marriage. In North America, where there is a Dravidian system, there is no positive cross-cousin marriage rule. In fact, cross-cousin marriage is not a structural reality. We are on a level below this phenomenon. Dravidian nomenclatures and this type of marriage are not linked; furthermore, it is only when the first fades away that the second really appears—in the full light of day, in its patrilateral form among the matrilineal Athapaskans, or as a negative of the matrilateral form among the patrilineal central Algonquins.

NOTES

This chapter was translated by Nora Scott. It is a completely revised version of a talk given by Emmanuel Désveaux at the roundtable, "Dravidian, Iroquois, and Crow-Omaha Kinship," held in Paris, June 3–5, 1993. It incorporates the initial results of the computer processing of the genealogical field data using the program GEN.PAR©, written by Marion Selz and P. Jeanet. Selz also participated in the formal analysis.

1. We must wait for the new edition of the *Handbook of American Indians* to see an accurate linguistic map of the region. We now speak of Northern Ojibwa (Rogers and Taylor 1981), who nevertheless exhibit fairly marked dialectal variations within the group. Only one of these dialects, Severn, has yet been studied in depth (Todd 1970).
2. The northernmost group today includes the following communities: Big Trout Lake, Kasabonika, Wunnimum Lake, Kingfisher Lake, Wapakeka (Angling Lake), Bearskin Lake, Sachigo, Muskrat Dam, and Wawakapewin (Long Dog Lake). Désveaux spent more than two years with this group some ten years ago (1984, 1988a) and had the good fortune to return in the summer of 1993, which gave him the chance to ask his informants some new questions inspired by the discussions that took place at the roundtable.
3. We have kept the name in our work (Désveaux 1984). The strong attachment the informants express for Big Trout Lake (for those who do not live there) cannot be dissociated from what might be called their "awareness of endogamy," in other words, their positive conception of a social space within which marriages are contracted. This awareness corresponds to reality, in that the corpus of 470 marriages (spread over three to five generations, depending on the lines, and including three-quarters of the population) compiled during our study shows a low rate of marriage outside the group: around 20 percent (Désveaux 1984:7). In fact, it appears that all of these northwestern Ontario groups—this time including the coastal Cree communities—and those of the adjacent parts of Manitoba are governed, above and beyond some linguistic and sociological differences, by the same strong penchant for endogamy, which distinguishes this region from the Labrador peninsula, where a high degree of exogamy seems to have long prevailed (Désveaux 1984:160–61).
4. Algonquian languages do not have a masculine and a feminine (the basic genders are animate versus inanimate); the word *ikwem,* meaning "girl" or "woman," or "female" when speaking of an animal, is added to mark the female gender of the main predicate. Its presence in the kinship nomenclature does not stem from any logic inherent in the system but from common sense.
5. In a Dravidian nomenclature, G^0 is a veritable pivotal point from the standpoint of the speaker's sex; reference to "uncles," "aunts," and parents-in-law is independent of ego's sex, while that of the "nephews" and "nieces," on the one hand, and the "sons-in-law" and "daughters-in-law, on the other, are reversed as a function of ego's sex.

6. It is not yet understood why this mark of seniority is reserved for males (see note 25).

7. To this must be added a category of sociological outsiders, the *peonuk*, a term that can be glossed as "foreigners" or "outsiders," but that actually designates "nonkin."

8. However, the difference induced by the speaker's sex for G^0 does not always appear in these monographs as clearly or systematically as in Big Trout Lake.

9. We have not included in this list the Emo Ojibwa, whose terminology is not exactly Dravidian: there is a slight difference between the terms for cross cousin and brother-in-law (Landes 1969[1939]:10).

10. These authors prefer to reconstruct the category of affines by opposition to a sociological principle of "incorporation."

11. Our reference corpus contains 470 marriages over an average range of four generations. Only 104 marriages are used here, the only relevant unions being those contracted between individuals for whom all four grandparents are known (which is the only way of determining if they are related as cousins). Also note the total absence from this corpus of marriage between first parallel cousins.

12. Strong (1929:279) comes up with a much higher rate for the Naskapi (five out of fourteen marriages). And yet he does not write "between first cousins," but only between "cross cousins." Furthermore, the interpretation of his data raises difficulties similar to those found with Hallowell's figures for Island Lake. Strong's "band" of fourteen marriages, or twenty-eight individuals, obviously does not constitute an endogamous entity. There have to be other marriages contracted elsewhere. In the end, the ratio of five out of fourteen is more suggestive of an endogamy indicator for the "band" in question than its rate of first-cross-cousin marriage. The same could be said of the five first-cousin marriages out of twenty-one that Dunning records for his generation II, the oldest of the three generations in his table.

13. Reverend Garret was the first white missionary to live full-time at Big Trout Lake. He arrived in 1924 and did not leave the community until 1949.

14. The trend is accompanied by terminological transformations (as was predicted in the case of the relation between nomenclature and system of marriage). At Big Trout Lake, the innovation consists of introducing new terms. For a male speaker, for instance, the close cross cousin (whose sister is therefore forbidden as spouse) will be called *nistes,* a term borrowed from the Shamattawa nomenclature, where it designates the elder brother and the parallel cousin (Turner and Wertman 1977:69).

15. After a period of acute "historicism," which denied Indian societies any aboriginality once they had been taken into the fur trade, an about-face occurred in favor of a more ethnographic vision of these societies and of the idea that, in the end, their structures had suffered little until their recent collapse under the blows of contemporary modernity. One of the merits of Ives's book (1990) is his strong defense of this thesis, which Désveaux (1988b), too, has always upheld on the more modest scale of northwestern Ontario.

16. Once again, Strong (1928:279), speaking of the Naskapi, breaks with the overall picture of northwestern Ontario: "Informants stated that among the Barren Ground, White Whale River, and Ungava Bands this form of marriage was considered most correct and was urged on the younger people by their elders." Allowances should be made in reading his account, which betrays his enthusiasm at having discovered a nomenclature and marriages that fit Rivers theoretical construction. At any rate, he was using secondhand information since he himself was staying with a group connected to the Davis Inlet Band.

17. We have used only those individuals whose two parents are known (see note 11).

18. Our informants confirmed that the ideal marriage is not sister exchange but the repetition of marriages between two sibling groups. Our genealogical records show little difference between the number of marriages by sister exchange (23) and those between two brothers and two sisters (18). At Berens River, according to Hallowell's (1975[1937]:236) informants, the ideal is that two brothers marry two sisters.

19. Strong (1929:283) recorded the same sort of affinal marking among the Naskapi. The two "brothers-in-law" tried to show each other their penis and scolded each other, each demanding the other's sister.

20. This is illustrated by the Campa of the Andean foothills (see chapter 10 of this volume).

21. I am intellectually indebted here to Lounsbury's (1964a) strategy for elucidating Iroquois systems, which Trautmann (1981) later adopted and applied to South Indian Dravidian systems. But where Lounsbury tried to find positive rules for generating (in Chomsky's sense) kinship terms, we have proceeded by elimination of all possibilities (in the mathematical sense) after having defined a minimum set of constraints.

22. The prohibition on incest puts ego's opposite-sex parent in the same category as ego. We can temporarily ignore the other parent.

23. For a similar expression of the same idea, see Héritier 1981:171.

24. Solution (γ) cannot be criticized for not being exactly ego-centered inasmuch as an individual of necessity has two parents, and so he has "one foot" in each gender.

25. For the same reason and referring to note 18, ego's same-sex parent belongs to his own division. The statistical balance is respected since we have parents on one side and in-laws on the other.

26. This explains why seniority in a sibling group is not discriminated from the male standpoint: a woman is neutral with respect to the formation of bands. Whichever rule pertains, co-residence of brothers or co-residence of brother and sister, two sisters can always belong to the same band (see note 6).

27. This was a good learning experience nevertheless, notably in the case of the Mackenzie Basin. It was by emphasizing the dialectic between "local band" and "regional band" and by talking about "socio-territorial entities" that Helm (1965) showed the emptiness of the idea of patrilocal band, the doctrinal core of Steward's vision of hunting bands. But short of a pure tautology (people have kin on both sides), the transformation of "locality" into "bilaterality" is a questionable enterprise.

28. Except on the individual level: in this instance, it is the classic figure, in Subarctic ethnography, of the shaman or the prophet that emerges on his own behalf (Désveaux 1991:122–25).

29. Alternatively, while we readily acknowledge that the increase in the density of populations that can be seen in the Great Lakes region compared with the Subarctic makes prohibition of cross-cousin marriage easier (whence the appearance of unilineal descent groups), we do not see how this makes it necessary.

30. Dreyfus-Gamelon (1993), Taylor (chapter 8), and Viveiros de Castro and Fausto (1993) all stress the importance of co-residence in the Dravidian systems of Amazonia. Lastly, a parallel can be seen in the choice of names. Among the central Algonquians as among the Ge, names are the prerogative of the clans or the stake in complex transmission strategies, but always in connection with clan membership.

31. Might this quasi-paranoid situation have the effect of reintroducing matrilateral marriage in order to mitigate the imbalances induced by patrilateral marriage, as is suggested by the Tsimshian and northern Tutchone cases?

7

Serial Redundancy in Amazonian Social Structure:
Is There a Method for Poststructuralist Comparison?

ALF HORNBORG

In surveying the ethnographic literature on indigenous social organization in low-land South America, one cannot fail to be intrigued by the tantalizing *redundancies* that seem to intertwine native models of society throughout this vast region. It is easy to appreciate the extent to which South American ethnography inspired Lévi-Strauss's pursuit of underlying "deep structures" shared by numerous empirical cases. Writing about the Gé linguistic family of central and eastern Brazil, Lévi-Strauss (1963:130) visualizes "a series of expressions, each partial and incomplete, of the same underlying structure, which they reproduce in several copies without ever completely exhausting its reality." The structuralist project was essentially a matter of formulating that "same underlying structure." In other words, it was founded on the assumption that the anthropologist's recognition of recurrent patterns was like catching sporadic glimpses of an invariant whole. However, regional congrui-ties in social classification have proved too elusive to be usefully captured in a single model. Needham (1971:13) has suggested that such structural redundancies were more like "serial likenesses," or, in Wittgenstein's words, like the overlapping of many fibers in a thread (Needham 1971:30). As this chapter explains, precisely this "seriality" may be a key to finding an epistemologically modest and nonreductionist mode of comparison, which balances formalism and relativism, structure and practice, continuity and change.

THEORETICAL POINTS OF DEPARTURE

A lasting contribution of Lévi-Strauss's structuralism, of course, is its epistemo-logical skepticism. But precisely this refusal to be content with any one representa-tion was what ultimately turned structuralism against itself. Poststructuralist an-thropologists argue that their own models cannot claim to appropriate "reality" any more than those that they try to retrieve from the natives. Structuralism itself was instrumental in bringing about this epistemological break. It was the "consuming fire" (Ardener 1985:65) that "expressed" the shift from scientific, universalist aspirations to a truly relativistic experience of cultural multiplicity. Now that the smoke from this traumatic holocaust is beginning to dissipate, however, we find ourselves as puzzled by structural congruities as Lévi-Strauss ever was. The intriguing redundancies in the ethnographic record are still there, and we must ask ourselves how to approach cross-cultural comparison without reducing the dynamic multiplicity of culture to appropriative, master narratives.

It is ironic that an accomplished comparativist such as Needham (1971:13) should conclude that detailed and large-scale comparison may be simply "impracticable," while dedicated ethnographers like Crocker (1977:256) and Seeger (1981:235–36) emphatically call for more comparative analyses. This mutual humility indicates that both approaches, formal comparison as well as an exploration of the "tautological hermeneutics" (Crocker 1977:256) of single societies, have their limitations. Shapiro (1984:13) sums up the situation by observing that insights gained from symbolic and interpretive approaches "must now be formulated in terms appropriate to focused and specific comparative research." This crucial but extremely problematic anthropological challenge nevertheless demands that we first clarify what we take to be the objectives of "comparative research."

If we are to compare, we must first agree on the nature of the phenomena we are comparing. Needham (1971:32) and Sperber (1985) argue convincingly that ethnography is the documentation of native *representations,* not of the behavioral realities for which they claim to stand. This basic premise of structuralism is shared by the mainstream of postmodernist anthropology. But there is another aspect, prominent particularly in Anglo-Saxon structuralism, that is not as widely accepted. Inasmuch as behavioral realities can at all be assumed to feature regularities, order, or structure, Needham has consistently proposed that such regularities are an *aspect* of (i.e., are generated and defined by) the native system of classification. In effect, social structure is unilaterally determined by, or even reducible to, a cognitive code. This aspect of structuralism has been challenged by what Ortner (1984) collectively labels "practice theory," that is, various recognitions (e.g., Bourdieu, Sahlins, Giddens) of the extent to which social behavior unfolds according to its own, generative logic. Individual strategies of action are certainly informed by shared systems of meaning, but there is always room for innovation yielding new, imperfectly recognized patterns. The elusive realm of social "performance" thus features a measure of autonomy, even opacity, vis-à-vis the "code." In this sense, the objection of "practice theory" against the most mentalist, Saussurian aspects of structuralism converges with earlier, materialist critiques and, in fact, with several explicit formulations by Lévi-Strauss himself (e.g., 1969:xxx–xxxiv).

One must assume that there are objective regularities in social behavior (what Sahlins has called "the structure of the practice"), while recognizing that they can only be perceived and codified in an imperfect and subjective way. Conversely, the implementation of the code ("the practice of the structure") is flexible and innovative. This mutual indeterminacy leaves code and performance each with the measure of freedom required in order to account for the *shifts of emphasis* referred to as "structural transformations." As Ortner (1984:146–47, 150) observes, the new emphasis on "practice" does not imply a denial of any determination by "the system" (structure, code), for the study of practice and the study of structure should be complementary rather than antagonistic. There is indeed a risk of reifying an inferred structure as a prescriptive code, but since behavior cannot be described or even visualized in terms other than structure, and since one can hardly deny that all human actors are to a certain extent guided by such organized visions, the anthropological pursuit of other people's representations will continue to be legitimate. Any attempt at emic, "ethnosociological" explication remains merely a *perspective,* but nonetheless becomes a *program* capable of bending behavior toward a certain inclination. It is in terms of this dialectic that I have tried to account for the variation in Amazonian kinship systems (Hornborg 1986/1988). Patrilineal descent, for instance, can be seen as a *hegemonization* of the male perspective, where there were originally separate, gender-specific views, as in "sex affiliation" or "parallel transmission."

Against this background, what can one make of serial redundancies in native representations? What do they represent? The debate on the *locus* of structure seemed to come to a stalemate when Lévi-Strauss (1969 [1949]:xxx) observed that cultural models are able to "duplicate" natural mechanisms because the brain itself belongs to nature. The *seriality* of structural congruities suggests indications of motion and change, rather than partial views of an invariant whole. The various representations of society documented throughout lowland South America appear to be segments of a *continuum,* and as such they may be assumed to correspond to real transformational processes. Traditional structuralism has focused on the mental operations through which reality is reconceptualized, but the least one can do is to *assume* that a continuum of such conceptualizations may correspond to a process of behavioral (rather than merely cognitive) modifications. The nature of these behavioral correlates can only be arrived at indirectly, since any representation (native or anthropological) can only amount to a particular perspective on a segment of a fluid and multifaceted process. Anthropologists may simply have to accept that they will always be caught midway in the dialectic between structure and practice. The "practice" position cannot avoid structural formulations in order to account for continuity, but structuralism must also be reconsidered in order to accommodate change. If structural redundancies in a series of native representations are merely taken to approximate universal structures of the human mind, rather than an elusive and mutable social reality, the point of orientation is fixed and unresponsive, and there can be no dialectical movement.

Lowland South American Ethnography: A Continuum of Serial Likenesses

This discussion concentrates on ten recurrent features of social classification in the South American lowlands, and the structural contiguities that suggest how they may be ordered along a transformational continuum. These features are (1) two-line or kin-affine (Dravidian) relationship terminologies, (2) the equivalence of alternate generations, (3) parallel transmission, (4) cross transmission, (5) affinal grandkin equations, (6) oblique marriage preferences, (7) unilateral cross-cousin marriage preferences, (8) lineal (Crow-Omaha) relationship terminologies, (9) unilineal transmission ("descent"), and (10) "Iroquois" relationship terminologies. These features seem to be structurally interrelated in various ways, and this entire spectrum may represent a chain of transitions between two polar sets of conditions defined in terms of the extent of social integration, patterns of postmarital residence, and the conceptualization of affinal relationships.

Dravidian Relationship Terminologies

During the past two decades, Louis Dumont's (1953) two-line or kin-affine interpretation of what is otherwise called the parallel/cross distinction in Dravidian terminologies from southern India has helped to shape anthropologists' understanding of social classification in lowland South America (Overing Kaplan 1973; Rivière 1973; Kensinger 1977, 1984a). Since kin and affines are distinguished only in the three medial generations, such a terminology seems an ideal "code" for regulating marriage exchange within cognatic, endogamous local groups (Overing Kaplan 1973). The fact that both parents are classified as kin testifies to its basically cognatic character, as does the transience and ego-centered nature of its "lineality." In terms of societal integration, it represents the "simplest" (Needham 1967:45) and "most atomistic" (Overing Kaplan 1975:194) system conceivable, and it is so fundamental to lowland South American culture that it has been advanced as its "structural definition" (Rivière 1973). Dravidian terminologies divide ego's social universe according to generation, sex, and kin-affine status, and the latter coincides with a consistent cross-versus-parallel distinction (Scheffler 1971). (There is often also a distinction of relative age, particularly among ego's siblings.) The merging of cross collaterals and affines in the three medial generations is its most significant feature (Buchler and Selby 1968:233), for this is an obvious correlate of a high incidence of brother-sister exchange marriage, which over time will imply a tendency toward "bilateral cross-cousin marriage" (see Trautmann 1981:23–24).

In Amazonia, Dravidian terminologies are particularly dominant among Caribs (Rivière 1977), Panoans (Siskind 1973:200; Dole 1979; Fields and Merrifield 1980; Kensinger 1984b), and Yanoama-speakers (Lizot 1971; Ramos and Albert 1977). Tukanoan terminologies have also been classified as Dravidian (Hugh-Jones 1979:76; Arhem 1981:36–37; Jackson 1984:160), but some of them seem to deviate from Dumont's classical definition in at least two ways. The patrilineal Barasana and Makuna both recognize separate affinal terms for male ego's wife, wife's parents, and children's spouses, and, although linguistics suggests differently, both apparently reverse the positions of MZ and FZ in the kin-affine dichotomy (Hugh-Jones 1979:79; Arhem 1981:37, 341–42).[1] These two deviations may be interrelated, since a patrilineal classification of FZ as kinswoman rather than affine renders the Dravidian equation FZ = WM more problematic than in cognatic systems.[2] The tendency to distinguish terminologically between FZ and WM in some Tukanoan societies may reflect the need to redefine patrilineal kinswomen as affines upon male ego's marriage with a patrilateral cross cousin. Consequently, their exogamous patrisib model seems to be pushing the Dravidian system toward a nonprescriptive, "Iroquois" derivative.[3]

The incongruity of these two types of dual classification (the ego-centered, cognatic, Dravidian form and the "socio-centered," unilineal one) is consistent with their complementary distribution in the South American lowlands. Dravidian terminologies are generally most intact where unilineal descent is weakest, such as among Guyana Caribs (Rivière 1984), Yanoama, and the Piaroa (Overing Kaplan 1973), whereas distinct affinal terms tend to occur wherever lineages or moieties are strong, as among Tukanoans, Gé, and Tupí.[4] A significant exception is found among the Panoans of eastern Peru.

Alternating Generations

Pano-speaking groups such as the Cashinahua, Sharanahua, and Mayoruna suggest a specific development of the Dravidian model (Hornborg 1993). They are almost unique in South America in having unilineal moieties but lacking separate affinal terms.[5] How, then, do they reconcile the affinal, Dravidian equation FZ = WM with a system of exogamous patrimoieties? Their solution is the Kariera model so well known from Australia. Panoan terminologies are perfectly aligned with a system of four "socio-centered" marriage classes (Fields and Merrifield 1980; Kensinger 1980, 1984b), which equate alternate generations of males (e.g., FF = male ego = SS) and females (e.g., MM = female ego = DD).[6] From the point of view of any ego, this system restricts the applicability of the kin-affine dichotomy to alternate generations only (G^{+2}, G^0, G^{-2}, etc.). In other words, even if FZ is grouped patrilineally with F, the category FZ/WM is "exempt" from the dual scheme and is neither exclusively kin or affine. The Kariera system, which is clearly a variant of the Dravidian pattern (Scheffler 1971:243, n. 12), seems to be a cognitive adaptation to the emergence of socio-centered kin-affine dichotomies in societies practicing genealogically close (e.g., bilateral cross-cousin) marriage.[7] As such, it could be seen as an alternative solution to the Iroquois one of introducing separate affinal terms.

Parallel Transmission

By emphasizing the equivalence of alternate generations, the Panoans exploit a logical regularity inherent in all Dravidian systems (see Trautmann 1981:197–99).[8] Another such logical regularity of Dravidian systems is the implicit principle of parallel transmission (or sex affiliation), which perpetuates two male (F to S) and two female (M to D) same-sex "lines" and restricts "affinity" primarily to relationships between persons of the same sex (Dumont 1953:35; Overing Kaplan 1973:562; Trautmann 1981:78–79, 174; Henley 1982:96; Journet 1993; also chapters 5, 6, and 10 of this volume).[9] Such a doubling of perspectives could be referred to as the *parallel transmission of affinal relationships*. This feature, too, would alleviate the contradictory status of FZ/WM among the Panoans, as a male ego's mother-in-law would not have to be considered an affine. Alternating generations and parallel (or bilineal)[10] transmission can in fact be seen merely as two perspectives on the same regularity, as bilateral cross-cousin marriage will merge the male and female "lines" in alternate generations (see Lawrence 1937; Murdock 1949:51–56; Lévi-Strauss 1969 [1949]:219, 1973:109–11).[11] I will argue that the coexistence of two complementary, gender-specific perspectives provides the seeds of unilineal reifications.

Cross Transmission

Another possible perspective derivable from bilateral marriage exchange is that of cross transmission (from MB to ZS and from FZ to BD), which is characteristic of the transfer of names among the Northern Gé. It could be seen as a transformation of parallel transmission (Scheffler and Lounsbury 1971:188–89; Lévi-Strauss 1973:110), or merely an alternative perspective on similar regularities in social reproduction. In a context of bilateral or patrilateral cross-cousin marriage, cross transmission is congruent with alternating generations (e.g., transmission from MB to ZS yields transmission from FF to SS), and Gé name-givers may just as well be grandparents as cross uncles and aunts. Names thus tend to recur in alternate generations (Seeger 1981:137). Name transmission among the Northern Gé is explicitly congruent with symmetric alliance. Lave (1979:20, 21, 31) notes that Krikatí naming is ideally a reciprocal exchange between cross-sex siblings (a brother naming his ZS and his sister naming her BD), as is, of course, bilateral cross-cousin marriage (see Shapiro 1985:3, 6–7). Among the Suyá, a man ideally marries the daughter of his *ngedi,* that is, a MB and a prototypical name-giver (Seeger 1981:129, 132, 261). Though Gé terminologies are far removed from the Dravidian pattern, its basic principles persist in recodified forms (alternating generations, parallel transmission, cross transmission). The connection between name transmission and marriage arrangements is fundamental and pervasive in this area of Brazil (see Nimuendajú 1942 on the Sherente). Among the Tupí-speaking Kagwahiv, naming and adoption into avunculocal residence combines with cross-cousin marriage as a culturally standardized mode of succession (Kracke 1984:107–8, 113). By naming it, a Kagwahiv brother explicitly claims his sister's child for betrothal to his own. Owing to uxorilocal residence, male ego would succeed his MB both as "brother" vis-à-vis the female matriline of his natal household, and as head of his postmarital household. Affinity and succession would be one, and it is obvious that a concept of matrilineal "descent" would only confuse the matter (but see de Heusch 1981:61, on identical conditions among the matrilineal Bemba of Zambia).[12]

Affinal Grandkin Equations

Gé name-givers, as already noted, are prototypically either grandparents or potential parents-in-law ("cross aunts" and "cross uncles"), and grandkin are generally equated with affinal categories (GrF = MB = SpF, GrM = FZ = SpM, GrCh = ZCh = ChSp). These are, in fact, the most common, transgenerational equations in South America and primarily seem to serve to widen the category of potential affines by effectively restricting consanguinity to the three medial generations. They seem to represent an important strategy for expanding ego's affinal categories in groups such as the Nambikwara, Waiwai, Trio, Sirionó, Txicáo, and Yanomam (on this last group, see Ramos and Albert 1977:82–83). Lévi-Strauss (1969 [1949]:121) observed that such equations are congruent with avuncular (ZD) marriage, and one might add that they are similarly conducive to other oblique marriages such as with FZ.

Oblique Marriage Preferences

Marriages with members of adjacent or alternate generations, respectively, seem to represent alternative and mutually exclusive means of expanding the range of genealogically close, potential spouses in Dravidian systems (Trautmann 1981:207, 235–36; Henley 1982:94–95, 104). The most common form of union between members of adjacent generations (oblique marriage) is between a man and his ZD. It is quite compatible with a Dravidian, two-line terminology (Lave 1966:196–97; Rivière 1966; Lévi-Strauss 1968; da Matta 1970:551; Needham 1972:16; Overing Kaplan 1984:153, n. 13), as it amounts to the assimilation of 0 and -1 generation, female affines. ZD marriage seems to have been a common strategy for avoiding bride-service among affines in predominantly uxorilocal societies such as the Guiana Caribs. Shapiro (1966:43–44) even speaks of "prescriptive" ZD marriage among some Tupí-speaking groups, where cross cousins and ZD are assimilated into a single category of potential spouses. The equation of cross cousins and ZD is common among Caribs and has also been documented, for instance, among the Gé-speaking Shavante (Maybury-Lewis 1967:216–17). Other, less common forms of oblique marriage are with a FZ, with a widowed MBW, or a secondary marriage with a WBD. FZ marriage, reported from the Bororo, for example, suggests a situation where female affines of G^0 are equated with those of G^{+1}, rather than G^{-1}.

Unilateral Cross-Cousin Marriage Preferences

Moore (1963:299) has suggested that oblique marriages illustrate "a kind of sexual succession" in that they "suggest which close relative (or relatives) in the generation above a young man or woman is the younger counterpart." Congruent with parallel transmission (the coexistence of inverse, male and female perspectives) is her observation that, from a female perspective, FZD succeeds FZ and MBD succeeds MBW, whereas, from a male perspective, ZD succeeds FZD and WBD succeeds MBD. Different oblique marriage preferences may thus be structurally associated with different unilateral cross-cousin preferences, depending on which principles of succession are emphasized and, one should add, on whether marriage ideals incline toward exogamy or endogamy. Discussing the Tupí-speaking Sirionó, Scheffler and Lounsbury (1971:175) suggest that parallel transmission in conjunction with exogamy would encourage marriage with the MBD rather than the FZD, as the relationship of a man to his FZD is "covertly equivalent to that of a man to his sister." Endogamous ideals, on the other hand, should favor the FZD.[13] Together, these two parameters (emphasis on male or female succession and on exogamy or endogamy) yield four structural combinations of oblique and unilateral cross-cousin marriage preferences, and Brazil offers empirical approximations of all four (table 7-1).

Table 7-1
Structural Equivalences of Male Ego's Potential Spouses under Different Regimes

Regime	Male Sucession	Female succession
Exogamy	MBD	MBD
	WBD	MBW
	Example: *Suyá*	Example: *Txicáo*
Endogamy	FZD	FZD
	ZD	FZ
	Example: *Sherente*	Example: *Bororo*

The Suyá, who are uxorilocal but whose political life emphasizes agnatic ties, prefer marriage with MBD, and include WBD in the marriageable category *hron* (W = BW = WBD) (Seeger 1981). The Txicáo, who seem to have very little agnatic cohesion with which to balance their uxorilocality, prescribe marriage with MBW or MBD (Menget 1977b). The uxorilocal but patrilineal Sherente may marry a FZD but not a MBD, and FZD is equated with ZD (kremzú) (Maybury-Lewis 1979b). The Bororo, finally, who strongly emphasize matrilateral succession (uxorilocality) but encourage "intimacy between a man and his father's group," rate FZ and FZD marriage as the most preferable (Crocker 1979:281, 292). It is noteworthy that elements of parallel transmission can be detected in all four of these groups, and that the Sherente and Bororo both have inclinations toward rank endogamy. It should also be noted that the two regimes associated with endogamy will generate Omaha and Crow equivalences, respectively. We may conclude that where Crow-Omaha equations represent positive marriage preferences, as among the Sherente and Bororo, they appear to be geared to endogamy.

It has often been observed that consistent ZD or FZ marriage will be equivalent to MBD marriage (Leach 1961:59–60, n. 2; Rivière 1966; Shapiro 1968:49; de Heusch 1981:42–43). Even where ZD marriage is generated as a structural complement to FZD marriage (see Moore 1963; de Heusch 1981:41–48; Trautmann 1981:206–7, 212–13), a high frequency of it may thus push toward the opposite practice.[14] Similarly paradoxical is the observation that consistent patrilateral cross-cousin marriage will be equivalent to classificatory matrilateral cross-cousin marriage, as FZD would tend to be a MMBDD (Needham 1962:109–10). Inversely, then, where a FZD preference is not explicit among the Gé (as it is for the Bororo and Karajá), a tendency toward patrilateral cross-cousin marriage may result from an ideal of matrilateral marriage combined with a prohibition of the actual MBD; this may have been the case for the Apinayé, Sherente, and Shavante (see Hornborg 1986/1988). The lineal kin equations that may be generated by oblique and MBD marriage (Omaha: MBD = M or Crow: MBD = D), by identifying MBD with incestuous categories, suggest that matrilateral cross-cousin marriage can be "self-extinguishing," producing a statistical predominance of FZD marriage (Eyde and Postal

1961). This is a possible interpretation for the Eastern Timbira (Krahó, Ramkoka-mekra, Kríkatí), among whom several terminological suggestions of MBD marriage are contradicted by a dislike for marriage to the actual MBD. In several Gé groups, FZD marriage is linked with cycles of alternating generations (the cyclical merging of male and female lines), as predicted by Lévi-Strauss (1969 [1949]:219; 1973:109–11).

Lineal (Crow-Omaha) Relationship Terminologies

Simply by distinguishing between patri- and matrilateral cross cousins, Crow-Omaha terminologies are congruent with unilateral marriage preferences.[15] The Crow-type relationship terminology of the Txicáo (Menget 1977b) is a perfect illustration of the congruity of Crow-Omaha terminologies and matrilateral cross-cousin marriage (Lane and Lane 1959; Eyde and Postal 1961). But by now one can see the many alternative series of congruities that lead from Dravidian to Crow-Omaha classification. The coexistence of Crow and Omaha equations in northern Gé groups such as the Kríkatí (Lave 1979:22) and Apinayé (da Matta 1973:291, 1979:123, 1982:126–27, 129) reflects their cross transmission of names (matrilineal for male names, patrilineal for female names), which in turn is congruent with parallel transmission and bilateral cross-cousin marriage, both of which are immanent in Dravidian terminologies. Crow-Omaha equations can also be logically generated from the affinal grandkin equations found in so many two-line terminologies throughout Amazonia. Or, one may say that affinal grandkin equations are conducive to Crow-Omaha.[16] Finally, of course, Crow-Omaha equations are congruent with oblique marriage (see Needham 1966a:27, 1972:24), which, as we have seen, is in itself compatible with Dravidian terminologies, and with various combinations of oblique and unilateral cross-cousin marriage, which again reflect principles of parallel transmission (Moore 1963).[17]

Moore's (1963) observations can be most economically summarized as follows: Crow-Omaha equations reflect the structural equivalence of ego and/or alter with his or her same-sex parent or child. Thus, male ego's FZD is equivalent to ZD if *he* identifies himself with his F, but with FZ if *she* is identified with her M. (Vice versa, male Ego's ZD is equivalent to FZD if he identifies himself with his S, and FZ to FZD if she is identified with her D.) Reciprocally, of course, female ego's MBS is equivalent to BS if *she* identifies herself with her M, but with MB if *he* is identified with his F. (And vice versa, female ego's BS is equivalent to MBS if she identifies herself with her D, and MB to MBS if he is identified with his S.)

The best way to understand the structural principles at work in generating Crow-Omaha equations is to see their "skewing" as the result of a *reification, or hegemonization,* of either the male or the female perspective in a Dravidian context of parallel transmission (figure 7-1). In the "gendered egocentricity" (Henley 1993) of such a Dravidian context, the series FZ-FZD-ZD and MB-MBS-BS represent, respectively, male and female ego's prototypically marriageable relatives in the three medial generations. A reification of the male or female perspective on succession, producing a patri- or matrilineal model embraced by both sexes, would truncate

Figure 7-1
From Dravidian to Crow-Omaha: "Core" Relationships from Male and Female
Perspectives and the Logic of Skewing as Geared to Reifications of Gendered
Perspectives (Unilineality)

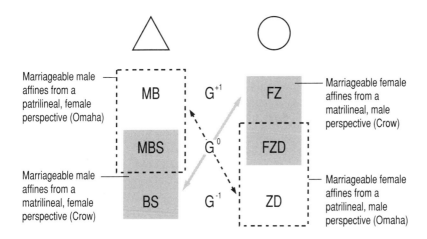

these series so as to produce Crow-Omaha skewing. A patrilineal model would
exclude male ego's FZ, leaving FZD = ZD (Omaha), whereas a matrilineal model
would exclude ZD, leaving FZ = FZD (Crow). The female perspective would similarly be truncated into MB = MBS (Omaha) or MBS = BS (Crow). Such processes
have evidently been operating among Gé-speakers such as the Sherente and Bororo,
where precisely these focal Crow-Omaha categories (FZD/ZD versus FZD/FZ) define
prototypical spouses for male ego (table 7-1).

Unilineal Transmission ("Descent")

Crow-Omaha terminologies have long been considered congruent with, and even
indicative of, unilineal "descent" (e.g., Tax 1937a:12–13; Murdock 1949:166–68;
Radcliffe-Brown 1952:70–78; Dole 1972:146–48), and there has been a tendency
to discuss these systems in terms of concrete groups such as "lineages" (Lévi-Strauss
1969 [1949]:xxxvi–xlii; Needham 1960:24, 1961:253; Moore 1963:308). More recently, the focus has shifted to less tangible principles of succession (Lounsbury
1964a:383–86; da Matta 1979:127), but the suggestion remains that the structural
derivations of unilineality are similar, irrespective of whether or not such principles
serve as the basis for recruitment to descent groups. Rivière (1980:538), for instance, asks "if the Northern Gé do not in fact have unilineal descent disguised as
name transmission." Instead of reifying "lineages" into solid entities, we should
think of descent as a mode of social classification like any other, no less mental in
origin (or material in its repercussions) than any other phenomenon of culture.

Whereas both cognation and parallel transmission represent sexual symmetry and equilibrium, unilineal principles imply that one of the sexes would abandon its own perspective, so to speak, in favor of a reification of the bias of the other. It has long been recognized that an inclination toward unilocal postmarital residence can be conducive to unilineal "descent" (Murdock 1949:59). To the cognatic and largely endogamous local groups of Guyana, choice of postmarital residence would not be a matter of great structural importance, and these groups are often classified as ambilocal. An abandonment of local group endogamy, however, would be the point at which a structural "choice" might have to be made between viri- or uxorilocality. Unilineality thus seems an aspect of supralocal integration. It is when the tangible boundaries set by local group endogamy dissolve that culturally construed, classificatory boundaries gain in importance. Whereas the Dravidian kin-affine dichotomy is egocentric, "internal" to the local group, and temporally transient (applicable only to the three medial generations), unilineality is a sociocentric reification of kin-affine boundaries, construing marriage as "external."[18] The 0-generation cross/parallel distinction, which in Dravidian systems expresses a transient, egocentric kin-affine dichotomy, provides a cognitive stepping-stone to unilineality (Hornborg 1987a). But, as mentioned earlier, there are many such stepping-stones along several paths.

The question remains whether these paths may have been traveled in both directions. Even if my presentation suggests a movement from Dravidian to Crow-Omaha, the elaborate social organization of the Gé seems to have more time-depth than that of the surviving groups of the tropical forest. Although I want to avoid "conjectural history," the atomistic societies of Guiana suggest contraction and devolution rather than archaism.[19] However typical of Amazonian societies such groups may appear today, they are very different from the populous chiefdoms that Gaspar de Carvajal encountered on the Napo River in 1542 (see Lathrap 1972). Groups surviving into the twentieth century are, without exception, strongly marginalized. Lathrap (1968:29) suggested that "most of the primitive groups inhabiting the tropical forest uplands away from the major flood plains can be interpreted as the wreckage of evolved agricultural societies forced into an environment unsuitable to the basic economic pattern." The typical Guiana system and that of the Gé should probably be understood as structurally opposite *logical possibilities* (see Rivière 1984:102) rather than as segments of an irreversible sequence. As long as they maintain the logic of an "elementary structure"—that is, as long as the relationship terminology codifies some kind of positive marriage preference—these movements (between Dravidian and Crow-Omaha) may permit a certain degree of reversibility.[20] As already noted, Crow-Omaha equations among groups such as the Sherente, Bororo, and Txicáo are indeed associated with positive, unilateral cross-cousin marriage preferences (on Jinghpaw Kachin kinship terminology, see Leach 1961; on Nasupo, see chapter 11 of this volume). Reversibility may be inherent in the contextuality of such classifications. The coexistence of separate modes of classification, such as different principles encoded in terms of reference and terms of address (see Basso 1970), would permit more or less dormant models to be reactivated when selected for by changing sociopolitical or demographic circumstances.

"Iroquois" Relationship Terminology

The label "Iroquois" has been used for bifurcate merging systems that (a) do *not* merge cross-collaterals and affines, and (b) employ a simplified (and structurally haphazard) mode of reckoning "crossness," whereby the sex of the closest linking relatives determines whether alter is "cross" or "parallel." Over time, feature (a) may encourage feature (b). In losing the consistent classification of cross-collaterals as affines (and introducing separate affinal terms), such "ex-Dravidian" systems can no longer maintain the logic by which cross and parallel are extended (Lounsbury 1964b:1079, n. 4; Scheffler 1971:233, 242, 244, 247, 252). Perhaps the fundamental difference between Dravidian and Iroquois is that in the former "crossness" is automatically defined by the transitivity of the kin/affine dichotomy, whereas the latter struggles with conscious *reckoning* of crossness and must resort to simplified shortcuts (i.e., ignoring the sex of intervening links in ascending generations). An "Iroquois system" cannot be *systematic* when it classifies as cross all children of paternal aunts and maternal uncles, and children of all opposite-sex members of ego's own generation, irrespective of whether these relatives themselves are cross or parallel. In South America, "ex-Dravidian" systems generally assume the form called "bifurcate generation" (Dole 1969), wherein the cross/parallel distinction tends to vanish in ego's generation. Trautmann and Barnes (chapter 2 of this volume) refer to such 0-generation "Hawaiianization" of Iroquois systems as "variant 3" of "Type B crossness," and it is found in Spier's Mackenzie Basin type, discussed by Ives and Asch (see chapters 4 and 5).

Here and elsewhere (Hornborg 1986/1988), I have, perhaps somewhat carelessly, used the term "Iroquois" for South American terminologies with feature (a) above; the data rarely permit us to identify the extent of feature (b). A good example of a system with both features, however, is provided by the Arawak-speaking Mehinaku (Gregor 1977). Here, as in many other cases from Amazonia (e.g., Basso 1970), the terms of reference distinguish between cross and parallel cousins, but the terms of address do not. The former terms are used to emphasize potential affinity and sexual relationships, the latter to overrule them by underscoring kinship ("brother," "sister"). The Mehinaku disagree on whether first cross cousins are marriageable (Gregor 1977:278, 288). All children of male ego's same-sex generation mates are "children," whereas all children of opposite-sex generation mates are "sister's children," a usage that is obviously directly linked to the generational cousin terminology.

Cases such as the Mehinaku, Kuikuru, and Kalapalo raise fundamental issues about whether to approach relationship terminologies from evolutionist or functional, "contextualist" perspectives. Although it is tempting to see the Mehinaku as a culture in the process of abandoning a Dravidian cross-cousin marriage prescription, in favor of a system codifying first-cousin exogamy through the use of generational cousin terms, most ethnographers today would hesitate to draw any conclusions about long-term change. They would emphasize the use of different kin terms in strategic manipulation of relationships and would not be looking for a single, consistent "system" for each culture. Indeed, there is a strong risk of reification here. Although it is still my conviction that "Iroquois" is, generally speaking, a "derelict" Dravidian mode of classification, we must take seriously the proposition that the two schemes can coexist in the same population, even when there is no clear transition taking place. Here, again, the contextuality of multiple, coexistent models (see chapter 5) may afford a measure of reversibility and a capacity to respond to varying circumstances. It is interesting to note that Dole (1969) and Ives (chapter 4) suggest diametrically opposite reasons for 0-generation "Hawaiianization," namely, pressures for local endogamy and for local exogamy, respectively. The expansion of consanguineal categories, which is the essence of Hawaiianization, suggests that a general association with exogamy is likely.

The simplified mode of reckoning crossness that has been called "Iroquois" or "Type B," can, of course, completely displace the "automatism" of Dravidian, kin-affine usages (in *all* contexts), and I would agree with Trautmann and Barnes (chapter 2) that this may be associated with larger aggregations of population. As the population expands, the Dravidian logic of exchange, unless compartmentalized into endogamous enclaves (see Yalman 1962), will tend to break down (see Schwerin 1983–84; Rivière 1984:108). "Type B" reckoning of crossness nevertheless "echoes" a basic premise of Dravidian systems, though applied in a new way: namely, the primacy of same-sex relationships. Gregor (1977:278–78) writes of the Mehinaku that "kinsmen linked by relatives of the same sex to ego are usually labeled by kinship terms that are also used within the nuclear family," whereas "kinsmen who trace their relationship through relatives of the opposite sex . . . may be described by a different nomenclature." In not reckoning with the sex of ascending links (a Dravidian system does not reckon with these links, either, because it does not have to, as their recognition is automatic), "Type B" applies the fundamental "same-or-opposite-sex?" criterion to the closest linking relatives only, which totally distorts the Dravidian logic *by trying consciously to reproduce it.* In other words, it is in trying to hold on to the defunct kin-affine dichotomy that "Type B" completes its process of deterioration (initiated through the adoption of a distinct terminology for affines). It seems that Crow-Omaha and Iroquois are two alternative trajectories of Dravidian (see chapter 11; Kronenfeld 1993), where the former may retain a measure of the "systematicity" of elementary structures (although now triadic and generalized rather than dualistic and restricted), whereas the latter represents a path toward complex structures in Lévi-Strauss's sense. This last conclusion harmonizes with the observations by Trautmann and Barnes (chapter 2), and by Ives (chapter 4), that the distribution of Iroquois and Dravidian in North America suggests a kind of center-periphery relationship. In the Amazon Basin, similarly, marginalized Dravidian-like systems (Carib, Yanoama, Tukano, Jívaro, Pano, etc.) surround the core of major floodplains occupied, prior to the European conquest, by Arawak- and Tupí-speaking chiefdoms whose modern descendants incline toward "Iroquois" modes of classification.

CONCLUSIONS

One aspect of my argument so far has been that there is a remarkable *redundancy* between all these Amazonian perspectives on society. The congruities seem to ex-

Figure 7-2
Social Redundancies in Amazonian Social Structure: The "Elementary"
Continuum

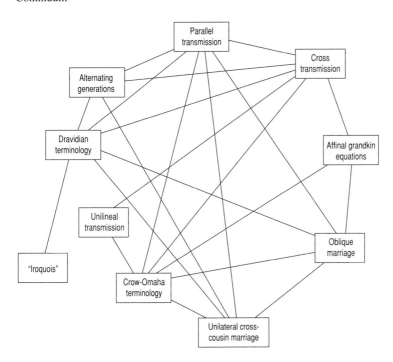

tend from one end of the spectrum to the other, and almost any feature can be seen
as structurally contiguous to (and derivative of) any other. Perhaps it is less of a
spectrum than a circle (figure 7-2). On the other hand, as indicated at the outset of
the chapter, there is a "seriality" in this continuum that suggests a *directionality,* or
at least a polarity, in the transformative sequence. The two ends of the spectrum
(Dravidian terminologies and unilineal systems) are structurally contradictory, and
some intervening links are necessary for the transition to occur.

Having browsed through this series of social models, one is certainly left with a
feeling of having moved in circles. But it has really been along a spiral of overlapping, cognitive reconnections, which in Amazonia have maintained a sense of continuity through what were quite clearly social (that is, also behavioral) transformations. What use do these seemingly tautological exercises have? At one level, they
help to illuminate the actual, ethnographic variation in Amazonian social structure.
More important, they remind anthropologists to maintain a position of epistemological modesty. As I have previously concluded (Hornborg 1986/1988:291), "Social structure can only be surmised through the systems of classification in which it
is imperfectly reflected, and by which it is indeterminately reproduced. . . . [W]e
must assume its objective existence but at the same time be content with perceiving

it only through the juxtaposition of its various subjective manifestations." Our perspectives can be no less partial than theirs. It would be a mistake to try to account for one model in terms of another, or for both in terms of a third. There can be no master narrative.[21] Yet, there are serial congruities between various representations. In allowing processes of social change to be traced indirectly, the more modest versions of structural comparison thus remain as rewarding and justifiable as ever.

My intention in this chapter was to move beyond the impasse of poststructuralist, postmodernist epistemology in order to get back to comparative research on social classification ("kinship"), but from a slightly modified point of departure. I am glad that "kinship" is receiving renewed attention, but one cannot pretend that the last twenty years of deconstruction have not occurred. It is now time to justify comparative research from an epistemological perspective that differs somewhat from the structuralism of the 1960s. What I have been suggesting might be called a "structuralism without master narratives."

There is an indeterminacy and a dialectic between classification (cognition, models, rules) and organization (behavior, practice, performance) that generates transformation, and both levels have their own logical inertia, but only classification is accessible in the "absolute" sense of *structure*.[22] Behavior "in itself" can only be approached by *imposing* the structure of a specific perspective. Series of partly overlapping models can be assumed *indirectly* to reflect behavioral transformations, although these remain epistemologically inaccessible except through the partial perspective of a structural explication. Redundancies and congruities can now be recognized, but it would be misleading to reduce serial likenesses to "a single structure" (see, e.g., Viveiros de Castro and Fausto 1993:161) or a "less determined general structure" (Henley 1993), for any new formulation would simply extend the series being examined.

I have tried to arrange a number of social models commonly reported from lowland South America according to their degree of mutual congruity but have found that there are a great number of possible links and transitions. In this comparative work, I have addressed all kinds of models, not only relationship terminologies but also marriage preferences, principles for succession, and so on. This approach has made it possible to suggest likely avenues of transition, and to link Dravidian and Crow-Omaha terminologies into a common transformational framework. I have given "Dravidian," "Crow," and "Omaha" minimal definitions, focusing on the structural logic of their core features. Dravidian is essentially synonymous with Needham's "prescriptive symmetric," defined by *the equation of cross-collaterals and affines in the three medial generations*. Crow-Omaha are defined by the effects of unilineal models on this basic scheme, generating oblique equations of categories that in the Dravidian system are affinal. For male ego, the core Crow equation is $FZ = FZD \neq ZD$ and the core Omaha equation is $FZ \neq FZD = ZD$. For female ego, they are $MB \neq MBS = BS$ and $MB = MBS \neq BS$, respectively.

I have suggested that structural reversibility hinges on the coexistence of alternative models or perspectives that can be activated according to varying circumstances. It is thus possible for an oscillation to occur between Dravidian and Crow or Omaha (as defined above), or between Dravidian and "bifurcate generation" (an

Amazonian version of Iroquois), *as long as the Dravidian usage is preserved in specific contexts* (e.g., as terms of reference where the terminology of address has been Hawaiianized). Circumstances that might stimulate such oscillations seem to include various kinds of pressures for local endogamy or local exogamy. We have seen that Crow-Omaha would tend to be associated with endogamy, whereas Hawaiianization may be associated with exogamy.

The continuous process of social self-explication (perhaps it could be called "ethnosociology"?) is in itself the major source of change. In trying to hold on to structural principles distilled from the elusive realities of social behavior, that is, in the *reification* or *objectification* of social practice, culture transforms itself. From a Dravidian universe of categories-cum-relationships, a number of implicit regularities can be drawn out, objectified, and codified into new forms that in turn may transcend the limits of that universe: (1) its focus on male ego's marriage to his FWBD suggests the embryo of matrilateral cross-cousin marriage (Txicào, Sirionó), or even Needham's "prescriptive asymmetric alliance"; (2) its implicit principles of parallel transmission (the coexistence of complementary, male and female perspectives on succession) provide matrices for unilocal residence and unilineal descent (Gé, Tukano); (3) its accommodation of oblique marriage points in the direction of Crow-Omaha systems (Sherente, Bororo); (4) the (alternative) emphasis on the equivalence of alternating generations sets the stage for systems of marriage sections (Pano); (5) its emphasis on reciprocity and dualism lays the foundation for dual organization (Gé, Tupí, Pano); and (6) the various Iroquois attempts at grasping its logic of cross and parallel tend to muddle it to oblivion.

The doubling of perspectives inherent in what I have referred to as the "parallel transmission of affinal relationships" poses a key problem for structuralist or essentialist approaches to kinship. Its crucial role in the transformation from Dravidian to Crow-Omaha, by definition impossible to represent in a single diagram, can only be appreciated if anthropologists are prepared to relinquish their "single-structure" approach to social reality.

NOTES

1. In the terminologies of the Barasana, Cubeo, and Bará, MZ is linguistically cognate to FB, and FZ is assimilated with WM among both the Cubeo and Bará (Goldman 1963:134–35; Jackson 1977:88–89; Hugh-Jones 1979:79).
2. By opposing *both* F and M (as "kin") to MB and FZ (as "affines"), Dravidian terminologies contradict unilineal descent (Shapiro 1970; Trautmann 1981:176, 197). This contradiction is often neglected, as when Buchler and Selby (1968:135) call Dravidian systems "patrilineal," or when Keesing (1975:108) includes FZ = WM in the Dravidian category of "kin," while classifying M as "affine."
3. I here define "Iroquois" negatively as an "ex-Dravidian" system (see the section " 'Iroquois' " Relationship Terminology" below). I doubt that a category of "Iroquois" systems can be defined in positive terms, in the sense of a recurring and specific structural logic.
4. This is not to deny the variation within linguistic families, for example, the occurrence of Carib or Tupí groups combining an apparent absence of unilineality with the presence of separate affinal terms (see chapter 15, n. 48), instances that may reflect specific historical

trajectories. I would be careful never to suggest *absolute* correlations of any kind, but the suggested *inclination* in difference between Caribs and Tupí remains clear. Nor does Viveiros's reminder (chapter 15, n. 48) that Dumont's Tamils are unilineal necessarily contradict my interpretation; the ambiguous position of the FZ in these contexts remains a structural fact, but there is no reason to suppose that people everywhere (and in as disparate circumstances as these!) will deal with this ambiguity in precisely the same manner. The ambiguity can be expected to be less acute, for instance, where (a) the endogamous group is large enough to provide enough alternatives other than marrying an actual FZD, and where (b) virilocal residence brings about the physical separation of male ego and his FZ (Hornborg 1993:105).

5. Outside the Pano family, the only group I am aware of that seems to combine exogamous moieties and a truly Dravidian terminology are the Tupí-speaking Kagwahiv (Kracke 1984:101–2).

6. In South America, marriage sections are unique to the Panoans, but it has elsewhere been observed that a male ego's marriage with his DD would be the result of an exchange of daughters between that man and his DH (J.-P. Dumont 1978:83; Henley 1982:117–18). This perspective is similar to a point made by Overing Kaplan (1984:140) about the connection between cross-cousin and ZD marriage: one is with the daughter of *father's* brother-in-law, the other is with the daughter of ego's *own* brother-in-law. Both ZD and DD marriage can thus be seen as extensions of reciprocity in two-line systems.

7. Henley (1993, n. 11) distorts my argument into a problem of "'cultural consistency' confronted by any patrilineal system," whereas I actually speak of a problem of *cognitive* consistency only where patriliny is combined with "cross-cousin marriage in small, endogamous groups" (Hornborg 1993:101). Henley bases his dismissal of my argument as "ethnographically ingenuous" on the fact that ego will "normally have both parents-in-law and children-in-law, i.e. affines, in adjacent generations as well." But this entirely misses my point. "Parents-in-law," "children-in-law," and the like are *English* categories; what does it mean to say that they are "affines" in a culture *that does not recognize any separate affinal terms?* I am talking about the cultural construction of affinity, whereas Henley sounds as if "affines" were an objective, cross-cultural constant. Finally, he is "not convinced that the need to maintain the congruity across generations of the kin:affine distinction represents a problem of 'cultural [*sic*] consistency' for indigenous actors rather than for theoretical model-builders!" I submit that if the cognitive delineation of social categories was not a problem for the actors, there would be no kinship systems (e.g., the whole phenomenon of "descent") for us to analyze.

8. Trautmann (1981:188–93) has shown that an extension of the cross/parallel logic of Dravidian systems into G^{+2} and G^{-2} puts male ego's FF, MM, and SCh into the "parallel" category, while MF, FM, and DCh are "cross." For female ego, DCh are "parallel," while SCh are "cross." I have found indications of alternate generations in almost half (22 of 48) of a sample of indigenous groups in lowland South America (Hornborg 1986/1988). Ideals relating to name transmission between alternate generations generally focus on "parallel" grandkin.

9. "Sex affiliation" is the term used by Williams (1932) for the Idutu-bia of Papua and, for example, by Lévi-Strauss (1973). "Parallel transmission" derives from Scheffler and Lounsbury (1971).

10. "Bilineal" or "double unilineal" transmission could be seen merely as another perspective on parallel transmission, as if the patri- and matrilineal continuities *reflected* the same-sex, male and female "lines," respectively. In central and eastern Brazil, the pervasive, "disharmonic" combination of patrilateral ceremonialism and uxorilocal residence provides a matrix for these principles of transmission. The cross transmission of names (see below) is yet another of their manifestations.

11. In surveying the literature on forty-eight lowland South American cultures (Hornborg 1986/ 1988), I discovered indications of parallel transmission in twenty-eight of these.

12. This merging of affinity and succession invalidates Lave's (1973) rejection of Scheffler and Lounsbury's articulation of parallel and cross transmission on the grounds that naming is fundamentally opposed to "kinship" (Hornborg 1986/1988:235–37).

13. Among the Idutu-bia of Papua, Williams (1932:58, 75–81) found "sex affiliation" linked to an ideal of FZD marriage.

14. Shapiro (1968) suggests that MBD marriage among the Sirionó was generated by avuncular (ZD) marriage, a practice redundantly codified in their terminology.

15. Of the twelve groups in our sample (Hornborg 1986/1988) that recognize Crow-Omaha equations (all of which are, incidentally, uxorilocal), at least ten express unilateral cross-cousin marriage preferences.

16. Merely as a matter of logical consistency, the equation DCh = ZCh should imply that ZCh = FZCh (Omaha). Similarly, the equations M = MBD and MB = MBS (both Omaha) can be generated from the equation MPa = WPa (i.e., MF = MB and MM = FZ), and the equations FZ = FZD, F = FZS, and Ch = MBCh (all Crow) from FPa = WPa (i.e., FF = MB and FM = FZ).

17. There are also other transgenerational equations, common particularly among Carib- and Tupí-speakers, that are congruent with ZD marriage, for example, MB = FZS, M = FZD, MBCh = ZCh.

18. Dual organization, however, represents a cohesive reaction to the combination of exogamy and uxorilocal residence (bride-service). Thus, whereas Gé moieties and Tukano patrisibs (both founded on unilocal residence) are associated with a similar conception of marriage as "external," the specific patterns of postmarital residence produce two very different kinds of society, based on different ways of solving problems of reciprocity. Among the Tukanoans, bride-service is feasible only within a restricted social range (see Arhem 1981:156–63). The norm is virilocal exchange marriages, but they frequently also resort to bride-capture. The moiety systems of the Gé, on the other hand, draw conceptually and spatially distinct sets of affines together into large, cohesive villages and life-long bride-service (Maybury-Lewis 1979a). In contrast to both these models, the cognatic, ambilocal systems of Guiana do not reify kin-affine distinctions but suppress them over time (Rivière 1984; Hornborg 1987b). This is the hallmark of the transient and egocentric dualism of Dravidian systems, or what Overing (1973) calls "alliance endogamy."

19. The Tukanoans of the northwest Amazon seem somewhat more "intact" in the sense of having been able to maintain lively supralocal exchange networks.

20. Kronenfeld (1993:28) similarly suggests that "the skewing overlay" on a Dravidian-type system "seems easily added or lost." Viveiros de Castro's conclusion (chapter 15), that "the transition between Amazonian-avuncular and 'semi-complex' regimes of the Central Brazilian type may be quite a lot shorter than was imagined," is very much in agreement with the general argument I have been advancing since the early 1980s (Hornborg 1986/ 1988). Recent contributions by Taylor (chapter 8 of this volume) and Henley (1993) have a similar thrust.

21. A concrete illustration of this is the impossibility of diagramming a symmetric alliance structure without producing a bias toward either the male or the female perspective. Herán's (1993a) presentation shows that even models that explicitly propose to avoid idiosyncrasies of representation other than those that are structurally relevant, must choose whether male or female succession is to be represented by vertical (as opposed to diagonal) lines. In trying to produce an unbiased model, similarly, Houseman and White (chapter 9 of this volume) must move into the realm of pure description. Their attempt to explicate structural principles (such as "sidedness"), however, immediately puts them in the same boat as everybody else who has tried to formulate "*the* underlying structure" of Amazonian society: they are adding

yet another perspective to the list of formulations that they are investigating. Although in other respects an instructive exercise, I do not believe that letting a computer work out "the marriage network itself . . . as a structured totality" (chapter 9) will solve this epistemological dilemma, since at some point the computer would have to be told what *to look for.*

22. It is crucial to remember that it is *models* we are talking about, which would preclude propositions such as Allen's (chapter 14), that a Dravidian system "consists formally (i.e. whether or not the members of the society recognize it) of two exogamous moieties," or Kronenfeld's (1993), that Dravidian-type terminologies imply a "moiety-like division of the society (whether overtly recognized or named or not)." Houseman and White (chapter 9) similarly speak of "dual organization" and "'exogamous' super-sets" in populations in which no such sociocentric groups are culturally recognized. I would recommend that we avoid reifying the polarized flows of genes and prestations generated by the transitivity of kin/affine terminological usages, except where such "groups" are part of a people's own conceptualizations.

8

Jivaro Kinship: "Simple" and "Complex" Formulas: A Dravidian Transformation Group

ANNE-CHRISTINE TAYLOR

This chapter provides a brief description of some of the synchronic variants of a kinship system (or a group of kinship systems) found in a set of tribal groups of South America remarkable for its cultural and sociological homogeneity. My aim was to study the variations of one so-called Dravidian-type kinship structure, their limits, and field of practice and in so doing to illuminate, negatively, as it were, the invariant aspects of this structure.

The mechanisms of tribal differentiation in these Jivaroan groups of Western Amazonia operate in two main areas: language and kinship. The differences systematically created from the elements provided by these two cultural subsystems constitute the main pillars of tribal identities. The Jivaroan group is divided into two blocs: the Jivaro proper and the Candoa. At present the first includes five recognized "tribes" or dialect groups: the Shuar, the Achuar, the Shiwiar, the Huambisa, and the Aguaruna. The second consists of two such groups: the Kandoshi and the Shapra. Within the Jivaro conglomerate, various levels of language are used to create differences as a function of the sociological units involved. At the *intratribal* level, these differences are of an essentially prosodic nature; at the *intertribal* level, they are both phonetic (altering either the vowels or the consonants) and lexical (term-for-term inversion in specific semantic areas: e.g., *pinink/tachau* = "beer bowl"/ "dish" in Achuar, but "dish"/"beer bowl" in Shuar). I strongly suspect that the linguistic differences between the two blocs work not only at the phonetic level but also *at the syntactical level* (see Taylor 1985). This hypothesis remains to be confirmed, however; the two dialect groups have in fact often been assigned to separate language families, so great is the phonetic and lexical distance between the Candoa and the Jivaro dialects.

As far as their kinship systems are concerned, the Jivaro bloc, strictly speaking, presents terminological variants of a predominantly Dravidian type ("two-line terminologies" with type A crossness, to use the Trautmann-Barnes formulation), combined with a symmetric prescriptive marriage rule. Intertribal variation plays on the genealogical and spatial distance between the prescribed spouses, and on the ideologically—but not statistically—preferred form of marriage. The Candoa bloc, on the other hand, features kinship systems that are apparently unique (as is their language), with no prescriptive marriage rule and with hybrid terminologies combining Eskimo, Iroquois, and Dravidian elements. At first glance, the Candoa systems seem to fall under the heading of "semicomplex" structures (given their "prohibitive" definition of marriage and their specific vocabulary for affines) or even, taking into account the absence of unilineal descent groups, to belong to the field of "complex" structures. It should be stressed, at this point, that all Jivaro-Candoa societies reckon descent bilaterally; their elementary social units are open kindred groups, more or less inclusive according to context and social circumstances.

For the sake of clarity and brevity, only three variants are examined here: the Achuar and the Aguaruna from the Jivaroan bloc and the Kandoshi from the Candoan bloc. I begin with the Achuar case for heuristic reasons, and not because I consider their system to be more "prototypical" or "original," in evolutionary terms, than that of the other Jivaroan groups.

THE ACHUAR VARIANT

The Achuar's basic territorial units (local groups) and their preferential zones of intermarriage are isomorphic. These units, which I call "endogamous nexi," comprise on average 100 to 150 persons, or some ten scattered households. The rule is that marriage takes place between close bilateral cross cousins; in indigenous terms, the potential spouse is designated by the reference term *wahe*, usually glossed as "child of the father's male affine" (FWBCh). Sister exchange is highly valorized and statistically very frequent; nevertheless, from the male standpoint, marriage is ideologically skewed toward FZD, the wife's father appearing, in this case, more strongly "affinalized" than if he were a consanguineal relation of ego's mother (MB). However, women reverse HF's valence and tend to define him in terms of mother's sibling. The residence pattern is "prolonged temporary uxorilocality" (an average of ten years). The following are among the special features of the Achuar system:

1. Genealogical closeness is valorized between the spouses, and even a strong symbolic assimilation of the spousal relation to that of opposite-sex siblings.
2. Sororal polygyny is generalized and quasi-"prescriptive"; this results in the matrimonial and residential dispersal of sets of brothers, who cannot share the same immediate affines (there is no *synchronic* repetition of marriage, then, but a necessary *diachronic* reiteration).
3. Notwithstanding the classificatory points of view of ego, his brothers and his parallel cousins are rigorously identical, as in all classical Dravidian systems (i.e., my cross cousin (*wahe*) is also cross cousin for B, FBS, MZS, etc.).

4. An operator of "kin distance" is present, and it divides according to context, recognized consanguineal or affinal relations into "real" (*nekas*) and "branch, peripheral" (*kana*).
5. Levirate (the inheritance, by a brother, of his deceased brother's wives), also quasi-prescriptive, is practiced.
6. There is fairly strong genealogical amnesia at G^{+2} (as a rule only the four grandparents—and sometimes not even these—can be recalled).

Lastly, it should be noted that the most frequent forms of "irregular" marriage are with classificatory "daughters" and "mothers," in other words, with terminological "consanguines" (either a wife of the deceased father or a daughter of an abducted wife), and very rarely with ZD or FZ (affines), the last two unions being regarded as particularly incestuous. In this, the Achuar (and the Shuar, whose kinship system is identical to that of the Achuar, except that there appears to be an ideological bias in favor of MB rather than FZH) clearly stand apart from many other Amazonian groups, notably those of the Guyanese area, who often combine cross-cousin and oblique marriage (i.e., between ego and FZ or ZD).

It is readily evident from inspection of table 8-1 that the Achuar terminology of reference corresponds to the most classic of "two-line terminologies," those that, within the last twenty years, have been associated with the Amazonian Dravidian systems. The vocative terminology, or terminology of address, however, shows significant departures from this pattern, which repay close examination. The principles that govern it may be summarized as follows:

1. For a male ego, all male relatives, affines or consanguines, keep their reference term.
2. For a female ego, all female relatives, consanguines or affines, are terminologically consanguinized (i.e., HM becomes M, etc.), except HZ.
3. With one exception, all cross-sex affinal relations are consanguinized by one partner and affinalized by the other (e.g., WM calls ego "son-in-law"—*aweru*, G^{-1} affine —, while he calls her "mother"—*nukua*, G^{+1} consanguine). The exception concerns relations between cross cousins, who call each other "brother/sister" (*umaru*) before marriage, and "cross cousin" (*waheru*) after marriage; in other words, once ego's female cross cousin marries alter, she is no longer "sister" but "female affine" (this is diagrammed in figure 8-1); the cross cousin married by ego is called "spouse."

In an earlier discussion (Taylor 1983), I analyzed how the asymmetric valence of male and female terms of address worked and explored the reasons for it. Briefly, the asymmetry corresponds to the marking of matrimonial projections for an ego (subsuming not only the prescribed marriage with the father's real brother-in-law's child [FZHCh and/or MBCh], but also the inheritance of deceased brothers' mar-

Table 8-1

Achuar Kin Terms

Reference terms		
Consanguines		Affines
G⁺²	*apachi, nukuchi* (FF, MF, MM, FM…)	
G⁺¹	*apa* (F, FB, FFBS…)	*iich* (MB, FZH, WF…)
	nuku (M, MZ, MZD…)	*tsatsar* (WM, FZ, MBW…)
G⁰	*unai*	*wahe*
	(opposite-sex sibling)	(af. G0, opposite sex)
	yachi	*sai*
	(sibling, m.s.)	(af. F0, m.)
	kai	*yuar*
	(sibling, w.s.)	(af. G0, w.)
G⁻¹	*uchi* (S, BS…/S, ZS…)	*awe* (BS, DH…/ZS, DH.)
	nawant (D, BD…/D, ZD…)	*awe* (BD, SW…/ZD, DH…)
G⁻²	*tiranki* (SS, SD, DS, DD…)	

Address terms		
Consanguines		Affines
G⁺²	*apachiru, nukuchiru*	
G⁺¹	*aparu*	*iichru, wearu*
	nukua	*nukua*
G⁰	*umaru*	*umaru* (before marriage)
		waherchi (after marriage with alter)
		nuaru/aishru (between spouses)
	yatsuru	*sairu*
	kairu	*yuaru*
G⁻¹	*uchiru*	*aweru*
	nawantru	*nawanta*
G⁻²	*tirankchiru*	

riage ties; whence the reciprocal affinalization of siblings of spouses), combined with a mechanism for neutralizing affinity designed to attenuate the "affinal" character of members of a co-resident endogamous kindred conceived in terms of a unit of consubstantiality.

The Achuar model thus offers a perfect fit with the "Dravidian" canon, and indeed doubly so: both in the sense of Trautmann and Barnes' "type A crossness" (cf. table 8-2) and in the sense defined by Dumont, inasmuch as it is explicitly founded, from the indigenous vantage point, on the transmission of an alliance relation that is always defined, man or woman speaking, in terms of male genealogical positions: while all women in this system are ambiguous from the standpoint of the affinity/

Figure 8-1
Consanguinization and Affinalization in Achuar Address

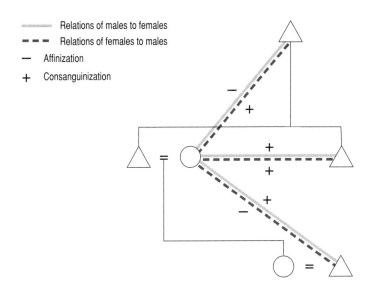

consanguinity opposition (except for "leviratic" female cross cousins), since they consanguinize their affines or are consanguinized by them, men, who anchor the relation, are always clearly defined as either affines or consanguines exclusively.

THE AGUARUNA VARIANT

The Aguaruna share with the Achuar the following features:

1. Intertwined bilateral kindreds forming an endogamous nexus, except that these units are considerably more extended than for the Achuar, since they comprise an average of three hundred persons, or from twenty to twenty-five households.
2. Sister exchange, sororal polygyny, inheritance of the brothers' wives and temporary prolonged uxorilocality.
3. Distinction between "close/real" and "peripheral" kin.

The prescriptive spouse, defined as the "child of the father's male affine," is here, too; marriage is said to take place between people who call each other *antsug,* a term that defines bilateral cross cousins in particular. A priori, then, *antsug* would be equivalent to the Achuar *wahe.* Nevertheless, there is clearly a discrepancy between the model given by informants, the model that "comes out" in the nomenclature, and the one that emerges from the statistics (Brown 1984; Guallart 1989).

Table 8-2

Comparison of Classifications of Distant Kin: Iroquois (Type B), Achuar-Dravidian (Type A), Awajun (Aguaruna), Kandoshi

Kintype	Type B	Type A	Awajun	Kandoshi
FFZS	F	X, G^{+1}	F	Col. G^+/nonkin
FFZD	X, G^{+1}	M	M	Col. G^+/nonkin
FFZSch	B, Z	X, G^0	XB, XZ	Col. G^0/nonkin
FFZDch	X, G^0	B, Z	XB, XZ	Col. G^0/nonkin
FFZSSch	S, D	X, G^{-1}	XCh	Col. G^0/nonkin
FFZSDch	X, G^{-1}	S, D	XCh	Col. G^0/nonkin
FFBDSch	S, D	X, G^{-1}	XCh	Col. G^0/nonkin
FFBDDch	X, G^{-1}	S, D	XCh	Col. G^0/nonkin
FZSch	S, D	X, G^{-1}	XCh	Col. G^0/nonkin
FZDch	X, G^{-1}	S, D	XCh	Col. G^0/nonkin
FMBS	F	X, G^{+1}	XF	Col. G^+/nonkin
FMBD	X, G^{+1}	M	M	Col. G^+/nonkin
FMBSch	B, Z	X, G^0	XB, XZ	Col. G^0/nonkin
FMBDch	X, G^0	B, Z	XB, XZ	Col. G^0/nonkin
MBSch	S, D	X, G^{-1}	XCh	Col. G^0/nonkin
MBDch	X, G^{-1}	S, D	XCh	Col. G^0/nonkin

From the schedule of Aguaruna reference terms in table 8-3, it is immediately obvious that this nomenclature differs noticeably from Achuar terminology. Although the terms for G^{+2} and G^{-2} are the same as those used by the Achuar (aside from phonetic permutations), classification for kin in G^{+1}, G^0, and G^{-1} is distinct:

1. In G^{+1} (m.s.), all men are "F" (*apag*), except MB (*diich*) and WF (*weag*); all women are "M" (*dukug*), except WM (*tsatsag*). For a male ego, there are therefore three male kin types in G^{+1} (F, MB, WF) and two female types (M, WM).

2. G^0, accordingly, also has five kin terms: "B," "Z," female "cross cousins" (*antsug*), male "cross cousins" (*saig*), and "spouses of B/Z" (*waheg*).

3. In G^{-1}, "S," and "D" (ego's children and those of his same-sex siblings) are opposed both to the "children of opposite-sex siblings" (*aweg*) and to the "children of opposite-sex cross cousins" (or children of *antsug*), who are called *ajika* (m.) and *nawasa* (w.).

Women's reference terms are the mirror image of men's: where men use three terms, women use two and vice versa. Here again, sexual dichotomy is seized upon as a device to transform affinal relations into consanguineal ones on one genealogical level while emphasizing this dichotomy in the adjacent generations.

Table 8-3

Aguaruna Terminology of Reference (Male Ego)

G⁺²		*apach/dukuch*	
		(MF, FF, MFB, FFB.../MM, FM, FMZ, MMMZ...)	
G⁺¹	*apag*	*diich*	*weag*
	F, FB, FZH...	MB	WF, HF
	dukug	*dukug*	*tsatsag*
	M, MZ, FZ...	MBW	WM, HM
G⁰	*yatsug*	*saig*	*waheg*
	B	FZS, MBS...	BW
	uban	*antsug*	
	Z, MZD, FBD	FZD, MBD	
G⁻¹	*uchin*	*aweg*	*ajika*
	S, BS...	ZS	MBDS, FZDS
	nawant	*aweg*	*nuwasa*
	D, BD	ZD	MBDD, FZDD
G⁻²		*tijan*	

The most striking aspect of this nomenclature is obviously the "marking" of MB, and the distinction—which is made explicit here while remaining latent for the Achuar—between MB and FZH. These two are often confused in practice owing to the frequency of marriage by sister exchange. This distinction, which is not mentioned in the Achuar's spontaneous description of the ideal marriage, becomes one of the main axes of the Aguaruna system, since it induces the third element in the terminology, the WF term. How can it be explained?

A close look at the genealogical data provided by the ethnographers who have studied the Aguaruna reveals a curious paradox: *antsug,* who are given as the ideal marriage partners, systematically avoid marrying each other, despite the ribald joking relationship they entertain. In fact, marriage occurs in statistically very significant proportions (50 percent of the 70 percent of marriages between "cousins") between *children of opposite-sex matrilateral cross cousins.* That being said, the matrilaterality of the marriage is more ideological than real, as the cross cousins in question are most often bilateral. Now these relatives destined to marry each other (children of *antsug*) call each other "B/Z" before marriage, as do the Achuar, but in this case with a genealogical "justification," for their respective fathers are indeed classificatory brothers and are called "F" by ego. But, and as among the Achuar, these "B/Z" are called *waheg* (opposite-sex cross cousin) as soon as they take a spouse. In sum, the real marriage does not occur at all between referential *antsug* (opposite-sex cross cousins), but between the children of *antsug,* that is, classificatory "brothers" and "sisters," who still regard themselves as *antsug* (cross cousins) *by virtue of the fact that ego's father and alter's mother are related as fictitious siblings.* In other words, cross cousins defined as matrilateral are assimilated to real opposite-sex siblings. If the Aguaruna claim to marry their *antsug* while avoiding

Figure 8-2

Aguaruna Terminology: Key Genealogical Positions

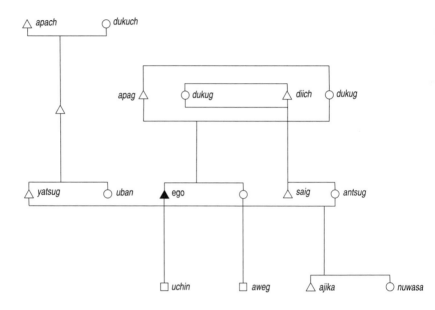

doing so, it is because they identify their form of marriage with that practiced by the Achuar (or to be more accurate, that of the Shuar, whose ideal marriage is ideologically skewed toward MBD), in other words with the exchange of children between brother and sister, or more precisely between brothers-in-law.

This appears quite clearly when examining the way vocative usages transform the vocabulary of affinity (figure 8-3). The terminology of address is indeed bipartite and reproduces, with the exception of a few details, the Achuar *reference* vocabulary: for instance, the special terms of address for ego's real affines in G^{+1} (WF and WM) are set aside because they are felt to be "too strong" (indigenous gloss) and replaced by the terms *diich* (reference MB) and *dukug* (M); the spouses of ego's children's also shed their specific terms (*ajika/nuwasa*), which are replaced by the reference term for "children of opposite-sex siblings" (*aweg*) (see figure 8-3).

Although Aguaruna terms of address reproduce the Achuar reference vocabulary, they also add a new element, namely, an incipient separation between lineals and collaterals, since F and M are distinguished from their siblings by the use of special diminutives. One finds the beginnings, too, of a rule of generational merging, ascendants in G^{+2} being assimilated to G^{+1} ("because of our love for them"). These features, which play a minor role for the Aguaruna, will move to the forefront in the Kandoshi kinship system.

Summarizing, then, union between real *antsug* (bilateral opposite-sex cross cousin) is indeed an Aguaruna "ideal" inasmuch as marriage is always perceived in

Figure 8-3
Transformations Introduced into Aguaruna Terminology of Address by Marriage

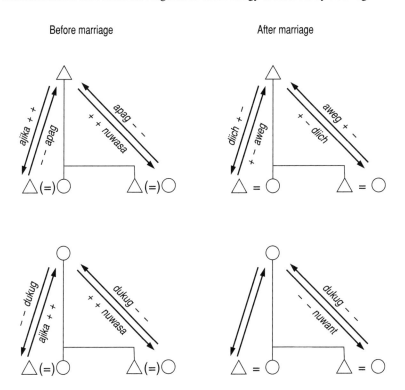

Before marriage   After marriage

terms of this structure. It is the position of bilateral first cross cousins that determines the repetition of the marriage, which is treated *terminologically* as though it were between close cross cousins (*antsug*) since once the marriage takes effect, the kin involved are reassigned to the positions of MB (FZH) and MBCh. In this sense we are indeed dealing with a "prescriptive" rule, not only because all marriages that take place are treated as though they followed the norm, but also because the rule is clearly embedded in the terminology, even if it is in a form that cannot be immediately deduced from the classificatory distribution of genealogical positions.

The consanguinization mechanisms inherent in all Jivaro kin systems operate here in a particularly complex manner because a third category has been introduced midway between the class of "real consanguines" and that of "real affines," and that is the category of "affinal consanguines" or "virtual affines" (since these people are affines only by virtue of past and future, not present, marriages). Paradoxically, this three-part division stems from a scrupulous adherence to the fundamentally two-part Dravidian logic: both because it supposes and reproduces a perennialized alliance relationship and because it plays exclusively on the necessary and sufficient distinction between affinity and consanguinity. The originality of the Aguaruna system is that it makes a radical distinction between conceptual principles and genealogical positions, which may well find themselves bisected by the affine/consanguine opposition rather than falling neatly into one or the other of the two categories. In this variant, for instance, some *men* are affected with the same ambivalence as some *women* in the Achuar model; in fact, MB occupies exactly the same place as FZ in the Achuar type, and his daughter (MBD) occupies Z's. This bivalence does not prevent MB—considered too "consanguineal" to be an "affine" in the Achuar system—from being given here as the term of the marriage alliance, his "closeness" being canceled out by the addition of an intermediary link, necessarily female (his daughter in the event), between him and ego. Alternatively, same-sex cross cousins and their parallel counterparts have, with respect to ego, the truly ambiguous status occupied by *all* Achuar women: the first because they are too consanguineal to be affines as they are the same sex as ego, the second, by the same token, because their consanguinity is too affinal. And that is why they do not appear as an anchor point of the alliance relationship, no more than the female matrilateral cross cousin (the real term of this relationship), simply because she is a woman (see figure 8-3). This goes to show that affinity and consanguinity are not contradictory, mutually exclusive predicates, as Dumont (1983a:166–67) maintains, not unparadoxically. Rather, they partake of an asymmetric complementary opposition, the terms of which can be at the same time ranked and inclusive/included (Viveiros de Castro and Fausto 1993).

Consider, now, the type of crossness at work in these nomenclatures. Formally, the terms of address fall more or less into type A, although the categorical distribution of the genealogical positions is atypical. The terminology of reference is harder to assign to one type or the other (see table 8-2), as it implies "type B crossness" (Iroquois) for certain genealogical positions, "type A crossness" for others, and neutralization of the difference for still others. These incongruities can be explained by the special character of Aguaruna marriage, which unites cousins who are "parallel" according to formal type A calculus, but who are "cross" cousins from a sociological standpoint inasmuch as the opposite-sex first-degree cross cousins who engendered them are *assimilated to siblings*.

The singular logic at work in the Aguaruna kinship system has one important consequence that should be pointed out: namely, it entails divorce between the classificatory "map" for ego and his same-sex real siblings, on the one hand, and that of his parallel cousins, on the other: points of view that are theoretically convergent in classical Dravidian systems and that are effectively so in the Shuar and Achuar types. In this case, however, ego and his real brothers have neither the same terminological MB nor the same real *antsug*, nor the same potential "prescriptive" wives as FBS or MZS (classificatory B). The point has its importance because it touches on one of the features that distinguishes the Dravidian and Iroquois systems of terminology, namely, the degree to which classificatory grids are individualized and therefore the heterogeneity of individuals' kinship worlds; in the Iroquois type, "two kinsmen who, from ego's standpoint, are respectively cross and parallel, can be both cross or both parallel from the standpoint of another kinsman of ego"

(Kronenfeld 1989:93; chapter 9 of this volume), a merger that is theoretically impossible in a classical Dravidian context.

In sum, if the Aguaruna variant is "Dravidian," it is less so in Trautmann's sense than in Dumont's, since its terminologies are governed much more by a sociological principle of transmission of an alliance relationship—marriage is always conceived over time, in terms of the marriages made in the ascending generations and projected in the subsequent ones—than by a classificatory method based on an algorithm using the cross/parallel distinction alone.

THE KANDOSHI VARIANT

Unlike other Jivaro groups, the Candoa dissociate the local-group and intermarriage zone. In effect, their local groups are strictly exogamous. They are also very small: as a general rule, they consist of no more than fifty to eighty persons. Furthermore, uxorilocality is not temporary here, but definitive. Nevertheless, some features typical of overall Jivaro social organization are also found here: bilateral descent reckoning; valorization of symmetrical exchange of female consanguines (but not necessarily "sisters"); "sororal" polygyny (quotation marks are needed here insofar as the category "sisters" is, as we shall see, much broader than in other Jivaro groups); and inheritance of "brothers'" wives. One important difference is the *synchronic* replication of marriage from the male point of view, scrupulously avoided in the other Jivaro groups. Among the Kandoshi, sets of brothers may share the same sets of effective affines, and this configuration is even explicitly sought and statistically frequent. On the other hand, *repetition* of the parents' marriage is excluded, since the cousins involved fall into the category of "close" kin whom it is forbidden to marry. In addition, while the Jivaro's ethnic social field is always divided into three categories—consanguines, affines, and nonkin or tribal enemies—the Candoa split theirs into four: close kin (genealogically and spatially), distant kin, nonkin, and tribal enemies (see figure 8-4). Here, the close/distant distinction, applied contextually to a binary kin classification among the other Jivaro, becomes the central axis of the system (Amadio and D'Emilio 1983; Surailles-Calonge 1992).

Marriage is prohibited between "close kin" *(maačriti),* disapproved but tolerated between "distant kin" *(kamindši),* and therefore implicitly biased toward "nonkin" *(tonari).* There is no question, then, of "prescriptive" marriage here, barring the redundant precept "one marries those who are marriageable."

Kandoshi reference nomenclature is "syntactically" if not "lexically" very different from that of the Jivaro (see figure 8-5).

The basic principles are as follows:

1. A strong distinction between lineal and collateral kin, the latter all being accounted for by two, and only two, classes (subdivided by sex): parents' or grandparents' siblings *(šibari/tatari)* and ego's or ego's children's siblings *(šuwanči/išari).*

Figure 8-4
Kandoshi Social Space

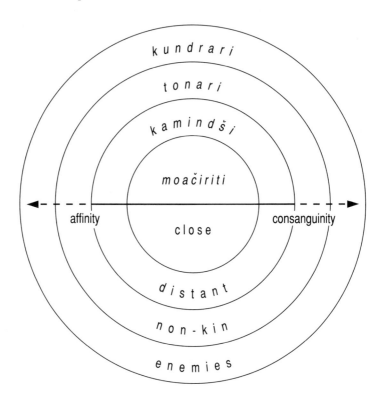

2. A clear distinction between these collaterals and their spouses, who, save two exceptions, all belong to a single class, whatever their genealogical level ("husbands/wives of siblings," *sambariri/masiči*).

In other words, ego uses descriptive terms for M, F, MM/MF, FF/FM, S, D, SpF, SpM, ChW, and ChH, and a massively classificatory nomenclature for all other recognized kin. The only two collateral genealogical positions receiving special treatment are those of FZH and, curiously enough, MZH, both designated by the term *šiiro* (very close to *saeru*, cross cousin/WB/ZH in Achuar; *saig* in Aguaruna), and that of WB/ZH (m.s.), designated by the term *širikama*. Note, in passing, the odd configuration of the terminology for effective affines of adjacent generations: for a man, the term *ngoširi* applies to WF and to SW or DH, the term *kumini* being reserved for WM; for a female ego, it is the inverse, the inclusive term being *kumini*, applied to HM and SW, while *ngoširi* is reserved for HF. But the symmetry is not perfect, for women use a specific term for DH *(paneari)*, the only term of the triad that is not reciprocal (see figure 8-6).

Figure 8-5
The Kandoshi Kinship Circle (Male Ego)

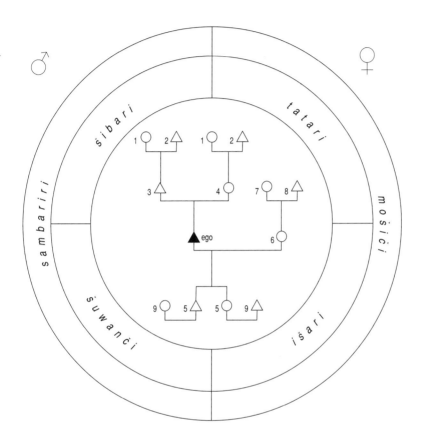

Key: 1. kumari MM, FM; 2. pačiri MF, FF; 3. apari F; 4 anieri M; 5. ipari Ch; 6 isanči W; 7. ngoširi WF; 8. kumini WM; 9. ngoširi DH, SW.

Furthermore, and unlike the case of the other Jivaro groups, Kandoshi vocative terminology is very close to the reference vocabulary, except that proper names are frequently used in place of the corresponding kin term, that "uncles" (*šibari,* male siblings of F, M, FF, FM, MF, MM) are called *iichi* (see *jiich/iichi* Achuar/Shuar: FZH, MB, SpF; Aguaruna *diich,* MB), and that collaterals' spouses are called *kunieta* (and reciprocally), a term derived from the Spanish *cuñado/cuñada* (brother-in-law/sister-in-law). In short, discrepancies between the two vocabularies appear in only two areas: that, after marriage and taking uxorilocality into account, of opposite-sex co-resident consanguines (*kunieta*) (i.e., potential spouses by levirate, which marks the relationship here just as it does in all other Jivaro groups) and that,

Figure 8-6

Kandoshi Terms of Address between Ego and Spouse's Parents and between
Ego and Child's Spouse

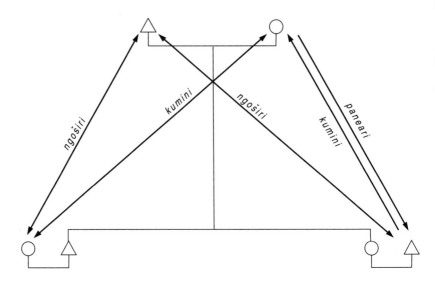

after marriage, of same-sex but non-co-resident "elder" collaterals. The meaning of
these vocatives is given below.

Although there is relatively little difference between address and reference for
the Kandoshi, compared with the other Jivaro systems, one mechanism, unknown
in the rest of this cultural group, needs to be mentioned, and that is genealogical
reclassification as a function of relative age. Any kinsperson may be shifted to a
different category in accordance with the age difference between him/her and ego:
for instance, FeB is an "uncle" (*šibari*), while FyB becomes a "brother" (*šuwanči*),
and so on. This flexibility affects "classificatory" terms only and obviously does not
concern ego's lineals or his effective affines. Application of this generational principle, together with vocative practices such as the use of proper names, fosters both
extreme "degenealogization" and singularization of individual classificatory grids.
On the cognitive level, these mechanisms nurture and explain the high degree of
genealogical amnesia—lateral rather than vertical, as in the other Jivaro groups—
reported among the Kandoshi.

Candoa kinship terminology is indeed strange, and at first glance has little in
common with the Jivaro systems. That being said, the differences between the two
groups of variants bear a family likeness with those that set apart the Jivaro variants
proper. Furthermore, many explicit features of the Candoa system are reminiscent
of latent elements of the Aguaruna model, such as the lineal/collateral distinction.
Both systems share a three-part classification, in particular, except that it works in
very different ways, and both have a specific vocabulary for real affines. But do
these formal similarities mean identical structures?

Consider Kandoshi marriage in practice. Because marriage is biased toward "nonkin nonenemies" (*tonari*), the matrimonial network would seem indefinitely expandable. And yet this openness is refuted by the statistics: the available genealogies (of which there are few, it is true; see Amadio and d'Emilio 1983) attest the existence of a few marriages between kin from the same local group three generations down the line, and above all a proliferation of marriages between residential groups having intermarried as a whole four generations before.

The possibility of closing the cycle after three generations has a simple explanation: taken in conjunction with uxorilocality, genealogical amnesia works in such a way that only three generations are needed for descendants of "close consanguines" (*maačiriti*) in G^{+2} to find themselves in the class of mutual "nonkin" (see figure 8-7). Once this is accepted, the next step is to ask whether the genealogical orientation of Candoa marriage is as open as it seems. Might not the "marking" of terms for WB/ZH and FZH (i.e., FWB) point to a tacit marriage preference? Concretely, by analogy with the Aguaruna model, one can imagine that the "selection" of patrilateral cross cousins (by marking their father) demarcates, in the same way as the Aguaruna's selection of matrilateral cross cousins (via MB), a zone of kin who *are forbidden as spouses for me, but who will beget my children's spouses.* This hypothesis has in fact statistical support: a genealogical study shows that a high proportion of marriages indeed results from the *širikama* relationship (WB-ZH) in G^{+2}.

And yet this confirmation is only part of the solution to the problem posed by the oddities of Candoa terminology. It is still necessary to determine whether the relative sex of the patrilateral cross cousins is a relevant factor in determining marriage (as it is for Aguaruna matrilateral cross cousins). Above all, we still need to understand *why* MZH *is given the same terminological marking as* FZH.

Is it possible to accept the a priori unlikely idea of an implicit bias toward *both* the descendants of patrilateral cross cousin and matrilateral parallel cousin? Theoretically, a structure of this type is perfectly conceivable, providing two of the pairs of cross-sex siblings necessary to make the model of repeated marriage between descendants of bilateral cross cousins work are replaced by two sets of same-sex siblings. This would produce a system in which each generation has two marriages between children of bilateral cross cousins and two between children of bilateral parallel cousins. But this theory does not seem to apply to the Candoshi data for the simple reason that the male progeny of FB/MZ normally follow the same matrimonial trajectory as male ego. It should not be forgotten that marriage here tends to take on a global collective character, with most "brothers" of each generation taking wives in the same local group; their descendants therefore cannot end up in the position of *tonari* (nonkin).

In view of the available data, marriage seems effectively biased toward the children of opposite-sex patrilateral cross cousins (symmetrically inverse, then, to the Aguaruna model), and not toward the children of same-sex cross cousins; as always, however, this orientation is more ideological than "mechanical," again because of "sister" exchange and the ensuing assimilation of MB/FZH. With respect to the Achuar variant, Kandoshi marriage adds an additional genealogical link, and

Figure 8-7

Reclassification of Kandoshi Kinship in Terms of Matrimonial and
Residential Trajectories

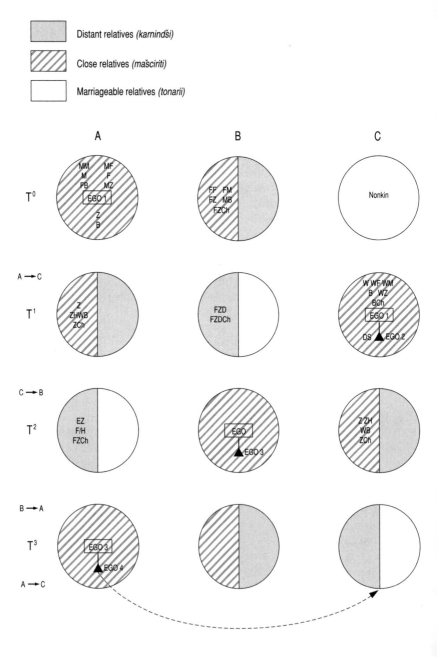

therefore one more notch, between ego and the recognized term of the alliance, in other words WB/ZH, *šiiro* (FZH) for ego's son, and WMF for ego's son's son. In this way, distance between cousins is maximized, since marriage, which is focused (as for the Achuar) on a totally "affinal" affine (FZH), is still delayed for a generation because of FZ's recognized "consanguinity" and consequently FZD's quasi-sibling status (nevertheless less "consanguineous" than FZS, precisely because she is cross sex with respect to ego). Briefly, in this configuration FZ takes the place of MB in the Achuar variant, while FZD takes over the position occupied by FZ (see figure 8-8).

Furthermore, marriage is always conceived of in terms of a collective trajectory, which explains in part why MZH is marked, being also and above all the *širikama* (brother-in-law) of my father's co-resident "brother." In sum, marriage is not thought of exclusively in terms of the father's marriage, but also and at the same time in terms of those of his brothers, no doubt a corollary of the "globalized" model of Kandoshi marriage. Once again, one finds a sharp but paradoxical divergence between ego's classificatory standpoint and that of ego's siblings. For the Aguaruna, however, the disjunction falls between ego (plus his brothers) and his parallel cousins. For the Kandoshi it divides ego and his brothers, despite their common matrimonial and residential trajectories, since the terminology explicitly combines even as it distinguishes the paths of the father's marriage (marking of FZH) and that of the father's "brother" (marking of MZH).

There is another reason for MZH's terminological privilege, though, which is the fact that, to prescriptive marriage between children of opposite-sex patrilateral cross cousins is added an alternative and complementary formula, that of marriage between descendants of same-sex cross cousins or opposite-sex parallel cousins in G^{+2}, that is, between ego and his MMMZSSD/MMFBSSD/FFFZSSD/FFMBSSD, or between ego's grandchildren and those of the female cross cousin's brother who gave him a daughter-in-law (see figure 8-8). In fact, if the closure between children of *širikama* in G^{+2} comes about (marriage between a member of group C and a member of group B, as in figure 8-7), in the *following* generation the marriage does indeed take place between children of a paternal *šiiro* (FZH) and a maternal *šiiro* (MZH) (i.e., between a member of group B and a member of group A, as in figure 8-7). This is yet another justification for the individualization of the term for MZH as well as FZH. In this way, Kandoshi nomenclature plays on the discrepancy between a "local" or individual perspective on marriage (bias toward children of opposite-sex patrilateral cross cousins, i.e., between FFZHDD/MMBSS) and a "global" perspective characteristic of the local group as a whole (marriage between descendants in parallel lines of two co-resident "brothers" in G^{+4}, or of two *pairs* of brothers-in-law, or *širikama*). Furthermore, the "desynchronization" of the *genealogical* and of the *spatial* conjunctions of an ego's kin has the effect of accentuating the apparent heterogeneity of the subsequent marriages with respect to those contracted by ascendants.

That the Kandoshi mark both phases of the alliance structure in their terminology (unlike the Aguaruna, who mark only the individual cycle), is not surprising: whereas their local kindred, unlike those of the other Jivaro, are exogamous, they

Figure 8-8
Kandoshi Marriage Models

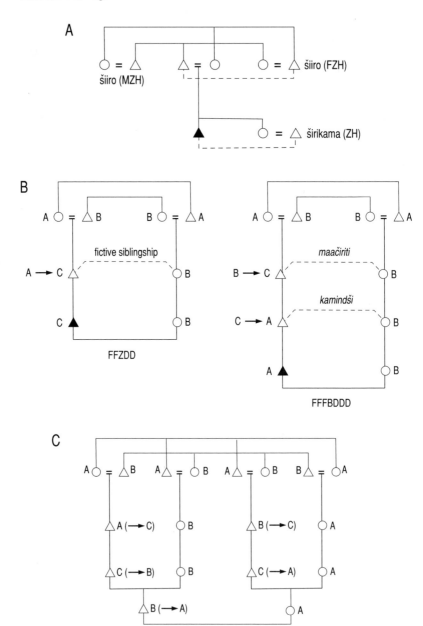

Key: A. The two šiiro, B. The two models of alliance, C. Conjunction of the two models.

have discontinuous matrimonial zones that remain relatively stable over time, as indicated by genealogical data. Now, if the FFZDD marriage bias absorbs the genealogical dilution, the tendency toward deferred repetition of global matrimonial exchanges (signaled by the marked term for MZH) effectively circumscribes the otherwise unlimited expansion of the matrimonial network. Consequently, and despite appearances, the Kandoshi do have *endogamous nexi* built around the marriage relationship and reproduced by it exactly as in the other Jivaro groups, except that the Candoa's nexi are considerably more extensive. Although data are lacking, one may suppose that a Kandoshi nexus includes six to seven local groups (although in theory three suffice), that is, between 400 and 600 persons. It is worth recalling that the Candoa, nearly wiped out in the seventeenth and eighteenth centuries by colonists settled in the upper Amazon and by the Jesuit *reducciones,* were probably more numerous than the actual Jivaro at the time of the conquest, and that they seem then to have had more massive and powerful war chieftaincies than the western Jivaro.

Odd as it may seem, the Kandoshi kinship system is not unique in the South Amerindian landscape. In the first place, it is likely that the kinship systems of certain Xingu groups, which associate bifurcate generational terminologies with avoidance of first-cousin marriage, belong to the same type as the Candoa system (Coelho de Souza 1995). Above all, the Kandoshi model bears a surprising resemblance to the Ngawbe (Guaymi) system described by Phillip D. Young (1970) and evoked by Franklin Tjon Sie Fat in chapter 3 of this volume. Like the Candoa, the Guaymi combine two marriage formulas, accompanied by purely "prohibitive" rules forbidding marriage between first cross cousins, classified as siblings. According to Young, marriage is usually biased toward FFZDD or FFZDDD, since the Guaymi, unlike the Jivaro, practice oblique marriage; nevertheless, the Guaymi also have shorter cycles, implying marriage with MMBDD. The two formulas complement each other: ego cannot marry a woman who would be *both* his FFZDD and his MMBDD. At the same time, sister exchange is strongly valorized, and so FFZDD is also FMBDD, just as MMBDD is also MFZDD. In other words, the Ngawbe marry either patrilateral second cousins (FFZDD / FMBDD) who are cross in the Iroquois type but parallel according to Dravidian computation, or matrilateral second cousins (MMBDD), who are cross *more dravidiano* and parallel *more iroquois.* By contrast, the Candoa lengthen one of the cycles: their first formula corresponds to the Guaymi "long" marriage, between patri(bi)lateral second cousins (FFZDD/FMBDD), and their second to marriage with a third cousin, at the same time MMMZSSD, MMFBSSD (cross by Iroquois calculation, parallel by Dravidian accounting), or FFFZSSD, FFMBSSSD (cross in Dravidian, parallel in Iroquois). In short, the Ngawbe model stands exactly halfway between the Aguaruna (biased toward MMBDD, a relatively "close" second cross cousin) and the Candoa, skewed either toward a relatively "distant" patrilateral cross cousin (FFZDD) or toward a relatively "close" matribilateral third cousin.

For the South American lowlands, there is nothing exceptional in the presence of alternative marriage models within a single system, or more accurately, a marriage formula comprised of two structurally linked parts. Two of the Jivaro subgroups seem to present this kind of structure: the Corrientes Shiwiar (Seymour-Smith 1988) and the Morona-Santiago Huambisa (Lena 1986–87), both of whom exhibit classic Dravidian reference terminologies and alternate between a Shuar-Achuar–type marriage of "close" bilateral cross cousins and a "distant" form of marriage with persons defined as "nonkin." According to F. M. Renard-Casevitz, the Matsiguenga (Arawak living in the eastern foothills of Peru) also have a dual marriage model (within the framework of preferential cross-cousin uxorilocal marriage): elder brothers usually opt for a close marriage (genealogically and above all spatially), younger brothers, for a (spatially) "distant" marriage. This divergence built into the matrimonial trajectory of same-sex siblings, whether real or classificatory, no doubt explains the "bi-ego-centered" and even multi-ego-centered character of some of the terminologies discussed: insofar as the two marriage formulas are interdependent, the classificatory grids (Dravidian or Iroquois) shed their strictly ego-centered aspect and incorporate tangentially and to varying degrees the perspectives of other members of the network, minimally that of the sisters (e.g., the Matsiguenga; see chapter 10), that of the classificatory brothers (Aguaruna), and eventually that of the real brothers (Kandoshi and perhaps Guaymi).

Properly speaking, then, the superficial similarities between the Candoa and the Jivaro variants do correspond to structural homologies. In particular, Kandoshi kinship has the same way of absorbing a marriage in one generation and projecting it "downward" that is, into the future. It also has the same way of using sexual dichotomy to neutralize or project affinity (I will not diagram the process here, but this feature shows up clearly in the terminological transformations affecting affinal genealogical positions over two generations. It also shows up when one superimposes the classificatory "maps" of a father and his son), the same nonambiguous characterization of nodal male genealogical positions: while female affines (and notably WM, who is clearly assimilated to a father's sister) may forswear their original consanguinity, the men who anchor the alliance must be either absolutely affines or absolutely consanguines, as is the case for the Achuar; and this logic indeed supposes a fundamental distinction between the two constituent axes of kinship. At the same time, in the Kandoshi model it is clearly not possible to define future affines, *except as "nonkin,"* inasmuch as their classification does not depend, a priori, on their being cross or parallel, but on their genealogical distance.

In sum, the Kandoshi system does indeed belong to the same set as the Jivaro. Like the other variants examined here, it is based on a representation, or an ideal of symmetric restricted exchange (the Jivaro "atom of kinship" would be ego, Z, ZH/ WB) with cross cousins, in the (Aguaruna and Kandoshi) "complex" formulas being assimilated to siblings, and on a rigorous distinction between affinity and consanguinity. This opposition can be skewed, however, by particular functional constraints that give a concentric twist to a structure customarily modeled as a two-part table. In the Kandoshi case, these constraints are the nonrelevance of the cross/parallel dichotomy for defining affinal terms and the intervention of reconsanguinization/deconsanguinization mechanisms linked to the necessity of transmitting the alliance relation on both individual and collective levels while erasing genealogical connections stemming from earlier marriages. All Jivaro systems thus

Figure 8-9
Jivaro Marriage Variants

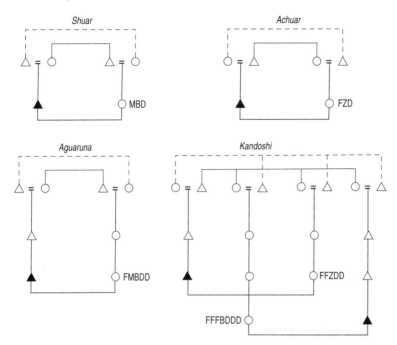

employ the same elements, work with the same logic, and utilize identical structures. All are governed by a concern for repeating a more or less genealogically distant marriage and perpetuating zones of intermarriage.

If I have harped on the cultural homogeneity of the Jivaro, I have done so because it is extraordinarily systematic at every level: the variants observed between the kinship systems are not a matter of either chance or history. It can even be shown by studying intratribal variants that demographic happenstance tends to exacerbate the distinctive features of the variant rather than to transform or efface them. Thus, despite their demographic collapse, none of the Candoa groups has reverted to a "simple formula," nor have the Shuar, on the rise for the last forty years and more, adopted the "rich formula" typical of the large Aguaruna nexi. The variations in their kinship models are thus stable and important components of Jivaro tribal identity.

Furthermore, all these systems clearly lie along an axis running from the "simplest" formula and the "closest" marriage (the Shuar model of marriage between close matribilateral cross cousins, which I have not discussed here) to the most "complex" formula and the most "distant" marriage (the Kandoshi model of marriage with the FFZDD or with a third cousin), associated with widening zones of intermarriage (which are also political units) (see figure 8-9).

In terms of the indigenous model, the discrepancies between the different formulas stem from the relative concentration or dilution of sameness between spouses and more generally between affines. It appears from this that full affinity in the Jivaro global model demands in all cases difference of sex in the horizontal relations between the "lines" involved in the marriage, such that the spouses' parents are always in a real or fictitious relation of opposite-sex siblings. This produces sameness of sex in vertical relations (except by definition between MB and his daughter), which has the effect of increasing the degree of "consanguinity" of the kin they unite, since any additional otherness (by change of sex) is avoided between descendants by parallel-sex filiation from an original brother-sister pair.

I believe I have now demonstrated that the variants of the Jivaro kinship system are all part of one "cultural" transformation group. But we still need to see if my two "rich formulas" (the Aguaruna and Kandoshi variants) can properly be regarded as Dravidian—in other words, if this set is also a transformation group of a single structural kinship type.

The Aguaruna variant, for its part, is obviously atypical of classical Dravidian systems. First of all, marriage takes place between "parallel" cousins (according to type A computation), who are nevertheless sociological and ideological "cross" cousins. Second, it shows the beginnings of a separate affinal nomenclature. That being said, Aguaruna kin classification is based on a perfectly clear and exhaustive distinction between affinity and consanguinity—*but not between affines and consanguines;* this distinction suffices to account for all of the oddities of the vocabulary. Furthermore, this variant always defines marriage in terms of past and future unions, with a view to replicating an alliance, and always in terms of the crucial male positions. From this standpoint, the Aguaruna variant corresponds perfectly to the spirit if not the letter of the Dravidian model as defined by Dumont.

Such cannot be said a priori for the Kandoshi variant: marriage is "prohibitive" rather than prescriptive, and the tripartite division of reference terms is not absorbed, as in the Aguaruna system, by a more classic binary vocabulary of address. This gives Kandoshi nomenclature an Iroquois shading, which is countered, however, by the apparent abolition of the cross/parallel distinction in favor of the division of "consanguines" into lineals and collaterals. Needless to say, things are far from clear when it comes to the opposition of Type A and B crossness; certain kin types (see table 8-2) are indeed classified according to the Iroquois model, but the terminological merging of generations masks the cross or parallel character of most genealogical positions. In fact, the Trautmann and Barnes opposition seems irrelevant to this context.

But what if a theoretical model of a "prescriptive marriage between children of bilateral cross cousins" is combined with a classificatory grid based on the necessary and sufficient distinction between affinity and consanguinity? It immediately becomes evident that it is perfectly logical to classify MBCh and FZCh as "consanguines," since ego cannot marry them even though they are cross kin; likewise, FZ and MB will be classified as consanguines because they cannot be real affines for ego in G^{+1}. It is therefore theoretically conceivable to have "Dravidian" nomenclatures that assimilate F = MB and M = FZ *providing they also hold:* F, FB,

MB, and so forth are *different* from FZH; and M, MZ, FZ are *different* from MBW. Likewise, in G^0, they may have B = MBS = FZS = FBS = MZS, and so on, *providing these are different from* ZH. This mode of classification distinguishes *only* between consanguines and affines: plainly, the boundary between the two types of kin does not fall in the same place as in the classic model because it splits away from the cross/parallel mechanism. Now this is exactly what transpires in the Kandoshi variant, except that it drastically simplifies the opposition, for functional reasons, by eliminating the criterion of genealogical level for all consanguines' affines, cross or parallel. Thus, insofar as the vocabulary is ego-centered and is built on a necessary and sufficient opposition between affinity and consanguinity (the only affinal positions given special terms are the spouses' parents or a child's spouse), and insofar as marriage is governed by a transgenerational view of the relationship (the vocabulary marks all of the genealogical positions through which the relation must pass, both individually and collectively so as to perennialize the zones of intermarriage), the Kandoshi model can be said rightfully to belong to the Dravidian corpus.

Consequently, the Jivaro macrogroup does constitute a transformation group of single kinship structure, and in this respect it is of considerable theoretical interest. Among the lessons that may be drawn, the first is that a profound structural link, which is in no way simple or univocal, does indeed exist between nomenclature and form of marriage. This is not, of course, a *one-to-one* correspondence between a typological model of terminology and a marriage formula. Nevertheless, a concrete terminological configuration always entertains a necessary relationship with the local marriage model, even though this relationship cannot be deduced solely from an analysis of the reference vocabulary; it appears only if the *whole* kinship terminology, both of reference and of address, is taken into account and a temporal dimension is introduced into the analysis. In other words, it is the interplay of the different vocabularies and their internal *transformations* that are really significant of the form of marriage, which is obviously a process and not a pure form. It follows that kinship typologies based solely on a synchronic consideration of reference terms are of scant interest from the sociological point of view.

In the same vein, the terminological features often regarded as symptomatic of a kinship system, have, if taken separately, a very limited diagnostic capacity and can even lead to typological aberrancies. For instance, in certain contexts, the presence of a limited but specific vocabulary for affines may not be the mark of an incipient "Iroquois system" but simply the product of a Dravidian logic working under the constraints of close kindred exogamy. In the same way, the presence of a "Hawaiian"-type G^0 terminology may be, rather than an indication of transition toward a "complex" system, the outcome of a perfectly elementary Dravidian alliance structure reproducing endogamous cognatic kindreds who think of themselves in terms of consanguinity. Lastly, the criterion of "type A crossness" does not in itself suffice to make a Dravidian system: although it may be true that all "type A's" are Dravidian (we still need to verify the type of crossness in so-called Crow-Omaha nomenclatures), all Dravidian terminologies do not necessarily imply type A computation. The Aguaruna and Kandoshi examples show that the distinction between affinity and consanguinity can work separately from the cross/parallel substratum and skew the system in unexpected directions, while strictly respecting the logic of complementary opposition between two principles and two only. That being said, Trautmann's criterion remains valid if a distinction is made between formal crossness and "sociological" or ideal crossness; in effect, the formally parallel kin found in the position of affines in the variants seen here are indeed "cross" kin, from the standpoint of both native ideology and function. But once again this sociological crossness appears only if the overall logic of the system is considered and can obviously not be deduced from the reference terminology. In short, I am willing to see Dravidian systems defined as "systems with Type A crossness" providing this crossness is given a "sociological," or a cultural, rather than a formal content; this proviso, however, robs Trautmann's distinction of much of its power as a simple and immediate diagnostic feature of kinship systems.

In sum, if one wishes to keep the category "Dravidian system" as an individual structural type, it seems that the only solution is to expand and complete the definition Dumont has given it: a system of transmission of the marriage relationship, which splits the recognized field of kinship into two and only two categories, affinity and consanguinity. This distinction obviously does not eliminate the ambiguity of certain genealogical (and therefore terminological) positions, certainly not the ambiguity of those that anchor the marriage relation. Ambiguity is even inherent in the system, since it must continually transmute close consanguines into affines, and vice versa; it is therefore a diachronic process before it is a classificatory grid. That is why the gap between the terminological registers is much more pronounced in Dravidian nomenclatures than in the Iroquois, which rarely exhibit the same wealth of teknonymous procedures that characterizes the bilateral Dravidian systems of Amazonia.

The whole problem is to define the status of this Dravidian type and explain how it relates to other systems of matrimonial exchange. Of particular interest are the Australian systems of symmetrical marriage using "sociocentric" Dravidian-like terminologies, and the Iroquois "ego-centered" systems, which imply a genealogical computation of crossness inverse to that of Dravidian terminologies while usually excluding, unless I am mistaken, marriage between close bilateral cross cousins, which is prototypical of the Dravidian model.

In the Amazonian context, I am inclined to think that the "Kariera"-type systems of the Panoan groups fall into the same structural type as the Dravidian, since their organization into "sections" is not organically related to marriage. Keeping in mind the nature of intra- and intertribal relations in the Pano group as a whole, it seems to me that this institution is superimposed on the marriage structure and combined with it, capable of integrating virtually any individual from the same macroethnic group. From this standpoint, the "section" system seems to function in a way that is homologous with the Panoan's social use of language, characterized on the intratribal level by a purely radical (in the proper sense of the term) "general language"; thus one Pano can always communicate with any other Pano, whatever the geographical and cultural distance between them, by means of a common system of roots. In other words, the Pano "sections" could be a sort of global sociological "grammar" separate from the alliance structure properly speaking, which would explain the fact that it is governed by a sociocentric point of view complementary to and not exclusive of the ego-centered viewpoint characteristic of the Dravidian system.

Regarding the relationship between "elementary" systems, to which the Dravidian model in principle belongs, and "(semi)complex" systems, to which the Iroquois model is supposed to belong, "rich" Dravidian systems such as the Aguaruna, and especially the Kandoshi system, raise some difficult questions even as they open up interesting avenues of investigation. The greater complexity of the Jivaro variants implies three orders of development:

1. A shift away from a "dual" structure and toward first a tripartite and then a concentric structure, the affinity/consanguinity distinction being gradually subsumed into the (spatial and/or geographical) close/distant distinction.
2. The progressive expansion of the intermarriage zones.
3. The progressive duplication of the perspectives combined in the terminology, resulting in increased individualization of the classificatory grids.

Can these facts be generalized? Are they, in other words, typical of a specifically Dravidian form of "complexity"?

If the Kandoshi variant belongs to the Dravidian structural type, it can be classified, in theory, as an "elementary" structure. Now the Candoa model clearly has one foot in "typological" complexity (that its workings are complex is obvious): by its marriage formula, by the "prohibitive" character of the way it expresses the marriage bias, by its combination of features drawn from separate "elementary structures," it indisputably resembles a "semicomplex" system (like those defined by Héritier). And one can even see that it would not take much to make it even more complex. For example, all that would be needed would be to get rid of the maternal *siiro's* (MZH) marking and the feature indicated by this marking, namely, the closure and perpetuation of the intermarriage zones, and to prevent (as the other Jivaro do) "brothers" from marrying within the same kin groups (thus to *simplify* the system in certain respects), in order to obtain a system in which expansion of the matrimonial network would theoretically be unlimited, and marriage would be, to use Viveiros de Castro's expression, (ideologically) patri-multibilateral. Does this mean that this variant should be regarded as a cognatic counterpart of the Crow-Omaha systems? Héritier has always maintained that a Crow or Omaha system could function without unilineal descent reckoning; that being said, Kandoshi terminology offers only a much attenuated and highly ambiguous version of the features usually associated with these kinship systems, since it utilizes neither strictly type A nor strictly type B crossness, and so although it may be "semicomplex," the term applies only to the form of marriage and not to the terminology.

And yet it is true that in all South Amerindian bilateral systems that, like the Candoa, orient marriage toward distant kin of the same generation (second or third cousins), the terminology tends to be skewed toward the Iroquois pole or, while remaining perfectly consistent, tends to combine, merge, or eliminate Trautmann and Barnes's two types of crossness. In other words, the matrimonial "complexification" of a Dravidian system seems incompatible with maintaining a strictly Dravidian crossness in a purely ego-centered terminology; the fact is, no one has yet discovered any true "Dravidian generational" systems that would be the counterpart of the "Iroquois generational" systems discussed by Tjon Sie Fat in chapter 3 of this volume, that is, forms that prohibit marriage between first cross cousins while systematically adhering to a type A crossness. If any such systems happen to exist on the Indian Subcontinent, I know of none in Amazonia, and I suspect that they are able to develop *only in the context of unilineal descent reckoning or sectional organization.* This is perhaps because the type A calculation is, as Tjon Sie Fat emphasizes, less "associative" than type B computation, and much more restrictive as far as permissible genealogical paths are concerned. It is such that, as soon as marriage takes on a "complex" character, it must either "go Iroquois," and shift toward a type B calculation or else bring in nongenealogical procedures for allocating kin, the organization by sections or lines taking over—automating as it were— the selection of permissible genealogical paths. Furthermore, if type A crossness places strong restrictions, from a terminological standpoint, on the field of cousins who are possible spouses, then it may be that true "Dravidian generational" systems will be found only in large societies where the terminological limitation is compensated by demographic abundance. In the end, given the same distant marriage formula, maintaining an ego-centered vantage point encounters functional limits sooner in the Dravidian (A) mode than in the Iroquois (B).

From this angle, the Dravidian and Iroquois systems no longer appear as truly distinct types, but rather as *modalities* of a common structure, associated with sister exchange and marriage between globally bilateral cousins (regardless of the ideological bias reflected by the native model), that is, associated with the *more or less deferred replication of an earlier alliance,* even if this is not apparent in the terminology or recognized in the indigenous model. In this framework, groups favoring marriage between what are considered "close" cousins—independently of the real degree of consanguinity between the spouses—whether they were cognatic or unilineal, would always have fairly Dravidian terminologies. Alternatively, those tending toward marriage between distant cousins defined as "nonkin" would fit into one of the two following options. They would have either ego-centered terminologies that were fairly Iroquois by their type of crossness or hybrid terminologies neutralizing the distinction between the two types of calculation in favor of a "sociological" crossness. In other words, "Iroquois generational" vocabularies—associated with "extended" symmetric exchange in which marriage, even where the spouses are defined as nonkin, reflects a previous alliance—would be nothing more than a complex variant of the Dravidian model. As a second option, they would have terminologies with type A crossness, but this would then be sociocentric (like the Australian systems) or semisociocentric (i.e., in association with unilineal organizations). Starting from this bifurcation, it is easy enough to imagine a series of structural transformations that, beginning with the "Iroquois generational" model, would lead, once more in the framework of an "extended" symmetric exchange with exchange of sisters, sometimes to full-blown generational systems in which all reference to the siblingship of the spouses' ascendants (or, more accurately, to an earlier alliance relationship) is eliminated, sometimes to out-and-out Iroquois unilineal systems (i.e., with an exclusively type B mode of calculation and a fully developed separate vocabulary for affines). Such systems would in all likelihood be correlated with a marriage system maximally extended in terms of length of cycles for the replication of earlier alliances and the genealogical conjunction of the two spouses. Another line of transformations would lead either to the most complex forms of sectional structures, such as those of the Aranda, or to systems retaining a Dravidian type A computation and an ego-centered vantage point, by combining lineage organization with terminological regrouping of genealogical positions normally distinguished in the classical Dravidian model. If it were to be confirmed that the Crow-Omaha type nomenclatures made use of type A crossness, these systems, with their characteristic skewing, would fit our hypothetical model very nicely.

It is true that this speculative construction of a set of transformations based on the *partial* dissociation of matrimonial and terminological systems breaks down the coherence of the "semicomplex" structural type. Yet, in contrast to the classic structural paradigm, it may shed light on the nature of the relations between Dravidian and Iroquois systems and bring out some general processes of complexification. All this makes it easier to grasp the passage from "elementary" forms of marriage and terminologies to their more complex modalities.

NOTE

This chapter was translated by Nora Scott. It is a revised version of a paper presented for the workshop on Dravidian and Iroquois systems organized by M. Godelier and T. Trautmann at the Maison Suger in 1993. It owes a great deal to subsequent discussions with the other participants, in particular M. Godelier, M. Houseman, and E. Viveiros de Castro, as well as to T. Trautmann's acute editorial comments. My thanks to all. This contribution synthesizes a chapter on Jivaro kinship in an unfinished Thèse d'Etat, which should be consulted for a more detailed description of the ethnographic material and of the analyses presented here.

9

Taking Sides: Marriage Networks and Dravidian Kinship in Lowland South America

MICHAEL HOUSEMAN AND DOUGLAS R. WHITE

Dual organization is a unifying concept underlying seemingly dissimilar alliance structures. An appropriate place to explore this idea is lowland South America, where dual organization is common. This chapter concentrates on the patterning of actual marriage networks in this region, with a view to identifying the invariant properties of such networks and then reconsidering the relationship between marriage network structure and other, categorical or jural features of social organization: notably, kinship terminologies, descent principles, and marriage rules. As a means to this end, we develop the concept of matrimonial "sidedness." In doing so, we derive new results concerning dual organization, which make possible a new understanding of Dravidianate systems.

The analysis makes use of published genealogical data on the Makuna (Arhem 1981), the Pakaa-Nova (Vilaça 1989), the Yanomamö (Chagnon 1974), the Trio (Rivière 1969), the Parakana (Fausto 1991), the Waimiri-Artroari (Silva 1995), the Guahibo (Metzger 1968), the Shavante (Maybury-Lewis 1967), and the Suya (Seeger 1981), as well as Hornborg's (1986/1988) comparative study of forty-eight lowland South American societies.

CLASSIFICATORY RULES AND THE NEED FOR ALTERNATIVE MODELS

Following Dumont (1953), Trautmann (1981, 1992) defines Dravidian kinship as a structural type (hereafter "Dravidianate") consisting of a set of terminological distinctions implying a rule of bilateral cross-cousin marriage. At the same time, he is quick to point out that as a cultural type relating to a particular set of concrete cases, this system varies considerably. In some instances, marriage with certain cross cousins (close, matrilateral, patrilateral) may be prohibited or less favored (close cross-kin marriage on the Indian subcontinent appears to range from 4 percent to 54 percent, with an average of about 22 percent; see Trautmann 1981:218). Thus, although marriages with close cross kin (i.e., MBD, FZD, ZD) are compatible with Dravidian terminology (Trautmann 1981:60–62), the marriage rule implied by Dravidian terminology is essentially a classificatory one. Indeed, marriages between first-degree cross-cousins may be few and far between, and in most if not all cases, a sizable proportion of marriages take place between persons who are not considered relatives at all.

In lowland South America, where two-line terminologies abound, the classificatory dimension of Dravidianate kinship is readily apparent. Here also, unions with certain cross cousins may be excluded or discouraged, and close cross-kin marriages often represent a small proportion of alliances. In our sample of nine Amazonian societies with Dravidianate characteristics, the percentage of blood marriages ranges from less than 1 percent to 37 percent, with an average of 11 percent, whereas the percentage of close cross-kin marriages (MBD, FZD, ZD, FZ) ranges from 0 percent to 18 percent, with an average of 5 percent (see table 9-2).

The classificatory nature of the Dravidianate bilateral cross-cousin marriage rule and the attested variability regarding the application of this rule has a simple but far-reaching implication, namely, that an "elementary" model of Dravidianate kinship—that is, one implicitly founded on an analytical reduction to a prototypical configuration of marriage between close kin—is fundamentally misleading. It would indeed seem more appropriate to try to grasp the functioning of Dravidanate systems by means of more complex types of models, specifically ones that incorporate a degree of indeterminacy commensurate with the genealogical uncertainty inherent in the partially indefinite marriage "rule" these systems are held to suppose. This is the type of model that we attempt to develop here.

Our approach to the problem of Dravidianate kinship contrasts sharply with that of the structuralist perspective that continues to dominate alliance theory. This perspective invites us to consider the (positive or negative) precepts governing various sorts of marriage between close relatives as models that, if applied repeatedly, will result in different types of properties of matrimonial networks. For the reasons already stated, we do not begin from such abstracted or reduced structures and thereby hope to avoid some of the common analytical pitfalls that follow from doing so, such as a reliance on static, ahistorical descriptions; the distinction between "mechanical" and "statistical" representations (Lévi-Strauss 1958:311); or what may well turn out to be a largely inappropriate emphasis on consanguineal unions. Instead, we focus on the marriage network itself, which we attempt to grasp as a structured whole. This makes it possible to represent the alliance system in a manner that is at once formal and statistical, and amenable to analysis from the perspective of both structure and historical change. After all, marriage practice is not informed by some ideal synchronic scheme (a "mechanical" model) and does not consist of a mere collection of individual behaviors (a "statistical" model). Rather, it is a dynamic coordination of such behaviors (a network model). Moreover, the recurrent features of this coordination are rather more loosely related to preferential or classificatory precepts than is usually (and often tacitly) supposed. Indeed, the very idea of a network model argues against the notion that action is to be analyzed in terms of preexisting normative or formal principles. It favors the idea of emergent characteristics arising from social interaction itself and governed by various feedback processes. Thus a systematic account of real kinship connectivities constitutes a necessary first step in the development of more realistic, albeit more complex, alliance models.

MATRIMONIAL SIDEDNESS IN AMAZONIA

The first task here, then, is to demonstrate that dual organization is a property of the marriage network as a whole.[1] This can be done through the reticulum of intermarried sibling sets, that is, the criss-crossing chains of brother-in-law or sister-in-law relationships within the (core) network. Only in the most restrictive case will such chains involve partners of the same generation only. Just a few marriages between people of adjacent generations are sufficient for a single ramifying sequence of interconnected sibling groups to encompass most of the network. Particularly interesting for this analysis are cases in which such affinal chains also join up to form closed marriage cycles: the number of sibling-in-law linkages taking place before closure is highly significant.

In most of our sample populations, practically the entire complex of intermarried sibling sets can be represented by a bipartite graph. That is, these sibling sets can be either exhaustively or overwhelmingly divided into two intermarrying supersets.[2] This means that the marriage cycles they make up always close at an even number of affinal connections. In other words, marriages do not take place between co-affines (i.e., affines of affines), or between co-affines of co-affines, or between co-affines of co-affines of co-affines, and so forth. We designate this bipartite ordering of sibling-in-law links by the term *dividedness*.

The prevalence of dividedness is a clear indication that the marriage networks concerned are ordered according to some type of dual principle. In the case of these Amazonian societies, however, a slightly different dynamic is involved: there is a clear tendency toward a bipartite ordering that is reiterated from one generation to the next along sexual lines, such that children of one or both sexes can be assigned to the same "exogamous" superset as their same-sex parent. Thus, with very few exceptions, the marriage network data of these populations can be adequately represented as two supersets of intermarrying patrilines or matrilines. We designate this bipartite, sex-linked alignment of marriage ties (figure 9-1) by the term *sidedness*.[3]

Figure 9-2 shows the network of intracommunity marriages for the Makuna of northwest Amazonia (Arhem 1981). The marriage graph is almost perfectly bipartite; it contains right and left sides organized in the male line (i.e., virisidedness, as we will call it, its opposite being uxorisidedness, and the two together being dual sidedness). The Makuna exemplify a general principle that matrimonial sidedness necessarily decays at some external boundary. As Arhem has emphasized (Arhem 1981:134–37), the dual division of the Makuna operates at the local level but cannot operate when pushed to intertribal marriages: Makuna persons assigned to op-

Figure 9-1
A Schematic of Sideness Organized in the Female Line (Uxorsidedness)

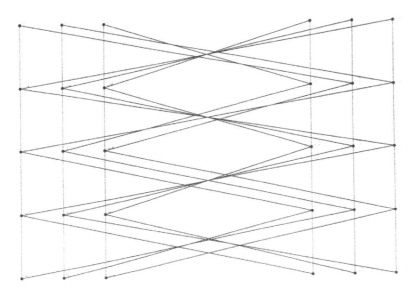

Note: Here, and in figures 9-2 to 9-10, in the interests of representing marriage networks in the most expedient fashion, certain aspects of conventional notation have been reversed. Male and female individuals are indicated by solid and dotted lines, respectively; marriages are indicated by points. Lines converging downward to a same point correspond to spouses (plural marriages are indicated by several lines emanating from the same point), whereas lines radiating downward from the same point correspond to sibling sets.

posing sides may have more geographically distant, non-Makuna affines in common. However, evidence of a lack of consistency at the external boundary is irrelevant to the assessment of sidedness, inasmuch as this boundary condition is a general one: side organization cannot contain the world of all marriages but describes only how marriage operates within a circumscribable network. Few societies fail to intermarry with other groups, but outside marriages are unlikely to preserve bipartite arrangements at this more inclusive level. Sidedness, then, is an essentially local phenomenon, implying a high degree of matrimonial closure.

Sidedness may be also internally bounded by progressive segmentation of the groups involved. This is illustrated by the genealogical data from Chagnon (1974) for the Yanamamö (Shamatari) village of Mishimishimaboweiteri (figure 9-3).

When the network of consanguineal and affinial ties among couples in the village is analyzed into blocks of regular equivalence (White and Reitz 1983), four quasi-exogamous supersets of patrilines emerge. The frequencies of intermarriage between these four blocks (A, B, C, D) are shown in the top part of table 9-1. In the bottom part, these frequencies are doubly normalized. This normalization provides comparable measures of endogamy versus exogamy across different societies (Rom-

Figure 9-2
Makuna Virisidedness

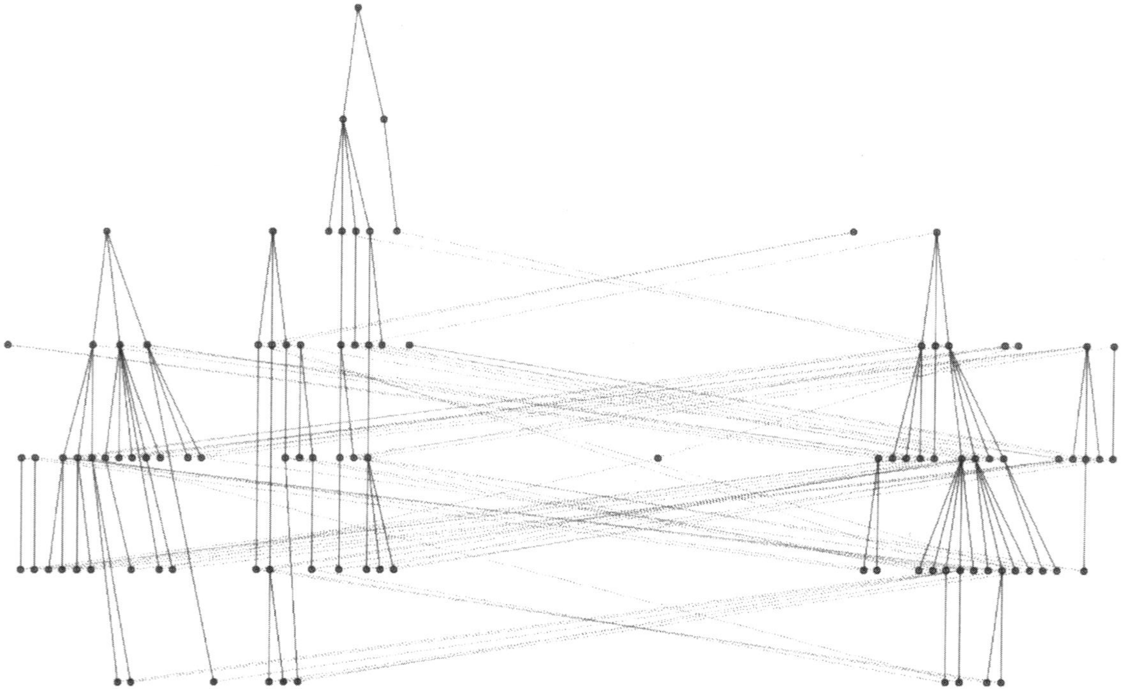

Figure 9-3
Yanomamo Virisidedness

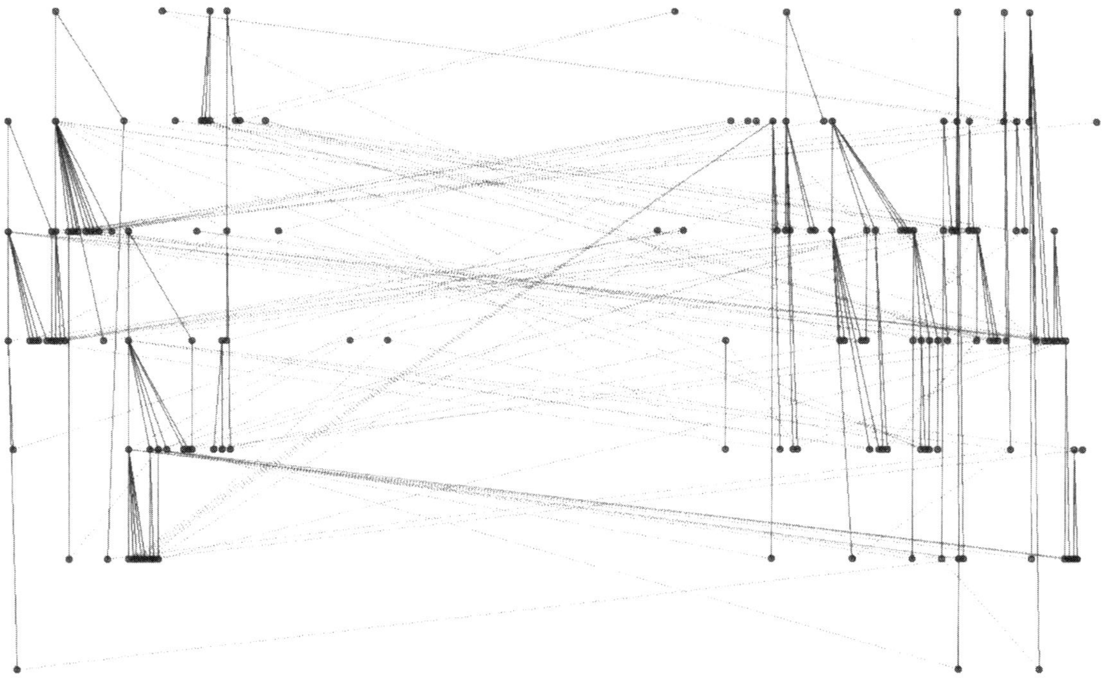

Table 9-1

Yanomamo Intermarriage

A. Absolute number

	A	B	C	D	Total
A	1	36	5	8	50
B	32	2	3	1	38
C	3	2	1	18	24
D	3	2	16	2	23
Total	39	42	25	39	135

B. Double normalized percentage

A	1.43	74.05	10.45	14.07	100.0
B	78.99	7.12	10.85	3.04	100.0
C	10.15	9.76	4.96	75.13	100.0
D	9.43	9.07	73.78	7.76	100.0
Total	100.0	100.0	100.0	100.0	100.0

Average of diagonals = 5.32%

Romney endogamy coefficient = $.0532 - (1 - .0532) \times - .89$

ney 1970). In the present case, an endogamy coefficient of -.89 indicates a strong tendency toward exogamy (exogamy = +.89) among the four supersets of patrilines. The supersets are paired, however: A intermarries with B, and C with D, to form two quasi-endogamous segments in the village with an intersegment endogamy coefficient of .80. If (A + B) and (C + D) were to split off from each other and marriages between them were not counted, the exogamy rates for the sidelike divisions they entail would be 96 percent and 92 percent, respectively (with an average of 95 percent). These rates of sidedness are remarkably high given the constant fissioning of Yanamamö groups: villages are continually being dissolved and reconstituted (e.g., every six to seven years), and constituent groups quite frequently separate into two, perhaps at a generational time scale of twenty years (Chagnon 1974).

Further examples of Amazonian virisided organization come from marriage data for the Pakaa-Nova, a Txapakuran-speaking group living on the Brazilian-Bolivian border (Vilaça 1989); the Parakana, a Túpi population of Brazil (Fausto 1990); the Carib Trio of Guinea (Rivière 1969); the Waimiri-Atroari, another Carib-speaking group of Northern Brazil (Silva 1993); the tropical forest-dwelling Guahibo of Southern Venezuela (Metzger 1968); the Shavante, Central Gé-speakers of Central Brazil (Maybury-Lewis 1967); and the Suyá, a Northern Gé population also of Central Brazil (Seeger 1981) (Figures 9-4, 9-5, 9-6, 9-7, 9-8, 9-9, and 9-10).

As a result of differences in local material and social conditions in which alliances are pursued, sidedness varies from group to group. Makuna sides, for ex-

Figure 9-4
Pakaa-Nova Virisidedness

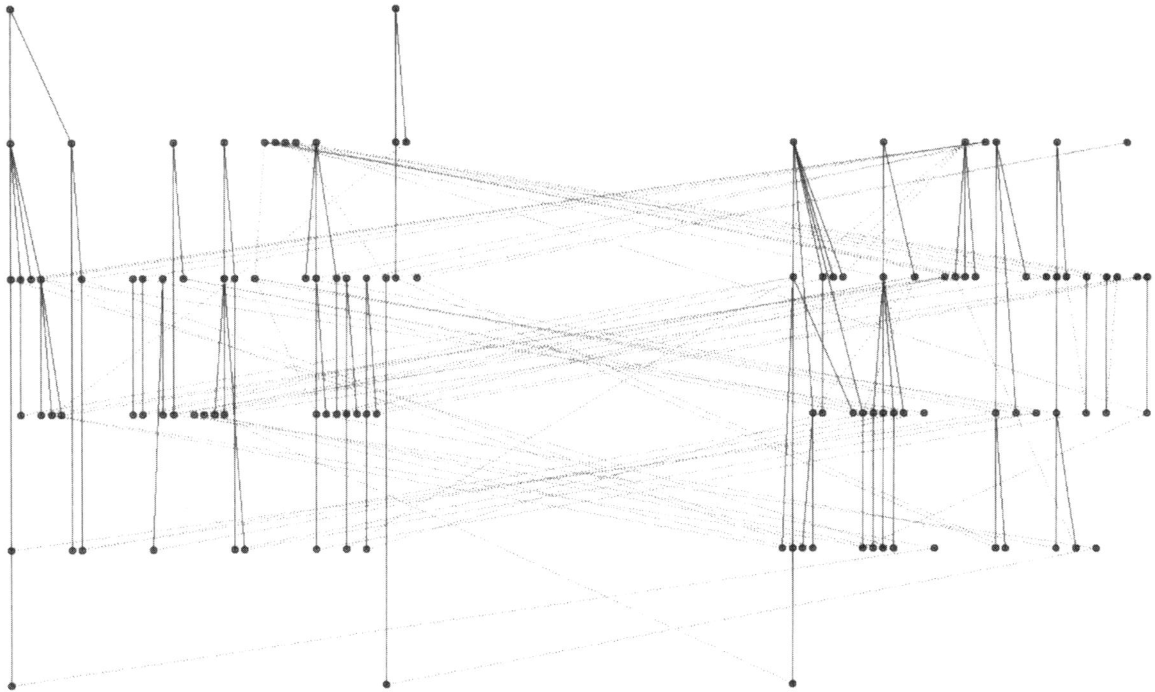

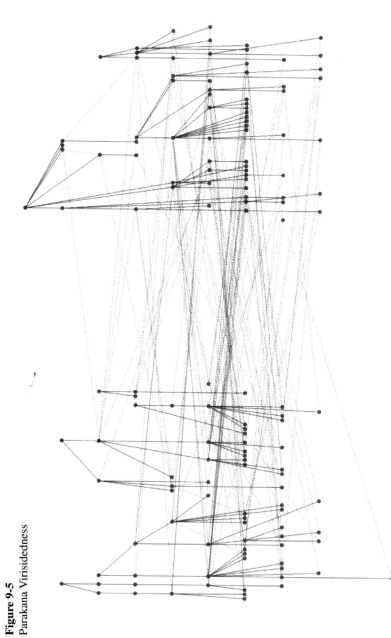

Figure 9-5
Parakana Virisidedness

Figure 9-6
Trio Virisidedness

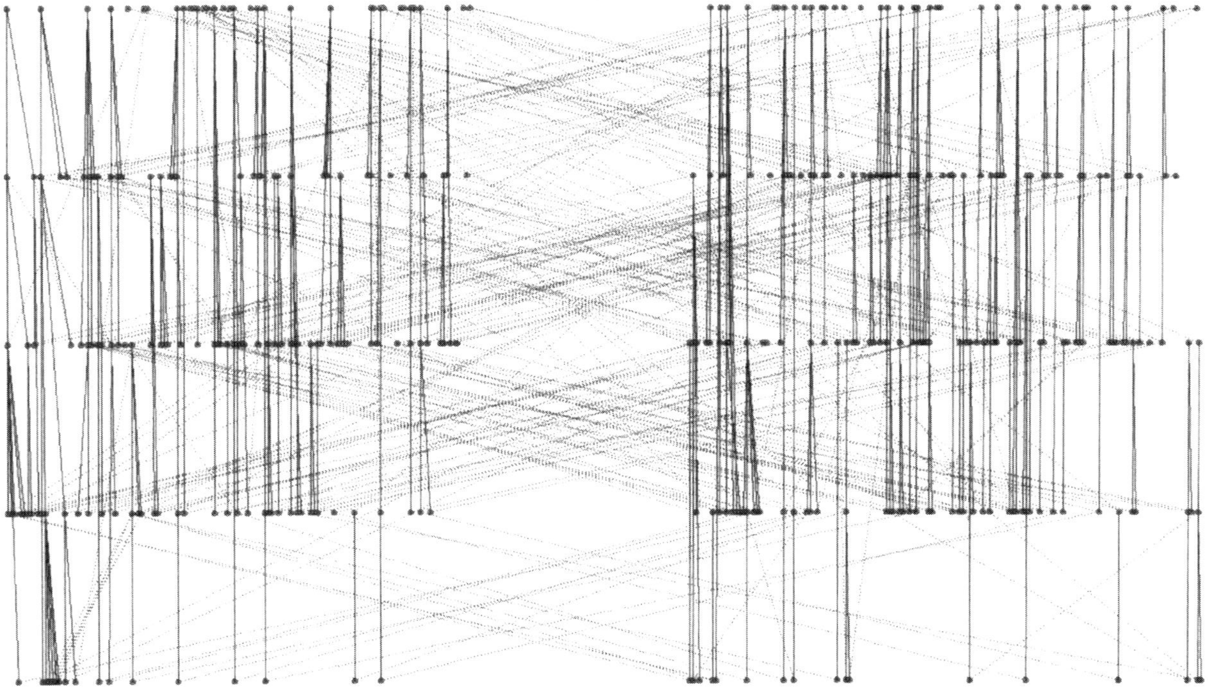

Figure 9-7
Waimiri-Atruari Virisisidedness

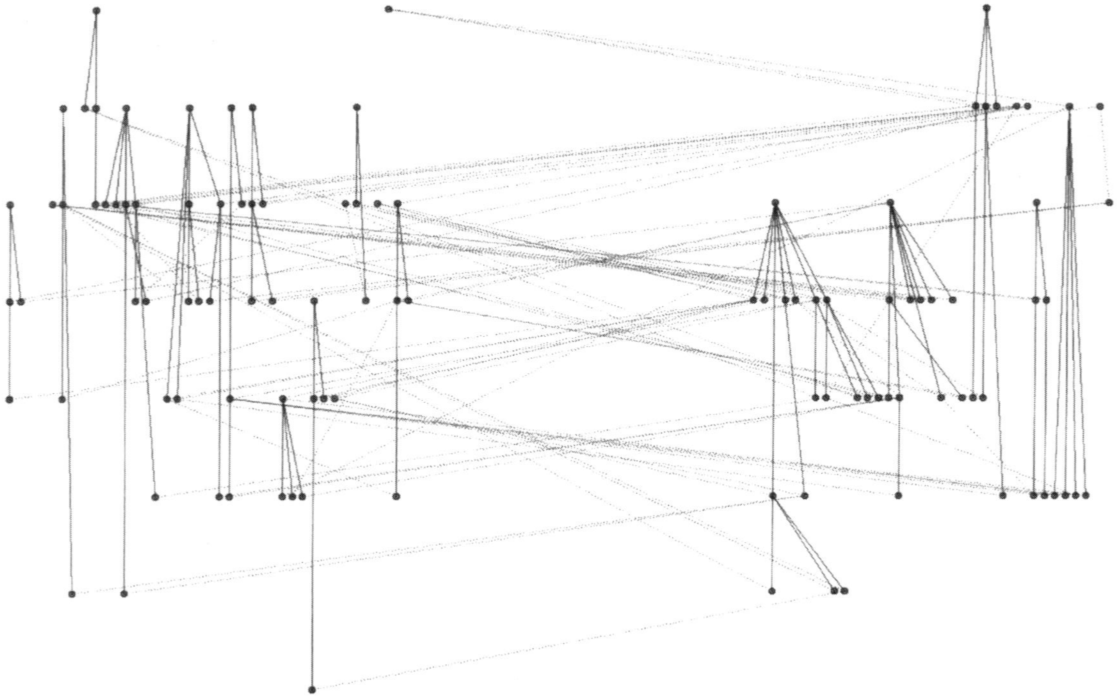

Figure 9-8
Guahibo Virisidedness

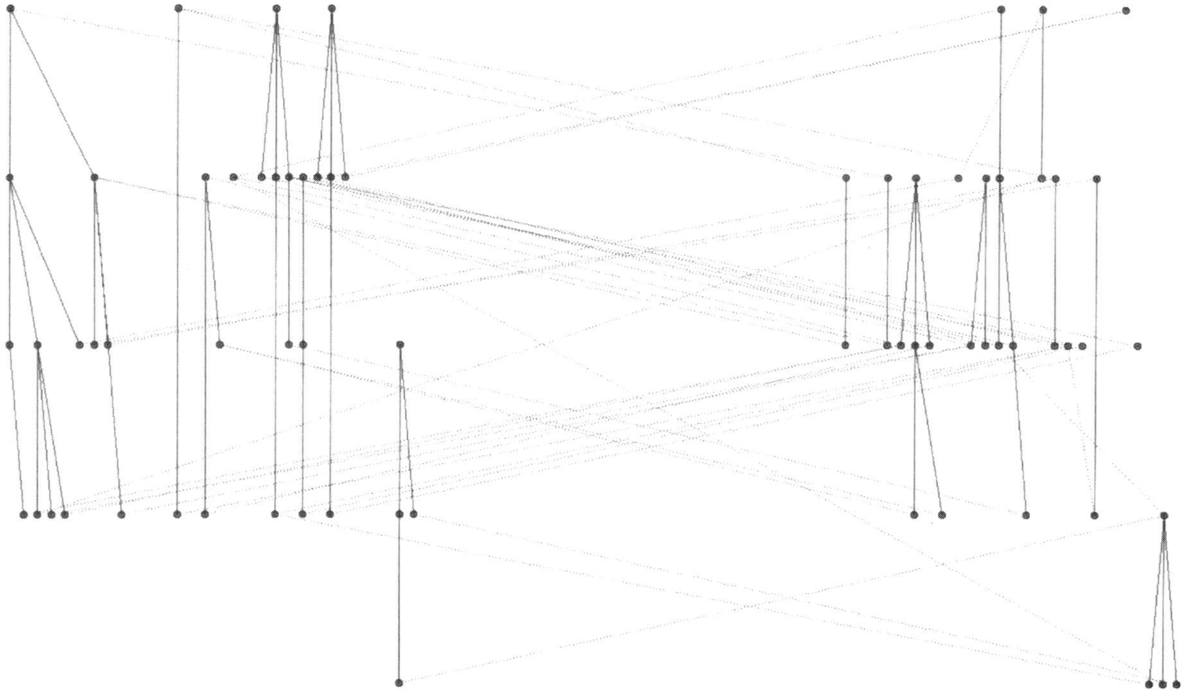

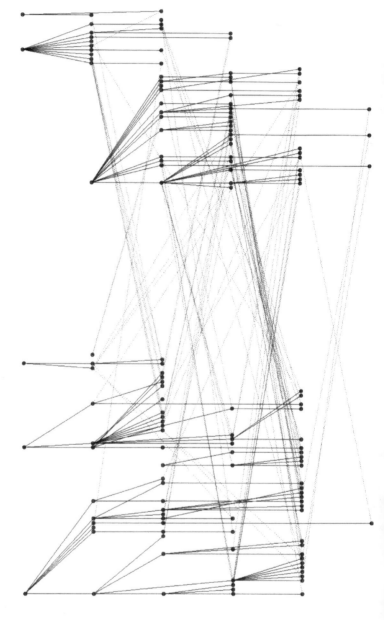

Figure 9-9
Shavante Virisidedness

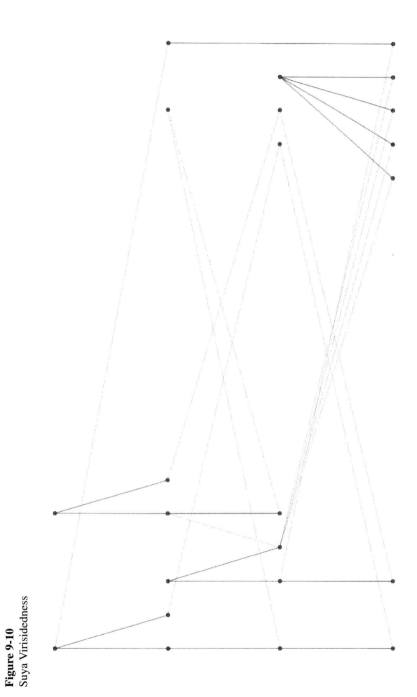

Figure 9-10
Suya Virisidedness

ample, consist of several deep lineage-like units (figure 9-2), and Trio sides of numerous shallow components (figure 9-6). Others, perhaps not as apparent, include a
greater proportion of consanguineal unions, oblique marriages, or sibling-in-law
cycles, which also differ in type. Table 9-2 provides an overview of several of these
differences for the Amazonian cases already mentioned. For purposes of comparison, this table also includes the marriage network of the Sinhalese village of Pul
Eliya (Leach 1971), a Dravidian case having both sidedness and dividedness (see
White and Houseman 1995); the network of the Polynesian island community of
Anuta (Feinberg 1982), which has dividedness but not sidedness (in contrast to the
Parakana marriage network which is sided but not divided); and that of the Tuareg
Udalen of Burkina Faso (Guinard 1984), which has neither sidedness nor divid-
edness.[4]

It is beyond the scope of this chapter to try to account for the various divergences that distinguish these populations. Rather, we wish to emphasize the recurrent pattern of (viri)sidedness that constitutes the larger statistical and structural
context for such local variations: a sex-linked bipartition of the marriage network.
Although the distribution of matrimonial sidedness in lowland South America cannot be fully assessed without more data, the available evidence suggests that it is
fairly extensive. In addition to the nine societies among which we have verified
sidedness empirically, there are at least ten others in Hornborg's (1988) survey for
which the available marriage data or the unambiguous presence of bipartite marriage arrangements suggest that sidedness is highly probable: the Nambikwara,
Mundurucu, Parintintin/Túpi-Cawahib, Amahuacu, Mayoruna, Sharanahua,
Cashinahua, Sanuma, Cuiva, and Karaja.[5] On the other hand, genealogical, normative, or classificatory material running contrary to a sided marriage pattern makes
sidedness seem unlikely among at least seven of the groups Hornborg surveyed—
the Witito, Bora/Mirana, Txicao, Kadiweu, Yanomam, and Mechinacu (Hornborg
1986/1988)—as well as among the Kandoshi (see chapter 8 of this volume). In the
remaining twenty-seven cases of Hornborg's sample, sidedness is possible, but there
are insufficient data to judge, although genealogical, normative or classificatory
elements suggest that sidedness may be likely for eight of them: the Bororo, Kalapalo,
Kuikuru, Barasana, Bara, Achuar/Shuar, Piaroa, and Warao. According to our esti-
mate then, at least 36 percent of the fifty-three Amazonian societies considered
(forty-eight in Hornborg [1986/1988], plus the Pakaa-Nova, Parakana, Waimiri-
Atroati, Guahibo, and Kandoshi) may be presumed to be sided. The overall frequency of sidedness for unambiguous cases ("verified" or "highly probable" versus
"unlikely") is 73 percent.

As these figures show, sidedness is a widespread feature of South American
lowland societies. What is the relationship between side organization and Dravidianate terminology?

SIDEDNESS AND DRAVIDIAN TERMINOLOGY

The particular characteristics of sidedness in any given community depend, of course,
on factors relating to group membership, such as residence, inheritance, and de-

Table 9-2

Dividedness and Sidedness in Several Societies

	N⁰ marriages in (core) network	% of blood mar- riages	% of close cross-kin marriages	N⁰ marriage cycles (% even cycles = dividedness)		Sidedness coefficient
Makuna	105	23%	14%	14	(100%)	.99 viri .82 uxori
Yanomamo	159	1%	0.6%	22	(86%)	.88 viri .73 uxori
Pakaa-nova	120	0.8%	0%	8	(100%)	.86 viri .81 uxori
Parakana	183	37%	18%	79	(78%)	.86 viri .62 uxori
Trio	389	4%	2%	17	(100%)	.87 viri .83 uxori
Waimiri-Atroati	108	7%	0.9%	21	(100%)	.83 viri .70 uxori
Guahibo	70	7%	3%	3	(100%)	.94 viri .86 uxori
Shavante	149	13%	1%	18	(94%)	.95 viri .72 uxor
Suya	23	4%	0%	3	(100%)	.93 viri .93 uxori
Pul Eliya	104	16%	9%	3	(100%)	.85 viri .87 uxori
Anuta	152	56%	0%	16	(100%)	.73 viri .75 uxori
Tuareg Udalen	282	44%	5%	63	(60%)	.62 viri .63 uxori

Sidedness coefficients are based on the number g of son links and f of daughter links, each of which may be located consistently (⁺) or inconsistently (⁻) with a sided pattern; thus there are four base counts: g^+, g^-, f^+, and f^-. These coefficients are in proportional reduction of variance form: $SC = ((g^+ + f^+) - (g^- + f^-)) / (g^+ + f^+ + g^- + f^-)$.

Shavante statistics concern San Macros, the largest Shavante village for which data are available (Maybury-Lewis 1967). Statistics for the village of Sao Domingos (124 marriages in the [core] network) are fairly similar: virisidedness = .95, uxori-sidedness = .79. Putative sibling ties have been counted as true sibling links, such that the percentage of blood marriages for the Shavante may be overestimated.

Biological fatherhood, as reported by the ethnographer, has been systematically accounted for in the case of the Waimiri-Atroari.

scent. These factors do not account for side organization itself, however. Thus, although virisidedness may be reenforced by agnatic descent, as, for example, in the case of the Makuna or the Shavante, its presence among these populations, as among the other, kindred-based societies in our sample, is due to other factors. Conversely, sidedness in itself does not imply any particular type of distribution of individuals into socially identified units. In short, sidedness, like dividedness, is an alliance structure.

At the same time, sidedness is a behavioral feature of alliance, not a classificatory one. It does not imply any global, "prescriptive" matrimonial scheme. Although the presence of exogamous moiety organization (as, e.g., among the Shavante) may act to accentuate sidedness, moieties and sides are not the same. Specifically, sidedness is not a synchronic structure, but a dischronic statistical regularity arising from the coordinate aggregation of actual marriage ties, aggregation that invariably contains a number of inconsistencies. Indeed, as our sample cases show (figures 9-2 to 9-10), sidedness is rarely (if ever) realized in an absolute or perfect fashion: it is an approximate rather than an inherent ordering. The sides to which individuals or descent lines will be assigned may vary according to the point of view adopted, that is, analytically speaking, according to which particular descent line is taken as the initial reference for determining the side membership of the remaining descent lines. This type of context-dependent variability does not apply in the case of moieties. In short, unlike moiety organization, sidedness is a "local" structure. It is perhaps worth emphasizing that this partly indefinite quality of sidedness is not indicative of disorder but is a correlative feature of its complexity: sidedness is best viewed not as a state or absolute condition defined by a specific (ideal) type of marriage, but as a process or relative condition underlying the integration of a diversity of (real) marriage choices into the orderly development of the network as a whole. Thus, as figures 9-2 to 9-10 illustrate, side organization accommodates or generates a wide spectrum of actual marriage ties. By the same token, as attested by the heterogeneity of the populations among whom sidedness is found (for more details, see Hornborg 1986/1988:222–26), it may be said to subsume a variety of categorical or normative systems, one of which is exogamous moiety organization.

As a property of the marriage network as a whole, sidedness is an emergent phenomenon, not a rule-driven one: sidedness does not imply any specific underlying principle. Parallel affiliation—that is, same-sex transmission, reported for twenty-eight of the forty-eight societies in Hornborg's sample, and according to him, "immanent in Dravidian kin terminologies" (1986/1988:237)—is logically consistent with sidedness, as is, for example, bilateral cross-cousin marriage. However, sidedness is no more governed by a "rule" of parallel affiliation (of marriage alignment) than it is regulated by a "rule" of bilateral cross-cousin marriage. At best, such "rules" represent alternative *partial* descriptions of sidedness. Their very incompleteness, relating to indeterminate aspects of sidedness itself, defines the limits of their explanatory role: the first "rule" ignores the crucial fact that sidedness (unlike moiety or descent group membership, for example) is not a transmittable property of individuals, but an ordering process characteristic of the network as such; the second "rule" passes over the genealogically unspecified (classificatory) character of the cross kin it purports to prescribe.

As a statistical feature of the marriage network arising from the synergistic concatenation of particular marriage choices, sidedness is neither a systemcentric matrimonial scheme (such as moiety organization) nor an egocentric marriage model (such as a bilateral cross-cousin marriage rule), but something in between: a "multiegocentric" (see chapter 8) or *multicentric* alliance structure. This analytically intermediate nature of sidedness is directly related to its relative ubiquity in Amazonia. Indeed, sidedness is an overdetermined aspect of the societies in which it is found. In other words, the reiteration of a sex-linked bipartite ordering of the marriage network from one generation to the next derives from the convergent influence of a variety of factors. Any number of two-line terminological schemes; various positive or negative marriage precepts favoring "crossed" categories; principles of parallel transmission involving names, statuses, or objects; instances of ceremonial dualism—all provide relational and conceptual constraints whose cumulative effect, when translated into action, contributes to sidedness (see also Hornborg 1986/1988:288). Reciprocally, an inclination of the evolving field of kin and affinal ties in the direction of a sex-linked bipartition tends to prompt the reiteration of such side-consistent classificatory and normative phenomena. One may thus suppose that sidedness, once in place, is more or less self-sustaining, persisting despite considerable changes in descent reckoning, residence or marriage preferences, terminological patterns, and so forth.[6]

Dravidianate terminology can be understood as an egocentric recoding of sidedness from the point of view of a participant in marriage alliances. Looking up to the senior generation, couples are already formed, either as one's own ancestors or collaterals, but classified as parallel or cross for sibling links. Hence the bifurcate (same-sex sibling) merging pattern (F = FB ≠ MB, M = MZ ≠ FZ) and its attendant 0 generation parallel/cross distinctions. Looking down from one's own generation, couples are yet to be formed, and only one member of each potential couple is ordinarily one's descendant: ego may be a participant in making new marriages for siblings or descendants.

In this perspective, Dravidianate terminology may be defined less as a thing in itself, than as a systematic expression of an ongoing positive relationship between a certain behavioral regularity, *sidedness,* on the one hand, and a particular classificatory principle, *egocentric crossness,* on the other. The latter, it should be stressed, is not equivalent to Type A ("Dravidian") crossness (see chapter 2), but rather to those features that Type A and Type B ("Iroquois") crossness have in common: bifurcate merging, a crossness calculus proceeding from senior generations to junior ones and applied to a limited number of generations, and a pattern in G^{-1} terms whereby husband and wife apply the same relationship term, or set of terms, to their mutual children, whereas brother and sister call their respective children by another term, or set of terms. On one level, this definition is but an empirically grounded, less "mechanical" and more complex rephrasing of Dumont's and Trautmann's original insight (contra Scheffler 1971) that the distinctiveness of Dravidian kinship lies in the supposed link between a set of linguistic categories and a certain type of marriage pattern (bilateral cross-cousin marriage). However, such a reformulation, precisely because it is at once more realistic and genealogically underspecified, can more easily account for both the observed variability of Dravidiante systems (within a given community and from one society to another) and their changes through time.

In sum, Dravidianate kinship occupies the structural space defined by the intersection of sidedness and egocentric crossness. This notion can best be understood by following the two (logical) paths leading out of Dravidianate, as determined by the elimination of one or the other of these two requisite features. The path that consists in maintaining sidedness but relinquishing egocentric crossness leads to the exogamous moiety systems typical of so many Australian Aboriginal societies (e.g., almost all of the populations mentioned in Scheffler 1978). In such systems, egocentric crossness disappears in favor of a more sociocentric recoding of sidedness in which moiety membership is the determinate factor. Although a bifurcate merging pattern remains for the +1 generation, as do attendant cross/parallel distinctions at zero generation, the crossness calculus is applied to a theoretically unlimited number of generations, and the -1 generation terms follow a quite different scheme: the husband and all his siblings apply one relationship term, or set of terms (generally glossed as "man's child") to his offspring, while the wife and all of her siblings apply another term, or set of terms ("woman's child") to these same offspring. Whereas the egocentric crossness pattern found in Dravidianate marks a distinction between individuals' consanguineal and affinial kin (M and F versus MB and FZ), the Australian sociocentric crossness pattern maps a distinction between "my group" (F, FZ, ♂Ch) and "other group" (M, MB, ♀Ch) (see Shapiro 1970:386; see also chapter 15 of this volume).[7]

The other path out of Dravidiante, in which egocentric crossness is maintained but sidedness is abandoned, leads to Iroquois-type systems. Here, the apparent absence of an overall structuring of the marriage network (see, e.g., Kronenfeld 1989, 1993) goes together with a simpler, one-generation-deep crossness calculus incompatible with side organization (cf. Trautmann 1981:86–87). Iroquois crossness may be said to be maximally societally inconsistent in the sense that in the Iroquois case, more than in the other terminological patterns examined here, "two relatives who are, respectively, cross and parallel, from ego's point of view, may be both cross or both parallel from the point of view of some other kinsman" (Kronenfeld 1989:93). Indeed, as Tjon Sie Fat (chapter 3) and Viveiros de Castro (chapter 15) indicate, whereas Australian crossness classifications are wholly coordinate—in Tjon Sie Fat's terms, Australian crossness is fully "associative," in that cross/parallel allocations are independent of the genealogical path taken: Dravidianate crossness is coordinate within generations alone, and Iroquois crossness is coordinate neither across generations nor within them. In Iroquois systems, in which unilineal descent is often present, and correlatively, in which matrilateral/patrilateral differences may be emphasized (Lounsbury 1964a), one should expect any existing bilateral marriage alliance patterns to conform, as Viveiros de Castro suggests, to a "concentric" rather than "diametric" (side-compatible) scheme.

The structural space corresponding to Dravidianate kinship thus opens onto Australian-type exogamous moiety systems, on the one hand, and to Iroquois "concentric" configurations, on the other. Either situation, presumably in the minority in lowland South America, is sure to provide precious indications regarding possible historical paths leading out of or into Dravidianate. Within Dravidianate itself, however, a great deal of variation remains. Both sidedness and egocentric crossness can be realized in a variety of ways, such that the association of these two features encompasses a diversity of particular social configurations. The latter may be thought of as so many arcs along possible "trajectories" (Hornborg 1986/1988) within this structural space. Both the unity of Dravidianate and the range of systems it includes can be better appreciated by looking at a few of these trajectories.

DEVIATIONS AND PERMUTATIONS

A first example is that of Panoan-speaking groups of southeastern Peru. Among these populations, names and decorative motifs are transmitted along agnatic lines from FF(B) to (B)SS for men and from FFZ/MM to (B)DD for women, thereby defining a system of alternative-generation namesake groups. Here, the dual organization implicit in a two-line ordering is horizontally bisected to form an overall "four-section" pattern similar to that of the Kariera of Australia.[8] In at least one case, and perhaps two (the Cashinahua [Hornborg 1986/1988:168 citing Kensinger 1977:235; d'Ans 1974:28–29] and the Mayoruna [Horborg 1986/1988:164, citing Fields and Merrifield 1980:5]), exogamous patrimoieties, each composed of two agnatically related namesake groups ("sections"), are expressly recognized; namesake group members marry persons from the equivalent namesake group of the opposite moiety. In the remaining cases, only the namesake groups are socially codified; the marriage pattern, however, remains the same.

Hornborg (1986/1988:241) has recently argued that

Panoan marriage classes represent an accommodation to the contradictory status of FZ as both consanguine (according to the patrimoiety model) and affine (according to the Dravidian terminology) in strongly endogamous societies featuring dual organization. The Kariera-type marriage classes circumvent the requirements of consistent sociocentric dualism by recognizing the kin-affine dichotomy in alternate generations only. Such systems of alternating generations thus seem half-way between cognatic "alliance endogamy" and "unilineal descent."

Although Hornborg is right about the intermediary character of these systems, his notions of "contradiction" or "cognitive inconsistency" (Hornborg 1993:101, 104) are something of a red herring. They are predicated on an unwarranted conflation of a dichotomy relating to group membership (same group versus different group), on the one hand, and a discrimination pertaining to the regulation of marriage (consanguinity/affinity), on the other (see chapter 15 of this volume). Panoan-speakers, like the Kariera but unlike most Australian Aboriginal populations, define affinity in an egocentric fashion: namesake groups are not, as such, directly involved in the regulation of marriage. Thus, among Panoans, alliance precepts are typically phrased egocentrically in terms of primary kin relations, and not in terms of section or moiety membership (alternative sociocentric phrasings may of course exist as well, as they do, e.g., among the Cashinahua [Kensinger 1984:227–32]).[9] Moreover, with moieties being recognized in only some cases, it is doubtful that Panoan namesake units represent unilineal descent categories at all. Indeed, Hornborg himself (1993:106) speaks of the "unilineal illusion" and suggests an alternative and equally satisfactory account of four-section structure, which is fully compatible with Dravidianate terminology, in terms of an egocentric system of parallel affiliation incorporating a principle of alternate generation (Hornborg 1993:104–5; for a similar model for the Kariera, see Dumont 1966). In short, moieties among Panoan-speakers—as among the Kariera—are to be appreciated as a secondary, optional sociocentric recoding of what remains an essentially egocentric, Dravidianate system.

Taking a quite different tack, one may observe that the most obvious feature of Dravidianate four-section systems is a systematic and across-the-board emphasis on generational distinctions, concomitantly applied to both kin and affines. How such an overall arrangement of sharply discriminated generational positions relates to particular social or material conditions or to other, ceremonial or cosmological considerations, remains unclear. On the level of alliance behavior, however, the implications are fairly straightforward: sidedness in the absence of oblique marriages.

Now, a sex-linked bipartite marriage network without oblique marriages, is at once virisided and uxorisided. Thus, the Panoan four-section system may be understood as a possible sociocentric recoding of the simultaneous presence of both viri- *and* uxorisidedness, that is, a *dual-sided* or *reversible* marriage network structure. This pattern is found not only among Pano groups but also in the network of first marriages among the Makuna (figure 9-2), who permit oblique marriages (ZD and WBD) for second wives only: if one eliminates the two such marriages that are recorded for the Makuna, figure 9-2 becomes dual-sided. In general, such a reversible network should be found in any population in which one mode of sidedness and same-generation marriage are combined. Indeed, these three features— virisidedness, uxorisidedness, and same-generation marriage—are interdependent. The presence of any two automatically implies the third.

This leads to the prediction that lowland societies with sidedness and same-generation marriage will recognize the principle of alternating generations inherent in such dual-sided systems. This hypothesis seems to be borne out by table 9-3, which shows the fifteen populations in Hornborg's (1986/1988) sample for which sidedness has been either verified or estimated as highly probable, as mentioned earlier. These populations have been ordered vertically according to whether they have a small or large proportion of oblique marriages (dual-sidedness versus simple sidedness), and horizontally according to whether they have or do not have alternative-generation name transmission, a clear indicator of the recognition of an alternating generation principle. All nine cases with few or no oblique marriages have

Table 9-3

Alternating Generation and Sidedness in Fifteen Amazonian Societies

	Alternating generation name inheritance	No alternating generation name inheritance
Sidedness with few or no oblique marriages.	Suya X^2* Shavante X^2 Karaja ‖^2 Cashinahua ‖^2 Mayoruna ‖^2 Sharanahua ‖^2 Amahuaca ‖^2 Makuna ‖^2 Cuiva +^{4}	Yanomamo –
Sidedness with frequent oblique marriages.		Parintintin – Nambicuara – Sanuma – Trio – Mundurucu +^{3}

Codes

Alternating generation name inheritance: ‖^2 FF–SS; X^2 MB–ZS with FZD marriage; +^{4} four-generation cycle.

No alternating generation name inheritance: +^{3} three-generation cycle; – not mentioned.

* The Suya have MB–ZS name transmission without FZD marriage, but use names in alternate generations (Hornborg 1988:80).

alternating two- (or four-) generation name inheritance, and all but one (83 percent) of the six societies without alternating two- (or four-) generation name inheritance have frequent oblique marriages.[10]

It should be stressed here that matrimonial "prescription" is extremely weak in dual-sided systems of the Panoan or Kariera variety: such systems imply no particular types of cousin marriages other than those (first, second, third, etc., cousins) that are consistent with sidedness. Restricting marriage to the same generation is isomorphic to classificatory cousin marriage of any type whatsoever. Thus, of twenty-four marriages in figure 9-1, for example (a dual-sided system), one is with a bilateral cross-cousin (FZD = MBD); six with FZD; four with MBD; two with MMBDD; one each with FMBSD, FFZSD, MFMBSDD, FMMBDSD; and seven with nonkin.

Societies having dual-sided marriage networks entailing purely classificatory cross-cousin marriages are, or course, perfectly feasible (e.g., almost all Australian

Aboriginal populations). However, the extent to which dual-sided societies, even single-sided societies, prohibiting first-cousin marriage and lacking some sort of sociocentric armature, actually exist, is still an open question. The issues involved here are highlighted by Tjon Sie Fat's recent demonstration (see chapter 3) that "Iroquois generational" terminologies—a full-fledged Type B crossness in which first (or first and second) cousins are merged with siblings and regarded as unmarriagable—are theoretically side-compatible. It remains to be seen whether sidedness does indeed occur in the marriage networks of such systems (e.g., the Arawakan Mehinacu [Gregor 1977:277]). If it does, this would suggest that the distinctiveness of Dravidianate consists not in the association of egocentric crossness and sidedness, but in the admission, under such conditions, of close-kin marriage, absent from the "Iroquois generational" alliance model. This would be in agreement with Trautmann's (1981:220) proposition that close cross-kin marriage is strongly favored in Dravidian systems. On the other hand, if sidedness is not found in "Iroquois generational" systems, this would imply that when close-kin marriage is excluded, the divergence between Type A (Dravidian) and Type B (Iroquois) crossness calculi is no longer structurally significant: in these conditions, as Taylor suggests in chapter 8, "formal" crossness gives way to a "sociological crossness" in which the consanguinity/affinity discrimination is disconnected from the genealogical cross/parallel opposition. In this respect, marriage network data of "Dravidian generational" populations (Tapirapé, Kadiwéu, Warao, etc.) would be equally demonstrative. Are they sided or not?

Tjon Sie Fat's demonstration also raises a similar question regarding another feature absent from his "Iroquois generational" alliance model, namely oblique marriage. To what degree is a presumption of oblique marriage not, as Good (1980) seems to maintain, an inherent feature of Dravidianate systems, notably as opposed to sociocentric side-compatible systems (e.g., of the Australian variety) in which oblique marriages are in principle excluded? Marriages into adjacent generations invariably bring to the fore the lack of consistency across generations that is the hallmark of Dravidian crossness. At the same time, such unions orient the marriage network away from reversible sidedness toward either a virisided or a uxorisided pattern, as explained earlier. In doing so, they provide, along with discriminations founded upon relative age or genealogical distance (see chapter 15), the grounds for a variety of distinctly egocentric (and therefore more complex) systematic resolutions of this inconsistency.

Another, fairly different type of trajectory within Dravidianate is that followed by Gé-speaking groups, many of whom have named moieties. In this case, however, it would seem that the sociocentric lineal principles thereby introduced are counteracted by a system of "crossed" name transmission. Names are typically passed from MB to ZS and from FZ to BD. As several authors (Melatti 1979; Lave 1979; Viveiros de Castro 1989; Lea 1992) have suggested, the onomastic identifications that this entails may result in Crow- or Omaha-type terminological equations in which FZS is identified with F (Crow), for example, or MBD is identified with M (Omaha).[11] This naming system, when combined with FZD marriage, is congruent with alternate generation naming found in a variety of populations and indicative of dual-sidedness (see table 9-4). Moreover, when envisaged from the point of view of alliance, such a cross transmission of names is fully consistent with side organization. As Hornborg suggests (1986/1988:236), the lines of matrilineally related males and partrilineally related females resulting from such a system can be seen as "structural 'shadows' of the system of parallel affiliation": "This structure [of name transmission] which in fact articulates cross-cousin marriage and parallel affiliation"— we would speak of sidedness—"is most consistently codified in Dravidian kin terminologies." In this light, it is significant that, as figures 9-8 and 9-9 show, both Gê populations in our sample, the Shavante (Maybury-Lewis 1967) and the Suya (Seeger 1981), have sided marriage networks.

A final example is provided by Tukano-speaking communities among whom exogamous unilineal descent groups are clearly present. Here, a strong (patri)lineal principle results in a number of Iroquois-type terminological characteristics such as separate affinial terms, a confusion of consanguines with agnates, and so forth (Hornborg 1986/1988: 172–84). This asymmetrical or unilateral tendency has the potential for the kind of nonassociativity or societal inconsistency previously evoked in connection with Iroquois configurations. At the same time, Tukano-speakers introduce a tripartite division of matrimonial exchange units into agnatic kin, affines, and co-affines (affines of affines), together with a relative avoidance of marriage between co-affinal groups, designated as "mother's [sister's] children" (see, e.g., Jackson 1977:87–89, 1983:88–123; Hugh-Jones 1979:76–106; Arhem 1981:137). This triadic structure in which co-affines are logically confused with kin has the result of continually reorienting the marriage network in the direction of an overall virisidedness. While working against the establishment of exclusive relations of symmetrical alliance on one level, this tripartite discrimination acts to integrate the resultant dispersal of alliances into a higher-order bipartite patterning of the network as a whole. Here, sidedness, if it exists, is realized in accordance with a diametric "multibilateral" model implying reciprocal FZD marriage (see Viveiros de Castro and Fausto 1993:156): a preference for FZD over MBD has been reported for both the Bara (Jackson 1977:87–89) and the Barasana (Hugh-Jones 1979:85).[12]

In this way, local conditions may bring about a variety of modifications or additions to the basic Dravidianate pattern: such as the presence of moieties, sections, unilineal descent groups, and Crow, Omaha, Hawaiian, or Iroquois terminological equations. As the above examples suggest, however, such variations are, first, consistent with side organization (although this remains to be verified), and second, subordinate to an egocentric recoding of this sex-linked bipartite marriage pattern. In other words, combining sidedness and egocentric crossness, they remain distinctly Dravidianate.

OBLIQUE MARRIAGES AND THE LATERALIZATION OF SIDEDNESS

A final point to mention concerns oblique marriages. It would seem that one of the traits of Dravidian systems is the regular occurrence of oblique marriages (Good 1980, 1993). This is also the case in many Dravidianate societies of lowland South America and, to varying degrees, in all of our sample marriage graphs (figures 9-2 through 9-10). The possibilities among Amazonian groups in Hornborg's (1986/

Table 9-4

Oblique Marriage (Even If Rare) and Postmarital Residence

	A: uxori-bias FZ, BD and/or MBDD marriage	Both A and B marriage	B: viri-bias ZD BDD and/or WBD marriage	
Strictly uxorial	Bororo: BD, FZ (through male ceremonial friend) Kraho: BD (rare) Sherente: MBDD (chiefs only)	Caingang: FZ, ZD Karaja: BD (6%), ZD (8%) Machinhuenga: FZ, ZD Warao: FZ, ZD	Sanuma: ZD	
Partly virilocal or bride-service		Amahuaca: FZ, ZD Waiwai: FZ, ZD	Achuar: ZD (rare) Barama River: ZD Barasana: ZD (rare) Karinya: ZD? Kuikuru: ZD Makuna: ZD, WBD Mayoruna:	BDD (rare) Mundurucu: ZD Mayoruna: BDD (rare) Mundurucu: ZD Nambicuara: ZD Pemon: ZD Pioria: ZD Parintintin: ZD Trio: ZD Tupinamba: ZD

Karaja: Pétesch (1992:379) gives rates of 13 percent for eBD marriage, 7 percent for ZD marriage and 2 per cent for MyZ marriage.

Achuar: Oblique marriage is exceptional. Taylor (1982:12) notes ZD marriages as a "semi-incestuous" endogamous extreme only among great–men. On the A side, however, such men may also marry classificatory daughters or the widow of a classificatory father. The latter are not considered here since the actual genealogical links are not stated.

Barasana: Barasana cases of true ZD marriage seem to be "justified by the need to complete an exchange when age and sibling–groups structure prevent a sister exchange" (C. Hugh–Jones 1997:102, cited in Hornborg 1998:178).

Makuna: Secondary marriages only.

Mayoruna: "Several men have wives both of their own generation as well as others of the grandchild generation" (Fields and Merrifield 1980:2–3). "An adult Mayoruna may ask his [...] (MB) or [...] (BZ, BD) for his or her daughter, implying that BDD would be one of the eligible kintypes of his second descending generation" (Hornborg 1988:166).

Pioria: "Incorrect," occasional, secondary marriages. "The reason why spouses are sought in the first descending generation is that by middle age, the sisters of Ego's [brothers–in–law] are all married. Instead of exchanging children, one of [them] marries the other's daughter [...] The compatibility of ZD marriage with a symmetric brother–in–law relationship has been similarly demonstrated among the Nambikuara" (Hornborg 1988:202, citing first Kaplan 1972:569, 1975:133, then Lévi-Strauss).

Tupinamba: "Uxorilocality was the explicit rule among the Tupinamba, but by marrying his ZD a man could avoid having to adopt the subordinate role of son–in–law in the household of his WF [...] [A] major rationale [of ZD marriage] may have been to legitimize virilocal residence in a strongly patrilineal [but uxorilocal] society" (Hornborg 1988:156).

1988) sample are: marriage with father's sister (FZ), with brother's daughter (BD), with sister's daughter (ZD), with brother's daughter's daughter (BDD), with mother's brother's daughter's daughter (MBDD), and with wife's brother's daughter (WBD). This obliquity can be the source of considerable gymnastics if one is trying to incorporate such marriages into a "mechanical" type of alliance model (see, e.g., Rivière 1969). Such marriages pose much less of a problem in the perspective adopted here: they remain clearly subordinate to an overall pattern of sidedness. However, the question remains: if oblique marriages are not to be understood as a basis for the elaboration of special alliance models, what is their significance?

As has already been mentioned, in cases where no oblique marriages occur, the marriage network can be appreciated equally as uxorisided or virisided. From this point of view, sidedness, in and of itself, gives preeminence neither to the male line nor to the female line. Rather, for a particular population at any given point in time, these lines may be stressed equally, or one may dominate the other. Indeed, as we have repeatedly emphasized, matrimonial sidedness does not constitute a timeless scheme, but rather a global ordering process dependent on existing marriage links. It is thus perfectly possible for a marriage network to display sidedness of one sort, say, virisidedness, up to a certain generation, and then, without ceasing to be a sex-linked bipartite ordering, to give way to a dual-sided or uxorisided pattern. Side structure, then, incorporates a further order of indeterminacy, as defined by the virtual simultaneity of these various sided configurations: viri-, uxori- and dual-sidedness are not so much separate organizational principles as they are different actualizations of a same basic *ambilateral* form. The temporary resolution of this indeterminacy into one of these three stable "solutions" depends largely on local conditions, apart from sidedness itself. What might these conditions be?

Given the fact that a situation of reversible or dual sidedness, in which equivalent stress is placed on male and on female lines, corresponds to a condition of same-generation marriage, it seems reasonable to suppose that the skewing of sidedness in favor of one or the other of these two lines of parallel affiliation is closely related to the recurrent presence of oblique marriages. There is a simple structural basis for this idea. Oblique marriages into an adjacent generation can be distinguished formally by the fact that, unlike same-generation marriages, they are not compatible with both viri- and uxorisidedness, but only with one or the other. Thus marriages with ZD, BDD, or WBD (or with FFZD, MBSD, or MBW) are consistent with virisidedness but not with uxorisidedness, whereas marriages with FZ, BD, or MBDD (or with MMBD, MMBDDD, or FZDD) are consistent with uxorisidedness but not with virisidedness.

Building on Moore's ideas (1963) regarding the possible connection between oblique marriage and same-sex succession, on the one hand, and unilateral cross-cousin marriage, on the other, Hornborg has stressed the role of oblique marriage in "disharmonic" systems in which residence and succession are organized along different same-sex lines:

In order for male Ego to stay together with his patrilineal kin in an uxorilocal society, he should marry his classificatory M, Z or ZD. In order for female Ego to remain with her matrilineal kin in a virilocal society, she should marry her classificatory F, B or BS (i.e. male Ego must marry his classificatory FZ, Z or D). It is not difficult to see that both systems will tend to encourage oblique marriage: ZD marriage in the former, and FZ marriage in the latter. (Hornborg 1986/1988:255)

Thus ZD marriage, the most common form of oblique marriage in South America, may be appreciated as "a likely strategy where there is a conflict between male patrilateral loyalties and requirements of uxorilocal residence . . . out of 18 societies in which marriages with ZD occur, at least 16 practice general or sporadic uxorilocality" (Hornborg 1986/1988:261).

Taking into consideration all reported types of oblique marriage, we have ordered the societies concerned according to whether the oblique marriages occurring among them are biased toward uxorisidedness, virisidedness, or both (table 9-4). The results, although largely in keeping with Hornborg's wider perspective, suggest that it is not so much conflictual conditions associated with disharmonic regimes (e.g., where general or sporadic uxorilocality prevails) that are important, as it is the presence/absence of comprehensive uxorilocality, and hence the impossibility/possibility of some sort of virilocal organization. Thus either uxori-biased oblique marriages or a combination of uxori-biased and viri-biased oblique marriages are found in strictly uxorilocal societies, whereas in those groups where virilocality, in some form or another, is present, only viri-biased oblique marriages occur.[13]

As suggested by a number of cases in table 9-4, oblique marriage may play an important role in the consolidation of individual power bases and the emergence of local leaders. Specifically, oblique marriages may be seen as strategic "bids" made by persons in positions of power in such a way as to support the same-sex line of affiliation consistent with their own residential groupings: either the male line (marriage with ZD, BDD, or WBD) or the female line (marriage with FZ, BD, or MBDD). From this point of view, it may be more accurate to see such arrangements as directed toward the realization of close-kin marriages that, additionally, break symmetry through the violation of one but not the other mode of sidedness. The aggregate consequence of these initiatives is to modulate the marriage network as a whole toward either viri-or uxorisidedness. This tendency may be presumed to be self-reinforcing: an inflection of the marriage network away from dual-sidedness—an inflection that can derive from other sources as well (see note 11) may in turn favor the realization of further viri- or uxori-biased oblique unions. Such an understanding of oblique marriage is congruent with the speculations offered in the preceding section regarding the importance of such marriages within the context of Dravidianate systems, that is, those entailing egocentric rather than (Australian-like) sociocentric sidedness.

CONCLUSION

Our goal has been to demonstrate the relevance of a particular approach to the analysis of alliance systems, in which primary importance is given to real matrimonial connections, and structure is conceived above all as an emergent patterning of the marriage network as a whole. Specifically, we have tried to show how the systematic examination of actual marriage ties can open the way to a fresh empirical study of dual organization. We have also proposed a network-based model of Dravidianate kinship: "multicentric" sidedness coupled with an egocentric crossness calculus. This is both a dominant structural type and a likely historical prototype for lowland South America: Amazonian alliance systems can be seen as a family of transformations building off this core connection between a certain behavioral regularity and a particular classificatory principle. Two levels of organization are involved here. The one concerns the considerable variability of detail that distinguishes these systems: such as the presence or absence of named moieties or namesake sections, of unilineal descent groups, of varying types of marriage preferences and prohibitions, and of Crow, Omaha, Hawaiian, or Iroquois terminological characteristics. The other pertains to the underlying formal feature to which this variability remains subordinated, namely, a sex-linked bipartition of the marriage network encoded in a an egocentric crossness.

NOTES

The order in which the authors' names appear is conventionally alphabetical and implies no precedence in authorship. Michael Houseman would like to thank the Davenport community (South Australia) and especially Alwyn McKenzie for their hospitality, as well as the Australian Institute of Aboriginal and Torres Strait Islander Studies (Canberra), especially Naru Ligthart and Kingsley Palmer, for having facilitated his research. Work by Douglas White on kinship and marriage graphs in 1991–92 was supported by the Maison des Sciences de l'Homme (Paris), the Maison Suger (Paris), and the French Ministère de la Recherche et de la Technologie, within the framework of an international and interdisciplinary working group on discrete structures in the social sciences created around the support and research facilities of the Maison Suger. Support for programming developments during 1992 was also provided by Alain Degenne's LASMAS research group at IRESCO (Paris) and the French Ministère de la Recherche. The authors would also like to thank Alf Hornborg, D. Legros, Anne-Christine Taylor and Eduardo Viveiros de Castro for their helpful comments.

1. Strictly speaking, we are concerned not with the network of all documented marriages for a given population, but with a subset of this network we call the *core*. This core network is made up of those marriages having a sufficient degree of interconnectedness to enable one to speak meaningfully of network structure. Specifically, it includes those unions whose partners are connected to each other by one or more prior consanguineal ties (consanguineous marriages), those unions whose partners are connected to each other by one or more prior affinal ties ("relinkages"—in French, *renchaînements*; see Jolas, Verdier, and Zonabend 1970), as well as, in the case of some networks, those unions that connect (sub)cores to each other. In other words, the core is essentially equivalent to the set of all marriages connected to at least two other marriages also in the core. For the notion of "core" and other concepts as used here, see Houseman and White (1996), and White and Houseman (n.d.).

2. We draw upon Hage and Haray's (1991) definition of the bipartite graph of marriage links between the members of different groups as the basic form of dual organization in alliance. Hage and Harary's approach to bipartite marriage graphs, however, suffers the defect of having to posit culturally defined groups between which relations of marriage or alliance are

defined. We apply the concept of bipartite graphs directly to the primary network of kinship relations. Thus the expression "superset" used here to indicate that the possibility of representing the marriage network by means of a bipartite graph does not, in itself, imply the existence of such bipartitions as culturally recognized units.

3. This formalism derives from Bertin (1967) and Guilbaud (1970). For a discussion, see Héran (1993b) and for a comparable system of notation, see White and Jorion (1992).

4. As the Anuta and Parakana cases suggest, sidedness, a vertically oriented bipartition, and dividedness, a horizontally oriented one, while often appearing together, may vary independently. This seemingly paradoxical state of affairs—the presence of sidedness without dividedness—appears to be linked among the Parakana to the prevalence of oblique marriages with close cross kin: 50 percent of blood marriages, that is, 18 percent of the total number of marriages in the (core) network, are with ZD, FBDD, FZSD, or MFBD; unions with ZD alone represent 30 percent of blood marriages and 11 percent of the total number of marriages.

5. Such inferences remain, of course, tentative. For the Nambikwara, see Hornborg (1986/1988:107) citing Lévi-Strauss (1948:77–79); for the Mundurucu, see Hornborg (1986/1988:152) citing Murphy (1956:418–30) and Murphy and Murphy (1974:72, 145–47); for the Parintintin, see Hornborg (1986/1988:154) citing Nimuendajú (1948:290) and Kracke (1984:99–100); for Pano-speaking groups, see this chapter and Hornborg (1986/1988:170–71). Specifically, for the Amahuaca, see Hornborg (1986/1988:163) citing Dole (1979:22–29); for the Mayoruna, see Hornborg (1986/1988:165) citing Fields and Merrifield (1980:26); for the Sharanahua, see Hornborg (1986/1988:167) citing Siskind (1973:199–202) and Torralba (1981:39–40); for the Cashinahua, see Hornborg (1986/1988:) citing d'Ans (1975:28–29) and Kensinger (1977:235, 1984); for the Sanuma, see Hornborg (1986/1988:191) citing Ramos (1974:172) and Ramos and Albert (1977:76); for the Cuiva, see Hornborg (1986/1988:218) citing Arcand (1977:28–30); and for the Karaja, see Pétesch (1991:379), who reports 96 percent of marriages with cross kin.

6. For a further discussion of sidedness, see Houseman and White (1995).

7. It should be noted that the Kariera seem to be one of the few Australian cases in which terminology appears to correspond to an egocentric crossness pattern: "The Kariera relationship terminology is of the bifurcate merging sort, and several anthropologists, including Radcliffe-Brown (1913) and myself (Shapiro 1970), have taken it to be similar to the [sociocentric exogamous moiety] scheme just considered. A re-analysis by Goodenough (1970:131–42), however, indicates we are all wrong. In Kariera, as in English, husband and wife apply the same terms to their mutual offspring, while another set of terms is applied to these offspring by their parents' opposite-sex siblings—mother's brother and father's sister" (Shapiro 1979:48–50).

8. See Hornborg 1986/1988:161–71. These populations include the Cashinahua (d'Ans 1975; Kensinger 1977), the Sharanahua (Siskind 1973; Torralba 1981), the Mayoruna (Fields and Merrifield 1980), and the Amahuaca (Dole 1979).

9. Shapiro (1979:49) makes a similar point regarding the Kariera, who also express their marriage rule in terms of primary kin relations. For him, the lack of correspondence between moiety divisions and terminological consanguinity/affinity distinctions merely indicates that the former are not relevant for the determination of marriage choice: "The salient dichotomy in Kariera is not own-moiety people/opposite-moiety people . . . but rather kin/affines, or—more accurately—those with whom one may not contract affinial relationships/those with whom one may do so."

10. Oblique marriage refers here to oblique *blood* marriages, the absence or presence of which is not quite the same as the absence or presence of dual-sidedness as a property of the marriage network as a whole. Although oblique blood marriages play an important role in orienting the marriage networks toward either viri- or uxorisidedness (see table 9-4), the absence of dual-sidedness does not necessarily imply the presence of oblique blood marriages. Thus, for

example, although very few oblique blood marriages occur among the Shavante and the Yanomamö, the marriage networks of these two populations are far from dual-sided (see table 9-3).

11. The Pakaa-Nova also have a very Crow-like terminology. It should be noted in passing that the compatibility of sidedness and Crow-Omaha systems is consistent with views that see such systems as potentially corresponding to a "super-Aranda" type model (Lévi-Strauss 1968:xix; Héritier 1981:122). See also Tjon Sie Fat's (990:223) ten-line bilateral model of the Samo case.

12. Sidedness remains to be empirically demonstrated for Tukano groups other than the Makuna. Among the Bara and the Barasana, for example, although there is no prohibition as such regarding marriage between lineages or longhouse communities certain of whose members are in a "mother's children" relationship, sisters' descendants ("mother's children") cannot marry, and de facto "mother's children" groups with whom marriages do not occur are in evidence. Here, the mechanics of sidedness are surely more complex than the "segmentary alliance" model proposed by Arhem (1981) for the Makuna. Specifically, they would seem to entail both the cumulative effects of a number of behavioral constraints touching on the strategic resolution of rival marriage claims (Jackson 1977), as well as a series of terminological and other slippages between different levels of social organization over time.

13. The significant exception to this pattern is the Waiwai (Hornborg 1986/1988:141, citing Fock 1963:134, 202); the others can be more or less disregarded; Ramos and Albert (1977:73, 76) consider the anomalous unions reported for the Sanuma to be "rather improper," and Dole (1979:31–33) treats the exceptional marriages among the Amahuaca as irregularities resulting from demographic stress.

10

On Double Language and the Relativity of Incest: The Campa Sociology of a Dravidian-Type Terminology

FRANCE-MARIE RENARD-CASEVITZ

This chapter examines one Amazonian society's rules of genealogical construc- tions and the diverging situational pathways to which they give rise as a function of gender. The issue is part of a broader debate on the discrepancy between the formal possibilities afforded by a global Dravidian typology and the concrete submodels governing kinship and marriage in a given society. The terminological submodel of interest here is that of the Matsiguenga, Jivaro, and Tukano. It can be considered a "pure" logical elaboration of the Dravidian model only when divorced from prac- tice; in fact, it exists, and goes on existing, by virtue of its modes of elaboration, incorporation, and operation, which are peculiar to a specific social body in the real world. Its very nature places it at the junction of other mutually dependent systems (marriage, descent, residence). Although it is the operator of the classification into consanguines and affines, the submodel comes to be embodied through rules exter- nal to the terminology alone and because of this exhibits a sensitivity to demo- graphic, historical-political, and cultural developments, as attested by a number of chapters in this volume.

An ego-centered system built on a Dravidian-type kinship terminology can in practice imply marked differences in the paths followed in defining the position of the spouses and the possibility or impossibility of their marriage. These divergences, which establish the relativity of incest and give the marriage norm a sociologically variable content, merit close attention, because they provide access to the passage- way between the "algebraic" logic of a general schedule of terms (for a survey of potentialities, see chapter 3 of this volume) and specific sociological systems. In the case examined here, the central question is what accounts for the differing genea- logical perspectives that are constant enough to seem relevant to the structure of the system? What principle or what regime switches on the terminological machinery? What does it say? How is it read?

The systems considered here govern kinship and marriage in an Amazonian group of some 80,000 persons residing in the forests on the eastern slope of the Peruvian

Andes. This group, known as the Campas, consists of four subgroups. One of these, the southern Matsiguenga, is the subject of this study. The kinship data presented in this chapter were collected during some sixty months over a period of more than twenty years. The sample consisted of adults (aged seventeen and older) and numbered nearly 8,000 living Matsiguenga (out of a population of more than 10,000), some 500 former Nomatsiguenga, and between 1,000 and 1,500 Ashaninga who have continued, over the past four generations, as in the past, to intermarry with the Matsiguenga according to an intertwining pattern of matrimonial networks that take in the entire Campa group and beyond.[1]

As I have explained elsewhere (Renard-Casevitz 1977), this group combines Dravidian-type terminology with bilateral descent reckoning; first matrilocal, then uxorilocal residence; preferential marriage with the patrilateral cross cousin (for a male ego); and a four-element sibling paradigm, made up of two sons and two daughters (the preferred number of children for a female ego, with a flexible double formula—eight children—in the case of Catholic monogamy with no birth control or with successive husbands).

Like many Amazonian systems, this one has little genealogical depth, but its patrilateral, multicentered formula opens the marriage system to space and time. In effect, there is no repetition of marriages between parallel siblings, whose matrimonial fates diverge, and there is no sister or brother exchange (except in the case of immigration in the first generation). As a result, the residential unit has four different alliance relations (through the children), which are managed by the members of the +1 generation (the minimum for ego according to the four-part paradigm: two sons-in-law from different places, two sons leaving to marry in different places), who eventually add these affinal groups to those of their own generation. One pair of cross siblings (son/daughter) marries nearby, or better, not far away, the other pair far away, genealogically and spatially (the distance might be 300 to 500 kilometers or more).[2] In fact, the networks are much more complex, because they combine the marriages of a local unit made up of clustered or scattered residential units of sisters and their husbands with married and marriageable children: this amounts to a minimum presence of eight local groups, according to the combinative logic of the marriage rules (four groups related to each other married with four other groups also related to each other), but in reality forms a chain of several dozen affinal and consanguineal groups extending across subregion, region, and province. These systems of kinship and marriage are open to history and to geopolitics, as reflected in the five centuries of partly documented Hispanic history.

At one point when I was studying these systems, I decided to rework certain aspects that I had left to one side and that are inherent to the nature of an ego-centered Dravidian system of terminology. I had noticed diverging genealogical structures for men and women, and marriages that could not be accounted for by neutrally aligning ascendants and collaterals equally and symmetrically in a bilateral pattern of descent,inasmuch as, following the patrilateral marriage model (male ego), the genealogies do not admit of all the paths that bilateral descent allows between spouses A and B. Whereas certain paths from A to B or from B to A are invariably taken, others are just as invariably not even considered or left unmentioned. Those regularly chosen were male paths for men and female paths for women; therefore, they were dependent on sexual duality.

These gendered biases have several consequences. First, all pathways between A and B are not equivalent. Second, in the logic of the Matsiguenga model of preferential patrilateral cross-cousin marriage (FZD marries MBS) combined with the gendered paths, there can be no marriage between bilateral cross cousins in any one generation (equivalent, symmetrical paths creating an equilibrium). Third, parallel lines play a clearly preponderant role in defining the positions of A and B (a recurring feature demonstrated in various Dravidian systems), such that men situate themselves primarily with respect to one or two agnates of the same sex, and women with respect to one or two female uterine relatives. It is this orientation "with an eye to" the paths as defined by ego's sex, this identification of one's position through the father for a man, the mother for a woman, that I call perspective, or more precisely, vantage point, and that is marked by gender. In this ego-centered system, ego clearly means either a man or a woman and implies the coexistence of two vantage points.

This finding led me to consider the implications for all ego-centered Dravidian-type terminologies of a system having two readings (a "men's" and a "women's") and two interpretations. It presents itself as a sort of two-part melody written in counterpoint and extends an invitation to enlarge the question to the whole set of ego-centered Dravidian-type terminologies that have a "men's" and a "women's" language. The two-colored checkerboard laid out by the nomenclature obviously evokes the many Dravidian systems that call upon different terms for the two sexes for a certain number of kin types and relative positions of members in the $+1$, 0, and -1 generations.

It should be noted that this discussion ignores all terminological systems with a single language, since they do not correspond to either the social reality of the case under consideration or to that of several neighboring Amazonian societies. Furthermore, those systems exclude the problematic of a double language that I have outlined.

Suppose one finds a nomenclature in which the vocabulary (address and reference) depends on ego's sex and in which there are two languages, a men's and a women's, which construct double-entry male/female systems. Once the existence of such a double language has been detected, one can look for its near and far boundaries and its ideological implications for various areas of a culture. These two languages are the means of expressing gendered points of view in the domains of kinship and marriage; they open up various *sociological* possibilities, whether or not these are realized:

Possibility A. The two languages are equivalent, convey contrasting points of view, and are mutually dependent and complementary; together, they construct the social world of kinship and affinity (and extend beyond this domain).[3]

Possibility B. The two languages are not equivalent. One is dependent on the other, as are the subsequent points of view. This possibil-

ity is automatically subdivided by simple inversion of the man/
woman relationship or by alternation of the dependency, according to
domain.

B1—M>F. The male language is globally dominant and imposes
a masculinized point of view (without going into unilineal
descent, patrilineages, and so forth there is a possibility, among
others, of evolution toward a sociocentric point of view).

B2—F>M. The female language is globally dominant and
imposes a feminized point of view.

B3—B1 and B2 switch back and forth between kinship and
marriage. If the language and the dominant vantage point
alternate between the two domains—for example, if it is feminized for kinship or residence, masculinized for marriage (a
configuration that seems fairly close to the outlook of Crocker's
Bororo)—a whole new series of subvariations unfolds.[4]

The formula of interest in the present case is the one that seems the least promising:
possibility A (although it is hard to tell the difference between A and certain configurations of B3).

To return to my field data: I had constructed my Matsiguenga genealogical questionnaires with ready-to-fill-in blanks. The advantage of these questionnaires was
their exhaustiveness, but in use, I found them to be ethnocentric. After the first
thousand or so interviews, the Matsiguenga would see me coming and, thanks to
the "grapevine," would be prepared to volunteer their genealogies and marriages,
as well as those of their parents and children. At that point, the vista changed considerably. The genealogies were no longer exhaustive; far from it. Eventually, I had
to devise a complementary set of questions to obtain further information. The answers to the various questions showed how the Matsiguenga themselves conceived
of their systems of kinship and marriage and put them into practice. They reflected
a genealogical foreshortening that was significant and sexually asymmetrical, as
well as two perspectives and two constantly privileged parallel paths. The
Matsiguenga term for kin, as opposed to affines, is *noneantabagetaera,* which means
"those by whom I have eyes everywhere." Although a single term, it delineates
nonsuperposable fields of application due to the nonoverlapping nature of the eyes.
Ego-centered by definition (*no* = I), these gendered eyes are turned first toward the
father, for a man; toward the mother, for a woman. Then they embrace a series of
ascendants and collaterals (descendants, whose own eyes are drawn to "I," are not
directly included in this category). The nonoverlapping nature of ego's point of
view is twofold: superimposed on the difference due to topographical position of
the residential unit is an internal difference due to sex.

Matsiguenga kinship is thus structured by two complementary points of view
using a single complex genealogy (mythical and real) spelled out man-fashion
(Kirisho) and woman-fashion (Nese) (for details, see Renard-Casevitz
1995:BIII:211–41). By way of illustration, consider the marriage between Nese and
Julio. It may surprise some who would construct the model of this marriage using

Figure 10-1
Possible Path from a Neutral Point of View, "F/D Incest"

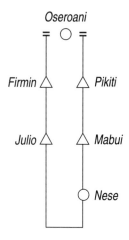

elements from a "neutralized" genealogical version that adds up male and female data gathered over time and in response to different objectives.

Shongabarini and Tyabebe are brothers. Shongabarini and Kyëtsa begat Mariaka, who begat Teresa, who had Nese among her daughters. Tyabebe and Sharita had among their daughters Oseroani. From her first marriage, Oseroani had Pikiti, father of Mabuitini, who was the father of Nese; and with her second husband she had Firmin, father of Julio who married Nese. Now compare an economical path provided by the "neutralized" version (figure 10-1) with the genealogical diagrams given, on the one hand, by Julio, situating himself with respect to his wife (figure 10-2) and, on the other hand, by Nese, who, in 1978, gave the same path (from the opposite vantage point) as Julio and, in 1991, an extended version transcribed here (figure 10-3).

If the marriage between Julio and Ines (Nese) is traced through their closest common relative (Mabuitini) via the shortest path, the result is terminological incest: Julio would have married his D (FBSD = BD = D), and vice versa, Ines, her F (FFBS = FB = F). However, the situation is incestuous with respect to an overall nongendered point of view or to a logic that turns the sexes into algebraical values. But this neutralized version does not exist for them, and each traces a marriage that follows the preferential model of union with a distant patrilateral cross cousin (for male vantage point, or matrilateral for females to manifest the obvious parallelism of paths). It should also be noted that, in their version, this distance is marked in two ways: (a) genealogically, in collateral lines descending from two sisters in G^{+2} for Julio and two brothers in G^{+3} for Nese, under the influence of Kirisho's ascending genealogy; and (b) spatially, by Julio's birth on the upper Pangoreni, where his father had married, and by his residence at Huallana (on the middle Picha nearly three days away), the home of his wife and her family. In this case, it is no exag-

Figure 10-2
Male Path: Patrilateral Marriage with a Not-close Relative, Male Ego (=Julio)

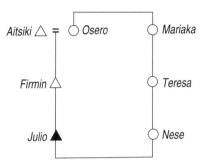

geration to speak of the relativity of incest. That is to say, in several cases, it exists only from a point of view that is irrelevant for the society and that the anthropologist introduces, thereby disregarding the double language that socially constitutes the domain of kinship.

A double-entry construction of Type A holds other implications. It is known that so-called Dravidian systems set up explicit or implicit moieties and an endogamous closure. With these cross-cutting points of view that structure the global view of society, the existence of moieties is explicit, but the fault line has shifted noticeably: there are not two opposite-gendered moieties dividing up society between them, but gendered moieties in apposition to each other: a male moiety facing a female moiety, each subdivided into at least three groups: ego's group flanked by two groups of affines stemming from the patrilateral marriage rule (here we find, turned on its head so to speak, the structure of the Indonesian model with three exchange groups analyzed by Lévi-Strauss 1958).

A perfect expression of these phenomena can be found in the checkerboard designs used by the Campa to decorate their objects. This checkerboard can be read on several levels: alternation of residential units of kin and affines, (i.e., fathers and fathers-in-law for a man, mothers and mothers-in-law for a woman); alternation of marriages over time; but also alternation for a young person of marriageable age whose same-generation relatives are spatially divided between "sisters" (for a male ego) or "brothers" (for a female ego) and potential spouses. This phenomenon is expressed by the affinal terminology. There is no one term as for kin, but as in the nomenclature, two points of view and two targeted terms applying sexual bipartition to the definition of marriage: *nagatomintiri,* "my affines," for a female ego, a term that translates literally as "those whose son I take"; *nagashintorira,* "my affines," for a male ego, which translates as "those whose daughter I take" (this refers, in effect, to a man-to-man or woman-to-woman affinal relation through the children, whereas for ego, each marriage renews the alliance between the two moieties).

And there are further implications: while, in matters of kinship and marriage, the social whole is constructed by the conjunction of two points of view alternately

Figure 10-3
Female Path: Matrilateral Marriage with a Distant Relative, Female Ego (=Nese)

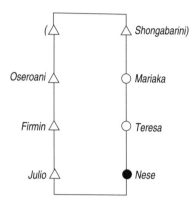

embedded and face to face, any general point of view bears traces of this and is constituted as the integration of two modes of apprehending the social field. In this way, the general point of view conjoins, at the local level, the male and female perspectives, and, at the global level, those of ego and alter (categories whose definition and extension vary with the degree of generality sought: subject, local group, province, and so forth).

At this point, one last, all-important implication arises: the division of society into moieties, one male and one female, introduces into the Dravidian systems, notoriously characterized by endogamous closure, a model that contradicts this closed system. It is open if not to the infinite, at least to the indefinite possibilities of the surrounding world. As far afield as men and women may be found, the system tends to place them in one moiety or the other and to incorporate them by means of marriage; they become the elements of a global system that is unconstrained by any unilineal descent system within genealogical recall and that will set about making them and their natal groups into consanguines by means of the delayed return favored by the patrilateral regime.

These sociological implications suggest an explanation for the Campa's extended matrimonial networks, whose outstanding feature is their lack of well-defined borders. Alliance with the Other—first with all the Campa subgroups, but also with other Amazonians, at one time with Andeans and Incas, and today with people from every horizon—is part of the dynamic of this system, which, by defining gendered moieties, sets up categories that may be extended indefinitely. This type of system is capable of embracing virtually everything it defines as human. It is the definition of human, as opposed to nonhuman (societies of animals, the dead, devils, or any group composed, as is human society, of two "races," after the Spanish *razas*, attributed by the Matisguenga to the male-female division), that constitutes the only insuperable barrier to marriage, to integration into the sphere of consanguinity and its endogamous reproduction.

NOTES

This chapter was translated by Nora Scott.

1. Through the regime of uxorilocal marriage, the Matsiguenga population of the Rio Urubamba for 1900–91 also integrated several whites from Cuzco, Quillabamba, Atalaya, and Pucallpa; one black for certain, and perhaps another; Andean mestizos; as well as dozens of Piro and in lesser numbers, Pano. Over the same period, Matsiguenga men married with the central Ashaninga, in small towns and cities along the jungle border, and with Piro and Pano women.

2. Here is an example of the marriages of the children of a couple living on the middle Koribeni (the husband was chief of the region for nearly a decade). A white man from Cuzco married Blanca. They kept a small dance hall on the other side of the newly constructed Koribeni bridge. T., from Chirumbia, married Gloria (spatially not near, 60 to 70 kilometers distant, but the regions are linked by numerous marriages). Asunta, the last daughter, married a close patrilateral cross cousin from the vicinity of Koribeni mission (Urubamba). One son, Jesus, married the daughter of the Poyentimari headman (200 kilometers away, but having one to several marriages per generation with the Koribeni region, river, and mission). Two of his brothers married nearby or not far away (Koribeni region, mission, and Sangobatea), and among the couple's adopted sons (seven orphans), the elder contracted a marriage even farther away, with a woman from Ticumpinea (downstream on the Pongo Maenike, some 230 kilometers from the middle Koribeni).

3. This does not mean we assume that the sociological values manipulated by these languages are equivalent. To illustrate this, say that the number of males and females in a society may be equivalent without implying the equivalence of the sex-age pyramids, the ratio of the sexes, or life expectancy. Or think of duets, canons, or counterpoint, which seize upon the difference between voices, the staggering of measures, the horizontal combining of notes, and create harmonies imparting highly varied roles to these components.

4. For a gendered interpretation of Bororo society, see, for example, Crocker (1969, 1985).

11

Dravidian and Iroquois in South Asia

ROBERT PARKIN

This chapter discusses the historical aspects of terminological data from South Asia. It is part of a continuing series of papers whose overall intention has been to demonstrate that a historical approach might obviate the difficulties encountered when comparing the very dissimilar terminological systems of South and North India from a purely synchronic perspective (see Parkin 1990, 1992b, 1992c). The present concern is not to go into these difficulties again (see Parkin 1990) but to improve the model of change presented earlier with the aid of interesting new evidence, some of which shows that at least one typologically "Iroquois" system exists in this region.

Such systems were originally assumed to be identical to typologically Dravidian ones, a conflation that even entered one of the textbook typologies (Murdock 1949). But Lounsbury (1964a) showed that although Iroquois terminologies do resemble Dravidian ones in their treatment of the nearest collaterals in the medial three levels, they treat further collaterals on an absolute-sex basis rather than on the relative-sex basis that the cross-parallel distinction depends on (see chapter 2 of this volume for a more detailed account). The discovery of an Iroquois system in South Asia has important implications for terminological change in the region, as is demonstrated here by comparing the Burushaski terminology with the Dravidian systems of the subcontinent, and also with North Indian, to which it also bears some similarities. A further link in the chain of transformations is provided by yet other data from the Himalayas.[1]

Ethnographers have always associated the South Asian region in part with Dravidian systems, but seldom with Iroquois systems. This may not reflect local realities so much as the bias of local traditions of ethnographic reporting. The relatively late identification, in the 1950s, of the Iroquois system as separate from Dravidian and its predominant association with North America in both the ethnographic and the theoretical literature may have discouraged the search for it in South Asia. Recently, however, I found that one example does exist on the periphery of the region. As this chapter explains, this evidence may also help to clarify the ways in which the nonprescriptive North Indian terminology differs from prescriptive South Indian or "Dravidian," as well as their possible historical links.

BURUSHO KINSHIP TERMINOLOGY

Several years ago, I suggested that the kinship terminology of the Burusho of the Karakorum region of northern Pakistan was basically Dravidian or two-line symmetric prescriptive (Parkin 1987). I am grateful to Peter Parkes for recently drawing to my attention a text (Ali 1983) I had then been ignorant of, one that contains data confirming my diagnosis so far as it went, but that also permits a more complete assessment of the present-day nature and possible history of the terminology. Ali is more interested in the descent and status systems of the Burusho than in marriage, and his treatment of the kinship terminology is a formal one, after the style ultimately of Harold Scheffler and more immediately of Anthony Carter, his doctoral supervisor. Nonetheless, those sympathetic to that approach can still see the modified two-line prescriptive pattern in his list of kinship terms (Ali 1983:45), at least in the core kin types. Because Ali worked in the Hunza valley, the terminology he records is in that dialect rather than either the closely related Nagir one, spoken in an adjacent valley, or Yasini, a remoter dialect spoken in the Yasin valley further east. It thus corresponds most closely to the dialect and terminology I had earlier marked "Bu," which in fact stood for the dialects of Hunza and Nagir taken together.

Before examining the terminology, however, it is important to look at the Burusho marriage system. Ali's data here are sketchy, but they are supplemented to some extent by another, slighter work by Hamid (1979:82), which has also only come to my attention recently. In this strongly Islamic environment, an ever-present possibility is the breakdown of clan exogamy in favor of patrilateral parallel cousin marriage. For the most part, the Burusho appear to have resisted this, despite their long having been Shiite or Ismailite (see Parkin 1987:160). According to Ali (1983:73, 74 n. 27), clan exogamy is the norm, and only royal and vizier clans indulge in FBD-FBS marriage to any extent; the rule of exogamy is confirmed by Hamid (1979), who also notes that divorce and the remarriage of divorcees and widows are allowed. It is still not clear whether there is a positive rule of marriage, although there are some interesting indications of a system not dissimilar to certain affinal alliance systems in central India. Ali (1983:44) mentions cross-cousin marriage only in passing but does not indicate whether this would include first cross cousins, especially since earlier sources appear to rule this out (see Parkin 1987). This interpretation would appear to be confirmed by Hamid (1979), who says that close kin are avoided in marriage. More important in the present context, he notes that affines are separated from matrikin both in Burusho normative behavior and in their terminology. The former are considered to be remoter than the latter and engage in less intimate and less long-term links with ego and his or her group (Ali 1983:291). The kin terms and their specifications are shown in table 11-1, in the spellings given by Ali.

Table 11-1

Kinship Terminology of the Burusho

Remoter Levels
pi   PaPa, PaPaPa, etc.
mis   ChCh, ChChCh, etc.

G^{+1} Level
u   F, FB, MZH, MH, FFBS, FMZS, MMZDH, FFFBSS; also FMBS, FFZS
mi   M, MZ, FBW, FW, MMZD, MFBD, FFBSW, MFFBSD; also MFZD, MMBD
ngo   MB, FZH, MFBS, MMZS, FFBDH, FMZDH; also MFZS, MMBS, FMBDH, FFZDH, HMB, WMB, HFZH, WFZH
ntso   FZ, MBW, FFBD, FMZD, MFBSW, MMZSW; also FFZD, FMBD, MFZSW, MMBSW, HFZ, WFZ, HMBW, WMBW
skir   SpF, SpFB, SpMZH
skus   SpM, SpMZ, SpFBW

G^{-1} Level
i   S, ssSbS, WS, HS, WZS, HBS, FBSSms, MZSSms, MMZDSSms, MZSDws, FBDSws, MMZDDSws; also FZSSms, MBSSms, FZDSws, MBDSws
ei   D, ssSbD, WD, HD, WZD, HBD, FBSDms, MZSDms, MMZDSDms, MZDDws, FBDDws, MMZDDDws; also FZSDms, MBSDms, FZDDws, MBDDws
saghun   osSbCh, WBCh, HZCh, FBDSh (m.s.), MZDCh (m.s.), FBCh (f.s.), (sic FBSCh [f.s.]?); also osSChSp, FZDCh (m.s.), MBDCh (m.s.), FZSCh (f.s.), MBSCh (f.s.)
rar   DH, BDHms, ZDHws, WZDH, HBDH, FBSDHms, FBDDHws
khakin   SW, BSWms, ZSWws, WZSW, HBSW, FBSSWms, FBDSWws

G^{0} Ego's Level
tcho   ssSb, PaChss, FFBSChss; also PaSbChss
lus   B (f.s.), PaS (f.s.), ZH (f.s.), HB (f.s.), FFBSS (f.s.); also PaSbS (f.s.)
yas   Z (m.s.), PaD (m.s.), BW (m.s.), WZ (m.s.), FFBSD (m.s.); also PaSbD (m.s.)
yar   H
yus   W
riik   WB, ZH (m.s.), HZ, BW (w.s.); also SpSbSp
sildir   ChSpF, ChSpFB, ChSpMZH
silgus   ChSpM, ChSpMZ, ChSpFBW

Source: Ali (1983).

Although slightly different from those given in other sources (see Parkin 1987:162), these spellings are easily recognizable.

As for the core specifications, that is, those nearest to ego, the data given above accord well with other sources on the whole, being fuller but not really contradictory. There are immediate differences to note in ego's level (see Parkin 1987:164). Ali's data continue to leave Adam Nayyar isolated as the only authority to give any relative-age terms. The latter's reporting of *acho* as SpSbSp also conflicts with Ali, who places such specifications under *riik. Acho* no longer appears to have the affinal specifications recorded by earlier authorities, which I had earlier viewed as being problematic because they were redundant to *riik*. Two other more general points have a bearing on my earlier observations. First, all cousins, not merely parallel ones and apparently of whatever degree (certainly first cousins), are equated with ego's siblings. Second, there is the regularity with which terms for primary affines are separated from those for cognates and the affines of cognates. The separation of affinal terms was recognized earlier, but the generational treatment of cousins in Burushaski was a supposition based on the evidence then available (Parkin 1987:166–67). Ali's data place the existence of both these important features in the Burushaski terminology beyond all doubt.

Neither circumstance should surprise ethnologists of South Asia. While the Dravidian systems of south India are famous for being reasonably pure examples of two-line symmetric prescriptive, at least in the three medial levels, elsewhere in India one frequently encounters apparently transitional forms that have a clear prescriptive basis but lean in a nonprescriptive direction. They are typically found in areas of contact with the nonprescriptive North Indian system that dominates the central area of South Asia. As I have often pointed out before (e.g., Parkin 1990, 1992a:chaps. 7, 8), certain tribal terminologies of central India exemplify these tendencies perfectly, as do some terminologies in the Himalayan region. One can almost certainly talk of an evolutionary trend in these cases. The Burushaski terminology, of the Karakorum further west, can now be added to their number on the basis of these two features, though it possibly differs with regard to remoter kin types in the levels adjacent to ego's, as explained later in the chapter.

These similarities are particularly evident among the Munda-speaking groups of southern Bihar and parts of Orissa. At least in the north of the Munda area, regular systems of affinal alliance exist that are conceived indigenously not as systems of cross-cousin marriage but as ones involving exchange among sibling pairs defined as being eSbSpySb to one another (i.e., eZHyZ and eBWyZ for male ego, eZHyB and eBWyB for female ego). This goes along with a system that does not allow the immediate renewal of alliances between the same two alliance groups but does allow renewal subsequently, after the lapse of at least one and, more typically, three generations. It also corresponds with the separation of affines from cross kin: if immediate renewal, through cross-cousin marriage, is not allowed, WF cannot also be MB (i.e., he cannot be the father of a cross cousin), nor can WB also be a cross cousin. It is the fact that prescriptive equations involving cognates nonetheless remain in the G^{+1} and G^{-1} levels of the terminology that suggests typological change and thus that the terminology is itself transitional when viewed from the viewpoint of global evolutionary trends. The generational pattern of ego's level, on the other hand, as well as the rule of delay before an alliance can be renewed, draws these tribal systems nearer to North Indian systems. These, though nonprescriptive terminologically and normally showing little signs of an affinal alliance system, sometimes have either an expectation of or a statistical tendency toward the repetition of alliances between the same groups within the same generation, though there is never any hint of a rule of renewal in the longer term. The Jat are an example of the former (Tiemann 1970), the people of Kangra an example of the latter (Parry 1979).

The significance of SbSpSb (siblings' spouses' siblings) as categories in a system of affinal alliance that exhibits some of the regularity of prescriptive systems should be explored a little further. A major question of interest is how far this can be seen as indicating a prescriptive system. Traditionally, observers of these groups have tended to be so concerned about establishing the presence or absence of "cross-cousin marriage" that they have not considered the possible existence of other formulations. In some cases, however, there is evidence of a specific category (Munda, Korwa *goi,* Santal *sangat,* Juang *saliray*) isolating SbSpSb specifications within the terminology, together with some indications, at least in the latter two cases, that the terms involved stipulate a marriage preference (McDougal 1963; Bouez 1985). Cross cousins are explicitly ruled out as marriage partners, but is this the insuperable problem it might seem? Certainly even the most radical structuralist approaches to such systems tend to assume the existence of cross-cousin marriage in practice, even if modified through the notion of classificatory relationships, and they would also insist on regular cognate-affine equations in the terminology. Some, indeed, would locate "prescription" in the terminology itself rather than see it as a property of the rules, despite the fact that this is what the word logically suggests (most obviously Needham 1973; this is my own practice, too). However, another aspect of this approach is to emphasize category over genealogy and to stress sensitivity to the indigenous representation over the requirements of analysis. One inference of this is that the Juang, for example, do not marry siblings' spouses' siblings, much less cross cousins, but *saliray* (their term for the stipulated category). In other words, one is possibly only restricting oneself in arriving at their own view of their marriage system when one translates it into apparently more readily understandable terms through the use of genealogical or other analytical denotata. The real problem in such cases is adequately to translate terms like *saliray* into analytical language. The solution is not difficult in all cases, but in some it certainly is.

SbSpSb categories are appropriate to the model of any situation in which groups of siblings intermarry. This is so where the marriages are taking place as a one-time event, never to be repeated. But they can also be applied to the marriage of cross cousins, even where they are expected to be repeated, generation after generation; what is different about the former is the absence, perhaps actually the nonrecognition, of vertical ties linking the referents genealogically. Given all these considerations, it is not immediately clear that the northern Munda systems should be considered nonprescriptive. Personally, I am content to remain agnostic for the time being, on the ground that adequate descriptions of kinship systems are at least as important as fitting them into analytical typologies. In any case, the potential interest of these groups for questions of terminological transformation in South Asia in no way depends on this question being decided.

IROQUOIS IN SOUTH ASIA

As already indicated, Ali's data show more than just the similarity between the Burushaski terminology and that of some Munda groups. Although the first group of specifications under each term in his list fit the two-line symmetric or "Dravidian" scheme (i.e., those for cognates; see table 11-1), those that appear after the word "also" (where this is given) do not. Apart from the fact that the terms for primary affines are separate from those for cross kin, the core, that is, the genealogically closest, specifications adhere to the formal two-line prescriptive model, although the extensions on the whole do not. Ali (1983:47) himself calls the pattern "Iroquois," his simultaneous reference to Scheffler indicating that he does not intend by this term a Dravidian or two-line prescriptive system.

A closer examination reveals that the pattern connected with these extensions actually corresponds to the "Cheyenne" variant of "Iroquois" rather than what might in this context be called "pure Iroquois." In this variant, while the G^{+1} and G^{-1} levels have Iroquois-type crossness, ego's level is generational (see Trautmann 1992). However, Burushaski also has the equations MB = FZH and FZ = MBW, a feature that betrays a prescriptive origin for the terminology despite all its other changes. It appears from Trautmann and Barnes (chapter 2) that such equations do occur in Iroquois and its variants as well as in Dravidian, and that they are compatible with all of them. This is welcome information, given the fact that traditional North Americanist discourse on the subject tends to ignore the treatment of PaSbSp specifications, despite their importance in allowing us to make some crucial distinctions between terminological types (e.g., those between prescriptive and nonprescriptive, or between symmetric and asymmetric prescription).[2]

The discovery that the Burushaski terminology proves to be an Iroquois variant was something of a surprise in the context of South Asia. Is it the only example? Note that Trautmann and Barnes give a second test of the difference between Dravidian and Iroquois, namely, whether cognate-affine equations occur in quantity or not. In their view, the equations have to be present for a terminology to be Dravidian; otherwise, Iroquois becomes a possibility. They do not say, rightly, that the absence of the equations as such defines a system as Iroquois: many other sorts of terminology that have nothing else in common regularly separate affines from cognates (Crow-Omaha, Hawaiian, cognatic). But how far are they really a necessary feature of a Dravidian terminology? They are always present in the ideal type, but is this always true ethnographically? One can certainly conceive of a terminology that is Dravidian and not Iroquois in its cognatic terminology but that regularly has separate affinal terms (e.g., MB = FZH ≠ SpF). In fact, such terminologies may be encountered quite frequently in South Asia, appearing, among others, in Munda (Parkin 1992:chap. 7), in Dumont's (1957) own field data from south India, and in a terminology recorded by Stirrat (1977) from Sri Lanka (discussed in Parkin 1992b,

1992c). Whether more of them, apart from Burushaski, are actually Iroquois rather than Dravidian would have to be tested specifically with regard to their treatment of the remoter cousins. This seems a surer criterion of the difference than the treatment of affines alone.

The North and Central Munda terminologies would, on the face of it, be a good place to start looking for further Iroquois features in South Asia. The generational nature of ego's level in most Munda terminologies, in which all first cousins and seemingly remoter ones, too, share terms with siblings, would rule out strict Iroquois, though it would allow the Cheyenne variant. Although a large number of terminologies have been recorded for these two branches of the language family, the sources available rarely give sufficient data on the sorts of extensions that would be relevant in deciding whether a particular terminology were or were not Iroquois. There are some very piecemeal exceptions, given below:[3]

1. Santal *kaka,* FyB, MyZH, FPaSbyS, step-F
2. Juang *atir,* FeB, MeZH, FMBS, though *atirae,* MeZ, FeBW, FMBD, FZHeZ, is consistent only with the Dravidian pattern
3. Ho *kaka,* FyB, MyZH, FFSbS, and *hatom,* FZ, MBW, SpM, FFSbD
4. Bhumij *kaka,* FyB, MyZH, FFBSy, FFZS, and *hatom,* FZ, MBW, FFZD
5. *putara,* eBS, FBSS (assuming m.s.) and *bhagina,* FBDS (assuming m.s.), perhaps connected with *bhanja,* osSbS, are consistent with both Iroquois and Dravidian patterns.

Apart from the single example above, McDougal's (1963, 1964) data on the Juang, which do give some cognatic extensions, clearly place them in a Dravidian, not in any sort of Iroquois pattern. As with other Munda terminologies, Juang has the intercognate equations one would expect of a Dravidian system but routinely gives primary affines separate terms from cross relatives, thus indicating that the mere separation of affinal terms is not diagnostic of Iroquois as against Dravidian.[4]

As for possible Iroquois features in South Asian terminologies that are lexically Dravidian, these are difficult to establish owing to the poor recording of wider collateral specifications. Only two of the terminologies listed by Trautmann (1981:117, 162) have data on extensions: Marathi non-Brahman (after Carter) and Coorg (after Emeneau). Data on the first are inadequate and therefore inconclusive with respect to G^{+1} and G^{-1}, but those concerning ego's level are just sufficient to indicate a Dravidian, not an Iroquois pattern. In the Coorg case, useful data are restricted to the +1 and −1 levels, but they also indicate a Dravidian, not an Iroquois pattern for the relevant categories. This is also true of the Tamil terminology recorded in Konku by Beck (1972:appendix F).

The paucity of data with respect to Dravidian is, of course, not the fault of Trautmann or his sources. However, it does show how a specific search for Iroquois patterns in South Asia has rarely been considered either necessary or interesting, because the cousin terminology will normally be expected to be generational here when it is not obviously Dravidian. The Burushaski terminology conforms to this rule in being generational in ego's level, but its adjacent levels have proved to be an exception to the norms of the region. This has only come to light through the ethnographer's (Ali's) decision to record the terms for wider collateral kin types in these levels, presumably because he was following the example of his supervisor, Carter. Given Ali's relative lack of interest in the terminology, we can only regard this as fortuitous.

NORTH INDIAN KINSHIP TERMINOLOGY

One other terminological pattern of special interest in South Asia is North Indian. Some light has already been shed on this system by Vatuk (1969), who has written one of the standard texts on the Hindi terminology, and Parry (1979), who has provided good comparative evidence, arranged explicitly in the same manner, from Kangra, northwest India (table 11-2 shows only Vatuk's data, which are somewhat fuller).

The North Indian terminological system has proved difficult to pin down, whether in its own terms or in comparison with the more clearly defined prescriptive systems of South India. I have suggested elsewhere (e.g., Parkin 1990, 1992a, 1992b) that a diachronic approach might prove more fruitful than the synchronic comparisons that are more usually attempted. The conceptual resources are certainly available to describe this terminology, if not actually to define it. It is clearly nonprescriptive: affinal terms are normally separate, and there are not even the intercognate equations (e.g., MB = FZH) that one encounters in, say, the North and Central Munda terminologies. The only exception to this statement, as Trautmann (1981:98ff.), has pointed out, is that certain affines who can be described as wife-giver's wife-takers and wife-taker's wife-givers of ego's level may be classed as siblings, though in a manner that is nonprescriptive (see Vatuk 1969). Ego's level with respect to cognates is generational, but the affinal area of this level usually exhibits a series of individual terms for each primary kin type. This is replicated in +1 and −1 for both cognates and affines, though gender is typically marked by what a linguist might consider morphological variation rather than terminological separation. In G^{+2} and G^{-2} also, each of the four minimal kin types receives a separate term.

It is tempting to call this last pattern "individualizing," but this expression is more usually applied to situations in which the kin types that are genealogically closest to ego (Pa, Sb, Ch) have separate terms in a terminology that is otherwise prescriptive, or at least classificatory. Allen (1989a:178) prefers to call the principle involved "zero-equation." That is, it is one in which terms and kin types, at least in parts of a terminology, have a one-to-one correspondence; Kryukov's (1972) "Arabic" type is also relevant here. A further distinction may be necessary, according to whether some "terms" do or do not take a descriptive, that is, circumlocutory phrasal form. However, that is not immediately relevant here.

In any event, it is not easy to conceive of this principle being applied right through a terminology, assuming that this covered a wide range of kin and did not, as with

Table 11-2
Hindi Kinship Terminology

G^{+2} Level		
bābā	FF	FFB, FMB, FFZH, FMZH, FZHF, FZHFB, FZHMB, FZHFZH, FZHMZH, MZHF, MZHFB, MZHMB, MZHFZH, MZHMZH
dādī	FM	W of *bābā*
nānā	MF	MFB, MMB, MFZH, MMZH, MBWF, MBWFB, MBWMB, MBWFZH, MBWMZH, FBWF, FBWB, FBWMB, FBWFZH, FBWMZH
nānī	MM	W of *nānā*
dādasarā	HFF/WFF	*bābā* of H/*bābā* of W
dādas	HFM/WFM	*dādī* of H/*dādī* of W
nānasarā	HMF/WMF	*nānā* of H/*nānā* of W
nānas	HMM/WMM	*nānī* of H/*nānī* of W
G^{+1} Level		
cācā/tāū	FyB/FeB	FFBS, FMBS, FFZS, FMZS, FZHBWB
cācī/tāī	FyBW/FeBW	W of *cācā/tāī*
māmā	MB	MFBS, MMBS, MFZS, MMZS, MBWB, MBWBWB, FBWB, FBWBWB, FBWBWZH, MZHBWB, MBWZH, MBWBWZH
māmī	MBW	W of *māmā*
buā	FZ	FFBD, FMBD, FFZD, FMZD, FZHZ, FZHBW, MZHZ
phūphā	FZH	H of *buā*
mausī	MZ	MZBD, MMBD, MFZD, MMZD, FBWZ, MZHBW, HBWM, ZHBWM, WZHM, BWZHM
mausā	MZH	H of *mausī*
māvsā	BWF/ZHF	F of *bhābhī,* F of *jījā* (see below)
māvsī	BWM/ZHM	M of *bhābhī,* M of *jījā* (see below)
mā, ammā, mātā (jī)	M	
bāp, pitā (jī)	F	
sasur	HF/WF	
sās	HM/WM	
pitasarā	HFyB/WFyB	*cācā* of H/*cācā* of W
pitas	HFyBW/WFyBW	*cācī* of H/*cācī* of W
tāyasarā	HFeB/WFeB	*tāū* of H/*tāū* of W
tāyas	HFeBW/WFeBW	*tāī* of H/*tāī* of W
maulasarā	HMB/WMB	*māmā* of H/*māmā* of W
maulas	HMBW/WMBW	*māmī* of H/*māmī* of W
phūphasarā	HFZH/WFZH	*phūphā* of H/*phūphā* of W
phūphas	HMZH/WMZH	*būā* of H/*būā* of W

Continued on next page

Table 11-2 continued

mausasarā	HMZH/WMZH	*mausā* of H/*mausā* of W
mausas	HMZ/WMZ	*mausī* of H/*mausī* of W

G^0 Level

bhāī*	B	FBS, MBS, FZS, MZS, HBWB, ZHBWB, WZHB, BWZH; BWBWZH (f.s.)
bhābhī/bhābahū	BW/yBW (m.s.)	W and WZ of *bhāī;* BWBW (f.s.), BWBWZ (f.s.)
bahen	Z	FBD, MBD, FZD, MZD, HBWZ, ZHBW, WZHZ, BWZHZ; ZHZHBW (m.s.)
jījā, bahenoī	ZH	H and HB of *bahen;* ZHZH (m.s.), ZHZHB (m.s.), ZHZHZH (m.s.)
sālā	WB	WFBS, WMBS, WFZS, WMZS, WBWB, WBWZH; BWB (m.s.), BWBWB (m.s.) BWBWZH (m.s.)
salhaj	WBW	W of *sālā*
sālī	WZ	WFBD, WMBD, WFZD, WMZD
sarhū	WZH	H of *sālī*
devar/jeṭh	HyB/HeB	HFBS, HMBS, HFZS, HMZS
daurānī/jeṭhānī	HyBW/HeBW	W of *devar/jeṭh*
nanad	HZ	HFBD, HMBD, HFZD, HMZD, HZHZ, HZHBW; ZHZ (f.s.), ZHZHZ (f.s.), ZHZHBW (f.s.)
nandoī	HZH	H of *nanad*
samdhī	SWF/DHF	F of *jāmāī*/F of *bahū* (see below)
samdhin	SWM/DHM	M of *jamāī*/M of *bahū* (see below)

G^{-1} Level

beṭā	S	(in certain circumstances includes *bhatījā* and *bhānjā*)
beṭī	D	(in certain circumstances includes *bhatījī* and *bhānjī*)
bhatījā	BS	S of *bhāī, sālā, devar/jeth*, BWB (f.s.), BWBWB (f.s.)
bhatījī	BD	D of same
bhānjā	ZS	S of *bahen, sālī, nanad,* ZHZ (m.s.) ZHZHZ (m.s.)
bhānjī	ZD	D of same
jamāī	DH	H of *beṭī, bhatījī, bhānjī, potī, dhevtī*
bahū	SW	W of *beṭā, bhatījā, bhānjā, potā, dhevtā*

G^{-2} Level

potā	SS	S of *bhatījā, bhānjā*
potī	SD	D of *bhatījī, bhānjā*
dhevtā	DS	S of *bhatījī, bhānjī*
dhevtī	DD	D of *bhatījī, bhānjī*

Source: Vatuk (1969).

us, recognize the largest number of individuals in the society as nonkin: otherwise, the number of terms required would have to be impossibly large. A closer examination of the North Indian terminologies recorded by Vatuk and Parry reveals that there are indeed terminological equations even for these supposedly individualizing terms. These equate primary kin types not with each other, as in a prescriptive or even to a limited extent a classificatory terminology (perhaps I should say here, with Needham, "lineal" terminology), but with a range of wider kin types that can clearly be seen as equivalents in some sense. I deliberately avoid using the term "classificatory" to describe them for the moment.

At the G^{+1} level, there are six terms for male cognates—F, FeB, FyB, MB, FZH, and MZH—which are therefore all terminologically distinct from one another. For the purposes of this demonstration, one can disregard relative age and reduce the set to five terms. Each term except that for F, which is a purely zero equation or individualizing term, has equations not with any other primary kin type (not even the equation F = FB obtains here), but with the same-sex cousins of the parent who provides the initial link from ego. In other words, the equation Sb = PaSbCh always applies in the formula used for these kin types, as it does in ego's level, which is generational. It applies equally in the affinal part of the terminology in all levels, in the sense that the terms for WB or SpMZ, for instance, also cover those cousins of W, SpM, and so on, who are of same sex as their siblings.

Thus in many areas of the terminology, this principle of sibling-cousin equivalence is applied in a manner that is internally coherent but that cannot be considered conventionally Hawaiian or generational. What one sees is its thoroughgoing application not only to ego's immediate siblings and cousins but to those of his parents and same-level affines too. This means that although the +1 level is not generational with regard to primary kin types—but quite the reverse, with separate terms for each, not just one for all—it can be considered generational with regard to kin types at a wider remove. This pattern is unique, as far as I know, and cannot be considered Iroquois or any of its variants any more than it can be considered Dravidian. However, it can logically be seen as a further development of the former, one that retains the equivalence of, for instance, PaSb and PaPaSbCh on a relative-sex basis (ego's parent to alter), but that no longer makes the intercognate equations that survive in Iroquois. At this stage I am remarking only on the logical possibility and am making no reference to historical possibilities.

One consideration is whether one can call these particular sorts of equivalences classificatory. The most usual definition of this term is that it describes lineal equations of the sort F = FB, with the assumption that equivalent kin types at a wider collateral distance are also included—in this instance FFBS, FFFBSS, and so forth. But this does not actually cover all its uses. One also talks freely of the "classificatory MBD," for example, in order to indicate that not only the actual MBD is being referred to but all her collateral equivalents, too. However, not even the actual MBD is likely to be equated with a primary kin type (which here could only be a sibling); if she were, she would be unlikely to be distinguished from parallel cousins in practice, and one would call the equation Hawaiian or generational, rather than classificatory. This shows that lineal-cognatic equations need not actually be present—and therefore that they cannot form part of the definition of the term "classificatory." Despite the usual definition, equations of the type FB = FFBS = FFFBSS, in which F has a separate term, are, according to this logic, as classificatory (in the sense of forming classes or merging genealogical positions) as those in which F is also a part of the equation. On this basis, then, the North Indian terminology is zero equation with respect to the lack of equivalence between primary kin types themselves, but classificatory in the sense that each of the latter (except F) is terminologically equated with a distinct set of equivalent kin types.

But this ignores the usual assumption that not all collateral kin types are equivalent in a classificatory equation: the principles of relative-sex designation and of same-sex sibling equivalence come into play. This applies no less to the idea of a classificatory MBD, since the actual MBD and her collateral equivalents who make up this category, although all cross kin to ego, are parallel kin to one another. But from the egocentric view of a terminology, parallel kin are linked with lineal kin and opposed to cross kin, who will also be affines if the terminology is prescriptive. This means that although FFBS (father's parallel cousin) is considered to be a classificatory equivalent of FB, FMBS (father's cross cousin) is not. An equation that covered all three specifications would not, in this view, be classificatory. This renders Iroquois and its subtypes, and also North Indian, not simply nonprescriptive but nonclassificatory, since they all equate (for instance) a parent's sibling with *all* that parent's same-sex cousins, cross as well as parallel.

TRANSFORMATIONS OF SOUTH ASIAN KINSHIP TERMINOLOGIES

Consider now the Burushaski terminology as the sole clear representative of typological Iroquois in South Asia, along with some other interesting and relevant evidence. To begin with, note the ways in which Burushaski is distinguished from North Indian. First, the former does not distinguish primary kin types from one another in the way that the latter does. Second, a related point, Burushaski has classificatory equations of the sort defined above: not even parental terms are individualizing (F = FB = FFBS = MZH, etc.). Third, although Burushaski has no cognate-affine equations, it does have the intercognate equations and distinctions for both cross and parallel kin that one would expect to find in a prescriptive terminology. Neither of these latter two features is characteristic of North Indian. What the two terminologies share, however, is the generational nature of ego's level and the treatment of second cousins in the +1 level. The second comparison depends on making allowance for the distinction from one another in North Indian but not in Burushaski of the primary kin types with whom these second cousins are equated.

Further east, in the similarly upland area of Kumaon, northwest India, a terminology has been recorded with a pattern that is clearly intermediate between these two. The data come from a recent German publication (Krengel 1989:196–97) in which the terminology is deliberately set out on the model used by Parry (who had himself adopted it from Vatuk) to facilitate comparison with other North Indian terminologies (see table 11-3). The treatment of first and second cousins and so on is the same as in these two earlier texts, that is, generational. What is different is the treatment of cognates in G^{+1} and G^{-1}. In $+1$, parallel kin are for the most part equated with one another in a manner characteristic of prescriptive systems: FeB = MeZH; FyB = MyZH; MeZ = FeBW (although MyZ ≠ FyBW). In -1, although the term for BS(f.s.) is not recorded, the equations Ch = ssSbCh = SpssSbCh are, and ZCh(m.s.) have separate terms. However, G^{+1} cross kin have separate terms not only from parallel kin but also from one another (i.e., MB ≠ FZH; FZ ≠ MBW), as is normally the case in North Indian.

The Kumaon terminology can thus be described as having a basically North Indian pattern with some, perhaps residual, prescriptive features. Certain North Dravidian terminologies of Bihar indicate an even further and later stage of transition from prescriptive to nonprescriptive in India. They have prescriptive equations only at the $+1$ level, and only in the most vestigial form; in addition, they exemplify what I have suggested elsewhere (Parkin 1988b:62ff.) about terminological redundancy indicating possible change. Since this point is still likely to be somewhat obscure, consider the Malpahariya G^{+1} consanguineal terminology (references are in Parkin 1992a, appendix 2):

jetha	FeB, MeZH; FeZH	mosa	MyZH
kaka	FyB, MyZH	mama	MB
jethi	MeZ, FeBW; FeZ	mami	MBW
kaki	FyBW	pisi	FyZ
mosi	MyZ	pisa	FyZH

One can see prescriptive equations here for the terms *jetha* and *jethi,* but contaminated, as it were, by extra specifications that would not belong there in any purer prescriptive system. *Kaka* and *mosa* especially should be compared. Both are MyZH, but it is *mosa* that one can expect to prevail in the struggle over this specification, for which it represents the standard north Indian term (e.g., Hindi *mausa*). This would mean the disappearance of another prescriptive equation, an assumption strengthened by the fact that *kaka,* FyB, MyZH, is normally only FyB in North Indian. In general, this part of the terminology appears to be moving toward the zero-equation structure of the typical North Indian terminology, in which each kin type has its own term. Here, in effect, one is able to predict terminological change because of the rich comparative evidence from elsewhere in the region.

The terminologies discussed here together with others that are typical of various parts of the South Indian region suggest two transformational paths. I have already broached this question in earlier work (Parkin 1990, 1992b) but take this opportunity to make some revisions. Each path starts from

1. Central Dravidian / Koraput Munda (two-line symmetric prescriptive terminologies in five levels and with alternating generation equations, thus differing in the last respect from Dravidian systems further south; see Parkin 1988b, 1992a).

Table 11-3
Kumaon Terminology

+1 Cognate Terminology

Lineal (consanguine, parallel)

ṭhulbaujyu	FeB, MeZH (big father)
kaka or *kāśabaujyu*	FyB, MyZH (little father)
thulljā	FeBW, MeZ (big mother)
kāki	FyBW
kaīj	MyZ

Nonlineal (affinal, cross)

bhin	FZH (eZH)
mam	MB
māmi	MBW
didi	FZ (eZ)

Full Kumaon Terminology

G⁺² Level

bubu	FF/MF	FFB, (FFZH), FMB, FMZH, MFB, (MFZH), MMB, MMZH, +Z of any *bubu*
āmā	FM/MM	W of any *bubu*
buṛ caur	HFF/WFF/HMF/ WFM/FZHP	any *bubu* of H/W
buṛ saśū	HFM/WFM/HMM/ WMM/FZHM	any *āmā* of H/W

G⁺¹ Level

ijā, ij	M	—
baujyu, bābu	F	—
ṭhulbaujyu/kaka	FeB/FyB	FFBS, FFZS, FMBS, FMZS
kāśabaujyu	MeZH/MyZH	MFBDH, MMBDH, MFZDH, MMZDH
thulijā/kāki	FeBW/FyBW MeZ	W of any *thulbaujyu/kaka* exception: MyZ = *kaīj*
mam	MB	MFBS, MFZS, MMZS, MMBS, FBWB
māmi	MBW	W of any *mam*
didi, pusyāṇi	FZ	FFZD, FFBD, FMBD, FMZD (classified with eZ)
bhin	FZH	H of any *didi*
caur	WF/HF	HFB, WFB, HMB, WMB, HMZH, WMZH, ZHF, ZHFB, BWF
saśū	WM/HM	W of any *caur*
dad/bhulā	eB/yB	FBS, FZS, MBS, MZS + H of any *sāi, jethau, nand, paūnī*
boji/bvāri	eBW/yBW	(yBW classified with SW)

Continued on next page

Table 11-3 continued

G⁺¹ Level

didi/bhulī	eZ/yZ	FBD, FZD, MBD, MZD + W of any *sāu, jethu,*
		javaī, bhin, (eZ classified with FZ, yZ classified
		with BD (f.s.))
bhin/javaī	eZH/yZH	BWB (f.s.), ZHB (eZH classified with FZH,
		yZH classified with DH)
jethu/sāu	WeB/WyB	WFBS, WMBS, WFZS, WMZS, BWB (m.s.)
		(WyB classified with WBS)
didi/bhulī	WeBW/WyBW	W of any *jethu/sāu*
jethau (paūṇī)/sāi	WeZ/WyZ + ZHZ	any Z of W and any Z of ZH
dad/bhuiā	WeZh/WyZH	any H of *jethau, sāi*
jithānā/dyor	HeB/HyB	HFBS, HMBS, HFZS, HMZS
jithānī/dyorāni	HeBW/HyBW	W of any *jithānā/dyor*
paūṇī/nand	HeZ/HyZ	HMBD, HFBD, HFZD, HMZD, ZHZ (f.s.),
		HFZ
dad/bhuiā	HeZH/HyZH	ZHZH, HFZH
samdi	SWF/DHF	F of any *javaī* or·*bvāri*
samdyaṇi	SWM/DHM	W of any *samdi*

G⁺¹ Level

cyal	S	BS (m.s.), WZS (WBS = *sāu*), ZS (f.s.), HBS
		(BS = *bhadyā*)
celi	D	BD (m.s.), WZD (WBD = *sāi*), ZD (f.s.), HBD
		(BD = *bhadye*)
bhānja	ZS (m/s)	HZS
bhānji	ZD (ms)	HZD
javaī	DH (yZH)	H of any *celi/bhānji/nātiṇi/bhulī:* including
		SWB, DHB, yZHB
bvāri	SW (yBW)	W of any *cyal/bhānja/nātī:* including SWZ,
		DHZ

G⁺¹ Level

nāti	SS/DS	
nātiṇi	SD/DD	

Source: Krengel (1989).

These lead to either

2. South Dravidian (two-line symmetric prescriptive in three levels, with a nonprescriptive pattern in G⁺² and G⁻² and no alternating generation equations).

or

3. North Munda (two-line symmetric prescriptive in G^{+1} and G^{-1} cognatic terminology, but with separate affinal terms; generational in ego's level).
4. Burushaski (similar to North Munda, but with Iroquois pattern for G^{+1} and G^{-1} cognates).
5. Kumaon (differs from Burushaski in having only residual prescriptive equations for G^{+1} and G^{-1} parallel kin types; primary cross kin in these levels have individualizing terms).
6. Malpahariya (evident breakup of remaining prescriptive features).
7. Standard North Indian (total removal of such features).

Proving the historicity of these transformations is the real challenge, something that will ultimately require much careful reconstructive work. But there are already some pieces of plausible evidence. The splitting of cognate-affine equations in Munda terminologies has generally been effected with the aid of loans from Indo-European (IE) languages (see Parkin 1992a:chap. 7), whose adoption was clearly a historical event or series of such events. The exact circumstances in which the Malpahariya terminology seems to be losing its remaining prescriptive features is another example (see Parkin 1992b, 1992c). There is more to discuss concerning the remains of such features in Kumaon, a terminology that is lexically IE and that exists in a frontier area between the prescriptive systems of the Himalayas and the nonprescriptive systems of the plains. This raises the possibility that it falls into the class of South Asian terminologies that appear to have kept a partly or wholly prescriptive pattern but to have switched lexis from another language—Dravidian, Munda, or Tibeto-Burman—into IE (e.g., Marathi, Konkani, Sinhalese, Shina; see Trautmann 1981:147ff.; Parkin 1987:167). Alternatively, there may simply have been some direct influence from neighboring prescriptive terminologies on some parts of it for reasons that are at present obscure. Another difficulty is the paucity of evidence at present for the existence of more terminologies similar to the Burushaski one in South Asia. As already demonstrated, there are some small indications of a Cheyenne pattern in certain Munda terminologies, and a dedicated search might reveal that these are not as isolated as they now appear to be. Conversely, it appears that possible transformational paths are neither identical nor preordained, and that history will not always have responded everywhere in the same manner.

Historically, two hypotheses can be proposed for South Asia. One is that the transformations I have suggested took place wholly within South Asia. Sufficient evidence exists within the region to support such a hypothesis, now that the Burushaski evidence is clearer and can be linked to at least one terminology, Kumaon, which is mostly but not entirely North Indian in structure. Arguing against this hypothesis is the fact that North Indian terminologies are overwhelmingly if not entirely IE lexically, and that this language family—South Asian examples such as those listed above excepted—cannot be identified with prescriptive systems at any point in its history, a history that is the deepest available for any language family. To chart a shift from prescription to nonprescription in South Asia, one would need to find a means of making IE terminologies prescriptive in the region. This is not

Figure 12-1
Location of Local Groups in India

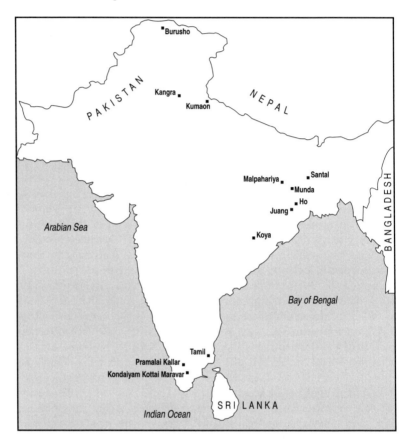

impossible, through the process of lexical transfer I have just mentioned. However, there is no evidence that this took place everywhere, only locally, and in regions of contact between IE and other language families.

The second hypothesis is therefore more likely. It is that however IE speakers arrived in the subcontinent, they brought with them terminologies that were already nonprescriptive. It may nonetheless be the case that the prescriptive systems they encountered there arrested their further development toward a more cognatic structure, in contrast to what appears to have been the development followed by linguistically cognate terminologies in Europe. It may well be that IE terminologies generally were at one stage in their history characteristically zero equation (with regard to primary kin types, at least), a pattern that can be discerned in the Latin terminology and that still survives in Scandinavian ones.[5] By its very nature, a zero-equation structure can logically only move toward the production of equations, and logically in more than one direction. One such direction would be to introduce classificatory and possibly also prescriptive equations. This, however, offends against the usual hypothesis that prescriptive precedes nonprescriptive (into which class zero equations fall), and classificatory precedes cognatic, in any transformational sequence. The other is to produce a cognatic pattern like that reflected in most modern European (non-Scandinavian) terminologies. As already noted, this seems to have been the most likely development in Europe itself. In South Asia, however, it did not take place, either because of the internal dynamics of Indo-European North Indian terminologies themselves or because of influence from the prescriptive terminologies of the region. In some cases, this influence clearly extended to producing prescription through lexical transfer, but in others it might have been restricted to preventing the further development of North Indian terminologies in a cognatic direction. Conversely, the presence of North Indian in the subcontinent might itself have had an effect in drawing certain lexically Dravidian, Munda, and Tibeto-Burman terminologies away from prescription, at least of the pure type that retains full cognate-affine equations. This change may have been effected through the disappearance or diminishing importance of positive marriage rules, itself reflecting the impact of high-status marriage practices that disapproved of marriage with any sort of cousin.

NOTES

1. Abbreviations for kin specifications are standard. In this discussion, I set aside my usual dislike of ethnonyms for designating terminological types of global significance and make frequent use of the expressions "Dravidian, Iroquois, Cheyenne, Hawaiian" and "Crow-Omaha" as alternatives. This is occasioned partly by the need, in a collection of this sort, to fall more into line with the terminology that most of the other contributors will be using and partly because not all of these types have yet acquired a generally accepted alternative that is ethnically neutral. This is especially true of Iroquois, Cheyenne, and Crow-Omaha (for Dravidian we have the expressions "two-line symmetric prescriptive" and for Hawaiian "generational," which I sometimes use, too, as appropriate). My use of all these terms is intended to refer to the terminological type (as conventionally defined) rather than the actual ethnographic terminology or the group that uses it, except where the context makes it clear that the latter is intended (mostly in respect of Dravidian, where the phrase "lexical Dravidian" in particular is often used to refer to Dravidian in the latter sense). I have avoided using Trautmann and Barnes's Type A and Type B for Dravidian and Iroquois (see chapter 2 in this volume), mainly because they refer only to the respective ways cross kin are treated rather than to systems as wholes.

2. Ali's data also amount to a decisive refutation of Pfeffer's (1984) hypothesis that the Burushaski terminology implies at least "four lines of regular exchange," solely on the basis that it separates affines from consanguines. Nothing in Adam Nayyar's data, on which Pfeffer actually based his analysis, suggests this hypothesis, and it must be rejected for similar reasons, as was the case for middle India (see Parkin 1993). That is to say, there are insufficient terms to establish four lines in the terminology, and the terms have the wrong specifications to establish proper descent lines to begin with. Ali's data, which were almost certainly too new to have been known to Pfeffer at the time of his study, are sufficiently full to put his hypothesis beyond all salvation.

3. Data are from Parkin (1984:chap. 6, tables 8 and 9; original sources listed at Parkin 1984:349).

4. There are also two examples from the related Mon-Khmer languages of Southeast Asia, namely Khasi (of Meghalaya, northeast India) and Bahnar (of the highlands of south-central Vietnam). I give the essential details below (data are from Parkin 1984:tables 14 and 19; original sources listed in Parkin 1984:350–51).

Khasi	kmie	M, MZ, MPaSbD, FBW
	kñi	MB, MPaSbS, FZH
	kpa kha	F, FB, FPaSbCh (*kpa* = MZH)

Bahnar
(western dialects)

	duc	FyZ, MyBW, Fy(PaSbD), My(PaSbS)W
	yang	MyZ, FyBW, My(PaSbD), Fy(PaSbS)W
	ka, me kra	FeZ, Fe(PaSbD)
	ma, ñô	MyB, FyZH, My(PaSbD)H, Fy(PaGSD)H
		(also MyZH, My(PaSbD)H)

5. The Polish terminology currently seems to be undergoing precisely this transformation (see Parkin 1995).

12

Transformations of Kinship Systems in Eastern Indonesia

JEAN-FRANÇOIS GUERMONPREZ

Eastern Indonesia, as it is understood here, takes in the islands beyond Bali and Lombok that dot the waters between Sulawesi, Australia, and New Guinea. The number and quality of the ethnographic publications over the past twenty years are such that this part of Indonesia is now better known than many other regions of island and mainland Southeast Asia. The marriage rules and practices of these Indonesian societies fall into the category of asymmetric systems. I have purposely used the neutral expression "asymmetric system" rather than "asymmetric connubium" or "generalized exchange" in order to call attention to the fact that the paradigms associated with the last two expressions are not entirely relevant to understanding Eastern Indonesian marriage practices.Since the emphasis here is primarily on kinship terminologies and their logical and historical transformations, I will not justify my choice of expression but merely define the asymmetric system of Eastern Indonesia by the contrasting matrimonial paths of a brother and sister, and by the fundamental importance of the relationship between maternal uncle and sister's children, the diachronic dimension of which is particularly manifest in rituals and is crucial to any understanding of these kinship systems.[1] This means relativizing the importance of marriage with the matrilateral cross-cousin (MBD), even though it is well attested in Eastern Indonesia and certain terminologies there are asymmetric prescriptive, which implies a rule of matrilateral cross-cousin marriage.

Historical linguistics has made great strides in the classification of Austronesian languages, an instrument indispensable to the diachronic study of Eastern Indonesian terminologies. With Blust's work, it is now generally accepted that all of the Austronesian languages spoken in New Guinea, Micronesia, and Melanesia, as well as all of the Polynesian languages, belong to the Eastern Malayo-Polynesian subgroup. These languages, together with the Austronesian languages of Eastern Indonesia, which belong to the Central Malayo-Polynesian subgroup, have a common ancestor: Proto-Central-Eastern-Malayo-Polynesian. At an even more inclusive level, all of the above languages come from Proto-Malayo-Polynesian, from which are also derived the Western Malayo-Polynesian languages spoken in the Philippines, Malaysia, Western Indonesia, Madagascar, and by a few ethnic minorities in Vietnam. Lastly, the Austronesian languages of Taiwan form a separate branch directly descended from Proto-Austronesian, like the Malayo-Polynesian languages (Blust 1984). Here it is only necessary to keep in mind that the languages spoken by the Austronesian groups of Eastern Indonesia all belong to the same linguistic subgroup, from which it can be inferred that their kinship terminologies share a common prototerminological ancestor, which was contemporary with Proto-Central-Malayo-Polynesian, a language spoken some 4,000 years ago by groups living probably in the vicinity of Seram (Blust 1984). Some emigrated from this site southward and settled the rest of the Moluccas, as well as the Lesser Sunda Islands. The result was the diversification of today's languages and societies.

Although all of the Eastern Indonesian groups dealt with here practice asymmetric marriage, not all of their kinship terminologies are asymmetric. On the contrary, most are of some other type. Some are symmetric, others combine symmetric and asymmetric features, and still others have cognatic features.[2] This presents a twofold difficulty: internal inconsistencies in the terminologies and dissonance between terminologies and actual marriage practices. As far as I can see, the only way to shed some light on this problem is to approach it from a diachronic perspective. A likely historical scenario might read as follows: at some time T_0, before the Eastern Indonesian languages began diverging, there was a single kinship system characterized by a given terminology and marriage rules and practices in accord with this kin classification; at a later time, T_1, after T_0 but before the languages diversified, the marriage rules and practices changed over to the asymmetric form. One of the aims of this chapter is to identify the semantic type of the terminology existing at the time of Proto-Central-Malayo-Polynesian. Another is to see if some logical constraints have governed the historical transformations of Eastern Indonesian terminologies.

Although this area of investigation is little traveled, it is not entirely uncharted. Needham's many contributions to the study of Indonesian terminologies are particularly well known. Although Needham does not express it in such explicitly historical terms, his viewpoint (Needham 1984) is that the prototerminology from which Eastern Indonesian terminologies derived was symmetric prescriptive. Since a thesis is all the more convincing if it can be successfully confronted with others, it initially seemed to me that Needham's position would be consolidated if a cognatic prototerminology could be shown to be impossible or, at least, unlikely. But it gradually became manifest that the opposite was true. Not only was it impossible to eliminate the cognatic solution but the latter proved more economical in accounting for the peculiarities of Eastern Indonesian terminologies and the diversity of the semantic types represented.[3]

Twenty-one terminologies have been included in this study. Because a close examination of such a large number would take too much space, only those of the southern Moluccas will be analyzed in detail here. Nevertheless this more manageable subset still gets to the heart of the problems posed more generally by the comparative analysis of Eastern Indonesian terminologies and the search for the proto-type. Having done this, I then look at the complete set of terminologies.

SOUTH MOLUCCAN TERMINOLOGIES

I chose the South Moluccas because they feature a small number of terminologies presenting sufficient contrasts and similarities; furthermore, they all belong to the same linguistic subgroup within the group of Central Malayo-Polynesian languages. These terminologies are those of the island of Tanebar-Evav, located in the Kei Archipelago (Barraud 1979), and the islands of Fordat (McKinnon 1983, 1991) and Yamdena (Pauwels 1984), in the Tanimbar Archipelago (see kinship terms in the appendix to this chapter). A fourth terminology, from Selaru Island, in the Tanimbar Archipelago, was recently recorded by Pauwels.[4] It is briefly discussed later in the chapter. The languages corresponding to the first three terminologies are derived from a protolanguage called "Proto-Tanimbar-Kei" (Collins 1983; Mills 1991). Accordingly, it can be assumed that these three terminologies share a common ancestral prototerminology.

Semantic Types

Kinship terms define equivalences (=) and differences(≠) within a set of genealogical positions. These equivalences and differences make it possible to establish what, for convenience, are called the "equations" that characterize the semantic type of a terminology. Following the typology of Needham and others, I call the basic types of equation symmetric lineal, asymmetric lineal, or nonlineal, and symmetric prescriptive, asymmetric prescriptive, or nonprescriptive.[5] The equation of male cousins, MBS = FZS ≠ FBS = MZS, for example, is called *symmetric lineal,* lineal because it distinguishes two "lines" of cousin (cross and parallel), symmetric because it merges both cross cousins, the matrilateral (MBS) and the patrilateral (FZS). The equation MBS ≠ FZS ≠ FBS = MZS is *asymmetric lineal* because it distinguishes the matrilateral and patrilateral cross cousins (making for three "lines"). The equation MBD = FZD = W/WZ is *symmetric prescriptive* because both female cross cousins are equated with the wife or the wife's sister, implying the logical equivalent of a rule of bilateral cross-cousin marriage, while the equation FZD ≠ MBD = W/WZ is *asymmetric prescriptive* because only the matrilateral female cross cousin is equated with the wife or the wife's sister. A given terminology can combine linear and prescriptive equations, linear and nonprescriptive equations (MBD ≠ W, WZ and FZD ≠ W, WZ), or nonlinear (MBS = FZS = FBS = MZS) and nonprescriptive equations, which are more simply called *cognatic* in the remainder of this discussion. Cognatic equations, then, are ones lacking a cross/parallel distinction and lacking merger of affinal kin with consanguines in a manner indicating a form of cross-cousin marriage; In other words, cognatic equations are "generational" in the Lowie-Kirchhoff sense and nonprescriptive, that is, having separate affinal terms.

For present purposes, I retain only the terms used by a male speaker in the three medial generations.[6] In the tables below, the letters on the right of the equations indicate their type: S for symmetric (linear or prescriptive), A for asymmetric (linear or prescriptive), and C for cognatic; (S) and (A) signal irregularities in a symmetric or asymmetric type; the notation SA means that an equation contains both symmetric and asymmetric features. The letters on the far right of each line identify the Moluccan terminologies (Kei, Yamdena, Fordat) satisfying the equations in that line.[7]

FIRST ASCENDING LEVEL (G^{+1})

1 F = FB = MZH ≠ MB = FZH	S	2 M = MZ = FBW ≠ FZ = MBW	S	K, Y, F
3 MB = FZH = WF	S	4 FZ = MBW = WM	S	Y, F
5 MB = FZH ≠ WF		(S)6 FZ = MBW ≠ WM	(S)	K

In this generation, the Yamdena and Fordat equations are symmetric lineal ("two lines") and prescriptive, while those of Kei are symmetric lineal but only partly prescriptive because of equations 5 and 6, which keep the spouse's parents distinct from the "aunts" and "uncles." We will say that the Yamdena and Fordat terminologies have the same semantic value in this generation, which will be designated by the letter S. The semantic value of the Kei terminology will be written as (S), the parentheses indicating the irregularities represented by equations 5 and 6.

REFERENCE LEVEL (G^0)

7 FZS = MBS ≠ FBS = MZS = B	S	8 FZD = FBD = MZD = Z ≠MBD	(A)	F
9 FZS = FBS = MZS = B ≠ MBS	(A)	10 FZD = FBD = MZD = Z ≠MBD	(A)	Y
11 FZS = MBS = FBS = MZS = B	C	12 FZD = MBD = FBD = MZD = Z	C	K
13 FZS = MBS = WB = ZH	S	14 FZD ≠ MBD = WZ = BW	A	F
15 FZS ≠ MBS = WB = ZH	SA	16 FZD ≠ MBD = WZ = BW	A	Y
17 FZS = MBS = B ≠ WB = ZH	C	18 FZD = MBD = Z ≠ WZ = BW	C	K

Because of its cognatic equations (11, 12, 17, 18), Kei terminology differs radically from the other two. The two share the asymmetric equations (8, 10, 14, 16) for the female specifications.[8] Equations 8 and 10 are irregularly asymmetric lineal, however, because FZD is equated with Z, FBD, MZD; this irregularity is not a universal trait of asymmetric systems, even though it is often interpreted as a logical expression of the interdiction of marrying a patrilateral female cross cousin. The male cross-cousin equations, on the other hand, are different. Fordat's are symmetric lineal (7) and prescriptive (13) while Yamdena's (9, 15) have both asymmetric (FZS ≠ MBS) and symmetric (WB = ZH) features. The divergence between these two terminologies comes in their way of classifying the father's sister's son, who in the case of Yamdena (9) is a "brother" (FZS = B) and in the case of Fordat (13) a "brother-in-law" (FZS = WB = ZH); to be sure, the Yamdena choice allows for a distinction to be made between the two kinds of cross cousin (FZS ≠ MBS), but equation 9 shows an odd combination of two "lines" and asymmetry.

In sum, the most remarkable characteristic of Fordat terminology is the contrast between its symmetric male equations and asymmetric female equations. The semantic value of this generation taken as a whole is then written SA. Although the Yamdena male equations are not as consistently symmetric as Fordat's, the semantic value of this generation is still composite rather than irregularly asymmetric; hence the notation (SA) with the parentheses indicating the irregularity of equation 9. Kei's semantic value for this generation is C.

FIRST DESCENDING LEVEL

19 ZS ≠ WBS = BS = S (A)	20 ZD = BD = D ≠ WBD	(A) Y, F
21 ZS = WBS = BS :S C	22 ZD = WBD = BD ≠ D	C K
23 ZS = DH : WBS A	24 ZD ≠ WBD = SW	A Y, F
25 ZS = WBS = BS ≠ DH C	26 ZD = WBD = BD ≠ SW	C K

Once again, the Kei equations are cognatic. Those for Yamdena and Fordat are asymmetric prescriptive, but two irregularities in lineality stand out: ZD = BD = D (20) and WBS = BS = S (19). The semantic value of these two terminologies is therefore (A) for this generation.

Finally, the semantic types of Moluccan terminologies can be described as a series of signs for the three generations in descending order (G^{+1}, G^0, G^{-1}) as follows:

Kei: (S) C C   Yamdena: S (SA) (A)   Fordat: S SA (A)

Through successive abstractions, we have obtained a simplified representation of a more complex reality. Having done this, it is easier to evaluate the variations exhibited by the Moluccan terminologies with respect to each other and to the canonical symmetric prescriptive (S S S) and asymmetric prescriptive (A A A) types, of which the South Indian and Kachin terminologies are more or less close variants. Because of their semantic heterogeneity, however, the Moluccan types cannot be regarded as simple variants of these canonical types. The existence of these heterogeneous types, so numerous in Eastern Indonesia, inevitably poses the problem of their existence in terms of historical transformations. In this sense, the Indonesian terminologies partake of those "turbulences" that Claude Lévi-Strauss (1983b:1231) proposed to take on when he observed that the anthropology of kinship had too long been limited to the study of ahistorical or purportedly ahistorical phenomena.

At this point, two preliminary observations can be made: each generational level follows its own independent historical evolution. This is particularly true of the levels at either end, since none of our three terminologies is of the X Y X type. Furthermore, the Fordat and Yamdena terminologies are two variants of the same basic type, while Kei's is of an altogether different make. This immediately raises the question of whether the Kei terminology represents an isolated or even aberrant historical evolution. The question is all the more pertinent as asymmetric marriage practices are just as clearly affirmed here as elsewhere in Eastern Indonesia.

Looking for Constant Features

Before going any further with this survey of the anomalies of Moluccan terminologies, it would be useful to point out certain aspects of their morphology and to identify a number of constant features. The contrast between generations is systematically marked in all three terminologies. This characteristic is so widespread among Austronesian groups that it can safely be attributed to the prototerminology contemporaneous with Proto-Austronesian. Thus any Austronesian terminology establishing transgenerational equivalences can be said to result from a specific local evolution. Such cases can be found in Eastern Indonesia, but they are restricted to one particular linguistic subgroup.

Except for Yamdena, relative age is relevant for same-sex siblings. In this respect, Yamdena is one of the exceptions in Eastern Indonesia. Yamdena terminology has lost a distinction that can rightfully be attributed to the prototype at the level of Proto-Central-Malayo-Polynesian.

Sexual difference is not systematically marked in the Moluccas. For instance, S and D are both designated by the same term in all three terminologies. In fact, this is a nearly universal feature of Eastern Indonesian terminologies and can therefore be attributed to the prototype. The complete absence of sexual distinction for Kei in the first descending generation (G^{-1}), together with the equation BS = BD = WBS = ZD for Fordat and Yamdena, would seem to indicate that, when this distinction is present (ZS ≠ ZD, WBS ≠ WBD) in the last two terminologies, it is more likely to be an effect of asymmetric prescription than a trait that has come down from the prototerminology.[9]

As is well known, the cross/parallel distinction is a constituent dimension of both symmetric and asymmetric types. Present in all three terminologies in the first ascending generation (G^{+1}), it is lacking for Kei in the other two, while Fordat and Yamdena present such irregularities of crossness as WBS = BS, ZD = BD. Thus no hypothesis can be advanced as to the presence or absence of this distinction in the prototype. In this respect, the terminologies of the Moluccas, and of Eastern Indonesia on the whole, pose a notably more difficult problem than Dravidian terminologies, which are characterized by the omnipresent dimension of the cross/parallel opposition in its symmetric form (see Trautmann 1981).

Asymmetric Prescription and Classificatory Anomalies

In the reference generation (G^0), asymmetric prescription is indicated in particular by the equation MBD = WZ = BW, common to Fordat and Yamdena. But we also find the equation FZD = Z. Assuming this last equivalence is dictated by the ban on patrilateral marriage, it should be pointed out that this solution leads to the transgression of two basic rules. In effect, the brother of ego's classificatory sister (FZD = Z) is not a "brother" but a brother-in-law (FZS = WB = ZH). In other words, the rule according to which a sibling's sibling is a sibling is not respected, nor is its complement according to which an affine's sibling is an affine. Actually, only Fordat transgresses these rules. Yamdena gets around them by classifying the patrilateral

Table 12-1

Equations Characteristic of Yamdena

Reference level (G^0)

1 FZD = Z : MBD = WZ = BWFZS = B : MBS = ZH = WB (SA)

2 FZD = Z : MBD = WZ = BWFZS = MBS = ZH = WB : B SA

3 FZD = MBD = WZ = BW : ZFZS = MBS = ZH = WB : B S

4 FZD = MBD = Z : WZ = BWFZS = MBS = B : ZH = WB C

First descending level (G^{-1})

5 WBD = SW : ZD = BD = BS = WBS : ZS = DH (A)

6 WBD = SW = ZD : BD = BS : WBS = ZS = DH   S

7 WBD = WBS = SW : BD = BS : ZD = ZS = DH   A

8 SW : WBD = ZD = BD = WBS = BS = S : DH   C

---

cross cousin as a "brother" (FZS = B), thus obliterating the cross/parallel opposition, for the father's sister's children then are no longer distinguished from those of the father's brother (FZCh = FBCh). Rather than use a special term to designate FZD (as, for example, the Kachin do), Fordat and Yamdena "choose" to identify her as a "sister" and to violate one classificatory rule or the other, the only advantage being the introduction into the kinship vocabulary of the prohibition on marrying this kinswoman.

In the first descending generation (G^{-1}), Fordat and Yamdena equations are identical (19, 20, 23, 24). They combine all of the aforementioned anomalies, so that the cross/parallel dimension is missing locally (ZD = BD, WBS = BS) and the affine/consanguine dichotomy runs through the two pairs of opposite-sex siblings, ZS –ZD and WBS –WBD. Are these anomalies again to be attributed to negative prescription, this time bearing on the sister's daughter (ZD =D) and the wife's brother's son (WBS = S), thus distinguishing this classificatory daughter and son from their opposite-sex siblings, who are spouses of a daughter or a son (ZS = DH, WBD = SW)? Perhaps. But then why is FZ not equated with M, inasmuch as the father's sister is also prohibited? There is, however, another explanation, which gives a simple and complete account of these anomalies. It results from a simple combinative exercise.

Logical Transformations, Historical Transformations

Let us take, for example, the equations characteristic of Yamdena in the last two generations (lines 1 and 5, table 12-1). The point of the exercise is to find all possible semantic combinations in each generation without changing the number of kinship terms. After eliminating certain unlikely combinations (e.g., WZ ≠ BW) and meaningless variants, we are left with the solutions in table 12-1.

At each of these two generational levels, one semantic value leads to another by way of an elementary transformation. Thus for each level, each line is a transformation of all others. In addition to the four values C, SA, (SA), and (A) proper to Moluccan terminologies, we obtain two new semantic values: S, the symmetric prescriptive form, in the two generations under consideration, and A, the asymmetric prescriptive form, in the last generation only. In this way we obtain four possible values for each level: C, S, SA, (SA) for the first, and C, S, A, (A) for the second. This makes sixteen separate semantic combinations for two levels. If we assume that value S remains constant in the first ascending generation (G^{+1}), we obtain sixteen separate semantic types differing in G^0 and G^{-1}. These sixteen contain the Fordat type (S, SA, (A)), the Yamdena type (S, (SA), (A)) and the S C C type, of which the Kei type, (S) C C, is an irregular variant. Eliminating the parentheses indicating irregular variants, there are still nine basic types: S C C, S C S, S C A, S S C, S S S, S S A, S SA C, S SA S, and S SA A. Several lessons can be drawn from this exercise.

First, assuming historical conditions such that we have a prototerminology belonging to one of the four types, S S S, S C S, S S C, and S C C, and a tendency to evolve toward asymmetry, and the constraint of a constant number of kinship terms— then the most asymmetric terminologies resulting from the transformations of one of these four prototypes will necessarily belong to types S SA (A) (Fordat), S (SA) (A) (Yamdena), or to types S SA A, S (SA) A, which are not attested for the Moluccas. In other words, type S C C is just as plausible a historical prototype as the symmetric prescriptive S S S. And if such is the case, the Kei type, (S) C C, is no less plausible. More generally, comparative analysis of Eastern Indonesian terminologies alone cannot support the conclusion that a cognatic or predominantly cognatic type is historically improbable or, even less, impossible. In order to eliminate these types and decide that the symmetric prescriptive type is the most likely candidate, additional data need to be introduced or different hypotheses made. This is not a superfluous point, in view of the fact that the thesis of a cognatic or predominantly cognatic prototerminology has not been seriously considered in recent studies on the evolution of Indonesian terminologies.[10]

Second, if we adopt a transformational perspective, as the Indonesian data require us to do, we see that the cognatic or predominantly cognatic terminologies are both like and unlike the symmetric prescriptive terminologies. Although they differ widely in structure, these types are nonetheless akin inasmuch as they form a single group of semantic combinations. In this way Indonesian terminologies invite us to relativize the idea that the cognatic type represents a unique or even abnormal configuration in the concert of terminologies.

Following the same train of thought, one might make a complementary observation. Indonesian terminologies are often presented in a symmetric or asymmetric table with the kinship terms listed in columns. While this is useful for symmetric and asymmetric terminologies, the method is less advisable in the case of composite terminologies such as those of Fordat and Yamdena in the Moluccas, or Endeh (A SA S) and West Manggarai (A SA A) on Flores (Needham 1968, 1970, 1980). When they are presented using a symmetric or an asymmetric matrix, the reader is naturally inclined to think that, notwithstanding a few details, these composite terminologies belong to the symmetric or asymmetric type. But types A SA S and A

S A A are not irregular variants of the S S S or A A A types.[11] These are distinct types in and of themselves, historically stable and structurally different from the symmetric and asymmetric types. In other words, it is important to distinguish two types of irregularities: accidental irregularities stemming from the peculiar history of each terminology, and irregularities that are too systematic to be accidental. To illustrate the first kind, I will take the classic example of a terminology that is symmetric prescriptive, except that the parents-in-law are designated by separate terms. In this case, we are indeed dealing with an irregular variant of the S S S type, and it is legitimate to list the kinship terms in a symmetric matrix. The second kind of irregularity is of an altogether different nature. These are irregularities recurring, as we have seen, in different languages that, moreover, belong to separate linguistic subgroups. To inscribe these composite terminologies in either a symmetric or an asymmetric matrix would be tantamount to confusing the two kinds of irregularity, which in turn would eliminate the possibility of understanding the logic of the historical transformations undergone by Indonesian terminologies. It was precisely the detailed examination of these composite terminologies that led me to assume that their apparent inconsistencies resulted from an underlying transformational logic.

Third, as I have tried to show, the "abnormal" terminologies of Yamdena and Fordat are the predictable, logical result of certain historical transformations, provided that the number of kinship terms remains constant.[12] This constraint, or "rule of economy of kin terms," raises a larger question: that of the logical and pragmatic modalities at work in the historical production of stable terminologies adapted to the needs of those concerned, but inconsistent from the standpoint of formal logic. Should this be surprising? In a historical context of transformational pressure, no committee of wise men met to decide rationally what transformations should be made in the group's kin classification. Under the special conditions of a propensity for change, it is understandable that formal logic may and sometimes even must undergo some rough handling. The Indonesian case shows that kin classifications, too, can be historical objects capable of evolving into complex forms in accordance with what are at least partly comprehensible modalities. As far as the Moluccas are concerned, it is reasonable to conclude that the rule of economy of terms was in all likelihood the logical and pragmatic modality that partially neutralized certain basic classificatory rules, resulting in the anomalies that characterize the terminologies of Fordat and Yamdena.

The foregoing analysis does not allow us to identify the Moluccan prototype. It simply circumscribes a certain number of possible types that must next be reduced by other means.

Identifying the Prototype

The crucial issue is not so much to pin down the prototype to the last detail but to make a choice between the symmetric type, on the one hand, and the cognatic type, on the other, as well as those types with cognatic features. What is the procedure, once all of the possibilities of formal terminological analysis have been exhausted? At this stage we could invoke Needham's general hypotheses and immediately conclude in favor of the symmetric type (Needham 1967:45–46, 1974:40, 1984:228–29). His first hypothesis states that cognatic terminologies are necessarily derived from terminologies that are symmetric or asymmetric; the second enables him to eliminate the possibility of an asymmetric prototype by assuming that terminologies necessarily evolve toward more complex forms. But one may also be reticent about resorting to such broad hypotheses, especially the first one, whose strength is also their weakness: the empirical problem of the historical transformations of Indonesian terminologies no longer arises since the solution is already given. Different and less axiomatic arguments can be advanced. Although there are notable differences in each society, marriage practices and rituals in Eastern Indonesia share so many basic features that it is highly unlikely that they resulted from independent innovations. If the marriage system was asymmetric before these societies began to go their separate ways, it follows that the prototerminology could not have been more asymmetric than the most asymmetric of the current terminologies. Indeed, the loss of certain asymmetric features would be an unlikely evolution in a stable regime of asymmetric alliance. Similarly, the prototerminology could not have had fewer cognatic features than the most cognatic of the current terminologies, for the acquisition of additional cognatic features would be no less aberrant. That leaves only two possible semantic types: S C C, of which Kei's terminology is a close variant, and C C C, the purely cognatic type not found in the Moluccas.

To sum up the two competing points of view: (1) either we resort to general hypotheses about the transformation of kinship systems, and the cognatic and asymmetric types are automatically eliminated, but in this case we need to find a plausible explanation for Kei's then aberrant terminology; or (2) we argue for the historical precedence of the asymmetric marriage system, which makes either a symmetric or an asymmetric prototype unlikely. In this case, the Kei terminology is no longer aberrant but simply more conservative than the terminologies of Yamdena and Fordat. I would add that nothing in the ethnography of Kei gives reason to suppose we are in the presence of an aberrant or unstable configuration (Barraud 1979). Because the defense of the cognatic hypothesis rests largely on the example of Kei, I will come back to this discussion having presented the rest of the Eastern Indonesian data (see the section "Identifying the Prototypes").

First, however, I consider how to go about a semantic reconstruction using the method successfully employed by Trautmann (1981:229–37) to reconstruct the Dravidian prototype. Trautmann borrowed his approach from historical linguistics. In this respect, it is useful to recall that reconstructing the meaning of a protomorpheme is usually more delicate than reconstructing the protomorpheme itself. Furthermore, reconstructing the meaning of kinship terms often presents specific difficulties because of their polysemia. In addition, a prototerm may have undergone such historical transformations that its meaning was not conserved in any of these reflexes. In this case, no semantic reconstruction is possible. Reconstructing the meaning of a prototerm in most cases means reconstructing the most probable meaning according to a process that may imply some subjective decisions on the part of the analyst. Whatever prestige linguistics may enjoy in the eyes of anthropologists, this method is far from always yielding the desired results.[13] Unlike a linguist and in accordance with the concerns of an anthropologist, Trautmann has not sought to reconstruct the Dravidian prototerms, but the prototype itself, using the semantic types of present-day Dravidian terminologies. In this perspective, the basic rule inherited from historical linguistics is that, if the same semantic type is found in at least two linguistic subgroups, then this type is a candidate for the prototype. It is therefore not so much the frequency of a type that counts as its distribution. The ideal case is obviously that of a frequently occurring type that is also represented in all of the linguistic subgroups.

In the case of the Moluccas, the situation is unfavorable because only three languages belong to the same linguistic subgroup, located on the lowest rung of the genetic classification of Eastern Indonesian languages. For the method to work, a much more inclusive level would be needed, that of the two major subgroups, which, since Esser's 1938 study, are known as "Sumba-Bima" and "Timor-Ambon." We must be content with simply improving the experimental conditions by bringing in a fourth Moluccan terminology, found on the island of Selaru, which, together with Fordat and Yamdena, belongs to the Tanimbar Archipelago. Although this island is geographically close to Yamdena and Fordat, its language diverges in so many ways that it cannot have come from Proto-Tanimbar-Kei (Collins 1983; Mills 1991). The language spoken on Selaru belongs to a second subgroup in the higher subgroup of South Moluccan languages, which themselves are part of the even more inclusive Timor-Ambon subgroup.

One noteworthy feature of Selaru terminology is that two terms are used to designate the father's sister's son: *wai* (FZS, B) and *mwana* (FZS, MBS). Such a terminology partakes of two semantic types: A (SA) (A) and A SA (A). In the first South Moluccan linguistic group, we have then types (S) C C (Kei), S S SA (A) (Fordat), S (SA) (A) (Yamdena), and, in the second, types A (SA) (A) and A SA (A) (Selaru). If the earlier method is applied, the semantic values are so distributed in the first ascending generation (G^{+1}) that nothing can be decided. On the other hand, there is justification for ascribing to the South Moluccan prototype value (A) in the last generation (G^{-1}) and values SA or (SA) in the reference generation (G^0). Thus the semantic reconstruction invites the conclusion that the prototerminology could not have been of the S C C type and that Kei's terminology is the result of a diverging evolution.

And yet this conclusion is wrong, for one simple reason. Under the transformational pressure present throughout Eastern Indonesia, it is inevitable that a certain number of terminologies from different linguistic subgroups evolved independently toward the asymmetric type. If this evolution had been uniform and complete, today there would be nothing but A A A type terminologies and it would be impossible to formulate any sensible hypothesis as to the nature of the prototype. Whereas the purpose of the criterion of type distribution is to eliminate the risk of drawing false conclusions from semantic convergences, the probability of which diminishes rapidly as soon as several linguistic subgroups come into play, the effect of the asymmetric drift robs this criterion of its usefulness.

The Indonesian and Dravidian cases are very different in this respect. Aside from a few exceptions that can be explained by the Indo-Aryan influence, Dravidian

Table 12-2

Simplified Characteristics of Twenty-one Terminologies

C C C	Savu, Roti
S C C	Ndao, Kei
S C S	Central Manggarai
S S C	Northern Tetum
S S S	Rembong, Alor, Pantar
A A A	Eastern Sumba, Boleng, Atoni, Tana, 'Ai[1], Kedang, Wailolong
S SA A	Yamdema, Fordat
A SA C	Ema
A SA S	Endeh
A SA A	Western Manggarai, Selaru

[1]In Tana 'Ai, however, some informants do not equate MBD with FZD, MBS with FZS, so their classification is asymmetric in the reference generation (Lewis 1988:198<en>201).

terminologies are variants of the symmetric prescriptive type. In the absence of semantic drift, the semantic reconstruction method can be applied with confidence, making it possible to go on, as Trautmann does, to single out the prototype from among the different variants of the symmetric type. Indonesia, however, is another case altogether. This method can be used legitimately only to reconstruct the equations of the prototerminology that are not exposed to the asymmetric drift. For instance, one may assign to South Moluccan prototerminology the equation WZ = BW as well as other secondary features that discriminate insufficiently between cognatic and symmetric prescriptive types. In short, semantic reconstruction, however useful it may be in other circumstances, cannot be employed here.

EASTERN INDONESIAN TERMINOLOGIES

I turn now to twenty-one terminologies of Eastern Indonesia.[14] Thirteen of these (Tana 'Ai, Wailolong, Alor, Pantar, Kedang, Roti, Atoni, Northern Tetum, Ema, Kei, Yamdena, Fordat, and Selaru) belong to the Timor-Ambon linguistic subgroup, and eight to the Sumba-Bima subgroup (Eastern Sumba, Ndao, Savu, Boleng, Western Manggarai, Central Manggarai, Rembong, Endeh).[15] It should be remembered that all of these terminologies exist alongside asymmetric marriage practices.[16]

Semantic Types

Proceeding as before, we have only to establish the classificatory equations characteristic of the twenty-one terminologies to construct their semantic types. Because the following analysis does not demand a detailed representation of the semantic types, the parentheses indicating irregularities can be dispensed with; hence the simplified procedure shown in table 12-2.[17]

The twenty-one terminologies correspond to ten distinct semantic types, seven of which are heterogeneous and three homogeneous (C C C, S S S, A A A). Five types have no asymmetric features, five types no cognatic features, and two types no symmetric features. Even though the earlier analysis of the Moluccan terminologies intimated this possibility, the diversity of the semantic types present in Eastern Indonesia is no less remarkable.

But does table 12-2 actually contain most of the existing types of Eastern Indonesia, or should we assume, on the contrary, that there are many others yet to be discovered? The number of semantic values taken by the different generations in descending order, are three, four, and three. Theoretically, then, there are thirty-six ($3 \times 4 \times 3$) possible types, twenty-six of which are not attested. In particular, types C A C, A C A, S A S, A S A are not represented in table 12-2. This suggests the existence of a rule stipulating incompatibility between the semantic values of adjacent levels. Just to see what happens, suppose that the values of two consecutive levels can never be C and A, C and SA, S and A. This eliminates twenty-three types. Four of the remaining thirteen types are C C S, C S C, C S S, and S SA S, which are at present unknown in Eastern Indonesia. But the other nine types (excluding A SA C) all figure in table 12-2. This pattern can hardly be accidental. It can therefore be assumed that the historical transformations in Indonesian terminologies have followed a rule of semantic incompatibility making it unlikely that adjacent levels will have values that are too different, such as C and A, C and SA, S and A.[18] Accordingly, we need to revise our remark based on the previous analysis of the Moluccan terminologies: adjacent generational levels are only relatively independent in their historical evolutions. If this is correct, it can be predicted that most of the terminologies remaining to be recorded, for example, in the North Moluccas and the Leti islands, will belong to one of these nine types.[19]

Next, it can be noted that the composite form SA appears in four of the ten types in table 12-2. In the Timor-Ambon subgroup, it is present in the Moluccas (Yamdena, Fordat, Selaru), but also on Timor (Ema), therefore in languages that are not only different but distantly related within this subgroup. In the Sumba-Bima subgroup, there are only two occurrences, both on Flores: Endeh and Western Manggarai. If we were to apply the semantic reconstruction method mechanically, the value SA could be attributed to the prototype in the reference generation (G^0). But in the context of asymmetric drift, the distribution of this value results, on the contrary, from independent evolutions. Moreover, in the reference generation, the asymmetric form A is found in only four cases (Boleng, Wailolong, Kedang, and Eastern Sumba). The fact that SA is more widely distributed than A supports the hypothesis formulated at the end of the section "Logical Transformations, Historical Transformations" inasmuch as the rule of economy of kinship terms makes SA a simpler solution and therefore historically more likely than A.

In this respect, it is useful to take a closer look at the four most asymmetric terminologies. Boleng has adopted a "clever" solution, distinguishing FZS and MBS by means of the terms *kesa* and *kela,* which differ by only one phoneme. The solution adopted by Kedang and Wailolong, on the other hand, is a thoroughgoing innovation. These two terminologies are characterized by cross-level equations.[20] Unlike the preceding example, the innovation was not an isolated lexical change, but a complete structural overhaul. It is a peculiar historical evolution, which has occurred only in certain related languages (Lamaholot) of the Timor-Ambon subgroup. Clearly, this solution does not require any new kinship terms; on the contrary, it leads to a reduction in their number. The Eastern Sumba solution is altogether different. As the Austronesian legacy of contrasting generations is conserved here, asymmetry, in the reference generation (G^0), is marked by an additional term that serves to distinguish father's sister's son from mother's brother's son. In addition, Sumba terminologies have the particularity of using descriptive expressions for certain genealogical positions.[21]

In sum, with the exception of Boleng, the most asymmetric terminologies are found in only two linguistic groups (Lamaholot and Sumba), at the lowest level of the genetic classification of languages, and close observation of these terminologies strongly suggests that they result from unique evolutions, diverging from the paths taken by the other terminologies. With respect to the reference generation, to say that Eastern Sumba's A form is more innovative and historically less probable than the SA form of the composite terminologies is also to say that there is a break between these two forms that does not occur between the forms SA and S, SA and C, S and C. This is precisely what could be expected, knowing that values C, S, and SA are part of the same set of semantic combinations whereas the value A is excluded in this generation (see "Logical Transformations, Historical Transformations"). This group is, however, less useful for understanding historical transformations in the other two generational levels, which are apparently more complex.

Identifying the Prototype

We can now resume the discussion interrupted at the end of the study of Moluccan terminologies (see "Identifying the Prototype"), keeping in mind that the prototerminology we are trying to identify was in use at the time Proto-Central-Malayo-Polynesian was a living language. The speakers of this language, from which all of Eastern Indonesia's Austronesian languages have derived, descended from migrants who had left the southern Philippines at an earlier time, while another branch of their descendants went on to people the shores of New Guinea and eventually the islands of the Pacific Ocean.

It will be recalled that the divergence between the two positions was due chiefly to the existence of type (S) C C (Kei) in the Moluccas and to the legitimacy of calling upon general hypotheses to illuminate what is primarily a historical question, even though in the absence of direct evidence the choice of the most likely prototype is inevitably based on logical arguments. As the cognatic type is obviously no more differentiated, or complex, than the symmetric and asymmetric types, the only way of eliminating the possibility of a cognatic prototype is to call upon Needham's first general hypothesis: cognatic terminologies are necessarily derived from previous symmetric or asymmetric terminologies. My objection is not one of principle, for it seems to me that the specificity of anthropology lies in its capacity to formulate general hypotheses. But, as long as their validity has not been seriously tested, general hypotheses are just intellectual constructions that satisfy our need for rational explanations.

The case of Eastern Indonesia casts doubt on precisely the scope of Needham's first general hypothesis. Whereas Needham (1984) had only one terminology at hand, that of Central Manggarai, which comprised only one cognatic generational level, table 12-2 contains seven terminologies having at least one cognatic generational level, which moreover are found in different linguistic groups. So it is no longer one single, supposedly aberrant evolution that needs to be explained, but seven (Savu, Roti, Ndao, Kei, Central Manggarai, Northern Tetum, and Ema). Unlike formal transformations, which analysts generate at their leisure on paper, historical transformations do not happen without motivation. In this respect, it is hard to imagine what social or cognitive motivations could be conjured up as an acceptable explanation for these seven terminologies evolving out of a symmetric prescriptive protototerminology after marriage practices have changed from symmetry to asymmetry. Needham's option of a symmetric prototype leaves a large remainder unexplained, with the additional difficulty that several terminologies would have evolved independently towards cognatic forms. In the present state of knowledge and in the framework of the historical scenario advanced at the beginning of this chapter, a symmetric prescriptive protototerminology is hardly plausible, and the most likely solution to the problem posed by Eastern Indonesian terminologies is that of a cognatic prototype.

Because this type has several subtypes, is it possible to narrow down the definition of this cognatic protototerminology? To explore this possibility would mean doing what I have abstained from doing until now, namely, turn to the kinship terms with the aim of reconstructing some prototerms. Since it would take too long to go through the process here, I will merely present the results, which turn out to be disappointing: in the two end generations, only three terms can be constructed with certainty: *ama, *ina, *anak,* the minimum specifications of which are, respectively, "father," "mother," and "child." The protototerminology for these two generations may also have included affinal terms or modifiers, but whatever traces there were that might have allowed their identification have disappeared. Likewise, it is difficult to say whether or not there were specific terms used to designate collaterals (MB, FB; MZ, FZ; ZCh, BCh). Nevertheless, since the terms for MB and FZ are quite often derived from those meaning F, FB and M, MZ, it seems likely that the prototype was characterized by the equations F = FB = MB and M = MZ = FZ (see Fox 1984:41). As for the reference generation (G^0), comparative analysis of the classificatory equations of the different terminologies suggests that, for this generation, the protototerminology was formally identical with that of Kei.

Finally, an objection comes to mind that needs to be answered. While the "conservatism" of certain groups explains the existence of the more or less cognatic terminologies in table 12-2, it is more surprising that purely or predominantly symmetric terminologies have come out of the transformation of a cognatic terminology under the transformational pressure of asymmetric marriage practices. This objection can be answered, first, by recalling that symmetric or predominantly symmetric terminologies obviously "function"; otherwise they would have been eliminated fairly rapidly. Furthermore, when certain contexts require distinguishing MB from FZH, MBS from FZS, WBS from ZS, it can be assumed that a discriminating modifier is added to the basic kinship term. As a matter of fact, all societies in Eastern Indonesia have expressions for "wife-givers" and "wife-takers," and, in all likelihood, these expressions are used when necessary to distinguish the two kinds of affines merged by the kinship vocabulary.[22]

In asymmetric marriage systems, where the matrilateral cross cousin is a potential wife and the patrilateral cross cousin is forbidden, one apparently more serious drawback of cognatic and symmetric terminologies is that the two types of female cross cousin are designated by the same term; in the first case, these cousins are "sisters," in the second, "wife's sisters." The advantage of the simple semantic shift represented by the equation $FZD = Z \neq MBD = WZ = BW$ seems so obvious that it may come as a surprise that several groups have retained the cognatic form (Savu, Roti, Ndao, Kei, Central Manggarai), whereas others have adopted the symmetric prescriptive solution (Tana'Ai, Alor, Pantar, Atoni). But, as already explained, equating FZD with Z leads one to violate certain fundamental classificatory rules. In this form, then, the asymmetric prescriptive solution is not obviously any more "logical" than the symmetric prescriptive and cognatic solutions.

CONCLUDING REMARKS

The comparative analysis of a set of terminologies is not a sterile exercise, contrary to what certain "post-modern" writers claim in their haste to declare this type of study mere illusion and thus to discard a long-standing tradition inaugurated in 1871 by Lewis Henry Morgan. And contrary to certain die-hard prejudices inherited from the structuralist and functionalist traditions, a diachronic approach to kinship systems is also legitimate.

The interest of the Eastern Indonesian example is that the kinship systems of this region have a history. This is no doubt fairly common, but it is particularly manifest here because of the large number of irregular terminologies and the frequent divergence between semantic type and marriage system. In speaking of this historical configuration, it is convenient to call upon the paradigm of "event-and-structure," the two protagonists of this history of Indonesian kinship. The contingent event, in the perspective of this discussion, was the shift from a "complex" form of marriage to a regime of asymmetric alliance; in the role of structure, a cognatic terminology, which, under the transformational pressure induced by this changeover, gave rise, in the course of a past composed of successive migrations and splits, to the diversified set of terminologies in use today. The challenge was to see if some order could be uncovered in the apparent disorder of these historical transformations. As I explained, some initially disconcerting classificatory anomalies can be attributed to a transformational logic constrained by "a rule of economy of kin terms." Furthermore, not all semantic types are apparently equally possible or probable and it is reasonable to assume that a rule of semantic incompatibility of adjacent generational levels reduced the otherwise wide-open field of variations. In counterpoint to a more universalist approach, this regional study shows that it is possible to shed some light on the structural history of kinship systems within groups speaking genetically linked languages.[23] In this respect, the Indonesian example serves to correct the general proposition that symmetric or asymmetric terminologies cannot possibly derive from cognatic terminologies and that cognatic kin classifications are always the result of irreversible historical transformations. This axiom may be convenient, but it is too simple to explain the histories of all cognatic systems.

Furthermore, the metamorphoses of kinship in Eastern Indonesia invite us to relativize, complexify, or even revise certain conceptions that are still more or less part of the anthropological tradition. For instance, it is no longer possible to believe, as was the case for decades, that Eastern Indonesian societies maintained an original asymmetric kinship system that had changed over to cognatic forms in the Philippines, Borneo, Sulawesi, Java, or on the Malay Peninsula and practically throughout Sumatra. Everything indicates, on the contrary, that the asymmetric connubium, as Dutch authors used to write, results from a historical development peculiar to these societies on the eastern fringes of Indonesia. Similarly, it would be unwise to accept as definitive truth the interpretation suggesting that the cognatic systems of Polynesia result from the transformations of formerly noncognatic systems. It is possible that the Eastern Polynesians were simply more conservative than the Austronesians of Melanesia, whose highly diverse kinship systems might be historical elaborations on a common cognatic legacy. According to this view, Eastern Indonesia and Melanesia would constitute a geographical area of historical innovations without equivalent in an otherwise largely cognatic Austronesian world. It would no doubt be fruitful and, at any rate, intellectually stimulating to compare the Eastern Indonesian and the Austronesian-speaking Melanesians, between whom a long-standing barrier has been maintained for arbitrary reasons.[24]

It has long been known that asymmetric systems are found above all in Southeast Asia and that most of these systems are found in Eastern Indonesia. In *The Elementary Structures of Kinship* (Lévi-Strauss 1967), asymmetric systems are given the conceptual status of a ahistorical type, or, as it were, an archetype. And yet it may be asked whether there exist in Southeast Asia asymmetric systems that were not the result of historical transformations. In the case of the Tibeto-Burmese-speaking groups, the most plausible hypothesis is that of a symmetric prescriptive prototerminology (Allen 1975, 1976), with the asymmetric systems, like that of the Kachin, being historically derived from a symmetric prescriptive protosystem. Thus as soon as enough information is available on Southeast Asian asymmetric systems, it becomes clear that they are not archetypes.

Alternatively, cognatic forms of kinship, at least in insular Southeast Asia, give no indication that they might be the result of historical transformations. The kinship terminologies, marriage rules, and rituals contain no "anomaly" that might suggest the existence of earlier noncognatic kinship systems. Furthermore, since the Javanese, the Balinese, and the Malays have basically the same cognatic kinship system as the groups in the interior of Borneo and the Philippines, the assumption that cognatic systems appeared with the emergence of the state and changes in the mode of production does not stand up for this part of the world. In short, the cognatic systems found in insular Southeast Asia are remarkably homogeneous and apparently quite stable. It is their stability that poses a problem, at least from a Lévi-Straussian standpoint. Indeed, if symmetric and asymmetric systems are in some way inscribed in the human mind, how is it that they did not "come to mind" in at least one of the numerous groups that have lived in Borneo and the Philippines for thousands of years? The classic kinship theories have produced a massive residue, cognatism, which has been conveniently attributed to "the complexities of history." As far as I can see, cognatism, at least in insular Southeast Asia, resists its purported historicity. And truly convincing arguments have yet to be found for denying cognatic forms the status of "elementary structures."

APPENDIX

Kinship terms: Kei, Yamdena, Fordat
I have listed below only those terms and specifications (m.s.) necessary and sufficient to establish the classificatory equations presented in the sections "Semantic Types."

Kei (Tanebar Evav)

yaman	F, FB, MZH
yaman turan	WF
renan	M, MZ, FBW
renan te	WM
memen	MB, FZH
avan	FZ, MBW
a'an	eB, FeBS, MeZS, MeBS, FeZS
a'an vat	eBW, WeZ
warin	yB, FyBS, MyZS, MyBS, FyZS
warin vat	yBW, WyZ
uran	Z, FBD, MZD, MBD, FZD
hoan	W
ifar	ZH, WB
yanan	Ch
yanan duan	BC, ZCh, WBCh
yanan turan	DH
yanan te	SW

Yamdena

ame	F, FB, MZH
ene	M, MZ, FBW
memi	MB, FZH, WF
abe	FZ, MBW, WM
wai	B, FBS, MZS, FZS, MBD, BW, WZ

ur	Z, FBD, MZD, FZD
fatnime	MBD
ifar	MBS, ZH, WB
sawan	W
anak	Ch, BCh, WBS, ZD
lengin	DH, ZS
ketim	SW, WBD

Fordat

yaman	F, FB, MZH
renan	M, MZ, FBW
memin	MB, FZH, WF
avan	FZ, MBW, WM
a'an	eB, FeBS, MeZS, MeBD, eBW, WeZ
warin	yB, FyBS, MyZS, MyBD, yBW, WyZ
ur	Z, FBD, MZD, FZD
fatnima	MBD
da'uk	FZS, MBS, ZH, WB
awan	W
yanan	Ch, BCh, WBS, ZD
ranetan	DH, ZS
etan	SW, WBD

Sources: Kei (Barraud 1979), Yamdena (Pauwels 1984), Fordat (McKinnon 1983, 1991).

NOTES

This chapter was translated by Nora Scott.

1. See in particular the ethnography of certain Moluccan societies in which, in marriage rituals, the temporal dimension of the MB-ZC relationship is especially well developed (Pauwels 1990; McKinnon 1991).
2. For the signification of "cognatic" in this context, see the section "Semantic Types" under "South Moluccan Terminologies."
3. To the best of my knowledge, the only writer supporting the asymmetric prescriptive prototerminology hypothesis today is Blust (1980, 1993). True, the reconstructions of this linguist concern the Proto-Austronesian (or Proto-Malayo-Polynesian) level, but the obvious implication is that the prototerminology corresponding to Proto-Central-Malayo-Polynesian was also asymmetric prescriptive.
4. My thanks go to Simonne Pauwels for having communicated the unpublished Selaru terminology.
5. It should be remembered, as Needham has often pointed out, that the terms "lineal" or "line" are used to qualify the form of certain classificatory equations as well as the overall morphology of a terminology; they have nothing to do with whether or not descent groups actually exist. However, it happens that all Eastern Indonesian societies mentioned in this paper have descent groups.

Figure 12-3
Location of Tribal Groups in Eastern Indonesia

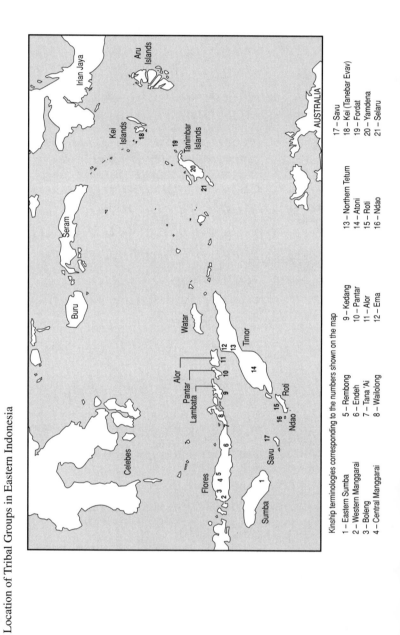

Kinship terminologies corresponding to the numbers shown on the map

1 – Eastern Sumba	5 – Rembong	9 – Kedang	13 – Northern Tetum	17 – Savu
2 – Western Manggarai	6 – Endeh	10 – Pantar	14 – Atoni	18 – Kei (Tanebar Evav)
3 – Boleng	7 – Tana 'Ai	11 – Alor	15 – Roti	19 – Fordat
4 – Central Manggarai	8 – Wailolong	12 – Ema	16 – Ndao	20 – Yamdena
				21 – Selaru

6. As usual in this kind of analysis, these three generations are retained because of their diagnostic value. The choice of the terms used by a male speaker results from the sources that often do not mention the terms used by a female speaker.

7. When the Kei and Fordat terminologies distinguish between elder and younger siblings, for the purpose of simplification I have written one equation instead of two. Obviously, this has no effect on the formal analysis of these terminologies.

8. These equations do not take into account the terms *fatnima* (Fordat) and *fatnime* (Yamdena), which enable the speaker to single out the matrilateral cross cousin when necessary.

9. It can also be noted that the equation $WZ = BW = B$ is common to Yamdena and Fordat, and that Kei presents a similar configuration. Sexual differentiation, elsewhere omnipresent in this generation (G^0), is absent here; moreover, opposite-sex affines are equated with same-sex siblings. In the Tanimbar Archipelago (also true for Selaru), a man calls his (elder or younger) sisters-in-law "brothers," and a woman calls her (elder or younger) brothers-in-law "sisters." Far from being a local innovation, this classificatory peculiarity is characteristic of other Eastern Indonesian terminologies (Western Manggarai, Central Manggarai, Rembong, Endeh, Tana 'Ai). It is also found in certain Austronesian-speaking Melanesian groups.

10. The exception is J. Fox (1984), who convincingly demonstrates that the cognatic hypothesis cannot be eliminated for the first ascending generation (see note 17). For the Savu and Ndao terminologies, see also the discussion between Fox (1987) and Forth (1988), which ended with the latter apparently conceding the plausibility of the cognatic hypothesis while maintaining his preference for the symmetric prescriptive thesis. At an earlier date, Fischer (1957:29), a Dutch anthropologist, also backed the cognatic hypothesis; but his argumentation consisted simply of referring to Murdock's (1949) ideas on the original form of kinship in the Malayo-Polynesian world; in the same period, the Leiden anthropologists apparently considered the opposite view of the original character of the asymmetric connubium to be self-evident.

11. Using (S) and (A) to designate the semantic values of the reference generation (G^0) in Endeh and Western Manggarai terminologies does not dissipate the risk of misunderstanding (Needham 1984:226, table 1). The notation SA has the advantage of avoiding ambiguity by pointing to the mixed character of the classificatory equations. Furthermore, both terminologies have, in this generation (G^0), exactly the same classificatory equations, making Needham's choice hard to understand.

12. If any explanation of these anomalies is to be acceptable, it should at least be based on the analysis of the terminologies and not rest on a teleological view of the evolution of historical transformations. One cannot be content then with an interpretation consisting of the assumption that the inconsistent terminologies in Eastern Indonesia represent a transitional phase in a series of transformations, the final stage of which is necessarily of an asymmetric prescriptive type. Aside from the fact that this does not explain anything at all, it is both arbitrary and rather unlikely to predict a logically happy ending to the history of Indonesian transformations in which the internal consistency of the terminologies would be recovered and a concordance reached between semantic types and marriage practices.

13. See in this respect Blust's (1980) discussion, which convinced neither anthropologists nor linguists that the Proto-Austronesian terminology was asymmetric prescriptive.

14. Needham's corpus (1984) has fifteen terminologies. I have added the four terminologies of the Moluccas and those of Savu, Ndao, Roti, and those of the Boleng, Tana'Ai, and North Tetum. Alternatively, I did not include the terminology of Komodo, which is too peculiar, nor the Endeh terminology of Mananga, which duplicates the Flores Endeh terminology. The absence of the Mambai (Timor) and the Lio (Flores) is due to the fact that I did not have access to these terminologies, which have not been published. Like Needham, I have classified together the various terminologies (all of which are asymmetric prescriptive) of eastern Sumba under the single heading "Eastern Sumba." Just as I was finishing this article,

the Nage (Flores) terminology was published (Forth 1993), adding to the number of predominantly cognatic terminologies.

15. Outside of the Moluccas, the islands from which the seventeen terminologies are taken are Sumba (Eastern Sumba), Savu, Ndao, Flores (Boleng, West and Central Manggarai, Rembong, Endeh, Tana'Ai, Wailolong), Lembata (Kedang), Pantar, Alor, Roti, and Timor (Atoni, North Tetum, Ema). I used the following sources: Fischer (1957) and Forth (1981) on Eastern Sumba; Kana (1983) on Savu; Fox (1987) on Ndao; Hicks (1990) on Boleng; Needham (1980) on West and Central Manggarai; Needham (1985) on Rembong; Needham (1968, 1970) on Endeh; Lewis (1988) on Tana'Ai; Barnes (1977) on Wailolong; Barnes (1974) on Kedang; Barnes (1974) on Pantar and Alor; Fox (1971, 1987) on Roti; Fischer (1957) and Schulte Nordholt (1971) on Antoni; Hicks (1990) on North Tetum; and Renard-Clamagirand (1982) and Barnes (1985) on Ema.

16. It is hard, however, to get a clear idea of the marriage practices on Alor and Pantar; Needham (1984) includes them in his list of societies practicing asymmetric marriage, while Barnes (1974) describes symmetric practices. In the case of Ndao, the sources available to me did not explicitly mention the nature of the marriage system. I have deduced it from the fact that (1) the language of Savu is understood by the inhabitants of Ndao, who (2) say they originally came from that island. Now on Savu, the ideal wife is the matrilateral cross cousin and sister exchange is forbidden (Kana 1983:134). It is therefore most likely that the Ndao marriage system is asymmetric.

17. Such a simplification has the disadvantage of erasing certain, often significant differences. For instance, the terminologies of Savu and Roti diverge from the pure cognatic type. The first one has a specific term (*makemone*) designating exclusively MB, whereas there is only one term (*ina*) for M, MZ, FZ. The Savu semantic type is therefore more accurately (C) C C. Furthermore, *makemone* is formed from *ama* (F, FB) and the modifier *kemone* (Fox 1987). This way of constructing terms designating MB and/or FZ is characteristic of a fairly large number of Eastern Indonesian terminologies. This observation lies at the heart of Fox's argument (1984), in which he rightly deduces that the possibility cannot be excluded that these terminologies are derived from terminologies that were cognatic in this generation. Roti, on the other hand, has two specific terms for FZ and MB, but also has F = FB = FZH, M = MZ = MBW. The second noncognatic feature results from singling out ZCh (*sele-dadi*). This expression is made from *sele*, "to plant," and *dadi*, "to grow" (Fox 1971:222); it illustrates the meaning of the MB-ZCh relationship on Roti and more generally throughout Eastern Indonesia: a flow of life running obliquely through the generations. Roti's semantic type is therefore more accurately expressed as (C) C (C). But this notation leaves out the fact that it is a basically cognatic terminology onto which has been grafted the asymmetric maternal uncle-sister's children relationship.

18. Unlikely but not impossible, because the Ema type is A SA C. However, Needham (1984:226) notes a semantic value of A for the last generation. Because Needham does not cite his source, it is possible that it is different from mine. In point of fact, the Ema ethnographer does not explicitly mention the terms for WBS, WBD (Renard-Clamagirand 1982:92–95). But the equation BCh = ZCh = Ch is clearly cognatic. Certain gaps and imprecisions in the Ema terminology nevertheless leave some doubt as to the semantic value of the last generation.

19. S SA S is also a likely type.

20. MB = MBS = MBSS, FZ = eZ, FZD= ZD, FZS = ZS (Barnes 1974:266, 1977:145). To construct the first type of cross-generational equivalences, the Lamaholot group terminologies often use a term that has cognates in other Indonesian languages usually meaning "grandparent" or "grandchild" (see Barnes 1979).

21. For example, *ana layia* (DH), *rai ana* (SW), *ana yera* (WBC) (Fischer 1957:11).

22. To my knowledge, the published ethnography on Eastern Indonesia contains no explicit information on this subject.

23. For what is meant by "structural history." see A.-C. Taylor (1988:esp. pp. 180–88).

24. To say that the prototerminology contemporary with Proto-Central-Malayo-Polynesian was cognatic implies that the same was probably true of the prototerminology of Proto-Central-Eastern-Malayo-Polynesian, which was the source of Melanesia's Austronesian languages. In this perspective, the evolutions of the kinship systems of Eastern Indonesia and Austronesian-speaking Melanesia are parallel problems, and to a certain extent historically linked. Furthermore, the Austronesian speakers who populated Eastern Indonesia were also in contact with indigenous non-Austronesian populations. Today these two linguistic families still exist side by side in certain parts of Eastern Indonesia. It is therefore quite possible that the historical evolution of the Indonesian kinship systems was not purely endogenous.

13

The Synchro-Diachronic Method and the Multidirectionality of Kinship Transformations

M. V. KRYUKOV

Nearly everyone engaged in kinship studies would agree that kinship systems are subject to change. So far there is no such unanimity regarding the question of whether transformations of kinship are of a sporadic nature or conform to some underlying developmental regularities that one can speculate about.

The nineteenth-century evolutionists adhered to the second supposition. Lewis Henry Morgan, one of the pioneers in the field of kinship studies, was convinced that kinship systems have evolved in a firmly established sequence, beginning with the Hawaiian (Malayan) type, which transformed into the Turanian (Iroquois) and then into the modern European (Aryan) one. Morgan used two criteria to determine the relative position of a given kinship type on the universal developmental scale. First, he believed that the most primitive ethnic groups must have a primordial kinship system, while the kinship system of the most developed groups must be the most advanced. On this ground Morgan assumed the Hawaiian type of kinship terminology to be the most ancient pattern because the Hawaiians among whom it was discovered seemed to him the most primitive of all peoples on earth.

Morgan was, of course, seriously mistaken about the primitivity of the Hawaiians. But modern social science appears to lack strict operational criteria to determine the relative progressiveness of one ethnic group over another. In any case, this approach to the problem of the historical sequence of kinship types is invalid.

The other basis on which to speculate about a possible chronological sequence among different types of kinship for Morgan was the fundamental idea inspired by his evolutionist way of thinking, namely the supposition that kinship systems display changes from simple to complex. The Hawaiian type (later called generational by Robert Lowie for its flattening of distinctions within each generation) looked the simplest of all systems known to Morgan, and he took this fact to confirm his assumption about the sequence of kinship terminologies.

Paul Kirchhoff challenged this view on the assumption that human ideas change from particular and concrete to general and abstract. Starting from this logical principle, Kirchhoff postulated the universal priority of a kinship type that had not been treated separately by Morgan, one identified by Lowie as bifurcate collateral, called "Type A" by Kirchhoff (recently labeled "zero equation" by Allen). The Chinese kinship terminology, corresponding to this type in the most elaborate way, differentiates among a maximum of kinship categories; it seemed to Kirchhoff the most particularistic and therefore the most ancient one. As the polar opposite of the Chinese Type A or bifurcate collateral type, the Hawaiian or generational type ("Type C" in Kirchhoff's classification) appeared to him an example of abstract thinking and was inferred to be the final point of the general current of development of kinship systems (Kirchhoff 1955).

Both Morgan and his early critics approached the problem of conjectured historical transformations of kinship systems with purely *logical* assumptions favoring one theoretical position or another, rather than basing them on *historical* evidence. There were, however, some exceptions.

LAVROVSKI'S APPROACH AND ITS FURTHER ELABORATION

One of these exceptions is an impressive contribution to kinship studies that is not widely known in the West. Just before Morgan's book, *Systems of Consanguinity and Affinity,* appeared, the Russian philologist P. A. Lavrovski published a work investigating the "original meaning" of Slavic kin terms. Lavrovski's objectives were somewhat limited, and the scope of his research was in no way comparable to that of Morgan. He certainly made no pretence of producing a typology of kinship terminologies. Although he provided many valuable observations on possible correlations between the structure of the kinship vocabulary and the underlying social structure, he did not treat the issue in a systematic way and thus did not arrive at a broader theoretical conception. Whereas Morgan's book marked the beginning of a new era of research in the social sciences and had great influence on later authors, Lavrovski's work on kinship was soon forgotten students of social anthropology, let alone the philologists.

Nevertheless, it was Lavrovski who first proposed and applied detailed procedures for tracing the regularities of transformation of kinship terminologies. Lavrovski deliberately refrained from following any a priori premises of logic as to the possible chronological sequences of variations among kinship systems. What he advocated repeatedly were certain specific historical methods to establish the development of changes of individual kin terms.

As a comparativist, Lavrovski made use of cross-cultural analysis of nomenclatures found in closely related Slavic languages and corresponding dialects. He then combined the synchronic comparison of variations in kinship terminology with diachronic observations. As he himself pointed out: "By no means was I intending to put aside historical evidences of terminological changes. On the contrary, my attention was exhaustively paid to any data of the sort I could discover; they were compared then with linguistic observations. I believe such a method may be of some importance" (Lavrovski 1867:4).

Using this method, Lavrovski studied all the available historical records containing Russian kin terms. It became evident to him that during the twelfth to fourteenth centuries A.D. the original Russian kinship nomenclature underwent a radical change, as some quite new terms came into existence in that period, while others became extinct. The main change, as Lavrovski put it, consisted of the essential simplification of kinship vocabulary, which he attributed to the dissolution of clan organization and the growing role of the nuclear family.

To give just a few examples, in early Russian usage there was a clear differentiation between paternal and maternal relatives: *stryi* (*stroi*) MB being distinguished from *ui* (*wui*) FB, and *strychich* MBS from *uichich* (*wuichich*) FBS. Later on, separate terms for parents' siblings distinguishing the father's and mother's side disappeared and new ones came into use that lumped parents' siblings (*dyadya* FB, MB; *tyotka* FZ, MZ). According to Lavrovski, the earliest evidence of the term *tyotka* is datable to 1178. This term is also found in birch bark inscriptions of the thirteenth to fourteenth centuries discovered recently in Novgorod and Pskov, while earlier records of the same sort discriminate between the two categories, as can be seen, for instance, from the following inscription found in Pskov: "all my *stroi* and all my *ui* and all my relatives of other sorts" (Marasinova, 1966:75).

It is obvious that through his study of Slavonic terms Lavrovski substantiated a historical shift in Russian from the bifurcate collateral into the lineal type of kinship terminology, using Lowie's classification, or from A to D as defined by Kirchhoff. What I call the *synchro-diachronic* method, created by Lavrovski more than a century ago, anticipated later developments in anthropological research and is still significant for related studies.

Contemporary authors writing on theoretical aspects of transformation of kinship types are inclined to agree that

historical and comparative tests lead to the same conclusion. The sociologist or functional anthropologist who suspects the one, and historian or historical anthropologist who suspects the other, may each exercise his private choice. The social scientist, presumably, can accept both and take comfort that they are in complete agreement. (Murdock 1949:352)

Nevertheless, tracing diachronic changes through the relevant historical records seems to be the most convincing way of verifying developmental regularities. To quote Frisch and Schutz: "Ideally, historical interpretations are the result of synchronic studies of various historical periods as revealed by documentary sources. . . . When available for remote periods of time, such documentary evidence provides the clearest and most reliable data" (Frisch and Schutz 1967:273). The problem here, however, is that the student of kinship is not normally in the privileged position of a sinologist, no other society can match Chinese data in historical length or chronological lucidity.

DEVELOPMENT OF THE CHINESE KINSHIP SYSTEM

The unparalleled bulk of Chinese written sources, covering a period of more than thirty centuries, can be used to investigate the history of Chinese kinship. To give an idea of the volume of sources at the disposal of a student of kinship, the database of official Chinese dynastic histories from the second century B.C. to the beginning of the twentieth century A.D. compiled in the Academia Sinica in Taipei includes texts totaling nearly 40 million characters. One important specificity of these materials is that most of them can be dated quite precisely (which is obviously not the case for the historic materials of some other countries with an ancient written tradition, such as India). Moreover, even in the earliest sources (the oracle bone inscriptions of the fourteenth to eleventh centuries B.C.), kinship terms are abundant, owing to the nature of the records, which are concerned mainly with ceremonial aspects of everyday life.

Some twenty years ago, I endeavored to develop a profile of the historical development of the Chinese kinship system using Lavrovski's method of synchronic analysis of terms found in Chinese dialects combined with consideration of diachronic changes in the kinship system as reflected in Chinese historical writings (Kryukov 1972). The following paragraphs summarize the results of this work.

As pointed out by Granet (1930:157), some kinship terms included in the vocabulary of the *Erya,* which dates back to the end of the first millennium B.C., can only be understood under the assumption of obligatory cross-cousin marriage. The most convincing item in this respect is *sheng* FZS, MBS, WB, ZH. Accordingly, *jiu* is both MB and HF, while *gu* stands for FZ and HM alongside of *waijiu* WF and *vaigu* WM. One may thus speculate that derivative terms *waijiu* and *waigu* originated in the elementary *jiu* MB, HF, WF, and *gu* FZ, HM, WM.

The latter supposition is substantiated by an examination of kinship terms used in inscriptions of the eleventh to seventh centuries B.C. All these are elementary, with reflections of obligatory cross-cousin marriage being even more obvious. This feature may also be inferred from the etymology of some key terms such as *chu* ZCh(m.s.), *zhi* BCh(w.s.), and *fu* SW. *Chu* means "to go away," *zhi* "to arrive," and *fu* "to return"; if I am a man, the children of my sisters are my relatives who "went away" as they belong to the other descent group (that of their father). On the other hand, if I am a woman, children of my brother are those who "arrived," being born to a woman of my husband's descent group. Again, from the point of view of a man, my son's wife "returned" to marry a man of my descent group. Since there is no distinction between F and FB, M and MZ, S and BS(m.s.), S and ZS(f.s.) and so forth, this ancient Chinese system may be identified as belonging to the Dravidian type. The terminology of the *Erya* is in fact of a transitional character: some remnants of the original system (such as *sheng, chu, zhi*) are still in use, but FB is already differentiated from F, MZ from M, WF from MB, and WM from FZ.

In the second century A.D., another vocabulary called *Shiming* recorded a further drift in the Chinese kinship nomenclature. No terms for cross cousins are included—a fact that must be taken as evidence of the former *sheng* no longer being used for FZS and MBS. As to the other connotation of *sheng,* that of WB, that is explicitly termed *waisheng* in the *Shiming. Sheng* appears in that book to have quite a new meaning, namely ZS, which had previously been attached to *chu* (the latter is also mentioned in the *Shiming*). A new elementary term, *zhang,* is introduced as a "vulgar form" of WF.

During the third to fifth centuries A.D., traits of a Dravidian type are no longer present in the Chinese kinship terminology. Thus by then it had completed the shift to a system of bifurcate collateral type, to which the modern Chinese nomenclature belongs.

The results of this study made it clear that the idea formulated by Lowie in the late 1920s—namely, that the bifurcate merging type of kinship had the bifurcate collateral model as its prototype—was wrong. The correlation of the two types appeared to be the reverse. In the written record of China it is possible to follow the whole process of a gradual shift from the original bifurcate merging to the later bifurcate collateral, which is now showing signs of moving toward the lineal type. Murdock's reconstruction of the transformation of the Chinese kinship system, which was based on "admittedly slight evidence" and assumed a Hawaiian prototype as a point of departure, also proved to be false (Kryukov 1972).

SOME FURTHER IMPLICATIONS

Obviously, no other ethnic group is in a position to compete with the objective conditions provided by the Chinese for the study of kinship using the synchro-diachronic method in the style of Lavrovski. But this does not mean that the approach is of no use in investigating the regularities of change in other kinship systems, as outlined below.

1. For one thing, historical records, although of much more limited chronological extent, are available for quite a number of societies. The kinship terminology of Latin is but one example. A survey of data in Latin sources of different periods makes it possible to reveal a bias rather similar to that traced in the Russian case. In classical Latin, in the parents' generation (G^{+1}), *avunculus* MB was clearly differentiated from *patruus* FB and from *pater* F, as well as *matertera* MZ from *amita* FZ and *mater* M. Accordingly, in G^0, *frater patruelis, filius avunculi, amitinus,* and *filius consobrinus* were used for FBS, MBS, FZS, and MZS. But in the colloquial speech of some centuries later, all these four kin categories began to be called *consobrini,* "cousins" (*Pandects* 38.10), while in the medieval Latin *avunculus* came to be used for both FB and MB (whence English "uncle"), so that in order to refer to FB specifically a new term emerged, *avunculus ex parte patris* (cf. English "uncle on the father's side"). This phrase would have seemed entirely meaningless and ridiculous for a Roman of Cicero's time.

2. Another possibility for applying the diachronic method is afforded by travelers or ethnographers who have recorded the kinship system of a given group several times at more or less long intervals of time. The terminology used by the inhabitants of Bongu village (Ray

Coast, New Guinea) provides an example. The first information about the Bongu kinship system was collected by the Russian anthropologist N. N. Miklukho-Maclay during his stay in Bongu in 1871–72, 1876–77, and 1883 (Miklukho-Maclay 1950:162–78). In 1896 A. Hanke, a German missionary, settled in Bongu and stayed there for several years; kinship terms were included in his dictionary of the Bongu language (Hanke 1909). Then in 1971 a Soviet expedition visited Bongu and recorded the current kinship terminology used by the villagers (Kryukov 1975:192). A comparison of the three lists of terms makes it obvious that during the last century the Bongu system has been undergoing a transformation from bifurcate-merging to bifurcate-collateral type.

3. In some cases, diachronic observations can be made through a comparison of the current kinship terminology and relevant data in myths, legends, popular aphorisms, and other aspects of oral tradition that usually embody archaic usage of terms. In Russian proverbs used as metaphors, one may come across a number of kinship terms that were once used extensively in everyday speech but that have vanished in the course of transformation of the kinship system. Every Russian today understands the allegoric sense of the saying "It is better to have nine *dever'* than one *zolovka*," but most would be unable to explain the precise meaning of these two terms, which were the ordinary words for HB and HZ, respectively, in former times.

4. When differences are observed between terms for reference and address, the latter usually represent innovations that will later be incorporated into the terminology of reference, too. The reason is that terms of address are a more dynamic segment of the system (Spoehr 1947:215). In the referential kinship vocabulary found in the Chinese *Book of Song* dating back to the first half of the first millennium B.C., the father's siblings are not differentiated from the father, both being called *fu*. But King Cheng-wang addressed Zhou-gong, his father's younger brother, using a different term, *shufu*, which later became a common appellation for FyB in the referential nomenclature (see below). Another direct testimony of the same regularity is provided in a story compiled by the beginning of the fifth century A.D. in which the following passage is found: "His wife ran to her mother-in-law (*gu*) and hailed her: 'Po!'" Some centuries later, *po* finally replaced original *gu* to refer to HM (Kryukov 1972:177, 205).

5. Sometimes it is possible to elicit important diachronic information in the field by interviewing informants of different age. Old people are able to provide some obsolete usages of terms whose meaning is already alien to the younger generation.

The lists of kin terms recorded recently among the Kam (an ethnic group on the Guangxi-Guizhou border in Southern China, ordinarily included in the Tai linguistic family) reveal certain dialectal variations. The terminology used by the Kam in Rongjiang county includes *liong* MB, FZH, SpF; *ba* FZ, MBW, SpM; *sao* FZS, MBS, WB, ZH; and *mai* FZD, MED, W, WZ, BW. But in Tianzhu the usage of *mai* is somewhat different, being a term for W only, while FZD, MBD, WZ, and BW are not discriminated terminologically from Z. There are two alternate possibilities regarding the developmental sequence of these two closely related systems: the Rongjiang variant can be interpreted as the result of transformation of the Tianzhu nomenclature, or the development may be assumed to have proceeded in the reverse direction, Rongjiang terminology being the starting point. Logically speaking, both assumptions are equally probable. Nevertheless, information provided by an old man who maintained, "When I was a little boy, we normally used *mai* to refer to daughters of *liong* and *ba*" (Long 1989) seems to be of decisive importance in judging the chronological priority of the Rongjiang nomenclature.

Studies employing synchro-diachronic kinship data should keep the following observations in mind.

First, when the terminologies being examined are used by a number of ethnic groups that are closely related linguistically but are now separated geographically, the common terms they use must be understood as the oldest layer of the vocabulary. Thus, although some Chinese scholars contend that *ani* FZ in the nomenclature of Naxi (Yongning county of Yunnan province in southwestern China) has emerged quite recently in response to the change from the neolocal to the patrilocal mode of residence, this may not be the case, since *ani* FB is found in a great number of Tibeto-Burman languages spoken in remote parts of Southeast Asia (by Tibetans, Kachin, Lolo, and others).

Second, it is important to remember that, morphologically, kinship terms may be classified as elementary, derivative, and descriptive. An elementary term is an irreducible item with a certain connotation; a derivative term is compounded from an elementary core and a modifying determinative that is not a kinship term by itself; a descriptive term is a more or less loose combination of several elementary terms (Murdock 1949:98).

Synchro-diachronic observations demonstrate that in the tide of attested temporal drift, derivative and descriptive terms invariably emerge as substitutes for earlier elementary ones. Sometimes derivative and descriptive terms may be later replaced by new elementary ones. In the history of Chinese kinship nomenclature, a derivative term *congzi* BS came into existence by the end of the first millennium B.C. to discriminate between S and BS in place of a previous *zi* S, BS as a part of the general drift from bifurcate merging to bifurcate collateral; later, a descriptive *xiongzi* (literally, "elder brother's son") was in use as an alternative for a period of time. In the third to fourth centuries A.D., the elementary term *zhi* extended its meaning to include both BS(f.s.) (its original connotation) and BS(m.s.), to be distinguished from *waisheng* ZS. Correspondingly, derivative terms *bofu* FeB and *shufu* FyB appeared by the middle of the first millennium B.C. as a modification of an original *fu*

F, FB (*bo* and *shu* being determinatives to specify relative age). In the fourth to fifth centuries A.D., *bo* and *shu* came to be used as elementary terms, which in contemporary colloquial speech are substituted for by the reduplicated forms *bobo* FeB and *shushu* FyB (Kryukov 1972:192, 201).

In the same way, it may be inferred that classical Latin *patruus* FB and *matertera* MZ are derivatives from *pater* F and *mater* M, and in their earlier usage probably included both F and FB, M and MZ, respectively. This consideration can be taken as evidence of a similar drift from bifurcate merging to bifurcate collateral. The regularity of derivative and descriptive terms normally originating from earlier elementary ones can be taken as internal evidence as to the relative position of the system under study on the chronological scale of transformation.

Third, loanwords also merit some attention. If a number of genetically related terminologies vary in a certain direction and do not include terms borrowed from other languages, a related system containing some loanwords is a later development. The reason is that borrowing is in many cases the simplest response to structural change, being an alternative way of using a new term to echo objective need. Thus *tyotka* appeared in the Russian kinship vocabulary as a response to the drift in categorization of relatives that demanded the emergence of a single "aunt" term for MZ, FZ, FBW, and MBW, which in this case was borrowed from Polish.

In other cases, borrowing turns out to be the result of intensive external influence under which the group in question may change its cultural layout drastically. Those categories of kin that are not in the course of drift may obtain new loanwords to denote them, too. The Chinese system, with its strong internal continuity, has not escaped the impact of outside intrusion. In the sixth to seventh centuries A.D., against the background of strong Turkic influences penetrating into many spheres of Chinese culture (such as costume and dwelling, customs, religion, decorative art, and language), the Turkic terms *aga* eB, *ata* F, among others, were absorbed into colloquial usage (Kryukov, Malyavin, Sofronov 1984:289). In both situations, however, be it a response to structural drift or a result of a powerful external influence, the occurrence of borrowed terms is a manifestation of a later development of an original kin vocabulary.

Fourth, in the process of transformation documented by historical evidence, a split might occur between subsystems used by male and female speakers. In the text of *Erya,* which reflects the state of transformation of Chinese system at the end of the first millennium B.C., there is a clear indication that new derivative terms *waiju* WF and *waigu* WM coexisted with the older elementary *ju* HF and *gu* HM (Kryukov 1972:234–35).

In the Tamil vocabulary, on the other hand, the subsystem of terms for females exemplifies countervailing innovations: *maman* is still used for MB, FZH, WF, while *mame* MBW is already differentiated from *attai* FZ, WM. It has long been observed that in patrilineal and patrilocal societies structural drift in the terminology used by females or designating female relatives could drop behind that of the males' subsystem, with a reverse situation if the prevailing rule of descent is matrilineal and mode of residence is patrilocal (Guo 1964). The Lolo-speaking groups of south-

western China demonstrate how these main principles of the synchro-diachronic
method can be used to provide a basis for judging the chronological sequence of
kinship systems.

LOLO KINSHIP TERMINOLOGY AND ITS DEVELOPMENT

Lolo is a general name embracing a number of linguistically related ethnic groups,
all of which belong to the Sino-Tibetan family. This ethnonym had been used by
Chinese scholars before 1949; thereafter Yi was adopted in mainland China as the
appellation of an officially acknowledged nationality, and such ethnic groups as
Lolopo, Nosupo, and Micipo were declared its subgroups.

A glance at the different kinds of sources relevant for the synchro-diachronic
analysis of Lolo kinship terminology might lead one to think that the prospect for
establishing a chronological sequence from the materials available is not very encouraging.

Pieces of Lolo folklore containing some miscellaneous information on kinship
vocabulary are published only in Chinese translation, making them useless for the
present study. Although the Lolo had their own system of writing and a considerable number of texts of a religious and ceremonial nature are available, the kinship
terms found in these manuscripts are in the main those of ascending generations,
while terms for parents' siblings, cousins, and nephews that are of high diagnostic
value for understanding the system's structure are lacking.

Some short lists of Lolo kinship terms recorded in the seventeenth and eighteenth centuries in different counties of Guizhou province are found in some local
Chinese historical records. The *Guizhou tongzhi,* for example, provides three sets
of terminology labeled as that of the "Lolo language," "Lolo language of Puan,"
and "Lolo language of Qianxi." The first of them contains eighteen terms and runs
as follows (pronunciation of the native terms is transcribed with Chinese characters
and is therefore sometimes distorted):

da	F
ami	M
dumo	FeB
popo	FyB
mimo	FeBW
mujiao	FyBW
ahei	FZ
ahu	WF
amo	eB
yegai	yB
amian e	BW
mei	yBW, yZ
ana	eZ

nizo	yZH
nawo	W
zo	S
zonu	BS
aman	D

The list of terms from Puan contains nine items and that from Qianxi fourteen. Neither contain cousin terms.

Unlike the lists of kinship terms from Quizhou, bilingual vocabularies of different variants of the Lolo language recorded in the eighteenth century in Sichuan and Yunnan and known under the name "Hua-yi yiyu" provide a lexicon written in both Chinese and Lolo characters. Five examples of such vocabularies are extant (Wen 1940:78–80). Unfortunately, the number of kinship terms in them is too limited to permit full-scale diachronic observations.

Of much greater value for our purposes are vocabularies of the Lolo language compiled by European missionaries at the end of the nineteenth century. The *Dictionnaire Français-Lolo, dialect Gni* by Paul Vial, providing valuable information of the kinship terminology of Sanipo (Vial 1909), and the "Essai de dictionnaire Lo-lo-Français, dialecte A-hi" by A. Lietard who was a missionary among the Asipo from 1898 to 1904 (Lietard 1911–12) are extremely important.

Relevant data belonging to the middle of this century are available for Nosupo (Lin 1946), Sanipo (Ma 1951), and Asipo (Yuan 1953). Information on Lolo terminology has recently been gathered from among the Sameipo, a local group of the Sanipo (Xie 1987), Nosupo (Harrell 1989), Nasupo (Yang 1985), Lipo (Harrell 1989), and Talu (Wang 1983).

The main body of material used in the analysis that follows was collected during my expeditions to the Lolo in 1989–92. My records include terminologies of Lisu (Miyi and Dechang counties of Sichuan province), which is officially considered to be a separate nationality, and of twenty-one Lolo groups now formally designated as subdivisions of the Yi nationality (Kryukov, 1989–92). Their locations are given in table 13-1.

Some kinship terms, such as *avu* (*agu*) for MB, *ani* for FZ, *zo* for S, are found in the vocabulary of all the groups listed above. Some other terms are specific for a number of groups only. The latter may be used as criteria for a genetic classification of the groups involved. I start with terms for siblings that are usually less affected by structural change, as well as those for siblings' spouses and children's spouses. A review of these terms makes it possible to differentiate between the following blocks of ethnic groups given in table 13-2 (nomenclatures with borrowed Chinese terms are not included).

According to the differences in the terms displayed in table 13-2, three blocks of ethnic groups can be isolated: Western (Lipo, Lolopo, Ganipo, Micipo, Talusu), Eastern (Nasupo, Naisupo, Alopo, Gapo, Depo), and Northeastern (Nosupo, Nesupo). From these data it also appears that Lolo groups belonging to the Western bloc have some connection with Lisu. This fact was realized by Chinese writers of the six-

Table 13-1

Locations of Twenty-one Lolo Groups

Group	Locality Sichuan	Locality Yunnan	Group	Locality Sichuan	Locality Yunnan
Nosupo	*Meigu*		*Lilu*	*Miyi*	
	Zhaojue		*Lipo*	*Renhe*	*Wuding*
	Xide			*Huili*	*Dayao*
Nesupo	*Buto*	*Yongsheng*	*Lolopo*		*Wuding*
Nasupo		*Wuding*			*Dayao*
		Luquan	*Laloba*		*Weishan*
Naisupo		*Wuding*	*Micipo*		*Wuding*
Talusu		*Yongsheng*			*Luquan*
Levu		*Yongsheng*	*Alopo*	*Huili*	*Wuding*
Lude		*Yongsheng*	*Depo*		*Wuding*
Nazha		*Yongsheng*	*Gapo*	*Huili*	*Luquan*
Tanglang		*Lijian*	*Sanipo*		*Wuding*
Nazu		*Yongsheng*	*Ganipo*		*Weishan*
Nilo	*Renhe*	*Yongsheng*			

teenth and seventeenth centuries who, while describing the ethnography of the Lisu, conjectured that "they are of Lolo's stock" or saw them as "a group which derived from Lolo" (Yang 1988:82).

Another point to note is that the structural characteristics of Lolo terminologies exhibit some important variations:

1. Most of them ignore the criterion of *collaterality*, making no distinction between lineal and collateral relatives in G^0; hence B = FBS = MZS and Z = FBD = MZD. However, some groups differentiate between lineal and collateral siblings using derivative terms for the latter, in which determinative *du* ("remote") is added to the core term (Lipo *ayu*/*nema* B, *ayudu*/*nemadu* FBS, MZS).

The lack of collaterality was relevant for the +1 generation at an earlier date, too, because in most Lolo systems terms for parents' siblings are derivative, with "father" and "mother" as a core to which is added a determinative "big" or "small" (Talusu *abu* F, *abula* FeB, *abuya* FyB; Nasupo *ade* F, *adewo* FeB, *adenyo* FyB). In some cases, however, items for FB and MZ are not elementary ones that derived from the corresponding determinatives (Alopo *anyo* FyB from *adenyo*) in the same way as Chinese *shufu* had been once replaced by *shu*. At the same time, some loan terms are used for relatives of the +1 generation (Alopo *dadie* FeB, borrowed from Chinese).

In G^{-1}, the differentiation between lineal and collateral occurs in some terminologies that apply derivative terms formed with the determinative *du* in the same way as those of G^0 (Lipo *zo* S, *zodu* BS).

Table 13-2

Variant Kinship Terms in Lolo Groups

Term	Group	Term	Group
1. eB		2. eZ	
ayi (aya, ayu)	*Talusu*	*adzi (adza, adzu)*	*Talusa*
	Nilo		*Lipo*
	Lisu		*Ganipo*
			Sanipo
amu	*Nasupo*	*ane*	*Nasupo*
	Naisupo		*Naisupo*
	Alopo		*Alopo*
			Gapo
			Depo
vuvu	*Nosupo*	*vymo*	*Nosupo*
	Nesupo		*Nesupo*
3. eBW		4. eZH	
alu	*Talusu*	*amu*	*Sanipo*
	Lipo		*Lipo*
	Ganipo		
	Lolopo		
ame	*Nasupo*	*anizo*	*Nasupo*
	Naisupo		*Alopo*
	Alopo		*Gapo*
	Gapo		*Depo*
	Depo		
zamo	*Nosupo*	*nimo savu*	*Nosupo*
	Naisupo		*Naisupo*
5. DH		6. SW	
mevu	*Lisu*	*cimo*	*Lisu*
	Talusu		*Lude*
	Lipo		*Lolopo*
	Nilo		*Lipo*
	Ganipo		*Ganipo*
	Laloba		
	Micipo		
sugu	*Nasupo*	*cisha*	*Nasupo*
	Naisupo		*Naisupo*
	Alopo		*Alopo*
	Gapo		*Gapo*
	Depo		*Depo*
am savu	*Nosupo*	*zamo*	*Nosupo*
	Nesupo		*Nesupo*

2. All Lolo terminologies adhere to the principle of *bifurcation* in G^{+1}; hence FZ ≠ MZ, MB ≠ FB (Lipo *ada* FZ, *amo* M, MZ; *avu* MB, *apo/abode* FB). The same principle is relevant for G^0 in the majority of Lolo systems, where FZS ≠FBS, MBS ≠ MZS and FZD ≠ FBD, MBD ≠ MZD (Lipo *hebe* FZS, *ayudu/nemadu* FBS; *ame* FZD, *adzudu/nemodu* FBD, MZD). Nevertheless, bifurcation is neglected in some terminologies that produce one term for both siblings and all sorts of cousins (Lude *azu/niazu* B, FBS, FZS, MZS, MBS). Terms for G^{-1} display bifurcation in some systems (Lipo *zodu* BS, *suve* ZS; Nosupo *zodu* BS, Nimo *zo*) while some others ignore it (Nasupo *zodu* BS, ZS).

The prevailing combination of the two principles (merging lineal and collateral kin and discriminating between those depending on the sex of the linking relative) is specific to the bifurcate merging type of kinship terminology. The only exception is a few systems (such as Lude) that demonstrate some evidence of change directed to formation of a vocabulary of generational type.

3. Lolo terminologies present different patterns relating to the principle of *affinity*. Some of them are more or less consistent in ignoring the difference between consanguineal and affinal relatives. The system of Lisu can be taken as one of the most obvious examples:

G^{+1}	ipa	F
	aupa	FeB, MeZH
	avo	FyB, MyZH
	ani	FZ, MBW, SpM
	ima	M
	auma	MZ, FBW
	avu	MB, FZH, SpF
G^0	iayi	eB, e(FBS), e(MZS)
	iniza	yB, y(FBS), y(MZS)
	inadzu	eZ, e(FBD), e(MZD)
	inima	yZ, y(FBD), y(MBD)
	mala	eBW
	iniza zamu y	BW
	iadzu mevu e	ZH
	mufu	FZS(m.s.), MBS(m.s.), yZH
	niehe	FZD(m.s.), MBD(m.s.)
	zagu	H
	zamu	W
G-1	iza	S, BS(m.s.)
	izama	Z
	icima	SW
	imevu	DH

This nomenclature reveals important diagnostic features specific to a subtype of bifurcate merging known as Dravidian in the contemporary literature on kinship.

As to the terms of G^{+1}, they correspond to the Dravidian model, making no distinction among FZ, MBW, and SpM, and among MB, FZH, and SpF. The situation in G^0 is somewhat different. Unlike the whole set of other terms in this system, two of the three terms for siblings' spouses are descriptive, which testifies to their later emergence. It is just these denotations that are covered by terms for cross cousins in a "standard" Dravidian nomenclature and partly preserved in Lisu *mufu* FZS, MBS, yZH. Thus it is certain that originally Lisu used a terminology in which *mufu* stood for FZS, MBS, ZH, WB. The direction of drift indicated by the three terms for siblings' spouses, contradictory to the rest of the nomenclature, is from Dravidian to Iroquois. That is, it remains bifurcate merging but splits consanguineal and affinal relatives.

Some groups under study are using terminologies mainly of Iroquois character. In Lipo vocabulary, *avu* is MB, whose wife was *ani* in Lisu. But now MBW in Lipo is *animo*, a term derivative from *ani* and therefore assumed to be a later development. By contrast, in Nazu *ani* still stands for both MBW and SpM, while *guma*, evidently borrowed from Chinese, is used to denote FZ; *avu* is MB and SpF, but FZH is called *gudie*, also a Chinese borrowing. Moreover, Chinese *jiujiu* and *jiuma* are introduced as alternative terms for MB and MBW. It testifies to the fact that a splitting of original categories combining MB, FZH, SpF and FZ, MBW, SpM was realized differently in Lipo and Nazu but went in the same direction, namely from Dravidian to Iroquois.

Another path of development is manifested in Nasupo terminology. This is a bifurcate merging nomenclature with consanguineal and affinal relatives coinciding in a systematic way, which, however, is quite different from that of Lisu:

G^{+1}	ade	F
	adewo	FeB, MeZH
	adenyo	FyB, MyZH
	ani	FZ, HM
	ame	M
	amewo	MeZ, FeBW
	amenyo	MyZ, FyBW
	avu	MB, WF
	ipo	FZH, HF
	asha	MBW, WM
G^0	amu	eB, e(FBS), e(MZS)
	ane	eZ, e(FBD), e(MZD)
	anizo y	B, yZ, yZH, yBW
	ame	eBW
	avusla	MBS, WB
	avumo	MBD, WZ
	anizo	FZS, eZH
	animo	FZD
	suvu	H, DH
	ci	W

G^{-1}	zo	S, BS
	amo	D, BD
	zodu	ZS
	amodu	ZD
	cisla	SW

As far as can be discerned, terminologies similar to that of Nasupo have not been ethnographically recorded before. At the same time, the Nasupo system appears similar to the type of kinship theoretically constructed by Parkin (1986:56), which he labeled asymmetric prescriptive, in contrast to symmetric prescriptive, or Dravidian, to which Lisu terminology clearly belongs. On the other hand, the Nasupo system concurs in its main points with that of the Kachin, differing from the latter only in the absence of intergenerational skewing. Since the Kachin terminology is normally considered to be of Omaha type, could not the Nasupo nomenclature be called Omaha-without-Skewing? If such a name seems to be too extravagant, there is still a need to acknowledge this type of kinship terminology, one that has not previously been taken into account by students of social anthropology and is not included in the current typologies of kinship systems. Following the tradition of naming kinship types after the ethnic groups in which they were found for the first time in a more or less consistent form, Nasupo may be accepted as the technical term for the asymmetric prescriptive type.

The difference between Dravidian and Nasupo types is obvious when one compares designata of terms in G^{+1} and G^0:

	Dravidian	*Nasupo*
G^{+1}	1. F, FB, MZH	1. F, FB, MZH
	2. M, MZ, FBW	2. M, MZ, FBW
	3. FZ, MBW, SpM, ZHM, BWM	3. FZ, ZHM, HM
	4. MB, FZH, SpF, ZHF, BWF	4a. MBW, BWM, WM
		4b. MB, BWF, WF
		4c. FZH, ZHF, HF
G^0	5. B, FBS, MZS	5. B, FBS, MZS
	6. Z, FBD, MZD	6. Z, FBD, MZD, DHM
	7. MBS, FZS, WB, ZH, SWF, DHF	7a. MBS, WB, SWF
		7b. FZS, ZH, DHF
	8. MBD, FZD, WZ, BW, SWM, DHM	8a. MBD, WZ, BW
		8b. FZD

Generally speaking, there are again two alternative possibilities to explain the structural differences between Dravidian and Nasupo. Dravidian may have been transformed into Nasupo, splitting the designata of its main terms, or Nasupo may have emerged from Dravidian by merging kin categories originally separate. If one approaches the problem from a purely logical point of view, both suppositions seem probable. But treating the dilemma historically one would immediately discover traces of transformation from Dravidian into Nasupo, while evidence of drift in the opposite direction is entirely lacking.

First of all, Nasupo terms for cross cousins appear to be later innovations in that they are found in other Lolo nomenclatures except a few that are geographically close to Nasupo (such as Alopo, Gapo, and Depo) are quite different from the distribution of such terms as *avu* MB, which is used widely by all Lolo groups and by Lisu as well.

Second, terms for cross cousins that are subject to change in the course of drift from one kinship type to another are derivative and descriptive ones in Nasupo. *Avusla* MBS is derived from *avu* MB (*sla* meaning "young"); *avumo* MBD, *anizo* FZS, and *animo* FZD are literally "daughter of *avu*," "son of *ani*," and "daughter of *ani*." Lisu terms for cross cousins, by contrast, are elementary.

Kinship terminologies of Nasupo type are specific for the Eastern bloc of Lolo groups and are unknown in the Western bloc. Nevertheless, there are some common terms both in the East and the West that may be taken as evidence in support of the hypothesis of a single origin of all Lolo groups. Among such common terms is *ame.* In the eastern Lolo nomenclatures, *ame* is used to denote eBW, but Lolopo and Micipo use *ame* MBD, FZD, while Lipo refers to female cross cousins as *amezo,* which derives from *ame.* This suggests that originally *ame* corresponded with Dravidian usage covering MBD, FZD, BW, and WZ. This term survived in some Western terminologies as an appellation for female cross cousins side by side with newly emergent terms for WZ and BW. Independently of this, eastern Lolo groups continued to use *ame* to denote BW, while new derivative or descriptive terms were constructed for cross cousins.

To sum up, Lolo provides historically attested evidence of a shift from a Dravidian prototype kinship system originally used by the remote ancestors of Lolo. Archaeological finds dating back to the Bronze Age indicate the presence of two cultural areas in Yunnan, one of them around Dali in the West and the other near Kunming in the East. It can be argued that these two cultural entities reflected the distinctions between two genetically akin populations, which later differentiated into modern Lolo groups.

Geography was not the only factor responsible for the separation of the two blocs of Lolo-speaking ethnic groups. For reasons that are not entirely clear, the social structure of ethnic groups of the Western and Eastern blocs developed in different directions.

In the Western bloc, the original symmetric prescriptive system, reflected in a kinship terminology of Dravidian type, was gradually dissolved, and there was a shift from Dravidian to Iroquois terminology. In the Eastern bloc, the transformation of Lolo social structure followed another direction: an asymmetric prescriptive system formed, which caused terminologies of a Nasupo type to emerge. The movement of a part of the western Lolo population to Sizhuan, which contributed to the geographical isolation of Nosupo and Nesupo groups, must have occurred before the internally consistent system of Nasupo type was formed, as no traces of asymmetric prescriptive features are found in these two nomenclatures. The Lolo terms recorded in the seventeenth to eighteenth centuries in Guizhou exhibit some evidence of belonging to the same pattern as Nasupo: *ahu* WF must stand for *avu*, and *amian* eBW is a distortion of *ame*. Both usages are found in the Nasupo vocabulary.

In addition, the changes in the original Dravidian system were followed by a partial transformation from Iroquois into Hawaiian—a process that can be clearly traced through diachronic comparison of Sanipo kinship vocabularies. By the end of the nineteenth century, special cross-cousin terms were used by the Sanipo of Lunan county, Yunnan (Vial 1909:102):

agniza (anizo)	MBS
agheza (avuzo)	FZS
amai (ame)	MBD, FZD

In 1991 the Sanipo of Wuding county, Yunnan—this being the Sanipo-Nasupo frontier—reported separate terms for male and female cross cousins (Kryukov 1989–92):

aniso	MBS
avuzo	FZS
anime	MBD
avume	FZD

But in the Sanipo hinterland, Ma Xueliang failed to find any terms for cross cousins as recently as the middle of this century (Ma 1951). In 1989 Xie Jian confirmed that Sameipo (a local group of Sanipo near Kunming) had no separate terms for cross cousins, and that all such earlier terms had been merged with siblings (Xie 1987:153).

DIRECTIONALITY OF DRIFT

The question that can now be posed is whether, in a global perspective, kinship systems have drifted in any particular direction. Having isolated three types of kinship, Morgan arranged them in a hypothetical sequence stressing the origin of Iroquois from Malayan. Later Rivers reversed the process, which nevertheless remained unilineal: from Iroquois to Malayan. Having established the existence of a fourth type, which he called a kindred one, Rivers refrained from speculating on the place of the latter among the others. Lowie admitted that the recognition of this bifurcate collateral type opened a new prospect—the derivation of bifurcate merging from bifurcate collateral. Here again, all existing items of an overall typology were thought of in a unidirectional sequence.

Gertrude Dole (1969) was perhaps the first kinship expert to assume that the direction of transformations of kinship systems was variable, and that the generational type was a rather exceptional product of adaptation to specific conditions under which exogamy of kin groups was impossible. One of the main findings of this study is that there are no traces of the generational type in Chinese kinship at any period of its history from the second millennium B.C. to the present time (Kryukov 1972:278). The assumption that drift in a protosystem might follow different directions is thus favored by Chinese historical evidence. Consequently, the interrelationships among the four Lowiean types (I, bifurcate merging; II, bifurcate collateral; III, generational; IV, lineal) can said to take the form shown in figure 13-1.

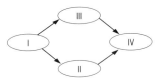

This sequence seemed logically acceptable from the point of view of consecutive changes relating to the two principles of *collaterality* and *bifurcation* embodied in these types, since there are two possible paths by which bifurcate merging (– collaterality and + bifurcation) can be transformed into lineal (+ –), one of them via generational (– –) and the other via bifurcate collateral (+ +). The interrelationships can therefore be redrawn, as shown in figure 13-2.

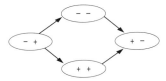

This scheme, introduced by Kryukov (1972), is still acceptable. But it cannot represent the whole range of the changes historically attested by applying the synchro-diachronic method to individual kinship systems since it does not take into account the third important criterion for isolating types of kinship, namely that of *affinity.*

As far as the criterion of affinity is concerned, three subvarieties of bifurcate merging can be identified: D, Dravidian, or symmetric prescriptive; N, Nasupo, or asymmetric prescriptive; and I, Iroquois, or nonprescriptive. The relationship among them can be traced by observing real historical transformations of a number of kinship systems, the Lolo case being just one concrete example (see figure 13-3).

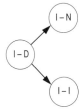

Consider now the criterion of *generation*. It seems obvious that the distortion of this criterion creates another subvariety of bifurcate merging, which is usually labeled Crow-Omaha. The interpretation of Crow-Omaha terminologies has been one of the most puzzling problems in the whole field of kinship studies. Unfortunately, that subject is beyond the scope of this chapter. It can be said, however, that if the Kachin kinship system is of an Omaha pattern (although not all experts on Omaha ethnography would agree with this statement), Crow-Omaha terminologies must be understood as derivatives of asymmetric prescriptive systems, but not symmetric prescriptive ones.

With these considerations in mind, it is now possible to propose a tentative typology of kinship systems in their developmental sequence. Figure 13-4 presents a further elaboration of the preceding diagrams of relations among the four Lowiean types, with the addition of the criteria of affinity (separate affinal terms) and generation (skewing or absence of skewing):

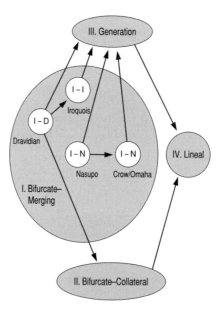

Structural drift within bifurcate merging has the Dravidian terminology as its starting point. No evidence of Dravidian having been formed as a result of the transformation of a system of any other type has been found so far. On the other hand, the possibility of change from Dravidian into Iroquois or Nasupo is attested in a number of cases. The position of Crow-Omaha may seem disputable, but to the present author's mind terminologies of Omaha type (at least those similar to Kachin) originated in systems of Nasupo type.

Iroquois and Nasupo are not indispensable links in the overall chain of structural changes of kinship systems. Dravidian might evolve directly into bifurcate collateral (Chinese) or generational type (as, for instance, in Eromanga terminology, which drifted from Dravidian type to an intermediate Dravidian-generational type [Kryukov 1971]). These findings lead to the following conclusions.

First, kinship systems are categories liable to drift. Types of kinship identified on certain structural grounds are not immobile parallel patterns. Rather, they change from one pattern into another, in accordance with certain regularities.

Second, the Dravidian subvariety of the bifurcate merging type is the starting point of change of kinship systems, and the lineal type is the final result of such drift. In this sense, changes in kinship, determined by the underlying development of social structure, have an overall direction, just as, according to Edward Sapir (1921:150, 155), "language moves down time in a current of its own making. It has a drift. . . . The linguistic drift has direction."

Third, Morgan's idea of arranging various types of kinship in a unilineal sequence is untenable. The Dravidian type cannot change into the lineal directly, so that the course of transformation may pass through one of several intermediate forms, some of which are later varieties of the same bifurcate merging, while others are either bifurcate collateral or generational types. As far as these intermediate links are concerned, the development path leading from the original Dravidian system may be treated as multidirectional.

Fourth, different sets of terms in adjacent generations are affected by the change from one pattern to another in a certain sequence, too. In view of the present knowledge of the mechanics of transformation, it appears that, contrary to Dole's (1957:117–18) postulate, the process of differentiation within the original system of kinship categories (Dravidian system changing into Nasupo, Iroquois, or bifurcate collateral) is such that terms of the +1 generation are the ones most sensitive to structural change. On the other hand, in the process of merging kinship categories (Dravidian transforming in the direction of generational, or bifurcate collateral to lineal) it is terms of G^0 that are first to react to structural drift.

Fifth, notwithstanding any perturbations in social conditions, a kinship system cannot regress and return to the format of a structural type that it once passed through. In this sense, the process of transformation of kinship systems may be assumed to be irreversible.

14

The Prehistory of Dravidian-Type Terminologies

N. J. ALLEN

In some respects anthropology has still to catch up with Morgan.
—Elisabeth Tooker, cited by Trautmann

How could Dravidian-type terminologies have come into existence? The answer could help anthropologists update Morgan's world-historical approach to human society, and thereby reformulate some of the stubborn traditional problems of kinship. But is this not simplistic? Has the whole history of anthropology since Morgan's day not made us too sophisticated to pose such gross questions? Has kinship itself not been deconstructed, and a fortiori the notion of kinship terminologies?

I do not find the notion of a kinship terminology seriously problematic. One can imagine a society in which mating occurs randomly and in which children, once out of the womb, have nothing further to do with a mother, let alone with father or siblings, so that the individual biological relationships that produce members of society are wholly irrelevant to other activities. However, no such society is known. The biological relationships are always given some significance (interpreted, built on, regulated, used, in various ways), and the language employed for these purposes always includes a more or less delimited set of terms that one can reasonably call a kinship terminology ("kinship" here covers affinity as well as consanguinity). Kinship terms are words that *can* be used to distinguish different types of relatives. The word "relative," many would object, is ethnocentric, but kinship terms often cover "unrelated" clansmen or the like, or are used metaphorically or manipulatively. Nevertheless, all languages *can* distinguish types of relatives (as in "she is my *x*, not my *y*").

To talk of a *type* of terminology raises more serious problems. Like other social phenomena, kinship terminologies vary continuously in time and space and do not fall into clear-cut categories. The solution, as is often the case in anthropology, is not to try ever harder to carve up the real world, but to set up ideal types or models, to which the real world approximates to a greater or lesser degree. By Dravidian-type terminologies I mean those whose structure conforms more or less to the simple symmetrical prescriptive ideal type, not only those belonging to the Dravidian language family. It is not necessary to discuss a priori the degree of conformity re-

Figure 14-1

Genealogical and Matrix Diagrams of Dravidian-type Systems

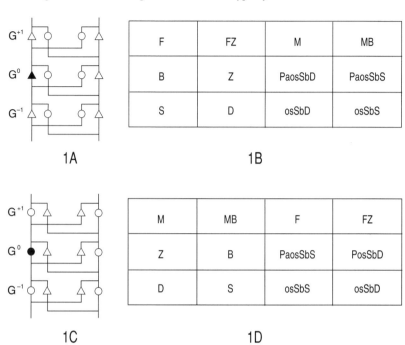

1A   1B

1C   1D

Note: 1A and 1B show male bias (male ego plus patrilineal columns), 1C and 1D show female bias.

quired, but before the origin of the type can be considered, it must be characterized. How is this to be done without prejudging the difficult issues?

DEFINING THE IDEAL DRAVIDIAN-TYPE TERMINOLOGY

Terminologies can hardly be discussed theoretically without drawing diagrams, and these may offer a better starting point than either verbal theorizing or the particu-larities of field data. The two main types of diagram are the genealogical and the matrix (figure 14-1).[1] Juxtaposing them emphasizes their congruence: there is a one-to-one relation between the "person symbols" (triangles and circles) of the one and the genealogical formulas in the boxes of the other. For brevity, I draw only the three central levels, but it is essential to give balanced treatment to male and female egos. The conventions will be familiar, but it may be useful to distinguish three readings of the genealogical diagrams.[2]

    1. *Minimal.* Each person symbol is read as a theoretical individual. In both dia-grams the structure thus consists of twelve individuals, six male and six female, organized in three rows ("generations"). The individuals are linked by three types

Figure 14-2

Dravidian-Type Genealogical Diagram Using Relative-Sex Symbols, and
Corresponding Matrix Using Sex-Neutral Formulas

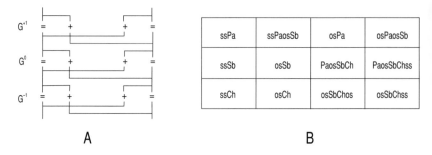

sSPa	sSPaosSb	osPa	osPaosSb
ssSb	osSb	PaosSbCh	PaosSbChss
ssCh	osCh	osSbChos	osSbChss

A   B

of relations, shown by lines: horizontally, within rows, by opposite-sex siblingship
and marriage; vertically, between rows, by filiation.[3] Each person in the lower two
rows is shown as marrying a bilateral cross cousin (PaosSbosCh). An obvious property of the structure is that ego is linked to any alter by a multiplicity of genealogical paths.

2. *Classificatory.* Each person symbol is read as embracing same-sex siblings:
the circle for M embraces MZ, the triangle for ego embraces his B, and so on. It is
as if the path from any person to his/her ssSb were shown by a siblingship line of
zero length. Logically, however, it makes no sense to stop at siblings: if F includes
FB, ego's triangle must embrace not only B (= FS), but also FBS, and remoter
parallel cousins; and analogously for each person symbol. Thus, if the diagram
extended indefinitely up and down the page, and if we posit perfect obedience to the
marriage rules, then the diagram covers all conceivable full relatives (as distinct
from half- and step-relatives), however remote they are.

3. *Sociocentric.* Person symbols are read not only as representing ego's relatives
but also and simultaneously as representing the members of sociocentric units, or
categories within such units. If society is endogamous and all members of society
are counted as relatives, figure 14-1a illustrates two exogamous patrimoieties exchanging women. Ego's triangle represents not only classificatory brothers but also
all members of ego's genealogical level within ego's moiety.

To change from male-bias diagram to female-bias, one simply swaps the person
symbols, replacing triangles with circles and vice versa. The male- and female-bias
diagrams share an underlying structure, whose depiction demands relative-sex symbols (figure 14-2).

Genealogical diagrams are fundamental aids to understanding the structure of
Dravidian-type terminologies since their lines *depict* the relations involved, but
matrix diagrams take one closer to the terminology. As drawn, each box in figure
14-1 contains only a single cognatic formula (though PaosSbD can be unpacked
into MBD + FZD). Even on the minimal reading (for which ego should be put in the
place of B or Z), one can start filling in other formulas in each box, one formula per
genealogical path, so that MB is supplemented with FZH, WF, and so on. The

Figure 14-3

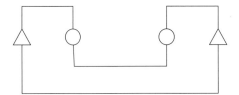

classificatory reading multiplies the possibilities (FBWB, WZF, etc.). Figure 14-2 can be filled in analogously, though the formulas soon grow cumbersome.

For the purposes of formal analysis, a particular kinship terminology is a list of words (signifiers) plus their specifications, but for theoretical purposes one can abstract from the lexical forms themselves and focus on the equations and discriminations made by them. Thus a *type* of terminology can be characterized by the *types* of equation and discrimination that it makes. How does this apply to the ideal Dravidian type? If we posit that types of relative falling in a single box of the matrix are equated, while those falling in different ones are discriminated, then we can define the ideal type as one that fits all relatives from the central levels into four boxes per level, each box containing one term and being related to a genealogical diagram as in figure 14-2.

However, the definition remains insufficiently precise, figure 14-2 being both arbitrary and ambiguous. Thus, to go back to the beginning, one can quite well redraw figure 14-1a, giving each row the form shown in figure 14-3 and adjusting the filiation lines accordingly. To make the matrix correspond, one now has to swap over the two right-hand columns of boxes in figure 14-1b, and the change can be carried through into figure 14-2.

One can also start from the matrix. Rather than thinking of it as a fixed grid into which specifications are poured in various ways, one can envisage it as a set of boxes, each with contents, which can be arranged in various ways on the page. This already applies to the male- and female-bias matrices of figure 14-1, which (if one ignores the position of ego) show exactly the same formulas, the same equations and discriminations, but in two contrasted layouts. But there are other possible layouts, too. Some analysts would prefer to swap the position of the FZ and M boxes in figure 14-1b, thereby keeping all primary relatives in the left half of the diagram.[4] Such diagrammatic variation has no effect on the semantic structure depicted and can be ignored in the definition of our ideal type.

A more significant issue concerns the boxes in figure 14-2b. Consider the top left-hand corner. If the diagram is read as it was introduced, namely, as illustrating the pattern underlying figures 14-1b and 14-1d, then the entry ssPa merely means that for male ego this box in the fixed grid contains the term for father while for female ego it contains the term for mother. However, these are two different terms, so that a single box no longer contains a single set of equations, as it did in figure 14-1.

On the other hand, we can also read figure 14-2b as if it bore to 14-2a the same relationship as the matrix diagrams bear to the genealogical in figure 14-1. This gives us a new terminology: the entry ssPa now represents a kinship term equating ♂F and ♀M, so that the term which I (a male) use for my father is the one my sister uses for her mother. Dravidian-type terminologies can classify relatives in adjacent generations either by the absolute sex of alter (which I call reading A or mode A) or by the relative sex of ego and alter (reading or mode R). In both cases, the models have twelve types of relative and twelve kinship terms, but they differ in the way male and female egos fit terms to relations.

In defining the ideal-type Dravidian terminology, there is no need to exclude the R mode; indeed, some might prefer it, in view of its logical purity. However, for most of us, absolute sex will be easier to work with since it is closer to what is ethnographically familiar and is more immediately susceptible to sociocentric interpretation.

ORIGIN OF DRAVIDIAN-TYPE TERMINOLOGIES

So how did Dravidian-type terminologies arise? In the absence of direct historical evidence, comparative/theoretical argument offers the only hope of an answer. The discussion cannot help being abstract, but I present it not as a contribution to mathematical anthropology but as an analysis of topics squarely in the mainstream of the discipline. Thus I hope the discussion is relevant not only to topics such as time, gender, lineality, and exchange but also to questions about the origins of human society—and hence perhaps (Allen 1994) of systematic cosmologies.

Over the past ten years I have tried to construct the outlines of a general evolutionary or world-historical theory of the domain of kinship and social structure. Allen (1982) presents a mode R version of what I see as the simplest possible configuration of the domain, using the image of a tribal dance and asking how the configuration might have developed. The influence of Durkheim's theory of the origin of religion is probably obvious, but there are virtually no references to the literature, either in that article or in the sketch of the whole theory (Allen 1986), which shifts to mode A. Allen (1989a), originally addressed to an audience of linguists, concentrates on terminologies, arguing for the historical reality and irreversibility of the semantic changes postulated in the theory. Allen (1989b), responding to Parkin (1988a), corrects a slip in his 1986 article, elaborates certain models, and includes some brief acknowledgments (particularly to Mauss, Hocart, and Granet). However, I try here, as far as possible, to present my argument without assuming knowledge of or access to my earlier works.

I suppose most contemporary anthropologists willing to advance an evolutionary schema would place Dravidian-type terminologies at or near its start. For instance, Kryukov (1972:64 and chapter 13 of this volume), having argued convincingly that Morgan was wrong in starting with the Hawaiian or generational type, presents the schema shown in figure 14-4. (I simplify by omitting mixed types. Kryukov's Iroquois includes my Dravidian type, and his Arabic is what I would call

Figure 14-4
Koryukov's Schema (simplified)

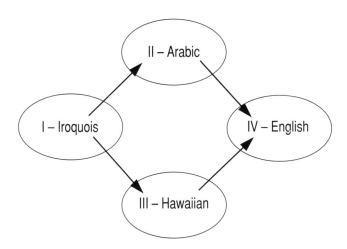

"zero-equation.")[5] In general, it is easy to conceive of changes leading *away* from the Dravidian type, and it is commonly done, for example, for the Sherpas (in an Omaha-type direction) by Allen (1976), or for the Mundas by Parkin (1992a); but the processes that might lead *toward* a Dravidian type are less obvious. Hence the special strategic importance of the type; I placed little emphasis on this in my theoretical discussions, though it was implicit in the earlier analyses of Tibeto-Burman terminologies.

One approach to the question of origins is to start from social structure and marriage rules and postulate that the terminology arose or adjusted so as to conform to them. I indicate four approaches of this kind, without trying to cite literature. (1) Two endogamous groups decide to fuse, and turn into two exogamous patri- or matrimoieties exchanging women. (2) A single endogamous group decides to split, with the same result. In either case, if patriliny is preferred, figure 14-1a can be reused with its sociocentric reading, each BZ pair now representing one generation within its moiety. (3) One starts from asymmetric (generalized) exchange taking place between enduring social units. In the neatest such model, MBD marriage links four patrilineal units arranged in a circle $a < b < c < d < a < \ldots$, so that each unit takes women from the unit on its right. Then the system folds in on itself, so that a and c merge, as do b and d, again producing two exogamous moieties.[6] (4) Sporadic exchange of sisters within an endogamous group becomes more and more regular, leading in the direction of prescriptive PaosSbCh marriage, but without any necessary involvement of sociostructural units.

Rather than criticizing such approaches, I explore what I take to be a more promising one. Could the Dravidian type of terminology have arisen from a *simpler type of terminology*?

Figure 14-5
A Tetradic Genealogical Diagram Using Relative-Sex Symbols

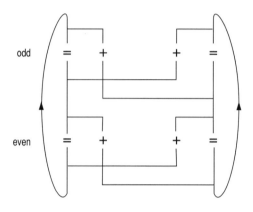

Note: The corresponding matrix diagrams can easily be worked out: the boxes for the odd level will have to contain specifications from G^{-1} as well as G^{+1}.

A Tetradic Terminology

The rows of figures 14-1 and 14-2 offer no real scope for simplification, but the columns do. The G^{+1} and G^{-1} levels in both cases are identical in form (four boxes, organized into two BZ pairs) and can readily be equated terminologically. I find it helpful to visualize a process of superimposition or infolding. The same process can be imagined for the G^{+2} and G^{-2} levels, which are folded in on the G^0 level. Eventually, all odd-numbered levels are superimposed, and all even ones likewise, leading to figure 14-5. I refer to diagrams resembling figure 14-5, and to structures congruent with them, as "tetradic."

What is to be made of this diagram? Before coming to modes A and R, we can, as before, distinguish degrees of "fullness." On the minimal reading, the eight individuals (4 + 4) are linked by the four intralevel horizontal relations and the two filiation relations. Unusually for a genealogical diagram, two of the latter are shown doubling back up the page so as to link parents *below* with children *above*. This produces a logical oddity: male ego's father in the top left quadrant is also ego's own son. The diagram makes little sense until it is read classificatorily.

On this reading, each person symbol includes not only same-sex siblings and parallel cousins but also equated members of alternate genealogical levels. Thus ego's father and son are equated (in the sense of being placed in the same category), but they are not presented as being *identical*. Consider also the symbol representing male ego's wife. In figure 14-1, the corresponding symbol represented PaosSbD and remoter cousins equated to the latter. In figure 14-5, it also covers FM(Z), (B)DD, and other specifications, some of them from remoter even-numbered levels. Not only does the diagram cover all possible full relatives of ego, past, present, or fu-

Figure 14-6
Tetradic Models

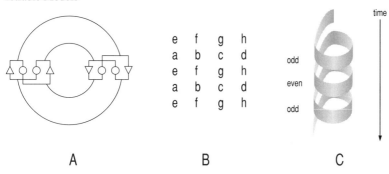

A   B   C

ture, but the "crystalline beauty" that Dumont (1983a:24) sees in Dravidian terminologies is perfected.

The sociocentric reading becomes obvious when we focus on the quadrants.
What we have is a picture of a four-section system, in the classical Australian sense.
The structure can be well expressed in the Maussian language of exchange. Those
in the upper row are parents of those in the lower, and by virtue of the recursive
filiation the lower are parents of the upper: the two "generation moieties" exchange
children (Allen 1995:56; Testart 1995:175). As for the horizontal intersection exchange rules, they raise a problem of analytical language. Some would say that, by
virtue of a cultural or biological universal, it is always men who exchange women;
but this is to introduce a sexual asymmetry which is wholly extrinsic to the *terminology*. It is better merely to say that sections exchange opposite-sex siblings or
"spouses-to-be."

One effect of the passage from figure 14-2 to figure 14-5 is to change the depiction of time. In figure 14-2 each new genealogical level is to be visualized either as
carrying ego further down the page or as pushing the existing levels further up the
page—each level recedes into the past as its members die off. In a sense, figure 14-
5 replaces this linear time by cyclical time (figure 14-6): after two generations, one
is back where one started. But in another sense, time is always necessarily linear,
and one may accordingly prefer to envisage an indefinitely tall stack of rows like
those of figure 14-2 and represent the "superimposition" of alternate rows by some
other diagrammatic device (figure 14-6b). The combination of linear and circular
time in tetradic models can be illustrated by a double-helix model, one helix for
each generation moiety (figure 14-6c).

Could figure 14-5 be yet further simplified? There are three possibilities: (1) to
conflate BZ pairs that are aligned vertically, leaving a distinction between descent
moieties cross-cut by sex; (2) to conflate BZ pairs aligned horizontally, leaving a
distinction between generation moieties cross-cut by sex; or (3) to conflate osSb,
simply leaving four sections. The diagram now merely illustrates the marriage and
recruitment rules of a four-section system and would hardly qualify as a "genealogical" diagram. However, the corresponding matrix represents a perfectly reason-

Figure 14-7
Splitting of the Odd Level of a Tetradic System

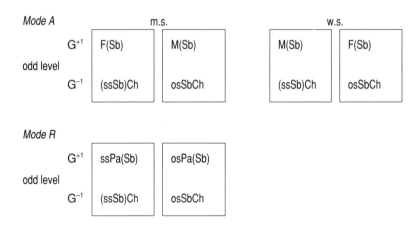

able kinship terminology. Whether operating in mode A or R, the four terms would not only classify all relatives but also constitute a nomenclature for the sections—albeit one that, being egocentric and relativistic, differs from an absolute nomenclature consisting of section *names* (a logically superfluous feature that a model-builder can introduce as and when convenient). Within this hypothetical tetradic society, the male-female distinction would, of course, continue to be made, when needed, by context or by periphrases. As a compromise between four-term and eight-term terminologies, one can posit four roots plus one (or two) gender affixes, but it is the four-term schema that is most convenient for theorizing. Reductions below four terms are imaginable but are not of much theoretical interest.

FROM TETRADIC TO DRAVIDIAN TYPE

Let us now reverse the perspective and consider the processes that would transform a tetradic terminology into a Dravidian-type one. To focus on terminology (and ignore time and exchange), the transformation consists simply of rupturing the alternate generation equations; but there is a logical difference between the odd and even levels. The odd level needs only a simple binary split between ascending and descending genealogical levels, but for the even level, if the split is binary, either it has to be between ego's level and G^{+2} taken together, or it has to involve a split of ego's level into elder and younger half-levels. If we start with the odd level of a four-term terminology, we only have to consider two equations per model, as shown in figure 14-7.

In both mode A and mode R, male ego equates his own children with F + FZ, and female ego equates hers with M + MB, but in A male and female egos use different terms to refer to the respective children, the same terms to a parent of given sex, while in R they do the reverse.[7] In other words, A treats male and female ego like siblings (who share parents but have different individuals as children), while R treats them like spouses (who share children but have different individuals as parents); in A the focus is on unmarried egos, in R on married ones. The difference could be shown in figure 14-5 by marking in bold the person symbols for the two egos: for A, the two symbols on the extreme left would be marked, for R the first and third symbols in the row.[8]

In order for the split to take place, new vocabulary is needed. Assuming the old terms are retained, will it be in the +1 or −1 levels? Or (to put it the other way around), if the new terms are differentiated by a suffix, which level would be the marked one? In general (Greenberg 1966:76), senior and elder are unmarked in relation to junior and younger, which suggests that the lexical innovation would affect the junior level.

Another question concerns the background of the split. A number of factors might have played a part, alone or in combination. Perhaps there existed individualizing (i.e., nonclassificatory) terms used only within the nuclear family and not in wider kinship contexts, terms such as *mama, papa, baby,* and *junior,* which could have helped in the development of a systematic split. Moreover, just as the even generation moiety contains more of ego's genealogically close age-mates than the odd moiety, so the odd moiety contains genealogically close age-mates of ego's parents and children; and this difference in age between *close* relatives in G^{+1} and G^{-1} could have been relevant. So could an earlier relative-age distinction in the even level, if one existed.

A more attractive option is to posit an elaborated tetradic structure. The literature regularly relates four-section systems having two BZ pairs per row to eight-section systems having four BZ pairs per row (Aranda type). But another possibility is to move, somehow (but how, exactly?), from four sections to an eight-section system having *two* BZ pairs in each of *four* rows (figure 14-8). Each generation moiety would have to split into two generation semimoieties. Even without modeling the details, one can envisage a corresponding terminology that put into semantic form the recursiveness shown by the arrows in figure 14-8. It would equate specifications separated by three genealogical levels, that is, +2 with −2 (PassPasb = SbssChCh), zero level with +4 and −4, +1 with −3 and +5, and so on. This elaborated tetradic structure does not become Dravidian-type until it loses its cyclical quality by rupturing the vertical equations. In this case, new vocabulary has already been introduced at the step from four to eight sections and is not needed at the equation-rupturing stage: the grandparent-grandchild equations could be left as an isolated survival, and remoter levels (starting with G^{+3}) could simply be excluded from the realm of relatives covered by single terms.

As for the even level, this transformational path splits it in the same process as it splits the odd, which seems to be the neatest solution. Another path would start with a binary split by relative age so that elder members of ego's genealogical level, together with ascending even-numbered levels, are contrasted with younger G^0 level plus descending even-numbered levels. But there are two difficulties. First, seniority by age is logically different from seniority by genealogical level. Not only may

Figure 14-8
More Tetradic Models

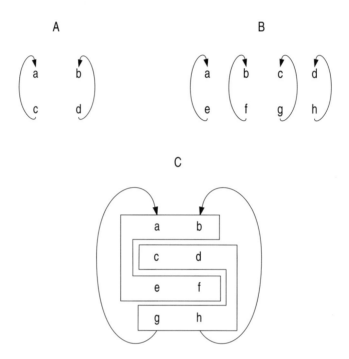

Note: A = simplified version of figure 14-5: a, b, c, d, stand for sections; B = elaborated tetradic model, Aranda-type; C = elaborated tetradic model, four-level type: interlocking outlines represent generation moieties, now subdivided into generation submoieties.

the two conflict (as when an uncle happens to be younger than his nephew), but they differ in character: the category "elder than I am" cannot contain exactly the same individuals for one sibling as it does for another, while the category "of my grandparents' genealogical level" normally does. Second, empirically, the frequency of PaPa-ChCh self-reciprocal terms or pairs of terms suggests that the *primary* binary split has often separated the G^0 level and G^{+2} (as in figure 14-8c), rather than elder/senior and younger/junior.

VARIANT TETRADIC STRUCTURES

Although all Dravidian-type terminologies may be supposed to derive from tetradic ones, and although figure 14-5 (reading A) doubtless provides the most obvious starting point, one must not oversimplify. Numerous systems qualify as tetradic in that they are isomorphic quadripartitions of the coextensive domains of ego's soci-

Figure 14-9
Basic Diagram for Circulatory Tetradic Models

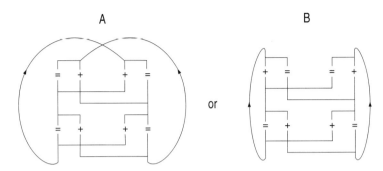

ety and ego's relatives. Let us review the main dimensions of variation, ignoring combinations.

1. We already know that the A and R readings of figure 14-5 are different terminologies.
2. One can redraw the four BZ pairs of figure 14-5 as four HW pairs and set up a corresponding four-term terminology. This, too, can easily be transformed into the Dravidian-type by appropriate splits.
3. More radically, one can generate a whole family of models based on figure 14-9. One could label this family circulatory, as distinct from oscillatory, since a line (e.g., the ascending patriline) circulates through all four sections rather than oscillating between two of them.[9] As is recognized by Campbell (1989:153ff.), building on Arcand's material from the Cuiva of Columbia, this type, too, is readily transformed into a Dravidian-type system.
4. Terminologies may treat differently linking relatives who are living and those who are dead, and tetradic models could take account of other divides in the life cycle, most obviously marriage. We might have B (married) ≠ B (unmarried), and so on. Conceivably, this could be relevant to the development of the odd-level split, in that G^{+1} level relatives are much more likely to be married than G^{-1}.
5. In view of the empirical association between bilateral cross-cousin marriage and ZD marriage both in South America and in South India (Rivière 1966; Good 1980), it is interesting to devise the corresponding oblique tetradic diagrams (figure 14-10; note the four BZ pairs). Perhaps some theoretical demographer could explore the parameters of a population conforming to this model.
6. "Elaborated" tetradic models contain more than four BZ pairs. Apart from the four-level model of figure 14-8, the Aranda-type model perhaps merits special mention since its most obvious transformation would bypass the Dravidian-type (figure 14-11). Suppose such a

Figure 14-10
Matrilineal and Patrilineal Displays of Tetradic Systems with ZD Prescription

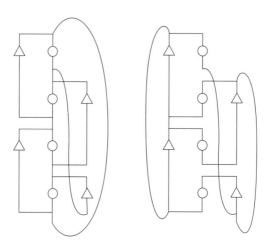

Note: The diagrams are typologically identical and differ only in placing of filiation lines. If drawn with relative-sex symbols, the diagrams would also cover FZ prescription.

system is given (say) a patrilineal slant. It already consists formally (i.e., whether or not the members of the society recognize it) of four exogamous semimoieties (*ae, cg,* etc.), and two exogamous moieties (*ae* + *bf* is one), and a change in the marriage rule could theoretically lead directly to four patriclans linked in circulating connubium by MBD marriage. One need not suppose that all kinship terminologies have passed through a Dravidian-type phase.

In view of all this variety, a phase of world history in which all terminologies were tetradic would not necessarily have displayed stasis and uniformity. One can imagine not only change over time, but also different terminologies used within a single society for different purposes. Nevertheless, the variation would have been confined within a framework set by the coextensiveness of society and the domain of relatives, by the congruence between egocentric divides and sociocentric, and by quadripartition, whether underlying or overt.

CROSSNESS

Supposing that tetradic terminologies *do* historically precede Dravidian-type ones, can they, in their abstract purity, help us to conceptualize the latter? Let us take the vexed notion of crossness ("so seminal for Dravidian systems," Trautmann 1981:47) and see whether it can be applied to tetradic models.

Figure 14-11
Transition from Aranda-Type Elaborated Tetradic System to Four-Line Circulating
Connumbium, Bypassing the Dravidian-Type System

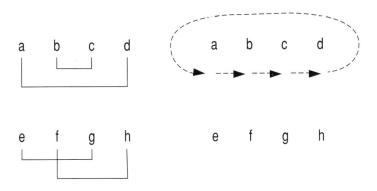

In most of the models, the even level is essentially unproblematic. Thus in what I call the "focal" model (figure 14-5, reading A), it is perfectly reasonable to think of the category containing ego's PaosSbCh as "cross," in contradistinction to the one containing ego's parallel cousins. *But is crossness in the odd level the same thing?*

In the G^{-1} level it seems natural to apply the label to osSbCh, to the cross niblings (i.e., cross nephews and nieces). Straightaway, however, we note a difference from the even level. I and my sister use a single term to cover our cross cousins, and both of us locate these relatives in the other half of the even level. But this coincidence of viewpoints does not apply to cross niblings. If I use *one* of the odd-level terms for them, and locate them in the diagonally opposite quadrant, my sister uses the *other* odd-level term for them and locates them in the other odd-level quadrant. The difference is not surprising since I have as cross cousins the same individuals as my sister does, but we do not share our cross niblings.

At first sight, reading R may seem to solve the difficulty. I and my sister use the same term for our respective cross niblings, and we both locate them in the quadrant diagonally opposite our own. However, it is not the same quadrant for both of us, for if male ego and female ego are to be shown on a single diagram they have to be located in different quadrants, so that the one diagonally opposite containing the cross-niblings will vary correspondingly. The discrepancy in relation to the even level has merely been displaced. Nothing a terminology can do can change the logical difference between the cross cousins I share with my sister and the cross niblings I do not.

The issues are very similar with the +1-level specifications. On reading A of figure 14-5, we are dealing with two terms equated with the cross niblings:

m.s.:   osSbCh = M(Sb), that is, osPa(Sb)
f.s.:   osSbCh = F(Sb), that is, osPa(Sb).

For me, my mother is the cross relative, for my sister it is her father, and conversely. On reading R, there is only a single term:

$$ossbCh = osPa(Sb)$$

but whereas I use it to cover my mother, my sister uses it to cover her (and my) father.

In talking about the +1 level, some analysts (e.g., Trautmann) would prefer to reserve the term "cross" for PaosSb (the reciprocal of ossbCh). In the focal model, which is "BZ-merging," PaosSb do not constitute a single category, but they do in the HW-merging type (§ V ii), where they are equated with SbosCh. However, the problem—that is, the difficulty of finding a notion of crossness applicable in the same way to odd and even levels—is again merely relocated. In an HW-merging model, the category of cross cousins is itself split: PaosSbosCh belong to ego's category, PaosSbssCh to the other one.[10]

I conclude that in tetradic models crossness can be used by the analyst to talk about particular groups of specifications (cross cousins, niblings, siblings, -parents, parents' cross siblings), but that it is not intrinsic to the fourfold structure. It cannot be used systematically to bisect the universe of relatives by assimilating one particular odd-level category to the even-level one containing cross-cousins. In fact the temptation to do so largely arises from the two-column layout from which we started in figure 14-1, and which led to the "four-square" layout of figure 14-5. Hence the advantage of the compass-point models that I have sometimes used previously and that display one of the "levels" vertically (in my practice, the even level, ego being located in the "south"—but the choice is unimportant).

The impossibility of finding an odd-level category that is intrinsically cross may seem paradoxical: the intersection divides within one generation moiety of figure 14-5 are identical with those in the other generation moiety, and if one of them produces an unproblematical parallel-cross distinction, why does not the other? The answer lies in the distinction between sociocentric and egocentric viewpoints. Sociocentrically, each generation moiety has exactly the same properties as the other, but it is precisely the introduction of an ego that makes the difference.

As one moves from tetradic to Dravidian-type terminologies, the rupture of the alternate-generation equations leaves unaffected the complications we have just described. The equations and discriminations of the terminology cannot be made to tell us which relatives or which terms in the G^{+1} level are to be called cross. This does not mean that no reasons can ever be found in particular cases for aligning one set of categories in a column or pair of columns and calling them cross. It does mean that the reasons for doing so have to come from outside the equations and discriminations, for example, from the predominant lineality, or from indigenous supercategories (the natives themselves could have a term for cross relatives), and these reasons need to be spelled out in each case. However, I suspect that attempts to construe Dravidian terminologies in purely binary terms (whether in terms of dual organization, kin and affines, or parallel and cross) will never be entirely satisfying.

TYPES OF ARGUMENT FOR AN EVOLUTIONARY SEQUENCE

The preceding section was based on the hypothesis that Dravidian-type terminologies derive from tetradic ones. But why should one accept that hypothesis? One reason, perhaps, is that it emanates from the wider hypothesis that *all* kinship terminologies derive from tetradic ones. (This view is equally compatible with monogenic or polygenic theories of human language and leaves open the choice between fan-shaped, tree-like, or strict unilineal models of derivation.) Because of the limitations of space, I can only point to lines of argument.

If one posits a primal type of kinship terminology, it has to be logically simple—no one supposes humanity started off by inventing Aranda- or Omaha-type terminologies. There seem to be only two directions in which to look for the logical simplicity, and here one can take a cue from Morgan. In spite of the complexities of his (and our) typologies, we have to look either to the classificatory pole, with its multiple equations, or to the descriptive pole, where equations may be absent.[11]

At the descriptive pole, the simplest terminology would resemble the "genealogical grid" in having one term per specification. It could even make do with just eight terms for the primary relatives (fewer if sex distinctions were neglected), and it could cover secondary and more distant ones, if at all, by stringing together the primary terms ("descriptively"). Such a construct is, of course, the regular conceptual starting point for analyzing terminologies by means of extension rules and can also be used as a basis for typologies that lack diachronic ambitions—thus Scheffler (1972:120) diagrams his typology with (roughly speaking) Estonian at the top left and Dravidian at the bottom right. But one finds the same idea in evolutionary contexts: Tooker (1992:369) suggests that the primary kin terms may have been invented just once, early in man's history, as "part of the proto-language from which all known languages descend." Logically, this extensionist view is not absolutely incompatible with tetradic theory, for the world history of terminologies *might* have consisted of a phase 1 dominated by the building up of equations and a phase 2 dominated by their dissolution. But we can turn at once to the classificatory pole and its contractionism.[12]

What types of arguments favor contractionism?

1. *Previous opinion.* As already mentioned, most evolutionary formulations start at or near the Dravidian type, and the focal tetradic terminology is little more than a simplified version of that type.
2. *Kinship and society.* Notoriously, small-scale societies tend to be "pervaded by kinship," and tetradic models, uniquely, make the two domains overlap perfectly (thus encouraging one to think also about isomorphic cosmic classifications).
3. *Levels of development.* In spite of obvious exceptions (hunter-gatherers with minimal equations, urban-industrial Dravidian-speakers), there does seem to be a *rough* correlation between modes of subsistence and types of terminology (see Dole 1972, whose notion of a "main sequence of development" seems to me reasonable).

Figure 14-12
Divergence of Egocentric and Sociocentric Phenomena as Societies Become Remote
from the Tetradic Starting Point

4. *History.* In particular cases, rightward shifts (i.e., ones leading away
   from the tetradic/Dravidian pole) can be demonstrated historically or
   argued for by comparison within linguistic families.
5. *Negative argument.* One seldom finds good evidence or strong
   arguments for leftward shifts, and I have previously tried to argue
   that they are implausible on semantic grounds. Apparent leftward
   shifts can result (as in India) when the equations and discriminations
   of a substratum mould an incoming language, pulling it typologically
   backwards, but I would welcome information on whether endogenous leftward shifts have ever been convincingly demonstrated.
6. *Survivals.* Assimilation of an individual to a grandparent by naming
   practices or by a doctrine of reincarnation is easily interpreted as a
   survival from tetradic society's thoroughgoing assimilation of
   alternate levels but is left obscure by extensionist theories.
7. *Coherence.* Although the focus here has been on terminologies,
   tetradic theory can be envisaged as shown in figure 14-12. The
   egocentric domain of kinship and the sociocentric domain of social
   structure tend to diverge, but at any point each is more or less closely
   related to the rules of marriage and recruitment. It may be that
   changes in these rules lie behind the main typological shifts (e.g.,
   loss of positive marriage rules relating to eventual loss of prescriptive equations), and that one line of argument can be based on the
   approximate linkage between terminologies and these other phenomena.

There may be other types of argument, too, but my main point is that the prehistory of Dravidian-type terminologies is best approached by thinking about the origin of all terminologies.

NOTES

1. I continue to use traditional genealogical notation, though there are many advantages to the
   new notation discussed at the conference by François Héran.
2. My only idiosyncracy is the use of brackets for optional symbols. F(B) means "father and/or
   father's brother."

3. At a finer level of analysis, filiation consists of the four distinct relations (F-S, F-D, M-S, M-D).
4. Here is a selection of layouts from the literature. I draw only the G^{+1} and G^{-1} rows, for male ego.

Barnard and Good 1984:56	F FZ M MB
	S D ZD ZS
Allen 1975:83	F M FZ MB
Keesing 1975:108	S ZD D ZS
Dumont 1983a:182	F M FZ MB
Campbell 1989:154	S D ZD ZS
Trautmann 1981:40	MB F M FZ
	ZS S D ZD
McDougal 1964:329	F MB FZ M
	S ZS ZD D

5. Iroquois-type terminologies differ from Dravidian-type ones in lacking cognate-affine equations and in the classification of PaPaSbCh(Ch) and PaSbChCh. Thus, where Iroquois equates Pass[PaSbCh]Ch with Sb, Paos[PaSbCh]Ch with PaosSbCh, the Dravidian type makes the parallel cousin/cross-cousin distinction within the square brackets, so that Pass[PassSbCh]Ch = Sb, Pass[PaosSbCh]Ch = PaosSbCh, and correspondingly for the formulae beginning Paos. In ignoring the parallel-cross distinction, the Iroquois type shows a covert Hawaiianization, comparable to the overt Hawaiianization of ego's generation noted by several conference contributors.
6. To start from a three-membered ring and postulate only a single merging is logically possible but less neat.
7. Since mode R is the less familiar, it may be worth unpacking the corresponding boxes in figure 14-7 into sex-specifying symbols. The resulting BZ pairs can be organized in terms of either absolute or relative sex:

	♂	♀	♀	♂		ss	os	os	ss
m.s.	F(B)	FZ	M(Z)	MB		F(B)	FZ	M(Z)	MB
f.s.	MB	M(Z)	FZ	F(B)		M(Z)	MB	F(B)	FZ
m.s.	(B)S	(B)D	ZD	ZS		(B)S	(B)D	ZD	ZS
f.s.	(D)S	(D)D	BD	BS		(D)D	(D)S	BS	BD

8. Theoretically (but implausibly!), one could imagine the two egos in different levels, so that the terms male ego uses for his even-level relatives are used by female ego for her odd-level relatives.
9. The existence of the type is indicated in the table of White (1963:82) under n = 4, Type I marriage prescription. I have previously called this family of models cyclical, but since all tetradic models are cyclical in some sense, the label might confuse.
10. As for the circulatory model of figure 14-9, the problem is certainly no less. Would a term equating osSbCh with ssPa(Sb) be cross or parallel?
11. I cannot here discuss the various types of "countertetradic" equations, that override the discriminations present in tetradic models. One example is the Iroquois-type equations mentioned in note 5.
12. Several sorts of contraction are relevant: contraction of the domain of relatives toward ego and away from society as a whole; contraction of the absolute size of the domain; contraction in the average number of specifications per term, that is, in the number of equations. The process is accompanied by loss of the "crystalline beauty" mentioned earlier.

15
Dravidian and Related Kinship Systems

EDUARDO VIVEIROS DE CASTRO

This chapter focuses on some kinship configurations recognized by anthropological lore—the "Dravidian," "Kariera," and "Iroquois" variants of bifurcate merging terminologies—in the light of the theory of marriage alliance developed by Lévi-Strauss, Dumont, and others. The first part deals with the formal differences among these terminological types and then moves on to two central conceptual pairs of kinship theory, namely, "parallel/cross" and "consanguinity/affinity." This is followed by a discussion of the possible matrimonial correlates of Iroquois-cross terminologies, along with a variant of the Dravidian type common in Lowland South America. Evidence for the ethnographic coexistence of Dravidian, Australian, and Iroquois schemes is presented next, and questions are raised about the idea that to each individual society there corresponds a single, unitary terminological model.[1]

ON TYPES AND MODELS

Of what use are ethnonymic labels to describe realities distant from eponymous societies? Many anthropologists object to ethnic labels because they say that institutional correlates are not always pertinent. Even when taken to refer to their own concrete eponyms, such labels are problematic. It has been suggested, for example, that perhaps the Iroquois did not have an "Iroquois" terminology (Kronenfeld 1989), or that the Dravidian paradigm established by Dumont and Trautmann is not generally applicable among the Dravidian peoples of South India (Good 1993). As this chapter explains, even the Kariera do not seem to have a "Kariera" terminology.[2]

However, more neutral naming has its problems, as well. Lowie's notion of "bifurcate merging," for example, supposes that the bifurcation present in the type is between maternal and paternal kin, which is not the case (Dumont 1983a [1953]:4). The notion of "two-section" or "two-line" systems, used for some time by Needham to refer to Dravidian systems, is also defective: apart from "section" evoking the Australian systems and "line" the notion of unilineality, hardly appropriate correlates, the Dravidian terminologies are distinguished from their analogues precisely because they do *not* contain "sections" or "lines." Meanwhile, Trautmann and Barnes's alphanumerical proposal (see chapter 2), which substitutes "Type A crossness" for "Dravidian" and "Type B crossness" (with its numbered variants 1, 2, 3, and 4) for "Iroquois," is not exactly a convenient model. And now, with Good's (1993; see also 1980) "beta version" of model A (which, according to him, is more widespread than Trautmann's and Dumont's "alpha version"), there is a risk of being drowned in ciphers.

It would be far more useful to have a structural definition appropriate to the types, Dravidian or otherwise, than to discuss their names. In other words, ethnologists need fewer "iconic" models, that is, models that are less dependent on the empirical generalization of paradigmatic cases. The Dravidian configurations of Trautmann, Dumont, or Good, for instance, should be seen as instantiations of a more abstract conceptual scheme, as particular cases—and not necessarily more "typical" for being Indian—of a Dravidianate model (or other preferred name) that, by definition, does not correspond to any of the empirical cases, for it describes the structure of these. Such a model, though it may derive from the analysis of ethnographic examples, cannot be the result of a comparative induction, but a construction capable of locating the concrete cases inside a series of transformations based on the determination of local constraints.

A brief word is in order here about the notion of "structure." Kinship models, as far as they can be considered "structural," contain both less and more information than the concrete systems they subsume: less, because they abstract particularities resulting from the coalescence of different dimensions in the ethnographic reality (language, ideologies, institutions)—as such, the models are relatively underspecified; more because they admit a number of transformational possibilities that cannot obtain simultaneously—and hence by incorporating distinct spatiotemporal states of a structure, are richer than any concrete system. Furthermore, the structures described by these models do not coincide with any particular "level" of the object. The distinctions between "concepts," "rules," and "behavior" (Schneider, in Trautmann 1981:21), or between the "categorical," "jural," and "behavioral" levels of kinship (Needham 1973), though perhaps methodologically useful, end up treating these aspects of a complex phenomenon as if they were real distinct objects and frequently confer on one among them the distinction of being the "true" locus of structure. Instead of reifying these stratifications of kinship, ethnologists should rather accept Lévi-Strauss's dictum that the observable phenomena "merely reproduce at the surface of action the deep structures that do not correspond to any of the three levels. Of these deep structures, these levels are merely the manifestations and indices, if they do not disguise or present misleading images of them" (Lévi-Strauss 1984:179–80).[3] That is to say, the structure can only be apprehended in the interface between the levels, in the differences or disjunctions between them. Indetermination and complexity are therefore intrinsic properties of a structural model, and not of its "passage" to the real: for the model does not coincide with the taxo-nomic or normative surface component, nor the real with individual or statistical behavior. A structure sets the limits of variation between different parts of a system. This chapter concentrates on the terminological dimension of kinship because of its manageability in a comparative analysis. Being relatively simple formal ob-jects that are capable of a variety of interpretations, terminologies are easy to com-pare. I assume, however, the existence of a complex correlation between the termi-nological, sociological, and ideological dimensions of kinship. I refuse the forced choice between the "reflectionist" attitude, according to which terminologies "ex-press" or "register" other social institutions, and the "autonomist" alternatives, be it those that are intent on insisting on the heterogeneity between different "levels" of the object or those that reduce terminological systems to their terms, and these to sociologically empty products of formal rules. I adopt the principle that "the func-tion of a kinship system [i.e., a terminology] is to generate marriage possibilities or impossibilities" (Lévi-Strauss 1966:14). Far from being, therefore, a passive effect or reflex of extrinsic causes or of more fundamental realities, a terminology "acts as an operating agent to a system of matrimonial exchange within a community" (Lévi-Strauss 1966:14). In contrast to the autonomists, I believe that kinship is a *system* of social reproduction; in contrast to the reflectionists, I do not think this system is a *totality* of a causal or an expressive type.[4]

This conception of terminology as an operating device of an alliance system is essential for the less iconic models proposed here to admit nontrivial interpreta-tions. Note that this conception is not restricted to "prescriptive" cases; when the emphasis is on the structurally secondary distinction between "prescription" and "preference," the levels of analysis of a model become confused with the concrete properties of particular systems. I contend that a matrimonial interpretation of "nonprescriptive" terminologies is possible. The prescriptive alliance models, apart from being "too holistic" (Scheffler 1971:253, recalling Schneider 1965), are too simplistic, as is Scheffler's formalism. In both cases, either an *immediate* relation between "marriage rule" and terminology is found, or *any* connection between kin-ship vocabulary and alliance structures is denied. But the relations between termi-nology and alliance certainly are not limited to the presence of spouse-equation rules.

BIFURCATIONS AND MERGERS OF THE "BIFURCATE MERGING" TYPE

A comprehensive history of the lumpings and splittings imputed to the "Dravidian," "Iroquois," and "Kariera" terminological types is obviously beyond the scope of this discussion. Let us take as our "base line" Murdock's (1949) general lumping of the three types under the name "Dakota-Iroquois." Lounsbury (1964a) was respon-sible for the first major split, between Iroquois and Dravidian, which he distin-guished by their crossness calculi after evaluating the "classical but erroneous an-thropological view" that related the "Iroquois-type kinship system" to membership in unilineal groups such as moieties or clans. After demonstrating that this was not the case, he observed:

There *do* exist systems which classify kin-types in the way that the Iroquois type was imagined to. These are the "Dravidian" type of systems. Interestingly, they are *not* generally founded on clan or moiety reckoning, but on a mode of bifurcation that, unlike the Iroquois, takes account of the sexes of all intervening links. The Dravidian and Iroquois . . . are systems premised on very different principles of reckoning, and deriving from social structures that are fundamentally unlike. (Lounsbury 1964a:211)

These remarks imply a conundrum: the Seneca (Iroquois), who may have had moieties and certainly had clans, used a terminology "transversal" to this morphology (classifying with the same terms relatives situated in different clans or moieties); Dravidian-type systems, though they present a crossness calculus (supposedly) identical to that generated by an algebra of inclusion in classes recruited by unilineal descent, are not "generally" associated with such institutions. Lounsbury does not say which social structure the Dravidian type would "derive" from.[5]

"Bifurcate merging" terminologies have been associated with unilineal institutions and with cross-cousin marriage ever since Fison and Tylor raised this possibility in the nineteenth century. In the case of India, the connection between Dravidian terminology and cross-cousin marriage rules dates at least to Rivers and is still accepted by most anthropologists; but many of them link this configuration to sociocentric morphologies, particularly to exogamous moieties or double unilineal exogamy systems. In the classic period of kinship theory, the similarity between the Dravidian and Australian systems (the so-called Kariera, in particular) was repeatedly affirmed: Radcliffe-Brown (1953) defined an "Australian-Dravidian" type, noting that its characteristic features were marriage with bilateral cross cousins and the absence of separate terms for affines; Lévi-Strauss ([1949]: 1969:99) underlined the "perfect harmony" present between classificatory terminologies without separate terms for affines, marriage between cross cousins, and dual organization.[6] Until the second major split, proposed by Dumont, the consensus seems to have been that the Australian and Dravidian patterns were identical.[7]

As is well known, it was Dumont ([1953, 1957] 1983a) who dissociated the Dravidian system from notions of "descent." In his view, marriage alliance, the structuring principle of Dravidian terminologies, is independent of any particular unilineal configuration, being simply inflected by these (where they exist) on the plane of its normative and empirical manifestations. Yalman's (1962, 1967) analyses of Sri Lanka's cognatic systems helped promote the dissociation. But it was Dumont's ([1970] 1983a) resurrection of an old debate with Radcliffe-Brown that consecrated the difference between the Indian "local formula" and the Australian "global formula."[8]

That debate revolved around the association of the Dravidian kinship vocabulary with moiety systems or principles of double unilineal exogamy.[9] Developing an observation made in 1953 (1983a:15 n. 9), Dumont argued that Dravidian and Kariera terminologies both express a relation of marriage alliance but differ in their classification of relatives in $G^{\pm2}$: the neutralization of the consanguine/affine opposition in these generations, in the Dravidian case, reveals a linear generational time and an ego-centered vision of alliance, whereas the maintaining of the opposition and the autoreciprocity of the terms in $G^{\pm2}$ (i.e., same terms for grandparents and grandchildren) in the Kariera case express a circular conception of time and a collective, sociocentric intermarriage relation between the terminological "moieties."

In 1981, however, Trautmann returned to Lounsbury's bifurcation and Radcliffe-Brown's merging: Dravidian and Kariera versus Iroquois. Affirming that Dravidian and Iroquois terminologies "are of fundamentally different types," Trautmann (1981:88) explains this difference by the presence (D) or absence (I) of a cross-cousin marriage rule, which manifests itself in the difference between the respective crossness calculi and the presence (I) or absence (D) of a separate affinal terminology. On the other hand, the cross/parallel classification of the Kariera system would be identical to the Dravidian (Trautmann 1981:88), being, like the latter, associated with a rule of cross-cousin marriage and the consequent absence of separate affinal terms.

The direct blow to Dumont's thesis would eventually come from an analysis of some Central Dravidian terminologies. Consolidating observations produced by different ethnographers, Trautmann proposed a "Dravidian model B," which, in contrast to the "model A" (South Dravidian) taken by Dumont as the paradigm of Dravidian, exhibits the "Kariera" bipartition in $G^{\pm2}$ (FF + MM / ♂SCh + ♀DCh as "parallel"; MF + FM / ♂DCh + ♀SCh as "cross"), which the French anthropologist had singled out as the crucial distinction between the two types. Trautmann concluded that the Kariera terminology is identical to that of Dravidian model B, and that the Kariera marriage classes could be seen as sociocentric transformations of supercategories present in certain Central Dravidian systems (1981:434–47, 237). The "local" and the "global" thus come together once more.[11]

There is no doubt that the Kariera terminology—the one reported by Radcliffe-Brown in 1913 and used by Dumont and Trautmann in their comparisons—and Dravidian B are perfectly isomorphic. Hence the question is this: does this terminology represent the general case usually called "Kariera"?

DRAVIDIAN AND AUSTRALIAN

When analyzing the Kariera vocabulary, Dumont notes that "a brother and sister designate as *ngaraia* [♂ZD = ♀BD] persons located in two different 'moieties,' which shows that the category is not contained in one 'section' or 'moiety' of the society" ([1970] 1983a:179). In other words, the Kariera nepotic terminology is identical to Dravidian: the reciprocal sets in $G^{\pm1}$ are F + M / Ch and MB + FZ / ♂ZCh + ♀BCh, which makes the Kariera terminological dualism, like the Dravidian, nonisomorphic to any sociocentric dualism.[12] But because Dumont is determined to establish the Dravidian/Kariera contrast, he emphasizes the difference in $G^{\pm2}$, which, as later research in India demonstrated, is not diagnostic. In any case, his general conclusion regarding Kariera terminology is somewhat disappointing, since it acknowledges the lack of a perfect fit between terminology and sociology:

There is obviously some relation between this dichotomy and that of the society into "moieties"—not in the sense that each of the two circles representing the vocabulary would correspond exactly to one of the "moieties" . . . but in the sense that on the one hand the society, on the other the vocabulary operate a dichotomy of the whole social body, and that the link between the two halves is the same in both cases—that is, intermarriage. (Dumont [1970] 1983a:183)

That same year, however, W. Shapiro used the general label "two-section" to compare a North American Dravidianate terminology—that of the Beaver Indians (Ridington 1969)—with Kariera and, more generally, Australian terminologies. In the Australian case, he notes, the categories "son" and "daughter" are not the same for a man and for his wife: "This, in fact, is one of the distinctive characteristics of nearly all known Australian relationship terminologies—that husband and wife never apply the same term to any one individual. Brother and sister, by contrast, usually do" (Shapiro 1970:384).

Shapiro takes a terminology from Arhem Land as his example. In fact, though he speaks of "Kariera," and refers to Radcliffe-Brown, he does not discuss that society's vocabulary.[13] This, as mentioned earlier, has a nepotic terminology of Dravidian type—or, for that matter, Iroquois, which is identical to Dravidian from the point of view of the reciprocal sets in $G^{\pm 1}$, though not from the point of view of the calculus that defines each set.[14] Judging the Australian/Dravidian differences in $G^{\pm 2}$ to be "sociologically trivial," Shapiro (1970:385) contrasts two schemes with only the three central generations, as in figure 15-1.

The author calls the left-hand columns of the diagrams "lineal section," and the right-hand ones "affinal section." Remarking that while the "Kariera" scheme can be represented as two patrisequences, the Beaver terminology "lacks a lineal structure altogether." He concludes:

Unlike the Kariera system, in which parents and parents-in-law, and child and child-in-law categories are divided equally between the sections, Beaver locates parent and child categories in one section, in-law categories in the other. . . . In short, the opposition between its sections is a "lineal"-affinal one *simpliciter,* whereas this opposition in Kariera is "diluted" by a descent-filiation element. (Shapiro 1970:386)

Shapiro suggests that the majority, "if not all," of two-section systems outside Australia have a structure similar to Beaver and suggests that the isomorphism between dual organization and "two-section" terminologies obtains only in the Australian type.

The contrast established here is clearly between a terminology structured by the consanguinity/affinity opposition (Dravidian) and another structured by a different opposition (Australian). The terms "lineal/affinal" are inadequate: only the Australian scheme can admit the term "lineal" for one of its "sections," since the Beaver type "lacks a lineal structure altogether." On the other hand, the Australian terminology does not seem to admit the label "affinal" for the opposite section—at least not in the same sense as the Dravidian type. By the same token, the notion of "section" cannot be applied the same way to both types: Dravidian terminology is in-

Figure 15-1
Australian and Dravidian

Australian ("Kariera")

F	FZ	MZ	MB
B	Z	MBD/FZD	MBS/FZS
BS	BD	ZD	ZS

"Dravidian" (Beaver)

F	M	FZ	MB
B	Z	MBD/FZD	MBS/FZS
S	D	♂ZD/♀BD	♂ZS/♀BD

consistent with moieties or its subdivision into sections. It is neither "two-line" nor "two-section"; and its reciprocal sets demonstrate that F and M are *relatives of the same type,* opposed as parallel relatives to FZ and MB, both cross.[15]

Shapiro's affirmation that "nearly all known Australian terminologies use a distinct nepotic classification"—yielding reciprocal sets F(B) + FZ / BCh and MB + M(Z) / ZCh[16]—is confirmed in *Australian Kin Classification* (Scheffler 1978), which presents these reciprocal sets in seven of the eight great terminological types analyzed in the book: "Kariera" (Scheffler chooses the Mari'ngar terminology as his example), Nyulnyul, Karadjeri, Arabana, Murngin, Walbiri, and Ngarinyin.[17]

The exception to the normal classification in $G^{\pm1}$ is the type Scheffler calls "Pitjanjara" (it is the same as Elkin's "Aluridja"), which is widespread in the Western Desert. It is a configuration identical to Trautmann and Barnes's variant 3 of "Type B crossness"—that is, it is an Iroquois terminology that has assimilated first cross cousins to siblings in G^0.[18] The crossness is unequivocally Type B: "Father's parallel and cross cousins are classified as 'father' and 'father's sister'; and mother's parallel and cross cousins are classified as 'mother' and 'mother's brother'" (Scheffler 1978:88). Classification in $G^{\pm2}$ is of Dravidian A or Iroquois type (FF = MF, MM = FM). The $G^{\pm1}$ or nepotic classification also shows the reciprocal sets F + M / Ch and MB + FZ / ♂ZCh + ♀BCh, which are quite different from the Australian ones given above. But the parallel/cross distinction can disappear in G^{-1}, all relatives from this generation being assimilated to Ch; the same distinction can be neutralized in G^{+1}, but only for mother's distant "brothers" and father's distant "sisters," designated as F and M.[19] This comes close to Trautmann and Barnes's "Type B variant 4," with its more pronounced "Hawaiian" profile.[20] All first and second cousins, assimilated to siblings, are matrimonially forbidden; cousins beyond this range can receive a specific designation, *watjira,* and are considered marriageable. Though these relatives are defined as children of distant "mother's brothers" and "father's sisters," Scheffler reports that *any* distant cousin would be *watjira,* independent of the parallel or cross status of his or her parent in relation to ego. Thus the cousin terminology is "Type B variant 3," but only for close cousins; for distant cousins, one finds either the classic identification between "opposite-sex cross cousin" and "spouse," or the assimilation of all distant cousins, "parallel" or "cross," to matrimonial partners, which inverts the prevailing situation for first and second cousins, all assimilated to siblings. In any case, the parameter of distance is fundamental to the classification.

The Pitjanjara exception has analogies with various South American cases, as explained below. For now, note that it closes the triangle in Australia: if Kariera terminology is "Dravidian," Pitjanjara-Aluridja is "Iroquois," while all other types proposed by Scheffler are variations on the "Kariera" scheme, which would be best called "Australian." Dravidian (model B) may be identical to Kariera, but Kariera is not identical to "Normal Australian."

The basic Australian terminological type *is* consistent with a sociocentric bipartition or quadripartition—that is, a logical consistency, not mutual implication or sociological causation. I agree with those who claim (as does Trautmann 1981:75–76) that kinship terminologies are necessarily egocentric—which does not mean they cannot bear markings of sociocentric institutional orderings—and I find the thesis according to which section systems are reifications of terminological super-classes (Scheffler 1978:chap. 12) quite acceptable. But such reifications do imply that the terminology is organized according to principles formally equivalent to a sociocentric calculus of marriage "classes."[21] The Dravidianate scheme, however, expresses a "method of relationships" irreducible to a "method of classes" (Lévi-Strauss 1969[1949]).

Criticizing a statement of Ridington's on the Beaver system, Shapiro observed:

He states that "The spouses of one's cross relatives must be in one's parallel category, and the spouses of parallel relatives in the cross category." But in view of the foregoing analysis this cannot be true, since the wife of "MB" (cross) is presumably "FZ" (also cross), and that of "F" (parallel) presumably "M" (parallel again). This remark indicates further a confusion on Ridington's part between the logic of Beaver social classification and that of Kariera—a confusion which, as I have noted, pervades much of the literature on two-section systems. (Shapiro 1970:385–86)

Trautmann also emphasizes this point for the Indian Dravidianate systems:

The classification of kinsmen in respect for crossness by kinsmen of adjacent generations is not coordinate. That is to say for the same individual kinsmen ego makes discriminations of cross and parallel in a way systematically at odds with the discrimination made by his father, or his mother, or indeed any other member of their generation. From his father's perspective, for example, ego's mother, her sisters, and her brothers, are all cross kin, whereas for ego his mother and her sisters are parallel, her brothers cross. The lack of isomorphic boundaries of crossness between kinsmen of successive generations shows that crossness is not of itself an affair of unilineal descent. (Trautmann 1981:47–48)

Dravidian categorical calculus, then, in contrast with Australian, is not coordinate across the generations. This translates as a relatively complex crossness algebra: Trautmann's rules 2, 4, 6, 8B, and 9B (1981:179–85, 190–93, reprinted in this volume's figure 1-4) express this phenomenon. The "Boolean" calculus (or "modulo 2 addition") obtaining in the classification in G^0, that is, Trautmann's Rule 1—"a person's same-generation affine's same-generation consanguine is that person's same-generation affine," and so on—cannot be applied without restriction as to generation and sex. The Australian "crossness" method, in turn, is quite simple: it is the well-known calculus of Kay (1965, 1967), which he erroneously imputed to the Dravidian systems. Such a calculus (where any B/Z pair has the same "crossness" index for any ego) only correctly predicts classifications in unilineal situations, or rather, it only allows one to predict if alter is "same" or "other" relative to ego, according to his/her inclusion (real or formal) in sociocentric categories—to be precise, in exogamous moieties (Tyler 1966). But, as Trautmann observed, this is precisely *not* the case in the Dravidian scheme. Kay's method only coincides with the Dravidian calculus when ego and alter are in the same generation; but it coincides with the Australian method without restriction as to generation. The problem, however, is that the Australian sections (or moieties) are *not* opposed as "parallel/ cross," or "consanguineal/affinal": the opposition F + FZ versus M + MB is not interpretable by these conceptual pairs, but *at most* in terms of an opposition that Dravidian systems *do not* use, namely, paternal versus maternal "moiety" or section. Thus Kay's method does not concern the notion of crossness: at most, it bears an extrinsic relation to this concept.[22]

Kay's "crossness" calculus is assumed directly by Kronenfeld in the article discussed by Trautmann and Barnes (chapter 2). Kronenfeld (1989:87, 88) says that "cross and parallel categories are *based on descent*," and that "the Dravidian system produces categories which are *consistent across generations* and which are *consistent* with moiety and lineage membership" (emphasis added). The three predicates that I stress are not true, as mentioned earlier—their affirmation in such a recent work proves the remarkable persistence of the "spell of descent" (Dumont [1966] 1983a:193) in the analysis of the Dravidian.[23]

BOXING THE CATEGORIES

In response to Dumont's pairing of F + M versus MB + FZ for Dravidian terminologies, Kathleen Gough (1959:202, 1966:334–35) proposed substituting the "consanguines/affines" opposition for "lineal or pseudo-lineal kin" versus "affines." Gough argued that the dichotomy "relates always to unilineal groups" and classified

Figure 15-2
The Dravidian Box According to Good

F	FZ	M	MB
B	Z	MBD/FZD	MBS/FZS
S	D	♂ZD/♀BD	♂ZS/♀BD

Source: Adapted from Good (1981: 116).

the father's sister together with the father. Keesing (1975:107–9) perpetuated the confusion between a Dumontian reading and a "two-section" or "descent-based" one. After noting that the Dravidian type "is often associated with exogamous moieties" (which is empirically false), he opposes "kin/affine" and "parallel/cross," saying that in Dravidian systems M is parallel and "affinal," the FZ being cross and "kin" (in a patrilineal situation); but soon after he presents a genealogical diagram (1975:fig. 30) in which M and MFBD are marked as "cross," MFZD as "parallel."[24]

Even authors who dissociate the Dravidian terminology from moieties or descent constructs invert the positions of M and FZ, on the basis of considerations one might call aesthetic (see, e.g., Good 1980, 1981; Barnard and Good 1984:56; and Allen 1975, and chapter 14 of this volume). Good (1981:114) went so far as to locate F and FZ in the "parallel" category, M and MB in the "cross," as in figure 15-2. (I give the kin type "markers" for the Tamil terms in the original; $G^{\pm 2}$ categories and G^0 relative age distinctions are not shown.)[25] This arrangement, which puts only sibling pairs on either side of the central axis—this "minor modification in the arrangement of female relatives" that would supposedly better express the alliance relation than the Dumont-Trautmann type of diagram (Good 1980:483, 479)—actually makes crossness a property coordinate across the generations and alliance a global and sociocentric relation, which seems not to be true for the Dravidian case.[26] Because the Good-Allen kind of diagram violates the structure of the reciprocal sets, placing the reciprocals in opposite divisions, it does not describe even the Australian classification, or an arbitrarily "patrilineal" situation (for in this case ♀BCh should be the same side as F + FZ and B + Z).

Discussing the different arrangements of the Dravidian box, Allen (chapter 14) argues that "the semantic structure of the terminology is not a function of the diagrams used to display it." That is undoubtedly so, but the real point is that *the diagrams should be a function of the semantic structure of the terminology*—or they cease to be models and become completely arbitrary. And the only intrinsic procedure for the initial determination of a terminological structure is the establishment of the reciprocal sets.[27]

Allen is, of course, conscious of the problem. In chapter 14 he tries to determine the logical (and historical) passage between the "Australian" and "Dravidian" configurations. He tries to minimize, but fails to neutralize, the difference that the two schemes manifest in $G^{\pm 1}$ and is forced to conclude that "crossness" means different things in odd and even generations, and even that crossness is not "intrinsic" to its tetradic protostructure.

These difficulties seem due to the fact that there is a formal discontinuity between an egocentric structure (in which oppositions are not coordinate across the generations), and a sociocentric structure (in which the social universe is consistently divided into two or more categories). Dumont's contrast between the local and global perspectives remains pertinent, although this is not to say that they cannot be present in the same concrete system.

Affinity

Dumont did contribute to a certain fuzziness in the Dravidian/Australian contrast. His marriage alliance theory, defining the *primary* meaning of the notion of affinity (and therefore of consanguinity) as a relation between individuals of the same sex (Dumont [1953, 1957] 1983:4–7, 73–76) would seem to suggest parallel unisexual "moieties" consistent across the Australian/Dravidian divide. If the equivalent treatment of F and M as consanguines proves that "the vocabulary has nothing to do with unilineal descent" (Dumont [1957] 1975:144 n. h), the definition of alliance as a same-sex relation would weaken this argument and open the door to the Australian "global solution"—which, it should be remembered, is equally an intermarriage formula. This would leave the author with only the supposed difference in $G^{\pm 2}$ to substantiate the opposition he was supporting.

For Dumont, the unisexual principle of marriage alliance was, above all, a way to solve the problems raised by his ethnographic object: societies with a perfectly "bilateral" vocabulary but with unilineal-unilocal groups and unilateral marriage preferences. Thus he describes the Pramalai Kallar, patrilineal and patrilocal, as follows: "The terminology here directs us to look at the father's sister as already married and as a mother of affinal cousins. Nevertheless she is at the same time to some extent kin, and it follows that she is less clearly and unambiguously an affine than the mother's brother" (Dumont [1957] 1983:78).

Among the Kondaiyam Kottai Maravar, matrilineal and patrilocal, it is the maternal uncle "who receives the ambiguous character which attaches to the father's sister among Pramalai Kallar . . . the foremost affine here is the father's sister" (Dumont [1957] 1983:79).

That is, in the first case, the focal pair of allies is F and MB; in the second, it is M and FZ. *One should not conclude from this idea, however, that alliance is a relation between same-sex affines, that it is only inherited by same-sex consanguines.*[28] Both the diagrams in which Dumont contrasts the Kallar and Maravar situations show, male egos in the descending generation ([1957] 1983:79). In the Maravar case, the intergenerational consanguinity tie connects an S to an M, and "the foremost" affinal relation links an FZ to a BWS, as in figure 15-3.[29]

As Dumont had pointed out earlier, in his Dravidian rendering of the atom of kinship in a "patrilineal" key:

Figure 15-3
Foremost Affinal Relations in Two Dravidian Systems

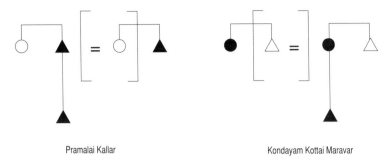

Pramalai Kallar   Kondayam Kottai Maravar

Source: Dumont (1983: 79).

Father and Ego are related by a link which excludes alliance, and which I propose to call "kin link." One qualification regarding sex must be added. . . . The two generations opposed to one another in the kin group are one generation of male siblings, and the generation of their children, both male and female. In other words, the distinction of sex, if it is the preliminary condition of the distinction of kin, is unrelated to the distinction of generation: this should be remembered. (Dumont [1953] 1983:11)[30]

This demonstrates, in my view, that Dumont does not reintroduce any sociocentric principle of descent in the construction of the concept of marriage alliance, contrary to what Yalman and others claimed. Also, the transmission of the alliance relationship does not suppose categories connected by unisexual links: inflections produced by supervenient unilineal institutions apart, children of *both* sexes inherit the alliance relationships of *both* parents.

Note, however, that curious definition of the FZ, in the Kallar patrilineal situation, as a *consanguineal* ("kin") relative "to some extent." The literature is rife with this confusion between the different phenomena we might call "kinship" (or "cognation"), "consanguinity," and "group affiliation."[31] Dumont does not escape it, either, although it is he who most alerted us to the necessity of not reducing "kinship" to "consanguinity" (Dumont 1971:13–15), and to the fact that Dravidian consanguinity "has, of course, nothing to do with actual groups" ([1957] 1983a:12).[32]

The Dravidian contrast between "consanguinity" and "affinity" *sensu* Dumont is a *matrimonial* and *categorical* opposition that does not involve any "cultural" notion of consanguinity as sharing of substance; neither does it suppose an opposition between "kinship" and "affinity." A relative like MZH is as consanguine as FB or F, MB as affinal as FZH and WF, and so forth. The relevant contrast here is FB = MZH versus MB = FZH; it is not the case, therefore, of an opposition of "consanguineal" kin, in the sense of relatives by birth, versus "affines," "in-laws," and "step-kin" (relatives by marriage)—in which case FB and MB would be jointly opposed to MZH and FZH, for example. The case may be that the ideologies of "blood relatedness" secondarily distinguish FB from MZH (and F from FB), or FBS from WZH, as designated kin, but these distinctions are neutralizable on the plane of terminological structure and marriage rules (identical reciprocals, equivalence as linking kin, etc.).

Consanguinity/affinity is not a descent-based distinction between "my group" and "other group," either—in which case FB and FZ would jointly oppose MZ and MB, for example. It *may* be the case that descent constructs complicate this simple opposition. In a matrilineal Dravidianate configuration, for example, it is likely that the MB will be a relative of the "self" category and FB an "other" relative; but this does *not* make the former a "consanguine" and the latter an "affine." The MB would at the same time be a matrilineal relative *and a terminological affine* (MB = WF); FB would be an agnatic relative *and a consanguine.* The terminological opposition consanguine/affine does not coincide with the sociological opposition agnatic/uterine. In cognatic Dravidianate systems like the ones widespread in Amazonia, on the other hand, FB and MB would both be cognates and *equally* remain consanguine in the first case, and affine in the second. Or in the case of a ZH who is a close cross cousin, an MBS, for example, he is at the same time a terminological affine and a "blood relative" (for the Achuar case, see Taylor 1989); on the other hand, a cognatically distant WBWB will be a "brother" without being a "true relative."

It is essential not to confuse the Dumontean consanguine/affine conceptual opposition with that between "relative" and "nonrelative," or between "agnatic" and "uterine," or between "same moiety" and "other moiety." Such confusion is dangerous *precisely* because the consanguine/affine contrast is frequently overdetermined by the other oppositions, which produce various torsions and tensions and define instability lines followed in the process of historical change (see Tyler 1984). Although they are distinct, the oppositions in question do possess certain homologies: "consanguine" evokes a concept of "same," and "affine" a concept of "other." In Dravidianate systems coupled with unilineal morphologies, relatives determined simultaneously as "same" (by group affiliation) and "affine" (by terminology and marriage rules: FZ in a patrilineal regime, MB in a matrilineal—or as "other" and "consanguine" (M in patriliny, F in matriliny) may come to be seen as "ambiguous," as Dumont observed. In cognatic environments, on the other hand, the opposition between consanguinity and affinity may be strongly overdetermined by a gradient of genealogical or residential distance.

CROSSNESS

It is quite likely that the Dravidianate opposition between consanguinity and affinity, and its implied calculus, are expressed only in pure fashion (*"simpliciter,"* as Shapiro would have it) in a few reference terminologies stripped of their quirks and considered outside of their institutional and pragmatic contexts. But on reflection, that somewhat contrived purity already contains a mixture: the assimilation of "consanguine" and "affine" to "parallel" and "cross," *concepts that presuppose an ultimate genealogical referent.*

Héritier (1981:175) noted that "once we leave the range of first cousins, there is no simple and universal criterion that would allow us to establish in objective terms the cross or parallel character of a relationship of consanguinity"—or of cognation, as I would prefer to say. This is true; but there is a "simple and universal" criterion to determine whether a relative is *terminologically* parallel or cross: it is his or her equivalence to primary genealogical relatives, that is, whether they are "objectively" parallel or cross. I would argue (with Taylor 1989 and chapter 8 of this volume), however, that this isomorphism between the *categorical* opposition consanguines/ affines and the *genealogical* opposition parallel/cross should not be seen as an essential identity—and normatively defining of the Dravidian type—but as a limiting case of a more complex relation that can "drift" in several directions, without this meaning an absolute autonomy between these conceptual pairs.

This raises the question of the primarily affinal content of the terminological categories that denote "cross" relatives, a thesis that is maintained by Dumont. There were specialists who disagreed with him on ethnographic grounds (e.g., Tyler, 1984:93 n. 2); others, confusing cognation with consanguinity and giving this last concept a substantialist, "emic" connotation, argued that Dravidian affines are "consanguines" before they are "affines" (Yalman, David, Carter). Because of such misunderstandings, Good (1980:481, 1981:115) prefers to refer to the Dravidian opposition as "parallel/cross," a formulation that Dumont had rejected as being genealogically biased and ethnocentric. Trautmann (1981:173ff.) also phrases the question in terms of parallel and cross—though he uses the symbols "C[onsanguine]" and "A[ffine]" in his equivalence rules (Trautmann 1981:178ff.). Even in the classic paradigm, the respective merits of these two oppositions are not obvious. As Trautmann demonstrates, what is distinctive about Dravidian crossness is precisely the marriage rule Dumont insisted on. The problem arises elsewhere: there are other crossness types that are generally considered not to be related to forms of alliance. One example is the "Iroquois" calculus. This would seem to suggest either that the parallel/cross opposition is independent of the consanguinity/affinity opposition (its equivalence in Dravidian then being contingent), or that the forms of crossness present in different "bifurcate merging" terminological types are completely heterogeneous.

Trautmann (1981:173–75, 184) is right in saying that Dravidian terminology as such does not authorize the "restricted" definition of affinity implied by the concept of "marriage alliance," and that Dumont is obliged to justify it by appealing to extraterminological institutions (marriage prestations, for example). But note that Trautmann's crossness calculus, as long as it depends on a "cross-cousin marriage rule," makes a relation of consanguinity between individuals of the same generation and opposite sex into the equivalent of a relation of affinity between individuals of the same sex and generation (Trautmann 1981:185). Only same-sex affines (and opposite-sex consanguines) produce affines in the next generation. Affines— terminological spouses—of opposite sex (and same-sex consanguines) produce consanguines. Alliance can only be projected generationally from a same-sex pair of affines (Silva 1995). In this sense, MB is primordially an affine of F, FZ of M, and so on. Whether this is "culturally" so in Dravidian India is another question.

What Dumont seems to be saying, however, is that the primary *structural meaning* of the *category* I translated as "MB" is *matrimonial.* That is, the "MB" is first and foremost "FZH = FWB = WF"; the real mother's brothers would simply be particular cases of this eminently affinal position. *Crossness is a specific manifestation of alliance, not the opposite.*

Some societies that seem to profess a Dumontean marriage alliance theory quite explicitly can be found in South America. Thus the "cross cousins" (prescriptive spouses) among the Piaroa of Venezuela are defined as father's or mother's same-sex affines' children, rather than as their opposite-sex siblings' children ([Overing] Kaplan 1975:137–38). Among the Achuar, more patrioriented (and polygynous) than the Piaroa, the spouse is conceived as the child of an ally of the father, not of a consanguine of the mother: the paradigmatic father-in-law is the FZH or the FWB, not the MB, who is nonetheless terminologically identical to the former two (Taylor 1989, and chapter 8 of this volume). It is precisely the cognatic character of the Achuar mother's brother (the fact that he is a "substantial relative" of the mother) that disqualifies him as a prototypical WF; in these circumstances, cognation, overdetermining the consanguinity/affinity opposition on the ideological (if not terminological) plane, partly dissociates the latter from the parallel/cross opposition and in doing so reveals it to be structurally primary.

The examples of the Piaroa and Achuar suggest that *the Dravidianate marriage rule aims for the reproduction of a former relationship between same-sex affines, but not necessarily or immediately of a former tie of opposite-sex siblingship; it is conditioned by previous alliances of relatives, not previous kinship between affines.* And if the marriage rule is the fundamental principle of Dravidianate terminological crossness, then Dumont's concept of an alliance relationship cannot be an "arbitrary device" (Trautmann 1981:174). Dumont is clear on this point: "To say that an alliance relationship is inherited is the same as to say that a certain marriage regulation is observed" ([1953] 1983:14).

It is essential to isolate the distinctive properties of alliance from its genealogical manifestations. If the Dravidianate scheme, like every terminology, "acts as an operating agent to a system of matrimonial exchange within a community," as Lévi-Strauss suggested, then it encodes a certain replicative pattern of alliances previously established by relatives—in the case of "elementary" systems, specifically by close consanguineal cognates. But *marrying like a relative* does not necessarily mean *marrying a relative* (Viveiros de Castro 1993b:126): the spouse's genealogical specification as "cross" is a limiting case of his categorical determination as "affine." Marriage with a cross cognate is the "elementary" reduction of an alliance replication structure that has no a priori determinate genealogical inscription: "The only relevant consideration in the definition of alliance structures is decidedly the possibility or impossibility of replicating former alliances" (Héritier 1981:99).[33]

Dumont's theory of "marriage alliance" is obviously structuralist inspired. It is, in fact, the structuralist theory of crossness. The asymmetry between the relations B/B (= Z/Z) and B/Z (= Z/B) expresses a fundamental structure of reciprocity connecting individuals of the same sex through individuals of the opposite sex (Lévi-Strauss [1949] 1969:115, 128). In this sense, "cross" and "parallel" have no other meaning than matrimonial, being nothing else but "consanguinity" and "affinity," relationships that, in a given generation—that is, in the synchronic dimension—can only exist sociologically between individuals of the same sex. In other words, the kinship categories applied to the opposite sex embody an essential ambiguity, being "tinged" by the values of consanguinity and of affinity. For a man, a sister is a consanguine who produces affines, a female cross cousin is an affine who produces consanguines; for each sex taken as a term, the opposite sex is purely a relation, or rather, a *conductor* of consanguinity and affinity relationships between individuals of the same sex.[34] The "parallel" or "cross" character of kinship relationships expresses first of all a difference in the relations established *with third parties* through these links. If the relationship brother/sister, as Héritier so aptly puts it (1981:171), is where "sibling identity turns into difference" ("l'identité des germains bascule dans la différence"), it is because that is where "la différence" becomes a necessary opening of the "natural" relation of siblingship to the "social" world of alliance.

By subordinating "crossness" to alliance, Dumont opened the way to a consideration of the Dravidianate systems that would permit the encompassing of the ethnographic ideal type of Southern India by a more general structure. But, by restricting the notion of alliance to systems with a "positive marriage rule," Dumont (1971) buttressed the position of Needham and his followers: he emptied the terminologies of any sociological content and turned them into mere cultural classifications, thus subordinating alliance to terminology. Dumont reads *The Elementary Structures* as legitimately bearing only a "local theory" valid for societies with "prescriptive" terminologies. The incest prohibition posed by Lévi-Strauss as the general principle of kinship, so Dumont's argument goes, would be excessively dependent on a "semi-empirical theory of exchange" guided by an imperative of social integration; it is necessary to replace it by the idea of "a distinctive opposition between consanguinity and marriage, or affinity" (Dumont 1971:131). Dumont (1971:133–34) thus proposes a theory or "mental integration" of conceptual oppositions: alliance and exchange are different things.

The problem is that it is difficult to imagine the content of the opposition between consanguinity and affinity, categories the very definition of which implies matrimonial exchange and the prohibition of incest, in the absence of a *general* alliance theory. The notion of "distinctive opposition" bypasses this problem: kinship is not phonology, and its constitutive oppositions cannot be founded on mere logical contrast. Dumont, it is true, concludes that Dravidian terminology expresses a "sociological theory of alliance"; but then it cannot be a theory of the diacritical opposition between categories the content of which should first be established. How can one construct an alliance theory on a purely cognitive basis? What imposes alliance? Is it legitimate to distinguish the "sociological" from the "mental" the way he does? Dumont's reading of *The Elementary Structures of Kinship* dismisses exchange as a "semiempirical" notion because it is the author himself who entertains a semiempirical conception of exchange, restricting it to matrimonial systems that manifest a "global formula."[35] Only thus can his affirmation that there are kinship systems that are not based on exchange (1971:134) be understood. The Lévi-Straussian concept of matrimonial reciprocity does not designate a contingent insti-

Figure 15-4
Australian Kin Classification

Sections 1–3		Sections 2–4	
FF	MM	FM	MF
FB	FZ	MZ	MB
B	Z	FZD/MBD	FZS/MBS
BS	BD	ZD	Z
♂SS/♀DS	♂SD/♀DD	♂DD/♀SD	♂DS/♀SS

tution, but the formal condition of the possibility of kinship. Dumont reduces exchange and alliance to institutions and then decrees that the "restricted" theory of *The Elementary Structures* is only applicable to societies provided with such devices.

ALTERNATE GENERATIONS

The different cases of self-reciprocity (explicit or revealed by the determination of superclasses) between alternate generations present in terminologies of Australian or Dravidian type are a sure index of classificatory principles that are less evident but equally operative in terminologies without self-reciprocals. In the Australian case, the simplest scheme inherent to the terminology leads to the following equations, corresponding to the four basic sections (Scheffler, 1978:446–49):

1. FF + MM = B + Z = ♂SCh + ♀DCh
2. MF + FM = FZCh/MBCh = ♂DCh + ♀SCh
3. F(B) = ♂(B)Ch, FZ = ♀BCh → [F + FZ = BCh]
4. MB = ♂ZCh, M(Z) = ♀(Z)Ch → [MB + M = ZCh].

To represent this scheme in a box-type diagram, an arbitrary decision needs to be made regarding the alignment of consecutive sections. Figure 15-4 shows a "patrilineal" arrangement.[36]

In Dravidian model B, equations 1 and 2 are identical to Australian. But the corresponding equations 3 and 4 should follow the reciprocal sets of any Dravidianate system:

Figure 15-5
Dravidian B Kin Classification

Classes 1–3'		Classes 2–4'	
FF	MM	FM	MF
FB	FZ	MZ	MB
B	Z	FZD/MBD	FZS/MBS
♂BS/♀ZS	♂BD/♀ZD	♂ZD/♀BD	♂ZS/♀BS
♂SS/♀DS	♂SD/♀DD	♂DD/♀SD	♂DS/♀SS

1. FF + MM = B + Z = ♂SCh + ♀DCh
2. MF + FM = FZCh/MBCh = ♂DCh + ♀SCh
3'. F(B) = ♂(B)Ch, M(Z) = ♀(Z)Ch → [F + M = Ch]
4'. MB = ♂ZCh, FZ = ♀BCh → [MB + FZ = ♂ZCh/♀BCh].

The "folding" of the alternate generations expressed in equations 1, 2, 3', and 4' does no more than consolidate the sets characteristic of Dravidianate terminologies: "Analysis into reciprocal sets establishes that a mother's brother and a man's sister child *fall in the same class,* and the classification rules I have given tend to show that *this is the same class in which spouses are found"* (Trautmann, 1981:185, italics added).

That is, equations 1 and 3' define the class of consanguineal (parallel) relatives, equations 2 and 4' the class of affinal (cross) relatives.[37] It is easy to see that classes 3' and 4' cannot be exogamous sections like their equivalents 3 and 4 of the Australian scheme, for they separate siblings and join spouses—they are egocentric classes, as may be seen in figure 15-5.

In *Dravidian Kinship,* Trautmann (1981:43, 141–42, 144) reports a few cases of equation 3'; in South America, one finds a Dravidian model B that contains, as well as equations 1 and 2, equation 4': FZ = ♂ZD/♀BD and MB = ♂ZS/♀BS. It is the Western Panare (Caribs of the Middle Orinoco) system analyzed by Henley (1993; see also 1972:89–103). Henley does not seem to think this equation distinguishes the Panare system from the Australian ("Kariera") type present among the Panoan peoples of Western Amazonia (where FZ = ♂D, M = ♂ZD), but the box diagram he draws separates consanguines and affines Dravidian-style in *all* generations.

Like other systems with self-reciprocals in alternate generations, that of the Panare matrimonially equates members of a same category: a man can marry the FM = DD

= FZD/MBD. But there happens the "major inconsistency" noted by Henley: the Western Panare say one should marry the child of a *wa'nene,* a category that covers the positions of FZ and ϑZD; by the cross-cousin marriage rule, however, ϑZDD = SD, this last one being a parallel relative by equation 1. The indigenous solution is pragmatic: "When a G-1 *wa'nene* is married to ego's own son or other close relative, her daughter is not regarded as marriageable but if the *wa'nene* is married to a more distant relative, her daughter is regarded as an entirely appropriate spouse for Ego" (Henley n.d.). This appeal to the parameter of genealogical distance recognizes the formal problem: the lack of coordination between the consanguine/affine distinctions across generations produces an inconsistency highlighted by the self-reciprocal FZ = ϑZD, potentially present in all Dravidian schemes. This suggests that Dravidian B is structurally unstable.

An analogous instability is also present in the avuncular variant of Dravidian model A (Rivière 1969; Good 1980; Fausto 1991), where there appear genealogical identities between "parallel" and "cross" kin like FZD = M, ϑZ = WM, ♀B = ♀DH, and terminological identities like ZD = y(MBD) = y(FZD) = y(MZ) (= WZ), which combine the formally contradictory principles of marriage with ZD (= MBD) and with FZD. The parameter of relative age (y(MBD)/y(FZD) ≠ e(MBD)/e(FZD)) and the lineal/collateral terminological split (M ≠ MZ) here work in a way that is similar to the genealogical difference ZDH ≠ S for the Panare.

Henley (n.d.) remarks that the Southern Panare, with an "even more conventionally Dravidianate" terminology than that of the Western Panare, do not make the equation FZ = ϑZD, but M = ϑZD. This, as the author acknowledges, is consistent with the use of parallel "sibling" terms for ϑSCh; but this is precisely the Australian equation 4, which is *not* consistent with the Dravidian dichotomy, for it equates a consanguine (M) to an affine (ϑZD).[38]

Tjon Sie Fat (chapter 3 of this volume) defined the crossness algebra for Dravidian model A, pointing out its restricted associativity. I suggest that model B, too, does not exhibit perfect associativity. Compare, for example, the Australian and Dravidian B classifications of a relative like FFZ. Using the alternate-generation structural equivalences, one would have, for the Australian, the following bracketing-independent reductions: F{FZ} = FD = Z or {FF}Z = BZ = Z. In the Dravidian, on the other hand, the equivalences (see equation 4') would generate two incompatible derivations: either F{FZ} = FZD = W or {FF}Z = BZ = Z.

Finally, the relation between Dravidian models A and B does *not* seem to be simply a question of the presence or absence of the crossness dimension in $G^{\pm2}$. Thus, if FFZ or MMB are *parallel* relatives in Dravidian B, they are *cross* in Dravidian A, as Tjon Sie Fat's multiplication tables and diagrams show. But if the model B equations (FFZ = MM, MMB = FF) can be said to express the cross-cousin marriage rule in $G^{\pm2}$, how are we to interpret the "cross" status of MMB and FFZ in model A? Note, however, that the "crossness" of these kin types is not terminologically realized in model A, where MMB = FF = MF, and FFZ = MM = FM.[39] The Dravidian type does not seem to manifest the "classic simplicity" that has so often been attributed to it.

Amazonia shows abundant examples of Dravidian A schemes; the Western Panare, in turn, is a case of Dravidian B in a cultural area (Guyana) dominated by the first

Figure 15-6
Cuiva Kin Classification

<table>
<tr><td colspan="2" align="center">"Sections" 1–3</td><td colspan="2" align="center">"Sections" 2–4</td></tr>
<tr><td align="center">MF</td><td align="center">FM</td><td align="center">MM</td><td align="center">FF</td></tr>
<tr><td align="center">MB</td><td align="center">MZ</td><td align="center">FZ</td><td align="center">FB</td></tr>
<tr><td align="center">B</td><td align="center">Z</td><td align="center">FZD/MBD</td><td align="center">FZS/MBS</td></tr>
<tr><td align="center">BS</td><td align="center">BD</td><td align="center">ZD</td><td align="center">ZS</td></tr>
<tr><td align="center">♂DS/♀SS</td><td align="center">♂DD/♀SD</td><td align="center">♂SD/♀DD</td><td align="center">♂SS/♀DS</td></tr>
</table>

type; among the already mentioned Panoan peoples of Eastern Amazonia, there are several examples of Australianoid terminologies, sometimes associated with named sections and moieties (see below). But this region also contains a rare, possibly unique, configuration: the terminology of the Cuiva (Guahibo), nomadic hunters and gatherers of the eastern plains of Colombia (Arcand 1977; see also Campbell 1989:142–63)—not far from the Western Panare. The Cuiva exemplify a third type of reduction by terminological self-reciprocity to four superclasses, which is a sort of "twisted Australian":

1′. FF + MM = FZCh/MBCh (= Sp) = ♂SCh + ♀DCh
2′. MF + FM = B + Z = ♂DCh + ♀SCh
3″. F(B) = ♂ZS + ♀(Z)S, FZ = ♂ZD + ♀(Z)D → [F + FZ = ZCh]
4″. MB = ♂(B)S + ♀BS, M(Z) = ♂(B)D + ♀BD → [MB + M = BCh].

This structure has a number of curious properties. Its nepotic terminology is of "Australian" type: H and W do not call their Ch by the same terms; B and Z use a single common term for ♂ZCh = ♀Ch and use another common term for ♂Ch = ♀BCh (see note 16). But the terms that designate F + FZ (= ♂ZCh + ♀Ch) and MB + M (2= ♂Ch + ♀BCh), are the same and not, as in the Australian case, MB + M (= ♂ZCh + ♀Ch) and F + FZ (= ♂Ch + ♀BCh). This suggests, along with the alternate equations of the even generations that twist the Australian equivalences in the same ropelike way, a sexually cross transmission of terminological statuses that is inconsistent, in contrast to the Australian case, with the alignment of the four sections in unilineal exogamous moieties, being, however (and contrary to the Dravidian case), equally inconsistent with a division into consanguines and affines. In figure 15-6, the symbols in italics show the cycling of terminological statuses from the MF and FF "lines," those in roman type the cycling of the FM and MM "lines"; in alternate generations, they mark the self-reciprocals.

The alliance scheme derivable from the Cuiva terminology is a sort of "super-Kariera," wherein a man reproduces his own terminological and sectional position through a patrilineal relative every four generations (male Ego = SSSS), instead of every two as in Kariera. In alternately male-female lines, the cycle obviously runs every two generations: MF—(MZ)—Ego—(BD)—♂DS/♀SS, FF—(FZ)—FZS/MBS—(ZD)—♂SS/♀DS, and so forth (see Arcand 1977:29–30).

Note that the Cuiva marry first bilateral cross cousins, that MB = WF, FZ = WM, and that they have neither sections nor descent constructs.[40] In fact (some analogous cases can be found among the Panoans of Amazonia, as discussed later), this self-reciprocal and "sociocentric" terminology of the Cuiva coexists with a perfectly Dravidianate terminological nucleus.

DRAVIDIAN AND IROQUOIS

I insisted above that Dravidian and Australian, despite some basic similarities of terminological calculus—in both types the cross cousins of F are "M" and "MB," those of M are "F" and "FZ," the children of a man's female cross cousins are "Ch," and so on—and their common "prescriptivity," present different terminological structures (each Australian odd-generation section or superclass includes consanguineal *and* affinal relatives). The question I turn to now is whether Dravidian and Iroquois are in fact two *fundamentally* different types (Trautmann 1981:88).

The crossness calculus and the presence or absence of separate affinal terms are the two factors usually taken as diagnostic of the Dravidian/Iroquois difference. For Dumont, the relation between these factors is one of identity (for "crossness" is affinity), in the Dravidian case: "The general and characteristic trait of terminologies associated with cross cousin marriage is an absence of distinct terms for affinal kin" (1971:114; see also [1953, 1957] 1983:12, 73–74). For Trautmann, the relation is equally intrinsic: the Dravidian calculus supposes a cross cousin marriage rule, and this has for a semantic equivalent an "opposite-sex cross cousin-spouse equation rule" (1981:55–56) that assimilates "cross" to "affine." The presence of separate affinal terms in the Iroquois-type terminologies would, in turn, be explained precisely by the absence of a rule of cross-cousin marriage (1981:85).

For Buchler and Selby (1968:234), who adopt Dumont's theory of Dravidian, Dravidian and Iroquois "are as different as a whale is from a fish."[41] They see the presence/absence of separate affinal terms as an absolute formal distinction (1968:233).[42] The master opposition in Dravidian systems would be "Cognates/Affines" (here is a typical example of the confusion between "kinship" and "consanguinity"), and marriage would be regulated by the "terminological code." The opposition in Iroquois systems would be "Cross/Parallel kin," and marriage would be regulated by "various social institutions" (Buchler and Selby 1968:233).

Scheffler (1971) seems to be the main discordant voice.[43] At the same time that he emphasizes the Dravidian/Iroquois difference as to crossness, he maintains that (1) the difference lies exclusively in the mode of extension of the "cross/parallel" opposition to distant collaterals—the definition of crossness would be identical in both types for the focal (primary) relatives; (2) there is another type of crossness (Kuma), logically "equidistant" from Dravidian and Iroquois; (3) there is no necessary relation between the crossness calculus and the Dravidianate affinal equations (in many Dravidian systems cross cousins are not marriageable; there are Dravidian cross systems with separate affinal terms; and there are Iroquois systems with cross-affinal equations); (4) consequently, there is no relation between Dravidian classifications and any type of marriage rule.

Trautmann (1981:61–62), however, demonstrated conclusively, against Scheffler, the logical relevance of the "opposite-sex cross cousin–spouse equation rule" (see also Overing Kaplan 1984) for Dravidian terminologies. But Trautmann's compelling demonstration of the concrete historical ancestrality of cross-cousin marriage (as a social institution) in India, that is, of a zero-point from which one can evaluate the "occasional ethnological inappropriateness of the bilateral cross cousin rule" (Trautmann 1981) is not of much help to anthropologists dealing with non-Indian Dravidianate systems.[44] From the general point of view of Dravidianate *as a morphological type,* this "historicist" hypothesis (perfectly justified in India, where we have documentary evidence for tens of centuries) taken in an absolute sense would be too strong and too simple. It would suppose an *original transparency between terminology and alliance* that was somehow lost in the course of history. This idea, besides presenting all the difficulties of infinite regression, accepts the genealogical interpretation of terminologies put forth by Scheffler, as well as the latter's requirement of an isomorphism between semantic rules and matrimonial norms (or even marriage statistics). If, as I maintain here, the consanguinity/affinity opposition logically encompasses that between "parallel" and "cross"—in other words, if the vocabulary of Dravidianate kinship is organized as a set of *categories* that indicate positions in a social field structured by *alliance*—its genealogical translation is contingent. Postulating a general, primeval coincidence between terminology and genealogical alliance (a position Trautmann, of course, does *not* assume in *Dravidian Kinship*) would amount to a kind of phylogenetic extensionism, giving, furthermore, an evolutionist slant to the notion of "elementary structure."

I also think that if Scheffler's conclusions are questionable—I, for one, do not accept them—this does not disqualify the problems he raised. Isolating Indian Dravidianate and saying that Scheffler's arguments are invalid because all "anomalies" *there* can be accounted for by historical contacts and changes, or insisting on the matrimonial opacity of the Iroquois type so as to maximize the contrast between it and the Dravidian—this seems a somewhat ad hoc defensive strategy.

In the first place, the radical distinction between Dravidian and Iroquois, insofar as it is based on the intrinsic relation between the crossness type and the presence/ absence of separate affinal terms, evokes the old and dubious opposition between "prescriptive" and "preferential" systems, as well as Needham's (and Dumont's) confusion between elementary structures and prescriptive systems. It opens the door for Scheffler's antialliance theses, by admitting that "crossness" is not, *in itself,* a phenomenon associated with alliance, whether because a "cross" relative is not always an affine, or because this notion in fact designates fundamentally different things in each terminological type, meaning affinity only in the Dravidian.

Second, the thesis of the *fundamental* difference between the types of crossness is ethnographically forced: among geographically close societies of a common linguistic and cultural basis, some present Dravidianate terminologies, some "Iroquois"; the sociological landscape of the Americas is full of examples of this phenomenon. There is also a notable internal variety to both types (greater than the two Dravidian "models" and four Iroquois "variants" proposed by Trautmann and Barnes), as well as a number of transitional forms in the ethnographic record; this suggests that we are still operating with models far too close to empirical paradigms arbitrarily chosen as ideal types. And finally, if Iroquois crossness (or Kuma, or other) does not admit correlation with a structure of matrimonial exchange, what then is its meaning? Would the curious resemblance between the classification of first cousins in Dravidian and Iroquois (variant 1) and the same structure of reciprocals in $G^{\pm 1}$ be accidental?

The radical heterogeneity argument is above all antieconomical. It is redundant in that it requires two different orders of reasons for Dravidian and Iroquois crossness: cousin marriage in the first case, and some purely semantic-cognitive dimension in the second (something like relative sex). It seems more interesting to work with the idea of a common basis for both types. Scheffler approximated Dravidian to Iroquois to refuse them any sociological correlate. The hypothesis I prefer, on the contrary, supposes that *all* types of "crossness" can be shown to be compatible with some regime of matrimonial exchange— which of course does not mean they can always be interpreted as "prescribing" marriage with a "cross" cognate: "the structure of exchange is not solidary with the prescription of a preferred spouse," as Lévi-Strauss ([1949] 1969:471) has already warned.[45]

I assume as a minimal definition of "crossness" the terminological marking of the difference between relationships traced through a same-sex sibling and those traced through an opposite-sex sibling. Short of reifying the difference between opposite-sex siblings and putting it as superior to the difference between same-sex affines—thus making the "chronological" anteriority of the first a logical anteriority, when in fact it is the *nonmarriageability* of the opposite-sex sibling that *defines* him or her as consanguine—"crossness" must be seen as a property derived from an alliance structure.[46] My hypothesis, therefore, is that it always carries a matrimonial implication, direct or indirect.

The absence of separate affinal terms is a feature often associated with Dravidian (and Australian) terminologies. As Parkin (chapter 11) observes, however, a terminology with Dravidian crossness and separate affinal terms is perfectly conceivable. If the *absence* of specific affinal terms can be a good indication of the "elementarity" of an kinship system, the *presence* of such terms does not guarantee its "complexity" in the sense of Lévi-Strauss, namely, that it is a system in which kinship plays no positive role in the choice of a spouse. In Amazonia, Dravidian-cross systems with an explicit preference for marriage to cognatically close bilateral cross cousins (or between MB and ZD) usually exhibit more or less complete sets of separate affinal terms (see, for instance, Jackson 1983:121–22; Rivière 1984:47–48, 61, 69; Seymour-Smith 1988:211–14; McCallum 1989:122–27; Fausto 1991; Viveiros de Castro 1992:397–99).[47] Here, in contrast to the Indian situation, it is not possible to solve the problem by pointing out allogenous influences (Trautmann 1981:122>en>24) or by determining a unilateral direction of change—and supposing an original state of prescriptive "purity" (see Viveiros de Castro and Fausto 1993; Henley n.d.).[48]

The essential point, Trautmann would contend, is that the affinal terms should be redundant with regard to the basic Dravidian discriminations, that is, they should not straddle the cells of the terminological box, particularly the cross/parallel divide. But the terminological separation of actual affines in a Dravidianate environment, even if logically redundant—which is not always the case—is never sociologically redundant. In the Amazonian situation, ethnographers have connected this feature to a tension between the marriage rule and the system of attitudes, and to the presence of a distinction between related and unrelated affines. What seems to be at play here is the fundamentally ambiguous character of affinity in Amazonia, an ambiguity that ends up actualizing a possibility inherent to any Dravidian scheme: the subdivision of its basic categories by the interference of other structural oppositions. Remember, too, the gradient-like character of this feature and its contextual complexity. It is common for an Amazonian terminology to mark only a few positions of actual affinity with specific terms, while others remain with the "prescriptive" equivalences. The type and number of marked positions vary from system to system: they can be distributed according to generational level, relative or absolute sex, the life-cycle positions of the parties involved, and the pragmatic and genealogical context of the use of the terms (Viveiros de Castro and Fausto 1993). Some systems mark actual affinity only in reference, using the terms of cognatic or virtual affinity in address; others admit specific affinal terms only for unrelated affines, and others, only for classificatory or "symbolic" affines (distant kin, ritual antagonists, strangers one has *not* married, enemies).

This leads to the inverse problem: the cases of Iroquois systems with affinal equations. Starting with the classic examples of the Cheyenne, Arapaho, and Kiowa-Apache (Eggan 1955b:43–45; McAllister, 1937:103–6), equations such as MB = FZH, FZ = MBW, FB = MZH, ZD = SW, and so forth, are not uncommon.[49] In this volume, Ives (chapter 4) shows other analogous cases in North America, and Parkin (chapter 11) in South Asia. In South America, the few available records of Iroquois-cross nomenclatures do not indicate whether such equations are made; interestingly, several terminologies of Central Brazil (Krahó, Apinayé, Kayapó, Bororo) that show intergenerational equations reminiscent of the Crow and Omaha types have the equations MB = FZH versus FB = MZH and FZ = MBW versus MZ = FBW (see Hornborg 1986/1988)—some of them also present among the Omaha (Barnes 1984:132–37) and the Fox (Tax 1937b:249–50).[50]

One possibility Trautmann and Barnes do not consider, but that Parkin (chapter 11) mentions for the Munda, is that such equations (in contrast to those of the type MB = WF) appear as much in Dravidian-cross as in Iroquois-cross systems because they imply "exclusive" sister exchange (nonrepeated in consecutive generations) as a conceptual model. The difference would be that Dravidianate terminologies encode in a "prescriptive" way a system of consecutive sister exchange—"cross-cousin marriage"—whereas the Iroquois configurations suggest a longer cycle of repeti-

Figure 15-7
Two Models of Prescriptive Second-Cousin Marriage

1. "Diametric"	2. "Concentric"
G^1 A ↔ B, C ↔ D	G^1 A ↔ B, C ↔ D
G^2 A ↔ D, B ↔ C	G^2 A ↔ D, B ↔ C
G^3 A ↔ B, C ↔ D	G^3 A ↔ C, B ↔ D
G^4 A ↔ D, B ↔ C	G^4 A ↔ B, C ↔ D

tion of the exchange, since cross cousins do not function terminologically as spouses there.

Therefore this is not a case of denying that Iroquois crossness is formally incompatible with close-cross cousin marriage, but of asking whether it, too, would not be associated with an alliance structure, of which Dravidian marriage would be a particular example. The question is whether it is possible to derive a marriage structure compatible with Iroquois crossness, and whether there is any relevant ethnographic evidence to this effect.

A "TYPE B" ALLIANCE MODEL

Since Dravidian and Iroquois classify first cousins identically, an alliance model that allows one to contrast Dravidian and Iroquois crossness must start from a situation in which marriages only take place between second cousins, which is equivalent to the exchange of sisters repeated in nonconsecutive generations. This requires a system with at least four objects (exchange units) *A, B, C, D*—according to the usual "elementary" convention whereby each unit is represented by a single brother/sister pair per generation. A system of this type that "proscribes" marriage with first cross cousins and "prescribes" bilateral exchange between the children of cousins, permits two solutions, as shown in figure 15-7.

The first is the well-known "Aranda" pattern: a structure of alliance replication between $2n$ matrimonial classes, of period 2, which respects the calculus "affine of affine = consanguine." It is a "double bilateral" scheme that admits the reduction $2n \leftrightarrow 2$. There are formally two exogamic "moieties": $\{A + C\} \leftrightarrow \{B + D\}$. The wife of a male ego is here a *Dravidian-cross* second cousin: W = MMBDD = FFZSD = MFZDD = FMBSD.[51]

In the second, period 3 solution, each unit exchanges with the three others sequentially in consecutive generations. Instead of the diametralism of the "Aranda" structure, this one is concentric or "multibilateral": each unit sees all the others distributed around itself as real or potential affines. Allies' allies are (or will be) allies, which is incompatible with a division of the society into two matrimonial superclasses. The marriageability (or crossness) of second cousins here follows the *Iroquois* calculus; the wife of a male ego is W = MMBSD = FFZDD = MFZSD = FMBDD.

Thus an "Iroquois-cross" marriage structure is formally conceivable, and it is not "two-sided" (see chapter 9) in the sense that the alliance network ideally derived from the terminology cannot be represented by a bipartite graph. From the ethnographic point of view, the alliance model above was proposed by Elkin for the Bardi of Australia. The Bardi had neither moieties nor sections, and their terminology was "Iroquois-cross" (MMBS = MB, FFZD = FZ, etc.), and not "Dravidian-Australian" (MMBS = F, FFZD = M, etc.). Elkin classifies it as an "Aluridja" type (Scheffler's "Pitjanjara"). Tjon Sie Fat (1990:196–200, 1993), in his algebraic typology of matrimonial exchange structures, uses it as an example of one of the automorphisms of the dihedral group—it is one of the simplest possible systems of restricted exchange, a category that covers the "semicomplex systems" of Héritier (1981) and probably the "exclusive straight sister exchange" of Muller (1980, 1982). Tjon Sie Fat also mentions (1993) Lucich's model for the Kokata and Aluridja, which would be identical to a Mundugumor alliance model he presents, which is an eight-line, period 4 structure with Iroquois-cross third-cousin marriage.[52]

Another example of what could be called "Type B restricted exchange" is the alliance system of the Umeda of New Guinea described by Alfred Gell (1975). The Umeda do not present any trace of "prescription" or even of preference for terminologically determined relatives; sister exchange between "nonkin" is the type of marriage really and ideologically favored. Gell proposes a structure with four "terminological" patrilines connected by symmetric exchange repeated every fourth generation (period 3), identical to the "concentric" solution shown above (Gell 1975:63–65; see also Gregory 1982:170, fig. 7.6; and Tjon Sie Fat 1993). The concentric and multilateral character of the Umeda social and matrimonial organization is, in fact, underlined by Gell (1975:43, 49, 83). More interesting, however, are the temporal dynamics that he reveals, which lead us far from the purely synchronic models of relationship between alliance categories found in "prescriptive" situations.

The four terminological lines of the Umeda model represent: (1) ego's group; (2) the groups of ego's real or potential affines (with whom his group exchanged or can exchange women in the present generation); (3) "allies," groups with whom ego's group exchanged women in the previous generation, not being able to do so in his generation—which is where the cross cousins are found; (4) allies from previous generations, or "residual allies," which is where the cross cousins of the F of Ego are found, that is, the children of cross cousins in ego's generation. Although in theory these residual allies are unmarriageable, since they are assimilated to cross cousins, Gell shows how relations of residual alliance turn into nonrelatedness and so are transformable into potential affinity.[53] The fourth category is the source of the second, in a cycle where the position of the groups connected by alliance shifts by one degree in every generation: "affines become allies, allies become residual allies, residual allies become unrelated marriageables, who can subsequently be incorporated into the scheme as affines" (Gell 1975:65).

Gell qualifies Lévi-Strauss's well-known aphorism concerning the difference between elementary and semicomplex systems, stating that in the Umeda case the marriage system does turn affines into kin (for the allies become unmarriageable), but the kinship terminology, by shifting the status of the groups related to ego's in each generation, turns kin into affines, or rather, potential affines. Such a contrapuntal relation between terminology and alliance offers a striking contrast with the unissonous coincidence these dimensions manifest in "elementary" models.

This relation rests on the border between "elementarity" and "complexity," as Gell observed. The temporal dynamics suggested for the Umeda can be approximated to models proposed for societies with Omaha terminologies (Bowden 1983; Houseman 1989) or for cases such as that of the Ho (Bouez 1989:14–15). Underlining the fact that sister exchange is compatible with elementary and "complex" regimes, Gell converges with a line of reflection that Muller (1980, 1982) pursued successfully and anticipates some key aspects of Héritier's theory (1981) on "semicomplex systems," as defined by the dispersion of same-sex kin and repetition of opposite-sex kin alliances.

Although I am reluctant to discuss examples from areas unfamiliar to me, it is important to mention that a fourth type of crossness—in addition to the Iroquois, Dravidian, and Kuma types proposed by Scheffler (1971; see Trautmann 1981:87–88)—can be found in New Guinea. It is the system of the Iafar, a group that belongs to the same regional system of the Umeda, in the West Sepik District. Juillerat (1977) classifies the terminology as "Iroquois," although the crossness calculus he establishes is quite different from that found by Lounsbury for the Seneca and Pospisil for the Kapauku:

1. Children of same-sex parallel cousins (MMZDCh, FFBSCh, MFBDCh, FMZSCh): parallel in Dravidian, Iroquois, Kuma, Iafar.
2. Children of opposite-sex parallel cousins (MMZSCh, FFBDCh, MFBSCh, FMZDCh): cross in Dravidian, Iroquois, Kuma, Iafar.
3. Children of same-sex cross cousins (MMBDCh, FFZSCh, MFZDCh, FMBSCh): parallel in Iroquois and Iafar, cross in Dravidian and Kuma.
4. Children of opposite-sex cross cousins (MMBSCh, FFZDCh, MFZSCh, FMBDCh): parallel in Dravidian and Iafar, cross in Iroquois and Kuma.[54]

Note that in the Iafar calculus the opposite-sex cross cousins of father and mother are not cross relatives of ego, as in the Iroquois and Kuma types, but parallel relatives ("F" and "M"), as in Dravidian (Juillerat 1977:26). The Iafar alliance system admits sister exchange. Juillerat (1986:294–311) considers it approximate to Héritier's "semicomplex" case, not only because of this feature but because of the structure of matrimonial prohibitions. Marriage between relatives seems possible only every fourth generation, as in the Umeda case, but here this means marriage to nonagnatic *third* cousins. Juillerat privileges a matrilateral cycle (also described by Gell [1975:70–76] as the "*mol* cycle" of the Umeda) between four units, wherein the male and female descendants in sexually parallel lines of a B/Z pair meet once more through the marriage of MMMBSSS to FFFZDDD (1975:301–2)—these are third cousins who are Dravidian- and Iroquois-cross, and who are marriageable as much in an Aranda scheme as in one of matrilateral exchange between four units (merged respectively, in these two elementary models, with FFZSS + MMBDD and with FZS + MBD). This is not strictly a case of "generalized exchange," however, since sister exchange seems to be preferred (Gell 1975:307–8); it is probably akin to the Aranda "matricycles."

The presence (or native perception) of "generalized" cycles in systems where sister exchange is the basic conceptual model shows that the "elementary" distinction between restricted exchange and generalized exchange (which did not easily account for the patrilateral formula) becomes somewhat hazy as soon as we move toward more complicated configurations. This can be seen in the Umeda and Iafar cases, in the pseudomatrilateral cycles of the Daribi (Wagner 1969) and of a few Australian systems (Murngin, Yir Yoront), as well as in some "semicomplex" African systems (Viveiros de Castro 1993b:131). This brings to mind three observations of Lévi-Strauss: (1) the combination of the principles of restricted and generalized exchange would be the basis of Crow-Omaha systems ([1949] 1969:465); (2) many terminologies from New Guinea float typologically between "Hawaiian," "Iroquois," and "Omaha"; (3) there is in New Guinea what he called a "disharmony" between the nomenclatures and the marriage rules, there being "Omaha" systems with "Iroquois" preferences (with this he seems to mean cousin marriage) and "Iroquois" systems with "Omaha" prohibitions (1984a:205).

Although the model proposed by Gell implies marriage to Iroquois-cross *second* cousins, Gell (1975:70) states that the matrimonial prohibitions cover *all* first and second cousins, real or classificatory, which seems contradictory—but the transition between "children of cross cousins" and "unrelated" marriageable people is clearly possible (Gell 1975:62). Like Juillerat, however, Gell thinks genealogically in terms of third cousins, saying, for example, that the FFFZSSD and MMMBDDD (1975:69, 73) are possible spouses given the logic of the terminology, and that the first is a preferential wife in another Sepik group (Gnau). Note that these kin types are third cousins Dravidian-cross, not Iroquois-cross, but that they are merged with the marriageable second cousins in the "Type B" model of the Umeda. Still, Gell mentions that in a few Gnau villages the preferred marriage is one generation closer, with FFZSD, also a Dravidian-cross cousin. On the other hand, Juillerat (1986:304, fig. 34) shows an example of genealogical "closure" (*bouclage*) among the Iafar, where the spouses are *Iroquois-cross* third cousins.

These variations in the degree to which cousin marriage is permitted and in the type of crossness involved may be inherent in the "Type B" symmetric alliance. Tjon Sie Fat (personal communication), reporting an observation of Alain Testart, pointed out a curious phenomenon: the "concentric" or "multibilateral" scheme shown above is in fact compatible with *Iroquois*-cross second cousins but the *third* cousins who are merged with the second cousins under the spouse category are always *Dravidian*-cross. In effect, in the model MMBSD/FFZDD/MFZSD/FMBDD = FFFZSSD/MMMBDDD and so forth. The "Aranda-diametric" scheme, in turn, is consistently Dravidian-cross for any degree of cousinship.[55] Perhaps this generational peculiarity of Iroquois-crossness bears some relation to another characteristic of the Type B alliance systems, also emphasized by Tjon Sie Fat (1990:196–

200) for the case of the Bardi and the Ngawbe: the presence of optional marriages or free variants. Thus, Tjon Sie Fat reports Dravidian-cross marriages among the Bardi (e.g., MMBDD in place of MMBSD) entailing a two-generational ("Aranda") instead of three-generational cycle of restricted exchange. Among the Ngawbe, the preference for the FFZDD (Iroquois-cross), which implies a three-generational alliance cycle, coexists with the optional marriage to MMBDD (Dravidian-cross, period 2).

This instability of the Bardoid structures suggests a relatively indeterminate or underspecified model in which both Iroquois-cross and Dravidian-cross second cousins may be married (thus suggesting a matrimonially "Kuma-cross" structure). The diametric Aranda scheme appears as an "attractor" since it is the shortest bilateral formula if first cross cousins are forbidden; but the concentric or multibilateral Iroquois-cross type scheme guarantees, on the other hand, a complete dyachronic scanning of the matrimonial field: every group different from that of ego can be affinalized.[56]

I do not know to what extent this "Iroquois" alliance model is of any use in the classic North American cases of Type B crossness. But there are at least two meridional examples of matrimonial preference for Iroquois-cross second cousins: that of the aforementioned Ngawbe (Western Guaymí, a Chibchan group from Panama: Young 1970, 1971), and that of some Jivaroan subgroups of the Amazon (Taylor 1989; chapter 8 of this volume).

The Ngawbe have a basically "Type B variant 3" terminology: bifurcate merging in G^{+1}, generational in G^0 (all first cousins and some types of second cousins are siblings), and "Iroquois" in G^{-1}: children of same-sex "siblings" are "son/daughter," children of opposite-sex "siblings" are "nephew/niece." In G^{+2} and G^{-2} the classification occurs in only one type of relative per sex. But there are some sexual and generational asymmetries and some interesting self-reciprocal equations (Young 1971:140–48). Thus, FZ (= MBW) and FZH (≠ MB) are equated to kin of G^{+2}, and, reciprocally, $\male$BCh = $\female$ChCh (note that B = FZS = MBS), which lends a certain "Crow" inflection to the scheme. The terms of G^0 for "sibling" are repeated in G^{-3} from the point of view of a male ego; for female ego, owing to the equations above, repetition takes place in alternate generations. The terms of G^{+3} are the same as those for G^{+2}.[57]

Ngawbe preferential marriage is the direct exchange of sisters (or ZD) between virilocal cognatic kin groups; in principle, an individual cannot marry any member of his kindred (an egocentric category), that is, anyone classified as "sister" (*ngawe*) or "brother" (*edaba*). The genealogical extension of these categories is so defined by Young (1970:86):

The degree of extension varies in practice with genealogical knowledge, which in turn is governed to some extent by factors of residence and intensity of social interaction. All first cousins are always referred to as *edaba* and *ngwae*, parallel second cousins (FFBChCh and MMZChCh) are usually included, second cross-cousins are often excluded, and all third cousins are generally excluded.

Figure 15-8
Eight Types of Crossness

	0.				1.				2.				3. Ngawbe			
G^2	0	0	1	1	0	0	1	1	0	0	1	1	0	0	1	1
G^1	0	1	0	1	0	1	0	1	0	1	0	1	0	1	0	1
G^0	0	0	0	0	0	0	0	1	0	0	1	0	0	0	1	1

	4. Yafar				5. Iroquois				6. Dravidian				7. Kuma			
G^2	0	0	1	1	0	0	1	1	0	0	1	1	0	0	1	1
G^1	0	1	0	1	0	1	0	1	0	1	0	1	0	1	0	1
G^0	0	1	0	0	0	1	0	1	0	1	1	0	0	1	1	1

Young (1970:89) then presents an alliance model virtually identical to the "Type B alliance" scheme of the Bardi and Umeda, with four units bilaterally exchanging sisters according to a cycle of period 3: the spouses in Young's model are Iroquois-cross second cousins. The definition of the "parallel second cousins" and the "second cross cousins" above, however, does not characterize a standard calculus of Iroquois crossness. In truth, there is a *fifth* type of crossness calculus here. Young suggests that a principle of "symmetric filiation" is at work in the Ngawbe system, where the men transmit patrifiliation, the women matrifiliation. This system of "double filiation" is similar to the "double descent" schemes so often proposed for the Australian systems. But here this double filiation excludes the first cross cousins, for it applies to the sharing of (any type of) filiation between ego and the *parents* of alter: "If a woman shares filiation with either parent of a man, she may not marry him; and conversely, if a man shares filiation with either parent of a woman, he may not marry her" (Young 1970:92). As the author demonstrates, this rule puts the FFZDD (= MMBSD, etc.) *and* the MMBDD (= FFZSD, etc.) as potentially marriageable and therefore structurally "cross": the first is Type B cross, the second Type A. Thus, there is a possibility of both a "Bardoid" and an "Arandoid" structure. In turn, the children of opposite-sex parallel cousins (MMZSCh, FFBDCh, MFBSCh, FMZDCh), which are cross in the four types of calculi indicated above (Dravidian, Iroquois, Kuma, Iafar), would here be "parallel second cousins," and therefore unmarriageable "siblings."

The ethnographic record of a fifth type of crossness suggests the existence of yet other types within the general pattern of bifurcate merging terminologies (nonskewed and sexually symmetrical). The diagram in figure 15-8 is an adaptation of those used by Scheffler (1971:248) and Trautmann (1981:87) for the classification of second cousins in the Iroquois, Dravidian and Kuma types, including the Iafar and

Ngawbe types. The symbols "0" and "1" designate, respectively, the *relative sex* (0 = same, 1 = opposite) of two siblings in G^2 and of their children in G^1, and the *crossness* or *marriageability* (0 = parallel/consanguine, 1 = cross/affine) of the cousins in G^0. I have ordered the types in a series numbered by the decimal equivalent of each binary string of 0's and 1's in G^0 in figure 15-8.

There are sixteen naturally possible cases; the remaining eight (numbered *8* to *15*) are obtained by substituting the 0's for 1's in G^0 in the first column of each of the types shown above. I took the first eight cases to be most "basic," however, for I believe that the children of same-sex children of same-sex siblings (the first column in each type) tend to be parallel in the overwhelming majority of terminologies; but nothing prevents a configuration such as "1111" (*15*) from existing ethnographically. It is a case in which all second cousins are marriageable (and no first cousins are so, or only the first cross cousins are so, etc.). Consider, for example, a "Hawaiian" (or an "Iroquois variant 3") situation in which the assimilation of cousins to siblingship goes only as far as first cousins. This would represent a type of "super-Kuma" crossness. I did not look for ethnographic examples of the first three types in figure 15-8; the first (*0*) is trivial, which suggests matrimonial prohibition of all second cousins (terminologically, it would be a "super-Iafar"; but this seems to be the case among the Iafar themselves, from the matrimonial point of view). Note that the Ngawbe case is in a way the opposite of the Iroquois: whereas in the latter relative sex is only taken into account in G^1, "coinciding" with the crossness in G^0, in the Ngawbe case relative sex is only important in G^2. The 0's and 1's could be erased in G^2 for Iroquois (as it is for Trautmann), and in G^1 for Ngawbe.

The kinship system of the Jivaro-Candoa groups, as analyzed by Anne-Christine Taylor in chapter 8, consists of very simple transformations, motivated by different constraints of demographic, morphological, and ideological type, that connect classically Dravidian systems (Shuar, Achuar) with structures matrimonially analogous to the Type B alliance model (Aguaruna, Candoa).

The Achuar exemplify a common Amazonian configuration: a Dravidian A terminology without separate affinal terms but with highly productive social/genealogical distance classifiers; marriage between cognatically close bilateral cross cousins (with a patrilateral slant) expressing a kindred-based, endogamous alliance structure; and complex divergences between vocative and referential nomenclatures, expressing a sexually marked dynamics of affinization and consanguinization.

The Aguaruna leave the binarism of the Achuar for a ternary scheme in the central generations, distinguishing (some) "cross" from "affinal" cognates. Close (first) bilateral cross cousins, although seen as ideal spouses, rarely marry; marriage tends to take place between the children of FZS and MBD, that is, one generation later than among the Achuar. We can see how the *ideological* identification between "sister" and "female cross cousin" of the Achuar (marked by a single vocative term for both types of relatives) becomes in the Aguaruna case a *sociological* identification: the Aguaruna FZS/MBD pair "functions" like the Achuar B/Z pair; the alliance between the offspring of B and Z is shifted one generation. Because sister exchange is the norm, these children of FZS and MBD tend to be bilateral cousins, but now Iroquois-cross: the matrimonially preferred FMBDD would also be FFZDD =

MMBSD = MFZSD. Close cross cognates cease to be virtual affines while still serving as links in the establishment of an alliance relation that, as among the Achuar, connects individuals of the same sex—but here, instead of having ZH and WB immediately transmitting their tie to the next generation, we have MBDH and WFZS; the husband of a cross cousin is not a "brother," but a "brother-in-law." This accounts for the terminological ternarism and at the same time for the maintenance of the central opposition between consanguinity and affinity, which begins to be commanded by the logic of proximity and distance already present in the Achuar case where, however, it is still terminologically (though not sociologically) inert. Furthermore, the affinal *address* terminology of the Aguaruna "Dravidianizes" its "Iroquois" marriage scheme, for the SpF is called "MB," the ChSp are called "nephew/niece," and so forth.

The striking feature among the Candoa (Kandoshi and Shapra) is the concentric classification of the matrimonial field in terms of kinship distance. Kandoshi terminology deviates noticeably from any of the classic types: it has separate terms for affinity and distinguishes between lineal and collateral relatives (both features were mentioned earlier in the Aguaruna case). Marriage with "close kin" is forbidden; with "distant kin" it is barely accepted and therefore oriented to "nonrelatives"; the exchange of "sisters" (co-resident female relatives) is the preferential form of marriage, globally uniting the small and numerous local groups, which, in contrast to the Achuar and Aguaruna local groups, are exogamous. Apparently the system has no intrinsic determination of alliances, which would take place in random dispersion. But Taylor (see figure 8-7) records a three-generation cycle in which "close kin" become "distant kin" and then "unrelated people" with whom marriage, and therefore renovation of the alliance between local groups, is possible: this dynamic is strikingly similar to that suggested by Gell for the Umeda and by Young for the Ngawbe. Chapter 8 proposes a model compatible with the Kandoshi terminological scheme, which features the marriage between children of opposite-sex patrilateral cross cousins; but spouses tend to be, as in the Aguaruna case, bilateral Iroquois-cross second cousins: the matrimonially preferred FFZDD would also be a FMBSD = MMBSD = MFZSD. The proposed scheme (figure 8-8) can be interpreted as a representation that is both partial (it does not matrimonially connect all the elements) and developed (each sibling set of the diagram contains *two* opposite-sex pairs) of the "Type B" scheme discussed here. The diagrammatic resemblances bring to mind the famous figure 38 of *L'Exercice de la parenté* (Héritier 1981:113), with the Kandoshi case suggesting a cognatic version of that "semicomplex" patrilineal alliance system. Taylor (chapter 8) explicitly mentions the possibility of the Kandoshi system fitting the semicomplex type of Héritier (and see Gell on the Umeda system).

Taylor concludes with considerations very close to those advanced above (which were largely inspired by the discussion in chapter 8) on the necessity of not reducing the opposition between consanguinity and affinity to its genealogical interpretation in terms of "parallel" and "cross." She proposes a distinction between "formal crossness" and "sociological crossness" that attempts to rivet the "Type B" marriage structures to Dumont's model, but that appositely subordinates terminology to alliance (a move not orthodoxically Dumontian). If this distinction is pertinent—and I believe it is—and if the Aguaruna and Kandoshi are, as chapter 8 suggests, "rich" variants of the Dravidianate, then the Ngawbe, Umeda, Iafar, and Bardi cases can also be thought of as variants of the same type. More generally, Type B crossness and the "elementary" diagrams that illustrate its matrimonial interpretation can thus be seen as a variant of Type A where the consanguinity/affinity opposition is freed from its immediate genealogical support (the Dravidianate crossness calculus). In this variant—of which the Type A can be seen as a *reduction,* not as an *origin*—the dynamics of alliance not only does not have a "prescriptive" encoding in the terminology but also does not necessarily depend on a specific genealogical preference. It is the result of a global differentiation of the social field into zones (defined by cognation, but also by residential distance, group affiliation, generational level) created by the previous states of the matrimonial system itself. Remember, too, that the Kandoshi, Aguaruna, Umeda, Ngawbe, or Iafar do not categorically "prescribe" or specifically designate as ideal spouses those relatives identified in models proposed by their ethnographers as probable occupants of the zones of the social field to which the alliances are directed: they represent only those *particular* cases, and not necessarily privileged ones, in which the general structure of alliance—of marriage, *like* a relative—produces a genealogical closure by permitting marriage *with* a relative.

All in all, Buchler and Selby's (1968) distinction between Dravidian marriage as regulated by the "terminological code" and Iroquois marriage as regulated by "various social institutions" is not pertinent: in both cases, marriage is regulated by the terminology *and* by "various social institutions." Equally, the distinction made by these authors between "cognates/affines" (Dravidian) and "cross/parallel" kin (Iroquois) is misleading. If the close cross relatives of the Iroquois systems are not *immediate* affines, they are *intermediate* affines, being between consanguinity and affinity. Being nonmarriageable cognates, they are, however, terms of a future alliance relationship, projected one or more generations ahead. Dravidian and Iroquois, Type A and Type B, are, as Trautmann and Barnes conclude (chapter 2), two phases of the same structure.

CONCENTRIC DRAVIDIANATE

Earlier in this chapter, I criticized Kronenfeld for affirming that the Dravidianate system produces categories that are consistent across generations and that are consistent with moiety and lineage membership. Kronenfeld relies on this idea to contrast Dravidian as a sociocentric system with Iroquois as an egocentric system: "The Iroquois-type cross/parallel distinction . . . is egocentric in the sense that two relatives who are, respectively, cross and parallel, from ego's point of view, may be both cross or both parallel from the point of view of some other kinsman" (Kronenfeld 1989:93).

The problem, of course, is that Kronenfeld's argument also applies to $G^{\pm 1}$ in Dravidian. Take, for example, M and MB: they are parallel (M) and cross (MB) from ego's point of view, but they are both cross from the point of view of ego's F or FF, and both parallel from the point of view of MF and MM, and so forth. The contrast attempted by the author would apply much better to an opposition between *Australian* and Iroquois. In fact, this seems to indicate that the Dravidianate scheme is in a way between Australian and Iroquois: the first would be its sociocentric and diametric re(ct)ification, the second its egocentric and concentric radi(c)alization. It is perhaps possible to order Australian, Dravidian, and Iroquois in terms of the algebra defined by Tjon Sie Fat: the Australian model seems to show full associativity (or "Kay-crossness"), the Dravidian partial associativity ("Trautmann-crossness"), and the Iroquois would be still less associative ("Lounsbury-crossness"). Perhaps the series should be unfolded in this order: Australian; Dravidian model B; Dravidian model A; Iroquois variants 1, 2, 3, 4. We would then have a gradient of associativity and "sociocentricity" (which should not be seen as possessing any evolutionary implication, logically or historically).

If Dravidian and Australian coincide in the way they "extend" crossness in G^0 and in the presence of spouse-equation rules, only Dravidian terminology is exhaustively organized by the opposition consanguinity/affinity—which does not mean that MB and FZ are not affinal kin in the Australian type, for they obviously are (e.g., MB = WF). In the Australian case as well as in the Iroquois, but in different ways and for different reasons, the matrimonial opposition consanguines/affines does not coincide with the other oppositions at work: the genealogical one between parallel and cross (Iroquois) or the sociological one between "self" and "other" (Australian). On the other hand, the classification in $G^{\pm 2}$ of Dravidian model A seems to "prepare" the Iroquois pattern: for example, in Australian and Dravidian model B, FFZ (= MM) and MMB (= FF) are distinguished from FM and MF as designated and linking kin; in Dravidian model A, they are distinguished only as linking kin; and in Iroquois, they are completely identified (see Scheffler 1978:137–38). This transition is analogous to that between Dravidian, Iroquois variant 1, and Iroquois variant 3 for G^0: cross cousins are distinguished from siblings as designated and linking kin (D), only as designated kin (I-1), and as fully identified with one another (I-3). One can conceive, in fact, of another terminological state of the Dravidianate, where cross cousins (of one or both sexes) would be distinguished from siblings only as linking kin, not as designated kin: such is the case of other Amazonian systems besides the Achuar (on the Aparaí, Ye'cuana, and Pemon, see Rivière 1984:46–47). Furthermore, Dravidian and Iroquois, though they use different crossness calculi, structure their terminologies in an analogous way, that differs from the Australian case. The *content* of the opposition "parallel/cross" is the same in Dravidian and Australian (i.e., consanguinity/affinity), but its *form* is distinct (different reciprocal sets), whereas in Dravidian and Iroquois the form is the same (identical reciprocal sets), but the content is distinct (the contrasts consanguine/ affine and parallel/cross do not coincide). We would then have something more than a unidimensional associativity gradient—a structure with several combinatory possibilities between multiple dimensions.

The concentric character of the Type B alliance model has been mentioned several times in this discussion. As noted earlier, the Pitjanjara used the parameter of distance as a terminological and matrimonial classificatory device; and Anne-Christine Taylor pointed to the role of kinship distance gradient for the Jivaro-Candoa and observed the concentric organization of the alliance structure. This leads me to suggest a new transitional configuration between Dravidian and Iroquois, which I call "concentric Dravidianate." It is a structure in which the consanguine/affine opposition is not quantitatively and qualitatively balanced.

In Shapiro's analysis, the emphasis is on two modes of extension of the "two-section" terminologies. One is supposedly characteristic of the Australian systems. It divides all of ego's social universe equally according to the classes "lineal" and "affinal." The other mode is the most widespread in the non-Australian systems; in it, "the 'lineal' terms are applied only to a small group of close kin; the affinal set, by contrast, is used more widely—not in reference to another positive social unit but to the remainder of society at large, even to strangers" (Shapiro 1970:386).

Almost all of Shapiro's examples of this mode of classification are Amazonian. In contrast, the classic Dravidian cases are seen as approximating the Australian situation, that is, with the consanguineal terms "applied more widely, to an extent approaching, perhaps, half of the society." Here Shapiro mentions the South Indian castes studied by Dumont, which observe the principle "the affine of my affine is kin to me."

The reference to India is certainly correct with regard to the terminological structure as such, but I do not know if it applies so well to the empirical calculus of affinity.[58] Even in Australia, the case of the Pitjanjara (and even more clearly of the Pintupi described by F. Myers [1986]) demonstrates that kinship distance can be decisive for the determination of affinity. But Shapiro characterizes the Amazonian situation perfectly.

In contrast to Dumont's Indian paradigm, the central opposition of the Amazonian Dravidianate systems operates according to a concentric regime (not a diametric one), that is, potentially ternary (not binary), dominated by a topological metric of distance (not a typological algebra of crossness), organized by gradable contrariety (and not by universal and mutually exclusive contradictories), and marked by a hierarchical opposition between consanguinity and affinity (not by a "equistatutory" and "distinctive" opposition).[59]

The balanced and circularly infinite alternation between consanguines and affines of the classic scheme (Trautmann 1981:41–42) is distorted in the "concentric Dravidianate" by gradients of genealogical or sociopolitical distance as well as by a general attitude of "masking" affinity, in such a way that consanguinity accumulates in the center of the social field, while affinity tends to spread over the periphery. This applies as much to kinship attitudes as to terminological usage. Close cognates, whether parallel (consanguines) or cross (virtual affines), are attitudinally consanguinized. Real affines, when they are not close cognates, tend to be treated and called as if they were (see the Aguaruna case above). In turn, the relatives who are technically consanguineal (parallel through calculus A) but who are distant from the genealogical, residential, or political points of view—that is, who did not reaffirm their ties with ego through similar alliances (marrying cognates close to ego's affines)—are reclassified as potential affines. Distance pushes relatives into the sphere of unrelatedness, which is defined by affinity. And there is the reciprocal of this affinization of distant consanguines: a proliferation of terms of "coaffinity" that are distinct from terms of consanguinity, and that are conceptually ambiguous, oscillating between the attributes of "brother" and "brother-in-law." Thus, if a WZH or a MBDH are not close cognates, they will tend to be classified by positions of coaffinity, which can eventually drift to terminological or even matrimonial affinity: canonically Dravidian systems like that of the Piaroa make the WZH a "brother-in-law," when he is not a real brother (Overing Kaplan 1984:154–55 n. 27).

Many of the superficially "Iroquois" features of Amazonian Dravidianate systems are a result of this consaguinization process of the close cross cognates, as in those terminologies where cross cousins are assimilated to siblings or the ♂ZCh to children, but where the calculus remains Type A. As Taylor showed, however, it does not take much for a system of this type to take in its entirety a more characteristically Iroquois cast: this is the case of the Aguaruna, and perhaps of the Upper Xingu groups—among which the terminology is unequivocally "Type B variant 1" (sometimes variant 3) and marriage to cognatically close cross cousins is frowned upon (though it takes place with some frequency).[60] The ideological consanguinization of close kin and the ideological affinization of distant kin can give place to a matrimonial regime in which distance becomes a positive vector in the orientation of the alliance field. But this does not mean that close cross cognates are completely assimilated to parallel cognates; on the contrary—and the Upper Xingu is a good example—because they remain potential affines, that is, affines with whom marriage has *not* taken place, first cross cousins receive the values of ambiguity and ritual hostility normally (in systems with close cognatic endogamy) invested in the occupants of the periphery of the social and matrimonial field.

The dynamics of concentric Dravidianate is not explained simply by the universal phenomenon of the weakening of the sociological content of the kinship categories as these are applied in a purely deductive way to people distant from ego. What takes place is a structural *interference* between a binary grid and a continuous scale, in such a way that the latter modifies the logic of the former, implying that the major divide of the Dravidian grid does not have a *stable genealogical meaning* in this regime. In place of the checkerboard pattern of the classic "two-section" morphologies (Australian, Indian Dravidianate) the pattern here consists of concentric circles, with consanguines surrounded by progressively more affinal categories, until the extreme sector of the social system is reached, at which point the category of enemies emerges, although it continues to be thought of—ritually, politically, mythologically—as being determined by potential affinity, or more than that, as embodying the very essence of affinity. This produces a fracture in the Amazonian notion of affinity, which could be summarized by saying that terms are separated from their relations: on one side are affines without affinity; on the other, affinity without affines. On one side, actual affinity is attracted to consanguinity: through local endogamy, reiterated symmetric exchange, patrilateral and avuncular "short-cycle" alliances, prescriptive terminological fictions, teknonymy, the ideologies of cognation and of conjugal consubstantiation, and matrimonial preferences expressed in terms of genealogical proximity. Affinity is reduced to the affines. On the other side, potential affinity, fundamentally collective or generic, opens kinship up to the outer world: in myth and in escatology, in war and in funerary ritual, in the imaginary worlds of sex without affinity or of affinity without sex. Affinity becomes a pure relation, which articulates terms precisely not connected by marriage. The true affine is one with whom one does not exchange women, but other things: dead bodies and rituals, names and goods, souls and heads. The effective affine is its weakened version, impure and local, contaminated really or virtually by consanguinity; the potential affine is the global and archetypical affine.

Amazonian ethnology makes many references to the political, ritual, and cosmological value of affinity. This goes beyond the general Lévi-Straussian principle of alliance as a condition of society. But remember that Lévi-Strauss is an Americanist, and that one of his first works set out to show how "a certain kinship tie, the brother-in-law relationship, once possessed a meaning among many South American tribes far transcending a simple expression of relationship" (1943:398), thus inaugurating the long series of references to the strategic character of affinity, to its mediating role between the local and the global, kinship and politics, the interior and the exterior (Rivière 1969, 1984:79–80; [Overing] Kaplan 1975, 1984; Dreyfus 1977:380; Turner 1979, 1984; Taylor 1983:345–47; Albert 1985). I would say that this central role of affinity, its capacity to transcend "a simple expression of relationship"—that is, to transcend kinship as such—gives it an encompassing value in the Amazonian systems, analogous to the value that descent would have in other societies (or anthropological models) of the world: the value of a model for the *socius*, an "idiom" that articulates and subordinates kinship to the sociopolitical and cosmological planes. The fission alluded to above between effective and potential affinity is at the origin of a hierarchic opposition between affinity and consanguinity: on the local level (or the "domestic" level, as the Africanists would say), which is the level where kinship is operative in the majority of Amazonian systems, affinity is attracted and encompassed by consanguinity; on the global level, potential affinity encompasses and circumscribes kinship. It is this inversion in the respective positions of consanguinity and affinity when one moves from the local to the global level that characterizes the opposition between the two categories as hierarchic (Dumont 1986).[61]

In societies where filiation encompasses alliance on a global level, "descent" is the main sociocosmological category—whose relation with filiation in a genealogical sense, as is well known, can be quite tenuous. In societies where, as in most Amazonian cases, alliance encompasses filiation on this global level, the dominant sociocosmological idiom is affinity. Amazonian kinship categories are thus in a relationship analogous to that maintained by the Nuer concepts of *mar* and *buth* (Evans-Pritchard 1951): just as *mar* kinship includes agnatic and uterine kin, so Amazonian cognatic kinship includes consanguines and affines; and just as *buth* begins only when agnation loses the cognatic and genealogical support of the *mar,* gaining ever more power as a sociological idiom the less "local" it becomes, so potential affinity begins where affinity loses its effective support in marriage and/or in co-residence. And just as Lienhardt (1961:46) spoke of a "transcendental fatherhood" manifested in the Divinity of the Dinka, one can speak in Amazonia of a "transcendental affinity"—in some cases, in a sense identical to that of Lienhardt (Viveiros de Castro 1992).

COEXISTENCES AND TRANSITIONS

The preceding analysis suggests that the regime of many Amazonian kinship systems (and of similar ones in other parts of the world) develops the ego-centered perspective of the Dravidianate matrix to the point of quantitative and qualitative imbalance between affinity and consanguinity, categories that thus become radically local and intransitive. If we associate this with the frequent presence of terms of coaffinity, with varied neutralizations of the basic dichotomy in G^0, with separate terms of affinity (which create a ternarism between parallels/cross/affines), and with the genealogical fluctuation of the crossness calculus according to parameters of a geopolitical type, then it can be concluded that we have before us a sociological (and sometimes terminological) variant of the Dravidianate, intermediary between classic Dravidianate—which "tends" toward the sociocentric variant of the Australian systems—and Iroquois systems.

Note, too, that the typological differentiation of the Dravidian, Australian, and Iroquois schemes (and their numerous subvarieties) does not imply that such configurations cannot coexist in the same society, defining different terminological "modes" (in the musical sense) or different levels of classification of the social field. The isolated occurrence (as much as a nonspecialist can judge) of the Dravidian scheme in Australia—among the Kariera, of all people—can be a sign as much of an authentic "Dravidian model B" on that continent, as of ethnographers' tendency to confuse two terminological modes of Kariera kinship: one, Dravidian, founded on the common "parallelism" of F and M versus the common crossness of FZ and MB; the other, Normal Australian, founded on the common allocation of each B/Z pair involved in symmetric exchange with a specific section (F + FZ and M + MB being members of opposite sections). The existence of the Aluridja terminologies and the Bardi alliance model also suggests that Australia has "Type B," Iroquois-cross systems, and that it may be possible to "move" from the Normal Australian sociocentric type to the Iroquois egocentric type. The case of the Pintupi, excellently analyzed by Myers (1986:180–218), shows the complex coexistence of two systems of kin categorization: one "formal," of Aranda or Walbiri type, with the terms divided according to sections and subsections, and marriage with MMBDD permitted (although marriage in the section of the first cross cousins is an "acceptable second choice"); the other "pragmatic," of "Western Desert Aluridja" type, with a generational terminology in G^0, founded on co-residence and the reckoning of distance (marriage with "distant people"—Myers 1986:185) and on a concentric cognatic ordering of the social field. These two terminologies (or terminological modes) clash on many points, starting with its different nepotic terminologies (Myers 1986:184, 192, 198). In fact, the Pintupi system seems to combine "Walbiri," "Aluridja" (Iroquois), and "Dravidian" features. For example (Myers 1986:195–96), if a MMBS is a socially close relative, he is assimilated to the consanguineal category of "father," in the Dravidian style (and I say Dravidian and not "four-section Normal Australian" because this distance metric operates together with the nepotic terminology of Dravidian-Iroquois type); but if it is a socially and geo-graphically distant relative, he is classified in the affinal category of WMB (≠F, Aranda style). One of the ways in which the Pintupi administer this "classification struggle" is especially interesting: Myers's diagram (1986:192) indicates that dis-tant collateral relatives (e.g., cousins descending from distant FFZ and MMB) are classified in the Aranda way, whereas close collaterals and lineals are classified in the Dravidian way. First cross cousins are ambiguous, sometimes defined (and classified) as "like siblings," sometimes as "like spouses" (1986: 199, 201, 208–9).

Myers affirms that the adoption of the subsection system in the Western Desert is recent, and that such a system is obviously superimposed on a more basic ego-centric grid. In fact, as many ethnographers on the continent have maintained, the sections always seem to be regularizations superimposed onto egocentric termi-nologies—and this leads to the conclusion that the Normal Australian pattern is an innovation added to a landscape probably of Dravidian and/or Iroquois type. Con-trary to Dumont (who argues that the "global formula" must precede the "local formula") and contrary to Allen, whose global-tetradic system is ancestral to all others, everything leads to the conclusion that the Normal Australian pattern is, as Trautmann suggested (1981:237), a sociocentric transformation of a Dravidian-type configurations—but it is necessary to insist that this "sociocentering" is a real *struc-tural transformation* of the terminology, and not a mere labeling of Dravidian B covert superclasses (since the latter do not coincide with Australian sections). This further suggests, as many have said, that the sections inflect the terminology and serve as a useful language to describe the marriage system, but that these inflections and this language are not effectively operative for the alliance dynamics, which remain ordered by an egocentric coding of the social space, and therefore by a structure of Dravidianate type.

The coexistence of sociocentric terminological schemes of the "section" type and Dravidianate schemes can also be seen in Amazonia. The previously mentioned case of the Cuiva is a good example. From what I know of the remaining Guahibo peoples (who are concentrated geographically), their basic terminology is of Dravidian model A type (Metzger and Morey 1983; Queixalós 1983), with no trace of the strange self-reciprocal equations of the Cuiva. Apart from that, the Cuiva themselves have an equally Dravidian A terminological nucleus (Arcand 1977), which is applied to close or lineal relatives, with a nepotic terminology of the type F + M/Ch, FZ + MB/♂ZCh + ♀BCh, and distinct terms for each generational level. The self-reciprocal terms of the "rope" structure seem to be preferentially applied to *collaterals* (FB/BCh, MZ/ZCh, FFZ, MMB, MFB, etc.) that, in the Dravidian key, are assimilated to lineal kin of their respective generations.[62]

The case of the Panoan peoples of Western Amazonia also illustrates this phe-nomenon of coexistence between global and local formulas. Some Panoan groups have purely Dravidian A terminologies and show no signs of moieties or sections, like the Katukina (Lima, 1994:42–46). The Amahuaca (Dole 1979), also without sections or moieties, combine a "concentric Dravidian" terminology with some Type

B equations (FMBD/FFZD = FZ) and a tendency to use sibling terms for cross cousins, but they also feature self-reciprocal equations of the Australian *or* Dravidian B *or* Cuiva type (♂F = S, ♀FZ = BCh, ♂ZS = F, ♂ZD = FZ).

The Matis (Erikson 1990:I, 110–46; II:415–31) have neither moieties nor named sections, but use a terminology almost purely Normal Australian in its reciprocal equations—in fact, like many other Panoan terminologies, it is even "purer" than the Australian terminological scheme, for all the kinship terms are self-reciprocal between alternate generations. This Australianoid terminology of the Matis derives, as in the case of the other Panoans who possess it, directly from the rules governing the transmission of names (FF = MMB ♀ SS, MM = FFZ ♀ DD); it is used above all in the *vocative* mode. In the *reference* terminology, there is a coexistence between Australian equations and a Dravidian nucleus: ChCh are distinguished from ♂BChCh (≠ ♂ZChCh) and from ♀ZChCh (≠ ♀BChCh); F and M use the same term for Ch, which is distinct from the self-reciprocal term for ♂BCh (= ♀BCh = FB + FZ) and for ♂ZCh (= ♀ZCh = MB + MZ). In other words, in a way analogous to the Cuiva and Pintupi cases, the *lineal* relatives are classified in Dravidian A style (with the exception of G^{+2}, which is always divided in the Dravidian B or Australian way), the *collaterals* in the Australian style. Also, classifiers of kinship distance or "intensity" are omnipresent and fundamental in the Matis case, as in all Panoan systems. Erikson (1990:I, 125) suggests that its eventual dominance can explain the existence of "Hawaiian" (more likely Type B variant 4) systems among some Panoans, as is the case of the Shipibo and Conibo.

The Cashinahua (Kensinger 1984b, 1991) have two moieties and four named sections: the sections are the sociocentric crystallization of the "namesake groups" created by the onomastic rule; the moieties are its patrilineal alignment. The Cashinahua *vocative* terminology is classically Australian and self-reciprocal, but the nepotic *reference* terminology is Dravidian, for the lineal relatives as well as for the collaterals: F(B) + M(Z) / ♂(B)Ch = ♀(Z)Ch; MB + FZ / ♀ZCh = ♀BCh [= ChSp]. The Marubo are divided into at least eleven matrilineal pairs of named ex-ogamous sections (Melatti 1977); they also present an Australian terminology associated to a Dravidian nucleus (F + M / Ch).

Finally, Townsley (1988) describes the Yaminahua as having three different structures of social classification: one, Dravidian, founded on a cognatic and concentric perception of the social field and on a logic of bodily reproduction, and manifested in the *reference* terminology for *lineals;* one, Australian, of diametric type, based on the onomastic reproduction between alternate generations, which configures nonnamed sections and is manifested in the *vocative* terminology; and one, dual, founded on a partition of the cosmos into named patrilineal moieties that transmit the spiritual aspect of the person.

Furthermore, many (though not all) Panoan terminologies exhibit more or less complete series of specific affinal designations: Katukina (Lima 1994:44–45); Sharanahua (Siskind 1973:79–80); Cashinahua (McCallum 1989:122, 127); Yaminahua (Calavia 1995:62–64); Marubo (Melatti 1977:101).[63]

If the examples above show the coexistence of Dravidian and Australian patterns, other South American cases present different combinations. The kinship systems of the Túpi-Guarani peoples were analyzed by Fausto (1991; see Viveiros de Castro and Fausto 1993) as divided into three basic types: (1) "Iroquois variant 3" configurations—bifurcated terminology in $G^{\pm1}$, generational in G^0, with marriage between distant "siblings," genealogically "cross" *or* "parallel" (Tapirapé, Tenetehara, Kaiowá);[64] (2) Dravidian A terminologies, with or without separate affinal terms (Wayãpi, Kagwahiv, Ka'apor, Kayabi, Asurini); and (3) terminologies marked by avuncular marriage equations (Parakanã, Tupinambá, ancient Guarani, Suruí). Note that some of the societies featuring Iroquois terminologies and distant marriage are numerically small, and that among those with avuncular marriage are the numerous and powerful Tupinambá and Guarani of the sixteenth century. The matrimonial regime of the Tupinambá was "hypo-Dravidian," which casts doubt on simple correlations between, Dravidianate terminologies, close endogamous marriage and small marginal societies, on one hand, and Iroquois terminologies, marriage with distant relatives, and demographically and economically affluent societies, on the other (Hornborg 1986/1988; Henley n.d.).

The Parakanã kinship system—the only avuncular case among the Túpi-Guarani that was studied in depth (Fausto 1991)—shows the coexistence between a marriage rule with the ZD (= MBD) and a marriage option frequently exercised with the FZD; it is common for a man to renounce his right over the ZD in favor of his own son.[65] This possibility is not, however, totally consistent with the genealogical or terminological identities of a pure avuncular pattern (FZ = MM, FZCh = MB + M, etc.). The Parakanã terminology avoids the assimilation of all female patrilateral cousins to the category of "M" (or rather, "MZ") by resorting to the criterion of relative seniority: cross cousins (patri- *and* matrilateral) older than ego are assimilated to mother's siblings, whereas the younger are identified with sister's children. As Fausto demonstrated, the system is in fact the result of the coexistence of two distinct structures, one "horizontal-Dravidian," the other "oblique-avuncular," which produces some complex effects: the nonequivalence between same-sex siblings (M ≠ MZ = e(FZD), MM ≠MMZ = FZ); the consequent appearance of a distinction between lineal relatives, classified in the Dravidian way, and collateral relatives, classified in the avuncular way—the same phenomenon described earlier for the Australian-Dravidian combination among the Panoans—and a distinction between the male and female terminological calculi.

The most important point, however, is that all Túpi-Guarani terminologies, as Fausto argued, are bifurcate-merging in $G^{\pm1}$, but *none* of them has *specific* terms for the cross cousins. In the case of the "Type B variant 3" examples, they are assimilated to siblings; in the avuncular cases, they are projected onto $G^{\pm1}$. And in the classic Dravidian cases, the terms for the cross cousins are words that mean "nonrelative," "potential affine," "enemy"—and this in the terminologies that do *not* have separate terms of affinity as well as in those that do. This suggests a general instability of the position of the cross cousins in the Túpi-Guarani systems, a sort of "0-value" that is filled differently in each of the three basic patterns.

Fausto's analysis suggested to me an ethnographic and theoretical generalization whose pertinence is yet to be tested. From the ethnographic point of view, it is possible that the "Iroquois variant 3" terminologies, or Dravidian A with generational neutralization in G^0, so widespread in Lowland South America (apart from the cases already mentioned, see the Kadiweu, Kiriri, Shipibo, Yaruro, and Warao, to take examples from different linguistic families), as well as the skewed terminologies of Central Brazil, normally classified in the "Crow-Omaha" typological family, are manifesting the same instability and the same terminological vacuum that marks the position of the cross cousins among the Túpi-Guarani. The "concentric Dravidianate" pattern would have as one of its properties precisely the liminal position of cross cousins, sometimes attracted by the consanguinity of siblings, sometimes repelled to the affinity of outsiders.

The connection with the terminologies of Central Brazil (normally associated with a matrimonial regime that forbids cousin marriage—but the ethnographies record a number of cases of patrilateral matrimonial preference) is not absurd. The transition between Amazonian-avuncular and "semicomplex" regimes of the Central Brazilian type may be much shorter than was imagined. First, the terminology of the famous Sirionó (Túpi-Guarani of Bolivia), where the FZD is matrimonially forbidden (classified in the "Crow" way as FZD = FZ = FM) and the MBD category is the prescribed one (MBD ≠ ZD, and this last one is also a forbidden relative), can be interpreted as a transformation of the avuncular marriage pattern characteristic of the Túpi-Guarani, especially since the data on the Yuqui, culturally very close to the Sirionó (Stearman 1989), reveal a clear avuncular preference. Note that the Sirionó pseudo-Crow terminology and matrilateral norm are almost identical to what Menget (1977b) found among the Txicáo, a Carib group of the Middle Xingu with strong overall similarities to Central Brazilian societies (Gé and Bororo). But, in the Txicáo case, the patrilateral cousins oscillate between a Sirionó-like classification and a Parakanã one (either FZD = FZ = FM, or FZD = MBD = W). Furthermore, the Txicáo permit the union between classificatory MB and ZD; the Caribs, along with the Túpian groups, are the classic representatives of avuncular marriage in Amazonia (the Trio, Guianese Caribs, present the same hybrid "horizontal-avuncular" structure of the Parakanã—Rivière 1969); and the Arara, immediate relatives of the Txicáo (Pinto 1989), have an avuncular-conjugal terminology and practice this form of union. Second, most of the Central Brazilian terminologies present two interesting peculiarities inside a general "Crow-Omaha" pattern. First, the skewed equations of cross cousins vary from group to group, sometimes producing "Crow," sometimes "Omaha" schemes—and within the *same* society, there may be cousin classifications of "Crow" *or* "Omaha" type (da Matta 1979; Ladeira 1982).[66] Second, there are symmetries that diverge notably from the unilateral skewing of the classic types: the systems of the Northern Gé assimilate *both* FZ and MB to the grandparents, and reciprocally, both ♂ZCh and ♀BCh are assimilated to grandchildren; this is neither Crow nor Omaha, but it is what is done by the Sirionó, Túpi-Mondé, the Yanomam, and other Amazonian groups, in particular those that have an avuncular matrimonial preference.

The theoretical generalization with which I close this discussion concerns the possibility of thinking of this 0-value of the cross cousins as characterizing one of those "less iconic" models I referred to at the outset. Next to a *genealogically* underspecified Dravidianate, in which the consanguinity/affinity opposition operates independently of the parallel/cross one—and therefore Type A schemes as well as Type B can be associated with a structure of bilateral alliance—one can imagine a *terminologically* underspecified Dravidianate, in which the position of cross kin in G^0 is a sort of "empty case" differentially filled in each particular configuration: sometimes in the canonical "Australian" or "Dravidian" semidiametric way; sometimes in the "concentric Dravidianate" way (with its bifurcate or generational variants in G^0); sometimes in the "Iroquois" way, in its several variants; sometimes in the avuncular way; and finally, sometimes through oblique cousin equations of the "Crow" and "Omaha" types. What remains stable and therefore defines the structural law of this model is the presence of a *nonneutralizable opposition* in G^{+1}: the opposition between consanguines and affines resulting from the symmetric exchange that has taken place in the generation immediately anterior to that of ego, and that commands the transmission of alliance in the subsequent generations.

It remains to be seen how far this idea can take us. One of its possible developments would lead to the reformulation of the typology that orders alliance systems in terms of "elementarity," "semicomplexity," and "complexity" (Viveiros de Castro 1990, 1993b). The two generalized models of the Dravidianate scheme—the metagenealogical generalization of A.-C. Taylor and the metaterminological one proposed here—imply that the notions of "elementary," "complex," and "semicomplex" do not mark an essential difference between types of systems, but of *regimes* or *modes* of alliance structures exhaustively described by the three elementary formulas of *The Elementary Structures,* or by their mathematical generalization achieved by Tjon Sie Fat (1990). The phenomenon of the greater or lesser "complexity" of an alliance system would thus be associated to the greater or lesser possibility of modeling it according to the postulates of the elementary schema: the structural identity (and hence the diagrammatic reduction) or nonidentity between same-sex siblings from the terminological and matrimonial points of view; the linear or nonlinear passage between local and global models of the alliance system;[66] the direct or indirect-only genealogical interpretation of the terminological discriminations; the determinate or indeterminate relation between the pattern of alliance replication and the genealogical closure of the matrimonial networks.

NOTES

1. Although this chapter derives from my research on Amazonian kinship systems and provides some examples taken from that region, it concentrates on more general problems—and here I apologize to the specialists for my reference to other ethnographic areas. I tried not to repeat what I have published elsewhere (see Viveiros de Castro 1993a; and Viveiros de Castro and Fausto 1993), considering that the present volume includes several substantial articles on South America. The present piece was written after the Maison Suger conference, but it originated in the discussions there and the reading of the original versions of many papers published here. Thus the occasional criticisms of other chapters in this volume are the effect of the inestimable stimulus to reflection they provided, and of my inevitably unfair advantage of being a late contributor. I thank Thomas Trautmann, Maurice Godelier, Franklin Tjon Sie Fat, Michael Houseman, and Carlos Fausto for the long discussions held

Figure 15-9
Location of Local Groups in South America

1. Ngawbe (Chibchan)
2. U'wa (Chibchan)
3. Cuiva (Guahibo)
4. Guahibo (Guahibo)
5. Yaruro (isolated)
6. Piaroa (Sáliva)
7. Panare (Carib)
8. Ye'cuana (Carib)
9. Yanomam (Yonomami)
10. Pemon (Carib)
11. Wapishana (Arawak)
12. Warao (isolated)
13. Trio (Carib)
14. Aparaí (Carib)
15. Wayâpi (Tupian)
16. Waimiri-Atroari (Carib)
17. Tukanoan groups
    (E. Tukanoan)
18. Achuar (Jivaro)

19. Shuar (Jivaro)
20. Aguaruna (Jivaro)
21. Kandoshi, Shapra (Candoa)
22. Matis (Panoan)
23. Marubo (Panoan)
24. Katukina (Panoan)
25. Yaminahua (Panoan)
26. Cashinahua (Panoan)
27. Sharanahua (Panoan)
28. Shipibo-Conibo (Panoan)
29. Amahuaca (Panoan)
30. Tupi-Mondé groups
    (Tupian)
31. Kagwahiv (Tupian)
32. Bakairi (Carib)
33. Mahinaku (Arawak)
34. Kuikuru (Carib)
35. Txicâo (Carib)
36. Kayabi (Tupian)

37. Kayapó (Ge)
38. Arara (Carib)
39. Parakanâ (Tupian)
40. Araweté (Tupian)
41. Asuriní (Tupian)
42. Tapirapé (Tupian)
43. Surauí (Tupian)
44. Tenetehara (Tupian)
45. Ka'apor (Tupian)
46. Krahó (Ge)
47. Apinayé (Ge)
48. Bororo (Bororo)
49. Siriono (Tupian)
50. Yuquí (Tupian)
51. Kadiweu (Guaykuru)
52. Kaiowá-Guarani (Tupian)
53. Guarani (Tupian)
54. Tupinambá (Tupian)
55. Kiriri (Kairiri)

Figure 15-10
Location of Tribal Groups in Australia

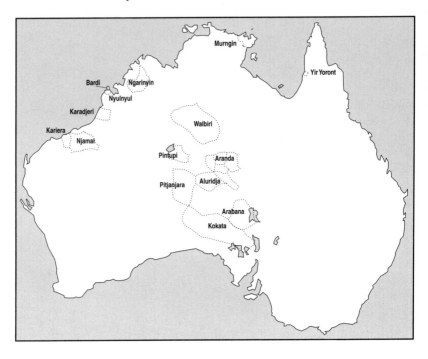

since the Suger meeting: their criticisms and suggestions contributed decisively to this chapter.

2. Being a South Americanist, I am rather tempted to choose more appropriate eponyms from my own continent: perhaps it would be better to change "Dravidian" to "Normal Amazonian," "Iroquois" to "Upper Xingu," and "Kariera" to "Cashinahua."

3. Lévi-Strauss (1984a:179) refers to a distinction of Leach's between "real behaviour, statistical norms and ideal rules" and an analogous scheme of Firth's, which derive, as do the previously mentioned distinctions of Schneider and Needham, from the classical Malinowskian distinction between "what people say about what they do, what they actually do, and what they think" (Kuper 1983:16).

4. Analysis of terminologies in terms of their functions in the interior of alliance systems does not of course preclude formalization in terms of equivalence rules; nor does it exclude the unraveling of its correlations with other dimensions of specific social realities: production relations, residential arrangements, developmental cycle of the domestic units, group incorporation, ideologies, and so on. But, between the reduction of terminologies to sociologically meaningless taxonomic principles (which makes comparison trivial) and its interpretation in culturally particularistic terms (which makes comparison impossible)— between an excessive extension and an excessive intention—there is enough space for an analysis in which form and meaning, logic and sociology, are apprehended in their mutual implication.

5. This is based on arguments virtually identical to those presented by Lounsbury in "the most famous footnote in anthropology" (see chapter 2 of this volume). Gertrude Dole (1957:164–

Figure 15-11
Location of Tribal Groups in Western Melanesia, New Guinea

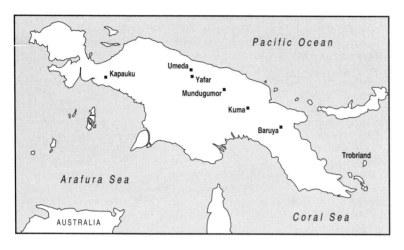

65, 178–79) opposes the "bifurcate merging kinship nomenclature" (Iroquois) to the type she calls, following Hocart, "Cross-Cousin nomenclature" (Dravidian). She thanks R. Carneiro for calling her attention to the difference between the types. It is not possible to know whether Carneiro and Dole knew of Lounsbury's paper, which though published only in 1964, had an earlier version publicly presented in 1956.

6. Lévi-Strauss, however, acknowledging an observation by Rivers, according to which there would be in Melanesia a complementary distribution between cross-cousin marriage and moiety systems, introduced the distinction between the "method of relationships" and the "method of classes." Bilateral cross-cousin marriage (method of relationships) is defined in *The Elementary Structures of Kinship* as a "procedure" or "tendency," in contrast to the "global formula" of dual organizations ([1949] 1969:101–3). But as dual organizations (method of classes) codify the same principle of restricted exchange present in cousin marriage (method of relationships), the local and global solutions are seen as interchangeable—and this leads Lévi-Strauss to concentrate on the "precision and clarity" ([1949] 1969:461) of the Australian "classes."

7. See, for instance, Buchler and Selby (1968:238), who illustrate Dravidian crossness by "two Dravidian-type systems: Kariera and Njamal."

8. This difference was soon generalized by the author in his critique of *The Elementary Structures of Kinship* (Dumont 1971).

9. In his 1957 article (see 1983a:36–104), Dumont still flirted with the question of double descent in India.

10. See Trautmann 1981:88–89, 175–76, 188–200, 235–37. Good (1980:479; 1981:115) and Tyler (1984:99), among others, also registered this problem for Dumont's theory.

11. Though he does not go so far as to state it, Trautmann seems to conceive the Proto-Dravidian system as having the bipartition in $G^{\pm2}$ (1981:232, 235–37). The same way Trautmann and Barnes (chapter 2) consider the "Iroquois variant 3" type as more coherent than the classic variant—for it assimilates cross cousins to siblings not only as linking kin, but as designated kin—so would model B in *Dravidian Kinship* be seen as somehow more logical than the Tamil variant, for it extends the fundamental contrast to all generations. We would thus obtain a maximum distancing between Dravidian (the strong version of which is

"model B") and Iroquois (the strong version of which is "variant 3"), and a minimum distancing between Dravidian and Kariera.

12. This same point was made by Goodenough (1970:133) about the Kariera vocabulary: "The terms for 'son' and 'daughter,' which are the same for male and female ego, cut across section and moiety lines."

13. In a further publication, Shapiro (1979:48–50) corrects himself and distinguishes the Kariera proper, as having F + M/Ch and so forth, from the common Australian pattern. I thank Michael Houseman for this piece of information.

14. This similarity derives from the classificatory principle Houseman and White (chapter 9) dub "egocentric crossness," shared by Dravidian and Iroquois.

15. Dravidian systems do not have two "lines" even in the purely terminological sense of "descent line" adopted by Radcliffe-Brown (Scheffler 1978:43–51). If the descent lines, as Leach ([1951] 1961:57) remarked, "are merely a diagrammatic device for displaying the categories of the kinship system in relation to a central individual [and] the number of basic descent lines in such a diagram depend merely upon how many different kinds of relatives are recognized in the grandfather's generation," then the Dravidian A scheme would be a "one-line system," for it only recognizes one type of relative (per sex) in G^{+2}.

16. The terms for G^{-1} are independent of ego's sex: $\male(B)Ch = \female BCh \neq \male ZCh = \female(Z)Ch$. Hereafter I will be using, except when explicitly indicated, "F" as including the positions of F and FB, "M" for M and MZ—I assume the same-sex sibling merging rule, that is, the structural identity between same-sex siblings characteristic of the "elementary" models (Lorrain 1975:127–29; Tjon Sie Fat 1990:40). The difference between the reciprocal sets in $G^{\pm1}$ can be visualized in the schemes below, where "a" and "b" stand for the terms used by the members of the ascending generation for those of the descending.

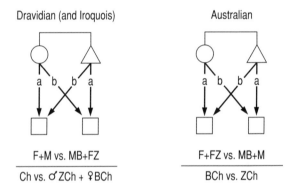

Dravidian (and Iroquois)   Australian

F+M vs. MB+FZ   F+FZ vs. MB+M
Ch vs. ♂ZCh + ♀BCh   BCh vs. ZCh

17. The author does not discuss the problem of the "ethnographic" Kariera with regard to the nepotic classification, which is even more curious given that he had already insisted, for the same reasons as Shapiro, on the impossibility of explaining Dravidian terminologies through "the moiety or two-section system hypothesis" (Scheffler 1971:233).

18. It is a very common variant in North America (once called "Cheyenne type") and in South America (once called, somewhat inappropriately, "Túpian type").

19. On this basis, Scheffler proposes two superclasses in G^{+1}: "father" (F + MB) and "mother" (M + FZ). This could suggest the third possible type of symmetric nepotic terminology with only two categories (see Trautmann 1981:176–77, for the three cases).

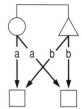

Here the reciprocal sets would be F + MB / ♂Ch + ♀ZCh and M + FZ / ♀Ch + ♀BCh. This is *not* exactly the Pitjanjara case, where, as I said, F and M use the same term for Ch (MB and FZ use the same terms equally for G⁻¹ kin: either "♂ZCh = ♀BCh," or simply "Ch"). But this could be the case of a "Hawaiian" terminology where the speaker's absolute sex would distinguish the terms for Alter in G⁻¹.

20. Scheffler (1978:113–18) compares the Pitjanjara type to the Iroquois but concludes that the similarities are superficial; because the latter has distinct cross-cousin categories, it would not make MB and FZ subclasses of "F" and "M," respectively. Considering, however, Trautmann and Barnes's "variant 3," it seems that the similarity between the types is perfectly admissible.

21. Even Scheffler, who in *Australian Kin Classification* devotes dozens of pages to denying any matrimonial correlate for Australian terminologies, has to admit that "the structures of section and subsection systems are consistent with the ways in which marriage is regulated (by kinship), and marriage appears to be regulated by such principles even though it is not" (1978:473).

22. Take, for example, the kin type ♂FFZSDD: it is a Dravidian-parallel relative ("D") and Iroquois-cross ("ZD"), independent of any descent rule; in Kay's method, she will be "cross" in a matrilineal context, "parallel" in a patrilineal context. In an "Australian" terminology, this relative will be, as in Dravidian, a "D"; if we have patrilineal moieties, she belongs to ego's moiety, if matrilineal moieties, to the opposite moiety—which has nothing to do with "parallel/cross," but with "same moiety/other moiety." It must be noted that the four-section Australian scheme is independent of the presence of moieties (Scheffler 1978:434, 446): the classification of relatives in each section and therefore the reciprocal sets are exactly the same if we have patrilineal or matrilineal moieties, or none; it is merely the "alignment" of the consecutive sections that would change (instead of FF—FB—B—BCh—SCh, etc., for the "patrilineal" case we would have FF—MB—B—ZCh—SCh, etc., in the matrilineal case).

23. Kronenfeld (1989:101 n. 5) rids himself of Scheffler's objection (1971:233) to the derivation of Dravidian terminologies from the moiety or two-section hypothesis saying that, even in a system of moieties, "cognitive ease considerations" would explain why F and M classify their joint offspring by the same terms: "a terminology can be 'consistent with' . . . a moiety system . . . without necessarily having to be an exact replica of it. The cross sex parent can 'know' that his or her 'children' are of the opposite ('they') group." It so happens, however, that these cognitive ease considerations do not explain why both cross-sex siblings of the parents classify their opposite-sex siblings' children jointly. Let us add, finally, that there are terminologies really "consistent with" a moiety system, that is, where F and M do *not* classify their joint offspring by the same term.

24. Misunderstandings concerning the Dravidian configuration have a tendency to proliferate in the literature. The well-known error of Buchler and Selby (1968:135) so castigated by Needham (1971:c–ci) reappears in *L'Exercice de la parenté* (Héritier 1981:176), charged with an extra imprecision. Thus, according to Héritier (she is referring to the Indian

Dravidianate), Dravidian systems "associate an Iroquois terminology and patriliny . . . with preferential matrilateral cross cousin marriage." Just to set the record straight: Dravidian terminologies do not belong to the Iroquois type; they are not necessarily associated with patriliny (in South India they are present in patrilineal *or matrilineal* societies, in Sri Lanka in *cognatic* societies); they are associated with "prescriptive" *bilateral* cross-cousin marriage, and with "preferential" matrilateral *or patrilateral* cross-cousin marriage (see Dumont [1957] 1983:36–104).

25. See Good (1980:479): "Though committed to the view that kinship terminologies are not directly related to the structures of social groups, Dumont nonetheless treats 'kinship' and 'affinity' as though they were attributes of groups rather than as merely Ego-centered modes of classification. Otherwise, how could he describe these attributes as having diachronic dimensions?" But on the same page the author argues in favor of his own diagram (where F + FZ is opposed to M + MB), saying that this would express better than Dumont's diagram the diachronic dimension of alliance, the very idea that he criticizes.

26. The debate over the universality of the principle of uniform reciprocals has no bearing on the present problem. It is curious to note that the excellent textbook of Barnard and Good (1984:49–53, 56) insists on the establishment of the reciprocal sets but at the same time presents a Dravidian box-type diagram in which they are violated (see also Good 1980:478, who takes Dumont to task for treating "the kinship terms in isolation from their reciprocals"). In the "small selection of layouts from the literature" presented by Allen (chapter 14) from the point of view of a male ego, the diagram of Barnard and Good shows a "patrilineal" situation (F + FZ / S + D, M + MB / ZD + ZS). Only those of Dumont, Trautmann, Campbell, and McDougal do not admit unilineal interpretations, from arbitrary arrangements. Allen does not see the problem of the reciprocals as a serious one: "In talking of the +1 level, some analysts (e.g. Trautmann) would prefer to reserve the term 'cross' for PosSb (*incidentally* [italics added] the reciprocal of ossSbCh)." Indeed.

27. I make this mistake elsewhere (Viveiros de Castro 1994:185).

28. What Dumont has in mind here are the different unilateral marriage preferences due to the weight of unilineal institutions: matrilateral marriage in the patrilineal groups, patrilateral in the matrilineal, with modulations dependent on the residence rule. MB is the main ally in the first case because F is the main consanguine, being the relative who transmits descent, and the same for FZ versus M (not FZH versus F, it should be noted) in the second case.

29. The same reasoning is repeated for the case of the "matrilineal" opposition M versus FZ: "The kin group arising here will be formed of a generation of female siblings, the mothers (opposed to their female affines), and of the generation of their children of both sexes" (Dumont 1983a:13; see diagram on the same page).

30. Some of my own previous work included.

31. There is a translation problem on which Dumont insisted (1971), but which he perpetuated, almost always writing "kin" in the English versions of his works, where in French he writes "consanguins" or "consanguinité." Trautmann, who criticizes the Dumontian choice of "kin" to designate "parallel" relatives (" 'consanguine' would have been a happier choice"— 1981:173), sometimes also uses the word "consanguine" with the meaning of "blood relative" (1981:24).

32. One of the points of my critique of Héritier (Viveiros de Castro 1990, 1993b, 1994) concerns precisely the nonadhesion, by the author of *L'Exercice de la parenté*, to this rule that she herself has stated. Héritier introduces considerations of genealogical closure (*bouclage*) of the marriage systems where the parameter of alliance replication (*redoublement*) should be "the only relevant consideration." I am not sure I am prepared to go as far as Houseman and White (chapter 9) in saying that the elementary models of alliance are "implicitly founded upon an analytical reduction to a prototypical configuration of marriage between close kin" and hence are "fundamentally misleading," but I agree with them entirely when they condemn the "largely inappropriate emphasis on consanguineal unions" that marks kinship

models in general. Though starting from quite different premises, I believe that the "less iconic models" I propose and the "network model" built by Houseman and White converge in a few respects, minimally in the refusal to opt between "autonomist" or "reflectionist" conceptions of the terminologies, and in the definition of the genealogical closure of concrete kinship systems as being a property structurally derived from the dynamics of the replication of alliances (see also Houseman and White 1995).

33. Note that in Dravidian A systems with avuncular marriage, or in those Dravidian B systems with marriage between MF and DD, the automatic allocation of opposite-sex relatives to categories of affinity and consanguinity is problematic: a man's sister or daughter can be a WM, a woman's brother or father can be a DH. More generally, in systems with avuncular marriage, only the relations *between* men are unequivocally either consanguineal or affinal (a FZD, for example, is genealogically or terminologically assimilated to an "M" or "MZ" by male *and* female ego). This "masculinization" of affinity in the avuncular systems is analyzed by Fausto (1991) for the Amazonian Parakanã; see also Houseman and White (chapter 9) on the "virisidedness" of systems with avuncular marriage.

34. If I understand Dumont correctly, the notion of "matrimonial exchange" would properly apply only to systems with global intermarriage formulas; Dumont interprets it as a morphological device of segmentary integration. The notion of "marriage alliance" is applicable more generally to every system with a "positive marriage rule" (prescriptive terminology), and appears as a device of "mental integration," that is, of replication of analytically (tautologically) defined conceptual oppositions.

35. In the following three box-type diagrams (figures 15-4, 15-5, 15-6), I use the symbols "FB," "MZ," BS," "BD," and so forth to indicate that we are dealing with classificatory positions that cover lineal and collateral kin, as well as to emphasize the distinction between classifications for which ego's relative sex is a parameter (Dravidian "♂BCh," "♀BCh," etc.) and those for which it is not (Australian "BCh," "ZCh," etc.).

36. Trautmann (1981:233) notes that no Central Dravidian terminology of his sample contains such simple equivalences. But Tyler (1984) proposes a Proto-Central Dravidian model with self-reciprocals in all alternate generations.

37. The diagrams of self-reciprocals in the alternate generations of Tyler's Proto-Central Dravidian (1984:97–98) do not allow one to clearly discern if the equations $G^{+1} = G^{-1}$ are of Dravidian or Australian type. But if they make FZ = ♂D, M = ♂ZD, then they are of the Australian type, which cannot be reduced to the "parallel/cross" opposition in the standard Dravidian sense.

38. See, for all this, Trautmann 1981:190–91. The problem of the Western Panare evoked above seems to be that they formulate their rule ("marriage with the child of a *wa'nene*") according to Trautmann's rule 9.3A, but its terminological calculus is of type 9.3B.

39. Cuiva marriage seems to take place only with members of the same generation (terminological or genealogical?)—Arcand (1977:25). In any case, note that the Western Panare inconsistency between terminology and marriage rule does not hold here: a man can marry his ZDD = SD, for she is in the same terminological class as his FZD/MBD. It is as if the Panare used a Dravidian B terminology and a Cuiva marriage rule.

40. See Lévi-Strauss (1966:18) on matrilateral versus Crow-Omaha systems; see also Schneider's version (1965:59), featuring apples and eggs instead of fish and whales, regarding the concept of "marriage" in the "segmental" and "segmentary" kinship paradigms.

41. But the presence of separate affinal terms only characterizes "virtually all" Iroquois systems (Buchler and Selby 1968:233); see also Buchler (1967:23): "presque tous les systèmes iroquois." These qualifications are important, as we shall see. Buchler and Selby (1968:233) choose most unfortunately when they use the positions of H and W to illustrate the absence of "distinct affinal assignments" in Dravidian. These are precisely the positions that virtually all of the Dravidianate systems distinguish terminologically as designated kin.

42. Echoed, for example, in Keesing 1975:110–11.

43. By this Trautmann means that in several Dravidianate systems unions with certain cross cousins (close, or bilateral, or patrilateral, or matrilateral) are forbidden or less preferred, and the fact that many terminologies of this type present separate affinal terms.

44. Lévi-Strauss's remark is amply illustrated by Tjon Sie Fat (1990:113, *passim*); see also Viveiros de Castro (1990), and Houseman and White (1994).

45. This is the problem with Héritier's "fundamental laws of kinship" (1981), which are supposedly prior to matrimonial exchange as a principle.

46. As is well known, in Dravidian India, in Australia, and elsewhere, the *terminological* identity between close cross kin and affinal kin may be accompanied by restrictions on its translation into *genealogical* identity. The Amazonian cases show, inversely, that a preferential genealogical identity can be associated with a terminological nonidentity. (For this useful distinction between terminological and genealogical identities, see Good 1980.)

47. Hornborg (1993), who relies on Buchler and Selby to affirm that "the defining feature of a Dravidian system is that the terms for cross-collaterals are the same as those for affines," explains the existence of separate sets of affinal terms in the Dravidianate systems of Amazonia through the presence of unilineal morphologies, which would cause the confusion between affinity/consanguinity and same group/other group. But Hornborg's contrast between patrilineal Tukanoans (with separate affinal terms) and cognatic Caribs (without them) bumps into Rivière's references (1984) to Carib systems with affinal terms, to say nothing of the many Túpi-Guarani cases where there are no traces of unilineality—a good example being the Araweté (Viveiros de Castro 1992). Recall that the Tamil castes studied by Dumont are all unilineal but do not have separate affinal terms: the FZ in a patrilineal situation can be "ambiguous" without having to be terminologically distinguished from the WM, and so forth.

48. These equations, by the way, seem to at least qualify the interpretation of the Iroquois crossness pattern in terms of paternal versus maternal "sides of the family" (Kronenfeld 1989:96), for they equate relatives on the maternal side (MB, MBW) with relatives on the paternal side (FZH, FZ): thus, there are "MB" on the paternal side.

49. Trautmann and Barnes make little of these equations in the Iroquois case, likening them to the English kinship system, where "the wife of an uncle is an aunt and the husband of an aunt is an uncle" (p.). This tongue-in-cheek remark is of course somewhat specious. The structure of G^{+1} in our system is F ≠ FB = MB = FZH = MZH and M ≠ MZ = FZ = MBW = FBW, whereas the Iroquois affinal equations are a subset of the Dravidian ones: F = FB = MZH ≠ MB = FZH and M = MZ = FBW ≠ FZ = MBW.

50. Suppose then that the other four types of daughters of cross cousins are "sisters," for they are nonmarriageable. The other eight types of second cousins—children of parallel cousins—are not representable in an elementary or "paleolithic" (Lévi-Strauss 1966:15–16) diagram, for they descend from same-sex siblings in the initial generation. In any case, they are classified identically in Dravidian and Iroquois calculi as to crossness.

51. We saw that Scheffler finds the similarities between the Pitjanjara and Iroquois types superficial (note 20); but he mentions the Bardi case (1978:538 n. 9) as a possible authentically "Iroquois" case in Australia. I did not have access to the texts of Elkin, Robinson, and Turner about the Bardi (or to Lucich's analysis of Kukata and Aluridja and McDowell's of Mundugumor—monographs on Oceania are not plentiful in Brazilian libraries). Apart from the references in Scheffler and Tjon Sie Fat, I was only able to consult Elkin's classic book ([1954] 1964). It is interesting to note that Elkin ([1954] 1964:77–78) remarks for the case of the Kokata (typologically close to the Bardi) that the alternate-generation equations express the possibility of marriage to MBDDD, but that this is only possible if the mother of this relative did not marry the S of ego, as the terminology also allows for (FMBDD = W). This is an inconsistency equivalent, in "Iroquois" terms, to that

pointed out by Henley for the Panare, in Dravidian B terms, where ZDD is marriageable only if genealogically ZD ≠ SW (see above).

52. The data in this monograph do not allow a clear typification of the Umeda terminology. Juillerat (1986:302) characterizes it as "Omaha."

53. The Kuma type, strictly speaking, is different from the other three, for the offspring of cross cousins are there called "cousin," not "nephew/niece"; reciprocally, parents' cross cousins are "cousin," not "uncle" and "aunt." There are thus three categories in G^{+1}: cousin, uncle/aunt, father/mother; and three in G^{-1}: cousin, nephew/niece, son/daughter. This strongly suggests marriage to "cousins." In Amazonia we find terminologies that would better represent this type of crossness: the Bakairi and Pemon (both Carib) classify the children of cross cousins of *both* sexes as nephew/niece (= children-in-law)—Oberg 1953:114; Thomas 1982:65. The Arawakan Wapishana, close neighbors to the Pemon, seem to share the same feature (Wilbert 1986:88, *passim*). It should be remarked that the Pemon and Wapishana are in the most classically Dravidianate area of Lowland South America: Northeastern Amazonia (Guyana).

54. Tjon Sie Fat's unpublished paper for the Cologne conference (1993) deals with third-cousin marriage types on sister exchange structures: he shows that the sixty-four third-cousin types (which are of course equally divided into sixteen Iroquois- and Dravidian-cross, sixteen I. & D. parallel, and thirty-two where D. and I. cross-classify for crossness) are reduced through the sister exchange in G^{+3} to only ten types, of which six are Dravidian-cross and only four Iroquois-cross. I do not know whether this asymmetry has anything to do with the "Testart-effect" (the partial-only compatibility of Bardi-like structures to Iroquois crossness). It should also be remarked that the Mundugumor "Iroquois compatibility" for third cousins also does not hold for the fourth cousins merged with the former; it is possible that all the structures of bilateral alliance with period 2 present this particularity, but I did not dare to test such conjecture.

55. In terms of their periods, the "Iroquois-concentric" scheme is one degree longer than "Aranda-diametric"; if one looks at the "matricycles," however, the situation is reversed: descendants in sexually parallel lines of a B/Z pair meet as H/W every three generations (period 2) in the concentric case, but only every four generations (period 3) in the diametric one.

56. The presence of self-reciprocals between nonadjacent generations in the case of non-Dravidian or Australian bifurcate merging terminologies deserves further study: see the U'wa (also Chibchan) of Colombia ($G^{-3} = G^{+1}$, $G^{+2} = G^{-2}$; Osborn 1982:50–63) and the Kiowa-Apache ($G^{+2} = G^{-2}$, $G^{+3} = G^{0e}$, $G^{-3} = G^{0y}$; McAllister 1937:103–11). In Amazonia, even in the sphere of the Dravidianate systems, there are transgenerational equations quite a lot more varied than the Australian or Dravidian B schemes: besides the already commented case of the Cuiva, see also the Piaroa ($G^{+3} = G^{0e}$, $G^{-3} = G^{0y}$; [Overing] Kaplan 1975:130), the Yanomam (all relatives of $G^{\pm2}$ and $G^{\pm3}$ are assimilated to cross/affinal relatives of $G^{\pm1}$ or of G^0, the variation taking place according to whether they are "real" or classificatory kin of the distal generations; see Albert 1985:221–35), and the Ye'cuana (all relatives of G^{+3} are assimilated to affines of G^{+1}, relatives of G^{-3} to affines of G^{-1}; male classificatory kin of G^{+2} are identified to cross cousins by male ego and to brothers by female ego, and inversely for the female kin of that generation; the classificatory relatives of G^{-2} are classified as cross cousins by male and female ego; see Arvello-Jimenez 1974:129–35, and Rivière 1984: 45–46).

57. There are Indian examples of the interference of extraterminological oppositions on the basic conceptual matrix of the Dravidianate. Dumont already showed that the "brother" category of the Pramalai Kallar was divided in co-resident FBCh versus MZCh dispersed in several lineages and localities. Among the Kondaiyam Kottai, ego's village would contain patrilocal brothers, matrilineal brothers, direct allies of ego, and allies of the "brothers"; but

these categories, although reducible to two (brothers and brothers-in-law) by Dravidian binary calculus, do not cover the whole social field in ego's generation: "a great number of people are undifferentiated: they may be at the same time brothers in a loose, merely local sense, and virtual affines, and it is only the nexus of individual alliances and their classificatory extensions which decides the question" (Dumont [1957] 1983:78). Or take the Koya case (Tyler 1966), where membership in patrilineal phratries inflects the crossness calculus in such a way that, if first and second cousins are equally divided into parallel and cross, from the third degree on, only cousins of the same phratry as ego's remain parallel: a FMMBSSS, who would be parallel by pure Dravidian calculus, will only be so in this case if ego belongs to the same phratry as his FMM; genealogical distance produces a quantitative preponderance of "cross," each phratry tending progressively to see all the others as "affines"—a situation reminiscent of a "Type B" model.

58. The following four paragraphs summarize part of what was published in Viveiros de Castro 1993a and Viveiros de Castro and Fausto 1993. For a thorough analysis of a "concentric Dravidianate" system of Amazonia, see Silva 1995 on the Waimiri-Atroari.

59. The possibility of a Type B alliance structure in the Upper Xingu is beginning to be investigated by M. Coelho de Souza (1995), who found traces of something similar to the Aguaruna case in a reference to the Mehinaku: although cross cousins are possible sexual partners, "sex *and marriage* is only proper for the *grandchildren of opposite-sex siblings*" (Gregor 1985:62, italics added); considering that Gregor also says that a "brother" and "sister" pair tend to arrange for their children to marry, this would suggest an "Iroquois" rather than an "Aranda" second-cousin marriage structure—the "brother/sister" pair actually being, in this case, opposite-sex cross-cousins.

60. It is not possible to discuss here the reasons that brought Dumont, the great champion of hierarchy in India and elsewhere, and critic of those who reduced the notion of opposition to its distinctive and symmetrical variant (1983), to see in the Dravidian systems "an island of equality in an ocean of caste" and to define the consanguinity/affinity contrast as "equistatutory" (1983a:vii, 166–67). See Viveiros de Castro 1993a:174, 202–4 n. 21.

61. Arcand (1977:31–32) favors a cosmological interpretation for the cross-"descent" scheme inherent to the self-reciprocal terminology: the operation of a principle according to which an element is always generated by another that is logically opposite to it; schemes analogous to the male-female-male "ropes" of the terminology would be found in Cuiva mythology, natural classifications, and so on.

62. The first ethnographer to call attention to the theoretical implications of Panoan affinal terminology is Lima (1994:44–45). The presence of separate affinal terms in so many Panoan groups seem directly to contradict Hornborg's (1993:103, 104) view that the fundamental feature of Dravidian, "Kariera," *and* Panoan systems is the consistent merger of affines and cross-collaterals. See note 49.

63. These three cases of "Type B variant 3" terminology among the Túpi are responsible, through a historical accident (they were the only three known to Wagley and Galvão [1946]), for the proposal of a "Túpian type," identical to the "Cheyenne type" of the specialists in North America. Dole (1969) later rechristened it "Bifurcate-generation type" and identified it among the Kuikúru (Carib) of the Upper Xingu.

64. The Túpi-Guarani data decidedly confirm the idea of a structural connection between avuncular and patrilateral marriage (against Good [1980:490; 1993], and with Lévi-Strauss [(1949) 1969:433] and Trautmann [1981:206]). But instead of the first being a derivative of the second, here the inverse is true: it is the patrilateral marriage that appears as an avuncular right relinquished in favor of a male ego's son.

65. See Maybury-Lewis (1979b:239): Gê terminologies are basically alike, differing only in how they classify the cross cousins. Oddly enough, however, the author takes this to mean that such variations are unimportant, since "they deal with something peripheral, like the cross-cousin category" (1979b:241). Such a position seems to echo the aversion often

manifested by Needhamites to the emphasis on cousin classification apparent in standard typologies. I beg to differ: from an alliance point of view, cross-cousin categories are anything but "peripheral," being so only if one sees kinship terminologies as pure cultural taxonomies with no sociological implications.

66. I am using a mathematical metaphor here: a linear relationship between two phenomena A and B connected by a function is one in which a change in A produces a proportional change in B, and a nonlinear relationship is one in which this does not hold. For instance, so-called chaotic phenomena are nonlinear in the sense that small changes in the initial conditions may provoke widely different evolutionary dynamics. Phase transitions are typically nonlinear processes: a small increase in heat changes water from the liquid to the gaseous phase at a certain temperature, while below that temperature the same small increase does not produce a big change. The point here is that there may conceivably be different types of alliance systems, some of them showing linear relationships between local and global levels (I would call these "elementary") and other, nonlinear relationships (I would call these "complex"). In the former case, the global alliance structure can be thought of as the marriage rule writ large; in the latter, it is much harder, and may even be inappropriate, to deduce the global properties of the alliance system from local rules such as "An A marries a B."

16

Afterword: Transformations and Lines of Evolution

MAURICE GODELIER

At several points in the introduction to this volume, the editors raised the issue of whether kinship terminologies and systems evolve. This is actually a two-pronged question. First, it asks whether, at a particular period in particular societies of a particular region, a certain type of kinship terminology has evolved and yielded, after a series of transformations that can be followed through space and time, to another type of terminology. And on a more abstract level—and given the fact that there are only a few different types of terminologies—is there any indication of irreversibility in these transformations, in the order in which one terminology replaces another? If such irreversibilities are found to exist, we may suppose that they imply some sort of directionality in the overall evolution of kinship systems along several possible lines of transformations. Second, if this is indeed the case, what type of kinship terminology and system, of those that are known or that can be reconstructed from those that exist, might have been the starting point for these various lines of evolution? What system gave rise, after a series of transformations, to terminologies having very different structures, which correspond to those that we are already familiar with or that may exist somewhere among those we have not yet analyzed?

Because I was the one who, during the Suger conference and on numerous occasions since, most insistently raised these questions about whether or not terminologies evolved, I was the one asked to attempt a reply. For this it seemed necessary to place this volume's theoretical findings within a global view of the domain of kinship, and to highlight their contributions as well as their shortcomings from that perspective.

But before starting, we need a definition of kinship, however provisional, that will allow us to delimit its domain. To make a long story short, kinship is the set of norms or rules that, in any given society, define the legitimate unions between the sexes and determine (in part) the status of the persons born of these unions. But kinship is not simply a matter of rules. When these norms function as true principles of action, they become the mental (*idéel*) condition, the departure point for establishing *real social relations* between individuals, and through them between the groups to which they belong. Kinship is a set of mental rules known (if not accepted) by all members of a society and of real social relations that correspond more or less to these norms and that link the individuals and groups by genealogical and/or categorical ties of filiation and marriage.

But like the god Janus, these norms have two faces: they forbid certain types of relations while allowing, and in some cases prescribing, others. For this reason, norms appear to both thought and action as positive or negative values, specifically attached to certain (allowed or forbidden) social relations and thus to the individual and collective behaviors that generate and then reproduce these relations. Of course, every society has practices that slight or even spurn the norms officially allowed. And these discrepancies or blatant contradictions between practice and norm are not without their signification, since they reflect the true deep-seated dynamics of a society and, in our case particularly, the dynamics of kinship relations.[1]

These prefatory remarks may seem self-evident. And indeed, their purpose is merely to help gauge the breadth and the complexity of the domain of kinship, since the preceding chapters discuss not only ideal norms but real practices, representations and values that may or may not be shared by all members of a society. As I will show, the stakes involved in all of this are important, but the importance varies according to the place and the weight of kinship in the way a given society functions. Kinship appears as a huge field of social and mental realities stretching between two poles. One is highly abstract: it concerns kinship terminologies and the marriage principles or rules they implicitly contain or that are associated with them. The other is highly concrete: it concerns individuals and their bodies, bodies marked by the position of the individual in kinship relations. Deeply embedded in them are the representations that legitimize these relations through an intimacy of blood, bone, flesh, and soul. Between these two poles lie all the economic, political, and symbolic stakes involved from the outset in the interplay of kinship relations or, conversely, that make use of these relations. The abstract pole, then, is the universe of the terminologies used in various societies to designate the relations an individual—man or woman—entertains with those whom society defines as kin, kin related by ties of filiation (sometimes descent) or by marriage. In saying this, I do not presuppose either that these interindividual ties correspond to real genealogical links or that they are purely categorical, and therefore merely conceptual and ideological. I will return to this point later. This abstract pole, made up of the set of terminologies systematically collected worldwide over more than a century, is one of the best studied aspects of kinship.

But in the past twenty years or so, anthropologists have forsaken this pole for the other one. This change occurred when theory took new turns in anthropology and the social sciences. Researchers began to pay serious attention to categories of society whose existence had until then commanded little interest and whose voice, as a consequence, had not really been heard. Foremost among these groups were women. Despite appearances to the contrary, those following this new course have not abandoned kinship as an object of study. Simply, the focus of analysis is no longer terminology. In reality, kinship continues to be explored, but now it is from the standpoint of its relationship with a person's body, male or female, the body of a dominated or a dominant person. That is to say, the central concern is no longer only kinship relations but the more encompassing field of the relations that empower certain persons in their society and exclude others. Everywhere, the body works like a ventriloquist's dummy, summoned to give voice to the order that reigns or should reign in a society, and not merely to attest to this order, but to testify for or against it. It is in this process that substances such as blood, semen, milk, and the like begin to speak, and deep within each person to hold forth in silent discourse on kinship and the social order. This is how the other pole of kinship deals with individuals in their most concrete intimacy. We are talking about kinship as a set of representations and issues that mark bodies, that embed themselves in these bodies; they do this by representing a transfer, between the sexes and the generations, of material and spiritual substances and forces, that are joined by the ranks and powers transmitted in some societies through kinship.

Rank, function, name, title, land, wealth, rights, and duties are all often inherited and transmitted through real or fictional kinship ties. This is where the distinction between filiation and descent—made by Meyer Fortes, E. R. Leach, and many others—is significant. What one inherits can, in effect, come exclusively from men or from women who are one's ascendants. This is possible only because there is some rule of descent that selects, from among all the ties of filiation that link an individual with his or her direct or indirect ascendants, a certain number who are thereby ascribed greater value than the rest. In a society that calculates descent patrilineally, land, titles, ritual functions, and so on are transmitted more or less automatically through men. This does not mean that nothing is handed down through women, or that the ties established through women are not recognized by individuals and by society. But in societies without a unilineal or a bilineal descent rule, or sociocentric rules that assign individuals at birth to a specific division, moiety, section, or subsection among which the entire society is parceled out, in so-called cognatic societies, then—and the bulk of societies having a Dravidian nomenclature are "cognatic"—many of the "things" that are transmitted tend to take the male or the female path indifferently. This is an important point, but the term "cognatic system" should not be allowed to obscure the fact that all kinship systems, of whatever sort, imply the existence of cognatic relations that converge toward, or diverge from, a male or a female ego. And in all societies, these cognatic ties are governed by the principles that, in a given society, define one's consanguines and one's affines, real or potential. On one hand, these rules can be socially marked or, on the other hand, can be entirely glossed over while existing implicitly.

This book presents only a few analyses of the relations between kinship and the body, and even then they are in a negative form. For instance, when Eduardo Viveiros de Castro shows (in chapter 15) that, in certain societies, representations of affinity can be completely disconnected from marriage alliances as they are really practiced, that the "pure" affine is the one to whom you have *not* given a woman or who has not given you one, it becomes clear that the notion of affinity can operate as a "category" used to classify individuals and groups situated at a certain distance from ego; and the distance may be such that there can be no true sharing of substances and forces, sharing that, as a rule, tends to be associated with the existence of kinship ties. As this example indicates, kinship can be used to talk about and deal with many things other than marriage and descent. At the same time, in all societies it functions as a rule for the appropriation of individuals, appropriation of children by the adults, who, in the society in question, are presented as their kin (and not necessarily their genitors), but also appropriation of kin by children, or appropriation of nonkin treated as kin by oneself and possibly by all those who are supposed to be the same as oneself. By now, it should be clear that what is at stake in kinship is necessarily more than questions of kinship alone.

This is a good opportunity to recall an essential point of theory, namely, that in no society does kinship suffice, through the relations it establishes and the groups it defines, to make a society. Although there was a time when researchers could concentrate on kinship—as G. P. Murdock did in *Social Structure* (1949:141 ff.), a book with an all-encompassing but misleading title since it dealt only with kinship—this vision of the relations between kinship and society seems to be a thing of the past. If I had to propose a definition of society that brought out the distance between kinship and society, I would say that society is a human group that claims first rights to the resources of a defined territory and that even if the individual component groups do not acknowledge a common origin, they do recognize themselves as sharing a common identity, at least with regard to neighboring societies. In order to go on living in their society, both the individuals and the groups that make up this society are called upon to act in such a way that they will reproduce the society as they reproduce their own numbers, and hence, up to a certain point, they will continually give it new life as they themselves endeavor to go on living.

If there is some meaning in this, it is that every society must, in one way or another, present itself as a whole that is greater than the individuals and groups that compose it. And these individuals and groups must aspire to reproduce their society as a whole by means of social practices that combine symbolic and material aspects. That is one of the functions of the moieties, sections, or subsections in most Australian societies, for example. Today it is widely thought that these divisions once provided the framework for a series of religious and political practices (to use our vocabulary) aimed at reproducing not only society in its totality, but the entire universe with all the plants and animals in it, which the rites were meant to reproduce and multiply. In a way, the division of Australian societies into moieties and sections was grounded in both kinship and something broader. M. J. Meggitt, C. G. von Brandenstein, and Harold Scheffler all agree in seeing sections as the divisions of society that correspond to superclasses present in kinship terminologies. This is why, despite their differences, a true congruence can be found between kinship terminologies and the sociocentric categories that cut across the whole of society.

But this is, if not a unique cultural universe, at least a rare case. Over the past ten years, anthropologists have discovered in the Panoan groups of Amazonia certain forms of terminology reminiscent of the moieties and sections of Australian societies (Hornborg 1993). Interestingly, these divisions correspond to rules for transmitting names, e.g., and therefore identities, and they overlay Dravidian-type terminological systems, of the kind that Tom Trautmann has dubbed "Dravidian B" and has shown to be the equivalent of a Kariera system. But such congruence between kinship terminologies and global divisions of society is rare. In India, for example, there is no congruence, no direct correspondence between kinship terminologies and the division into caste and subcaste that constitutes the global architecture of Indian society, whatever the nature of the kinship systems—Indo-European, Munda, or Dravidian—found in the populations divided into these castes from the north to the south of this subcontinent (Testart 1966; von Brandenstein 1970; Meggitt 1972; Scheffler 1978).

Paradoxically, another example of this distance and difference between kinship and society is found in the Shoshone and Paiute societies, which Julian Steward nonetheless used as the model of societies in which the family constitutes what he called the general level of integration of society. And yet he also showed that among the Shoshone these families, who are dispersed for the better part of the year, gathered in one spot during the season when natural resources were plentiful to perform initiation ceremonies, worship, and plan future marriages. During this time, the society was entirely present to itself—physically, socially, and symbolically; it was something more and something other than the sum of all the families gathered together. It is therefore not merely an accident that the members of these societies then made the decisions necessary for their own reproduction and thereby that of the society. From this purportedly extreme case, I conclude that nowhere do kinship relations alone suffice to make a society. Moreover, nowhere can kinship be reduced to the family. Articulated with kinship, there must also be social relations of some kind that enable people to represent society in its identity and to manage relations and conflicts between the particular groups that constitute this society, such that this identity is preserved, as are the relations between humans and the powers that seem to rule the universe, that seem to be the source of the prosperity or the disasters that succeed each other in the life of societies. Such relations, which overspill kinship and enable the society to exist as a whole in relation to its members and in relation to the gods, are what our Western culture calls political-religious relations.

This is not to deny that in many societies kinship relations between individuals and groups assume a great diversity of those functions that we in the West classify as economic, political, or religious. In the present work, John Ives (chapter 4), Michael Asch (chapter 5), and Emmanuel Désveaux and Marion Selz (chapter 6) show that the "band," the prevailing kind of organization among the Ojibwa and other Subarctic populations, is formed around a pair of opposite- or same-sex siblings (two brothers, for example); and because of this the kinship relations linking individuals within these bands constitute the social basis for organizing their hunting and gathering activities and game sharing, and for coping with the vagaries of nature and the conflicts of interest that sooner or later pit individuals against one another and threaten the existence of the band. It is also the kinship relations between individuals and members of other bands that enable them to resolve these conflicts by offering everyone the opportunity to leave their band to join another.

But while it is easy to say that kinship may take on various economic and political functions, should one also suppose there is some correspondence between a given mode of production and a given system of kinship? This was one of the questions that preoccupied anthropologists inspired by Marxism, either directly (as in the case of Maurice Godelier, Claude Meillassoux, Emmanuel Terray) or indirectly (as in the case of Marshall Sahlins). Their findings, however, seem to contradict their original hypothesis and show that there is no direct correlation between a set mode of production and a given kinship system. To borrow an example used by Michael Kryukov in chapter 13, the kinship terminology currently used in Western Europe (in England, France, and Germany, among others) is of Eskimo type and seems to have resulted from transformations of ancient Roman terminology, in Latin, which in turn was of so-called (bifurcate collateral) Sudanese type. Historical documents indicate that the transformation came about gradually (at the end of late antiquity, between the sixth and the eleventh centuries), at a time when the structures of European feudal society were slowly taking shape. These structures consisted of a hierarchy of lords and vassals who wielded power and exercised the right of ownership over the masses of generally non-free peasants and craftsmen. It is therefore likely that some correlation exists between the formation of feudal society and the mutations in the Latin system of kinship. But as yet this correlation has not been clearly demonstrated. Alternatively, it seems the Eskimo terminology that became generalized in this period continued down to the European countries just mentioned, whereas there have been two successive social systems, a feudal mode of production and government, replaced by a capitalist mode.

Changes have clearly taken place within kinship terminologies and systems, and these changes somehow reflect transformations in the societies in areas other than kinship—in economic, political, or religious realities. Family functions change faster than the kinship nomenclatures, but these nomenclatures can also change in order to adapt to other changes. At the same time, adaptation does not signify direct, structural correspondence, and even less the simultaneous appearance of two conjoined realities. One comes to the same conclusion starting from another reality, religion. To take an example, Christianity appeared in the ancient Middle East some ten centuries before the formation of European feudal society and sixteen centuries before the appearance and subsequent expansion of capitalist relations, once again in Europe. For the past two thousand years, this religion, the birth of which had nothing to do with feudalism or capitalism, became and has remained, through its various transformations, the dominant religion of the Western world. But this does not mean that kinship or religion do not entertain any relations with the other areas of human practice, that they are quasi-autonomous spheres of society. The point is merely that there is no direct correspondence between these domains. And this is because each one has its own finalities. Those of kinship are first of all to define ways of socially regulating marriage alliances and filiations among individuals. To take the example of European kinship once more, the work of historians such as Georges Duby (1981) or Jack Goody's (1983) attempt to reconstruct the evolution of the family and marriage in Europe demonstrates that certain factors, in the wake of the "Germanic invasions," caused family groups, including those of the aristocracy, to shrink and reduced them to houses and family lines that no longer had anything in common with structures organized by clans and lineages, if indeed these ever existed. And finally, all kinship units, those of the aristocracy as well as other social classes, were forced to bow to Church-imposed monogamy and to the transformation of marriage into a sacrament, a ritual act no longer celebrated by families uniting with each other, but by the church that united them. All of these changes probably favored the emergence in Europe of an Eskimo-type terminology. But since this type is found in Borneo as well as in New Guinea or in northern America among the Inuit, on a global scale the so-called Eskimo terminology shows no direct relations with any given mode of production or with any given religion.

If this is true, then how are we to treat changes in kinship terminologies and systems? Where are we to look for the reasons for these changes? This is the question at the heart of this volume. But how should it be formulated? Are the observed transformations erratic, contingent, without fixed direction, or do they follow a certain line with no going back—broadly speaking, are they irreversible? If this is the case—and the preceding chapters provide proof to this effect—then terminologies not only change, they evolve. Now the cat is out of the bag. Not only do terminologies disappear or change in the sense of yielding to others, but those that replace them are not and cannot be just any terminology. If this were to be confirmed, kinship terminologies could be said to succeed each other along certain possible lines of evolution, laid out by the action of a few transformation rules. Furthermore, these transformations would be such that the new forms of terminology replacing the old ones would deviate ever further in structure from the starting point; the movement would be characterized by a tendency, a drift that never returns to the starting point. Specific information in this volume attests to the existence of such drifts.

But before considering whether kinship terminologies and systems evolve, I would like to draw attention to a fact that poses a problem of major theoretical importance: there are very few kinship terminologies in the world. All of the kinship terminologies in the languages spoken by the ten thousand great and small societies into which humankind is divided today are variants of fewer than ten types of terminologies. By "type" I mean the principles of construction and the logical structure of the specialized vocabulary used in a language to designate the set of individuals who are linked with ego—an abstract individual characterized only by male or female gender—by filiation or by marriage relations, and who because of these links are placed in the same categories as ego or in separate categories. Furthermore, ego is not necessarily *only one* individual. The term can designate a set of individuals belonging to the same class because they are in an equivalent relationship to other individuals. Ego can designate an individual and also the set of same-sex siblings or, extending outward, an individual and the set of same-sex siblings and same-sex parallel cousins, if we are dealing with a so-called bifurcate merging classificatory system, and so on.

The type to which a specific terminology expressed in a specific language belongs becomes apparent, then, when the nature of the relations designated by the words in the kinship vocabulary has been identified and when the principles that define these relations and organize them into a system have been discovered. So kinship terminologies are maps, linguistic and logical, which, by means of a few words, or signs, designate a subset of social relations having to do with filiation and alliance that constitute a set of real or possible relations whose number is always much greater than the number of words used to designate them.[2] These logical-linguistic maps are used by every member of a society to situate him- or herself with respect to all other members of the society, according to whether or not they are kin, and therefore in order to know what to expect of the others and what the others expect in return.

As Tom Trautmann (1987) stressed in his book on Morgan, the linguists are not the first to have apprehended the semantic content of kinship vocabularies and to have shown how these sets of terms form a system. It was Morgan who first posited that the semantic content of these sets and their systematic character had something to do with "laws of marriage," the rules that, in any society, classify the degrees of kinship and stipulate whom an individual may or may not marry. Kinship termi-nologies, then, are linguistic realities in which essential social realities are present and are represented; and these realities are the rules that determine who is kin and then which individuals, kin or nonkin, one may or may not marry. In short, these realities all revolve around the prohibition of incest. Certain terminologies do more than simply define whom ego may not marry. They indicate whom he or she should (preference) or must (prescription) marry. For instance, Dravidian terminology is structured by a law that prescribes marriage with a bilateral cross cousin. Australian systems go on to distinguish between cross cousins, who are marriageable, and parallel cousins, who are not, but the classification is no longer ego-centered; it rests on the existence of marriage classes into which all members of society are automatically placed at birth. Iroquois terminologies also distinguish between par-allel and cross kin, but, unlike Dravidian terminologies, they contain no rule oblig-ing marriage with a cross cousin. The parallel/cross distinction exists, but in a lim-ited form, and attests to the fact that Iroquois systems still make "sister" exchange, the exchange of women, an essential principle of marriage.

To reiterate, kinship terminologies incorporate, in an abstract conceptual man-ner, some of the elements that form the content of a society's filiation and marriage relations. And these relations are articulated and associated with the reproduction of other relations insofar as there are present and active within them elements of the social relations that organize a society's economy and power. However, kinship terminologies in themselves have no *direct* connection with the social relations that organize production and government. Nevertheless, in societies where descent is reckoned unilineally or bilineally, relations of filiation, which are by their essence bilateral, are subjected to the action of these descent principles, which as a rule serve to regulate the transmission and circulation of the basic components of the social organization of production and power: land, herds, weapons, titles, rank, func-tions, and so on. But recall, too, that kinship terminologies, in themselves, say *noth-ing* about the existence of the descent rules that may govern a society or about their nature, that is, whether they are patri-, matri- or bilineal or undifferentiated. This distinction between filiation and descent is, as I said earlier, one of the basic contributions made by Meyer Fortes and other descent theoreticians, and it seems to have survived the assaults of the often fair criticism that has been directed at this theory.[3]

As we know, the Iroquois followed a matrilineal descent principle in the organization of their kin groups and their society. But the so-called Iroquois terminology is not linked to this descent rule, and Iroquois terminologies are found in patrilineal societies (the Baruya of New Guinea) and cognatic societies (the Ngabwe of Panama, whose terminology Franklin Tjon Sie Fat designates as Iroquois-3). To be sure, as Anne-Christine Taylor forcefully reminds us in chapter 8, terminology analysis must not be reduced to the analysis of reference terms alone; terminologies of address must also be taken into account, as they often differ from the former on important terms and contribute valuable information, not contained in the reference terminologies, on the dynamics of the kinship system, on the direction in which it is heading, that is, on the evolution in progress. Fred Eggan, for example, has noted that nineteenth-century Crow reference terminology was indeed of the Crow type, but that their address terminology contained many so-called Hawaiian features. We will return to the question of whether the presence of these so-called Hawaiian features is or is not an indication that a kinship terminology—whether it be Dravidian, Iroquois, Crow, or Omaha—is in the process of evolving toward a Hawaiian-type terminology. My answer will be no.

Let us now return to the problem of the number of identified types of kinship terminologies and their possible evolutions. Their number has grown since G. P. Murdock first proposed his classification in *Social Structure*, in 1949. Murdock, elaborating on the hypotheses set out independently by Robert Lowie and by Paul Kirchhoff, had grouped all known terminologies into four configurations, which he presented as permutations of the combination of two rules for distinguishing kin: collaterality and bifurcation.

These four configurations corresponded to six major types of terminology. The configuration combining collaterality and bifurcation corresponded to the Sudanese-type terminologies (for example, the ancient Roman system, the Russian system, the Chinese system). The configuration combining bifurcation and absence of collaterality corresponded to Dravidian, Iroquois, and Crow-Omaha, which have been the principal focus of this book. The configuration combining collaterality and absence of bifurcation corresponded the Eskimo terminologies. And the configuration that distinguished neither collaterality nor bifurcation but stressed generation corresponded the so-called Hawaiian terminologies. Of course, all of these systems are based on a distinction between genders and generations. Nevertheless, in certain systems the generation distinction can be partly neutralized, as is the case in the so-called Crow-Omaha systems.

But these different types of terminologies can also be grouped according to whether or not they contain a specific vocabulary for designating relations by marriage. Under this criterion, the terminology splits into two groups. One does not have separate terms for affines; it includes most Dravidian-type terminologies and practically all those of the so-called Australian type. The other has a specific vocabulary for designating affines; it takes in all of the remaining kinship terminolo-

Table 16-1

Four Configurations of Terminology Types

Types	Collaterality	Bifurcation	Terminologies
Bifurcate collateral	+	+	Sudanese
Bifurcate merging	–	+	Dravidian, Iroquois, Crow/Omaha, Australian
Generational	–	–	Hawaiian
Lineal	+	–	Eskimo

gies. In the case of Iroquois terminologies, the parallel/cross distinction exists, but cross kin are not identified with affines as they are in Dravidian systems. Nevertheless, certain Iroquois systems have equations that give MB = FZH = WF, as in Dravidian systems.

In table 16-1, I have placed the Australian, as well as the Dravidian, Iroquois, and Crow-Omaha systems, under the heading "bifurcate merging." This position reflects the findings of the analyses reported in this book and enables the reader to determine the theoretical advances over the past twenty years. But the table is still highly simplified with respect to the greater number of terminologies that have been identified to date. Indeed, the types known as Kuma and Yafar (from the name of two New Guinea tribes), along with Ngawbe (a group of Indians in Panama) can now be considered full-fledged stable types (on the same footing as those previously recognized). These new types were identified and situated with respect to Dravidian and Iroquois by two contributors to this volume, working independently: Viveiros de Castro and Tjon Sie Fat. Viveiros de Castro was the first to have constructed a general typology of all possible definitions of second-cousin crossness, that is, of G^0 kin linked to a pair of apical siblings in G^{+2}. He begins his construction by combining two criteria: the relative sex of the G^{+2} apical sibling pair and the relative sex of the kin of ego and alter in G^{+1}. Combining these two binary oppositions yields sixteen possible types of crossness for classifying second cousins. And of these sixteen possibilities, five were consistent with actual systems collected in the field: Dravidian, Kuma, Iroquois, Ngabwe, and Yafar. This typology is a major discovery that should inspire new studies, for it has still not been shown that the sixteen types of crossness correspond to as many canonical—that is, independent—types.

Using a different approach and a purely algebraic method, Tjon Sie Fat came to complementary conclusions about the same types of terminologies. Beginning with the possible ways of combining A and C, relations of affinity and consanguinity, he was able to differentiate, first of all for the class of Dravidian and Iroquois models, all possible forms of crossness in G^{+1} and G^{-1}. He also showed that these distinctions were valid for those Iroquois varieties identified as Yafar, Kuma, and the rest. But whereas Viveiros de Castro's method yielded an exhaustive inventory of forms of crossness, but without defining the position of each possibility in a table of transformations that included stages and therefore distances between these forms, that of Tjon Sie Fat, which was based on the construction of a hypercube, yielded important complementary information. It showed, for example, that the Yafar and Kuma terminologies both lay midway between the Dravidian and the Iroquois typologies, although *not on the same possible transformation path,* but on separate paths. He therefore introduced a measure of distance for the possible transformations that completed Viveiros de Castro's general table of forms of crossness. It was also surprising to discover that the structure of Yafar terminology was the same as that of the Red Knife, a North American Indian group whose terminology had already been identified by Trautmann and R. H. Barnes as being a realization of their type B variant 2 terminology (type B = Iroquois). The convergence and the complementarity of the findings of these two studies show yet again that one of the tasks of anthropology is to make social phenomena intelligible, by using a comparative approach based on the construction of different patterns of possible structural transformations. In this regard, it is worth noting the role that references to the enthnography of new Guinea and Australia have played in the work of Viveiros de Castro and Tjon Sie Fat.

The landscape of Dravidian systems has also been altered. Trautmann has identified two types of Dravidian systems, which he calls Dravidian A (which corresponds for the most part to the South Indian terminologies) and Dravidian B (in which the Dravidian parallel/cross opposition is extended beyond the three medial generations to G^{+2} and G^{-2}). Surprisingly enough, this Dravidian B seems to correspond to the terminology of the Australian Kariera group. Another surprise is that, starting from Trautmann's demonstration of the existence of a Dravidian B, Viveiros de Castro showed that Kariera terminology corresponded exactly to this type but that it was in fact different from the terminology listed as "Kariera" in ethnology handbooks, which assumed the Kariera model to be complementary, and opposed to the Aranda model.

Another major discovery concerning Dravidian systems was also made by Viveiros de Castro and in part by Taylor. In chapter 15 Viveiros de Castro has shown the deep-lying features that distinguish the Dravidian structures of the Amazonian societies from the Dravidian structures of India. The latter have a "diametric" structure that divides the other members of society surrounding ego into consanguines and affines, whereas the Amazonian terminologies are "concentric." Viveiros de Castro and Taylor (chapter 8) divide the whole society into three, rather than two, groups: consanguines, true affines, and potential or "pure" affines, whom one does not marry but with whom one exchanges names, heads, goods, and everything but women. I will come back to this point.

When one compares Indian Dravidians with Subarctic North American Dravidians, Louis Dumont's hypothesis of the transmission of marriage alliances between same-sex affines appears meaningful only for the Indian groups. There is no trace of this in Subarctic America for the simple reason that the bands that constitute the local co-residence and cooperation units among the Ojibwa and other groups have no genealogical depth. They are formed around a pair of same-sex siblings (two brothers) or a pair of opposite-sex siblings, as Ives, Asch, and Désveaux have shown. But these bands, whether they are endogamous or exogamous, break up after a generation and cease to exist. Such fluid dynamics leave no room to inherit alliances. And yet this formula, which in Dumont's view should characterize all Dravidian systems, is also found in certain Amazonian groups, such as the Shuar, analyzed by Taylor. Among the unexpected discoveries that make our representations of kinship even more complex, I would also mention Robert Parkin's demonstration (in chapter 11) of the existence of an Iroquois system on the Indian subcontinent, whereas this type of system was thought to be completely absent from this part of the world. This is the Burushaski terminology, which, in complete contrast to the Indo-European systems in the north of India, seems to have classificatory equations of the type F = FB, and which distinguishes between parallel and cross kin without equating cross kin and affines. In short, we now have more terminology types identified than we did twenty years ago. But these new types all fall somewhere between those that had previously been identified. Hence this series of discoveries tends to substantiate the idea that all the terminologies now known represent different configurations stabilized at various points along different lines of evolution.

So here we are, back to the question of whether kinship terminologies evolve, except that now we recognize the problem needs to be approached on two levels. The first is the local and regional level, which can be reconstructed from historical documents, from the findings of ethnographic work built up over the last two centuries. The second is the purely abstract level. Keeping in mind the information we have collected on regional forms and lines of evolution that are historically verifiable (level one), at this level we attempt to formulate hypotheses on the nature of the terminologies that may have been, thousands of years ago, the starting point for subsequent evolutions, some moments of which have been successfully reconstituted for a locality and a historical time. This second level of inquiry can never be anything but a purely theoretical reconstruction, with no other means of verification than the identification of a logical convergence and consistency between the type of terminology reconstructed as the starting point and what we know of the nature of the terminologies now identified, and, when these are known, of their local evolutions.

Consider the problem at the regional level. In such an endeavor to reconstruct the evolutions of terminologies, Kryukov (chapter 13) has underscored the importance of privileging those societies for which we have accumulated considerable historical documentation. A case in point is China, which provides us with hundreds of texts covering some two thousand years. These texts include systematic inventories of kinship vocabulary not only for the Han but also for so-called minority peoples such as the Lolo. India, too, furnishes a large amount of written material, as do the societies of Western Europe. For China, Kryukov has reconstituted the stages of evolution beginning with an ancient system of Dravidian type, as he believes, that was transformed among the Han into a Sudanese system; the structure of this system still exists despite the appearance, in recent centuries, of "Eskimo" features. Alternatively, peoples such as the Lolo provide a historically attested example of a prescriptive symmetric Dravidian system evolving in two directions: on the one hand, toward a nonprescriptive Iroquois-type terminology (found in the western Lolo groups) and, on the other hand, toward a prescriptive asymmetric terminology among the eastern Lolo, especially the Nasupo. The latter type distinguishes between wife-givers and wife-takers in a manner consistent with a form of generalized exchange and found equally among the Kachin. For Western Europe, the reconstruction of the evolution of the ancient Roman system into the present Eskimo-type European systems seems to be confirmed.

Removing ourselves to America, we see coexisting in Amazonia terminologies of Dravidian and Iroquois type and even, in the Pano groups analyzed by Alf Hornborg in chapter 7, sociocentric terminologies of Australian type. But it is important to point out that several contributors to this volume fail to agree on how certain Amazonian terminologies should be interpreted. In a study of three Jivaro groups, Taylor, for instance, reveals huge differences between, on the one hand, the typically Dravidian terminology of the Shuar, which contains the classic equation of marriage with the bilateral cross cousin, a rule that the Shuar seem to follow in practice, and, on the other hand, the two terminologies of the Aguaruna and the Kandoshi, especially the latter, which forbid marrying close cousins or replicating one's parents' marriage and which have a large number of Iroquois-like features. Taylor drew two conclusions from her analyses: first, she found in these three terminologies an increasing discrepancy between affinity and consanguinity as categories or as genealogical relations. Her position converges with that of Viveiros de Castro. But she also concludes that these three terminologies are transformations of a single basic Dravidian system, the original form of which was like the Shuar system, but whose two other forms, the Aguaruna and Kandoshi systems, are so deformed with respect to a Dravidian logic that one would be hard put to decipher their underlying structure, which nevertheless is still of Dravidian type. Neither Viveiros de Castro, Tjon Sie Fat, nor I share this conclusion. Indeed, the Aguaruna have a terminology similar to that of the Yafar (midway between Dravidian and Iroquois), and the Kandoshi have a complex type of Iroquois terminology known as "Ngabwe." However, we see this as an exemplary case of a group of related societies, languages, and cultures in which there has been a local evolution of a Dravidian system. That system was preserved in some of these societies, but in others it evolved toward Iroquois forms.

If this is the case, one cannot conclude, as Taylor does, that the Aguaruna and Kandoshi terminologies are Dravidian terminologies that have become so deformed as to be unrecognizable. They are, on the contrary, two normal Iroquois terminologies resulting from transformations of an originally Dravidian terminology. In epistemological terms, this would be an example of a structure that, as a consequence of transformations, has been replaced by other structures, each having its own but different logic. At either end of this line of evolution, then, we would have, not a Dravidian structure to begin with and one of its unrecognizable varieties at the other end, but a Dravidian structure to begin with and a type of Iroquois structure at the other end. At either end of this line are two different basic structures. What they would obviously have in common would be that they are both of the bifurcate merging type, each combined with a marriage rule of sister exchange, but they would differ by their definition and the extension given to parallel and cross-kin categories and, beyond that, to the categories of consanguinity and affinity.

Ives and Asch provide a comparable example in the case of Ojibwa groups having Dravidian terminologies in North America, in the Subarctic zone, and Iroquois terminologies further south. The Eika also illustrate the very rare case of a Dravidian system in which the parallel/cross distinction extends to G^{+2} and G^{-2}. This is, in all likelihood, an example of Dravidian B, which resembles Kariera terminology with sociocentric dimensions. The Eika, it should be remembered, had a complex moiety organization.

In the case of Australia, the table of terminologies has become much more complex. Terminologies such as those of the Bardi and the Aluridja, which seemed odd to specialists like Elkin, actually appear to fit the Iroquois model. The Kariera are no longer Kariera, but now appear to be type-B Dravidians. In Australia, then, Dravidian, Iroquois, and Australian terminologies have all managed to develop and now coexist. The question here, then, is what kind of relations exist between Australian and Dravidian terminologies? A consensus seems to be emerging on this issue. For Viveiros de Castro, Australian systems are a "singular" transformation of Dravidian systems whose structure has been deeply altered and reorganized by the imposition of sociocentric categories, which cut across the entire society and divide its members between two, four, or eight categories, depending on whether the systems are organized into moieties, sections, or subsections. The primary purpose of these divisions would be to organize initiations, which are ritual action on nature and on man, reactivation of the acts that founded the cosmic order, of Dreamtime. The Australian structures are exceptional in that these social divisions are consistent with the superclasses contained implicitly in the kinship terminologies. This consistency gives the terminologies the "crystalline beauty" that Lévi-Strauss spoke about. His admiration stems from the fact that, as he said, one can always use two methods for classifying kin as marriageable and unmarriageable, the method of (genealogical) relations and the method of (matrimonial) classes. Furthermore, in the case of Australian terminologies, one can, up to a certain point, use one or the other with practically the same results. The two seem to correspond.

If this hypothesis about the "Dravidian" basis of Australian terminologies were to be confirmed, we would have two possible transformations for Dravidian terminologies, starting from one basic ego-centered diametric form. One would be a transformation of Dravidian terminologies into an Australian type, after their structure had been remodeled by the impact of superimposed sociocentric divisions. The other, occurring in Amazonia, would be a transformation of diametric Dravidian terminologies into concentric ones that would give rise to an overall division of society according to a ternary and not a binary or dualist rule.

Two problems remain. Despite the fact that some authors suggest, as Ives does when he speaks of the Mackenzie Indian terminology, that there are some Dravidian systems in North America in which the parallel/cross distinction has completely disappeared in G^0 (known as generational G^0), this does not seem to be substantiated by the findings of Tjon Sie Fat, Viveiros de Castro, or Taylor, who say they have found no convincing examples of this in Amazonia or elsewhere. It would seem, then, that cancellation of the parallel/cross distinction in G^0 occurs only in certain types of Iroquois systems and is consistent with a rule forbidding marriage with close cousins but allowing replication of marriages after two or three generations. Here we would have Iroquois-type systems that maintain the ideal marriage rule of direct exchange of women, but that prohibit renewing this exchange before a lapse of several generations. These generational Iroquois systems would be examples of what Lévi-Strauss has called semicomplex kinship systems, in which the exchange of women remains a basic principle but marriage is governed by negative rules of nonrenewal of alliances before a certain number of generations. This is the case of the Yafar, Kuma, Ngabwe, and other similar systems. The expression "Hawaiianization" is often used in this volume to refer to these generational G^0 Iroquois systems. This formula does not really seem to fill the bill, though, for it gives the impression that the transformation in G^0 is the starting point for an evolution that would lead these Iroquois systems to become full-fledged Hawaiian terminologies. But in order for that to happen the merging of terms that characterizes Hawaiian systems would have to appear, as Kryukov points out, in G^{+1} and not in G^0. We should therefore not speak of the Hawaiianization of Iroquois systems (and even less of Dravidian ones). We have not yet found the processes that led to the appearance of full-fledged Hawaiian terminologies, nor do we know the systems in which they originated or the transformations by which they developed.

Another major problem touched on in this volume concerns the Crow-Omaha terminologies. These seem to be close to the Iroquois terminologies in that they contain a separate terminology for affines. They are thought to be based on the interplay of a series of marriage prohibitions, which, depending on the variety, go as far as to forbid ego to marry in four lines, that of F, M, FM, and MM (see the work of Floyd Lounsbury and Françoise Héritier). Nevertheless, Crow-Omaha systems allow and sometimes even encourage the renewal of marriages after a certain number of generations, which is also true of generational Iroquois terminologies. This is the case of the Samo of Burkina Faso, whose Omaha terminology has been closely studied by Héritier. Furthermore, the skewing scheme of Crow-Omaha terminologies neutralizes the generation difference for some kinship positions. This gives the impression that Crow-Omaha terminologies are close to the Iroquois terminologies and could even be derived from them. But this book shows that the difference between Dravidian and Iroquois terminologies can be clearly defined only when the differences between the ways the two systems define parallel and cross kin are understood. To resolve this question, it would be necessary to identify the type of crossness calculus that was specific to Crow-Omaha systems, if one existed. And that has not yet been done.

The skewing in Crow-Omaha terminologies raises another problem. Is this skewing necessary to their logic, and is it part of their definition? Or is it a secondary feature that can be found in association with other types of terminologies? In fact, skewed patterns can be found in Iroquois or even Hawaiian terminologies, as in the case of the Fanti, analyzed by David Kronenfeld. Must one therefore conclude, as Scheffler and Lounsbury did, that skewing alone does not define a system as Crow-Omaha?

The analysis of Crow-Omaha systems needs to be pursued, but for the moment Tjon Sie Fat has gone the farthest with this task.[4] For the construction of his formal model of all of the varieties of Dravidian, Iroquois, Kuma, and other terminologies, Tjon Sie Fat (chapter 3) has posited that these started from a bilateral mode of classification for primary kinship relations. A child is related as "parallel" kin *to both* parents (F,M) and to its siblings (B,Z). "Crossness" is then introduced when it comes to classifying the nephews/nieces such that the children of opposite-sex siblings are for ego cross, and not parallel, kin. The converse classification means that in G^{+1}, parents' opposite-sex siblings are also cross. Other specifications can be added: for instance, affinal categories that may or may not correspond to a subset of the cross category. Here, Tjon Sie Fat suggests that if, instead of linking a child with its two parents, one decides that ego, as well as his/her brothers and sisters, is linked exclusively with *only one* parent, the father or the mother, then a binary mode of classification is generalized that, in its unskewed forms, would correspond to the Australian models with moieties. And indeed a series of terminological structures is generated that is identical to or homologous with the classic "moiety" systems, and therefore compatible with the rule of sister exchange and cross-cousin marriage in its various forms.

If a principle of lineal invariance is added to this unilineal principle of consanguinity—for instance, if the MBCh is classified with MB and M, which implies that on the paternal side the FZCh is classified with nephews and nieces—then skewing is introduced into the terminology, and the different Crow-Omaha kinship structures are generated as described by Lounsbury and Scheffler. This hypothesis would generate two terminological sets: on the one hand, a set organized according to unilateral reckoning of cross/parallel kin, which would apply to Australian, Crow-Omaha, and other such systems; and, on the other hand, a set organized according to bilateral reckoning, which would apply to Iroquois and Dravidian systems. Tjon Sie Fat suggests that this perspective would make it possible to account for many of the cases recorded by Lounsbury and Scheffler in which an Omaha pattern is found to be combined with equations of the type MB = WF, MBD = Sp, and so forth, which are also found in classic Dravidian terminologies containing the bilateral cross-cousin marriage rule. Proceeding in this direction, one might also encounter the case of the Kachir, which Lounsbury identified as Omaha. And once again the problem would arise of whether the formal structure of Crow-Omaha terminologies is necessarily associated with the existence of a certain number of specific marriage prohibitions. This is the position taken by Héritier, and by Copet-Rougier, who, following Lévi-Strauss (1965), associate Crow-Omaha terminologies with alliance systems involving a large number of marriage prohibitions combined with a principle of exchange of women between lines that cannot be repeated before a certain number of generations. The debate continues. According to Tjon Sie Fat, it is no accident that Crow-Omaha systems resemble Iroquois systems of the Ngabwe or Mundugumor type and that at the same time they sometimes give the impression of being consistent with Australian systems, to the extent that Lévi-Strauss and Héritier have spoken of super-Aranda models.[5]

Tjon Sie Fat's present position suggests a closer association than specialists usually recognize between Crow-Omaha terminologies and the presence of unilineal descent rules in societies where these terminologies are found. But for the time being, this is only a suggestion. Strictly speaking, Tjon Sie Fat's position points to a connection between Crow-Omaha terminologies and a unilineal principle of consanguinity, which is not the same thing as a unilineal descent principle. Furthermore, we should keep in mind that many anthropologists stress two facts: first, that Crow-Omaha structures can be found in cognatic societies, and, second, that in those Crow-Omaha societies with unilineal descent rules, some of the marriage prohibitions apply to cognatic relationships (which are not, however, usually named in the terminology). This, too, remains an open question.

Before turning from the regional or local level to the global one and the question of the evolution of kinship terminologies from this perspective, we need to return to the two essential points brought out by Viveiros de Castro: first, that cognation, consanguinity, and affinity should not be confused, and, second, that the categories of consanguinity and affinity are opposed, but in such a way that, depending on the context, one also encompasses the other. For Viveiros de Castro, cognation is synonymous with "relatedness," in other words, with the existence of a connection between two individuals stemming from any kinship relation, whether filiation, siblingship, or marriage. From this perspective, a cognate is a relative, whatever the nature of the kinship tie. In Western European kinship systems (of Eskimo type), the field of cognatic relations is congruent with that of relations of consanguinity.[6] But this is not the case in Dravidian systems. In Dravidian reckoning, many cognates are real or potential affines. For instance, MB and FZ are cognates, but they are not consanguines in the Dravidian sense of the term. As far as categories go, they are affines. MB is as close a cognate as FB, but in a Dravidian system, MB is an affine and FB a consanguine. MBD is a wife (W) and FBD is a sister (Z). And vice versa, many people classified in a Dravidian system as consanguines are not cognates, since the rule governing Dravidian systems is ideally that $CC = C$; $AA = C$; $CA = A$; $AC = A$.[7] And so one can find in Dravidian systems noncognates who are nevertheless classified as consanguines or as affines.

Therefore the notion of consanguinity as it obtains in Euro-American kinship systems is entirely different from that implied by Dravidian systems. And cognation is neutral where consanguinity and affinity are concerned, insofar as the latter has to do with the marriageability or nonmarriageability of individuals. For Viveiros de Castro, the parallel/cross distinction appears ultimately as a genealogical reduction of the opposition between the categories of consanguines and affines, in other words, between marriageables and unmarriageables. Therefore, in Dravidian systems a bond of "consanguinity" between individuals does not necessarily mean that they are connected by blood ties. In these systems, consanguinity and affinity are definitions of categories that are in part translated into genealogical relationships. Nevertheless, despite the clarity of these distinctions, it must not be forgotten that, in certain Dravidian systems, some ambiguity continues to weigh on the status of close affines, and that, for example, FZ (who belongs to the *category* of affines) will be treated *culturally* as a consanguine before her marriage with MB and as an affine afterward.

As Viveiros de Castro indicates, there is in these three types of (bifurcate merging) terminologies—Australian, Dravidian, and Iroquois—an opposition that cannot be neutralized in G^{+1}. This opposition stems from a systematic exchange of spouses occurring in the generation before ego and concerns the subsequent generations insofar as a repetition of this marriage may be allowed either immediately or only after a lapse of two or more generations. Whether renewal of the marriage is immediate or deferred, but in a cyclical fashion, would indicate a passage from what Lévi-Strauss has called elementary structures of kinship to semicomplex structures, two types generated by different marriage regimes. Thus the parallel/cross opposition would be merely one particular aspect of a more general terminological and sociological opposition between consanguinity and affinity, cross and parallel kin being, with respect to ego, two subsets of the two kin categories, consanguines and affines, two subsets corresponding to the members of these categories who are genealogically related to ego.

Viveiros de Castro's hypothesis suggests the existence of a twofold opposition between Australian, Dravidian, and Iroquois systems. In Australian and Dravidian systems, he sees a different form but similar content, insofar as, in both cases, the parallel/cross distinction overlays the consanguinity/affinity distinction. Alternatively, in Dravidian and Iroquois systems, he sees the same form but opposing content, since in Iroquois systems, the consanguinity/affinity opposition no longer coincides with the parallel/cross distinction.

Viveiros de Castro also shows, for Amazonian systems, the processes by which the categories of consanguinity and affinity may become radically disconnected from any genealogical relation at all. This is diametrically opposed to Dumont's view, which is based on India's Dravidian systems. In Amazonia, the "pure" affine is the alien, the enemy with whom women will never be exchanged. The real affine, who lives close by in the same highly endogamous local group, tends, on the contrary, to be treated as a consanguine. Detached in this way from any connection with matrimonial exchange, affinity becomes a language, a way of bringing into the kin group people and groups who are not affines, consanguines, or cognates, in short, those who are nonkin, aliens, and possibly even enemies. In a two-stroke movement, then, these Dravidian societies tend to make consanguines of all affines living with consanguines in local groups that are cognatic and highly endogamous and to make affines of aliens and enemies who live on the periphery of society, but who are brought in by the extension of an affinal relation entirely severed from marriage.

In Amazonia, we are at the opposite pole from India and the operation of the Dravidian systems encountered there. The Dravidian classifications of Amazonia are no longer truly dualist and symmetric with respect to ego. They have become ternary and concentric. Why is this? It seems to me that the reason lies outside the kinship domain. Here, we are looking at societies in which war or various forms of cannibalism or headhunting were traditional practice. Paradoxically, one had to kill and physically absorb an enemy in order to establish one's own identity and to gain prestige in one's own group. The enemies killed and eaten thus contributed, without the need for marriage alliances, an essential part of the individual's identity and a decisive component in the power he exercised in his own society. From a certain point of view, this "pure" affinity without marriage is inconceivable without a cosmic and sociological vision of personal identity in which war and ingestion of alien enemies become the equivalent of marriage and birth for the construction of individual and collective identity.

It is probably this cultural horizon that illuminates the conclusions of the formal analyses carried out by Viveiros de Castro and Taylor on the way the consanguinity/affinity opposition operates in the various Amazonian societies on which they report. Ultimately, in this type of casteless and stateless society, it is a kinship category, affinity, that is used to think society as a whole, to conceive relations between inside and outside, in short, to think the political sphere beyond kinship. And to extend Viveiros de Castro's reasoning, it may be no accident that, in African societies lacking a state, castes, or classes (i.e., lacking the institutions that usually represent society directly as a whole and are a central feature of the political and religious spheres), in acephalous societies in which kinship is organized by unilineal descent rules and not by fluid cognatic principles, it is consanguinity, hypostasized in the form of descent from a common male or female ancestor, that becomes the language by which society is designated in its wholeness. Consanguinity in these African societies thereby would assume the same function as affinity in the cognatic Dravidian societies of Amazonia.

At last, we are ready to consider the evolution of all kinship terminologies on a global scale, and as a series of types of terminology that are known to be small in number but are thought to have differentiated from one or several starting terminologies. Here we are working on a purely speculative plane with no possibility of direct verification. And yet, such an attempt can and must be guided by the lessons of the available local evolutions, which can be historically verified. The bulk of these cases seem to present themselves as a succession of different transformations, all starting from a terminology that is almost Dravidianate. Using the different analyses that appear in this book, we can draw up the following inventory.

According to one hypothesis, some Dravidian systems developed into sociocentric Australian systems. According to another hypothesis, some Dravidian systems developed into Sudanese and then into Eskimo systems. There are also numerous examples of the transformation of Dravidian systems into different varieties of Iroquois systems. Yet another hypothesis is that some Dravidian systems developed into asymmetric systems of the Kachin type. There is also some evidence of possible transformations of Iroquois systems into Crow-Omaha type. Jean-François Guermonprez (chapter 12), however, introduces a discordant note, since he posits the transformation of cognatic systems of Malayo-Polynesian type into asymmetric systems. Although his thesis has sparked a good deal of debate, Guermonprez firmly believes that an asymmetric marriage rule excluding on principle reciprocal exchange between wife-givers and wife-takers must have become generalized in Indonesia and Southeast Asia by superimposing itself on what was originally a large number of different terminologies. However, it also seems likely that all of the Austronesian-speaking groups that gave rise to the Polynesian populations, on the one hand, and to the Malay and Malgache groups, on the other, took with them as they migrated kinship systems of a cognatic type that have either Hawaiian terminologies (Polynesia) or Eskimo-type terminologies (Malaysia). But that is all we know about these historical processes. As yet there has been no systematic study of Hawaiian or Eskimo terminologies. Likewise, we still lack a detailed study of the so-called Sudanese terminologies and their evolutions.

In our present state of knowledge (or ignorance), we may still venture to suggest that the kinship terminologies that were the remote source of those recorded over more than a century in the thousands of local societies that populate our planet may have possessed structures "analogous" to those of the surviving Dravidian or even Australian systems in operation today. In one respect, this is the hypothesis submitted by Nick Allen (chapter 14). However, Allen's model is one of a tetradic system that may have been at the origin of not only the sociocentric Australian systems and the ego-centered Dravidian systems, but also of other systems of Kachin, Cuiva, or some other type. His approach, as he emphasizes, is a purely logical one. It consists of elaborating the model of a very small number of kinship relations, assuming the prohibition of incest between siblings and the exchange of women, or, he says—and this is very important—of children (which is not the same thing); this model would operate on the basis of ego-centered relations as well as on the basis of marriage classes not centered on ego. Allen has attempted, then, to model a protosystem containing in principle the two possibilities, which could subsequently split up and generate diverging evolutions. This starting point was doomed to be short-lived, however, since in most societies, kinship does not globally coincide with society, or at least no longer does. As a consequence, the evolution of terminologies would have taken several forms in accordance with the growing discrepancy between kinship structures and the overall organization of society.

This observation allows us to return to what could be a persuasive factor in our attempt to show the existence of directionality in evolution processes, namely, the presence or absence in a kinship terminology of a separate and specific vocabulary for affines. Would not the presence of such a vocabulary indicate the existence of directionality in the processes that bring about transformations in terminologies? I would say yes. And to justify this assertion, I call on the example of Iroquois terminologies. Unlike Dravidian terminologies, these, as we know, do not merge cross collaterals and affines, and for determining collaterals' crossness they use a calculus that disregards the gender of kin between ego and alter in the ascending generations. Alter's crossness is determined by the sex of his or her closest kin. Now there seems to be a link between these two features of Iroquois systems. In effect, once cross kin and real or potential affines are no longer merged but placed in partly or even wholly separate categories, there is no longer any use for rules for determining crossness in the three (and sometimes more) medial generations of the terminologies, as is the case in Dravidian terminologies. In this respect, the Iroquois mode of reckoning crossness requires only one criterion, the gender of the last intermediary relative between ego and alter in G^{+1}.

If this is so, one may suppose that a Dravidian system would become Iroquois upon the disappearance of the (bilateral) cross-cousin marriage rule implicit in Dravidian terminologies. And this transformation seems to be irreversible. Once there is a separate terminology for affines that distinguishes them from cross kin, it seems impossible to back up and once again merge cross kin and affines under the same terms. Concretely, this would mean that the specific term for wife's father in an Iroquois terminology would disappear and that the term for mother's brother (MB) would once again designate the wife's father as well (MB = WF = SpF, and so on).

But if the transformation of a Dravidian terminology into an Iroquois one shows irreversibility, this would confirm the de facto existence of directionality in this line of evolution. Is it possible now to go further and advance the general hypothesis that all terminologies having separate sets of terms for affines are the result of processes of this type, that is, irreversible ones? This would concern not only the Iroquois and Crow-Omaha terminologies, but also the Sudanese, Hawaiian, and Eskimo systems, which use specialized vocabulary to designate affines. A general hypothesis of this type would imply, automatically as it were, that the five terminology types were different transformations of previous types analogous to today's Dravidian or even Australian terminologies. Yet this hypothesis absolutely fails to tell us what transformations led to these five terminologies, at least one of which—the Eskimo system in Europe— we have found stems from a transformation of the ancient Latin Sudanese type of terminology.

This way of posing the problem of the starting point of the lines of evolution of the various terminologies is totally different from Morgan's approach. On the basis of what appear to be purely ideological criteria, Morgan chose the Hawaiian terminologies as the starting point for all the other transformations or evolutions. As Kruykov points out in chapter 13, Morgan believed that the Hawaiian terminologies—which generalize the notion of brother, sister, father, mother to all sorts of persons in collateral branches—attest to now vanished practices of group marriages, which were the mark of humankind's first steps away from its animal state, away from generalized incestuous promiscuity, which, according to Morgan and other thinkers of his time, characterized the sexual life of animals.

The last question implied by any type of terminology and kinship relations concerns the origin of the incest prohibition and the establishment of marriage exchange between individuals and groups: in short, the question of the emergence of the typically human aspects of kinship relations. Asking this question once again forces us to submit theoretical hypotheses that cannot be directly verified and that may at best indirectly converge with the known facts. I will briefly summarize the explanations advanced by Freud and Lévi-Strauss for the emergence of kinship relations. Freud's explanation, in *Totem and Taboo* (1913), rested on the myth of the murder, by his sons, of a chief of a primitive horde. The chief wielded absolute power over the members of his group, which was a sort of vast consanguine extended family and had absolute sexual monopoly on his women and daughters. The story is well known. After killing the father, the sons, instead of sharing their mothers and sisters among themselves, decided to forgo satisfying their incestuous desire for fear that one by one they would all meet their father's fate. By renouncing the women closest to them, they were forced to seek women outside the horde and therefore to practice exogamy and the exchange of women. We see that Freud's speculations already contained the hypothesis Lévi-Strauss was to develop half a century later in his *Elementary Structures of Kinship* (1947). But Lévi-Strauss makes no mention of Freud in this work and he does not attribute any specific place to sexuality, except to recall that, inasmuch as women are the object of men's desire, they constituted a possible exchange value between men. Lévi-Strauss therefore does not explain the incest taboo as a response to the need to bring sexuality under collective and individual management so that society as such may be reproduced as a whole. His hypothesis is a purely sociological one:

As Tylor has shown almost a century ago, the ultimate explanation is probably that mankind had understood very early that, in order to free itself from a wild struggle for existence, it was confronted with the very simple choice of "either marrying-out or being killed-out." The alternative was between biological families living in juxtaposition and endeavoring to remain closed, self-perpetuating units, over-ridden by their fears, hatreds and ignorances, and the systematic establishment, through the incest prohibition, of links of intermarriage between them, thus succeeding to build, out of the artificial bonds of affinity, a true human society, despite, and even in contradiction to, the isolating influence of consanguinity. (Lévi-Strauss 1956:278)

For Lévi-Strauss, then, the primordial problem was not the social management of sexuality but the moralization of social life. What is surprising in the descriptions imagined by Freud and Lévi-Strauss of our distant ancestors' mode of life is that *they did not live in society,* not in communities or bands made up of several families cooperating to reproduce themselves together on a given territory; they lived *in isolated families.* Their vision of the social life of our ancestors is one of scattered hordes, families isolated both biologically and socially, perpetuating themselves on their own and therefore through incest, and torn by fear and hatred of other family members. In both visions, in the beginning was the family, but not society. Society would have arisen later from a contract, according to which everyone, men and women, agreed to forgo incest and, the men alone agreed to exchange women among themselves and for themselves.

Without doubt, Lévi-Strauss's theory threw a new light on the nature of kinship relations, insofar as it endeavored to explain by a single hypothesis three different facts strung together into a sort of syllogism. To prohibit incest within the family is to commit the group to exogamy; and to commit the group to exogamy is to require everyone to exchange women, since each man, by forbidding himself to marry the women of his own group, undertakes to give them to others and expects the others to do the same. Nevertheless, this proposition involves a logical and ideological *coup de force,* for to say that prohibiting incest imposes exchange does not mean that it necessarily or automatically imposes the exchange of women among men.

In fact, forbidding incest opens up three logical possibilities. Either men exchange women among themselves, which signifies that they dominate women in society in general as well as in the field of kinship and marriage; or women exchange men, their brothers, among themselves, and the existence of such societies has been demonstrated with the case of the Rhades of Vietnam or the Tetum of Timor (unknown at the time Lévi-Strauss was writing his *Elementary Structures of Kinship*). Or, third, whole families exchange men and women, who come together and found new families; in this case marriage rests on an exchange in which it cannot be said that one gender exchanges the other for its own benefit. This is the case in many of today's European societies, but other examples can be found in Asia or in America. We are therefore obliged to conclude that, while kinship is always based on exchange, the exchange of women is not the only form possible and is therefore not a universal principle whose origin must be sought outside of society in man's biological nature.[8] Whatever the outcome of this debate may be, if kinship is always exchange, it is also always filiation. And, depending on the society, filiation may or may not be structured by descent rules that select certain relations rather than others for the purpose of transmitting rank, power, or identity. And in any case, filiation is transmission, and transmission is not "exchange."

But to return to the basic fact, to the internal relationship that seems to exist between kinship and the incest prohibition, we, too, are going to pose the fundamental question about the origin of the incest taboo (Godelier 1986). The incest prohibition first of all forbids (hetero- and homo-) sexual relations between close kin or between all those who are assimilated to close kin. Several conditions need to have been present at some (pre-)historical time for such a prohibition to have had meaning and to have been reproduced down to the present day, whatever its forms or the breadth of its field of application. How can we represent for ourselves these conditions, which concern not only the inaccessible past, but are such that they continue to exist and to be compelling in the present? We picture these conditions in the following manner, which is a sort of logical induction enabling us to reconstruct this origin, to effect a logical regression toward this time.

It seems to me that prohibition of incest makes sense only if it was imposed on a humankind *already living in societies,* and that these societies were something other than large closed consanguine families (like the gorilla families under the exclusive authority of the silverback male), reproducing incestuously. Human society must therefore already have been divided into groups of individuals of both genders and several generations; it must have been a whole that was not reducible to even the far-reaching limits of a large consanguine family. These societies, therefore, must *already have contained more or less stable families* that made up the parts of society, without the whole (a human band exercising its control over a territory) to which these families belonged being reducible to the sole sum of these parts. And since the incest taboo concerns sex, human sexuality had to have come to the point in its evolution where it in some way it presented *a threat* to the reproduction of society as such, *as a whole.* And this opposition between sexuality and society obliged the human groups to intervene in their sexual practices and to bring them under both collective and individual management. In a way, human sexuality had to have come to a point where it was perceived as asocial or even antisocial in some of its aspects. What, then, could have been the features that, in the course of the evolution of human sexuality, compelled humankind to intervene and to begin managing sexual practice?

I suggest that the reason for this was the emergence and development of a human sexuality that had been freed from the seasonal constraints of nature, a sexuality that took over the human body in its entirety, a *generalized* sexuality operating more by internal representation than by external stimulation, a cerebralized sexuality that was perhaps the outcome of the development of the human brain, itself connected with the freeing of the hands, the increased complexity of activities and social relations, and so forth. This is what seems to have occurred in the phenomenon known as the loss of oestrus in the human female, which was the result of an evolution lost in time, not a specific event but a gradual transformation of the socialized human body. And if it had become socially necessary to intervene in this generalized sexuality, this intervention had to occur as soon as the individual was born and in the first stages of socialization. In human primate societies, probably unlike those of chimpanzees, the socialization units must already have taken the form of more or less stable families, but probably not because of any sexual attachment or lasting feelings. It was probably because a sexual and generational division of labor had grown up, independently of sexuality, which did not exist in the other primate societies, a division of labor between hunting and gathering that sharpened with the domestication of fire and the necessity of sharing out the raw and the cooked. Such a division could not help but create reciprocal forms of material, social, and affective dependence between the sexes, dependence and reciprocity that was not to be confused with sexual attachment but that could be associated with it. Here, too, these forms of division of labor and cooperation could not have arisen without a development of the brain enabling humans to apprehend not only relations but relations between relations. That is to say, humans developed the capacity to decontextualize relations and to anticipate long-term consequences of individuals' behavior in society and thus the consequences of their actions on the reproduction of society itself (Godelier 1996).

In my view, we need to presuppose the existence and combination of this series of conditions—living in society, societies that were not extended consanguine families but territorial bands made up of a certain number of social units dedicated to procreation and childraising (families), units rendered more or less stable by the development of a social division of labor between the sexes unknown in other primate societies—for the prohibition of incest within "families" to have any meaning. We would need to assume that the type of generalized sexuality specific to humans—which became one of their defining features (alongside articulate speech, the social division of labor, and others)—could have constituted a permanent threat to ongoing relations of cooperation (and authority) within the family and between families, insofar as all families were led to cooperate in various ways in order to reproduce their society as a whole, as the encompassing unit that ultimately was the general and common condition of their existence and of that of each individual. For two things are largely confirmed in the relations between sexuality and society. The first is that, among primates, there are two sources of recurring conflict: access to food and sex (the level of conflict increasing when females are in oestrus), to which a third must be added, defense of a common territory where the individuals can indeed procure food and reproduce. But the "generalized" sexuality of humans is potentially a source of even greater conflict than the other primates' seasonal sexuality directly controlled by nature, and therefore a source of conflict that would constitute a threat to the complex forms of cooperation that had evolved in the human protosocieties, between individuals of both genders and between the families making up the territorial groups.

This is why, I think, humans are the only species compelled to manage socially, in other words collectively *and* individually, sexuality in both of its dimensions, namely, desire and reproduction. The incest prohibition is a particular but fundamental aspect of this social management of sexuality. For whatever the reservations and shadings imposed by the complexity of the facts, the incest taboo applies first and foremost to sexual relations within the family. And—a second fact that seems to be confirmed—wherever incest is condemned and at the same time practiced (which leaves aside the singular cases in which it is, on the contrary, imposed and positively valorized, as was the case of the incestuous "royal" marriages among the Inca and the Hawaiians, for example), it potentially or really subverts, across the board, relations of cooperation and authority within the family. For when incest is practiced, all of the individual kinship positions gradually merge and fuse with one another and in the end are abolished, since the same individual can end up being, for instance, the son and the husband of his mother as well as the brother of the sons and daughters born of this union.

In this theoretical perspective, the incest taboo appears to be founded not on biological reasons but on an objective universal social necessity: that of subordinating human sexuality to the process of producing and reproducing society, which is always something more and other than a simple adding up of families. Furthermore, this subordination of sexuality to the reproduction of society reaches well beyond the prohibition of incest; it extends to forbidding sexual relations with animals, with corpses, and so on.[9]

But the fundamental point is that the prohibition of incest is, as so many myths repeat and so many theories affirm, the source of *specifically human* kinship relations, of relations that, as they developed, gradually encompassed and redefined the units of procreation and socialization, in other words, the families that existed before the relations emerged. From the moment the rule states that one does not reproduce with one's own, and this rule obtains for all generations and in generation after generation, the problem becomes how to remember one's kin, one's ascendants, in order to know with whom one can legitimately "become related by marriage," in the eyes of others (and oneself), in other words, in the eyes of the society one belongs to.

But preserving the memory of past generations in order to know how to act toward present generations brings out simultaneously the two dimensions, the two axes along which all kinship systems are constructed and all terminologies expressed: the axis of memory, filiation; and the axis of action, choice, the marriage axis. It is from the time incest became prohibited that, with respect to every individual and every group of individuals, society found itself split into two sides, into two categories: those one can marry and those one cannot marry, marriageables and unmarriageables. This is the principle that structures every kinship system and that underlies all distinctions and oppositions: parallel/cross, consanguine/affine, unmarriageable/marriageable. The emergence of human kinship relations has divided all society in accordance with rules that have created categories that not only transcend the boundaries of the family but that subject it to their logic, a logic that encompasses and redefines the family each time. The phenomenon is particularly clear when one sees how a unilineal—patrilineal or matrilineal—descent principle assigns individuals, at their birth, a completely different status and future depending on their gender, on whether titles, land, and identity are transmitted by women or by men. The family organization can never be the same in all instances because it is remodeled each time by the logic of the kinship relations that underpin it. For the constitution of a new family is a moment in the reproduction of kinship relations and the condition of the continuation of the kinship system (and of the terminology) of which these relations are a part. It is in this sense that kinship penetrates every corner of society, and yet there is no society in which social life can be reduced to relations and phenomena of kinship.

Of course, the movement that culminated in the emergence of the incest prohibition and its generalization may have begun well before the appearance of articulate speech and may have relied on various forms of protolanguage for its development. But it could not reach fulfillment, in the appearance of the kinship terminologies and systems known today, without articulate speech and the capacities for abstraction that enabled humans to generalize the notions of marriageable and unmarriageable, and to concretize them and to specify them in such distinctions as cross and parallel kin, for instance. There had to be some kind of language that went beyond gestures and sounds associated with a specific concrete context. There had to be some language capable of conveying abstractions, relations completely detached from the physical context in which the individual is speaking, in sum, relations that refer to other relations, past, present, or future, between individuals, relations between relations. This is what is designated by the terms of kinship terminologies. Without the ability to represent relations between relations, it is impossible to construct systems with sections and subsections, like those of Australia.

Moreover, we have indirect evidence of this protohistoric development in the first attested tombs, which probably date back more than 100,000 years. For men do not bury their enemies but their kin, and men do not bury the dead unless they think that, in some form or other, in some way or other, they go on living after death, in an invisible world or at least in the not directly visible part of the universe. That is to say, men do not bury their dead unless they have some representation of the material and immaterial components of the human person, of man's place in the cosmos and of the division of the universe into at least two parts, a visible part and an invisible part peopled by familiar or unfamiliar beings, visible or invisible, who are supposedly endowed with very different capacities for acting on the fate of humans. Archaeology and paleontology shed a glimmer of light on this protohistory of kinship. But it will never be possible genuinely to reconstruct all the stages of this history, which may have resulted, thousands of years ago, in kinship systems involving the exchange of women and/or children, as well as a general division of society with respect to an abstract but gendered ego, into marriageable and unmarriageable individuals, a division found in all human societies, a large portion of these systems being of Dravidian type for the reasons I have suggested (or of Iroquois type if the repetition of the same marriages generation after generation was no longer considered necessary).

It is therefore possible to think, with some justification, that the first human kinship systems must have seen the light of day even before articulate speech became fully developed. And it is possible to imagine that the incest prohibition, which became a general rule in small societies in which all members knew each other, had the effect of generalizing the practice of exchanging human beings—men, women, and children—within these societies and between them. As a consequence, the exchange of human beings became the basic rule of all kinship systems. That the same exchange should be repeated between the same partners from one generation to the next, as in Australian systems, or at more or less regular intervals, as in Iroquois systems, are particular applications of an initial general principle, which is the fact of having to exchange. It is in this perspective that it may be possible to shed some light on the fact that nowhere, not even in Australian societies where kinship seems to permeate the whole social fabric, does it constitute the whole of society, and that it always deploys itself between two poles: one highly abstract pole, that of kinship terminologies in which the individual is assigned his or her role, but as an abstraction, distinguished only by gender; and the other, most personal pole imaginable, that of the representations of body and soul, of shared substances and forces, of identities. The history of humankind had its beginning in this endeavor to bring sexuality under some kind of control, for man is the only species that not only lives in society, like other social animals, but produces society in order to live.

NOTES

This chapter was translated by Nora Scott.

1. Everyone can observe that the same norms can be interpreted in several ways, or gotten around in several manners, or even sometimes openly violated (such as marrying a parallel cousin, a "sister," or a "brother" in a society where this is forbidden). But this is part of the analysis of the strategies elected by individuals and groups for achieving their goals, taking into account the rules of their society, which are in principle known by everyone who needs to know them, even if, as we have seen, there are sometimes differences between the women's terminology and the men's (see chapter 10). But this is not the object of our book. I would add, however, that analyzing kinship in terms of strategies, as Pierre Bourdieu did for Kabyle marriages, makes a positive contribution but in no way disproves and much less destroys Lévi-Strauss's analyses of the structures of kinship terminologies and the different marriage rules to which these structures formally correspond. Individual strategies cannot, by dint of repetition and confirmation, generate a Dravidian or a Hawaiian terminology that becomes common to all members of a society because it is embedded in their language and their representations. On the contrary, it is when one is familiar with the features of an Australian or Dravidian—or whatever—kinship system that one can grasp the strategies of individuals and groups and look for the reasons that move them to follow the ideal rules supposed to guide their actions or to deviate from them, or even to dispense with them altogether. And these

reasons are never formally stated. They lie with the economic, political, or other realities that are at stake in these strategies.

2. It seems that no terminology in the world has more than forty words for the different kinship relations and positions it designates.

3. Scheffler sides with Meyer Fortes on this point, and I agree with him. But we part ways when he maintains, in the teeth of evidence, that Dravidian or Australian kinship terminologies are not structured by marriage laws, and that there is no connection between the presence of some form of cross/parallel distinction and the implicit existence of a marriage rule. In this volume, Scheffler's position is shared by Emmanuel Désveaux (see chapter 6).

4. From here on I will be summarizing a personal communication by Franklin E. Tjon Sie Fat.

5. End of Tjon Sie Fat's personal communication.

6. *Cognate* comes from the Latin *cognatus,* which comes from *cum-gnatus. Natus* comes from *nascor* (to be born). In Latin, *cognatus* designates someone related by birth to ego, on both the paternal (agnatic) and the maternal (uterine) sides. This is also the definition of the French term "cognat" and of the English term "cognate."

7. Eduardo Viveiros de Castro, personal communication.

8. Probably because of the many criticisms addressed to his famous definition of kinship as the exchange of women by men and for men, as well as his deduction that, while other exchange formulas are possible, they do not correspond to any fact on the ground, Lévi-Strauss has since, and on several occasions, amended his original propositions and recognized their theoretical and ideological shortcomings.

9. Cf. the Abominations in the Old Testament book of Leviticus.

Bibliography

Ahearn, Laura
    1994   *Consent and Coercion: Changing Marriage Practices among Magars in Nepal.* Unpublished Ph.D. dissertation, University of Michigan, Ann Arbor.

Aikens, C. Melvin, and Younger T. Witherspoon
    1986   Great Basin Numic Prehistory: Linguistics, Archaeology and Environment. In *Anthropology of the Desert West: Essays in Honor of Jesse D. Jennings,* edited by Carol J. Condie and Don D. Fowler. Anthropological Papers No. 110. University of Utah, Salt Lake City.

Albert, Bruce
    1985   *Temps du sang, temps des cendres: représentation de la maladie, système rituel et espace politique chez les Yanomami du sud-est (Amazonie brésilienne).* Unpublished doctoral dissertation, Université de Paris X–Nanterre.

Ali, Tahir
    1983   *The Burusho of Hunza: Social Structure and Household Viability in a Mountain Desert Kingdom.* University Microfilms International, Ann Arbor, Mich.

Allen, N. J.
    1975   Byansi Kinship Terminology: A Study in Symmetry. *Man* 10:80–94.
    1976   Sherpa Kinship Terminology in Diachronic Perspective. *Man* 11:569–587.
    1982   A Dance of Relatives. *Journal of the Anthropological Society of Oxford* 13:139–146.
    1986   Tetradic Theory: An Approach to Kinship. *Journal of the Anthropological Society of Oxford* 17:87–109.
    1989a   The Evolution of Kinship Terminologies. *Lingua* 77:173–185.
    1989b   Assimilation of Alternate Generations. *Journal of the Anthropological Society of Oxford* 20:45–55.
    1994   Primitive Classification: The Argument and Its Validity. In *Debating Durkheim,* edited by W. Pickering and H. Martins. Routledge, London.
    1995   The Division of Labour and the Notion of Primitive Society: A Maussian Perspective. *Social Anthropology* 3:49–59.

Amadio, M., and d'Emilio
    1983   La alianza entre los Candoshi Murato del Alto Amazonas. *Amazonia Peruana* 5/9:23–36.

Arcand, Bernard
 1977 The Logic of Cuiva Kinship. In *Actes du XLIIe Congrès International des Américanistes,* edited by Joanna Overing Kaplan, vol. 2, pp. 19–34. Société des Américanistes, Paris.

Ardener, E.
 1985 Social Anthropology and the Decline of Modernism. In *Reason and Morality,* edited by Joanna Overing Kaplan, pp. 47–70. Tavistock, London.

Arhem, Kaj
 1981 *Makuna Social Organization: A Study in Descent, Alliance, and the Formation of Corporate Groups in the North-Western Amazon.* Uppsala Studies in Cultural Anthropology No. 4. Almqvist & Wiksell, Stockholm.

Arvello-Jiménez, Nelly
 1974 *Relaciones políticas en una sociedad tribal: estudio de los Ye'cuana, indígenas del Amazonas venezoelano.* Instituto Indigenista Interamericano, Mexico.

Asch, Michael
 1972 *A Social Behavioral Approach to Music Analysis: The Case of the Slavey Drum Dance.* Unpublished Ph.D. dissertation, Columbia University, New York.
 1980 Steps toward the Analysis of Aboriginal Athapaskan Social Organization. *Arctic Anthropology* 17(2):46–51.
 1988 *Kinship and the Drum Dance in a Northern Dene Community.* Circumpolar Research Series. Boreal Institute for Northern Studies, Edmonton, Alta.

Atkins, J. R.
 1974a On the Fundamental Consanguineal Numbers and Their Structural Basis. *American Ethnologist* 1:1–31.
 1974b Consanguineal Distance Measures: A Mathematical Analysis. In *Mathematical Models of Social and Cognitive Structures,* edited by Paul A. Ballonoff. University of Illinois Press, Urbana.
 1974c GRAFIK: A Multipurpose Kinship Metalanguage. In *Genealogical Mathematics,* edited by Paul A. Ballonoff. Mouton, Paris.

Ballonoff, Paul A. (editor)
 1974 *Genetics and Social Structure: Mathematical Structuralism in Population Genetics and Social Theory.* Dowden, Hutchinson and Ross, Stroudsburg, Pa.

Barnard, Alan, and Anthony Good
 1984 *Research Practices in the Study of Kinship.* ASA Research Methods in Social Anthropology No. 2. Academic Press, London.

Barnes, R. H.
 1974 Two Terminologies of Symmetric Prescriptive Alliance from Pantar and Alor in Eastern Indonesia. *Sociologus* 23:71–89.
 1975 Editor's Introduction to Josef Kohler, *On the Prehistory of Marriage: Totemism, Group Marriage, Mother Right.* University of Chicago Press, Chicago.
 1977 Alliance and Categories in Wailolong, East Flores. *Sociologus* 27:133–157.
 1979 Lord, Ancestor and Affine: An Austronesian Relationship Name. *Nusa* 7:19–34.
 1984 *Two Crows Denies It: A History of Controversy in Omaha Sociology.* University of Nebraska Press, Lincoln.
 1985 Tanebar-Evav and Ema: Variation within the Eastern Indonesian Field of Study. *Journal of the Anthropological Society of Oxford* 16:209–224.
 1995 Lounsbury's Analysis of Republican Pawnee Terminology: Comparison with Lushbaugh's Original Data. *Plains Anthropologist,* in press.

Barraud, Cécile
  1979   *Tanebar-Evav.* Cambridge University Press, Cambridge.
Basso, Ellen
  1970   Xingu Carib Kinship Terminology and Marriage: Another View. *Southwestern Journal of Anthropology* 26:402–416.
Beck, Brenda
  1972   *Peasant Society in Konku.* University of British Columbia Press, Vancouver.
Berthe, L.
  1970   Parenté, pouvoir et mode de production. In *Echanges et communications,* edited by J. Pouillon and P. Maranda, pp. 707–738. Mouton, Paris.
Bertin, J.
  1967   Les réseaux. *Sémiologie Graphique: Les diagrammes—les réseaux—les cartes.* L'Ecole des Hautes Etudes en Sciences Sociales et Gauthiers-Villars, Paris.
Bettinger, Robert L.
  1983   Aboriginal Sociopolitical Organization in Owens Valley: Beyond the Family Band. In *The Development of Political Organization in Native North America.* Proceedings of the American Ethnological Society, edited by Elisabeth Tooker and Morton H. Fried, pp. 45–58. American Ethnological Society, Washington, D.C.
Bloch, Maurice
  1971   The Moral and Tactical Meaning of Kinship Terms. *Man* (n.s.) 6:79–87.
Blust, R. A.
  1980   Early Austronesian Social Organization: The Evidence of Language. *Current Anthropology* 21:205–247.
  1984   The Austronesian Homeland: A Linguistic Perspective. *Asian Perspectives* 26:45–67.
  1993   Austronesian Sibling Terms and Culture History. *Bijdragen tot de Taal-, Land- en Volkenkunde* 149:22–76.
Bouez, Serge
  1985   *Réciprocité et hiérarchie: L'Alliance chez les Hos et les Santal de l'Inde.* Société de l'Ethnographie, Paris.
  1989   L'Alliance classificatoire chez les Ho: préférence ou prescription. In *Les Complexités de l'alliance, I: les systèmes semi-complexes,* edited by F. Héritier-Augé and E. Copet-Rougier, pp. 1–22. Archives contemporaines, Paris.
Bourdieu, Pierre
  1977 (1972)   *Outline of a Theory of Practice (Equisse d'une théorie de la pratique, précédé de trois études d'ethnologie kabyle)* translated by Richard Nice. Cambridge Studies in Social Anthropology. Cambridge University Press, Cambridge.
Bowden, Ross
  1983   Kwoma Terminology and Marriage Alliance: The "Omaha" Problem revisited. *Man* 18 (4):745–765.
Boyd, J. P.
  1991   Social Semigroups: A Unified Theory of Scaling and Blockmodelling as Applied to Social Networks. George Mason University Press, Fairfax, Va.
Brandenstein, C. G. von
  1970.   The Meaning of Section and Subsection names. *Oceania* 41:39–49.
Brown, M.
  1984   *Una paz incierta. Historia y cultura de las comunidades aguarunas frente al impacto de la carretera marginal.* Centro de Antropología Aplicada de la Amazonía Peruana, Lima.

Buchler, Ira
    1967   L'Analyse formelle des terminologies de parenté iroquoises. *L'Homme* 7(1):5–31.
Buchler, Ira, and Henry Selby
    1968   *Kinship and Social Organization: An Introduction to Theory and Method.* Macmillan, London.
Calavia, Oscar
    1995   *O Nome e o tempo dos Yaminawa.* Unpublished doctoral dissertation, Universidade de São Paulo.
Callender, Charles
    1962   *Social Organization of the Central Algonkian Indians.* Unpublished Ph.D. dissertation, Department of Anthropology, University of Chicago.
    1978   Great Lakes-Riverine Sociopolitical Organization. In *Northeast,* edited by Bruce Trigger, pp. 610–621. Handbook of the North American Indians, vol. 15, William C. Sturtevant, general editor. Smithsonian Institution Press, Washington, D.C.
Campbell, Alan
    1989   *To Square with Genesis: Causal Statements and Shamanic Ideas in Wayãpí.* Edinburgh University Press, Edinburgh.
Carsten, Janet, and Stephen Hugh-Jones (editors)
    1995   *About the House: Lévi-Strauss and Beyond.* Cambridge University Press, Cambridge.
Chagnon, N.
    1974   *Studying the Yanomamö.* Holt, Rinehart and Winston, New York.
    1968   *Yanamamö. The Fierce People.* Holt, Rinehart and Winston, New York.
Coelho de Souza, Marcela
    1995   Da complexidade do elementar: para uma reconsideração do parentesco xinguano. In *Antropologia do parentesco: estudos ameríndios,* edited by E. Viveiros de Castro. Editora da Universidade Federal do Rio de Janeiro, Rio de Janeiro.
Collier, Jane Fishburne, and Sylvia Junko Yanagisako
    1987   Toward a Unified Analysis of Gender and Kinship. In *Gender and Kinship: Essays toward a Unified Analysis,* edited by Collier and Yanagisako. Stanford University Press, Stanford.
Collins, J. T.
    1983   *The Historical Relationships of the Languages of Central Maluku, Indonesia.* P.L. Series D, No. 47. Australian National University, Canberra.
Crocker, J. C.
    1969   Reciprocity and Hierarchy among the Eastern Bororo. *Man* 4:44–58.
    1977   Why Are the Bororo Matrilineal? In *Actes du XLIIe Congrès International des Américanistes,* vol. 2, edited by Joanna Overing Kaplan, pp. 245–258. Société des Américanistes, Paris.
    1979   Selves and Alters among the Eastern Bororo. In *Dialectical Societies: The Gê and Bororo of Central Brazil,* edited by D. H. P. Maybury-Lewis, pp. 249–300. Harvard University Press, Cambridge, Mass.
    1985   My Brother the Parrot. In *Animal, Myth and Metaphors in South America,* edited by G. Urton. University of Utah Press, Salt Lake City.
Curtis, Edward S.
    1928   *The North American Indian,* vol. 18. Edited by Frederick Webb Hodge. Johnson Reprint Corporation, 1970.
D'Ans, A.-M.
    1974   Estructura semantica des parentesco Machiguenga (Arawak). *Revista des Museo Nacional* 40:343–361.

De Laguna, Frederica, and Catherine McClellan
    1981   Ahtna. In *Subarctic*, edited by June Helm, pp. 641–663. Handbook of North
            American Indians, vol. 6, William C. Sturtevant, general editor. Smithsonian
            Institution Press, Washington, D.C.
DeMallie, Raymond
    1979   Change in American Indian Kinship Systems: The Dakota. In *Currents in
            Anthropology: Essays in Honor of Sol Tax*, edited by Robert Hinshaw.
            Mouton, The Hague.
Dempsey, Hugh A.
    1982   History and Identification of Blood Bands. In *Plains Indian Studies. A
            Collection of Essays in Honor of John C. Ewers*, edited by Douglas H.
            Ubelaker and Herman J. Viola, pp. 94–104. Smithsonian Contributions to
            Anthropology. Smithsonian Institution Press, Washington, D.C.
Désveaux, Emmanuel
    1984   La mythologie des Indians de Big Trout Lake (nord-ouest de l'Ontario,
            Canada). Paris, Ecole des Hautes Etudes en Sciences Sociales. Thèse de
            doctorat de Troisième cycle, 2 vols.
    1988a   *Sous le signe de l'ours, mythe et temporalité chez les Ojibwa septentrionaux.*
            Editions de la Maison des Sciences de l'Homme, Paris.
    1988b   Récit individuel et destin collectif. *L'Homme* 28(2–3):184–198.
    1991   Fragment d'une tradition orale. *L'Homme* 119:119–126.
Dole, Gertrude
    1957   *The Development of Patterns of Kinship Nomenclature.* Unpublished Ph.D.
            dissertation, University of Michigan, Ann Arbor.
    1969   Generation Kinship Nomenclature as an Adaptation to Endogamy. *Southwest-
            ern Journal of Anthropology* 25(2):105–123.
    1972   Developmental Sequences of Kinship Patterns. In *Kinship Studies in the
            Morgan Centennial Year*, edited by P. Reining, pp. 134–166. Anthropological
            Society of Washington, Washington, D.C.
    1979   Pattern and Variation in Amahuaca Kin Terminology. In *Social Correlates of
            Kin Terminology*, edited by K. M. Kensinger, pp. 13–36. Bennington College,
            Bennington, Vt.
Donald, Leland, and Marion Tighe
    1987   A Formal Analysis of Three Apachean Kinship Terminologies. In *Themes in
            Ethnology and Culture History: Essays in Honor of David F. Aberle*, edited by
            Leland Donald, 34–80. Folklore Institute, Archana Publications, Meerut.
Dorsey, J. O.
    1884   *Omaha Sociology.* Third Annual Report of the Bureau of Ethnology, 1881–82,
            pp. 205–307. Washington, D.C.
Dreyfus-Gamelon, Simone
    1977   Note sur l'espace des relations sociales et de parenté: propositions pour un
            modèle sud-américain de structure de l'alliance symétrique. In *Actes du XLIIᵉ
            Congrès International des Américanistes*, edited by Joanna Overing Kaplan,
            vol. 2, pp. 379–385. Société des Américanistes, Paris.
    1993   Systèmes dravidiens à filiation cognatique en Amazonie. Paper presented at
            the Maison Suger Conference on Kinship Systems, Paris.
Driedger, Linda
    1989   *Kinship, Marriage and Residence in Fort Resolution, N.W.T.* Master's thesis,
            University of Alberta.
Duby, Georges
    1981.   *The Knight, the Lady and the Priest: the Making of Modern Marriage in
            Medieval France.* Pantheon Books, New York.

Dumont, Jean-Paul
    1978   *The Headman and I.* University of Texas Press, Austin.
Dumont, Louis
    1953   The Dravidian Kinship Terminology as an Expression of Marriage. *Man* 54:34–39.
    1957   *Une Sous-caste de l'Inde du Sud: organisation sociale et religion des Pramalai Kallar.* Mouton, Paris.
    1961   Marriage in India: The Present State of the Question. I. Marriage Alliance in South–East India and Ceylon. *Contributions to Indian Sociology* 5:75–95.
    1966   Descent or Intermarriage? A Relational View of Australian Section Systems. *Southwestern Journal of Anthropology* 22:31–50.
    1971   *Introduction à deux théories d'anthropologie sociale: groupes de filiation et alliance de mariage.* Mouton, Paris.
    1975 (1953, 1957, 1966, 1970)   *Dravidien et Kariera: l'alliance de mariage dans l'Inde du sud, et en Australie.* Mouton, Paris.
    1983a (1953, 1957, 1966, 1970)   *Affinity as Value: Marriage Alliance in South India, with Comparative Essays on Australia.* University of Chicago Press, Chicago.
    1983b   La Valeur chez les modernes et les autres. In L. Dumont, *Essais sur l'individualisme: une perspective anthropologique sur l'idéologie moderne,* pp. 222–262. Seuil, Paris.
    1986   *Essays on Individualism: Modern Ideology in Anthropological Perspective.* Chicago University Press, Chicago.
Dunning, Robert William
    1959   *Social and Economic Change among the Northern Ojibwa.* University of Toronto Press, Toronto.
Dyen, Isadore, and David F. Aberle
    1974   *Lexical Reconstruction. The Case of the Proto-Athapaskan Kinship System.* Cambridge University Press, Cambridge.
Eggan, Fred
    1950   *Social Organization of the Western Pueblos.* University of Chicago Press, Chicago.
    1955a   Social Anthropology: Methods and Results. In *Social Anthropology of North American Tribes,* edited by Fred Eggan, pp. 485–551. University of Chicago Press, Chicago.
    1955b   The Cheyenne and Arapaho Kinship System. In *Social Anthropology of North America Tribes,* edited by Fred Eggan, pp. 35–95. University of Chicago Press, Chicago.
    1955 [1937] (editor)   *Social Anthropology of the North American Tribes.* University of Chicago Press, Chicago.
    1966   *The American Indian. Perspectives for the Study of Social Change.* Aldine, Chicago.
    1980   Shoshone Kinship Structures and Their Significance for Anthropological Theory. *Journal of the Steward Anthropological Society* 11(2):165–193.
Elford, Leon W., and Marjorie Elford
    1981   *English-Chipewyan Dictionary.* Northern Canada Evangelical Mission, Prince Albert, Sask.
Elkin, A. P.
    1939   Kinship in South Australia. *Oceania* 10:196–234.
    1940   Kinship in South Australia: General Survey and Summary. *Oceania* 10:368–388.
    1964 [1954]   *The Australian Aborigines.* Doubleday, Garden City, N.Y.

Engels, Friedich
    1972 [1884]   *The Origin of the Family, Private Property and the State, in the Light of the Researches of Lewis H. Morgan (Der Ursprung der Familie, des Privateigenthums und des Staats, im Anschluss an L. H. Morgan's Forschungen)*, translated by Aleck West, Introduction and notes by Eleanor Burke Leacock. International Publishers, New York.
Erikson, Philippe
    1990   Le Matis d'Amazonie: parure du corps, identité ethnique et organisation sociale. Doctoral thesis, Université de Paris X, Nanterre.
Esser, S. J.
    1938   Talen. In *Atlas van Tropisch Nederland*. M. Nijhoff, Gravenhage.
Etherington, I. M. H.
    1939a   On Non-associative Combinations. *Proceedings of the Royal Society of Edinburgh* 59:153–162.
    1939b   Genetic Algebras. *Proceedings of the Royal Society of Edinburgh* 59:242–258.
    1941a   Duplication of Linear Algebras. *Proceedings of the Edinburgh Mathematical Society,* Series 2, 6, part 4:222–230.
    1941b   Non-associative Algebra and the Symbolism of Genetics. *Proceedings of the Royal Society of Edinburgh* 61:24–42.
Evans-Pritchard, Edward
    1951   *Kinship and Marriage among the Nuer.* Clarendon, Oxford.
Eyde, D. B., and P. M. Postal
    1961   Avunculocality and Incest: The Development of Unilateral Cross-Cousin Marriage and Crow-Omaha Kinship Systems. *American Anthropologist* 63:747–771.
Fausto, Carlos
    1991   *O sistema de parentesco parakana: casamento avuncular e dravidianato na Amazônia.* Master's thesis, Museu Nacional, Rio de Janeiro.
Feinberg, R.
    1982   *Anuta. Social Structure of a Polynesian Island.* Brigham Young University Press, Laiee, Hawaii.
Fiedel, S. J.
    1987   Algonquian Origins: A Problem in Archaeological Linguistic Correlation. *Archaeology of Eastern North America* 15:1–11.
Fields, H. L., and W. R. Merrifield
    1980   Mayoruna (Panoan) Kinship. *Ethnology* XIX:1–28
Fischer, H. Th.
    1957   Some Notes on Kinship Systems and Relationship Terms of Sumba, Manggarai and South Timor. *I.A.E.* 48:1–31.
Flannery, Regina
    1938   Cross-Cousin Marriage among the Cree and Montagnais of James Bay. *Anthropological Quarterly* 11:29–33.
Fock, Niels
    1963   Waiwai: Religion and Society of an Amazonian tribe. National-muséets Skrifter Ethnografisk Raekke No. 7. National Museum, Copenhagen.
Forbis, Richard G.
    1977   *Cluny, An Ancient Fortified Village in Alberta.* Department of Archaeology Occasional Papers No. 4. University of Calgary, Calgary, Alta.
Forth, Gregory L.
    1981   *Rindi: An Ethnographic Study of a Traditional Domain in Eastern Sumba.* M. Nijhoff, The Hague.

1988   Prescription Gained or Retained?: Analytical Observations on the Relationship Terminology of Ndao, Eastern Indonesia. *Sociologus* 38:166–183.

1990   From Symmetry to Asymmetry: An Evolutionary Interpretation of Eastern Sumbanese Relationship Terminology. *Anthropos* 85:373–392.

1993   Nage Kin Terms: A New Form of Eastern Indonesian Social Classification. *Bijdragen tot de Taal-, Land- en Volkenkunde* 149:94–123.

Fowler, Catherine S.

1972   Some Ecological Clues to Proto-Numic Homelands. In *Great Basin Cultural Ecology: A Symposium,* edited by Don D. Fowler, pp. 105–121. Desert Research Institute Publications in the Social Sciences No. 8, Reno, Nev.

Fox, J.

1971   Sister's Child as Plant: Metaphors in an Idiom of Consanguinity. In *Rethinking Kinship and Marriage,* edited by R. Needham, pp. 219–252. Tavistock, London.

1984   Possible Models of Early Austronesian Social Organization. *Asian Perspectives* 26:36–43.

1987   "Between Savu and Roti": The Transformations of Social Categories on the Island of Ndao. In *A Word of Language,* edited by D. Laycock and W. Winter, pp. 195–203. P.L. Series C. 100. Australian National University, Canberra.

Friedman, Johnathan

1974   Marxism, Structuralism and Vulgar Materialism. *Man* 9:444–469.

Frish, Jack A., and Noel W. Schutz

1967   Componential Analysis and Semantic Reconstruction: The Proto Central Yuman Kinship System. *Ethnology* 6:272–293.

Gell, Alfred

1975   *Metamorphosis of the Cassowaries: Umeda Society, Language and Ritual.* Athlone, London.

Gibson, Kathleen R., Mary Ellen Thames, and Kathryn T. Molohon

1991   Mating Patterns and Genetic Structure of Two Native North American Communities in Northern Ontario. In *Papers of the Twenty-Second Algonquian Conference,* edited by W. Cowan, pp. 145–156. Carleton University, Ottawa.

Gifford, Edward W.

1917   Tubatulabal and Kawaiisu Kinship Terms. *University of California Publications in American Archaeology and Ethnology* 12(6):219–248.

1922   Californian Kinship Terminologies. *University of California Publications in American Archaeology and Ethnology* 18:1–285.

Gladwin, Thomas

1948   Comanche Kin Behavior. *American Anthropologist* 50:73–94.

Godelier, Maurice

1972   *Rationality and Irrationality in Economics.* Trans. B. Pearce. New York: Monthly Review Press.

1986   Incest Taboo and the Evolution of Society. In *Evolution and Its Influence,* edited by Alan Grafen, pp. 63–92. Oxford University Press, London.

1990   Inceste, parenté, pouvoir. *Psychanalystes* 36:33–51.

1993   L'Occident, miroir brisé: Une évaluation partielle de l'anthropologie sociale assortie de quelques perspectives. *Revue Annales* 48(5):183–1207.

1995   Is Social Anthropology Indissolubly Linked to the West, Its Birthplace? *International Social Science Journal* 47:141–158.

1996a   *L'Enigme du Don.* Fayard, Paris.

1996b   Meurtre du père ou sacrifice de la sexualité. In *Approches anthropologiques et psychanalytiques,* edited by Maurice Godelier and Jacques Hassoun, pp. 21–52. Les Cahiers d'Arcanes, Paris.

Goddard, Ives
1978   Central Algonquian Languages. In *Northeast,* edited by Bruce G. Trigger, pp. 583–587. Handbook of North American Indians, vol. 15, William C. Sturtevant, general editor. Smithsonian Institution, Washington, D.C.

Goddard, Pliny E.
1916   The Beaver Indians. *Anthropological Papers of the American Museum of Natural History* 10:202–293.

Goldman, Irving
1963   *The Cubeo Indians of the Northwest Amazon.* 2d ed. University of Illinois Press, Urbana.

Good, Anthony
1980   Elder Sister's Daughter Marriage in South Asia. *Journal of Anthropological Research* 36:474–500.
1981   Prescription, Preference, and Practice: Marriage Patterns among the Kondaiyankottai Maravar of South India. *Man* (n.s.) 16:109–129.
1993   On the Non-existence of "Dravidian Kinship." Paper presented at the Maison Suger Conference on Kinship Systems, Paris.

Goodenough, Ward
1970   *Description and Comparison in Cultural Anthropology.* Cambridge University Press, Cambridge.

Goody, Jack
1983   *The Development of the Family and Marriage in Europe.* Cambridge University Press, Cambridge, England.
1990   *The Oriental, the Ancient and the Primitive: Systems of Marriage and the Family in the Pre-industrial Societies of Eurasia.* Cambridge University Press, Cambridge.

Goss, James A.
1977   Linguistic Tools for the Great Basin Prehistorian. In *Models and Great Basin Prehistory. A Symposium,* edited by Don D. Fowler, pp. 49–70. Desert Research Institute Publications in the Social Sciences, Reno, Nev.

Gough, Kathleen
1959   Review of Louis Dumont. *Une Sous-caste d'Inde du Sud. Man* 59, art. 323, pp. 202–203.
1966   Review of Louis Dumont. *Une Sous-caste d'Inde du Sud* and *Hierarchy and Marriage Alliance in South Indian Kinship. Current Anthropology,* 7(3):332–335.

Graburn, Nelson H. H.
1975   Naskapi Family and Kinship. *Western Canadian Journal of Anthropology* 5, pp. 56–84.

Granet, Marcel
1930   *Chinese Civilization.* Routledge and Kegan Paul, London.
1939   Catégories matrimoniales et relations de proximité dans la Chine ancienne. *Annales sociologiques,* série B, fasc. 1–3.

Greechie, R. J., and M. Ottenheimer
1974   An Introduction to a Mathematical Approach to the Study of Kinship. In *Genealogical Mathematics,* edited by Paul A. Ballonoff. Mouton, Paris.

Greenberg, Joseph
1966   *Language Universals: With Special Reference to Feature Hierarchies.* Mouton, The Hague.

Gregor, Thomas
   1977   *Mehinaku: The Drama of Daily Life in a Brazilian Indian Village.* University
           of Chicago Press, Chicago.
   1985   *Anxious Pleasures: The Sexual Lives of an Amazonian People.* University of
           Chicago Press, Chicago.
Gregory, Chris
   1982   *Gifts and Commodities.* Academic Press, London.
Gruhn, Ruth
   1987   Aboriginal Culture History through Linguistics and Archaeology in the Great
           Basin. *Idaho Archaeologist* 10(1):3–8.
Guallart, J. M.
   1989   *El mundo magico de los Aguaruna.* CAAAP, Lima.
Guedon, Marie-Françoise
   1974   *People of Tetlin, Why Are You Singing?* Mercury Series, Ethnology Division
           Paper No. 9. National Museums of Canada, Ottawa.
Guilbaud, G. Th.
   1970   Système parental et matrimonial au Nord Ambrym. *Journal de la Société des
           Océanistes* 26:9–32.
Guignard, E.
   1984   *Les Touareg Udalen: Faits et modèles de parenté.* L'Harmattan, Paris.
Guo, Mingkun
   1964   *Chgoku-no kazokusei oyobi gengo-no kenky* (Chinese Family Organization
           and Language). Tokyo.
Hage, P., and F. Harary
   1991   *Exchange in Oceania: A Graph Theoretic Analysis.* Oxford: Clarendon Press.
Hallowell, A. Irving
   1928a   Recent Changes in the Kinship Terminology of the St. Francis Abenaki. *Atti
           del XXII Congresso Internazionale degli Americanisti,* 97–145.
   1928b   Was Cross-Cousin Marriage Practised by the North-Central Algonkian?
           Transactions of the XXIII International Congress of Americanists, pp. 519–
           544.
   1932   Kinship Terms and Cross-Cousin Marriage of the Montagnais-Naskapi and the
           Cree. *American Anthropologist* 43:171–199.
   1937   Cross-Cousin Marriage in the Lake Winnipeg Area. In *Contributions to
           Anthropology: Selected Papers of A. Irving Hallowell,* pp. 317–350.
           University of Chicago Press, Chicago.
   1975   *Contributions to Anthropology: Selected Papers of A. Irving Hallowell.*
           University of Chicago Press, Chicago.
   1992   *The Ojibwa of Berens River, Manitoba: Ethnography into History,* edited by
           Jennifer S. H. Brown. Harcourt Brace Jovanovich College Publishers, Fort
           Worth.
Hamid, S. Shahid
   1979   *Karakuram Hunza: The Land of Just Enough.* Ma'aref, Karachi.
Hanke, A.
   1909   *Grammatik und Vokabularium der Bongu-Sprache.* G. Reimer, Berlin.
Hanks, Lucien M., and Jane Richardson Hanks
   1945   *Observations on Northern Blackfoot Kinship.* Monographs of the American
           Ethnological Society No. 9. J. J. Augustin, New York.
Hanna, Margaret G.
   1976   *The Moose Bay Burial Mound, EdMq-1.* Anthropological Series,
           Saskatchewan Museum of Natural History No 3. Regina, Sask.

1984 Do You Take This Woman? Economics and Marriage in a Late Prehistoric Band. *Plains Anthropologist* 29(104):115–129.

Hara, Hiroko Sue
1980 *The Hare Indians and Their World.* Mercury Series, Ethnology Service Paper No. 63. National Museums of Canada, Ottawa.

Harrell, S.
1989 Ethnicity and Kinship Terms among Two Kinds of Yi. *Ethnicity and Ethnic Groups in China,* edited by Chien Chao and N. Tapp. *New Asia Bulletin* 8:179–197.

Hassrick, Royal B.
1944 Teton Dakota Kinship System. *American Anthropologist* (n.s.) 46:338–347.

Hawkes, K.
1976 *Binumarien: Kinship and Cooperation in a New Guinea Highlands Community.* Ph.D. dissertation, University of Washington. University Microfilms, Ann Arbor.

Held, Jan Garett
1935 *The Mahabharata: An Ethnological Study.* K. Paul, Trench, Trubner, London.

Helm, June
1960 Kin Terms of the Arctic Drainage Dene: Hare, Slavey, Chipewyan. *American Anthropologist* 62(2):279–295.

1961 *The Lynx Point People: The Dynamics of a Northern Athapaskan Band.* National Museum of Canada Bulletin 176. Ottawa.

1965 Bilaterality in the Socio-Territorial Organization of the Arctic Drainage Dene. *Ethnology* 4:361–385.

1968a The Nature of Dogrib Socio-territorial Groups. In *Man the Hunter,* edited by R. B. Lee and I. DeVore, pp. 118–125. Aldine, Chicago.

1968b The Statistics of Kin in Marriage: A Non-Australian Example. In *Man the Hunter,* edited by R. B. Lee and I. DeVore, pp. 216–217. Aldine, Chicago.

1969a *Remarks on the Methodology of Band Composition Analysis.* National Museum of Canada Bulletin 228:212–217.

1969b *A Method of Statistical Analysis of Primary Relative Bonds in Community Composition.* National Museum of Canada Bulletin 228:218–230.

1989 Review of *Kinship and the Drum Dance in a Northern Dene Community* by Michael Asch. *American Anthropologist* 91:489f.

Helm, June, and Beryl C. Gillespie
1981 Dogrib Oral Traditions as History: War and Peace in the 1820s. *Journal of Anthropological Research* 37(1):8–27.

Henley, Paul
1982 *The Panare: Tradition and Change on the Amazonian frontier.* Yale University Press, New Haven.

1993 South Indian Models in the Amazonian Lowlands. Unpublished.

Herán, François
1993a On Kinship Annotation. Paper presented at the Maison Suger Conference on Kinship Systems, Paris.

1993b *Figures et legèndes de la parenté.* Recherches et documents de l'INED. Institut National des Etudes Démographiques, Paris.

Héritier, Françoise
1981 *L'Exercice de la parenté.* Hautes Études/Gallimard Le Seuil, Paris.

1994a *De l'inceste.* Editions Odile Jacob, Paris.

1994b. *Les Deux soeurs et leur mère.* Editions Odile Jacob, Paris.

Héritier-Augé, Françoise, and Elisabeth Copet-Rougier (editors)
1991–94 *Les complexités de l'alliance.* 4 vols. Vol. 1: *Les systèmes semi-complexes;*

vol. 2: *Les Systèmes complexes d'alliance matrimoniale*; vol. 3: *Economie, politique et fondements symbolique (Afrique)*; vol. 4: *Economie, politique et fondements symbolique.*) Editions des Archives Contemporaines, Paris.

Heusch, Luca de
    1981   A Defense and Illustration of the Structures of Kinship. In *Why Marry Her?* pp. 29–81. Cambridge University Press, Cambridge.

Hickerson, Harold
    1967   A Note of Inquiry on Hockett's Reconstruction of PCA. *American Anthropologist* 69:362–363.

Hicks, David
    1990   *Kinship and Religion in Eastern Indonesia.* Acta Universitatis Gothoburgensis, Göteborg.

Hill, Jane H.
    1992   The Flower World of Old Uto-Aztecan. *Journal of Anthropological Research* 48(2):117–144.

Hockett, Charles F.
    1964   The Proto Central Algonquian Kinship System. In *Explorations in Cultural Anthropology: Essays in Honor of George Peter Murdock,* edited by Ward H. Goodenough, pp. 239–257. McGraw-Hill, New York.

Hoebel, E. Adamson
    1939   Comanche and H3kandika Shoshone Relationship Systems. *American Anthropologist* 41:440–457.

Hornborg, Alf
    1986/1988   *Dualism and Hierarchy in Lowland South America: Trajectories of indigenous social organization.* Uppsala Studies in Cultural Anthropology 9. Almqvist & Wiksell, Stockholm.
    1987a   Lineality in Two-Line Relationship Terminologies. *American Anthropologist* 89:454–456.
    1987b   Review of *Individual and Society in Guiana: A Comparative Study of Amerindian Social Organization,* by P. Rivière. *Ethnos* 52:410–412.
    1993   Panoan Marriage Sections: A Comparative Perspective. *Ethnology* 32:101–108.

Houseman, Michael
    1989   Les Structures de l'alliance chez les Beti: analyse critique du fonctionnement matrimonial dans les systèmes semi-complexes. In *Les Complexités de l'alliance. I: Les systèmes semi-complexes,* edited by F. Héritier–Augé and E. Copet-Rougier, pp. 149–177. Archives contemporaines, Paris.

Houseman, Michael, and Douglas White
    1995   Sidedness. Unpublished.
    1996   Structures réticulaires de la pratique matrimoniale. *L'Homme* 139, in press.

Hugh-Jones, C.
    1977   *Social Classification among the South American Indians of the Vaupés Region of Colombia.* Unpublished doctoral dissertation, University of Cambridge.
    1979   *From the Milk River.* Cambridge University Press, Cambridge.

Ives, John W.
    1985   *Northern Athapaskan Social and Economic Variability.* Unpublished Ph.D. dissertation, University of Michigan, Ann Arbor.
    1987   The Tsimshian Are Carrier. In *Ethnicity and Culture, Proceedings of the Eighteenth Annual Conference of the Archaeological Association of Calgary,* edited by R. Auger, M. F. Glass, S. MacEachern, and P. H. McCartney, pp. 209–225. University of Calgary Archaeological Association, Calgary, Alta.
    1988   On the Relationships Linking Social Structures, Local Group Size, and

Economic Strategies. In *Diet and Subsistence: Current Archaeological Perspectives, Proceedings of the Nineteenth Annual Conference of the Archaeological Association of Calgary,* edited by B. V. Kennedy and G. M. LeMoine, pp. 66–79. University of Calgary Archaeological Association, Calgary, Alta.

1990   *A Theory of Northern Athapaskan Prehistory.* Westview Press, Boulder, Colo.
1992   Regular Transformations in North American Kin Systems of Dravidian and Iroquois Structural Type. Paper presented at the Conference on Kinship in Asia, Institute of Ethnology and Anthropology, Russian Academy of Sciences, Moscow.
1993   The Ten Thousand Years before the Fur Trade in Northeastern Alberta. In *The Uncovered Past: Roots of Northern Alberta Societies,* edited by Patricia A. McCormack and R. Geoffrey Ironside, pp. 5–31. Circumpolar Research Series No. 3. Canadian Circumpolar Institute, University of Alberta, Edmonton, Alta.

Jackson, Jean E.
1977   Bará Zero Generation Terminology and Marriage. *Ethnology* 16:83–104.
1983   *The Fish People: Linguistic Exogamy and Tukanoan Identity in Northwest Amazonia.* Cambridge University Press, Cambridge.
1984   Vaupés Marriage Practices. In Kensinger 1984a:156–179.

Jamous, Raymond
1991   *La relation frère-soeur; parenté et rites chez les Meo de l'Inde du Nord.* Editions de l'Ecole des Hautes Etudes en Sciences Sociales, Paris.

Jenness, Diamond
1938   The Sarcee Indians of Alberta. *National Museum of Canada Bulletin* 90:1–98.

Jolas, T., Y. Verdier, and F. Zonabend
1970   Parler famille. *L'Homme* 10(3):5–26.

Journet, Nicholas
1993   L'expression de l'affinité dans la terminologie de parenté curripaco. Paper presented at the Maison Suger Conference on Kinship Systems, Paris.

Josselin de Jong, J. P. B. de
1983   The Malay Archipelago as a Field of Ethnological Study [1935]. In *Structural Anthropology in the Netherlands,* edited by P. E. Josselin de Jong, pp. 164–182. Foris Publications, Dordrecht.

Juillerat, Bernard
1977   Terminologie de parenté Iafar (Nouvelle-Guinée) Etude formelle d'un système dakota-iroquois. *L'Homme* 21:5–38.
1981   Organisation dualiste et compléementaritée sexuelle dans le sépik occidental. *L'Homme* 21(2):5–38.
1986   *Les Enfants du sang: société, reproduction et imaginaire en Nouvelle Guinée.* Editions de la Maison des Sciences de l'Homme, Paris.

Kaestle, F. A.
1995   Mitochondrial DNA evidence for the identity of the descendants of the prehistoric Stillwater Marsh population. In *Bioarchaeology of the Stillwater Marsh: Prehistoric Human Adaptation in the Western Great Basin,* edited by Clark Spencer Larsen and Robert L. Kelly, pp. 73–80. American Museum of Natural History, Anthropological Papers, No. 77.

Kana, Nico L.
1983   *Dunia Orang Savu.* Jakarta, Sinar Harapan.

Kay, Paul
1965   A Generalization of the Cross/Parallel Distinction. *American Anthropologist* 67:30–43.
1967   On the Multiplicity of Cross/Parallel Distinctions. *American Anthropologist* 69:83–85.

1975   The Generative Analysis of Kinship Semantics: A Reanalysis of the Seneca
        Data. *Foundations of Language* 13:201–214.
Keesing, Roger M.
    1975   *Kin Groups and Social Structure.* Holt, Rinehart & Winston, New York.
Kennedy, Brenda
    1981   *Marriage Patterns in an Archaic Population: A Study of Skeletal Remains from
            Port au Choix, Newfoundland.* Mercury Series, Archaeological Survey of
            Canada Paper Number 104. National Museum of Man, Ottawa.
Kensinger, Kenneth M.
    1977   Cashinahua Notions of Social Time and Social Space. In *Actes du 42e
            Congrès International des Américanistes* II, edited by B. Albert et al. Société
            des Américanistes, Paris.
    1980   The Dialectics of Person and Self in Cashinahua Society. Paper presented at
            the 79th Annual Meeting of the American Anthropological Association.
            Washington, D.C.
    1984a   (editor) *Marriage Practices in Lowland South America.* University of Illinois
            Press, Urbana.
    1984b   An Emic Model of Cashinahua Marriage. In *Marriage Practices in Lowland
            South America,* edited by K. M. Kensinger, pp. 221–251. University of Illinois
            Press, Urbana.
    1991   Panoan Kinship Terminology and Social Organization: Dravidian or Kariera,
            or Something Else? Paper present at the symposium Classic Panoan Topics in
            the Light of Recent Research, 47th International Congress of Americanists,
            Tulane University, New Orleans.
Kirchhoff, Paul
    1932   Verwandtschaftsbezeichnungen und Verwandtenheirat. *Zeitschrift für
            Ethnologie* 64:41–72.
    1955   The Principles of Clanship in Human Society. *Davidson Journal of Anthropol-
            ogy* 1(1):1–10.
Kracke, W. H.
    1984   Kagwahiv Moieties: Form without Function? In *Marriage Practices in
            Lowland South America,* edited by K. M. Kensinger, pp. 99–124. University
            of Illinois Press, Urbana.
Krauss, Michael E.
    n.d.   The Proto-Athapaskan and Eyak Kinship Term System. Ms. on file with the
            author.
Krauss, Michael E., and Victor K. Golla
    1981   Northern Athapaskan Languages. In *Subarctic,* edited by J. Helm, pp. 67–85.
            Handbook of North American Indians, vol. 6, William C. Sturtevant, general
            editor. Smithsonian Institution, Washington, D.C.
Krengel, Monika
    1989   *Sozialstruktur in Kumaon: Bergbauern im Himalaya.* Franz Steiner Verlag,
            Wiesbaden.
Kronenfeld, David B.
    1973   Fanti Kinship: The Structure of Terminology and Behavior. *American
            Anthropologist* 75:1577–1595.
    1980a   A Formal Analysis of Fanti Kinship Terminology (Ghana). *Anthropos* 75:586–
            608.
    1980b   Patricularistic or Universalistic Analysis of Fanti Kin-Terminology: The
            Alternative Goals of Terminological Analysis. *Man* (n.s.) 15:151–169.
    1989   Morgan vs. Dorsey on the Omaha Cross/Parallel Contrast: Theoretical
            Implications. *L'Homme* 29(1):76–106.
    1993   The Explanation of Kin Terminologies. Unpublished.

Kryukov, M. V.
1971   Expedition to the South Pacific. Unpublished field notes.
1972   *Sistema rodstva kitaitsev* (The Chinese kinship system). Nauka, Moscow.
1975   Moxhno li saglyanut'v glub' istorii Bongu: L Ocherk sistemy rodstva (An insight into the Bonguans' past: Survey of the kinship system). *Na beregu Maklaya* (On the Maclay Coast). Nauka, Moscow.
1989–1992   Among the Lolo. Unpublished field notes.
Kryukov, M. V., V. V. Malyavin, and M. V. Sofronov
1984   *Kitaiskiy etnos v srednie veka* (Chinese ethnos during the medieval era). Nauka, Moscow.

Kuper, Adam
1983   *Anthropology and Anthropologists: The Modern British School.* Rev. ed. Routledge & Kegan Paul, London.

Ladeira, Maria Elisa
1982   *A troca de nomes e a troca de cônjuges: uma contribuição ao estudo do parentesco timbira.* Master's thesis, Universidade de São Paulo.

Lamb, S. M.
1958   Linguistic Prehistory of the Great Basin. *International Journal of American Linguistics* 24:95–100.

Landes, Ruth
1937   *Ojibwa Sociology.* Columbia University Contributions to Anthropology, vol. 29. Columbia University Press, New York.
1969 [1938]   *The Ojibwa Woman.* AMS Press, New York.

Lane, R., and B. Lane
1959   On the Development of Dakota-Iroquois and Crow-Omaha Kinship Terminologies. *Southwestern Journal of Anthropology* 15:254–265.

Lathrap, Donald W.
1968   The Hunting Economies of the Tropical Forest Zone of South America. In *Man the Hunter,* edited by R. B. Lee and I. DeVore, pp. 23–29. Aldine, Chicago.
1972   Alternative Models of Population Movements in the Tropical Lowlands of South America. *Actas y Memorias del XXXIX Congreso Internacional de Americanistas* 4:13–23. Instituto de Estudios Peruanos, Lima.

Lathrap, Donald W., and Rudolph Troike
1984   California Historical Linguistics and Archaeology. *Journal of the Steward Anthropological Society* 15(1 & 2):99–157.

Lave, J. C.
1966   A Formal Analysis of Preferential Marriage with the Sister's Daughter. *Man* 1:185–200.
1973   A Comment on a Study in Structural Semantics: The Sirionó Kinship System. *American Anthropologist* 75:314–317.
1979   Cycles and Trends in Kríkatí Naming Practices. In *Dialectical Societies: The Gê and Bororo of Central Brazil,* edited by D. H. P. Maybury-Lewis, pp. 16–44. Harvard University Press, Cambridge, Mass.

Lavrovski, P. A.
1867   *Korennoye znachenie v nazvaniyakh rodstva u slavyan* (The original meaning of Slavic kinship terms). Tip. Imp. academii nauk, St. Petersburg.

Lawrence, W. E.
1937   Alternating Generations in Australia. In *Studies in the Science of Society,* edited by G. P. Murdock, pp. 319–354. Yale University Press, New Haven, Conn.

Lea, Vanessa
    1992   Mebengokre (Kayapo) Onomastics: A Facet of Houses as Total Facts in Central Brazil. *Man* 27(1):129–153.

Leach, E. R.
    1961   *Rethinking Anthropology.* University of London/Athelone.
    1961(1951)   The Structural Implications of Matrilateral Cross-Cousin Marriage. In *Rethinking Anthropology,* edited by E. Leach, pp. 54–104. Athlone, London.
    1971   *Pul Eliya. A Village in Ceylon.* Cambridge University Press, Cambridge.

Leacock, Eleanor, and Richard Lee
    1982   *Politics and History in Band Societies.* Cambridge University Press, Cambridge.

Lebar, Frank M.
    1972   *Ethnic Groups of Insular Southeast Asia.* Vol. 1. Human Relations Area Files Press, New Haven.

Lehman, F. K., and K. Witz
    1974   Prolegomena to a Formal Theory of Kinship. In *Genealogical Mathematics,* edited by P. Ballonoff. Mouton, Paris.

Lena, S.
    1986–87   Compte rendu de mission dans un sous–groupe jivaro: les Huambisa du Rio Santiago (Amazonas. Pérou). Mémoire de Diplôme d'Etudes Approfondies, Ecole des Hautes Etudes en Sciences Sociales, Paris. Mimeo.

Lesser, Alexander
    1928   Some Aspects of Siouan Kinship. *23rd International Congress of Americanists,* 563–571.

Lévi-Strauss, Claude
    1943   The Social Use of Kinship Terms among Brazilian Indians. *American Anthropologist* 45(3):398–409.
    1948   *La vie familiale et sociale des Nambicuara.* Société des Américanistes, Paris.
    1949   *Les structures élémentaires de la parenté.* Presses universitaires de France, Paris.
    1956.   The Family. In *Man, Culture and Society,* edited H. Shapiro and G. Dole, pp. 261–285. Oxford University Press, London.
    1958   *Anthropologie structurale.* Plon, Paris.
    1963   Social Structures of Central and Eastern Brazil. In *Structural Anthropology,* pp. 120–31. Allen Lane, London.
    1965   The Future of Kinship Studies. The Huxley Memorial Lecture, 1965. *Proceedings of the Royal Anthropological Institute* 13–21.
    1966   The Future of Kinship Studies. The Huxley Memorial Lecture 1965. *Proceedings of the Royal Anthropological Institute of Great Britain and Ireland for 1965*: 13–22.
    1967   *Les Structures élémentaires de la parenté.* Mouton, Paris.
    1968   The Social Use of Kinship Terms among Brazilian Indians. In *Marriage, Family, and Residence,* edited by P. Bohannan and J. Middleton, pp. 169–183. Garden City, N.Y.: Natural History Press.
    1968   *Les structures élémentaires de la parenté.* 2d ed. Plon, Paris.
    1969 [1949]   *The Elementary Structures of Kinship (Les Structures élémentaires de la parenté).* Rev. ed. Translated by James Harle Bell and John Richard von Sturmer, edited by Rodney Needham. Eyre & Spottiswoode, London.
    1973   Reflections on the Atom of Kinship. In *Structural Anthropology* 2, pp. 82–112. Penguin Books, Harmondsworth.
    1979   *La Voie des masques.* Plon, Paris.

1983a   *The Way of the Masks*. Jonathan Cape, London.
1983b   Histoire et ethnologie. *Annales* 38:1217–1231.
1984a   *Paroles données*. Plon, Paris.
1984b   On Indonesia. In *Anthropology and Myth: Lectures 1951–1982* (*Paroles données* 1984), translated by Roy Willis, pp. 153–159. Basil Blackwell, Oxford.

Lewis, E. Douglas
1988   *People of the Source: The Social and Ceremonial Order of Tana Wai Brama on Flores*. Foris Publications, Dordrecht.

Lewis, Ioan M.
1994   *Blood and Bone: The Call of Kinship in Somali Society*. Red Sea Press, Laurenceville, N.J.

Lienhardt, Godfrey
1961   *Divinity and Experience: The Religion of the Dinka*. Clarendon, Oxford.

Lietard, A.
1911–12   Essai de dictionaire Lo-lo-Français, dialecte A-hi. *T'oung Pao* série 2, 12:1–37, 123–156, 316–346, 544–558.

Liljeblad, Sven, and Catherine S. Fowler
1986   Owens Valley Paiute. In *Great Basin,* edited by Warren L. D'Azevedo, pp. 412–434. Handbook of North American Indians, vol. 11, general editor William C. Sturtevant. Smithsonian Institution, Washington, D.C.

Lima, Edilene C. de
1994   *Katukina: História e organização social de um grupo Pano do Alto Juruá*. Master's thesis, Universidade de São Paulo.

Lin, Yaohua
1946   Kinship System of the Lolo. *Harvard Journal of Asiatic Studies* 9.

Lint, J. H. van, and R. M. Wilson
1992   *A Course in Combinatorics*. Cambridge University Press, Cambridge.

Lizot, J.
1971   Remarques sur le vocabulaire de parenté Yanómami. *L'Homme* 11:25–38.

Lorrain, François
1975   *Réseaux sociaux et classifications sociales: essai sur l'algèbre et la géométrie des structures sociales*. Hermann, Paris.

Lounsbury, Floyd G.
1956   A Semantic Analysis of the Pawnee Kinship Usage. *Language* 32:158–194.
1964a   The Structural Analysis of Kinship Semantics. In *Proceedings of the Ninth International Congress of Linguists,* edited by Horace G. Lunt, pp. 1073–1093. Mouton, The Hague.
1964b   A Formal Account of the Crow and Omaha-type Kinship Terminologies. In *Explorations in Cultural Anthropology,* edited by W. H. Goodenough, pp. 351–393. McGraw-Hill, New York.

Lowie, Robert H.
1928   A Note on Relationship Terminologies. *American Anthropologist* 30:263–267.

Lucich, P.
1987   *Genealogical Symmetry: Rational Foundations of Australian Kinship*. Light Stone Publications. Armidale, New South Wales.
1991   Beyond Formalism: Group Theory in the Symmetries of Culture. *Journal of Mathematical Sociology* 16:221–264.

Ma, Xueliang
1951   *Sani yiyu yanjiu* (A study of Sani, a Yi dialect). Shangwu, Shanghai.

McAllister, J. Gilbert
1937   Kiowa-Apache Social Organization. In *Social Anthropology of the North*

American Tribes, edited by Fred Eggan, pp. 99–172. University of Chicago Press, Chicago.

McCallum, Cecilia

    1989   *Gender, Personhood and Social Organization amongst the Cashinahua of Western Amazonia.* Unpublished doctoral dissertation, London School of Economics.

McDonnell, Roger F.

    1975   *Kasini Society: Some Aspects of the Social Organization of an Athapaskan Culture between 1900 and 1950.* Unpublished Ph.D. dissertation, Department of Anthropology and Sociology, University of British Columbia.

McDougal, Charles

    1963   *The Social Structure of the Hill Juang.* University Microfilms, Ann Arbor.

    1964   Juang Categories and Joking Relationships. *Southwestern Journal of Anthropology* 20:319–345.

McDowell, Nancy

    1991   *The Mundugumor. From the Field Notes of Margaret Mead and Reo Fortune.* Smithsonian Institution Press, Washington, D.C.

McKinnon, Susan

    1991   *From a Shattered Sun: Hierarchy, Gender, and Alliance in the Tanimbar Islands.* University of Wisconsin Press. Madison.

    1983   *Hierarchy, Alliance, and Exchange in the Tanimbar Islands.* Unpublished Ph.D. dissertation, University of Chicago.

MacLane, S.

    1990   The Reasonable Effectiveness of Mathematical Reasoning. In *Mathematics and Science,* edited by Ronald E. Mickens. World Scientific, Singapore.

MacNeish, June Helm

    1960   Kin Terms of the Arctic Drainage Dene: Hare, Slavey, Chipewyan. *American Anthropologist* 62(2):201–488.

Mandelbaum, David G.

    1979   *The Plains Cree. An Ethnographic, Historical and Comparative Study.* Canadian Plains Studies No. 9. Canadian Plains Research Center, University of Regina, Regina, Saskatchewan.

Marasinova, L. M.

    1966   *Novye pskovskie gramoty XIV–XV vekov* (Newly discovered Pskov inscriptions of the 14–15th centuries). Izd-vo Moskovskogo un-ta, Moscow.

Marx, Karl

    1972   *The Ethnological Notebooks of Karl Marx (studies of Morgan, Phear, Maine, Lubbock).* Transcribed and edited by Lawrence Krader. Van Gorcum & Co., Assen.

Matta, Roberto da

    1970   Review of *Marriage among the Trio,* by P. Rivière. *Man* 5:550–551.

    1973   A Reconsideration of Apinayé Social Morphology. In *Peoples and Cultures of Native South America,* edited by D. R. Gross, pp. 277–291. Doubleday/ Natural History Press, Garden City, N.Y.

    1979   The Apinayé Relationship System: Terminology and Ideology. In *Dialectical Societies: The Gê and Bororo of Central Brazil,* edited by D. H. P. Maybury-Lewis, pp. 83–127. Harvard University Press, Cambridge, Mass.

    1982   *A Divided World.* Harvard University Press, Cambridge, Mass.

Maybury-Lewis, D. H. P.

    1967   *Akwé-Shavante Society.* Oxford: Clarendon Press.

    1979a   (editor) *Dialectical Societies: The Gê and Bororo of Central Brazil.* Cambridge, Mass.: Harvard University Press.

1979b   Cultural Categories of the Central Gé. In Maybury-Lewis 1979a:218–246.

Maxwell, Joseph A.

1979   The Evolution of Plains Indian Kin Terminologies: A Non-reflectionist Account. *Plains Anthropologist* 23(79):13–29.

Meggitt, M. J.

1972.   "Understanding Australian Aboriginal Society: Kinship Systems or Cultural Categories?" In *Kinship Studies in the Morgan Centennial Year,* edited by Princilla Reining, pp. 64–87. Anthropological Society of Washington, Washington, D.C.

Melatti, Julio Cesar

1977   Estrutura social marubo: um sistema australiano na Amazônia. *Anuário Antropológico* 76:83–120.

1979   The Relationship System of the Kraho. In *Dialectical Societies: The Gê and the Bororo of Central Brazil,* edited by D. H. P. Maybury-Lewis. Harvard University Press, Cambridge, Mass.

Menget, Patrick

1977a   Au nom des autres: classification des relations sociales chez les Txicão du Haut-Xingu. Thèse de 3ème cycle, Université de Paris X, Nanterre.

1977b   Adresse et référence dans la classification sociale Txicáo. In *Actes du XLIIe Congrès International des Américanistes II,* edited by Joanna Overling Kaplan, vol. 2, pp. 323–339. Société des Américanistes, Paris.

Metzger, Donald

1968   *Social Organization of Guahibo Indians.* Unpublished Ph.D. dissertation, University of Pittsburgh.

Metzger, Donald J., and Robert V. Morey

1983   Los Hiwi (Guahibo). In *Los Aborigenes de Venezuela,* vol. 2: *Etnologia contemporánea I,* edited by W. Coppens, pp. 125–216. Fundación La Salle de Ciencias Naturales, Instituto Caribe de Antropología y Sociología. Monte Avila Editores, Caracas.

Meyer, David

1984   The Development of the Marriage Isolate among the Pas Mountain Indians. *Western Canadian Anthropologist* 1:2–10.

Michelson, Truman

1916   Notes on the Piegan System of Consanguinity. In *Holmes Anniversary Volume,* edited by F. W. Hodge, pp. 320–333. J. W. Bryan Press, Washington, D.C.

Mickens, R. E. (editor)

1990   *Mathematics and Science.* World Scientific, Singapore.

Miklukho-Maclay, N. N.

1950   *Sobranie sochineniy* (Selected works), vol. 1. Moskow: Nauka

Miller, Wick R.

1986   Numic Languages. In *Great Basin,* edited by Warren L. D'Azevedo, pp. 98–106. Handbook of North American Indians, vol. 11, general editor, William C. Sturtevant. Smithsonian Institution, Washington, D.C.

Mills, R. F.

1991   Tanimbar-Kei: An Eastern Indonesian Subgroup. In *Currents in Pacific Linguistics,* edited by Robert Blust. Series D, 117. Australian National University, Canberra.

Moore, John H.

1994   Putting Anthropology Back Together Again: The Ethnogenetic Critique of Cladistic Theory. *American Anthropologist* 96(4):925–948.

Moore, Sally Falk

1963   Oblique and Asymmetrical Cross-Cousin Marriage and Crow-Omaha Terminology. *American Anthropologist* 65:296–311.

Morgan, L. H.
    1871   *Systems of Consanguinity and Affinity of the Human Family.* Smithsonian Contributions to Knowledge, vol. 17. Smithsonian Institution, Washington, D.C.
    1877   *Ancient Society, or Researches in the Lines of Human Progress from Savagery through Barbarism to Civilization.* Reprint with a foreword by Elisabeth Tooker. University of Arizona Press, Tucson.

Muller, Jean–Claude
    1980   Straight Sister-Exchange and the Transition from Elementary to Complex Structures. *American Ethnologist* 7(3):518–528.
    1982   *Du Bon usage du sexe et du mariage. Structures matrimoniales du haut plateau nigérian.* Paris/Québec: L'Harmattan / Serge Fleury.

Murdock, George Peter
    1949   *Social Structure.* Reprint. New York: Free Press.

Murphy, Robert F.
    1956   Matrilocality and Patrilineality in Mundurucu Society. *American Anthropologist* 58:414–434.
    1967   Tuareg Kinship. *American Anthropologist* 69:163–170.

Murphy, Robert, and Julian Steward
    1956   Tappers and Trappers: Parallel Processes in Acculturation. *Economic and Cultural Change* 4:393–408.

Murphy, Yolanda, and Robert Frank Murphy
    1974   *Women of the Forest.* New York: Columbia University Press.

Myers, Fred
    1986   *Pintupi Country, Pintupi Self: Sentiment, Place, and Politics among Western Desert Aborigines.* Smithsonian Institution Press, Washington, D.C.
    1988   Critical Trends in the Study of Hunter-Gatherers. In *Annual Review of Anthropology,* vol. 17, edited by B. Siegel, A. Beals, and S. Tyler, pp. 261–282. Annual Reviews Inc., Palo Alto.

Needham, Rodney
    1960   Lineal Equations in a Two-Section System: A Problem in the Social Structure of Mota (Banks Island). *Journal of the Polynesian Society* 69:23–30.
    1961   An Analytical Note on the Structure of Sirionó Society. *Southwestern Journal of Anthropology* 17:239–255.
    1962   *Structure and Sentiment.* University of Chicago Press, Chicago.
    1966a   Age, Category, and Descent. *Bijdragen tot de Taal-, Land- en Volkenkunde* 122:1–35.
    1966b   Terminology and Alliance: I. Garo, Manggarai. *Sociologus* 16:141–157.
    1967   Terminology and Alliance: II. Mapuche; Conclusions. *Sociologus* 17:39–54.
    1968   Endeh: Terminology, Alliance, and Analysis. *Bijdragen tot de Taal-, Land- en Volkenkunde* 124:305–335.
    1970   Endeh, II Test and Confirmation. *Bijdragen tot de Taal-, Land- en Volkenkunde* 126:247–258.
    1971   Remarks on the Analysis of Kinship and Marriage. In *Rethinking Kinship and Marriage,* edited by R. Needham. ASA Monographs 11:xiii–cxvii. Tavistock, London.
    1972   Prologue. In *Terminologia, alianza matrimonial y cambio en la sociedad Warao,* by M. M. Suárez. Caracas.
    1973   Prescription. *Oceania* 43 166–181.
    1974   The Evolution of Social Classification: A Commentary on the Warao Case. *Bijdragen tot de Taal-, Land- en Volkenkunde* 130:16–43.
    1980   Diversity, Structure, and Aspect in Manggarai Social Classification. In *Man,*

Meaning and History, edited by R. Schefold, J. Schoorl, and J. Tennekes, pp. 53–81. M. Nijhoff, The Hague.

1984   The Transformation of Prescriptive Systems in Eastern Indonesia. In *Unity in Diversity,* edited by P. E. de Josselin de Jong, pp. 221–33. Foris Publications, Dordrecht.

1985   Prescription and Variation in Rembong, Western Flores. *Bijdragen tot de Taal-, Land- end Volkenkunde* 141:275–87.

Nicholson, B. A.

1994a   Interactive Dynamics of Intrusive Horticultural Groups Coalescing in South-Central Manitoba during the Late Prehistoric Period—The Vickers Focus. *North American Archaeologist* 15(2):103–127.

1994b   Orientation of Burials and Patterning in the Selection of Sites of Late Prehistoric Burial Mounds in South-Central Manitoba. *Plains Anthropologist* 39(148):161–171.

Neuman, Robert W.

1975   *The Sonota Complex and Associated Sites on the Northern Great Plains.* Nebraska State Historical Society, Publications in Anthropology No. 6. Lincoln, Nebraska.

Nimuendajú, Curt

1942   *The Serente.* The Southwest Museum, Los Angeles.

1948   The Cawahib, Parintintin and Their Neighbors. In *The Tropical Forest Tribes,* edited by J. H. Steward. Handbook of South American Indians III. Bureau of American Ethnology Bulletin No. 143. Smithsonian Institution, Washington.

Norbeck, Edward

1963   Lewis Henry Morgan and Japanese Terms of Relationship: Profit through Error. *Southwestern Journal of Anthropology* 19:208–215.

Oberg, Kalervo

1953   *Indian Tribes of Northern Mato Grosso, Brazil.* Institute of Social Anthropology, Publication No. 15. Smithsonian Institution, Washington, D.C.

O'Laughlin, Bridget

1975   Marxist Approaches in Anthropology. In *Annual Review of Anthropology,* vol. 4, edited by B. Siegel, A. Beals, and S. Tyler, pp. 341–370. Annual Reviews Inc., Palo Alto.

Opler, Morris E.

1937   An Outline of Chiricahua Apache Social Organization. In *Social Anthropology of the North American Tribes,* edited by Fred Eggan, pp. 173–242. Chicago: University of Chicago Press.

Ortner, Sherry B.

1984   Theory in Anthropology since the Sixties. *Comparative Studies in Society and History* 26:126–166.

Osborn, Ann

1982   Mythology and Social Structure of the U'wa of Colombia. Unpublished doctoral dissertation, University of Oxford.

Overing Kaplan, Joanna

1972   Cognation, Endogamy, and Teknonymy: The Pioria Example. *Southwestern Journal of Anthropology* 28:282–297.

1973   Endogamy and the Marriage Alliance: A Note on Continuity in Kindred-Based Groups. *Man* 8:555–570.

1975   *The Piaroa, a People of the Orinoco Basin: A Study in Kinship and Marriage.* Clarendon Press, Oxford.

1984   Dualisms as an Expression of Differences and Danger: Marriage Exchange and Reciprocity among the Piaroa of Venezuela. In *Marriage Practices in Lowland South America,* edited by K. M. Kensinger, pp. 127–155. University of Illinois Press, Urbana.

Overing Kaplan, Joanna (editor)
    1977   *Social Time and Social Space in Lowland South American Societies.* Vol. 2: *Actes du XLIIe Congrès International des Américanistes.* Société des Américanistes, Paris.

Parkin, Robert
    1984   *Kinship and Marriage in the Austroasiatic-speaking World: A Comparative Analysis.* Unpublished D.Phil. dissertation, Oxford.
    1985   Munda Kinship Terminologies. *Man* 20:705–721.
    1986   Prescriptive Alliance in Southeast Asia: The Austroasiatic Evidence. *Sociologus* (n.s.) 36(1):52–64.
    1987   Kin Classification in the Karakorum. *Man* 22(1):57–70.
    1988a   Reincarnation and Alternate Generation Equivalence in Middle India. *Journal of Anthropological Research* 44(1):1–20.
    1988b   Prescription and Transformation in Mon-Khmer Kinship Terminologies. *Sociologus* 38(1):55–68.
    1990   Terminology and Alliance in India: Tribal Systems and the North-South Problem. *Contributions to Indian Sociology* (n.s.) 24:61–76.
    1992a   *The Munda of Central India: An Account of their Social Organization.* Oxford University Press, New Delhi.
    1992b   Dispersed Alliance and Terminological Change in South Asia. *Journal of the Anthropological Society of Oxford* 23(3):253–262.
    1992c   Dispersed Alliance and Terminological Change in South Asia. Paper presented at the Conference on Kinship in Asia, Russian Academy of Sciences, Moscow.
    1993   Middle Indian Kinship: A Critique of Georg Pfeffer's Interpretation. *Anthropos* 88(4–6):323–336.
    1995   The Contemporary Evolution of Polish Kinship Terminology. Forthcoming in *Sociologus* 45(2).

Parry, Jonathan
    1979   *Caste and Kinship in Kangra.* Routledge & Kegan Paul, London.

Pauwels, S.
    1984   *Comment mon beau-frère devient mon allié. Organisation sociale et rituels à Jamdena.* Thèse de doctorat de troisième cycle, Université de Paris VII.
    1990   La Relation frère-sour et la temporalité dans une société d'Indonésie orientale. *L'Homme* 30:7–29.

Pétesch, N.
    1992   *La pirogue de sable. Mose de représentation et d'organisation d'une société du fleuve: les Karaja de l'Araguaia (Brésil Central).* Thèse, Université de Paris XM—Nanterre.

Pfeffer, Georg
    1982   *Status and Affinity in Middle India.* Franz Steiner Verlag, Wiesbaden.
    1984   Kin Classification in Hunza. *Journal of Central Asia* 7(2):57–67.

Pinto, Márnio T.
    1989   *Os Arara: tempo, espaço e relações sociais em um povo karibe.* Master's thesis, Museu Nacional, Rio de Janeiro.

Pospisil, Leopold
    1959–60   The Kapauku Papuans and Their Kinship Organization. *Oceania* 30:188–205.

Proulx, Paul
    1984   Two Models of Algonquian Linguistic Prehistory: Diffusion versus Genetic Subgrouping. *Anthropological Linguistics* 26:393–434.

Queixalós, Francisco
    1983   Sex and Grammar in Sikuani (Guahibo) Kinship Terminology. Reprinted from
            Anthropological Linguistics, Summer:162–177.
Radcliffe-Brown, A. R.
    1913   Three Tribes of Western Australia. Journal of the Royal Anthropological
            Institute 48:143–94.
    1965 [1935]   Patrilineal and Matrilineal Succession. In Structure and
            Function in Primitive Society, edited by A. R. Brown. Free Press, New York.
    1952   Structure and Function in Primitive Society. Cohen & West, London.
    1953   Dravidian Kinship Terminology. Man 53, art. 169.
    1968   The Study of Kinship Systems (1941). In Structure and Function in Primitive
            Society, edited by A. R. Brown, pp. 49–89. Free Press, New York.
Ramos, A. R.
    1974   How the Sanuma Acquire Their Names. Ethnology 13:171–185.
Ramos, A. R., and B. Albert
    1977   Yanoama Descent and Affinity: The Sanumá/Yanomam Contrast. In Actes du
            XLIIe Congrès International des Américanistes, edited by Joanna Overing
            Kaplan, vol. 2, pp. 71–90. Société des Américanistes, Paris.
Reay, Marie
    1959   The Kuma. Melbourne University Press, Melbourne.
Renard-Casevitz, France-Marie
    1977   Du proche au loin. In Actes du XLII$_e$ Congrès International des
            Américanistes, edited by Joanna Overing Kaplan, vol. 2, pp. 121–140. Société
            des Américanistes, Paris.
    1995   Idéologie matsiguenga: du local au global. In Les Hommes vêtus, pp. 211–
            241. Unpublished Doctorat d'Etat, Paris.
Renard-Clamagirand, B.
    1982   Marobo. Selaf, Paris.
Ridington, Robin
    1968   The Environmental Context of Beaver Indian Behavior. Unpublished Ph.D.
            dissertation, Department of Anthropology, Harvard University, Cambridge,
            Mass.
    1969   Kin Categories versus Kin Groups: A Two Section System without Sections.
            Ethnology 8(4):460–467.
Rivers, W. H. R.
    1914   Kinship and Social Organisation. Constable & Co., London.
    1968 (1914)   Kinship and Social Organisation. With commentaries by
            Raymond Firth and David M. Schneider. London School of Economics
            Monographs on Social Anthropology no 34. Reprint. Athlone Press, London.
Rivière, Peter
    1966   A Note on Marriage with the Sister's Daughter. Man 1:550–556.
    1969   Marriage among the Trio: A Principle of Social Organization. Clarendon,
            Oxford.
    1973   The Lowland South America Culture Area: Towards a Structural Definition.
            Paper presented at the 72d Annual Meeting of the American Anthropological
            Association. New Orleans.
    1977   Some Problems in the Comparative Study of Carib Societies. In Carib-
            Speaking Indians, edited by E. B. Basso, pp. 39–42. University of Arizona
            Press, Tempe.
    1980   Dialectical Societies (Review Article). Man 15:533–540.
    1984   Individual and Society in Guiana. Cambridge University Press, Cambridge.
Rogers, Edward S.
    1962   The Round Lake Ojibway. Royal Ontario Museum, Art and Archeology

Division, Occasional Paper 5. Ontario Department of Lands and Forests, Toronto.

Rogers, Edward S., and J. Garth Taylor
1981   Northern Ojibwa. In *Subarctic,* edited by J. Helm, pp. 231–243, Handbook of North American Indians, vol. 6, general editor, William C. Sturtevant. Smithsonian Institution, Washington, D.C.

Romney, A. Kimball
1967   Kinship and Family. In *Social Anthropology,* edited by Manning Nash, pp. 207–237. Handbook of Middle American Indians, vol. 6, general editor, Robert Wauchope. University of Texas Press, Austin.
1970   Measuring Endogamy. In *Explorations in Mathematical Anthropology,* edited by P. Kay. Cambridge, Mass.: MIT Press.

Rossignol, Rev. M.
1938   Cross-Cousin Marriage among the Saskatchewan Cree. *Anthropological Quarterly* 11:26–28.

Rubel, Paula G., and Abraham Rosman
1983   The Evolution of Exchange Structures and Ranking: Some Northwest Coast and Athapaskan Examples. *Journal of Anthropological Research* 38(1):1–25.

Rushforth, Scott
1977   *Kinship and Social Organization among the Great Bear Lake Indians: A Cultural Decision-Making Model.* Unpublished Ph.D. dissertation, Department of Anthropology, University of Arizona, Tempe.

Salzmann, Zdenek
1959   Arapaho Kinship Terms and Two Related Ethnolinguistic Observations. *Anthropological Linguistics* 1:6–10.

Sapir, Edward
1921   *Language: An Introduction to the Study of Speech.* Harcourt, Brace, New York.

Schafer, Richard D.
1966   *An Introduction to Nonassociative Algebras.* Academic Press, New York.

Scheffler, Harold W.
1971   Dravidian-Iroquois: The Melanesian Evidence. In *Anthropology in Oceania: Essays Presented to Ian Hogbin,* edited by L. R. Hiatt and C. Jayawardena, pp. 231–254. Angus and Robertson, Sydney.
1978   *Australian Kin Classification.* Cambridge University Press, Cambridge.

Scheffler, Harold W., and Floyd G. Lounsbury
1971   *A Study in Structural Semantics: The Sirionó Kinship System.* Prentice-Hall, Englewood Cliffs, N.J.
1972   Systems of Kin Classification: A Structural Typology. In *Kinship Studies in the Morgan Centennial Year,* edited by P. Reining, pp. 113–33. Anthropological Society of Washington, Washington, D.C.

Schefold, Reimar
1988   *Lia: das grosse Ritual auf der Mentawai-Inseln (Indonesien).* Reimar, Berlin.

Schneider, David M.
1965   Some Muddles in the Models, or, How the System Really Works. In *The Relevance of Models for Social Anthropology,* edited by M. Banton, pp. 25–86. Tavistock, London.
1972   What Is Kinship All About? In *Kinship studies in the Morgan centennial year,* edited by Priscilla Reining, pp. 32–63. Anthropological Society of Washington, Washington, D.C.
1984   *A Critique of the Study of Kinship.* University of Michigan Press, Ann Arbor.

Schulte Nordholt, H. G.
1971   *The Political System of the Atoni of Timor.* M. Nijhoff, The Hague.

Schwerin, K. H.
    1983–84   The Kin-Integration System among Caribs. In *Themes in Political Organiza-
               tion: The Caribs and their Neighbours. Antropologica,* edited by A. B. Colson
               and H. D. Heinen, pp. 59–62:125–153.
Seeger, A.
    1981   *Nature and Society in Central Brazil.* Harvard University Press, Cambridge,
            Mass.
Service, Elman
    1971   *Primitive Social Organization.* 2d ed. Random House, New York.
Seymour-Smith, Charlotte
    1988   *Shiwiar: Identidad étnica y cambio en el río Corrientes.* Ediciones Abya-Yala/
            Centro Amazónico de Antropología y Aplicación Práctica, Quito.
Shapiro, Judith R.
    1984   Marriage Rules, Marriage Exchange, and the Definition of Marriage in
            Lowland South American Societies. In *Marriage Practices in Lowland South
            America,* edited by Kenneth M. Kensinger, 1–30. University of Illinois Press,
            Urbana.
    1985   The Sibling Relationship in Lowland South America: General Considerations.
            In *The Sibling Relationship in Lowland South America,* edited by K. M.
            Kensinger, pp. 1–7. Bennington College.
    1986   Kinship. In *Great Basin,* edited by Warren L. D'Azevedo, pp. 620–629.
            Handbook of North American Indians, vol. 11, general editor, William C.
            Sturtevant. Smithsonian Institution, Washington, D.C.
Shapiro, Warren
    1966   Secondary Unions and Kinship Terminology: The Case of Avuncular
            Marriage. *Bijdragen tot de Taal-, Land- en Volkenkunde* 122:82–89.
    1968   Kinship and Marriage in Sirionó Society: A Re-Examination. *Bijdragen tot de
            Taal-, Land-en Volkenkunde* 124:40–55.
    1970   The Ethnography of Two-Section Systems. *Ethnology* 9:380–388.
    1979   *Social Organization in Aboriginal Australia.* Australian National University
            Press. Canberra.
Sharp, Henry S.
    1979   *Chipewyan Marriage.* Mercury Series, Ethnology Service Paper No. 58.
            National Museum of Man, Ottawa.
Shimkin, D. E.
    1941   The Uto-Aztecan System of Kinship Terminology. *American Anthropologist*
            43:223–245.
Silva, Márcio F. da
    1995   Sistemas dravidianos na Amazônia: o caso waimiri-atroari. In *Antropologia do
            parentesco: estudos ameríndios,* edited by E. Viveiros de Castro. Rio de
            Janeiro: Editora da Universidade Federal do Rio de Janeiro, in press.
Siskind, Jane
    1973   *To Hunt in the Morning.* Oxford University Press, London.
Smith, David Glenn, Robert L. Bettinger, and Becky K. Rolfs
    1995   Serum Albumin Phenotypes at Stillwater: Implications for Population History
            in the Great Basin. In *Bioarchaeology of the Stillwater Marsh: Prehistoric
            Human Adaptation in the Western Great Basin,* edited by Clark Spencer
            Larsen and Robert L. Kelly, pp. 68–72. American Museum of Natural History,
            Anthropological Papers, No. 77.
Sperber, Dan
    1985   *On Anthropological Knowledge.* Cambridge University Press, Cambridge.

Spier, Leslie
    1925   *The Distribution of Kinship Systems in North America.* University of
            Washington Publications in Anthropology, vols. 1–2, pp. 69–88. Seattle:
            University of Washington Press.
Spoehr, Alexander
    1947   Changing Kinship Systems: A Study in the Acculturation of the Creeks, ·
            Cherokee, and Chocktaw. *Field Museum of Natural History. Anthropological
            Series* 33(4):153–235.
Stearman, Allyn
    1989   *Yuquí: Forest Nomads in a Changing World.* Holt, Rinehart & Winston, New
            York.
Steward, Julian
    1933   Ethnography of the Owens Valley Paiute. *University of California Publica-
            tions in Archaeology and Ethnology* 33(5):233–350.
    1938   *Basin-Plateau Aboriginal Sociopolitical Groups.* Bureau of American
            Ethnology Bulletin No. 120. Smithsonian Institution, Washington, D.C.
    1955   The Concept and Method of Cultural Ecology. In *Theory of Culture Change,*
            pp. 30–42. University of Illinois Press. Champaign.
Stirrat, R. L.
    1977   Dravidian and Non-Dravidian Kinship Terminologies in Sri Lanka. *Contribu-
            tions to Indian Sociology* (n.s.) 11:271–93.
Strong, William Duncan
    1929   Cross-Cousin Marriage in the Culture of the Northeastern Algonkian. In
            American Anthropologist (n.s.) 31:277–288.
Surailles-Calonge, A.
    1992   A propos de l'ethnographie des Candoshi et des Shapra. *Journal de la Société
            des Américanistes* 72(2):47–58.
Tax, Sol
    1937a   Some Problems of Social Organization. In *Social Anthropology of North
            American Tribes,* edited by Fred Eggan, pp. 3–32. University of Chicago
            Press, Chicago.
    1937b   The Social Organization of the Fox Indians. In *Social Anthropology of North
            American Tribes,* edited by Fred Eggan, pp. 243–284. University of Chicago
            Press, Chicago.
Taylor, Anne–Christine
    1982   The Marriage Alliance and Its Transformations in Jivaroan Societies. Paper
            presented at the 44th International Congress of Americanists. Manchester.
    1983   The Marriage Alliance and Its Structural Variations in Jivaroan Societies.
            Social Science Information 22(3):351–353.
    1985   L'art de la réduction. Les mécanismes de la différentiation tribale dans
            l'ensemble jivaro. *Journal de la Société des Américanistes* 71:159–189.
    1988   Les Modèles d'intelligibilité de l'histoire. In *Les Idées de l'anthropologie,*
            edited by Ph. Descola, G. Lenclud, C. Severi, and A.-C. Taylor, pp. 151–192.
            A. Colin, Paris.
    1989   La parenté jivaro. Unpublished.
Testart, Alain
    1966   *La Parenté Australienne: Etude morphologique.* Editions du CNRS, Paris.
    1993   Quelques considérations sur le temps dans la parenté et le mariage entre
            cousins croisés. Paper presented at the Maison Suger Conference on Kinship
            Systems, Paris.
    1992   La réversibilité du temps et le mariage des cousins croisés. *Social Anthropol-
            ogy* 1(1a):73–78.

1995   Age et génération chez les Aborigènes australiens. *L'Homme* 134:171–178.

Thomas, David H.
1982   *Order without Government: The Society of the Pemon Indians of Venezuela.* University of Illinois Press, Urbana.

1983   On Steward's Models of Shoshonean Sociopolitical Organization: A Great Bias in the Basin? In *The Development of Political Organization in Native North America, 1979 Proceedings of the American Ethnological Society,* edited by Elisabeth Tooker and Morton H. Fried, pp. 59–68. American Ethnological Society, Washington, D.C.

Tiemann, Gunther
1970   The Four-*got* Rule among the Jat of Harayana in Northern India. *Anthropos* 65:166–177.

Tjon Sie Fat, Franklin
1990   *Representing Kinship: Simple Models of Elementary Structures.* Faculty of Social Sciences, Leiden University, Leiden.

1993   Local Rules, Global Structures: Models of Exclusive Straight Sister-Exchange. Paper prepared for the conference Kinship and Exchange: New Perspectives, University of Cologne.

1994   Walks around the Hypercube: "Iroquois-Dravidian" Transformations. Unpublished.

1995   Rewriting the Rules: Operator Algebras and the Structural Analysis of Kinship Semantics. Unpublished.

Todd, Evelyn M.
1970   *A Grammar of the Ojibwa Language: The Severn Dialect.* Unpublished Ph.D. dissertation, University of North Carolina, Chapel Hill.

Tooker, Elisabeth
1992   Lewis H. Morgan and His Contemporaries. *American Anthropologist* (n.s.) 94:357–375.

Torralba, P. A.
1981   Sharanahua. *Antisuyo I* 4:37–83.

Townsley, Graham
1988   *Ideas of Order and Patterns of Change in Yaminahua Society.* Unpublished doctoral dissertation, Cambridge University.

Trautmann, Thomas R.
1981   *Dravidian Kinship.* Cambridge Studies in Social Anthropology vol. 36. Cambridge University Press, Cambridge.

1987   *Lewis Henry Morgan and the Invention of Kinship.* University of California Press, Berkeley.

1992   Dravidian Kinship as a Cultural Type and as a Structural Type. Paper presented at the Conferenceon Kinship in Asia, Russian Academy of Sciences, Moscow.

Trautmann, Thomas R., and R. H. Barnes
1991   Dravidian and Iroquois. Paper presented at the Iroquois Conference, Rensselaerville, N.Y.

Turner, David H., and Paul Wertman
1977   *Shamattawa: The Structure of Social Relations in a Northern Algonkian Band.* Mercury Series, Canadian Ethnology Series Paper No. 36. National Museum of Man, Ottawa.

Turner, Terence
1979   Kinship, Household, and Community Structure among the Kayapó. In *Dialectical Societies: The Gê and Bororo of Central Brazil,* edited by D. H. P. Maybury-Lewis, pp. 179–214. Harvard University Press, Cambridge, Mass.

1984   Dual Opposition, Hierarchy, and Value: Moiety Structure and Symbolic Polarity in Central Brazil and Elsewhere. In *Différences, valeurs, hiérarchie (textes offerts à Louis Dumont)*, edited by J.–C.Galey, pp. 335–70. Ecole des Hautes Etudes en Sciences Sociales. Paris.

Tyler, Stephen A.
1966   Parallel/Cross: An Evaluation of Definitions. *Southwestern Journal of Anthropology* 22:416–432.
1984   Change in Dravidian Kinship. In *Différences, valeurs, hiérarchie: textes offerts à Louis Dumont*, edited by J.–C. Galey, pp. 91–115. Ecole des Hautes Etudes en Sciences Sociales, Paris.

Tylor, E. B.
1889 [1871] *Primitive culture*, 2 vols. Henry Holt, New York.
1889   On a Method of Investigating the Development of Institutions: Applied to Laws of Marriage and Descent. *Journal of the Anthropological Institute* 18:245–72.

VanStone, James W.
1965   *The Changing Culture of the Snowdrift Chipewyan*. National Museum of Canada Bulletin 209. Ottawa.

Vatuk, Sylvia
1969   A Structural Analysis of the Hindi Kinship Terminology. *Contributions to Indian Sociology* (n.s.) 3:94–115.

Vial, Paul
1909   *Dictionnaire Français-Lolo, dialecte Gni*. Société des Missions-Etrangères, Hong Kong.

Vickers, J. Roderick
1994   Cultures of the Northwestern Plains: From the Boreal Forest Edge to the Milk River. In *Plains Indians*, A.D. *500–1500. The Archaeological Past of Historic Groups*, edited by Karl H. Schlesier, pp. 3–33. University of Oklahoma Press, Norman.

Vilaça, A. N.
1989   Comendo como gente: formas do canibalismo wari (Pakaa-Nova). Dissertaçao de Mestrado, PPGAS/Museu Naçional, Rio de Janeiro.

Viveiros de Castro, Eduardo
1989   Onamastique, terminologie de parenté et préférence matrimoniale chez les Gê (Brésil Central). Paper presented at the Séminaire général, University of Paris X—Nanterre.
1990   Princípios e parâmetros: um comentário a *L'Exercice de la parenté*. *Comunicação do PPGAS* No. 17. Museu Naçional.
1992   *From the Enemy's Point of View: Humanity and Divinity in an Amazonian society*. University of Chicago Press, Chicago.
1993a   Alguns aspectos da afinidade no dravidianato amazônico. In *Amazônia: etnologia e história indígena*, edited by E. Viveiros de Castro and M. Carneiro da Cunha, pp. 150–210. Núcleo de História Indígena e do Indigenismo (USP), FAPESP, Sao Paulo.
1993b   Structures, régimes, stratégies. *L'Homme* 125, xxxiii(1):117–137.
1994   Une Mauvaise querelle. *L'Homme* 129, xxxiv(1):181–191.

Viveiros de Castro, Eduardo, and Carlos Fausto
1993   La Puissance et l'acte: la parenté dans les basses terres de l'Amérique du Sud. *L'Homme*, 126–128, xxxiii(2–4):141–170.

Wagley, Charles, and Eduardo Galvão
1946   O parentesco tupi-guarani. *Boletim do Museu Naçional* 6:1–24.

Wagner, Roy
    1969   Marriage among the Daribi. In *Pigs, Pearlshells, and Women: Marriage in the New Guinea Highlands,* edited by R. M. Glasse and M. J. Meggitt, pp. 56–76. Prentice-Hall, Englewood Cliffs, N.J.

Walker, James R.
    1914   Oglala Kinship Terms. *American Anthropologist* (n.s.) 16:96–109.

Wang, Ningsheng
    1983   Yunnan yongsheng yizu (taluren) de yanshi hunyin xingtai (Primitive Marriage System among the Yi (Talu) of Yongsheng, Yunnan). *Xinan minzu yanjiu* (Studies of Nationalities of Southwestern China). Siguan minzu, Chengdu.

Wells, David G.
    1986   *The Penguin Dictionary of Curious and Interesting Numbers.* Penguin Books, Harmondsworth.

Wen, Yu
    1940   "Lolo yiyu" yanjiu (A study of vocabulary of the Lolo language). *Huazi ziehe dazue zhongguo wenhua yznjiusuo jikzn* 1.1:77–94.

Wheeler, C. J.
    1982   An Inquiry into the Proto-Algonquian System of Social Classification and Marriage: A Possible System of Symmetric Prescriptive Alliance in a Lake Forest Archaic Culture during the Third Millennium B.C. *Journal of the Anthropological Society of Oxford* 13:165–174.

White, Douglas R., and Michael Houseman
    n.d.   Ambilateral Sides and Property Flows among the Sinhalese: Refiguring the Ethnography of Dravidian Kinship and Exchange. In *Kinship, Networks and Exchange,* edited by T. Schweizer and D. R. White, in press.
    n.d.   Kinship Networks and the Balance Principle. Unpublished.

White, Douglas R., and Paul Jorion
    1992   Representing and Analysing Kinship: A Network Approach. *Current Anthropology* 33:454–63.

White, Douglas R., and K. P. Reitz
    1983   Graph and Semigroup Homomorphisms. *Social Networks* 5(2):193–234.

White, H. C.
    1963   *An Anatomy of Kinship.* Prentice-Hall, Englewood Cliffs, N.J.

Wigner, E. P.
    1960   The Unreasonable Effectiveness of Mathematics in the Natural Sciences. *Communications in Pure and Applied Mathematics* 13:1–14.

Wilbert, Johannes
    1986   Contributions to Wapishana Kinship Nomenclature. *Antropologica,* 65:77–100.

Williams, F. E.
    1932   Sex Affiliation and Its Implications. *Journal of the Royal Anthropological Institute* 62:51–81.

Wilmsen, Edwin
    1989   *We Are Here: Politics of Aboriginal Land Tenure.* University of California Press, Berkeley.

Wissler, Clark
    1911   Social Organization and Ritualistic Ceremonies of the Blackfoot Indians. *The American Museum of Natural History Anthropological Papers* 7:3–64.

Wobst, H. Martin
    1974   Boundary Conditions for Paleolithic Social Systems: A Simulation Approach. *American Antiquity* 39:147–178.

1976 Locational Relationships in Paleolithic Society. *Journal of Human Evolution* 5:49–58.

van Wouden, F. A. E.
 1968 *Types of Social Structure in Eastern Indonesia [1935].* M. Nijhoff, The Hague.

Xie, Jian
 1987 *Kunming dongjiao de sameizu* (Samei of the eastern suburbs of Kunming). Zhongwen daxue, Hong Kong.

Yalman, Nur
 1962 The Structure of the Sinhalese Kindred: A Re-Examination of the Dravidian Terminology. *American Anthropologist* 64:548–575.
 1967 *Under the Bo Tree. Studies in Caste, Kinship and Marriage in the Interior of Ceylon.* University of California Press, Berkeley.

Yang, Hesen
 1985 Wuding yizu fengshi tusi gailiu de liuwangshe yicon shehui diaocha (Sociological survey of Yi villages, Wuding Country, inhabited by refugees of the Fen Clan). *Yizu wenhua* 1:84–123.

1988 Chuxiong yi chou minzu yuanliu (Origin of nationalities in Yi region of Chuxiong). *Yizu wenhua* 4:80–91.

Young, David A., and Robert L. Bettinger
 1992 The Numic Spread: A Computer Simulation. *American Antiquity* 57(1):85–99.

Young, Phillip D.
 1970 A Structural Model of Ngawbe Marriage. *Ethnology* 9(1):85–95.
 1971 *Ngawbe: Tradition and Change among the Western Guaymí of Panama.* University of Illinois Press, Urbana.

Yuan, Jiahua
 1953 *Axi shange* (Folksongs of Asi). Shangwu, Shanghai.

Zhevlakov, K. A., A. M. Slin'ko, I. P. Shestakov, and A. I. Shirshov
 1982 *Rings That Are Nearly Associative.* Academic Press, New York.

Zimmermann, Francis
 1993 *Enquête sur la parenté.* Presses Universitaires de France, Paris.

Index

Achuar, 188–91, 238, 346, 362

Address terminologies, 189–90, 194–95, 199–200, 394

Affinal section, 337

Affinity/affines: in alternating generations, 172; Amazonian notion of, 355, 367–68, 403; crossness and, 33–34; Dravidian, 33–34, 81, 342–44; grandkin as, 173–74, 176; parallel transmission of, 172–73; terminology for as evidence for directionality in kinship evolution, 405–6

Aguaruna, 191–97, 201, 203, 208, 362–63

Ahtna, 106

Algonquian: center/periphery pattern in, 134; Central, 53; cross-cousin marriage, 51, 52, 106–9, 126; crossness, 106–11, 126; prehistory, 128–29; proto-, 126–28

Ali, Tahir, 253, 255

Allen, N. J., 341–42

Alliance: crossness and, 346, 353; Kandoshi, 203–5; local group, 119–21, 135; marriage, 148–49n.10, 345–46, 381n.34; multicentric, 231; sidedness and, 230; in South Asia, 255, 256; "Type B," 356–64

Alternating generation principle, 234–35

Aluridja, Northern, 80

Amahuaca, 370–71

Amazonia: affinity in, 355, 367–68, 403; Crow-Omaha in, 373; Dravidian in, 171–72, 245, 366–68, 403–4

Apache, Western, 17

Aranda, 356, 360

Arapaho, 34, 35, 108–9

Asch, Michael, 100, 118, 161–62

Associativity, 60, 61, 62, 85

Asymmetric system, 271

Athapaskan (Dene), 52; cross-cousin marriage, 96, 117, 125; crossness in Mackenzie Basin, 97–98, 99–106; origin and migration of, 123–24; proto-, 123, 124

Atkins, J. R., 63

Australian systems: contrasted with Dravidian, 337–39, 340, 342–44, 348, 365, 379n.22; modes of extension in, 366; as sociocentric system, 365; as transformed Dravidian, 370, 399

Bahnar, 270n.4

Bands, 129, 161–62. See also Hunter-gatherer societies

Barasana, 238

Bardi, 357, 360

Barnes, R. H., 22, 77

Beaver, 102–4, 105, 119, 144, 157, 337–38

Bettinger, Robert L., 137

Bifurcate collateral terminologies, 9, 298

Bifurcate merging terminologies, 9, 298, 311, 335, 395

Bilaterality, 162

Blackfoot, 109–11

Boleng, 283, 284

Bongu, 298–99

Bororo, 175

Boyd, J. P., 62

Buchler, Ira, 352, 364

Burushaski, 257–59, 263, 397

Burusho, 253–55

Callender, Charles, 52

Campa, 245–50

Candoa, 187, 188. *See also* Kandoshi
Carib, 174
Cashinahua, 371
Cheyenne, 34, 35, 108, 257, 258
Chinese, 295, 296–98, 299, 300–301
Chipewyan, 96, 105–6
Classificatory systems, 6–7
Cognatic terminologies, 273, 280, 284–85, 287–88
Cognation, 402
Comanche, 114–15, 116
Consanguine, 63, 402
Cree, 106–7, 108
Cross-cousin marriage: affected by acculturation, 155–56; Aguaruna, 193–96; Algonquian, 51, 52, 106–9, 126; ancient Chinese, 297; asymmetric, 83; Athapaskan, 96, 117, 125; bilateral, 30, 81, 83, 99, 116, 119, 125, 134, 173, 188, 201, 206, 208, 214; close, 236; demographic cause for, 155; Dravidian, 7–8, 81, 83, 99, 117–18, 214–15, 335; Dravidian and Iroquois contrasted, 356–64; Kandoshi, 201, 203, 205; Ngawbe, 205; Ojibwa, 154–57; problems of, 163; prohibition of, 163, 164; pseudo-, 113–14, 117, 133; Shoshone/Numic, 113–17, 131, 132; Slavey, 144; unilateral, 116, 163, 174–76, 178, 193, 271
Crossness: affines and, 33–34; Aguaruna, 196; algebraic models of, 63–86; Algonquian, 106–11, 126; alliance and, 346, 353; Athapaskan, 97–98, 99–106; defined, 30, 354; Dravidian, 8, 18, 64, 66, 70, 83, 85, 231–32, 344–47; in early North America, 134–36; in early Uto-Aztecan, 131; egocentric, 231, 232; equivalence rules for, 19; erosion of, 125; formal vs. "sociological," 210; hypercube modeling of, 10–12, 18–24; Iroquois, 9, 33, 60, 65, 66–67, 69, 71, 73, 81, 92n.7, 179, 232, 236, 355–57, 359; marriage and, 346, 354; Ngambe, 87; in tetradic models, 326–28; types of, 30–34, 361–62, 395–96; uneven distribution of, 16–17; used to define intermediates between Dravidian and Iroquois, 10–12, 20–25. *See also* Cross-cousin marriage
Crow, 10, 129
Cross-parallel discrimination. *See* Crossness
Crow-Omaha system, 211; in Amazonia, 373; associated with endogamy, 175, 183; "crossed" name transmission and, 236; defined, 182; derivation of, 312; skewing of, 17, 134, 400–401; unilateral marriage preference

and, 176–77; unilineal consanguinity and, 402
Cuiva (Guahibo), 351–52, 370

Dakota, 52
DeMallie, Raymond, 58n.11
Dempsey, Hugh A., 111
Descent: distinguished from filiation, 393–94; unilineal, 177–78
Descriptive systems, 7
Dividedness, 216, 229
Dole, Gertrude, 310
Donald, Leland, 17–18
Dorsey, J. O., 27–29
Dravidian/Dravidianate system (Type A): affinal terminology in, 33–34, 81, 342–44; algebraic model of, 60, 63–70, 72–73, 77, 81–86; in Amazonia, 171–72, 245, 366–68, 403–4; box, 341; complexity of, 92n.7; concentric, 366–67, 373; consanguinity and affinity contrasted in, 342–44; consanguinity in, 402–3; contrasted with Australian, 336–39, 340, 342–44, 348, 365, 379n.22; contrasted with Crow-Omaha, 182–83; contrasted with Iroquois, 9, 11, 27, 30–32, 67–72, 81, 83–85, 179, 212–13, 252, 257, 331n.5, 334–35, 352–64, 380n.24; cross-cousin marriage in, 7–8, 81, 83, 99, 117–18, 214–15, 335; cross cousin role in, 148; crossness, 8, 18, 64, 66, 70, 83, 85, 231–32, 344–47; defined, 209–10; distribution of, 6; formal analysis of, 157–61; history of concept, 334–36; ideal, 314–18; Jivaro, 187, 190, 197, 208, 211; lack of cross cousin marriage rule in, 165; Mackenzie Basin Dene, 97–99, 102, 104, 106, 117, 141–42, 143–44, 147, 161–62; as marginalized system, 180; marriage alliance and, 345–46; models A and B of, 348–50, 396; Morgan's errors about, 40, 44–46; in North America, 51, 52, 54–55, 134–36; Northern Ojibwa, 150–57; oblique marriage in, 237–40; origin of, 318–30; Panoan, 210; as prototype in North America, 134–36; sidedness in, 228–37; as sociocentric system, 364; as stable type, 12, 20; transformation paths from, 163–64, 178, 182–83, 264, 266–67, 308–9, 312–13, 370, 399, 404; transformation to Iroquois of, 232, 398–99, 405–6; varieties of, 10, 117–18
Dual organization, 185n.18, 214, 216, 233–36, 240. *See also* Moieties
Dumont, Louis; on Dravidian/Australian con-

trast, 335–36, 342–43; on Dravidian crossness, 18, 171, 345–46; on Dravidian vs. Iroquois, 352; on inheritance of kinship, 162; on Kariera, 336–37; on marriage alliance, 335, 346–47; on Pramalai Kallar, 383–84n.57

Dunning, Robert William, 156

Eggan, Fred, 34; on Arapaho, 108–9, 126; on Crow, 129; on early Uto-Aztecan, 131; on Owens Valley Paiute, 133; on Shoshone, 116–17

Elkin, A. P., 78, 80, 357, 382n51

Endogamy: Beaver, 102–4; conditions favoring, 119; Cree, 107; Crow-Omaha system associated with, 175, 183; rank, 175; social isolation through, 120

Eskimo system, 10, 391, 392, 394

Exchange: asymmetric, 319; as basis of kinship, 408; contrasted with alliance, 347; restricted vs. generalized, 359

Exogamy: clan, 253; conditions favoring, 119; "Hawaiianization" and, 180; Mackenzie Basin, 100, 102, 104

Eyak, 106, 123

Fanti, 55

Fausto, Carlos, 372

Filiation: distinguished from descent, 393–94

Fordat, 273, 274, 275, 276, 277, 289

Fowler, Catherine S., 130

Fox, 28, 29, 163

Fox, J., 292n.17

Freud, Sigmund, 406–7

Frisch, Jack A., 296

Gé, 173, 175, 176, 185n.18, 373

Gell, Alfred, 357–58, 359

Genealogical amnesia, 200

Gnau, 359

Good, Anthony, 341, 380n.25

Gough, Kathleen, 340–41

Gregor, Chris, 180

Guahibo, 225

Hallowell, A. Irving, 51, 107, 155, 156

Hamid, S. Shahid, 253

Hanks, Jane Richardson, 109

Hanks, Lucien M., 109

Hanna, Margaret G., 121

Hawaiian system, 10, 294, 295, 394, 400, 406

Helm, June, 100–102, 141, 148n.4

Henley, Paul, 184n.7, 349, 350

Héritier, Françoise, 345, 346, 347, 358, 380n.32

Hickerson, Harold, 126

Hill, Jane H., 137

Hindi (North India), 259, 260–63

Hockett, Charles F., 126

Hoebel, E. Adamson, 116

Hopi, 131

Hornborg, Alf, 228, 233, 234, 237, 239–40, 382n.47

Hunter-gatherer societies: archaeological predictions about, 120–21; developmental processes in, 118–20; kinship in, 94–95; Subarctic, 95–96

Iafar. *See* Yafar

Incest, 248–49, 347, 407–8, 409, 410

Indo-European languages, 267–68

Indonesian, Eastern: prototype terminology, 284–85; semantic types, 282–84; tribal group locations, 290

Iroquois system (Type B): affinal terminology in, 34; algebraic model of, 65, 67–69, 71–77, 78, 84; associated with large population aggregations, 180; contrasted with Dravidian, 9, 11, 27, 30–32, 67–72, 81, 83–85, 179, 212–13, 252, 257, 331n.5, 334–35, 352–64; 380n.24; crossness, 9, 33, 60, 65, 66–67, 69, 71, 73, 81, 92n.7, 179, 232, 236, 355–57, 359; as egocentric system, 364–65; generational, 73–74, 77, 87, 88, 89, 236, 400; as later development in North America, 134, 135, 136; Morgan on, 29–30, 40–42, 43, 44, 50, 57n.9; in North America, 34–39, 40, 41–42, 43, 44, 48, 52, 54–55; origin of, 55, 179–80, 312; in South and Southeast Asia, 56, 257–59; as stable type, 12, 20; as transformed Dravidian, 232, 398–99, 405–6; validity of, 29; variants, 10, 22–23, 33, 73–80, 87–89

Ives, John W., 52

Jacker, Edward, 35–38, 52

Jivaro, 187, 207–9, 211. *See also* Achuar; Aguaruna

Juillerat, Bernard, 88, 358–59

Kagwahiv, 173

Kam, 300

Kandoshi, 197–205, 206–7, 208–9, 211, 363

Karaja, 238

Kariera, 172, 242n.7, 336–37, 369, 396

Kaska, Ross River, 120

Kaw (Kansa), 49–50

Kay, Paul, 340
Keesing, Roger M., 341
Kei, 273, 274, 275, 276, 280, 288
Kennedy, Brenda, 121
Khasi, 270n.4
Kinship: the body and, 388; defined, 4, 386–87; distinguishing behavior, rules, and categories in, 4–5, 333; origin of, 406–11
Kinship analysis: algebraic modeling in, 60–62; future of, 3–4, 16–18; history of, 1–3; study of past with, 3; uneven development of, 17–18
Kinship systems: directionality in, 310–13; elementary, semicomplex, and complex, 357–58, 374; exchange as basic rule of, 412; four configurations of, 394–95; language requirement of, 411; marriage and, 410–11; mode of production and, 391–92; prehistory of, 411–12; tetradic, 320–30. *See also* Affinity/affines; Crossness; Kinship terminology; *name of specific system*
Kinship terminology: asymmetric, 287; center/periphery pattern for, 134; descent not linked to, 394; evolution of, 392, 397–99, 404–6; gender specific languages for, 246–50; generational, 9; historic documentation of change in, 295–96, 298–301; lineal, 9; as linguistic map, 393; matrimonial alliance interpretation of, 334, 346; pan-societal categories and, 389–90; prescriptive, 256, 264, 267, 268; problems with names for, 332–33; reality of, 5; reconstructing, 280–81; rule of economy of, 279, 286; semantic types of, 273; typologies of, 5–6, 9–16; uneven distribution of types, 16–17. *See also* Bifurcate merging terminologies; Bifurcate collateral terminologies; Cognatic terminologies; Kinship systems; Merging; Reclassification/recalculation; Sidedness; Skewing
Kiowa Apache, 138n.4
Kirchhoff, Paul, 9, 294–95
Kondaiyam Kottai Maravar, 342, 343
Koya, 384n.57
Kronenfeld, David B., 61; on Dravidian crossness, 340, 379n.23; on Dravidian vs. Iroquois, 364–65; on errors in Morgan's data, 27–29, 50, 56n.1; on Fanti, 55
Kryukov, M. V., 318–19
Kukata, 78, 80
Kuma, 10, 11, 12, 20, 89–90, 383n.53
Kumoan, 263–64, 265–66

Lamb, S. M., 129–30
Lathrap, Donald W., 178
Latin, 298, 301
Lavrovski, P. A., 295–96
Leach, E. R., 378n.15
Levirate, 189, 191, 197
Lévi-Strauss, Claude: on classificatory terminologies, 335; on function of kinship, 334; on method of relationships vs. method of classes, 377n.6; on "Omaha," 359; on origin of incest taboo, 407; on structures, 168, 169, 170, 333; three kinds of kinship systems of, 142–43
Lienhardt, Godfrey, 368–69
Lineality, 8
Lineal section, 337
Lipo, 307
Lisu, 306–7
Loanwords, 301, 307
Lolo, 302–10
Lounsbury, Floyd, 10, 27, 54, 174, 334–35
Lowie, Robert, 9

McAllister, J. Gilbert, 138n.4
Mackenzie Basin system, 141, 144; crossness in, 97–98, 99–106. *See also* Slavey
Makuna, 216–17, 218, 234
Malpahariya, 264
Mandelbaum, David G., 108
Marriage: asymmetric, 286; crossness and, 346, 354; dual-sided, 234–36; oblique, 174, 176, 236, 237–40; third bilateral cousin, 87. *See also* Alliance; Cross-cousin marriage; Endogamy; Exogamy
Matis, 371
Matsiguenga, 206, 245–50
Mayoruma, 238
Mehinaku, 179, 180
Merging: generational, 78, 80; rule, 30. *See also* Bifurcate merging terminologies
Meyer, David, 107
Miller, Wick R., 130
Moieties, 236, 319; Cashinahua, 371, Fox, 163–64; kinship terminologies consistent with, 379n.23, Matsiguenga, 249, 250; Panoan, 172, 233
Moluccan, South, 273–77; prototype of, 279–82; transformation of, 277–79
Montagnais-Naskapi, 107–8
Moore, Sally Falk, 174, 176
Morgan, L. H., 393; changing awareness

Dravidian vs. Iroquois, 40–48, 50–52; on development of kinship systems, 294; distinguishes classificatory and descriptive kinship systems, 6–7; importance of Ojibwa to, 39–40; on Iroquois (Seneca) kinship, 1–2, 29–30, 40–42, 43, 44, 50, 57n.9; kinship terminologies published by, 22–24; legacy of, 25n.1; on Omaha kinship, 27–29, 48–50; papers of, 34–35; possible errors/bias of, 28–29, 33, 46, 50, 54
Munda, 255, 258, 267
Mundugumor, 87–88, 89, 90–91
Murdock, George, 10, 296
Myers, Fred, 369–70

Naming/name transmission, 173, 176, 234–35, 236–37
Nasupo, 307–9, 312
Navajo, 17
Naxi, 300
Nazu, 307
Needham, Rodney, 168, 169, 272, 284–85
Ngawbe, 10, 86–87, 88, 205, 360–61
Norms, 387
Nuer, 368
Numic, 111–17, 129–33, 137

Ojibwa, 16; bands, 390; cross-cousin marriage, 52, 154–57; as example of Iroquois (Type B) crossness, 35–40; Northern, 150–57; terminological adjustments in, 156–57
Omaha, 10, 27–29, 48–52. *See also* Crow-Omaha system
Ortner, Sherry B., 169, 170

Paiute, Owens Valley, 132–33
Pakaa-Nova, 221
Panare, Western, 349–50
Panoan, 172, 210, 233–35, 370–71
Parakanā, 222, 372
Piaroa, 346
Pintupi, 80, 369–70
Pioria, 238
Pitjantjara, 80, 338–39
Polygyny, sororal, 188, 191, 197
Postmarital residence, 178
Potawatomi, 163–64
Pramalai Kallar, 342, 343
Prescriptive systems. *See under* Kinship terminology

Radcliffe-Brown, A. R., 335
Reay, Marie, 90

Reciprocal sets, 380n.26
Reclassification/recalculation: genealogical, 200; Ojibwa, 156–57; Slavey, 144, 145
Red Knife. *See* Chipewyan
Reification, 176–77, 183
Ridington, Robin, 102–4, 157
Riggs, S. R., 42–43, 52
Rivers, W. H. R., 96, 154
Rivière, Peter, 177
Rogers, Edward S., 156
Roti, 292n.17
Rushforth, Scott, 142
Russian, 295–96, 299, 301

Sanipo, 310
Sapir, Edward, 313
Sarsi, 106
Savu, 292n.17
Scheffler, Harold W., 174; on Dravidian/Iroquois, 59–60, 352–53; on kinship terminologies and marriage, 379n.21; on Kuma, 89–90; on Pitjantjara, 80, 338
Schneider, David, 2
Schutz, Noel W., 296
Scudder, Ezekiel C., 46
Selaru, 281
Selby, Henry, 352, 364
Self-reciprocity, 348
Seneca, 1, 27, 40–42, 54
Serrano, 131
Sexuality, 408–10
Shapiro, Warren, 242n.9, 337, 339
Shavante, 226, 229
Sherente, 175
Shimkin, D. E., 130–31
Shoshone, 112–17, 390
Sidedness: alliance and, 230; defined, 216, 237; Dravidian terminologies and, 228–33, 234–37; as local phenomenon, 217; oblique marriage and, 237–40; self-sustaining, 231; viri-, 218–28; Yanomamö, 220
Sirionó, 174, 373
Sister exchange, 89; Jivaro, 188, 191; Kuma, 90; Mundugumor, 87; Ngawbe, 360; Umeda, 357–58; Yafar, 88
Skewing, 10, 17, 29, 134, 176–77, 400–401
Slavey: crossness, 97–98, 100, 101, 142–44; developmental processes, 103; as exemplar of Mackenzie Basin kinship type, 141; exogamy, 100, 101–2, 104, 119–20, 144; kinship knowledge, 145–46; local groups/bands, 104, 105, 119–20, 162; recalculation of kinship relations in, 144, 145

Spier, Leslie, 100
Steward, Julian, 112–14, 116, 390
Strong, William Duncan, 107, 166n.12, 166n.16
Structuralism/structure, 168–69, 182, 333–34
Sudanese system, 10, 394
Sumba, Eastern, 284
Suyá, 175, 227
Symmetric filiation, 86–87

Tamil, 44–46, 47, 301
Tighe, Marion, 17–18
Timbira, Eastern, 176
Tjon Sie Fat, Franklin E., 10–11, 18, 25n.8, 357, 359–60
Trautmann, Thomas R.: on Dravidian, 63, 81–83, 85–86, 99, 214, 336, 339–40, 345, 349; on Dravidian vs. Iroquois crossness, 22, 352, 353; on Iroquois, 77; reconstruction of Dravidian prototype by, 60, 280–81
Trio, 223
Tsimshian, 125
Tubatulabal, 131
Tukanoan, 171–72, 185n.18, 237
Túpi-Guarani, 372–73

Tupinamba, 238, 372
Two-section systems, 337–38. *See also* Dual organization
Txicáo, 175, 373
Tylor, E. B., 7

Uto-Aztecan, 130–31, 137

Viveiros de Castro, Eduardo, 10, 25–26n.8

Waimiri-Atroari, 224
Wheeler, C. J., 126
Wigner, Eugene, 59
Winnebago, 48–49
Wirangu, 80
Wissler, Clark, 109

Yafar (Iafar) system, 10, 11, 12, 20, 88–89, 358–59
Yamdena, 273, 274, 275, 276–78, 288–89
Yaminahua, 371
Yanamamö, 217, 219, 220
Young, David A., 137
Young, Phillip D., 86–87, 360–61